Caesar Rules

For centuries, Roman emperors ruled a vast empire. Yet, at least officially, the emperor did not exist. No one knew exactly what titles he possessed, how he could be portrayed, what exactly he had to do or how the succession was organised. Everyone knew, however, that the emperor held ultimate power over the empire. There were also expectations about what he should do and be, although these varied throughout the empire and also evolved over time. How did these expectations develop and change? To what degree could an emperor deviate from the prevailing norms? And what role did major developments in Roman society – such as the rise of Christianity or the choice of Constantinople as the new capital – play in the ways in which emperors could exercise their rule? This ambitious and engaging book describes the surprising stability of the Roman Empire over more than six centuries of history.

Olivier Hekster is Professor of Ancient History at the Radboud Institute for Culture and History, Radboud University Nijmegen. He is chair of the international network 'Impact of Empire', and a member of the Royal Netherlands Academy of Arts and Sciences and the Academia Europaea. His publications include *Emperors and Ancestors: Roman Power and the Constraints of Tradition* (2015).

Caesar Rules

The Emperor in the Changing Roman World
(c. 50 BC–AD 565)

OLIVIER HEKSTER
Radboud University Nijmegen

Shaftesbury Road, Cambridge CB2 8EA, United Kingdom

One Liberty Plaza, 20th Floor, New York, NY 10006, USA

477 Williamstown Road, Port Melbourne, VIC 3207, Australia

314–321, 3rd Floor, Plot 3, Splendor Forum, Jasola District Centre, New Delhi – 110025, India

103 Penang Road, #05–06/07, Visioncrest Commercial, Singapore 238467

Cambridge University Press is part of Cambridge University Press & Assessment, a department of the University of Cambridge.

We share the University's mission to contribute to society through the pursuit of education, learning and research at the highest international levels of excellence.

www.cambridge.org
Information on this title: www.cambridge.org/9781009226790

DOI: 10.1017/9781009226776

© Cambridge University Press & Assessment 2023

This publication is in copyright. Subject to statutory exception and to the provisions of relevant collective licensing agreements, no reproduction of any part may take place without the written permission of Cambridge University Press & Assessment.

First published 2023

Printed in the United Kingdom by TJ Books Limited, Padstow Cornwall

A catalogue record for this publication is available from the British Library.

Library of Congress Cataloging-in-Publication Data
Names: Hekster, Olivier, author.
Title: Caesar rules : the Emperor in the changing Roman world (c. 50 BC–AD 565) / Olivier Hekster, Radboud University Nijmegen.
Other titles: Emperor in the changing Roman world (c. 50 BC–AD 565)
Description: Cambridge, United Kingdom ; New York, NY : Cambridge University Press, [2022] | Includes bibliographical references and index.
Identifiers: LCCN 2022030481 (print) | LCCN 2022030482 (ebook) | ISBN 9781009226790 (hardback) | ISBN 9781009226769 (paperback) | ISBN 9781009226776 (epub)
Subjects: LCSH: Emperors–Rome. | Rome–Politics and government–Empire, 30 B.C.-476 A.D. | BISAC: HISTORY / Ancient / General
Classification: LCC DG274 .C34 2022 (print) | LCC DG274 (ebook) | DDC 937/.06–dc23/eng/20220629
LC record available at https://lccn.loc.gov/2022030481
LC ebook record available at https://lccn.loc.gov/2022030482

ISBN 978-1-009-22679-0 Hardback

Cambridge University Press & Assessment has no responsibility for the persistence or accuracy of URLs for external or third-party internet websites referred to in this publication and does not guarantee that any content on such websites is, or will remain, accurate or appropriate.

To the memory of Fergus Millar (1935–2019)

Anything that happens, happens.

Anything that, in happening, causes something else to happen, causes something else to happen.

Anything that, in happening, causes itself to happen again, happens again.

It doesn't necessarily do it in chronological order, though.
　　　　　　　　　　　Douglas Adams, *Mostly Harmless* (1992)

You must know that, although I have used the term 'expectations' more than once, you are not endowed with expectations only.
　　　　　　　　　　　Charles Dickens, *Great Expectations* (1861)

Contents

List of Figures [*page* ix]
List of Maps [xi]
List of Graphs [xii]
Preface [xiii]
Timeline [xvi]
List of Abbreviations [xxi]

Introduction: Emperors and Expectations [1]
  Emperors in Their World [1]
  Writing a History of Emperorship [4]
  Different Emperors at Different Times [8]
  Between Coercion and Communication [10]
  Great Expectations [13]
  Remember, Remember... [17]

1 Portraying the Roman Emperor [23]
  Roman Emperors and the Dangers of Appearing Regal [23]
  Indicators of Imperial Power and the Importance of Expectations [27]
  Naming the Emperor: Titles and Forms of Address [30]
  Depicting the Emperor: Portrait, Reliefs and Statuary [45]
  Denoting the Emperor (1): The Power of Dress [69]
  Denoting the Emperor (2): The Importance of the Crown [81]
  Denoting the Emperor (3): The Sceptre [90]
  The Creation of an Imperial Image? [102]

2 Playing Imperial Roles [106]
  Emperors and the Codification of Imperial Roles [106]
  The Emperor and His Military Role [109]
  The Emperor and His Religious Role [133]
  The Emperor and His Civic Role [156]
  Combining Imperial Roles: Exemplary Emperors [169]

3 Being around the Emperor [183]
  Institutional Entourage: Senators and Bishops [184]
  Closeness to Rule: The Emperor's Men at Court [209]
  The Imperial Family [226]
  Emperors and Entourage [254]

4 The Emperor in the Capital and Provinces   [260]
  Emperors in Their Capitals   [263]
  Expectations of a Civic Ruler   [285]
  Expectations of a Military Ruler   [293]
  Expectations of a Religious Ruler   [309]
  Emperors in Their Provinces   [317]

Conclusions: Emperors in a Changing World   [326]

Appendix   [334]
  The Julio-Claudians   [334]
  The Flavians   [334]
  The adoptive and antonine emperors   [335]
  The Severi   [335]
  The Tetrarchy   [335]
  The Constantinian dynasty   [336]
  The Valentinian dynasty   [336]
Glossary   [337]
Bibliography   [340]
Index of Persons and Places   [393]
General Index   [399]

Figures

0.1	Remembering Trajan	[*page* 21]
1.1	To kill a king	[25]
1.2	Portrait of Caesar on a coin	[28]
1.3	Justinian enthroned	[30]
1.4	The names of Augustus and his heirs	[31]
1.5	Pompey's image	[49]
1.6	Augustus' new imagery	[50]
1.7	Vespasian and the qualities of age	[52]
1.8–1.9	Different images of Gallienus	[55]
1.10	Emperors in gold	[60]
1.11	Emperor and Senate	[64]
1.12	The seated ruler	[68]
1.13	Caligula in purple	[72]
1.14	Opulent emperorship	[76]
1.15	Emperor and dignitary	[78]
1.16	King David as Roman emperor	[79]
1.17	A very imperial image of Hadrian	[86]
1.18	Constantine's radiate crown	[88]
1.19–1.20	Magisterial or imperial sceptre?	[93]
1.21	Augustus as Jupiter	[94]
1.22	Claudius as Jupiter	[97]
1.23	Victory of the cross	[101]
1.24	Crowned by the hand of God	[102]
1.25	An impressive puppet emperor	[103]
2.1	Proclaiming peace	[111]
2.2	From victory to angel	[114]
2.3	To triumph or not?	[117]
2.4	Military Hadrian	[123]
2.5	The victorious ruler	[126]
2.6	Caracalla as a priest	[137]
2.7	Trajan as an orator	[159]
2.8	Constantine as *civilis princeps*	[166]
2.9	Different roles on one coin	[173]

2.10	Trajan among the gods	[180]
3.1	The emperor's virtues	[185]
3.2	The absent emperor in Rome	[191]
3.3	Constantine at Nicaea	[205]
3.4	Agrippina and Nero	[229]
3.5	Victory through vow	[234]
3.6	The emperor and empress together	[238]
3.7	The hierarchical place of the empress	[241]
3.8	Stilicho's family	[251]
3.9	The continued role of the Senate	[257]
4.1–4.2	Rome and New Rome	[277]
4.3	Constantine as founder	[281]
4.4	Imperial might against the provinces	[296]
4.5	A local image of the belligerent emperor	[297]
4.6	An emperor subjugating local tribes	[301]
4.7	Roman victory, provincial style	[303]
4.8	Provinces in their own right	[305]
4.9	The emperor and local gods	[312]
4.10	Emperors or gods?	[313]
4.11	The Roman empire as a foreign country	[319]
5.1	Late-antique splendour	[328]

Maps

0.1 The Roman empire   [*page* 6–7]
2.1 Justinian's empire   [132]
4.1 Rome's imperial fora   [271]
4.2 The traditional topography of Constantinople   [280]

Graphs

1.1 Imperial titulature on central coinage   [*page* 33]
1.2 Imperial headgear on central coinage   [84]
1.3 Sceptres on central coinage   [99]
2.1 Military messages on central coinage   [113]
2.2a Reverse themes on central coinage (per dynasty)   [171]
2.2b Reverse themes on central coinage (reign-by-reign)   [172]
2.3 Reverse themes on *aurei*   [175]
3.1a Number of coins struck for empresses   [236]
3.1b Messages on coins struck for empresses   [236]

Preface

This book brings together almost twenty-five years of thinking, reading and writing about Roman emperorship. In that time I have been helped along by many friends, colleagues, students and teachers. Looking back over the years, it becomes apparent how much of humanities research is teamwork, with insights taking shape in conversation – more or less heated – or written debate. Many of the ideas in this book, moreover, found their origins whilst I was teaching or being taught. So before acknowledging the help of those who directly eased the writing of this book, I want to take the opportunity to thank all my students for their ceaseless questions and repeated requests to explain myself more clearly. I also want to thank my teachers over the years. They are too many to mention all. Some stand out. First and foremost, Fergus Millar, to whom I owe so much. This book is, in many ways, a continuation of a conversation we've had since I entered his rooms at Brasenose College, Oxford, in 1998. Even then, remarkably, he took me seriously, correcting my many errors but never trying to make me change my point of view. That we can no longer have this discussion, nor coffee at the Oxford Playhouse or the Oriental Institute, still saddens me profoundly. It is with immense gratitude that I dedicate this book to his memory. Others were important too. That material culture plays such a pronounced part in my research is mainly thanks to Margareta Steinby, Bert Smith, Chris Howgego and Eric Moormann, who at various stages introduced me to the value (and pitfalls) of different categories of ancient sources. Luuk de Blois, John Rich and the late Thomas Wiedemann introduced me to the intricacies of Roman leadership and challenged me to develop my own points of view. To all of them, my thanks.

At a different level, this book is the end product of a generous five-year research programme that was financed by the Dutch Research Council (NWO). It allowed a team of dedicated scholars to jointly explore the role of 'constraints and tradition' in the formulation of Roman power. Their research underlies countless observations in this book, as testified in the notes and bibliography. Many thanks, therefore, to Sam Heijnen, Ketty Iannantuono, Dennis Jussen and Daniel Syrbe for our close cooperation over the past years; to Sven Betjes for the same and for providing me with numerous numismatic graphs; and to Erika Manders for her ideas and friendship, but especially for keeping us all on track and effectively running the project. Working on a shared subject with so many enthusiastic and intelligent colleagues has been strikingly productive, and more importantly, it has been fun. My Nijmegen colleagues Lien Foubert, Nathalie de Haan, Stephan Mols, Danielle Slootjes (now in Amsterdam) and especially Maaike van Berkel have created the context in which we were able to work productively and discussed ideas and concepts with us at regular occasions. The Faculty of Arts at the Radboud University has been systematically supportive in allowing me time to write. I cannot think of a better place in which to work.

Most of this book was written during the time of the COVID pandemic. This has made me appreciate more than before the importance of a good research library, notwithstanding the ever-increasing availability of digitised books and articles. I am extremely grateful to Johannes Hahn and Hans Beck for hosting me at Münster several times in the past year, for allowing me access to the splendid libraries in the Fürstenberghaus and for our discussions about Roman emperors and football. Other colleagues were kind enough to send me forthcoming work, answer questions or suggest relevant literature. Many thanks to Rhiannon Ash, Hennig Börm, Lien Foubert, Corey Ellinthorpe, Sander Evers, Danielle Slootjes and Shaun Tougher. Before COVID restrictions made travel nearly impossible, I was able to discuss many aspects of this book at lectures and workshops in Amsterdam, Chicago, Durham, Giessen, Pamplona, Nijmegen, Münster, Pavia, Toronto, Tübingen and Vienna. Comments on the various papers that I presented there have had a profound impact on this book. Willy Piron's work in obtaining images and the rights to publish them has been a great support, as has Sven Betjes' work in creating indexes and getting the book ready for production. Michael Sharp was an exemplary editor, and his enthusiasm for the project has been more important than he probably realises. Also at CUP, Katie Idle, Natasha Burton and Franklin Mathews Jebaraj guided the complicated process of turning a manuscript into a book, and the sharp eye of Rosemary Morlin corrected a worrying number of inconsistencies. My heartfelt thanks to all of them.

During the actual writing of the book, I have been helped immensely by several friends and colleagues, who went out of their way to read and comment upon one or more chapters. Their advice has improved the book beyond measure. So my heartfelt thanks to Cailan Davenport, Jaś Elsner, Angela Hug, Ben Kelly, Eric Moormann, Miguel John Versluys and, above all, Jo Quinn, who read various drafts of all of the chapters with amazing cheer and eye for detail. Jo's impact on this book has been immense – the least of which is that I will never use the verb 'to impact' again.

As ever, I was able to count on Thijs Goverde, Edwin van Meerkerk and Ted Kaizer to discuss life, the Roman world and everything, and on Birgit, Hannah and Leonie for unreserved support – even if that meant being away from home for stretches of time to work in the Münster libraries. They are unlikely to read this book, but without them I could not have written it.

Timeline

Emperors and Prominent Usurpers[1]

Augustus	28/27 BC–AD 14
Tiberius	14–37
Gaius (Caligula)	37–41
Claudius	41–54
Nero	54–68
Galba	68–9
Otho	69
Vitellius	69
Vespasian	69–79
Titus	79–81
Domitian	81–96
Nerva	96–8
Trajan	98–117
Hadrian	117–38
Antoninus Pius	138–61
Marcus Aurelius	161–80
Avidius Cassius	175
Lucius Verus	161–9
Commodus	176–92
Pertinax	193
Didius Julianus	193
Septimius Severus	193–211
Pescennius Niger	193–4
Clodius Albinus	193–7
Caracalla	198–217
Geta	209–11
Macrinus	217–18
Diadumenianus	218
Elagabalus	218–22

---

[1] Men appointed as Augustus by a ruling Augustus or accepted by the Senate have been included as emperors. For Tetrarchic emperors, years indicate their elevation to 'Caesar'. Prominent other rulers and selected usurpers are included to provide an overview.

Severus Alexander	222–35
L. Seius Sallustius	225(?)–7(?)
Maximinus Thrax	235–8
Magnus	235
Gordian I	238
Gordian II	238
Balbinus	238
Pupienus	238
Gordian III	238–44
Sabinianus	240
Philip Arabs	244–9
Pacatianus	248
Jotapianus	249–?
Silbannacus	c. 249
Sponsianus	?
Decius	249–51
L. (?) Priscus	250
Herennius Decius	251
Hostilianus	251
Trebonianus Gallus	251–3
Uranius Antoninus	253
Volusianus	251–3
Aemilianus	253
Valerian	253–60
Gallienus	253–68
Macrianus	260–1
Quietus	260–1
Valens	261
Aureolus	268

Palmyrene Empire (260–72)

Septimius Odaenathus	260–7
Vaballathus	267–72
Zenobia	267–72
Antiochus	272

Gallic Empire (260–74)

Postumus	260–9
Laelianus	269
Marius	269
Victorinus	269–71
Tetricus I	271–4
Tetricus II	273–4

Claudius II Gothicus	268–70
Quintillus	270
Aurelian	270–5
Domitian (II)	271
Urbanus	271/2
Septimius	271/2
Tacitus	275–6
Florianus	276
Probus	276–82
Saturninus	280
Bonosus	280–1
Proculus	280–1
Carus	282–3
Carinus	283–5
Numerianus	283–4
Marcus Aur. Julianus	283
Sabinus Julianus	284/5
Diocletian	284–305
Domitius Domitianus	297
Maximian	285–310
Amandus	285

British Empire (286–96)
Carausius	286–93
Allectus	293–6

Galerius	293–311
Constantius	293–306
Maximinus Daia	305–13
Severus II	305–7
Constantine I	306–37
Maxentius	306–12
Domitius Alexander	308–11
Licinius	308–24
Valerius Valens	314
Martinianus	324
Constantine II	337–40
Constans	337–50
Constantius II	337–61
Magnentius	350–3
Nepotianus	350
Vetranio	350
Julian	360–3

Jovian	363–4
Valentinian I	364–75
Valens	364–78
Procopius	365–6
Gratian	367–83
Valentinian II	375–92
Magnus Maximus	383–8
Flavius Victor	384/387–8
Theodosius I	379–95
Eugenius	392–4

Emperors of the West (395–476)

Honorius	395–423
Constantine III	409–11
Constans II	409–11
Maximus	409–11
Priscus Attalus	409–10
	414–15
Jovinus	411–13
Constantius III	421
Joannes	423–5
Valentinian III	425–55
Petronius Maximus	455
Avitus	455–6
Majorian	457–61
Libius Severus	461–5
Anthemius	467–72
Olybrius	472
Glycerius	473–4
Julius Nepos	474–5
Romulus Augustus	475–6

Rulers of Italy

Odoacer	476–93
Theodoric	493–526
Athalaric	526–34
Theodahad	534–6
Vitigis	536–40
Totila	541–52

Emperors of the East (395–565)

Arcadius	395–408
Theodosius II	408–50

Marcian	450–7
Leo I	457–74
Leo II	474
Zeno	474–91
Leontius	484–8
Basiliscus	475–6
Anastasius I	491–518
Justin I	518–27
Justinian I	527–65

Persian Kings

Shapur I	240–70
Shapur II	309–79
Khusro I	531–79

Abbreviations

AE	= *L'Année épigraphique* (Paris 1888–)
AJA	= *American Journal of Archaeology*
ANRW	= H. Temporini / W. Haase (eds.), *Aufstieg und Niedergang der römischen Welt* (Berlin 1972–98)
AntTard	= *Antiquité Tardive*
BCEA	= *Bulletin canadien des études anciennes*
BJ	= *Bonner Jahrbuch*
BMCRE	= H. Mattingly, *Coins of the Roman Empire in the British Museum* (London 1965)
CAH	= *Cambridge Ancient History*
CIL	= *Corpus Inscriptionum Latinarum* (Berlin 1863–)
CIS	= *Corpus Inscriptionum Semiticarum* (Paris 1881–1962)
CPhil	= *Classical Philology*
CQ	= *Classical Quarterly*
HSCP	= *Harvard Studies in Classical Philology*
IAM	= *Inscriptions antiques du Maroc* (Paris 1966–2003)
ICret	= M. Guarducci (ed.), *Inscriptiones Creticae* (Rome 1935–50)
ILAlg.	= S. Gsell (ed.), *Inscriptions latines de l'Algérie* (Paris–Algiers 1922, 1957)
I.Eph.	= H. Wankel (ed.), *Die Inschriften von Ephesos* (Bonn 1979–84)
IG	= *Inscriptiones Graecae* (Berlin 1873–)
IGLS	= L. Jalabert/ R. Mouterde, *Inscriptions Grecques et Latines de la Syrie* (Paris 1929–)
ILS	= *Inscriptiones Latinae Selectae* (Berlin 1892–1916)
IMEM	= *Proceedings of the Workshop of the International Network Impact of Empire (Roman Empire c. 200 B.C.–A.D. 476)*
JAHA	= *Journal of Ancient History and Archaeology*
JDAI	= *Jahrbuch des Deutschen Archäologischen Instituts*
JRA	= *Journal of Roman Archaeology*
JRH	= *Journal of Religious History*
JRS	= *Journal of Roman Studies*

LSA	= Last Statues of Antiquities
LTUR	= *Lexicon Topographicum Urbis Romae* (Rome 1993–2000)
MAAR	= *Memoirs of the American Academy in Rome*
MDAI (R)	= *Mitteilungen des Deutschen Archäologischen Instituts* (Rome)
MEFRA	= *Melanges de l'École Francaise de Rome – Antiquité*
NC	= *Numismatic Chronicle*
OCRE	= Online Coins of the Roman Empire
OGIS	= Wilhelm Dittenberger (ed.), *Orientis Graeci Inscriptiones Selectae* (Leipzig 1903–5)
PanLat	= *Panegyrici Latini*
PBSR	= *Papers of the British School in Rome*
P.Col.	= W. L. Westerman/C. W. Keyes (eds), *Columbia Papyri* (New York–Atlanta 1929–98)
P.Coll.Youtie	= A. E. Hanson (ed.), *Collectanea Papyrologica: Texts Published in Honor of H. C. Youtie* (Bonn 1979)
PIR	= *Prosopographia Imperii Romani*
PLRE	= *The Prosopography of the Later Roman Empire*
P.Oxy	= B. P. Grenfell/A. S. Hunt, *The Oxyrhynchus Papyri* (London 1898–)
REA	= *Revue des Études Anciennes*
REAL	= A. Pauly/G. Wissowa/W. Kroll, *Real-Encyclopädie der klassischen Altertumswissenschaft* (1893–)
RGDA	= *Res Gestae Divi Augusti*
RIC	= H. Mattingly (ed.), *Roman Imperial Coinage* (London 1913–56)
RIPD	= Roman Imperial Portraits Dataset
RMD	= M. M. Roxan, *Roman Military Diplomas* (London 1978–2006)
RN	= *Revue Numismatique*
RPC	= *Roman Provincial Coinage* (London 1992–)
RPh	= *Revue de Philologie*
RRC	= M. Crawford, *Roman Republican Coinage* (Cambridge 1974)
RSC	= H. A. Seaby/D. A. Sear/R. Loosley/C. E. King, *Roman Silver Coins* (London 1952–89)
SB	= F. Preisigke, *Sammelbuch griechischer Urkunden aus Aegypten* (1913–2016)

SCPP	= W. Eck/A. Caballos/F. Fernández, *Das Senatus Consultum de Cn. Pisone Patre* (Munich 1996)
SEG	= *Supplementum Epigraphicum Graecum*
SIG	= W. Dittenberger (ed.), *Sylloge Inscriptionum Graecorum* (Leipzig 1915–24)
SNG Levante	= *Sylloge Nummorum Graecorum, Levante-Cilicia*
SO	= *Symbolae Osloenses. Norwegian Journal of Greek and Latin Studies*
TAPA	= *Transactions of the American Philological Association*
ZPE	= *Zeitschrift für Papyrologie und Epigraphik*

Abbreviations of the works of ancient authors follow the *Oxford Classical Dictionary*.

Introduction

Emperors and Expectations

Emperors in Their World

Roman emperors ruled their world. They did so from the moment that emperorship was established in Rome up to the fall of the Roman empire. This seems self-evident, but almost everything in the previous two sentences is subject to debate. There was no clearly articulated concept for 'emperor' in the Roman world, which makes it hard to firmly state when Roman emperorship started. Was it during Caesar's reign, as he was the first sole ruler of the Roman world since the mythological kings? Or during the rule of his adoptive son, the later Augustus, under whom the institutional basis for a supreme position of power was created that would be the foundation of Roman rule for centuries? The accession of Tiberius was the first example of proper succession, which brought its own problems for an office that did not exist in a system in which magisterial offices could not be inherited.[1] It could also be argued that Roman 'emperorship' only started under Caligula, who had little military and administrative experience when he came to power but still received all the honours and powers that effectively constituted Roman leadership immediately after the death of his predecessor Tiberius. It is even possible to push the 'official' start of emperorship forward to the start of Galba's reign, because that was the first moment that someone from outside Augustus' household was given 'imperial' powers.[2] The end of Roman emperorship (and of the Roman empire)

---

[1] The literature on the beginning of Roman emperorship is immense. Suetonius starts his biographies of Rome's first sole rulers with Caesar. On Caesar's and Augustus' positions in the state see below p. 24–25. Tiberius' accession is discussed in Vel. Pat. 2.124–5, Tac. *Ann.* 1.7, 1.12 and Dio 57.2. An extraordinary newly found inscription shows the importance of military loyalty to the new ruler before anything was resolved by the Senate: P. Rothenhöfer, 'Emperor Tiberius and his *Praecipua Legionum Cura* in a New Bronze Tablet from AD 14', *Gephyra* 19 (2020), 101–10 and now especially A. Caballos Rufino, 'Un senadoconsulto del año 14 DC en un epígrafe bético', *ZPE* 219 (2021), 305–26.

[2] On Caligula receiving powers *en bloc*: A. Barrett, *Caligula. The Abuse of Power* (London – New York 2015²), 73–80. The legal basis of power was formalised in a so-called *Lex de Imperio*. The one for Vespasian is transmitted to us: B. Levick, 'The *Lex de Imperio Vespasiani*: The Parts and the Whole', in: L. C. Colognesi / E. Tassi Scandone (eds.), *La Lex de Imperio Vespasiani e la Roma dei Flavi* (Rome 2009), 11–22 and below p. 34.

is even more difficult to properly date. In the Roman west, Romulus Augustulus, who was deposed by Odoacer in 476, is often described as the last Roman emperor, but nearly a century later, the eastern emperor Justinian ruled in the Italian peninsula. Even when the west was finally and definitively lost to Roman power, the various kings who followed in the emperors' footsteps fulfilled much the same function as emperors, and were often addressed by similar titles and visualised in similar images.[3] In the eastern parts of the Roman empire, moreover, emperors continued to reign until the fall of Constantinople in 1453. By then the empire had shrunk dramatically in size, and the changes in its socio-political and cultural set-up were such that historians talk about the Byzantine rather than the Roman empire, although the inhabitants themselves did no such thing, and continued to describe themselves as Romans.[4]

So there is no clear definition of what a Roman emperor was, nor an undisputed date for the beginning or end of Roman emperorship. Still, for a very long time a series of individuals were nominally in charge of one of the largest political units that world history has seen. It had been created through massive military expansion, and although from the early third century onwards all free inhabitants were awarded Roman citizenship, the diversity of the peoples who had been coerced and incorporated into the Roman world remained continuously visible. Rome ruled an empire.[5] Up to the first century BC, this territory was governed through what is often described as a 'mixed constitution', which incorporated aristocratic, democratic and monarchic elements of rule. This Roman constitution had evolved and shifted substantially over time, but it excluded sole rule, except for clearly delineated periods of crisis, in which a 'dictator' could take sole decisions.[6] When the problems facing the ever-expanding empire

---

[3] Clear historical overviews are provided by M. Kulikowski, *The Tragedy of Empire. From Constantine to the Destruction of Roman Italy* (Cambridge [Mass.] 2019), esp. 214–30 and P. Heather, *The Fall of the Roman Empire. A New History of Rome and the Barbarians* (Oxford 2006), esp. 430–59. See further below p. 35.

[4] C. Wickham, *Framing the Middle Ages. Europe and the Mediterranean 400–800* (Oxford 2005), 29–32, points out how *byzantios* was only used to refer to inhabitants of the capital. For everyone else *romanus* or *rhomaios* was used.

[5] J. Burbank/ F. Cooper, *Empires in World History. Power and the Politics of Difference* (Princeton – Oxford 2010), 8 for the definition of 'empire'. On the awarding of citizenship through the co-called *Constitutio Antoniniana* (AD 212): A. Imrie, *The Antonine Constitution. An Edict for the Caracallan Empire* (Leiden – Boston 2018).

[6] A. Lintott, *The Constitution of the Roman Republic* (Oxford 1999), 1–2, 109–13; 191–213. The most important ancient discussion of the mixed constitution is Polybius, *Histories* 6.11–18. Illustrative for the notion that sole rule was excluded in the Republic: Tac. *Ann.* 1.1: 'freedom and the consulship were established by L. Brutus. Dictatorships were taken up only on occasion'.

put pressure on its political system, the office of dictator changed to a more autocratic form. Its time limit was removed, and individuals were awarded a dictatorship for 'bringing stability to the political order' (*rei publicae constituendae*).[7] Ultimately, this would lead to civil war, Caesar's sole rule, more civil war and then Augustus' long reign – from which point onwards sole rule became the norm. From 50 BC onwards – brief periods aside – a sole man ruled an empire. These men were differentiated from other rulers, from 27 BC by the name Augustus, by both the Romans and those who came to be subjected by them. There was no doubt that they outranked the monarchs of neighbouring kingdoms, with the exception of the ruler of the adjacent Parthian (and later Sasanian) empire. It makes sense, then, to call these Roman rulers 'emperors', even if the Romans themselves did not.[8]

The change towards a political system in which one man ruled supreme was substantial. It also turned out to be effective, in the sense that for approximately 500 years in the west, and about a millennium longer in the east, emperorship was virtually unchallenged as a mode of rule, even if individual rulers were often challenged and deposed.[9] How was this new role incorporated into the existing structures of the Roman empire? And how could the position continue to function and flourish notwithstanding the massive changes that the empire underwent over the centuries? The transition to a Christian empire may be the most obvious of these, but there were other pronounced shifts. Militarily, Rome changed from an expansionist empire which expected to defeat its enemies to a territory defending its borders and negotiating with enemies. Geographically, the eastern part of the empire gained ever more importance, through the incorporation of eastern local elites and ultimately the move towards Constantinople as imperial residence and capital. There were major shifts in the organisation

---

[7] App. *BC*. 1.98.459; 1.99.462; L. Gasperini, 'Su alcuni epigrafi di Taranto romano', in: M. Raoss (ed.), *II miscellanea greca e romana II* (Rome 1968), 379–97; L. Gasperini, 'Ancora sul frammento 'cesariano' di Taranto', *Epigrafica* 33 (1971), 48–59; A. Baroni, 'La titolatura della dittatura di Silla', *Athenaeum* 95 (2007), 775–92; Lintott, *The Constitution*, 113.

[8] On periods of shared Roman emperorship, see below pp. 43 and 246–247. On the Parthians and Sasanians, and their relation to Rome: B. Dignas/ E. Winter, *Rome and Persia in Late Antiquity: Neighbours and Rivals* (Cambridge 2007), 9–44; M. Canepa, *The Two Eyes of the Earth. Art and Ritual between Rome and Sasanian Iran* (Berkeley – Los Angeles – London 2009). Note that if we call the Roman ruler 'emperor' rather than Augustus, we should call the Persian rulers likewise. Placing an eastern king of kings against a Roman emperor says more about modern historiography than about ancient conceptions of rule.

[9] In his ongoing project 'New Blood: Rome's Emperors in Global Perspective', Walter Scheidel argues that the frequency with which individual Roman rulers were disposed is exceptional when compared to other monarchical systems of rule.

of the empire as well, both in its territorial divisions and in the status of people who were placed in charge of administrative zones. Throughout all these changes, emperors retained their position as head of state.

Looking at the Roman empire over a long period of time, it is noticeable how often society was in political and cultural flux. For emperorship to endure, it must change with it. Yet, in ancient Rome, change and innovation were claimed to be suspect. A key notion was custom (*mos*), the way things were done at a given time, or even better, ancestral custom (*mos maiorum*), the way things had previously been done.[10] That was not an absolute. Romans were aware of change. The great second-century historian Tacitus, for instance, described how Emperor Claudius explained his proposal to allow members of the Gallic elite into the senate by quoting precedent, only then to note how 'what today we defend by examples will be among the examples'.[11] Claudius defended his innovation by presenting it as a continuity of existing practices, even if in extended form. That extension, however, could influence later practice. How was emperorship itself formulated and perceived on such a tightrope between (necessary) adaptation and the need for continuity? In other words, how was power presented and perceived in a society that was supposed to be dominated by tradition, but politically and culturally in flux? This book looks at emperorship over a long period of time in order to address this question.

Writing a History of Emperorship

This is a book discussing Roman emperorship over a period of more than 600 years. It cannot aim for completeness. Instead, it focuses primarily on the presentation and perception of emperorship, although it will argue that these had major repercussions for the emperors' behaviour. It does so by looking at how emperors were named and portrayed (Chapter 1), at the three main roles they had to fulfil; that of military leader, religious leader and divine figure, and as a civic ruler (Chapter 2), at the individuals and groups with whom emperors were expected to surround themselves (Chapter 3), and at the impact of (local) monuments, ceremonies and traditions on the perception of the emperors and their main roles in

---

[10] Lintott, *Constitution*, 4–6; A. Wallace-Hadrill, *Rome's Cultural Revolution* (Cambridge – New York 2008), 215–218.

[11] Tac. *Ann.* 11.24. The original speech of Claudius is transmitted through *CIL* 13.1668. It includes many references to earlier Roman history.

Rome, Constantinople, and the wider Roman world (Chapter 4; for the location of the various places mentioned in this book, see Map 0.1).

In order to explore these four themes, the book uses a wide variety of source material. Centrally issued coinage (also called imperial coinage) has survived in substantial numbers for the entirety of the period. It forms a useful starting point to establish a baseline of developments in the emperor's names and titles (through the legend), image (through the portrait), and role (through the scenes on the reverse of coins).[12] Central coins can often be contrasted to so-called provincial coinage, issued by autonomous cities or kings who had allied themselves to Rome.[13] Statues and other sculptural portraits of the emperor are also transmitted in large quantities, as are inscriptions and papyri referring to the emperor. All of these can be used to look at developments over time, though all have their peculiarities, limits and drawbacks which need to be taken into account before drawing historical conclusions.[14] Narrative reliefs, paintings and large-scale imperial architecture are similarly important to the argument, and they must have dominated the (urban) landscapes of the Roman world, thus playing a major part in transmitting the emperor's roles. There are also objects which were of more precious materials, such as gems or ivory diptychs, which have therefore been transmitted in much smaller numbers and were only accessible to a limited audience in antiquity. In that sense, they showed more private images of the emperor, or at least images that could be targeted to a specific group. The precious objects help to show how wide the range of possibilities for imperial representation could be as long as you knew who the audience would be. And of course much of our evidence is literary (the

---

[12] R. Wolters, 'Die Geschwindigkeit der Zeit und die Gefahr der Bilder: Münzbilder und Münzpropaganda in der römischen Kaiserzeit', in: G. Weber/ M. Zimmermann (eds.), *Propaganda – Selbstdarstellung – Repräsentation im römischen Kaiserreich des 1. Jhs. n. Chr.* (Stuttgart 2003), 175–204; 190–1, 195; M. Crawford, 'Roman Imperial Cointypes and the Formation of Public Opinion', in: C. Brooke/ B. Stewart/ J. Pollard/ T. Volk (eds.), *Studies in Numismatic Method: Presented to Philip Grierson* (Cambridge 1983), 54–5. The analysis of coin types has been facilitated enormously through the digitisation of material in the 'Online Coins of the Roman Empire' database (OCRE): http://numismatics.org/ocre/. On the use of OCRE as a research tool, see now S. Betjes, *The Mind of the Mint. Continuity and Change in Roman Imperial Coin Design from Augustus to Zeno (31 BCE–491 CE)* (PhD Nijmegen 2021), 38–44.

[13] These coins are systematically presented on https://rpc.ashmus.ox.ac.uk/, which also supplies an introduction to the use of this material, with selected bibliography. See further below p. 318–320.

[14] Roman imperial statues are now assembled in the 'Roman Imperial Portraits Dataset' (RIPD): https://doi.org/10.17026/dans-2ca-hxmd and https://imperialportraits.rich.ru.nl/, and the 'Last Statues of Antiquity' dataset (LSA): http://laststatues.classics.ox.ac.uk/. For inscriptions see especially the 'Epigraphik-Datenbank Clauss-Slaby' (EDCS): http://db.edcs.eu/epigr/ and for papyri the 'Papyrological Navigator' (PN): https://papyri.info/.

Map 0.1 The Roman empire

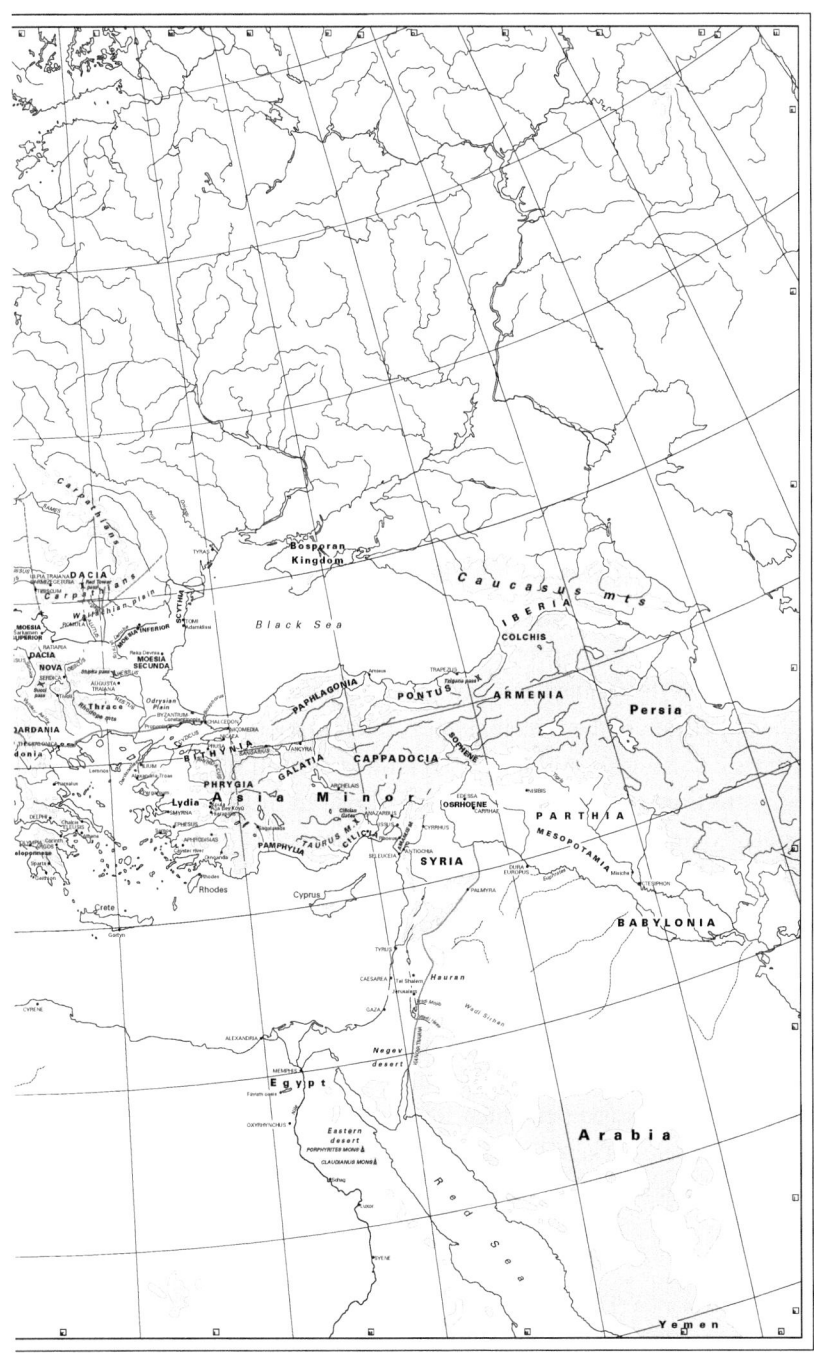

documentary evidence from inscriptions and papyri aside). Throughout the book, testimonies from classical historians are used to (re)construct events and opinions. Equally important, however, are letters sent to and by emperors, legal texts (often issued by the emperor) and laudatory speeches (often delivered before the emperor). Like the material evidence, these texts have their peculiarities and limits, and throughout the book I will try to explain why I think that a certain text (or a certain object) can help us understand what an emperor did, or was expected to do. Ample citation of the literary sources and images of the material ones will hopefully help the reader to follow that argument.

This is a book about emperors, but no monarch rules on his or her own.[15] Empresses were important, as were imperial heirs, and they will receive much attention (especially in Chapter 3). But others, such as generals, senators, *equites*, bishops, local elites, friendly (and not-so-friendly) kings, philosophers and eunuchs mattered too. The emperor's relationship with soldiers and the crowds in Rome and Constantinople was an essential component of his rule (see especially Chapter 4), but it is difficult to find evidence for how these people, or people in the provinces of lower social status, such as the farmers and day labourers who must have made up most of the population of the Roman empire, thought about their emperor. There are texts discussing what soldiers and crowds did and wanted, but very few, if any, are from their perspective. I have tried to include as many of such 'popular' viewpoints as possible into the argument.[16]

Different Emperors at Different Times

The period which this book deals with starts when Caesar obtained sole power. It ends at the death of Justinian the Great in 565. The beginning marks the first occasion at which Rome was ruled by someone who could be called emperor. There had been sole rulers before Caesar, but not since the time of the legendary kings (when there had been a Roman city state

---

[15] The possible exception is the king in Antoine de Saint-Exupéry's *Le Petit Prince*. But even he is much relieved when he finally encounters a subject.
[16] On 'popular' perceptions of emperors: K. Kröss, *Die politische Rolle der stadtrömischen Plebs in der Kaiserzeit* (Leiden – Boston 2017), 271–84; C. Courier, *La Plèbe de Rome et sa culture (fin du IIe siècle av. c–fin du Ie siècle ap. J.-C.)* (Rome 2014). An important analysis of the way in which art and monuments may have been perceived by non-elites: J. R. Clarke, *Art in the Lives of Ordinary Romans. Visual Representation and Non-Elite Viewers in Italy, 100 BC–AD 315* (Berkeley – Los Angeles – London 2006).

rather than an empire) had someone attempted to gain sole control permanently. After Caesar, sole rule became the norm. The reign of Justinian forms the last period in which a Roman emperor aimed to rule a united eastern and western Roman empire. That reign also saw the abolition of the consulate, abolishing a post that had been central to Rome for over a millennium. Justinian even argued that Roman history had always been dominated by monarchs, showing how sole rule had become a self-evident part of the Roman past.[17] Roman systems of rule, then, shifted significantly during the reigns of Caesar and Justinian. This is clear with the benefit of hindsight but was also recognised by people at the time. Still, any demarcation of time is somewhat arbitrary, and neither beginning nor end date of this book indicates a moment of absolute change. Caesar's position was the result of a long-lasting process, and after Justinian's death sole leaders continued to rule the Romans. Rulers in Constantinople remained Roman emperors. Kings and popes in Rome and Ravenna, and powerful leaders of Gaul would continue to make use of imagery and titulature that placed them in line with (earlier) Roman emperors. Being the 'true' Roman monarch apparently bestowed legitimacy well after 565.

A substantial part of the six centuries with which this book deals is firmly placed in what is called late antiquity (usually dating from the very late third century to either the sixth or early eighth centuries). There has been an enormous amount of scholarly attention on this period in the past decades, much of it focusing on emperorship. Recent work still has to position itself in relation to Sabine MacCormack's magisterial *Art and Ceremony in Late Antiquity*, which appeared forty years ago.[18] She described the late-antique emperor as a figure of a much more exalted status than the rulers of the first two centuries of the principate, as was expressed through images and ceremony. Throughout the book, however, she emphasised that this had been a gradual transformation of existing notions and traditions. For MacCormack, that transformation first took shape during the reigns of Diocletian (organised in a so-called Tetrarchy) and Constantine. Later scholarship has refined MacCormack's ideas, and especially discussions about late-antique panegyric have developed our understanding of the emperor in the later Roman world enormously. Yet the notion remains that Roman emperorship and imperial ideology were wholly reformulated under Diocletian and Constantine (though making use of existing traditions), reacting to the instabilities of the third

---

[17] Justinian, *Novella*, 47. See below p. 194.
[18] S. MacCormack, *Art and Ceremony in Late Antiquity* (Berkeley – Los Angeles – London 1981).

century.[19] This book will argue, instead, that the ruler's exalted status was an integral element of emperorship from the very beginning. It existed alongside the emperor's more 'senatorial' status and his roles as civil, military and religious ruler. From Caesar onwards, Roman emperorship meant different things to different people in different contexts. The balance between these various aspects of emperorship changed over time, but this was neither a linear process, nor a systematic one.

One reason why scholarship has so strongly emphasised the difference between emperors in the early and later Roman empire, and indeed the related difference between pagan and Christian emperorship, is the intellectual need for categorisation. It is easier to think in defined units. But any attempt to define such a category, for instance through periodisation, leads to the risk of lumping; overemphasising the similarities within the period under discussion. At the same time, there is the risk of splitting: continuously emphasising differences between more narrowly defined categories, up to the point that everything is unique and patterns cannot be established.[20] By widening the historical scope, this book aims to avoid some of these pitfalls. There is of course the real risk that it replaces one form of periodisation with another. Yet it hopes to show that it is important to look at Roman emperorship (and indeed Roman history in general) through an historical analysis that bridges the early empire/late antiquity divide.

Between Coercion and Communication

Throughout the period under discussion, emperors and their subjects paid attention to the presentation and perception of power. This was important for the longevity of Roman rule. Legitimation and acceptance of just rule

---

[19] J. W. Drijvers/ M. McEvoy, 'Introduction', in: J. W. Drijvers/ M. McEvoy (eds.), *Envisioning the Roman Emperor in Speech and Word in Late Antiquity* (= *Journal of Late Antiquity* 14) (Baltimore 2021), 2–8, 2. Recent important works on late-antique emperorship often focusing on the fourth and fifth centuries and supplying discussion of earlier bibliography are: M. P. García Ruiz/ A. J. Quiroga Puertas (eds.), *Emperors and Emperorship in Late Antiquity: Images and Narratives* (Leiden – Boston 2021); K. Cyprian Coda/ M. S. de Leeuw/ F. Schultz (eds.), *Gaining and Losing Imperial Favour in Late Antiquity* (Leiden – Boston 2019); D. W. P. Burgersdijk/A. J. Ross (eds.) *Imagining Emperors in the Later Roman Empire* (Leiden – Boston 2018); J. Wienand (ed.), *Contested Monarchy: Integrating the Roman Empire in the Fourth Century AD* (Oxford – New York 2015). On the Tetrarchy, below p. 43.

[20] J. Berg, 'Lumping and Splitting', *Science* 359 (2018), 1309. The concepts were first applied to the field of history by J. H. Hexter, *On Historians: Reappraisals of Some of the Makers of Modern History* (Cambridge [Mass.] 1979), 227–51.

played an important part in keeping imperial control. There was coercion too. Roman emperors were military leaders, something that was made public from the beginning of imperial rule. Augustus (and his successors) started letters to the Senate with the emphatic phrase 'If you are in good health, it is well. I and my army are in good health'. Many monuments throughout Roman territory further recalled the emperor's capacity for unleashing violence.[21] Emperors were also located at the centre of an economy of favours, forging bonds of loyalty with the people who mattered to run the empire.[22] Force and patronage, in other words, were important modes through which emperors managed to maintain their position. Yet, these were not enough. In his influential *Imperial Ideology and Provincial Loyalty in the Roman Empire*, Cliff Ando has persuasively argued that an important reason for the relative lack of resistance against Roman domination, and hence for its longevity, was that conquered peoples were convinced of the benefits of subjugation to the Romans and therefore accepted it, incorporating Roman notions and points of view into their own discourses. At the same time, these newly formulated discourses had an impact on Rome and its inhabitants. Consensus rather than fear guaranteed Roman dominion.[23] One point is that substantive rebellions (especially if simultaneous in different areas) would have stretched the relatively small number of soldiers. For much of Roman imperial history, Roman armed forces numbered about 350,000 men.[24] But more importantly our evidence suggests that many more people in the empire came to accept being part of the Roman empire rather than rebelling against it. The threat of violence may well have been a factor in this, as were the practical benefits given to those who cooperated with Rome, but broadcasting those potential threats or advantages to the population of the empire is part of the presentation of power.

---

[21] Dio, 69.14.3; J. Reynolds, *Aphrodisias and Rome: Documents From the Excavation of the Theater at Aphrodisias* (London 1982), documents no. 6, 12; J. B. Campbell, *The Emperor and the Roman Army, 31 B.C.–A.D. 235* (Oxford 1984), 148–56. See further below pp. 120–121 and 296–305.

[22] J. E. Lendon, *Empire of Honour. The Art of Government in the Roman World* (Oxford 1997), 107–60; A. Winterling, 'Die Freundschaft der römischen Kaiser', in: A. Winterling (ed.), *Zwischen Strukturgeschichte und Biographie. Probleme und Perspektiven einer römischen Kaisergeschichte (Augustus bis Commodus)* (Munich 2011), 207–32 with discussion of previous historiography.

[23] C. Ando, *Imperial Ideology and Provincial Loyalty in the Roman Empire* (Berkeley – Los Angeles – London 2000).

[24] Up to the *Constitutio Antoniniana* of 212 these included approximately 200,000 auxiliary forces, consisting of non-Romans. In the later period, tribes pressing on Roman frontiers were regularly settled inside Roman territory, acting as a (military) buffer against other peoples. For numerical comparison: the active personnel in the modern military forces of China is 2,350,000, of France 203,650, of India 1,442,900, of Russia 900,000, of the UK 148,450 and of the USA 1,379,800: IIIS, *The Military Balance 2020* (London – New York 2020), 26.

A similar argument can be made for the continuity of the office of emperor. Of course people adhered to their ruler because of what he could do for or to them. But only a relatively small number of people would experience this first hand. So for most of the inhabitants of the empire the perception and belief that the emperor could help or hurt them was more important than his practical actions. This does not diminish the importance of force or patronage as essential components of the stability of the emperor's position. Still, the power that the emperor held needed to be communicated to be understood. This is one of the reasons that the emperor's image was highly visible in military contexts. Images were depicted, of course on standards which were proudly borne before legions, but also on specially made glass *phalerae*, which were distributed to centurions and lower-ranking soldiers in the period from Augustus to Claudius, probably as an experiment in bonding with these groups of soldiers. In all branches of the army, then, individuals constantly carried the image of the emperor, reminding the troops of their ultimate leader.[25]

Imperial imagery and the discourses surrounding emperors often emphasised the emperor's (military) power. This was one way to create and keep support. Equally important, however, was the notion that emperors had a right to rule. Emperorship was at least partly accepted because the various groups and people who constituted Roman society thought that the position of the emperor was legitimate. There was much discussion about right and wrong behaviour of specific emperors, but little if any consistent subversion of imperial authority as such.[26] This did not mean that emperors could do as they please. Rather, they had to continuously re-affirm the underlying notion that emperorship was just, and, moreover, that they were the right individual to hold the office. As time moved on, individual emperors had to increasingly live up to the positive reputation of their predecessors, and avoid the pitfalls that had made other predecessors unpopular – or even saw them killed. The fact that emperorship was ill defined allowed for some

---

[25] J. Stäcker, *Princeps und Miles: Studien zum Bindungs- und Nahverhältnis von Kaiser und Soldat im 1. und 2. Jahrhundert n. Chr. (Spudasmata 91)* (Olms 2003), 160–6, 179–86, 198–205; D. Richter, *Das römische Heer auf den Trajanssäule. Propaganda und Realität* (Mannheim – Möhnesee 2004), 300–38; E. Dabrowa, 'Le Uexillum sur les monnaies coloniales (IIe-IIIe s. aprés J.-C.)', *Latomus* 63 (2004), 394–405. See for this point already O. Hekster, 'Fighting for Rome: The Emperor as a Military Leader', in: L. de Blois/ E. Lo Cascio (eds.), *The Impact of the Roman Army (200 BC–AD 476): Economic, Social, Political, Religious and Cultural Aspects* (Leiden – Boston 2007), 91–105.

[26] On the relation between power and legitimacy, see especially D. Beetham, *The Legitimation of Power* (Basingstoke – New York 2013²), esp. 42–63. On the acceptance of imperial imagery and the hierarchy which it implied: M. Hellström/ A. Russel, 'Introduction: Imperial Imagery and the Role of Social Dynamics', in: A. Russell/ M. Hellström (eds.), *The Social Dynamics of Roman Imperial Imagery* (Cambridge 2020), 1–24; 21.

flexibility in who came to power, and for experimentation in how to take up the role. Yet experimentation carried risks. Various groups of people had expectations of what a good emperor needed to be and do. Deviating from those expectations could lead to antagonism.[27] At the same time, the expectations of different groups in different regions varied, and could at first sight even be mutually exclusive. The emperor needed to (appear to) be different things to different people. Alongside the tension between adaptation and continuity, then, Roman emperors faced tension between different expectations from different groups who had to support their claim to power.

This was not a one-way process. Emperors needed to relate to the expectations of their subjects, but those subjects also had to adjust to the massive changes in Roman society and how these affected the political landscape in which they lived, with the emperor at the pinnacle of society. Roman rulers were continuously repositioned within existing worldviews, not only by rulers who needed to legitimate themselves, but also by subjects who had to understand the world in which they were living. How did that process work? Communication was an important part of it. Through images, written texts, spoken stories and ceremonies the emperor related to his subjects, and his subjects confirmed and shared in his authority. This went well beyond reminding people of the emperor's powers. By communicating the image and role of the emperor, these were reproduced to the world at large and changed meaning in the process. Communication, after all, goes beyond reproducing a message and can also transform or even produce meaning.[28] The presentation of emperorship continuously (re)shaped the office of the emperor. How that presentation developed over time tells us much about how emperorship changed – or remained constant – during the many centuries of Roman rule. It lies therefore at the core of this book.

Great Expectations

Expectations influenced Roman emperorship. So how did they take shape? One way was through the behaviour of earlier emperors. The actions and the

---

[27] The most often-used examples for this process are 'mad' emperors like Caligula, Nero, Commodus and Elagabalus who antagonised the senatorial elite who wrote history. But Nerva did not live up to the expectations of his soldiers, who effectively forced him to adopt Trajan as his heir and Justianian's attempts to shift power away from circus factions led to a major revolt. See below pp. 74–5, 153 and p. 268.

[28] R. T. Craig, 'Communication Theory as a Field', *Communication Theory* 9 (1999), 119–61; 125; J. W. Carey, 'A Cultural Approach to Communication', in: J. W. Carey, *Communication as Culture: Essays on Media and Society* (New York - London 2009²), 11–28; 19.

consequent reputations of Caesar and Augustus formed a framework within which later rulers had to operate. This framework was, however, not absolute. Individual rulers could and did deviate from earlier ones. Occasionally they had to. Caesar had gained his position through major military victories and Augustus by ending civil war. Later emperors who lacked that sort of experience could not simply follow precedent. This at least partly explains the very different representational choices, in the very early empire, of Caligula and Nero.[29] Massive changes in society were also responsible for new patterns of behaviour and representation. There was, for instance, no real Roman precedent for the position of an emperor in a religious system with one supreme god, yet after the conversion of Constantine emperorship needed to be formulated in those terms, without alienating too many subjects. Similarly, emperors in the third and fifth centuries had to respond to a situation in which the empire was under threat, whereas the capacity for conquest had been one of the cornerstones of successful emperorship before.[30] The reactions to these new situations created new precedents, both positive and negative. Some behaviour turned out to be acceptable; some created too much criticism to be repeated. The history of Roman emperorship was one of trial and error. Yet, what we will see throughout this book was how rapidly an emperor's behaviour could become normalised. Anything, after all, happens for the first time only once, as long as people remember that it happened. Afterwards, there was precedent to which people could refer. Sometimes new types of behaviour by emperors backfired, at least among important groups, as it did for Caligula and Nero, whose reigns were cut short because of the discontent that they generated. Yet even in their failure, they influenced the perception of sole rule and created new possibilities for successors, as long as these stopped short of fully copying the behaviour of Caligula or Nero. Being less bad than a hated predecessor could be seen as a step forward. This book will regularly highlight the importance of the range, or bandwidth, of emperors' behaviour, and how that range shifted under the influence of (normalised) actions by subsequent emperors.

Of course, there had not always been emperorship, and in various parts of the empire, Roman rule itself was an innovation. Imperial precedent was not always the most important factor in what people expected their ruler to be.

---

[29] Below p. 51, 87.

[30] On the conversion of Constantine and its consequences for emperorship: R. van Dam, *The Roman Revolution of Constantine* (Cambridge 2007), 221–353. On the third- and fifth-century crises: L. de Blois, *Image and Reality of Roman Imperial Power in the Third Century AD. The Impact of War* (Abingdon – New York 2019), 37–131, 226–53; A. D. Lee, *From Rome to Byzantium AD 363 to 565: The Transformation of Ancient Rome* (Edinburgh 2013), 81–133, 159–95.

Pre-existing (local) traditions also shaped the expectations that people had of Roman emperors. Those traditions, and their impact, are often difficult to define. Indeed, the notion of what exactly 'tradition' is has been much discussed, especially how it differs from 'custom' or 'habit'. These differences are on the whole concerned with viewpoint and awareness. When people are aware of existing practices and consciously place themselves within or outside the framework that these create, they identify themselves as standing in a tradition and that goes beyond following customary patterns of behaviour. Often, however, people simply follow 'implicit cultural knowledge, rooted in the tradition of the past', without explicit reference to (or even awareness of) historical origins.[31] For expectations of rulership, both pre-existing traditions and customs matter. Important for our literary sources are various historical and rhetorical traditions, going back to Greek authors writing about tyrants and good rule, or Roman Republican authors writing about kingship, mostly in negative terms. These certainly mattered to the writing elite of the empire, for whom these literary traditions were often a lens through which they perceived (or at least described) the emperors' behaviour. That behaviour of emperors, however, may have in turn influenced how these (literary) traditions were interpreted.[32]

There were also non-literary traditions and traditional modes of behaviour that were relevant, such as local ways of depicting rulers or modes through which they could be worshipped.[33] These, too, could change under Roman influence. Some traditions were hijacked and some neglected. Sometimes new or heavily adapted practices (especially rituals) were presented as traditional in a process that has come to be known as 'invented tradition'.[34] Yet, this need not always have been a conscious process.

---

[31] R. Osborne, 'Introduction: For Tradition as an Analytical Category', *World Archaeology* 40 (2018), 281–94; 283–8; J. Fejfer/ M. Moltesen/ A. Rathje, 'Introduction', in: J. Fejfer/ M. Moltesen/ A. Rathje (eds.), *Tradition: Transmission of Culture in the Ancient World* (Copenhagen: Museum Tusculum Press 2015), 9–16; T. Hölscher, *Visual Power in Ancient Greece and Rome: Between Art and Social Reality* (Oakland 2018), 12, 100.

[32] See for instance A. J. S. Spawforth, *Greece and the Augustan Cultural Revolution. Greek Culture in the Roman World* (Cambridge – New York 2012), who convincingly argues that Roman interpretations of Greek notions changed these notions, which in their changed forms trickled down throughout the empire, even back to the Greek world.

[33] Most discussed in this context is the imperial cult, often in combination with the notion of *proskynesis* (prostration) of the worshipper before (images of) the emperor. On the continuing importance and adaptation of the Hellenistic ruler cult in the Roman empire, see: C. F. Norena, 'Ritual and Memory: Hellenistic Ruler Cults in the Roman Empire', in: K. Galinsky/ K. Lapatin (eds.), *Cultural Memories in the Roman Empire* (Los Angeles 2015), 86–100. See further below pp. 260–261, 310.

[34] E. Hobsbawm, 'Introduction: Inventing Traditions', in: E. Hobsbawm/ T. Ranger (eds.), *The invention of Tradition* (Cambridge 1983), 1–14; 1–2; A. W. Busch/ M. J. Versluys, 'Indigenous

Instead, it seems worthwhile to at least sometimes interpret references to 'traditional' connotations of a new monarchical system of rule as an attempt by emperor and subjects to come to understand the new situation, and each other. In some contexts, pre-existing notions helped the formulation of power in new situations; in others they hindered them. People aimed to place new situations in known contexts, identifying and elaborating traditions to understand new situations.[35] Customs and traditions, then, influenced what people would expect their (new) emperor to be and do, but the incorporation of Roman emperorship in the political landscape in turn had an impact on how people perceived their past.

Traditions and customs differed from one place to the next. They also differed, or at least mattered differently, for different echelons of society. How to differentiate these groups is not always easy. This book will often use the shorthand 'elite' placed against 'the people'. That does not properly reflect Roman practice, which distinguished between various *ordines*, groups sharing political and social status, the membership of which depended on a range of criteria. So within what this book calls elite, there were often pronounced differences. Senators took up a different position in the state than *equites*, and provincial magistrates (part of the elite at a local level) differed from the elites in Rome and Constantinople. Where these differences are relevant, they will be signposted, and on occasion the book will differentiate between members of, for instance, the provincial elite, the military elite or the senatorial elite. But that there was a relatively small group in the capital and other towns of the empire who held much more status, wealth and influence than the rest of the population, and that this group often had time to read and write is clear.[36] Traditions that may have mattered little to farmers, day labourers or soldiers were often important to them.

Rhetorical traditions, for instance, were enormously significant for high-status orators who wanted to find forms in which to praise their ruler. The continuation of certain political offices was important for those who had historically held such offices. But for many in society, who were not likely

---

Pasts and the Roman Present', in: D. Boschung/ A. Busch/ M. J. Versluys (eds.), *Reinventing the Invention of Tradition? Indigenous Pasts and the Roman Present* (Paderborn 2015), 7–15; 11 and O. Hekster, 'Identifying Tradition. Augustus and the Constraints of Formulating Sole Rule', *Politica Antica* 7 (2017), 47–60; 48–9.

[35] This point was already made in Hekster, 'Identifying tradition', 56 and is related to the concept of anchoring as explored by OIKOS, the Dutch national research school in classical studies: I. Sluiter, 'Anchoring Innovation: a Classical Research Agenda', *European Review* 25 (2017), 1–19; www.anchoringinnovation.nl/.

[36] C. Davenport, *A History of the Roman Equestrian Order* (Cambridge 2019), 6, 8–9. For the notion of elites or elite status groups in a general sense, see: P. Crone, *Pre-Industrial Societies: Anatomy of the Pre-Modern World* (Oxford 2003²), 101–4.

ever to hold office, nor to speak before the emperor (if they were even literate), neither point was particularly relevant. That the man who ruled their world was depicted in a way that fitted precedent will have been much more pertinent to them, or that he allowed their traditional patterns of worship to continue – something that of course became a point of dispute when Christianity became the dominant religion.

Consequently, people from these different echelons of society will have had different expectations about what their emperor should do or be. Because literary evidence has long been the main source material for analysing Roman history, the perspective of the writing elite on Roman emperorship and individual emperors has dominated scholarship. Indeed, the seminal work on Roman emperors, Fergus Millar's monumental *The Emperor in the Roman World*, in many ways looks at emperorship from the point of view of Roman and local elites. It is a foundational work and meticulous in its analysis of how the emperor related to equestrians and senators at Rome, councillors and city associations in the provinces, and to bishops and priests once Christianity became an important religious movement. Millar's much-quoted *dictum*, 'the emperor was what the emperor did', sketches a world in which emperors responded to continuous requests by large numbers of subjects for favours and judgements. Yet *The Emperor in the Roman World* does not look at the Roman emperor as a military leader, or as an object of worship.[37] Nor does it look at the many images of the emperor that were visible throughout the empire. These doubtless had an impact on how most people perceived their ruler and on the expectations they held about what emperors should be and do. Emperors had to relate to these expectations. In other words, the emperor was, also, what people expected him to be, and that was to a large extent dependent on what previous emperors were seen or said to have done. That, of course, makes it important to understand how different people came to remember previous emperors and their actions, and how these memories were transmitted and developed over the centuries.

Remember, Remember …

How did people remember their emperors? The behaviour of previous rulers mattered and set precedent. Individual rulers, and even their

---

[37] F. Millar, *The Emperor in the Roman World (31 BC–AD 337)* (London 1992²), citation from p. 6. The relation between emperors and various networks of local elites is now set out in G. Woolf, 'The Rulers Ruled', in: K. Berthelot (ed.), *Reconsidering Roman Power. Roman, Greek, Jewish and Christian Perceptions and Reactions* (Rome 2020), 85–100.

specific acts could form a positive or negative example for later emperors.[38] The notion of memory was an important one in Roman culture, causing rulers to be aware that their name and reputation would be transmitted over time. Moreover, Romans held the view that memory's chief purpose was to shape the future. By recalling exemplary behaviour, later men would be encouraged to follow in their forefathers' footsteps.[39] All of this implies that people were able to recall those rulers and their behaviour. This is uncomplicated for immediate predecessors. But how was the reputation of specific emperors remembered after several generations? Substantial information was transmitted by contemporary and later authors, ranging from flattering poems to juicy anecdotes about perverse behaviour. The trustworthiness of this – often anecdotal – evidence is debated. Emperors were described either positively or negatively, with the author's point of view a deciding factor in how a ruler's behaviour was described. For the transmission of an emperor's reputation, that trustworthiness is less important than the fact that certain stories were written down and thus made permanent for posterity. The accounts of historians like Suetonius, Tacitus and Cassius Dio were still read in late antiquity, as were laudatory speeches like the one Pliny made in favour of Trajan. They were one way in which emperors lived on in memory. These literary accounts, however, were only relevant to a limited group of people, even if that group might have been enlarged by the incorporation of certain texts into the Roman educational system.[40] The bulk of Roman subjects, possibly even including substantial parts of the local elites, will

---

[38] M. Roller, *Models from the Past in Roman Culture. A World of Exempla* (Cambridge 2018), 3–23; S. Bell, 'Role Models in the Roman World', in: S. Bell/ I. L. Hansen (eds.), *Role Models in the Roman World. Identity and Assimilation* (Ann Arbor 2008), 1–39; 1–19. See further below p. 178–179.

[39] The literature on the application of 'memory studies' on Roman history is enormous. The assembled articles in K. Galinsky (ed.), *Memoria Romana. Memory in Rome and Rome in Memory* (Ann Arbor 2014) and Galinsky/ Lapatin, *Cultural Memories* form a good starting point, with J. Weisweiler, 'Making Masters, Makings Subjects: Imperial Ideology and Memory Policy in the Early Roman Empire and the Later Roman State', in: Galinsky/ Lapatin *Cultural Memories*, 66–85 especially pertinent for this book. On the Roman conception of memory, see C. Baroin, *Se souvenir à Rome: formes, representations et pratiques de la mémoire* (Paris 2003).

[40] B. Baldwin, 'Tacitus, the *Panegyrici Latini*, and the *Historia Augusta*', *Eranos* 78 (1980), 175–8; R. McKitterick, *History and Memory in the Carolingian World* (Cambridge 2004), 223–6, 236–9, 247; B. Gibson/ R. Rees (eds.), *Pliny the Younger in Late Antiquity* (Baltimore 2013) = *Arethusa* 46 (2013), 141–57. On the relative continuity of literate education over time: T. Morgan, *Literate Education in the Hellenistic and Roman Worlds* (Cambridge 1998), 46; E. J. Watts, *City and School in Late Antique Athens and Alexandria* (Berkeley – Los Angeles – London 2006), 2–21. On levels of literacy in the ancient world: A. Kolb (ed.), *Literacy in Ancient Everyday Life* (Berlin – Boston 2018).

not have read the historical accounts, poems and speeches through which modern scholarship (re)constructs the lives of long-dead Roman emperors.

Written-down accounts were far from the only way through which imperial reputations were handed down. The Roman world was a visual one. Images on coins, paintings, and reliefs, statues, busts and enormous monuments, often attributed by name, dominated surroundings. These objects formed a visual world, a memoryscape in which Roman subjects lived and moved, and in which they continuously encountered their past and current rulers.[41] These images and monuments gave a variety of reflections on a long sequence of Roman emperors. How people encountered and interpreted these images will have differed markedly from one context to the next. They could be intended and perceived as an expression of ideology, but also as markers of a specific group identity, or reflections of individuals' status by linking themselves to their ruler. Geographical and chronological contexts mattered. Images, after all, were influenced by local traditions and the specific contexts in which they were seen. They also continued to be seen and adapted as time went on. Not only, then, did different groups have different expectations of certain imperial images and interpret one image in very different ways; even a single individual may have perceived an image differently in different contexts.[42] Yet, these images will have continuously influenced (in various ways) how people remembered the events and emperors that were commemorated. After all, individual and collective memories are to a large extent shaped by external stimuli. The images of all those past emperors and their actions will also have created some sort of 'prospective memory'. In other words, they massively influenced expectations that people had of their emperors. As Jan Assmann memorably pointed out: 'The past is not simply "received" by the present. The present is "haunted" by the past and the past is modelled, invented, reinvented, and reconstructed by the present'.[43] The importance of physical surroundings on

---

[41] Hölscher, *Visual Power*, 95–6, 254. On the notion of memoryscape and its impact on Roman subjects: Weisweiler, 'Making Masters, Making Subjects', 67–75.

[42] This point was already made in O. Hekster, 'When Was an Imperial Image', in: Russell/ Hellström, *Social Dynamics*, 274–88; 283–5, from which some formulations are taken. It provides (pp. 275–81) a historiographical overview of the main debates surrounding Roman imperial imagery, with references.

[43] J. Assmann, *Moses the Egyptian. The Memory of Egypt in Western Monotheism* (Cambridge [Mass.] 1997), 9, taken up by M. J. Versluys, 'Haunting Traditions. The (Material) Presences of Egypt in the Roman World', in: Boschung/ Busch/ Versluys, *Reinventing the Invention of Tradition?*, 127–58. On the notion of prospective memory: M. L. Popkin, *The Architecture of the Roman Triumph. Monuments, Memory and Identity* (Cambridge 2016), 14–15, 80–1 with further references.

how people thought of their emperors, and through that on the development of emperorship has not been sufficiently taken into account when discussing emperorship. It is a major point of departure for this book.

Not all these images would have called individual emperors to mind. Rather, there was some sort of standardisation of images on public monuments and coins which was strongly linked to emperorship in a more abstract sense. This repertoire of specific themes and scenes depicted the ruler in his military, religious and civil roles. Such stock images became, as it were, set pieces in a visual language through which emperorship could be communicated and constructed.[44] In this way, these images commemorated emperorship more than individual men. They strongly influenced the way people conceived of emperorship, as fixed visual vocabulary was not easy to change, which meant that emperors were depicted in ways that had to relate to how their predecessors were depicted. Still, the memory of individual rulers and other members of the imperial family could also be transmitted visually. It seems at least likely that, for instance, monuments like the columns of Marcus Aurelius or Trajan at Rome, with colossal statues of the emperor on top and narrative friezes of their major campaigns spiralling up (Figure 0.1) would be identifiable to a wider audience, and continuously recall these emperors' actions. Similarly, victory arches like those of Augustus, Titus, Septimius Severus and Constantine are likely to have been known under the name of the emperor for whom they were erected. This would have applied to a range of monuments and other objects in the wider Roman empire.[45] Coins even included the name of the emperor, empress or heir for whom they had been minted, creating monuments in miniature for a sequence of identifiable rulers.[46] The close

---

[44] G. Seelentag, *Taten und Tugenden Traians. Herrschaftsdarstellung im Principat* (Stuttgart 2004), 303; T. Hölscher, 'Historical Representations of the Roman Republic: The Repertory of Coinage in Comparison with Other Art Media', in: N. T. Elkins/ S. Krmnicek (eds.), *'Art in the Round'. New Approaches to Ancient Coin Iconography* (Rahden 2014), 22-37; 25-6; J. Trimble, 'Communicating with Images in the Roman Empire', in: F. S. Naiden/ R. Talbert (eds.), *Mercury's Wings. Exploring Modes of Communication in the Ancient World* (Oxford 2017), 106-27; 113; G. Seelentag, 'Antoninus Pius und die Herrschaftsdarstellung des 2. Jhs.', in: C. Michels/ P. F. Mittag, (eds.) *Jenseits des Narrativs. Antoninus Pius in den nicht-literarischen Quellen* (Stuttgart 2017), 19-30.
[45] Cf. Hölscher, *Visual Power*, 60.
[46] The importance of the commemorative function of coins, and the notion of 'monuments in miniature': A. Cheung, 'The Political Significance of Roman Imperial Coin Types', *SchwMbll* 48 (1998), 53-61; 56-8. Later re-use of earlier coin types with explicit links to the rulers for whom original coins were struck strengthens this point: S. Betjes, 'Moneta, the Memory of Roman Coinage: The Storage of Dies (or Coins) at the Mint of Rome', *Journal of Archaeological Numismatics*, forthcoming.

Figure 0.1 Remembering Trajan: 113, Rome, Marble column (h 35.07 m). The column with its 200 m. long helical frieze recalls Trajan's Dacian wars. The emperor's name is highly visible on a dedicatory inscription, and he figures fifty-eight times in the narrative relief. A massive statue on top of the column, and the position of the column in Trajan's Forum made abundantly clear who was commemorated.
Source: CKD – Radboud University Nijmegen, photo Diane Kuster

attention paid to memory sanctions for emperors who had lost so much support that successors wanted to distance themselves from them further shows how aware the Romans were of the relation between image and memory.[47]

All of this makes it likely that for many people in the empire, even centuries later, Augustus was a figure with whom certain stories were connected, and whose image at least some people (and not necessarily only those in Rome) would be able to recognise. People may even have been able to connect someone like Agrippina not only to the lurid stories that surrounded her, but also to the statues, reliefs and coins that showed her face, often with her name nearby on a pedestal inscription or coin legend.[48] Not all rulers or members of the imperial family will have made the same impression. Different emperors will have been remembered differently in different areas. It is for instance likely that people from Lepcis Magna were especially aware of Septimius Severus, even centuries after his death, since he had been born in the town and monumentalised it after coming to power.[49] How detailed knowledge of a specific emperor will have been remains unclear. But emperors, even long-dead ones, were often more than just a name. When late-antique senators acclaimed new emperors as 'better than Trajan' or bishops hailed the emperor Marcian and his wife Pulcheria as the 'new Constantine' and the 'new Helena' they employed memories of earlier rulers to highlight specific aspects of the emperors' behaviour.[50] How did such interactions between memories, traditions and expectations help or hinder the presentation and perception of power in a changing Roman society? That is what this book sets out to answer.

---

[47] H. I. Flower, *The Art of Forgetting. Disgrace and Oblivion in Roman Political Culture* (Chapel Hill 2006); J. de Jong, 'Memoria, Morality, and Mnemonic Hegemony of Roman Emperors', *JAHA* 6 (2019), 17–26.

[48] This does not only apply to emperors or empresses. E. J. Graham, 'Becoming Persons, Becoming Ancestors: Personhood, Memory and the Corpse in Roman Rituals of Social Remembrance', *Archaeological Dialogues* 16 (2009), 51–74 has convincingly argued how the memory of M. Nonius Balbus at Herculaneum changed through the town's topography and monuments. On the relation between visualization and memory in the Roman world, see: J. Elsner/ M. Squire, 'Sight and Memory. The Visual Art of Roman Mnemonics', in: M. Squire (ed.), *Sight and the Ancient Senses* (London – New York 2016), 180–204, 185–91, 215. Trimble, 'Communicating with Images', 107 argues in favour of high levels of 'visual literacy' in the Roman empire.

[49] Below p. 289. [50] Eutr. *Brev.* 8.5.3; *Acts of Chalcedon*, 6.11. See below pp. 178 and 232.

1 | Portraying the Roman Emperor

Roman Emperors and the Dangers of Appearing Regal

Roman emperors embodied their world. They were the supreme commanders of the armies, the lynchpin between men and gods, and the ultimate authority of law and justice.[1] All of this is well testified, with anecdotes and images describing the emperor as a sought-out figure, the centre of a group, dominating his surroundings. Such a central figure in the state needed to be instantly recognisable as being superior to all others. This was made difficult by the fact that his position needed to be presented as emphatically different from Hellenistic kingship. For many inhabitants of the empire, and certainly for senators in Rome, kings were a problem. Romans compared the relation between the king and his subjects to that of a master and his slaves and prided themselves on not having a monarch.[2] Indeed, addressing an opponent as (would-be) king was a strong invective in the late Roman republic. The rulers of the so-called regal period of ancient Rome (c. 753–509 BC) had many problematic connotations, many of them to do with abuse of power. The last king, Tarquinius Superbus, had become the negative example par excellence.[3] These problems with kingly

---

[1] See K. Hopkins, *Conquerors and Slaves: Sociological Studies in Roman History, Volume 1* (Cambridge 1978), 197–242, with C. Ando, *Imperial Ideology and Provincial Loyalty in the Roman Empire* (Berkeley – Los Angeles – London 2000). For Roman emperors and war images, see T. Hölscher, 'Images of War in Greece and Rome: Between Military Practice, Public Memory and Cultural Symbolism', *JRS* 94 (2004), 1–17; for the emperor as supreme priest, see A. Cameron, '*Pontifex maximus*: From Augustus to Gratian – and Beyond', in: Maijastina Kahlos (ed.), *Emperors and the Divine: Rome and its Influence* (Helsinki 2016), 139–59. For the emperor in his legal capacity, see K. Tuori, *The Emperor of Law* (Oxford 2016); O. Hekster, 'Imperial Justice? The Absence of Images of Roman Emperors in a Legal Role', *Classical Quarterly* 69 (2020), 247–60.

[2] M. Roller, *Constructing Autocracy: Aristocrats and Emperors in Julio-Claudian Rome* (Princeton 2003), 213–64; Roller, *Models from the Past*, 253–9; E. Dench, *Empire and Political Cultures in the Roman World* (Cambridge 2018), 24–7, suggesting that I *Mac.* 8.11–16 'not one of them has put on a crown or worn purple as a mark of pride' echoes Roman notions.

[3] Y. Baraz, 'Discourse of Kingship in Late Republican Invective', in: N. Panou/H. Schadee (eds.), *Evil Lords. Theories and Representations of Tyranny from Antiquity to the Renaissance* (Oxford 2018), 43–60. But cf. C. Sigmund, *'Königtum' in der politischen Kultur des spätrepublikanischen Rom* (Berlin–Boston 2014), 53–168, on a more positive attitude to kingship in the Republic.

status were recognised by Julius Caesar when he became a dominant force in Roman politics. He publicly refused the crown that was famously offered to him by Mark Antony, and is said to have responded to be being hailed a king (*rex*) by stating, 'I am not called Rex but Caesar', a not particularly good pun on *rex* as it is both the Latin word for king and a Roman *cognomen* (surname).[4] His claims not to want kingship were not enough, as his obviously superior position in the Roman state was a major factor in his assassination in 44 BC. It is not a coincidence that Caesar's assassins are said to have used 'liberty' as their slogan. They further emphasised this message by minting coins that showed the *pileus*, a cap indicating freedman status and through it liberty, between two daggers, and EID(IBVS) MAR(TIIS) (Ides of March) in the legend. It is ironical that the obverse of this coin shows the portrait of Brutus, identified by name, considering that depicting his portrait on coins had been an indication of Caesar's superior position. Even more emphatically anti-monarchical were coins struck for Brutus with Victory standing on a broken sceptre and breaking a diadem (Figure 1.1).[5] Demonstrating superior power was a risk. At the same time, there was no denying the power held by Caesar or by the sole rulers who followed in his footsteps.

That was a clear warning for Caesar's adoptive son. Octavian, who would later accept the name Augustus, gained supremacy in the Roman state after years of civil war.[6] At the battle of Actium (31 BC), his great opponents Mark Antony and Cleopatra VII were defeated. This did not mean that Octavian instantly made his new position clear. There was a decade of developments in which the new ruler's position was formulated, reformulated and normalised. This may have been either a cunning strategy by Augustus, who hid his 'autocratic aspirations' behind a Republican

---

[4] Suetonius, *Life of Caesar*, 79.2. E. Rawson, 'Caesar's Heritage: Hellenistic Kings and Their Roman Equals', *JRS* 65 (1975), 148–59, 159, perceptively argues that for Caesar the title of king was only 'worth turning down'.

[5] *RRC* 508/3; *RRC* 507/2; H. Börm, 'Antimonarchic Discourse in Antiquity: A Very Short Introduction', in: H. Börm (ed.), *Antimonarchic Discourse in Antiquity* (Stuttgart 2015), 9–24, 16; W. J. Tatum, *Always I Am Caesar* (Oxford – Malden 2008), 59, 141–3. Cf. *RRC*, 435/1, from 53 BC, showing a sceptre and a diadem placed under a curule chair, suggesting a rejection of regal symbols in favour of traditional Roman symbols of state, possibly in the context of Pompey's increased power.

[6] See also R. Syme, 'Imperator Caesar: A Study in Nomenclature', *Historia* 7 (1958), 172–88 (= *Roman Papers* I, Oxford 1979, 361–77), on how the changing name of the young ruler reflected his position. See also F. Millar, 'The First Revolution: Imperator Caesar, 36–28 BC', in A. Giovannini (ed.) *La Révolution romaine après Ronald Syme: Entretiens sur l'Antiquité Classique* 46 (Geneva 2000), 1–30.

Figure 1.1 To kill a king: 43–42 BC, travelling mint. Silver denarius (3.88 g): CASCA LONGVS (the name of the moneyer), surrounding an image of Neptune/BRVTVS IMP on either side of an image of Victory. The image of Victory, holding a palm branch and breaking a diadem while standing on top of a broken sceptre, was clear: peace was restored by the death of a would-be king. RRC 507/2
Source: ANS 1905.5, 7.30, American Numismatic Society

façade, paying lip service to (invented) Roman traditions in the process, or a much more organic process in which subjects and ruler alike tried to adapt to a new political landscape.[7] Yet, whoever was behind the process, the slow adaptation of the new ruler's position shows that it needed time before acceptable forms of addressing him were found. That need not mean that people were unaware of where real power lay. There was no doubt that Augustus was in control of the empire.[8] But he could not easily use the trappings of power associated to kingship. From the beginning of Roman emperorship, there was a potential tension between the recognisable supreme position of the ruler and the problematic connotations that came with the notion of kingship.

---

[7] Conscious manipulation: F. J. Vervaet, 'Arrogating Despotic Power through Deceit: The Pompeian Model for Augustan *dissimulatio*', in: A. J. Turner/K. O. Chong-Gossard/F. J. Vervaet (eds.), *Private and Public Lies: The Discourse of Despotism and Deceit in the Greco-Roman World* (Leiden – Boston 2010), 133–66, 165; J. W. Rich, 'Consensus Rituals and the Origins of the Principate', in: J.-L. Ferrary/J. Scheid (eds.), *Il princeps romano: autocrate o magistrato? Fattori giuridica e fattori sociali del potere imperiale da Augusto a Commodo* (Pavia 2015), 101–38, 115. 'Organic' process: C. Moatti, 'Historicité et altéronomie: un autre regard sur l'histoire', *Politica Antica* 1 (2011), 107–18; O. Hekster, 'Identifying Tradition. Augustus and the Constraint of Formulating Sole Rule', *Politica Antica* 7 (2017), 47–60, 51–2.

[8] F. Millar, 'State and Subject: The Impact of Monarchy', in: F. Millar/E. Segal (eds.), *Caesar Augustus: Seven Aspects* (Oxford 1984), 37–60.

The choice to address the ruler as 'princeps' is a case in point. It is first attested by the poet Horace in 27 BC, possibly following an imperial hint.[9] It was a nice traditional title with connotations of power. Cicero had described the influential politicians Scipio and Cato as *principes*. By 27 BC, addressing someone as *princeps* was established usage for leading men of the state, but also for individuals recognised as pre-eminent in that state. Just before Horace's address, in 29/8 BC, Octavian had been designated *princeps senatus*.[10] In time, this formulation shifted towards a more formal means of addressing the ruler. In 9 BC, the emperor's confidant Paullus Fabius Maximus used the term in a letter to the assembly of Asia in which he suggested that Augustus' birthday should become a feast day.[11] By 5/4 BC, at the latest, *princeps* was in formal use, as is clear from Augustus' fifth Cyrene edict. In it, the emperor could cite a decree of the senate that mentioned 'Imperator Caesar Augustus, our princeps'.[12]

Clearly, by this stage, *princeps* had become a way to denote the superior power of the ruler. That it was necessary to develop such a new formulation shows both the need to have a way to address someone in a position of supreme power and the difficulties in finding a sufficiently non-monarchical term. Tellingly, the ultimate solution was one in which an existent term was reshaped. That placed the position of the ruler into a context that people already knew and so made it easier to understand and accept the emperor's new position in the political landscape – for rulers and subjects alike. Similarly, the name Augustus, by which the ruler would be known from 28/7 BC onwards, was not a new invention but a term with precedent, even if it had not been used as a name before. There are stories

---

[9] Hor. *Carm.* 1.2.50, 21.14, *Epist.* 2.1.256. Cf. Prop. 4.6.46; Ovid, *Fasti* 2.142; J. W. Rich, 'Making the Emergency Permanent: "Auctoritas, Potestas" and the Evolution of the Principate of Augustus', in: Y. Rivière (ed.), *Des réformes augustéennes* (Rome 2012), 29–113, 38n5. For the notion of Augustus' subjects taking the hint, see B. Levick, *Augustus: Image and Substance* (Harlow 2010), 74.

[10] Cic. *Rep.* 1.34; *Nat Deor.* 3.11. Cf. Cic. *Planc.* 20; Diodorus 31.24; Corn. Nepos, *Cato* 2.2. For a full overview of Republican *principes*, see L. Wickert, 'Princeps (civitatis)', *REAL* 22 (1954), 1998–2296, 2014–29, with references for Pompey cited in 2022–4. Cf. J. A. Lobur, *Consensus, Concordia, and the Formation of Roman Imperial Ideology* (London–New York 2008), 33, 229n145. On the differentiation between *princeps* and *princeps senatus*, see A. Cooley, *Res Gestae Divi Augusti: Text, Translation, and Commentary* (Cambridge 2009), 160–1, though her observations do not exclude the possibility that the *term* princeps could have been inspired by the *position* of 'princeps senatus'. Cf. G. Rowe, 'Reconsidering the Auctoritas of Augustus', *JRS* 103 (2013), 11–15.

[11] *OGIS* 2.458.

[12] *SEG* IX.9, lines 86–7, using the Greek *hegemon*, which doubtlessly translates as *princeps* (as it does in the *RGDA*).

in ancient literature that the name Romulus was also considered, but dismissed for its regal connotations. This once again shows the problems that the notion of kingship posed to the new ruler.[13]

Indicators of Imperial Power and the Importance of Expectations

Certainly at the beginning of the principate, the emperor needed to be recognisably in supreme power, but not as a king. How could that problem be solved? An important avenue was the adaptation of existing (Republican) prototypes to shape the formulations and iconography through which absolute rule was portrayed.[14] Whether this adaptation was done by subjects who tried to formulate the position of the new ruler in terms that they understood, or by the Roman emperor (or those surrounding him) in order to avoid the semblance of monarchy, is often hard to say. It is likely that both played their part. Importantly, the original meaning of the prototypes did not entirely disappear in their 'imperial' adaptation. The senatorial background of the word *princeps* would continue to influence the way in which emperors were supposed to behave. Once chosen, the new emperor had to relate to the expectations that such a 'traditional' title brought with it – however much it had been adapted to the new situation. To an extent, this is how all communication works. Words do transmit not only messages but also normative values. In the act of communicating messages, shared meaning is produced and reproduced.[15] In this light, it

---

[13] Precedent for Augustus: Ennius, *Annales* 4.5: 'augusto augurio'. On Romulus as name for the new emperor: Suet, *Aug.* 7.2; Florus, 2.34.66; Dio, 53.16.7. Note also Augustan bronze coins showing Numa Pompilius on the reverse, *RIC* I^2 Augustus 390–6, with A. Turner, 'The Importance of Numa Pompilius: A Reconsideration of Augustan Coins', *Open Library of Humanities* 2 (2016), http://doi.org/10.16995/olh.58.

[14] M. Koortbojian, *The Divinization of Caesar and Augustus: Precedents, Consequences, Implications* (Cambridge 2013), 9, noting how the image of Divus Julius 'was amalgamated from a series of models, whose roles in Roman tradition were well established yet rarely – if ever – the subject of such appropriation', with similar observations on the cult statue (p. 49) and augural images (pp. 50–78). Likewise, A. L. Kuttner, *Dynasty and Empire in the Age of Augustus: The Case of the Boscoreale Cups* (Berkeley – Los Angeles 1995), 172–98, rightfully emphasises the importance of Republican prototypes for imperial imagery. Cf. Lobur, *Consensus*, 8, and already P. Zanker, *The Power of Images in the Age of Augustus* (Ann Arbor 1988).

[15] M. Griffin, 'Sociocultural Perspectives on Visual Communication', *Journal of Visual Literacy* 22 (2002), 29–52. Cf. the various articles in L. Albornoz (ed.), *Power, Media, Culture. A Critical View from the Political Economy of Communication* (London – New York 2015), esp. C. Bolaño, 'Communication and Epistemological Struggle' (189–99) and V. Mosco, 'The Political Economy of Communication: A Living Tradition' (35–57). See above, p. 13.

Figure 1.2 Portrait of Caesar on a coin. Rome, March 44 BC. Silver denarius (3.77 g). CAESAR IMP; laureate head of Caesar, with depictions of priestly objects (*lituus* and *culullus*) / M. METTIVS; figure of Venus, holding Victory, sceptre and shield. RRC 480/3
Source: Heritage Auctions, 7-9-2011, lot 23260

seems unhelpful to dismiss a term like *princeps* as a Republican 'façade'.[16] Rather, it was a way for Roman subjects to formulate and understand a changing political landscape.

Such adaptations of terms and images could take shape at a remarkable speed. A prime example is the way portraiture on coins developed. It is easy to forget how revolutionary it was for Caesar to have his face on Roman coins. He was the first living Roman to be so depicted (Figure 1.2). Even if iconographically the coins looked like earlier Roman coins, it was easy for opponents to suggest that Caesar aimed for kingship or divinity. After all, the faces on earlier coins in the east had been of Hellenistic kings, whereas portraits on Roman coins had been those of gods. Yet, in the civil war following Caesar's assassination, the various Roman contestants were represented on coinage as a matter of course.[17] By the time Augustus gained

---

[16] On the notion of a Republican façade, see F. J. Vervaet, 'Arrogating Despotic Power through Deceit: The Pompeian Model for Augustan *Dissimulatio*', in: A. J. Turner/K. O. Chong-Gossard/F. J. Vervaet (eds), *Private and Public Lies. The Discourse of Despotism and Deceit in the Greco-Roman World* (Leiden – Boston 2010), 133–66, 165, and already N. K. Mackie, '*Res Publica Restituta*. A Roman Myth', in: C. Deroux (ed.), *Studies in Latin Literature and Roman History* 4 (Brussels 1986), 303–40.

[17] C. Rowan, *From Caesar to Augustus (c. 49 BC–AD 14). Using Coins as Sources* (Cambridge 2018), 33–8, 57–79; Koortbojian, *The Divinization of Caesar and Augustus*, 94. B. Woytek, 'Heads and Busts on Roman Coins: Some Remarks on the Morphology of Numismatic Portraiture', *Revue numismatique*, 171 (2014), 45–71, notes the similarities between early imperial coin portraits and Roman elite funerary masks. This would be another way to show how these coin portraits appealed to existing modes of representation.

sole supremacy, being portrayed on coinage had become a standard Roman practice and was apparently no longer strictly associated with Hellenistic kingship or divinity. After something has happened for the first time, it creates a precedent, which can but need not become common habit.

This rapid adaptation did not mean that the new emperor could be depicted on coins in whatever way suited him. There was still a need to be recognisable, but also to avoid looking like a king. After all, as stated above, one of the reasons for Caesar's death had been that he appeared too monarchical. Shifts in what was deemed tolerable for a Roman ruler were certainly possible, sometimes even rapid, but going beyond the range of acceptable behaviour carried real risks with it. This meant that Roman traditions, and the expectations that these created, formed a framework in which rule had to take shape.

Within this framework, several indicators of imperial status appeared over time. First, a distinctive titulature took shape, both for Roman emperors and for people immediately surrounding them. There were forms of address that were specific to individual emperors, and titles that increasingly defined emperorship. None of this, however, appears to have happened very systematically. Second, there developed specific modes of depicting emperors on coinage, in relief sculpture and paintings and through statuary. For instance, size mattered. Only emperors and gods were to be represented larger-than-life size.[18] Increasingly, also, one could recognise emperors on imagery because they were the only ones depicted seated on a throne. Over time, the image of the enthroned emperor became a prominent way of showing the position and sovereignty of the ruler.[19] This would ultimately even lead to coinage under Justinian (527–65) showing an enthroned effigy of the

---

[18] B. Ruck, *Die Grossen dieser Welt: Kolossalporträts im antiken Rom* (Heidelberg 2007), 201–4, 228; H. Cancik, 'Größe und Kolossalität als religiöse und aesthetische Kategorien. Versuch einer Begriffsbestimmung am Beispiel von Statius, Silvae I: Equus Maximus Domitiani Imperatoris', *Genres in Visual Representations: Visible Religion* 7 (1990), 51–65. But note J. Mylonopoulos, 'Divine Images versus Cult Images. An Endless Story about Theories, Methods, and Terminologies', in: J. Mylonopoulos (ed.), *Divine Images and Human Imaginations in Ancient Greece and Rome* (Leiden – Boston 2009), 1–19, 10.

[19] B. Kiilerich, 'The Image of Anicia Juliana in the Vienna Dioscurides. Flattery or Appropriation of Imperial Imagery', *SO* 76 (2001), 169–90, 177, with further references. Seated togate statues were a Julio-Claudian innovation, as argued by Kuttner, *Dynasty and Empire*, 37–44. On representations of the emperor at Rome, see also S. Benoist, 'Images, effigies et corps du prince à Rome: une mise en scène du discours impérial dans la cité', in: D. Carrangeot/B. Laurioux/V. Puech (eds), *Rituels et cérémonies de cour de l'Empire romain à l'âge baroque* (Septentrion 2018), 25–37.

Figure 1.3 Justinian enthroned. Antioch, 529–33. Bronze follis (8.1 g–31 mm): D N IVSTINIANVS P P AVG. Full image of the emperor on the throne, holding sceptre and cross-topped globe/Large M between star and crescent, with cross and mintmarks.
Source: Sear, *Byzantine Coins and Their Values* no. 214
Source: MA-shops, 2-9-2021, lot MA-ID: 21302156

emperor on the obverse (Figure 1.3).[20] Emperors were allowed to be seated, but everyone else had to stand. Third, certain symbolic trappings of power over time became linked to emperorship, such as the imperial cloak, crowns and sceptres. These 'powerful props' remained potentially controversial: a crown or ornate jewellery could easily call regal associations to mind. The fourth-century author Eutropius explicitly notes how Diocletian's request to be adorated and his choice to wear precious stones were 'suited rather to royal usages than to Roman liberty'. The increasingly common way of denoting rule by the use of Tyrian purple (in *toga picta* and *tunica palmata*) was one mode in which new symbolism could take shape.[21]

Naming the Emperor: Titles and Forms of Address

If one traces imperial titulature over time, a number of points stand out. An obvious one which is not always taken sufficiently into account is how clearly dominant the names used by the emperors were from the very beginning of imperial rule. They may have tried to avoid regal

---

[20] T. Vorderstrasse, 'Coinage of Justin II and its Imitations. Historical, Papyrological, Numismatic and Archaeological Sources', *Anatolica* 35 (2009), 15–35, 16.
[21] Eutr. 9.26; M. Bradley, *Colour and Meaning in Ancient Rome* (Cambridge 2009), 206–8. See below p. 69–77.

Figure 1.4 The names of Augustus and his heirs: Lugdunum, 2 BC–AD 4. Aureus (7.77 g.–20 mm): laureate portrait of Augustus, surrounded by the legend CAESAR AVGVSTVS DIVI F PATER PATRIAE. Augustus' name changed during his reign, but continuously expressed his superiority/ togate images of Augustus' grandsons and heirs Gaius and Lucius Caesar with shield and spear, with depictions of priestly objects (*simpulum* and *lituus*). Surrounding the image are the full titles of the princes: C L CAESARES AVGVSTI F COS DESIG PRINC IVVENT. *RIC* I (2nd ed.) Augustus 206
Source: ANS 1905.57.282, American Numismatic Society

connotations, but their dominance was there for all to see. The formal name of the first emperors, regularly inscribed on coins or on stone was *Imperator Augustus Caesar, divi filius*, which can be roughly translated as 'Consecrated commander, Caesar, son of a god' (Figure 1.4).[22] Going by *princeps* may have softened the blow, but there must have been little doubt as to who was in control. Caesar was, of course, a family name, which through its use by emperors who were unrelated to Rome's first dynasty over time became an integral part of the imperial title, denoting an intended successor, at least up to the fourth century. Its inclusion emphasised how dynastic Roman emperorship was from the very beginning and throughout the ages.[23]

Imperial nomenclature developed over time. Importantly, through a wide range of inscriptions, papyri and the legends on coinage, it is possible to trace this development in detail for the entire period that this book focuses on. This makes emperors' names and titles a useful indicator of how the presentation of emperorship shifted from one dynasty to another,

---

[22] Syme, 'Imperator Caesar'; Millar, 'The First Revolution'.
[23] O. Hekster, *Emperors and Ancestors. Roman Rulers and the Constraints of Tradition* (Oxford 2015), 10.

and under the influence of major societal shifts. Looking at the imperial nomenclature on central coinage up to the very end of the fifth century (Graph 1.1), there is some striking continuity, but also some noticeable change. Coin legends form an interesting starting point, since coinage was the most flexible medium at imperial disposal – messages on coins could be fairly easily adjusted to central demands and shifts in representational emphasis.[24] So what happens over time with the most frequently recurrent elements of the emperors' name on coins?

Clearly, at least in coin legends, *Augustus* was *the* defining element in the imperial name, with almost all central coins that were struck for the emperor (about 75 per cent of all coins, with the remainder almost exclusively struck for other members of the imperial family) including that title. When there were more claimants to the position of Augustus in the empire, the abbreviation AUGG (or even AUGGG or AUGGGG) could indicate as much, which was a useful way to indicate the position of one claimant without denying the status of another, as happened, for instance, in the third-century Gallic and Britannic empires.[25]

Imperator was an important element from the beginning up to the reign of Constantine, as was *Caesar*, though not quite so systematically included. Other parts of the imperial name were more open to change. *Pontifex Maximus* (Greatest Pontiff) and *Tribunicia Potestas* (Power of the Tribune) are noticeably present on coins up to the mid-third century and *consul* is one of the dominant elements of the imperial name from the middle of the first to the end of the second century. They are replaced over time, however, with *Dominus Noster* (our lord) becoming, with *Augustus*, the dominant form of address throughout the fourth and fifth centuries. The epithet *Pius Felix* (Pious and Fortunate) appears on coinage in the later second century, and becomes standard on coinage from the late-third to early-fourth century onwards.

It is tempting to link shifts in these recurrent elements of the emperor's name to political and cultural shifts in the Roman empire. Society changed, and these changes had an impact on how Roman subjects recognised and addressed their emperors. For instance, consul, the supreme political office of the Roman republic, became systematically incorporated as part of the imperial address in the reign of Vespasian (69–79). This was the start of a

---

[24] Hekster, *Emperors and Ancestors*, 317.
[25] M. Lyne, 'Some New Coin Types of Carausius and Allectus and the History of the British Provinces AD 286–96. *The Numismatic Chronicle* 163 (2003), 147–68; 163–4; P. Grierson/ M. Mays, *Catalogue of Late Roman Coins in the Dumbarton Oaks Collection and in the Whittemore Collection. From Arcadius and Honorius to the Accession of Anastasius* (Cambridge [Mass.] – London 1992), 85–6.

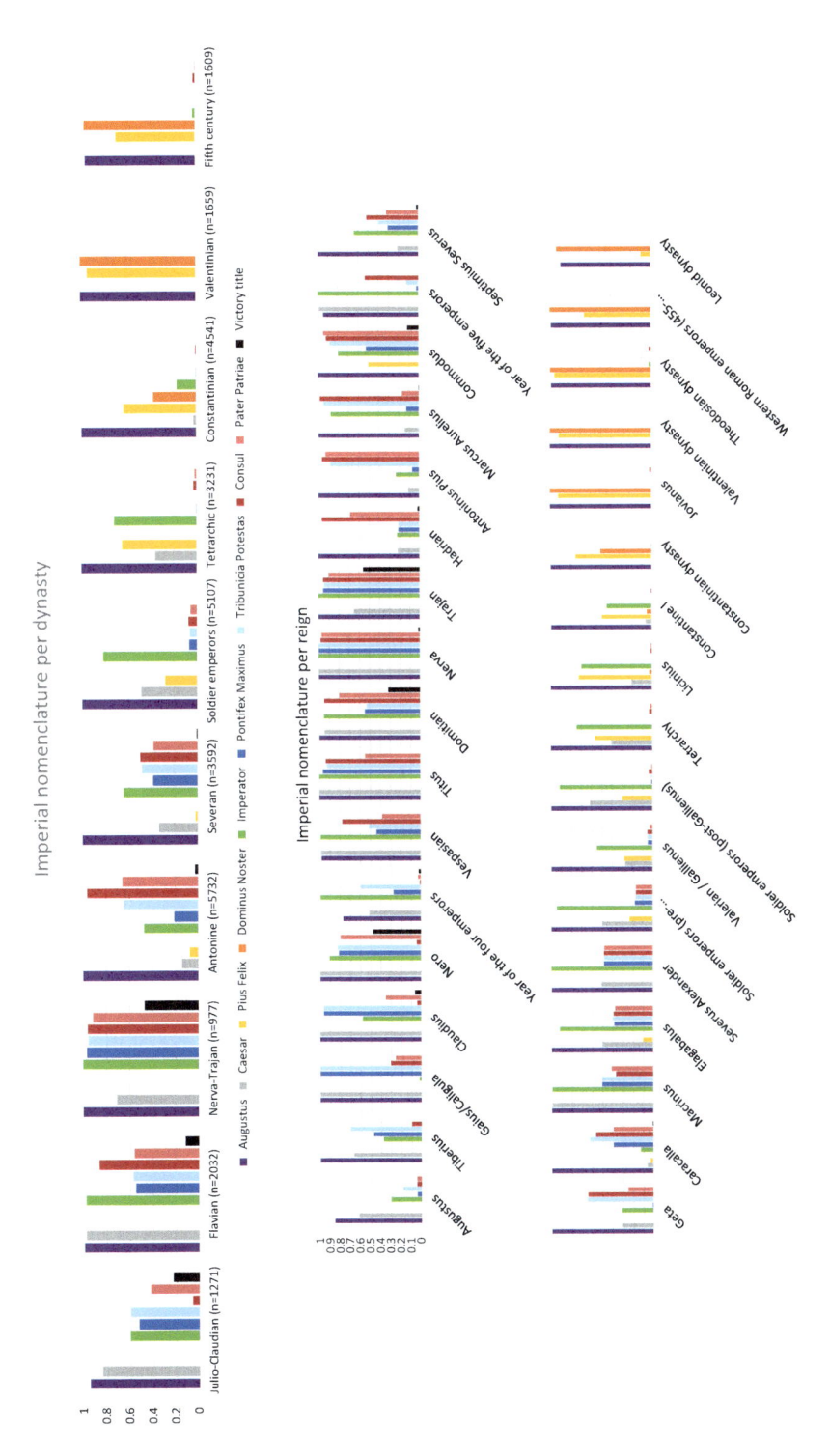

Graph 1.1 Imperial titulature on central coinage

new dynasty that could not easily legitimise itself through reference to the first emperor.[26] The fact that at the beginning of the reign the so-called *Lex de Imperio Vespasiani* was issued, transmitted through a surviving bronze inscription listing the legal formulations of imperial powers, suggests discussion about the basis of emperorship at the time, which might be one reason to stress his role as consul more systematically.[27] When, during the course of the third century AD, outside assailants started to threaten the empire, the emperor's military capacity became the essential qualification for holding power, and the legal basis became much less important.[28] Consequently, *consul* disappeared as a core element of the emperor's titulature. Roughly the same trajectory can be seen for *Tribunicia Potestas*, which indicated that the emperors held the power of the people's tribune – which had been an important element of imperial powers from Augustus onwards. Instead of these references to Republican precedent that had been so important in establishing emperorship, it became important to stress the emperor's military prowess. His support by the gods also became more prominent, for instance through naming the emperor's divine luck.

The shift in the way in which the emperor was named from the fourth century onwards may likewise be linked to major changes in state and society. Rather than continuing with the standard elements *Imperator Caesar Augustus*, which had been the official names (*praenomen, nomen* and *cognomen*) of the first emperor and were taken up as defining aspects of the imperial name, the emperor became *Dominus Noster,* and was more than ever before described as *Pius Felix*. This period also saw major changes in the empire, as its territory was effectively divided into an eastern and western half after the death of Theodosius in 395. Especially in the west, the position of the emperor weakened due to barbarian conquests of parts of his territory and the increasing influence of a few extremely wealthy senatorial families.[29] Moreover, in the course of the fourth century, the empire moved decisively towards Christianity as the dominant religion.[30] It is likely that the changing ways of defining the emperor reflect the

---

[26] B. Levick, *Vespasian* (London – New York 2017²), 83–4.
[27] *ILS* 244. The seminal article remains P. A. Brunt, 'Lex de Imperio Vespasiani', *JRS* 67 (1977), 95–111. On probable earlier laws of accession: P. Buongiorno, *Claudio, il principe inatteso* (Palermo 2017), 59–62.
[28] De Blois, *Image and Reality*, 177–86, 231–46.
[29] See A. H. M. Jones, *The Later Roman Empire, 284–602* (Oxford 1964), 523–62. See further below p. 191–194 on the relation between emperor and senators in the later empire.
[30] Still seminal: R. MacMullen, *Christianizing the Roman Empire: (A.D. 100–400)* (New Haven 1984), though modern literature on the subject is enormous.

new political situation and societal norms. At the same time, it is worth stressing the relative continuity, not only through the continuation of the title Augustus, but also because there was ample precedent in Roman history for addressing leading men as *Pius*, *Felix* or *Dominus*. In fact, inscriptions show that emperors were already (generally) described as *dominus* (lord) rather than *optimus* (best) from the late-second century onwards, anticipating the standardisation of *Dominus Noster* on coins.[31]

The importance of continuity is also reflected in the coinage of the so-called western kingdoms, such as that of the Vandals and the Visigoths. They modelled their coins, including the legends, so closely on Roman imperial coins that they are often referred to as 'pseudo-imperial' or 'imitation' coins.[32] Even after Romulus Augustulus was deposed as the last western emperor in 476, the Visigoth king Euric continued to copy Roman issues. Only in 573 would Visigoth kings place their own names on coins, with *Rex* or *Rex Inclitus* as the legend.[33]

In the eastern empire, too, there was a substantial stability in the imperial form of address, up to an important innovation by Justinian II in 690. From then on, Christ rather than the emperor appeared on the obverse of coins, and the imperial image on the reverse was accompanied by *Servus Christi* (Servant of Christ).[34] This was a major innovation which made visible a changed relationship between emperor and church. That it took so long for imperial coins to recognise this shift – bringing it beyond the period that this book deals with – once more emphasises the relative continuity of imperial address on coinage up to that moment.

Growing Christianity may have been a factor in a less noticeable but much earlier shift in the imperial name. The combination of epithets Pius Felix was systematically abbreviated on coins as PF, and it appears that after the conversion of the empire, the preferred Christian reading of that abbreviation became *Perpetua Felicitas*, losing the pagan connotations

---

[31] C. Noreña, *Imperial Ideals in the Roman West. Representation, Circulation, Power* (Cambridge 2011), 284–97.

[32] A. Kurt, *Minting, State, and Economy in the Visigothic Kingdom: From Settlement in Aquitaine through the First Decade of the Muslim Conquest of Spain* (Amsterdam 2020), 34–6; P. Grierson, *Coins of Medieval Europe* (London 1991), 3–6; R. Naismith, 'Gold Coinage and its Use in the Post-Roman West', *Speculum* 89 (2014), 273–306.

[33] Kurt, *Minting, State and Economy*, 86–9. The parallels to the title *Pontifex Inclitus*, which came to replace Pontifex Maximus, is noticeable: see below p. 139.

[34] M. Humphreys, 'The 'War of Images' Revisited. Justinian II's Coinage Reform and the Caliphate', *The Numismatic Chronicle* 173 (2013), 229–44; 232–9.

while retaining the traditional abbreviation.[35] This may not have been enough in the east, where PF disappears from coin legends under the Leonid dynasty (457–518) although it remained part of the western Roman emperors' titulature up to the deposition of Romulus Augustulus. It is tempting to suggest a linguistic reason, with the Latin reading as an insufficient alternative for the Greek-speaking eastern empire.[36] The disappearance of *Pontifex Maximus* from coin legends cannot easily be linked to upcoming Christianity, as it anticipates Constantine's conversion by about a century. In inscriptions, however, the title continued much longer as part of the imperial name, before being changed into *Pontifex Inclitus* (Honourable Pontiff), a title that was still used for the emperors Valentinian III (425–55) and Marcian (450–7).[37] This, like the new meaning of the abbreviation PF, shows how something that closely resembled the old could shed associations that no longer fitted the times.

That *Pontifex Maximus* remained part of imperial titulature in inscriptions much longer than on coins shows the first of two ways in which it is too limiting to look only at recurring elements in imperial coin legends when trying to understand how individual emperors were addressed. There were, after all, many other types of documents in which names and forms of address for emperors recur. The second is that focusing on recurring elements obscures that names and portraits also identified individually. They were, in other words, not solely defined as emperor, but also as a specific individual who was emperor.

As to the first point; our surviving evidence for imperial names includes provincial coins, papyri, and all sorts of inscriptions.[38] The emperor was

---

[35] S. Betjes, *The Mind of the Mint*, 118–28 and J.-P. Callu,'Pia Felix', *RN* 155 (2000), 189–207; 206. See further below p. 138. The preferred reading need not have been the only reading, and Pius Felix could also be employed in a Christian context, as Euseb. *Laud. Const.* 7.12 shows: J. R. Fears, 'The Theology of Victory at Rome: Approaches and Problems', *ANRW* II.17.2 (1981), 736–826; 749–52, 822–3.

[36] F. Millar, *A Greek Roman Empire. Power and Belief under Theodosius II (408–450)* (Berkeley – Los Angeles 2006), 20–5; 93–7 for Greek as the increasingly dominant language in the Eastern Empire at all levels. Note the confusion on some fifth-century coins caused by an insufficient knowledge of Latin: J. P. C. Kent, 'Coin Inscriptions and Language', in: D. F. Clark/ M. M. Roxan/ J. J. Wilk (eds.), *The Later Roman Empire Today* (London – New York 1992), 9–18; R. Schlösser, 'Römischen Münzen als Quelle für das Vulgärlatein', *Quaderni Ticinesi* 18 (1989), 319–35.

[37] R. Dijkstra/ D. van Espelo, 'Anchoring Pontifical Authority: A Reconsideration of the Papal Employment of the Title *Pontifex maximus*', *JRH* 41 (2017), 312–25; 315–17; A. Cameron, 'Pontifex Maximus: from Augustus to Gratian – and Beyond', in: M. Kahlos (ed.), *Emperors and the Divine – Rome and its Influence* (Helsinki 2016), 139–59, with references to earlier literature. See below p. 135 on the emperor's expected role as religious intermediary.

[38] See above, pp. 5–8.

addressed by a variety of subjects in legal text, letters, historiographical treatises and speeches. When looking at these, the image is less clear-cut than the overview above suggests. *Augustus* is the defining title in inscriptions too, mostly translated as σεβαστός (*sebastos*) in Greek. Regularly, however, the title was transliterated as Αὔγουστος, and increasingly also as βασιλεύς (*basileus*), which meant 'king' and was a translation of the Latin *rex*.[39] Taking a wider view and including so-called unofficial titulature shows even more diversity, if not almost total chaos, in the way emperors are addressed. Numerous names, titles, honorifics and epithets that are not found on the coins struck by imperial mints are linked to emperors as a matter of course in inscriptions, papyri, and in historiographical and panegyrical texts.

A recent analysis of so-called unofficial titles from Augustus to Severus Alexander (31 BC–AD 235) shows how titles like Optimus (Princeps), αὐτοκράτωρ μέγιστος, θεός, Ὀλύμπιος (*autokrator megistos, theos, Olympios*) and a variety of superlatives occur as a matter of course.[40] The range of titles and honorifics in these inscriptions can differ enormously, showing more leeway in addressing the emperor than modern scholars often assume. The exception to this flexibility are the so-called military *diplomata*, which are highly systematic in their inclusion of specific imperial titles, and are therefore often used to trace the 'official' name of an emperor – the ancient equivalent of having a modern document notarised properly.[41] Yet, for much of our epigraphic evidence, local differentiation and wide variations from reign to reign are most noticeable. Still, there may have been some increase in military and divine epithets over time.[42] That local appellations occasionally went too far is clear from a fascinating inscription from Hierapolis, in which the emperor Antoninus Pius was described as γῆς καί θαλάσσης δεσπότην ('lord over land and sea') only for the last word to be exchanged for the less dominant κύριον, still expressing dominance, but less forcefully. After Hierapolis had started, others followed suit, and addressing

---

[39] D. Kienast/ W. Eck/ M. Heil, *Römische Kaisertabelle. Grundzüge einer römischen Kaiserchronologie* (Darmstadt 2017⁶), 21. It seems that the transliteration Αὔγουστος in documentary inscriptions became more common from the reign of Constantine onwards: R. W. B. Salway, 'Constantine *Augoustous* (not *Sebastos*)', in: J. Drinkwater/ R. W. B. Salway (eds.), *Wolf Liebeschuetz Reflected. Essays Presented by Colleagues, Friends, and Pupils* (London 2007), 37–50.

[40] S. Bönisch-Meyer, *Dialogangebote. Die Anrede des Kaisers jenseits der offiziellen Titulatur* (Leiden – Boston 2021), 430–526 based on roughly a thousand inscriptions, ca. 400 in Latin and ca. 600 in Greek.

[41] Hekster, *Emperors and Ancestors*, 32–3.   [42] Bönisch-Meyer, *Dialogangebote*, 420.

the emperor as δεσπότης became more common in inscriptions.[43] There was no total flexibility, but the range of how to address the emperor was substantial, and could widen over time.

So-called provincial coins, struck under the auspices of members of local elites, show some of the same flexibility in imperial nomenclature as the inscriptions do. Obverse legends became increasingly diverse in the first two centuries AD, and could be different from one region to the next. Still *Augustus*/ σεβαστός and *Caesar*/ Καῖσαρ were fairly fixed elements, and from the reign of Vespasian onwards *Imperator*/ αὐτοκράτωρ came into regular use.[44] Though there was a wide variety in honorifics that were added to the imperial names, at least parts of the general pattern that could be seen in central coin legends can be traced in provincial coinage too, with shifts when the new Flavian dynasty was established under Vespasian, and more military and religious honorifics in the course of the third century.[45]

Papyri addressing emperors, of which vast quantities have survived, can usefully be linked to titles on coins and in inscriptions.[46] Noticeably, the core elements of the imperial name remained the same, at least for the period up to the death of Constantine in 337.[47] There seems, however, to have been a trend towards addressing emperors with increasingly elaborate epithets, perhaps comparable to the superlatives in the epigraphic evidence.[48] There is also a rough trend towards fewer inclusions of 'Republican' titles. In the third century, new military and religious epithets appeared at the same time as these aspects of imperial power were emphasised on coins.[49] Under Constantine and his successors yet another epithet, *perpetuus* (αἰώνιος; *aionios*) was introduced. Finally, there is a noticeable change in how *dominus* is increasingly translated into Greek as δεσπότης

---

[43] T. Ritti, 'Antonino Pio, "Padrone della terra e del mare". Una nuova inscrizione onorario da Hierapolis di Frigia', *Annali di archeologia e storia antica* 9-10 (2002-2003), 271-81, with further references. Christoph Michels kindly referred me to *Dig.* 14.2.9 (Volusius Maecianus) in which Antoninus refers to himself as '*kyrios* of the world'.

[44] V. Heuchert, 'The Chronological Development of Roman Provincial Coin Iconography', in: C. Howgego/ V. Heuchert/ A. Burnett (eds.), *Coinage and Identity in the Roman Provinces* (Oxford 2005), 29-56; 47.

[45] Bönisch-Meyer, *Dialogangebote*, 530-3.

[46] J. de Jong, 'More than Words: Imperial Discourse in Greek Papyri', *Cahiers du Centre Gustave Glotz* 25 (2014), 243-61; 249; Bönisch, *Dialogangebote*, 533-6.

[47] R. S. Bagnall/ K. A. Worp, *Chronological Systems of Byzantine Egypt* (Leiden - Boston 2004²), 45, also noting the absence of papyri dating by the regnal year of the ruling emperor for the period 337-537.

[48] J. de Jong 'Emperor Meets Gods. Divine Discourse in Greek Papyri from Roman Egypt', in: M. Kahlos (ed), *Emperors and the Divine - Rome and its Influence* (Helsinki 2016), 22-55; 35.

[49] De Jong, 'More than Words', 254-6; de Jong, 'Emperor Meets Gods', 36-9.

(*despotes*), which as we saw above includes strong notions of supremacy and ownership, rather than the earlier (less dominant) κύριος.[50] As in the epigraphic and Roman provincial evidence, the imperial name is more fluid in papyri than on central coinage, but the general development of imperial address seems similar. This greater fluidity may be (partly) explained by the greater space on papyri and inscriptions than was the case for the spatially delineated legend on coins, and by greater access to papyri and inscriptions. Many scribes could produce a text but only a very few people decided what was on coins.[51] That makes the similarities of the developments in the different sources even more noticeable.

A second reason why looking only at recurring elements of imperial names and titles is insufficient to analyse how emperors could be addressed and recognised is that it ignores those elements that were specific to individual emperors. Perhaps most importantly, all emperors following Augustus held their own *praenomen*, such as Tiberius (14–37), Claudius (41–54) or Constantine (311–37). These names were important markers on coins, papyri and inscriptions. They were so well known that they could often be abbreviated. Such names were regularly not the names with which emperors were born. Names could be changed upon accession, such as Diocles, who latinised his name to Diocletian when he became emperor (284–305).[52] These names are how individual emperors were mostly identified in ancient historiography, by authors such as (amongst very many others) Tacitus, Plutarch, Dio Cassius, Ammianus Marcellinus or Procopius.

Alongside their proper names, ancient authors also identified emperors through specific nicknames, often in derogatory ways. A good example is the way in which Cassius Dio uses the negative names 'Sardanapalus', 'Pseudo-Antoninus' or 'the Assyrian' when describing the reign of the emperor commonly known as Elagabalus (218–222), whose 'real' imperial name was Marcus Aurelius Antoninus. Nor was Dio the only one to use such nicknames for the emperor, who is named as 'the unholy little Antoninus' in a contemporary papyrus.[53] Indeed, in the ancient world,

---

[50] Bagnall/ Worp, *Chronological Systems*, 45; D. Hagedorn/ K. A. Worp, 'Von *kyrios* zu *despotès*. Eine Bemerkung zur Kaisertitulatur im 3/4. Jhdt.', *ZPE* 39 (1980), 165–77.

[51] The discussion on who was responsible for the creation and selection of coin types is immense. See for an overview and convincing suggestions: L. M. G. F. E. Claes, 'A Note on the Coin Type Selection by the A Rationibus', *Latomus* 73 (2014), 163–73.

[52] Kienast/ Eck/ Heil, *Römische Kaisertabelle*, 53–329, with references to sources for the names of all emperors from Augustus to Theodosius.

[53] *P. Oxy.* 46. 3299. Cf. *P. Oxy* 46.3298; J. Osgood, 'Cassius Dio's Secret History of Elagabalus", in: J. Madsen/ C. H. Lange (eds.), *Cassius Dio: Greek Intellectual and Roman Politician* (Leiden – Boston 2016), 177–190; 180–3; C. Bruun, 'Roman Emperors in Popular Jargon: Searching for

the Romans seem to have been noticeable for the frequency with which they gave nicknames to their rulers, often referring to effeminacy and apparently extreme (sexual) preferences.[54] But not all nicknames were negative, and it appears that several emperors wanted to be called by particular nicknames and that soldiers in particular often used monikers, perhaps to stress an informal relation between the emperor and his troops.[55] This illustrates the complexities of understanding how emperors were addressed. Nicknames can define a ruler as much as 'official' names.

Emperors also had a 'dynastic' name, such as Flavius or Severus. Like a *praenomen*, this name could be changed, most obviously through adoption. This was often more a political statement than a legal process. Septimius Severus (193–211), effectively founder of a new dynasty, adopted himself as Marcus Aurelius' (161–80) son fifteen years after that emperor had died. Severus changed his elder son's name into Marcus Aurelius Antoninus in the process, although the latter is better known through his military nickname Caracalla (211–17).[56] These fictitious adoptions to strengthen imperial claims occurred regularly in the fourth century, with several emperors assuming the name Valerius or Flavius as a matter of course.[57] This increased adoption of existing imperial names shows the importance of dynastic considerations in Rome. At the same time, there was often no male heir to succeed, with a noticeable dearth for over 150 years after the death of Theodosius II (402–50), whose elevation to co-Augustus at the age of one highlights the importance of dynastic legitimacy.[58] Usurpers therefore boosted their status by appropriating famous dynastic names or by marrying into the dynasty they had just replaced, or into the one before.[59]

However important specific names, titles and honorifics were to emphasise imperial status and to differentiate the emperor from anyone else

---

Contemporary Nicknames (1)', in: L. de Blois et al. (eds.) *The Representation and Perception of Roman Imperial Power* (Amsterdam 2003), 69–98; 87; A. V. Makhlaiuk, 'Emperors' Nicknames and Roman Political Humour', *Klio* 102 (2020), 202–23; 223–4, 226.

[54] Plut. *Cor.* 11.3–4; Makhlaiuk, 'Emperors' Nicknames', 216–7, 223.
[55] Bruun, 'Contemporary Nicknames', 9; Makhlaiuk, 'Emperors' Nicknames; 228–9, both with references.
[56] Hekster, *Emperors and Ancestors*, 209–17.
[57] Kienast/ Eck/ Heil, *Römische Kaisertabelle*, 19.
[58] G. Dagron, *Emperor and Priest. The Imperial Office in Byzantium* (Cambridge 2003), 26–7; J. Szidat, *Usurpator Tanti Nominis. Kaiser und Usurpator in der Spätantike (337–476 n. Chr.)* (Stuttgart 2010), 165–82. On the role of 'child emperors', see esp. M. McEvoy, *Child Emperor Rule in the Late Roman West, AD 367–455* (Oxford 2013), and below p. 129.
[59] Dagron, *Emperor and Priest*, 40; Szidat, *Usurpator*, 200.

in the realm, there were also regular occasions in which an individual emperor was named differently. Contemporary authors who were writing about a reigning emperor could simply speak of 'Caesar'. This type of address may have become more elaborate over time. In a famous *panegyric* to Trajan (98–117), Pliny the Younger addressed the emperor as 'Caesar'. In the later so-called *Panegyrici Latini* (289–389) there seems to have been some inflation in how to address the emperor. The emperor could be addressed as 'sacritissimus imperator' (most sacred imperator), but 'imperator Augusti', 'Caesar invictus' (unconquered Caesar), and 'Augustus venerabilis' (reverent Augustus) also featured with some frequency.[60]

The associations that addressing the emperor as Caesar brought with it could vary substantially. Context played an important role. The most splendid ambiguities can be found in the work of Optatian (died sometime between 333–5). In one poem, he addresses Constantine with the line 'holy Caesar (*sancte Caesar*), in your serenity take pity on your poet'. At first sight, this looks like a fairly old-fashioned appeal to the emperor, reminiscent of Horace's *Odes*. Yet Optatian's poems need to be seen to be understood, as they are spectacular when visually laid out on the page. When the poem is written out in grid form, the word 'Caesar' forms the centre of a cross. In another poem, the title *Constantinus Pius et Aeternus imperator* forms the vertical axis of a Chi-Rho sign, which had great symbolic importance to Constantine. Even apparently traditional formulations could gain new meaning.[61] At other times, orators seem to use traditional names and titles to emphasise how traditionally Roman the emperor was, ignoring the apparent inflation of titles. The fourth-century rhetorician Libanius addresses the emperors Julian (360–3) and Theodosius (379–95) with ὦ βασιλεῦ, without superlatives. A panegyric from 397 by the poet Claudian for the western emperor Honorius (393–423) described how the latter had

---

[60] M.-C. L'Huillier, *L'Empire des mots. Orateurs gaulois et empereurs romains, 3e et 4e siècles* (Paris 1992), 453–5 for references and precise numbers. Cf. C. Ware, 'Panegyric and the Discourse of Praise in Late Antiquity', *JRS* 109 (2019), 291–304 for a recent overview of scholarship on panegyric discourse.

[61] Optat. *Carm.* 2 and *Carm* 14 with visualisations in M. Squire/ J. Wienand (eds.), *Morphogrammata. The Lettered Art of Optatian. Figuring Cultural Transformations in the Age of Constantine* (Paderborn 2017), 28, 39, plate 1; J. Elsner/ J. Henderson, 'Envoi: A Diptych', in: Squire/ Wienand, *Morphogrammata*, 495–515; 497–8, 503. See M. Squire, 'Optatian and Is Lettered Art', in: Squire/ Wienand, *Morphogrammata*, 55–120; 96–7 on Optatian's appropriation of classical terminology to formulate Christian concepts. On Constantine and the Chi-Rho sign, see below, p. 100.

changed from 'Caesar' into 'princeps' (without any adjectives) and had become the equal of his brother Arcadius (383–408), the eastern emperor.[62] Much later still, a letter from the eastern emperor Anastasius (491–518) to the Roman Senate includes all the 'republican' titles of *consul, proconsul, tribunicia potestas,* and *pater patriae*.[63]

At the same time, the statesman and scholar Cassiodorus (c. 485–c. 585) could write a letter to that very emperor, addressing him as 'most clement emperor' (*clementissime imperator*) and 'most dutiful of princes' (*piissime principum*).[64] The letter was written in the name of King Theodoric, who as king of the Ostrogothic Kingdom (493–526) and regent of the Visigoths (511–26) ruled much of the western empire. Theodoric seems to have been extremely careful in the use of his own titles, and Cassiodorus assiduously avoided calling the western king *Augustus*. Yet, a public inscription from the Via Appia, near Terracina, could still address him as 'Our lord (*dominus noster*) the glorious and famous king (*rex*) Theodoric, perpetual emperor (*semper Augustus*) ... propagator of the Roman name'.[65] For the people who set up the inscription, almost certainly members of the local elite, Theodoric, like his predecessor Odovacer (476–93) who had deposed the 'last' western emperor Romulus Augustulus (475–6), was rightful ruler, and hence *Augustus*.[66]

Clearly, the original Augustan ways of denoting emperorship as *Imperator Caesar Augustus* or as *princeps* retained their importance for over 500 years, at all levels of society. Moreover, the addition of superlatives to the imperial titles can be placed in a wider pattern; it runs parallel to the creation of elaborate titles for a range of (political and religious) positions during the late-fourth and fifth centuries. If non-imperial officeholders could be *gloriosissimus, magnificentissimus, eloquentissimus, eminentissimus* or *excellentissimus*, it need hardly surprise that the emperor, too, became *piissimus*.[67]

---

[62] Lib. *Or.* 12.2, 13.1; Claudian, *Panegyric on the Fourth Consulate of Honorius*, 170–1: 'mutatur principe Caesar; protinus aequaris fratri'.

[63] *Collectio Avellana*. no. 113.

[64] Cassiodorus, *Variae* I, 1, 1–2; M. S. Bjornlie, 'Audience and Rhetorical Presentation in the *Variae* of Cassiodorus', *Revue belge de philologie et d'histoire* 92 (2014), 187–207; 194–5.

[65] *CIL* 10.6850-2; L. E. Tacoma, *Roman Political Culture. Seven Studies of the Senate and City Councils of Italy from the First to the sixth Century AD* (Oxford 2020), 218–21.

[66] S. Fanning, 'Odovacer 'Rex', Regal Terminology, and the Question of the End of the Western Roman Empire', *Medieval Prosopography* 24 (2003), 46–55 for an analysis of Odovacer's imperial profile.

[67] E. M. Schoolman, 'Vir Clarissimus and Roman Titles in the Early Middle Ages: Survival and Continuity in Ravenna and the Latin West', *Medieval Prosopography* 32 (2017), 1–39; 6–13.

Tracing forms of imperial address over time, if only cursorily, in various types of sources allows for two main observations, the first about continuity and change. There was substantial stability in the use of central elements, certainly in the Latin appellations. When, during the so-called Tetrarchy (293–306), the empire was ruled by four men who in a form of collegiate emperorship held different parts of the realm, the two senior emperors were named *Augustus* and the two junior ones *Caesar*, embedding the new system through traditional titulature.[68]

The translation of the different terms into Greek showed some flexibility throughout Roman history, and one can trace some shifts in emphasis of the various titles in different media, but at the core there was pronounced continuity over centuries. More variance, however, existed in the use of additional elements to the imperial name, both titles and honorifics. For some of these extra elements, there seem to have been chronological developments that can be linked to political and societal changes in the empire. Noticeable shifts can be traced during the period of the Flavian dynasty, an increased emphasis on military and religious epithets when the empire faced difficulties in the third century, and a transition of the 'pagan' elements in imperial nomenclature in the fourth and fifth century. Yet, not all media and all regions followed the same pattern, and not all patterns were linear. The disappearance of 'Republican' elements from central coinage, for instance, seems to have had little impact on how emperors were addressed in panegyric speeches. It seems likely that the core elements of how emperors were addressed became synonymous with emperorship as such, and became defining features.

Additional titles and honorifics could be more easily adapted to time and place, linked to changing societal norms, and adhering to what people expected of their emperor in very different contexts. Not everything was possible, however, when adapting these titles and epithets. It seems that there were certain conventions and expectations that were kept in mind, as the shift of *Pontifex Maximus* to *Pontifex Inclitus*, the new meaning of the abbreviation PF, or the development of *Dominus Noster* on both inscriptions and coins showed. The dominance of specific epithets for different emperors in one region suggests that local traditions played an important role, too, when naming the emperor.[69] People, it seems, could choose from

---

[68] O. Hekster/ S. Betjes/ S. Heijnen/ K. Iannantuono/ D. Jussen/ E. E. J. Manders/ D. Syrbe, 'Accommodating Political Change under the Tetrarchy (293–306)', *Klio* 101 (2019), 610–39; 611.

[69] Bönisch-Meyer, *Dialogangebote*, 396–7, 403–13.

an array of names, titles and honorifics when addressing the emperor, with regional variations, and an extension of the range over time.

This leads to the second main observation.[70] It is extremely difficult to establish an 'official' imperial name at any given moment. The legend on central coinage differed from the titulature on military *diplomata*, which was in turn different from what was written on (legal) papyrus texts or from how emperors were directly addressed in speeches or letters. Certain emperors preferred to be called by nicknames. What, then, set an 'official' title apart from an 'unofficial' one? There seems not to be a single ancient source which says some such distinction existed. So why is this an important differentiation in modern research?[71] If there is no real system as to which titles were included in 'official' documents (mostly defined as either centrally issued documents, and/or documents with a legal status), and if 'non-official' documents (which include letters to the emperor) could apparently even make up titles for the emperor, what then defined how emperors could be addressed? Rather than looking for formal structures, it might be more useful to think of the imperial name as established, or even better, permanently negotiated, in some sort of dialogue between ruler and different groups of subjects, with a range of possibilities.[72]

Many titles and epithets seem to describe what people expected or wanted the emperor to be. This becomes explicit when the statesman and orator Symmachus addressed the then ten-year old emperor Gratian (367–83) as *Novi saeculi spes parta* (longed-for hope of a new age).[73] But epigraphic appellations to Septimius Severus as *indulgentissimus et clementissimus princeps dominus noster* (kindest and mildest prince, our lord) function in a very similar way, expressing expectations of what the emperor should be.[74]

---

[70] The argument set out here is massively influenced by a discussion on this subject with Mike Peachin.

[71] There is a strong argument that 'official' titles are those voted by the Senate, though that still does not include all relevant nomenclature: B. Parsi, *Désignation et investiture de l'empereur romain* (Paris: Sirey 1963); R. Talbert, *The Senate of Imperial Rome* (Princeton 1987) 354–71; Bönisch-Meyer, *Dialogangebote*. 11–15.

[72] The notion of the imperial name as a dialogue is rightfully emphasised by Bönisch-Meyer, *Dialogangebote*, 11–15, although she still stresses the importance of an official/non-official divide when looking at imperial titles.

[73] Symmachus, *Oration* III, 2, with G. Kelly, 'Pliny and Symmachus', *Arethusa* 46 (2013) 261–87; 277 and McEvoy, *Child Emperor Rule*, 51–2 on the difficulties of praising a child emperor.

[74] *CIL* 10.7274 (Panhormus, Sicilia; 198). Cf. *CIL* 10.7343 and 2.4020. Already Augustus was *Diligentissimus et Indulgentissimus* (*CIL* 9.5420), Trajan, Hadrian, Antoninus Pius, Commodus and Septimius Severus all *Indulgentissimus* (*CIL* 6.1492; 12.1797; 11.1424; 8.8702; 5.27), Antoninus also *Optimus et Indulgentissimus* (*I.Eph.* II 282), as was Marcus Aurelius (*CIL* 14.4003). The epithet was more common under Caracalla, who was referred to as *dominus*

Other parts of the nomenclature – like the inclusion of Republican titles under Vespasian, or fictitious cognomina in the late empire – indicated how emperors tried to boost their legitimacy or popularity.

Naming the emperor meant defining him. Considering the size of the empire and the diversity of its population, it may not be surprising that people's expectations of the emperor's role and character varied substantially. Whether someone named the emperor as 'most pious princeps' or as 'unconquered saviour' may tell us much about the person addressing the ruler. That both forms of address were possible, sometimes even for the same emperor, may be more indicative of how multifaceted and ill-defined Roman emperorship was.[75] Yet, in all its flexibility and experimentation, only the emperor was *Augustus*. The name of Rome's first emperor continued to define the institution. This was the name that was unique to the emperor and used by all of them for over 500 years.

Depicting the Emperor: Portrait, Reliefs and Statuary

Names and titles were essential to address emperors and were visible throughout the empire. They did not show what an emperor looked like. To distribute the physical image of individual emperors, there were imperial portraits in sculptural or painted displays, and on coinage. These portraits, often carved from marble or cast in bronze, were nearly omnipresent in Roman society: in public squares, temples, theatres, villas, and many other places. The number of statues must have been staggering.[76] Portraits played a crucial role in visualising the emperor, often placing him in a specific context in historical reliefs or paintings. The imperial titulature on coin legends, at least for the first three centuries of imperial rule, usually surrounded a recognisable imperial

---

indulgentissimus quite frequently: *CIL* 6.1052; 6.1060; 10.7276; 17.4/1, 54; 17.4/1, 68–9; 17.4/1, 90; 17.4/1, 100; 17.4/1, 226. Cf 6.1082; 12.6531; 8.10305; 8.22384; 8.6307; 8.6998–7000; 8.7972; 8.19493; *ILAlg*.II 1, 3592: Bönisch-Meyer, *Dialogangebote*, 432–3, 454–5, 458–9, 474–5, 486–9, 505–6, 514–17, 520–3.

[75] See p. 239–240 on the names and forms of address for imperial women.
[76] M. Pfanner, 'Über das Herstellen von Porträts. Ein Beitrag zu Rationalisierungsmaßnahmen und Produktionsmechanismen von Massenware im späten Hellenismus und in der römischen Kaiserzeit', *Jahrbuch des Deutschen Archäologischen Instituts* 104 (1989), 157–257, 178–9 estimates that there were between 25,000 and 50,000 original portraits of Augustus alone. See also J. Fejfer, *Roman Portraits in Context* (Berlin 2008), 384–9 and 393–4. Tac. *Ann*. 1.73, suggests that there were likenesses of Augustus in all households. Cf. P. Stewart, *Statues in Roman Society. Representation and Response* (Oxford 2003), 118–56 on the impact on public life of this 'other population of Rome'.

face (Figure 1.4, above). Statues and busts were almost invariably placed on bases which provided their audiences with additional information, such as the emperor's names.[77] In this way the emperor was known to the many inhabitants of the Roman empire who would never be able to see him in person.

The specific physical features and depicted hairstyle of the portraits of individual emperors were surprisingly consistent throughout the empire. That made an emperor recognisable to the many people in the empire, wherever they would encounter such a portrait. The reason for this was that the vast majority of portraits were replicas or adaptations of a common prototype developed at the imperial centre. Who designed the prototype remains unclear, but it seems probable that sudden innovations in portraiture will have needed to be approved by the ruler, or someone close to him.[78] Of course not all portraits were equally similar to that prototype. Portraits on cameos that circulated at the imperial court and those on coins that were commissioned by central mints were probably closest to imperial wishes.[79] Likewise, portraits in and around imperial residences and in military contexts will have cohered closely to a central 'portrait type'.[80] In all likelihood, a plaster or clay copy of the prototype of the emperor's portrait was distributed throughout the Roman empire to form the point of reference for locally constructed portraits.[81]

There is some evidence that portraits were sent out to the provinces at the beginning of a reign, or on specific occasions, though most references for this come from the fourth century and later.[82] Most Roman emperors, like many monarchs before and after them, had different portraits designed for them during the course of their reign. From the beginning of the twentieth century onwards, these so-called portrait types have been systematically catalogued, allowing us an overview of the vast majority – if not perhaps all – of Roman

---

[77] J. M. Højte, *Roman Imperial Statue Bases: from Augustus to Commodus* (Aarhus 2005).
[78] K. Fittschen, 'Zum angeblichen Bildnis des Lucius Verus im Thermen-Museum', *Jahrbuch des Deutschen Archäologischen Instituts* 86 (1971), 214–52; 220–4; D. Boschung, *Die Bildnisse des Augustus, Das römische Herrscherbild* Vol. 1 (2) (Berlin 1993), 8–10; K. Fittschen, 'Methodological Approaches to the Dating and Identification of Roman Portraits', in: B. Borg (ed.) *A Companion to Roman Art* (Hoboken 2015), 52–70.
[79] R. von den Hoff, 'Kaiserbildnisse als Kaisergeschichte(n): Prolegomena zu einem medialen Konzept römischer Herrscherporträts', in: Winterling, *Zwischen Strukturgeschichte und Biographie*, 15–44, 22–6. On the problems of comparison, see Fejfer, *Roman Portraits*, 411.
[80] Von den Hoff, 'Kaiserbildnisse', 23–4.
[81] Pfanner, 'Über das Herstellen von Porträts'; Von den Hoff, 'Kaiserbildnisse', 20–1; Fittschen, 'Methodological Approaches', 56.
[82] Ando, *Imperial Ideology*, 229–31. For the earlier empire, references are scarcer, but it seems likely that when Tacitus mentions how Tiberius was 'shown to all the legions' (*Annales* 1.3.3) it is the image he is talking about, rather than the man himself travelling to all legionary camps.

imperial portrait types. Sometimes it is possible to date these new types, either because they can be traced through changes on the portraits on coins, or because names or titles on statue bases allow for a precise historical context.[83]

Not all portraits in parts of the empire that were more remote will have been equally close to what was intended. In a very well-known aside in a letter to the emperor Hadrian, Arrian of Nicomedia describes seeing a statue of the emperor on the shore of the Black Sea, at Trapezus (in Cappadocia) which was 'rather fitting in its posture', but 'neither did it resemble you, nor was it very beautiful'.[84] Likewise, when Marcus Cornelius Fronto writes to Marcus Aurelius (161–80) on how his portraits can be found everywhere, he also notes that these images were often badly carved and very dissimilar.[85] A survey of probable representations of Hadrian and Trajan in Greece and Asia Minor suggests that there were many portraits that differed more or less radically from the centrally issued images. Local considerations often influenced how an emperor was depicted, much as was the case for how he was named.[86] There is, then, a risk that the portraits that are so assiduously catalogued form only a part of the surviving corpus, since they exclude those images that do not cohere to the standardised image of an emperor, leading us to overestimate how systematic images were dispersed.[87]

It does seem clear, however, that there was at least an attempt to disseminate such a systematic image of the emperor. Noticeably, the patterns of new types are very different for one emperor or the other – both in how often new types were designed and in how substantial the shifts of the imperial portrait within one reign could be. Still, it is possible to trace some sort of pattern when looking at the development of imperial portraiture from the early empire to Justinian.

---

[83] This research has been the prime focus of scholars from the German school of portrait studies, accumulating in a famous series of catalogues, called *Das römische Herrscherbild*. The new digital *Roman Imperial Portraits Dataset (RIPD)* (https://doi.org/10.17026/dans-2ca-hxmd) forms the basis for quantitative statements about portraits in this book. See S. Heijnen/ O. Hekster/ T. Hermsen, 'Roman Imperial Portraits Dataset (RIPD)', *Research Data Journal for the Humanities and Social Science* 7 (2022). 1–14.

[84] Arrian, *Periplus*, 1.3–4; P. Zanker, *Provinzielle Kaiserporträts. Zur Rezeption der Selbstdarstellung des Princeps* (Munich 1987), 7.

[85] Fronto, *Ad M. Caesarem* 4.12.4

[86] L. A. Riccardi, 'Uncanonical Imperial Portraits in the Eastern Roman Provinces: The Case of the Kanellopoulos Emperor', *Hesperia* 69 (2000), 105–32.

[87] Digital approaches to imperial portraits may be able to compensate for this bias: J. Pollini, 'Die Umarbeitung römischer Kaiserbildnisse: Deutungsprobleme und neue Lösungsansätze mit Hilfe digitaler Technologie', in: T. Greub, *Revisionen des Porträts. Jenseits von Mimesis und Repräsentation* (Leiden – Boston 2020), 243–70; D. Srirangacher Ramesh/ S. Heijnen/ O. Hekster/ L. Spreeuwers/ F. de Wit, 'Facial Recognition as a Tool to Identify Roman Emperors. Towards a New Methodology', *Humanities and Social Sciences Communications* 9.78 (2022).

Like imperial names and titles, portraits and statues changed over time. Also, like names and titles, different portraits made use of different ways in which individuals had been presented in earlier Roman history – or even of ways in which people outside of the Roman empire, like Hellenistic kings, had been presented – and in doing so may have triggered associations with these historical figures, and with the context in which they had lived. Of course, portraying Roman leaders pre-empted Roman emperorship, but not by much. Depicting living men in monumental art on a large scale only took off in Rome during the late republic. Before that time, depicting someone too prominently was seen as too regal and therefore problematic, as criticism of Marius and Sulla's imagery makes clear.[88] In the late-Republican struggles for power, the likes of Pompey the Great (106–48 BC) and Julius Caesar started to project their image more systematically, in order to show their status and prestige to a wide audience.[89] In doing so, they mixed traditional Roman ways of depicting people with elements of Hellenistic regal portraits. Pompey's image, for instance, copied the hairstyle of Alexander the Great, but combined it with recognisable features, making it less idealised than any surviving Alexander portrait (Figure 1.5).[90] Alexander was a potent symbol of heroic leadership, making it fashionable to incorporate elements of Alexander's noticeable portraiture into the imagery of powerful leaders. Throughout Roman imperial history, Alexander remained an important paradigm for rule, not only in the Greek east but in the whole Mediterranean world. Caesar's portraits, like those of Pompey, combined different styles, mixing idealised and recognisably individual features. There was, however, great variation between the various surviving portraits, with some emphasising the more realistic 'veristic' style much more than others.[91]

The scale at which portraits of Caesar began to circulate in the empire was already unheard of, certainly after they appeared on coinage, the first time that a living individual was depicted on the obverse of Roman coins.[92] Yet, a true systemisation of portraiture in much larger numbers only started under Augustus. The speed with which a specific portrait of the new ruler became known throughout the empire was remarkable, and was

---

[88] See above p. 23; Stewart, *Statues in Roman Society*, 28–35.
[89] See especially L. Giuliani, *Bildnis und Botschaft: hermeneutische Untersuchungen zur Bildniskunst der römischen Republik* (Frankfurt am Main 1986).
[90] Giuliani, *Bildnis und Botschaft*, 56–105.
[91] Koortbojian, *The Divinization of Caesar and Augustus*, 100–10; P. Zanker, 'The Irritating Statues and Contradictory Portraits of Julius Caesar', in: M. Griffin (ed.), *A Companion to Julius Caesar* (Malden – Oxford 2009), 288–314.
[92] See above p. 28.

Figure 1.5 Pompey's image: Marble head (h. 25 cm), from the tomb of the Licinii Crassi (Porta Salaria), Rome, c. 10, Ny Carlsberg Glyptothek, Copenhagen, inv. no. 733. The portrait shows Pompey in a recognisably Roman way, indicating age and experience, but with the hairstyle of Alexander the Great
Source: CKD – Radboud University Nijmegen

helped by circulating it on coins.[93] This was a new type of imagery, inspired at least as much by classical Greece as by Roman and Hellenistic precedents (Figure 1.6).[94] Remarkably, the portrait would not change substantially for the rest of Augustus' life, presenting him as an idealised youth even when he was into his seventies. That sort of continuity will have made it very easy for people to recognise the image of the emperor, but much less helpful to recognise the emperor in person from his portraits.

Augustus' smooth and ageless imperial image would set the standard for a substantial period of time. Even posthumous portraits of Caesar came to

---

[93] A. Burnett, 'The Augustan Revolution Seen from the Mints of the Provinces', *JRS* 101 (2011), 1–30.
[94] Zanker, *Power of Images*, 98–100; T. Hölscher, 'Greek Styles and GreekAart in Augustan Rome: Issues of the Present Versus Records of the Past' in: J. I. Porter (ed.), *Classical Pasts: The Classical Traditions of Greece and Rome* (Princeton 2006), 237–59; 243; G. Adornato, 'The Dilemma of the Prima Porta Augustus: Polykleitos or not Polykleitos?', in: G. Adornato/ I. Bald Romano/ G. Cirucci/ A. Poggio (eds.), *Restaging Greek Artworks in Roman Times. Archeologia e arte antica* (Milan 2018), 245–74.

Figure 1.6 Augustus' new imagery: Marble statue of Augustus in cuirass (h. 2.06 m), from the Villa of Livia (Prima Porta), c. 20, Musei Vaticani, Braccio Nuovo. Inv. No. 2290. Throughout his life, and even after his death, Augustus was portrayed as a young man with idealised looks that recall Classical Greek examples
Source: CKD – Radboud University Nijmegen

resemble Augustus' classicising portrait, as did the portraits of Augustus' grandsons Gaius and Lucius, both of whom had been considered as heirs before they died in youth.[95] The images of Augustus' ultimate successor Tiberius, and those of his successors Caligula (37–41) and Claudius were likewise beardless and with a hairstyle that was very similar to the other members of the so-called Julio-Claudian dynasty. The portraits of Caligula, Claudius and Nero did, however, show age much more than Augustus' portraits had, making them more realistic, although it remains unclear why.

All Julio-Claudian portraits were clearly images of individual rulers, but they also expressed continuity of emperorship through their reproduction of highly recognisable physiognomic details of their predecessors' portraits. Looking at these portraits, people would be able to know who their emperor was, and instantly know that he was a member of the ruling Augustan household.[96] This 'visual alignment' of images was an important element in formulating early emperorship. The emperor Nero (54–68) tried to present himself in a more monarchical way, with less emphasis on his Augustan lineage. But his portraiture initially still followed Julio-Claudian precedent, and even when he changed that, it was less a completely new style than a moving away from what had become the norm. It seems that the well-known smooth and youthful Julio-Claudian portraiture still underlay the new imagery, although the thick neck, much broader face and near-radiate hairstyle was very different from that of Augustan portraiture.[97]

A more substantial change, however, took place during the civil wars that marked the end of the Augustan dynasty (68–9) and at the beginning of the Flavian dynasty. Much like we noted in the development of imperial titulature, references to the first emperor became less important and were replaced by notions that held Republican connotations.[98] A form of realism that had been important in Republican imagery was reintroduced into

---

[95] Zanker, 'The Irritating Statues and Contradictory Portraits of Julius Caesar', 310; K. Lorenz, 'Writing Histories from Roman Imperial Portraiture: The Case of the Julio-Claudian Princes', in: C. M. Draycott/ R. Raja/ K. Welch/ W. T. Wootton (eds.), *Visual Histories of the Classical World: Essays in Honour of R. R. R. Smith* (Turnhout 2018), 171–80.

[96] Fejfer, *Roman Portraits*, 272, referring back to A. K. Massner, *Bildnisangleichung: Untersuchung zur Entstehungs- und Wirkungsgeschichte der Augustusporträts (43 v. Chr.–68 n. Chr.)* (Berlin 1982), 42–141.

[97] E. Winsor-Leach, 'The Politics of Self-Presentation. Pliny's "Letters" and Roman Portrait Sculpture' *ClAnt* 91 (1990), 14–39; 25; E. La Rocca, 'Nero's Image: The Four Portrait Types', in: S. Bartsch/ K. Freudenburg/ C. Littlewood (eds.), The *Cambridge Companion to the Age of Nero* (Cambridge 2017), 354–8; C. Vout, 'Art and the Decadent City', in: Bartsch/ Freudenburg/ Littlewood, *The Age of Nero*, 179–94. Fejfer, *Roman Portraits*, 273 considers it 'a completely new style'.

[98] See above, p. 32.

Figure 1.7 Vespasian and the qualities of age: Marble head (h. 45.7 cm), from Carthage c. 70–80, British Museum, London, 1850,0304.35. At the beginning of his reign, Vespasian's portrait returned to a Republican representation of age and experience. Later portraits looked more like Julio-Claudian portraits
Source: © The Trustees of the British Museum

Flavian portraiture. It suggested the experience and (military) qualities that came with age (Figure 1.7).[99] The change in imagery was not, however, absolute. Recently, Heijnen has argued convincingly that the most dramatic aspects of the Flavian shift in portraiture were short-lived. When Vespasian had secured his position, his portraiture began to again look more like Julio-Claudian imagery. New portraits appeared in which the emperor looked younger, his face was smoother and receding hairline much

---

[99] R. M. Schneider, 'Gegenbilder im römischen Kaiserporträt: Die neuen Gesichter Neros und Vespasians', in: M. Büchsel / P. Schmidt (eds.), *Das Porträt vor der Erfindung des Porträts* (Mainz 2003), 59–76; S. E. Wood, 'Public Images of the Flavian Dynasty: Sculpture and Coinage,' in A. Zissos (ed.), *A Companion to the Flavian Age of Imperial Rome* (Malden – Oxford 2016), 129–47; 131; J. Fejfer, 'The Image of the Emperor: Seeing Domitian', in: A. Raimondi Cominesi/ N. de Haan/ E. M. Moormann/ C. Stocks (eds.), *God on Earth: Emperor Domitian. The Re-invention of Rome at the End of the 1st Century AD* (Leiden 2021), 73–82; C. Vout, 'Portraiture and Memory Sanctions', in: Raimondi Cominesi et al., *God on Earth*, 175–80.

less pronounced.[100] There were still marked Flavian elements in the portrait (such as a pronounced jaw and bulking forehead) which allowed the portraits of Vespasian's sons Titus and (79–81) Domitian (81–96) to resemble those of their father. But the portraits of the Flavians were not a world away from Julio-Claudian imagery.

This mix between continuing recognised practice while incorporating different elements in designing imperial portraits continues throughout Roman history up to the mid-fourth century. Imperial portraiture reflects political shifts and attempts by emperors to present themselves differently from their predecessors. In doing so, various established modes of representation are used, with new elements occasionally added into the mix. Famously, Hadrian (117–38) was the first emperor to be portrayed with a beard (Figure 2.4, below). Frequently, this is attributed to that emperor's interest in Greece but it may equally be linked to Hadrian's attention to the provinces in a more general sense, or even have been an attempt to look more military.[101] Noticeably, the beard figures on portraits that do not age during a twenty-year reign, recalling Augustus' portraiture. That does not negate the newness of depicting an emperor with a beard, but it shows how such new elements were formulated within a developing range of possibilities. These new elements were often picked up by successors and incorporated into an emerging repertoire. For almost a century after Hadrian, emperors of the Antonine and Severan dynasty were shown with a full beard. By that stage, it is unlikely that the beard referred to something so specific as 'Greekness', if it ever did. Rather, it will have indicated continuity of a certain mode of emperorship. In this representational repertoire, Augustus' portrait remained a clear point of reference. Much like Vespasian could use the Republican exaggerated realism to show how he was a different kind of ruler than his predecessor Nero, so later emperors could return to a more or less 'pure' Augustan style to refer to a preferred mode of emperorship. The portraits of emperors such as Trajan (98–117) and Constantine are perhaps the most explicit examples of this pattern.

Portraits of emperors were not just there to allow people to recognise an individual ruler, they also formed a visual vocabulary that expressed the

---

[100] S. Heijnen, *Portraying Change. The Representation of Roman Emperors in Freestanding Sculpture (ca. 50 BC–ca. 400 AD)* (PhD Nijmegen 2021), 55–6, with fig. 10 a–b.
[101] P. Zanker, *Die Maske des Sokrates: Das Bild des Intellektuellen in der antiken Kunst* (Munich 1995), 206–12; C. Vout, 'What's in a Beard? Rethinking Hadrian's Hellenism', in: S. Goldhill/ R. Osborne (eds.), *Rethinking Revolutions through Ancient Greece* (Cambridge 2006), 96–123; 99–119; S. Heijnen, 'Living Up to Expectations: Hadrian's Military Representation in Freestanding Sculpture', *BABESCH* 95 (2020), 195–212.

kind of emperor that was depicted. In the third century, military elements like stubble or a short beard and very short cropped hair often featured on emperors' portraits.[102] But short hair could also be combined with the full beard of the Antonines and Severans, which made reference to a more 'senatorial' status, as happened on portraits of Macrinus (217–18) and Pupienus (238).[103] An extreme case of mixing messages can be seen during the reign of Gallienus (253–68), in whose reign the Roman empire faced dire difficulties, including the capture of his father Valerian (253–60) by the new-Persians, the proclamation of a Gallic counter-empire (260–74) and a similar claim from Palmyra, led by Queen Zenobia (270–2).[104] In one surviving colossal portrait from Rome, Gallienus closely resembles Hadrian, but in a different portrait, also from Rome, the emperor is portrayed very differently, as a charismatic youth, incorporating elements of the portraiture of Alexander the Great and Augustus (Figures 1.8-9). These portraits transmitted different messages, probably to different groups of people.[105] More than with the imperial name, there seems to have been one clearly defined imperial portrait, but some variation was possible.

Over time, it seems that the importance of expressing forms of emperorship through portraiture became more important than depicting individual emperors. An important step in this trajectory was during the Tetrarchy, the new 'rule of four' which made it necessary to publicise the fact that different rulers were in charge simultaneously. Naming two emperors as *Augusti* and two as *Caesares* was one way of embedding this new system of government in traditional terminology.[106] Visual alignment of the portraits of the rulers was another way of making people understand the new political structure. Such assimilation of portraiture was not new in itself – it was the standard way to express continuity of a ruler with his predecessors – but under the Tetrarchy the four rulers so closely resembled one another that it was difficult to tell one from the other. With their square heads, stubble and short hair, they were

---

[102] M. Bergmann, *Studien zum römischen Porträt des 3. Jahrhunderts nach Christus* (Bonn 1977); S. Heijnen/ E. M. Moormann, 'A Portrait Head of Severus Alexander at Delft', *AA* 2020, 163–70; 165–7; D. E. E. Kleiner, *Roman sculpture* (New Haven – London 1992), 361–76; O. Hekster, *Rome and its Empire, AD 193–284* (Edinburgh 2008), 59–60.

[103] It is probably not coincidental that the third-century historian Herodian comments that Macrinus took Marcus as an example and stresses the senatorial status of Pupienus (Hdn. 5.2.4; 8.7.3–5).

[104] De Blois, *Image and Reality*, 76–91, with references.

[105] L. de Blois, *The Policy of Emperor Gallienus* (Leiden 1976), 197; K. Fittschen, 'Das Bildnis des Kaisers Gallien aus Milreu: zum Problem der Bildnistypologie', *Madrider Mitteilungen* 34 (1993), 210–27; Canepa, *Two Eyes of the Earth*, 80–1.

[106] See above, p. 43. On the importance of formulating the new power structure in familiar terms: Hekster et al. 'Accommodating Political Change', 610–39.

Depicting the Emperor: Portrait, Reliefs, Statuary 55

Figures 1.8–1.9 Different images of Gallienus: Two portraits of Gallienus from Rome show him in entirely different ways, representing different views of emperorship. One colossal statue closely recalls portraits of Hadrian, whereas the other is much more idealised, emphasising the emperor as a young beauty, much like images of Alexander the Great and Augustus had done
(Figure 1.8) Marble bust (h. 53 cm.) from Rome, c. 265–8, Ny Carlsberg Glyptotek, Copenhagen, inv. 832
Source: CKD – Radboud University Nijmegen
(Figure 1.9) Marble bust (h. 38 cm), from Rome, 261–8, Rome, Museo Nazionale Romano – Museo delle Terme / Thermenmuseum, inv. 17147.
Source: CKD – Radboud University Nijmegen

instantly recognisable as 'soldier emperors'.[107] But who was who was much more difficult to determine. Context still often made it possible to understand which of the four rulers was intended, and there were differences between the image of the *Caesares* and of the *Augusti*, creating a sort of 'double duality' which fitted precedent much better than a rule of four.[108] The Tetrarchic

---

[107] R. Rees, 'Images and Image: A Re-Examination of Tetrarchic Iconography', *Greece & Rome* 40 (1993),181–200; M. Bergmann, 'Bildnisse der Tetrarchenzeit', in: A. Demandt / J. Engemann (eds.), *Imperator Caesar Flavius Constantinus. Konstantin der Grosse. Ausstellungskatalog* (Mainz 2007), 58–73.
[108] Hekster et al., 'Accommodating Political Change', 626–33.

experiment was not successful, and led first to civil war and then the sole reign of Constantine. Constantine's portrait mixed elements of earlier imperial styles (especially those of Augustus and Trajan) with the Tetrachs' large eyes. So did the portraits of his sons, up to the point that it is difficult to distinguish one son from the other – or from their father.[109] Constantine's image became so dominant under his successors that, apart from the brief reign of Julian the Apostate (361–3) who sported a beard, it became increasingly difficult to tell different emperors apart.[110]

After Constantine's death, then, there increasingly was one rather homogenous imperial image, strongly linked to a Constantinian prototype, rather than a range of possibilities from which to design individualised portraits. The emperors of the Valentinian and Theodosian dynasty (364–457) all had similar features with perhaps slightly different hair. Individualised elements were still regularly added, but some of the fifth- and sixth-century emperors are difficult to identify from their portrait if no name is added.[111] There is never any doubt that these are images of emperors. From Constantine onwards, diadems were regularly added to emperors' images and only emperors could wear these, although not all images of emperors showed diadems.[112] This was only one of the explicit references to kingship which were added to representations of Roman emperors in the Constantinian period and beyond. Explicit monarchical references had apparently become much less problematic in depicting Roman rule, partly through increased interactions with the Sasanian empire and exposure to eastern tradition. Romans had always been aware that there were alternative paradigms of rulership, as the continuous popularity of images of Alexander makes clear. Closer relations with the Sasanian court brought these alternative models closer to home.[113] But in these very late-antique images, the echoes of

---

[109] E. Varner 'Innovation and Orthodoxy in the Portraiture of Constantine and His Sons', in: N. J. Baker-Brian/ S. Tougher (eds.), *The Sons of Constantine, AD 337–361. In the Shadows of Constantine and Julian* (London 2020), 97–132, esp. 98–106.

[110] This included a formalisation as to who was allowed to dedicate imperial statues, with bronze portraits even requiring the permission of the emperor himself: B. Ward-Perkins, 'The End of the Statue Habit, AD 284–620', in: R. R. R. Smith / B. Ward-Perkins (eds.), *The Last Statues of Antiquity* (Oxford 2016), 295–308; 303–4, 307.

[111] R. R. R. Smith, 'Late Antique Portraits in a Public Context: Honorific Statuary at Aphrodisias in Caria, A.D. 300–600'. *JRS* 89 (1999), 155–89; 182–3; F. Guidetti, 'Between Expressionism and Classicism: Stylistic Choices as Means of Legitimisation in Late Fourth-Century Imperial Portraits', in: M. P. García Ruiz / A. J. Quiroga Puertas (eds.), *Emperors and Emperorship in Late Antiquity. Images and Narratives* (Leiden – Boston 2021), 139–76.

[112] F. Kolb, *Herrscherideologie in der Spätantike* (Berlin 2001), 76–9. See below p. 81–100 on the development of imperial attributes.

[113] Canepa, *Two Eyes of the Earth*, with 199 on the diadem. Börm, 'Antimonarchic Discourse', 18.

Augustan portraiture were still visible. Even in a wholly changed society, some continuity in visual language remained.

Some of this continuity can also be traced in the way people discussed what seeing the emperor in person entailed. What should an emperor look like, in the eyes of his subject? For this, we can look for references in ancient biography, historiography and panegyric. Importantly, all of these genres assumed a link between physical appearance and character, often described as 'physiognomic consciousness'.[114] This is, in many ways, similar to Hellenistic theories of appropriate royal appearance, which can be roughly summarised as claiming that what makes a king is simply looking like one.[115] There was, then, much cultural continuity beyond what is commonly defined as Roman. In any case, describing or portraying an emperor was not value neutral. Rhetorical references to physical appearance could be used for positive or negative effect.[116] In such descriptions, the facial features played a prominent role. This is already a relevant theme in speeches from the Roman republic, with Cicero emphasising the importance of describing someone's face, and especially their eyes.[117] Eyes were especially said to show character, as handbooks on rhetoric and on physiognomy make clear.[118] This attention to eyes can be traced in various descriptions of emperors throughout Roman history, from Suetonius to Ammianus and beyond: Augustus is said to have had 'clear, bright eyes', whereas Julian's eyes were 'fine and full of fire, a sign of his sharp mind'.[119] The eyes of Theodosius II (408–50) were 'black and

---

[114] E. C. Evans, *Physiognomics in the Ancient World* (Philadelphia 1969), 5–6, with over 2,000 examples in the appendices. See also M. Bradley/ E. Varner, 'Roman Noses', in: M. Bradley (ed.), *Smell and the Ancient Senses* (London – New York 2014), 171–80.

[115] R. R. R. Smith, *Hellenistic Royal Portraits* (Oxford 1988), 50–3; O. Hekster/ R. Fowler, 'Imagining Kings: From Persia to Rome', in: O. Hekster/ R. Fowler (eds.), *Imaginary Kings: Royal Images in the Ancient Near East, Greece and Rome* (Stuttgart 2005), 9–38; 25–8.

[116] J. Trimble, 'Corpore Enormi. The Rhetoric of Physical Appearance in Suetonius and Imperial Portrait Statuary', in: J. Elsner/ M. Meyer (eds.), *Art and Rhetoric in Roman Culture* (Cambridge 2014), 115–54; G. F. Chiai, 'Good Emperors, Bad Emperors: The Function of Physiognomic Representation in Suetonius' De Vita Caesarum and Common Sense Physiognomics', in: J. C. Johnson/ A. Stavru (eds.), *Visualizing the Invisible with the Human Body. Physiognomy and Ekphrasis in the Ancient World* (Berlin – Boston 2019), 203–26.

[117] Cic. *De Orat.* 3.221; A. Corbeill, *Nature Embodied: Gesture in Ancient Rome* (Princeton – Oxford: Princeton University Press 2004), 140–68; D. Jussen, 'The Marks of a Ruler: The Face of the Roman Emperor in Fourth-Century Imperial Panegyric', *Hermes* 149 (2021), 304–25.

[118] For example Polemon A4, B1. On physiognomy, see esp. S. Swain (ed.), *Seeing the Face, Seeing the Soul. Polemon's Physiognomy from Classical Antiquity to Medieval Islam* (Oxford 2007).

[119] Suet. *Aug.* 79.1; Amm. Marc. 25.4.22. H. V. Canter, 'Personal Appearance in the Biography of the Roman Emperors', *Studies in Philology*, 25 (1928), 385–99; 399; C. Head, 'Physical Descriptions of the Emperors in Byzantine Historical Writing', *Byzantion*, 50 (1980), 226–40; 227–8.

sharp-sighted' and Leo I (457–74) 'had vigorous eyes'.[120] It is tempting to link this emphasis on eyes in literary discussions of the emperor's character to an increased focus on the eyes in Roman imperial portraiture. From around the period of the Tetrarchy onwards, emperors were depicted with very large eyes, although technical considerations of marble cutting may also have played their role.[121]

It was not only eyes. Other facial features, like mouth, cheeks, necks, noses and hair, also received attention, although more rarely.[122] Referring to emperors' expressions (frowning, blushing, crying, but also 'calmness of eye') was yet a different way in which orators could bring the emperors' face and character together.[123] It is difficult to see real developments over time here, and even more difficult to link those to changes in imperial portraiture. What we can see instead is continuation of the underlying idea that physical features and character were linked, and a fairly stable set of positive and negative aspects of appearance. Stature was of importance, too, and is often named in physical descriptions of Roman rulers. Emperors could be tall, well-proportioned, stooped, thin or sluggish.[124] Again, we see a continuation in time as to which build had positive or negative connotations. This continuation made it possible to link an emperor to an eminent predecessor by comparing features or figure. Theodosius, for instance, was said to have resembled Trajan in 'manners and physique', as was clear from 'many writings and pictures'.[125] Portraits may have changed over time, but the key characteristics that they meant to communicate seem to have been surprisingly stable.

The image that imperial portraits disseminated was not limited to that of character. They also radiated power through sheer numbers, by the choice of certain materials and the size of portraits. As to material, it is important to remember that though the vast majority of surviving imperial portraits are marble ones, there must have been substantial numbers of portraits in gold, silver, ivory, glass and porphyry.[126] Those materials held divine associations

---

[120] Leo Gramm. *Chronographia* (ed. Bonn) 1842, 107, 113; Head, 'Physical Description', 228.
[121] J. Elsner, 'Physiognomics: Art and Text', in: Swain, *Seeing the Face*, 204–24; 216.
[122] Evans, *Physiognomics*, 14, 16, 50; Jussen, 'The Marks of a Ruler', figure 1. For the period from Constantine onwards: Head, 'Physical Descriptions', with the comments by B. Baldwin, 'Physical Descriptions of Byzantine Emperors', *Byzantion* 51 (1981), 8–21.
[123] *Pan. Lat.* VI (7) 4.4; Jussen, 'The Marks of a Ruler'.
[124] Canter, 'Personal Appearance', 387, 397–8, with references.
[125] *Epitome de Caesaribus*, 48.6. Theodosius explicitly compared himself to Trajan, which may well have influenced the passage. See below p. 179–180.
[126] Heijnen, *Portraying Change*, 22 notes how almost 92 per cent of the surviving imperial portraits are marble and just over 4 per cent are bronze. Portraits in costly materials are almost absent from the corpus, since their high value often led to reuse. See G. Lahusen, 'Zu römischen

from at least the Hellenistic era onwards.[127] The choice to portray emperors in these materials would therefore have made their elevated position instantly obvious. Ancient authors often claim that particular emperors who wanted to emphasise their supremacy used 'divine' materials, but it is much more likely that this was common imperial practice.[128] There are surviving ivory portraits of Augustus, Septimius Severus and Julian, and surviving gold statues of Marcus Aurelius, Septimius Severus, Licinius I and II and Valentinian (Figure 1.10).[129] This is certainly not a list of emperors known for exaggerated claims of superiority. Imperial portraits could stress superior status from the beginning of the principate onwards.

Of the more valuable portrait materials, porphyry had a special position. It became known to the Romans in AD 18, and a porphyry statue was brought to Rome for the first time during the reign of Claudius, who seems not to have approved.[130] Under Trajan and Hadrian, however, and again from the reign of Diocletian onwards, porphyry statues became popular at the Roman court. In fact, imperial porphyry was the exclusive prerogative of the court, probably because of its purple colour which had strong regal connotations.[131] All preserved Roman porphyry statues, even the ones without heads or inscriptions, can safely be attributed to the imperial house.[132] Its prominence in the very late third and early fourth century once again confirms the shift in imperial portraiture taking place in those decades.

Statuen und Bildnissen aus Gold und Silber', *ZPE* 218 (1999), 251–66, emphasising the process of gilding statues.

[127] H. Niemeyer, *Studien zur statuarischen Darstellung der römischen Kaiser* (Berlin 1968), 19.

[128] Niemeyer, *Studien zur statuarischen Darstellung*, 20; T. Pekáry, *Das Römische Herrscherbild*, III, *Das Römische Kaiserbildnis in Staat, Kult und Gesellschaft, dargestellt an Hand der Schriftquellen* (Berlin 1985), 69; 78.

[129] New York, Metropolitan Museum of Art, inv. 23.160.78; Rome, Museo Nazionale Romano, Palazzo Massimo alle Terme, inv. 517382; Rome, Museo Nazionale Romano, Palazzo Massimo alle Terme (*RIPD* nos. 114, 1634, 2114); Lausanne, Musée d'Archéologie et d'Histoire, inv. 39/134; Komotini, Archaeological Museum, inv. 207; Geneva, private collection; Houston (Texas), Collection Ferrel; Conques, Abbatiale Sainte-Foy de Conques (*RIPD* nos. 1191, 1578, 2102, 2108, 2118). See A. D. Pury-Gysel, *Die Goldbüste des Septimius Severus: Gold- und Silberbüstenrömischer Kaiser* (Basel 2017).

[130] Plin. *NH* 36.11; J. Bingen, 'The Imperial Roman Site of the Mons Claudianus (Eastern Desert of Egypt)', *Diogenes* 61 (2016), 7–17.

[131] On purple as an imperial colour, see below p. 69–80.

[132] M. M. Abu El-Enen/ J. Lorenz/ K. A. Ali, 'A New Look on Imperial Porphyry: A Famous Ancient Dimension Stone from the Eastern Desert of Egypt – Petrogenesis and Cultural Relevance', *International Journal of Earth Sciences* 107 (2018), 2393–408; 2396; R. Amedick, 'Immortal Ambitions. Sarcophagi and Social Distinction in Roman Culture', in O. Hekster/ S. T. A. M. Mols (eds.), *Cultural Messages in the Greco-Roman World* (Leuven 2010), 33–46; 41–2.

Figure 1.10 Emperors in gold: Gold bust (h. 33.5 cm) from Avenges (Switzerland) c. 180, Lausanne, Musée d' Archéologie et d' Histoire, inv. 39/134. Precious-metal imperial portraits emphasised the emperor's elevated status. Most have been melted down, but surviving examples, like this one of Marcus Aurelius, show that not only 'bad' emperors were depicted through materials that held strongly divine associations
Source: CKD – Radboud University Nijmegen

Apart from costly material, the size of a portrait could indicate power. From the very early empire onwards, larger-than-life-size portraits of rulers are preserved. This mattered. In earlier times, only gods could be depicted as larger than life.[133] That Roman rulers could be shown in this way indicated their superhuman status. There are surviving portraits of Caesar that are a little over life size, but in all likelihood these are posthumous, when Caesar had officially become a god.[134] A truly colossal portrait of Augustus (the height of the head is approximately 250 cm) possibly formed part of a statue that stood on top of the Mausoleum at Rome.

---

[133] Above p. 29.
[134] For example Antikensammlung Berlin, Sk 342 (41 cm high). On Caesar's divinisation and the impact on his portrait see: Koortbojian, *The Divinization of Caesar and Augustus*, 94–128.

A smaller one, but still colossal (the height of the head is more than 90 cm) was erected at Lepcis Magna in the reign of Tiberius. By this stage the first emperor had been deified and become Divus Augustus, like Caesar had become Divus Julius and many succeeding emperors would become *divi*.[135] But at roughly the same time, when Tiberius was still very much alive, only a somewhat smaller portrait of the ruling emperor (with a height of almost 75 cm) was also erected in Lepcis Magna.[136] The number of surviving colossal portraits is relatively small, so it is difficult to trace a development over time and see if these colossal statues increased in frequency or size.[137] Yet it is clear that from the very beginning of the principate, the superior status of the emperor could be emphasised through the size of his portraits.

Size was not the only similarity between imperial portraits and images of the gods. Postures and features of imperial statues often mirrored statues of the gods, and imperial statues could include divine attributes.[138] Much like divine statues, also, people thought that imperial statues held the presence of the figure that they represented, as indicated by stories about moving or listening statues.[139] Moreover, as Simon Price already noted decades ago, there was substantial overlap between the terminology of imperial and divine statues.[140] It was also possible to claim asylum at statues of the emperor, like at those of gods. That right was confirmed in the various codifications of Roman law, up to and including those of Theodosius and Justinian.[141] This continuation well into the Christian empire shows how what had started as divine connotations of imperial statues had become an act onto its own. The advent of Christianity clearly had an effect on

---

[135] El-Beida; Archaeological Museum; Vatican Musea, Rome, inv. 5168; D. Kreikenbom, *Griechische und römische Kolossalporträts bis zum späten ersten Jahrhundert nach Christus* (Berlin 1992) 160–1; cat. no. III 10; I. Gradel, *Emperor Worship and Roman Religion* (Oxford 2002), 261–371. On *divi*, see below p. 145–7.

[136] Kreikenbom, *Griechische und römische Kolossalporträts*, 186–7, no. III 4.

[137] But see Ruck, *Die Grossen dieser Welt*, 205–28 for developments between the Republic and third century, and 229–68 for the later Roman empire.

[138] S. F. R. Price, *Rituals and Power. The Roman Imperial Cult in Asia Minor* (Cambridge 1984), 180–1; M. Fuchs, 'Römer in Göttern- und Heldenpose', *JRA* 3 (1990), 279–85; S. T. A. M. Mols/ E. M. Moormann/ O. Hekster, 'From Phidias to Constantine: The Portrait Historié in Classical Antiquity', in: V. Manuth/ R. van Leeuwen/ J. Koldeweij (eds.) *Example or Alter Ego? Aspects of the Portrait Historié in Western Art from Antiquity to the Present* (Turnhout 2016), 19–63; 36–42.

[139] M.-J. Versluys, 'Art', in: R. Osborne (ed.), *A Cultural History of Objects in Antiquity* (London 2021), 115–33.

[140] Price, *Rituals and Power*, 177.

[141] Legally defined as '*ad statuas principum confugiunt*', Gaius, *Inst.* 1.53, but also in more general terms as '*ad statuas confugere*', *Dig* [Ulpian], 21.1.19,1; *Cod.Theod.* 9.44.1; *Cod.Iust.* 1. 25.1; *Dig.* 47.10.38; 48.19.28.7; Kitzinger, 'The Cult of Images', 122–3.

imperial imagery, but established practice remained important, especially if it was possible to remove the more prominent pagan associations.

Those associations were, however, a cause of Christian concern. A law of 425 explicitly states that 'if Our images are shown at plays or games, they shall demonstrate that Our divinity and glory live only in the hearts and the secret places of the minds of those who attend. A worship in excess of human dignity shall be reserved for the Supreme Divinity'.[142] Apparently there was a need to prevent such excessive worship. Attention bestowed upon the images of the emperors was too close to idolatry for comfort.[143] Yet even in the Christian empire, the link between emperor and portrait retained its importance. Recognising someone's portrait was a way of recognising their right of rule. Theodosius I is said to have publicly exhibited the portrait of his erstwhile opponent Magnus Maximus (383–8) in Alexandria to show that he accepted the latter's claim to rule the western empire. Coins celebrating the CONCORDIA AVGGG depicted both Theodosius' and Maximus' portraits.[144] Recognising co-emperors by accepting their portrait became especially important when the empire was formally divided into an eastern and western half. The ceremonial reception and distribution of laureate portraits became a way to denote joint rule, as illustrated when Leo I accepted the claim of Anthemius (467–72) as the new emperor in Rome by commanding that their laureate portraits should be exhibited together, and that Anthemius' portrait should be sent to all cities of the empire.[145]

Again, we see in late antiquity a formalisation of dealing with the imperial image that takes its cue from earlier practice. Placing a portrait on coins had been an indication of imperial claims, or the recognition of such claims, throughout the history of imperial Rome.[146] Imperial portraits were not just objects but were believed to have a direct bond with the emperors whom they depicted.[147] In this way, sculptural and painted portraits had already functioned as substitutes for the real rulers for a long time. This is one reason why the face of the emperor was present in almost all judicial contexts, through the imperial standards that flanked the

---

[142] Cod. Theod. 15.4.1 (translation C. Pharr 1952); Cod.Iust. 1.24.2.
[143] K. Marsengill, 'The Christian Reception of Sculpture in Late Antiquity and the Historical Reception of Late-Antique Christian Sculpture', *Journal of the Bible and its Reception* 1 (2014), 67–101; 85–7.
[144] Zosimus 4.37.3; *RIC* IX Trier no. 83a–b; Ando, *Imperial Ideology*, 249.
[145] *De Ceremoniis*, 1.87; Ando, *Imperial Ideology*, 250.
[146] Ando, *Imperial Ideology*, 246; O. Hekster, 'Imagining Power. Reality gaps in the Roman Empire', *BABESCH* 86 (2011), 111–24; 111–12, with references.
[147] J. Elsner, *Art and the Roman Viewer. The Transformation of Art from the Pagan World to Christianity* (Cambridge 1995), 170.

magistrate who spoke law. The presence of the imperial portrait bestowed legitimacy on the proceedings.[148] There is also substantial evidence for laudatory speeches held before of an imperial portrait that address the ruler as if he were present.[149] This incorporated presence was uncomfortable for Christianity, but could also be used to explain dogmatic difficulties. St Basil (c. 330–79) directly relates it to contemporary discussions about the nature of the Trinity: 'The imperial image, too, is called the emperor; and yet there are not two emperors: neither is the power cut asunder nor the glory divided. And as the authority which holds sway over us is one, so the glorification we address to it is one and not many, since the honour shown to the image is transmitted to its model'.[150]

The assimilation of the notion of an imperial 'presence' into discussions of matters of faith shows how traditional ideas could be employed to make new religious structures understandable to the population of the Roman empire. The formalisation of a ceremonial acceptance of laureate portraits likewise used existing practices surrounding imperial statues to ease political change. It is often emphasised how much emperorship changed in late antiquity. Yet, these changes incorporated and continued many earlier practices and beliefs. There were substantial shifts in shape and ceremony, but there were also many essential earlier elements that were included into the new shape that emperorship took. There was continuous tension in Roman imperial history between the need to adapt the emperor's image to societal changes and the risk of alienating a population that had grown used to certain standards and practices. At the same time, these expectations and conventions could also be used to adapt to change. Vespasian's use of Republican imagery, like Constantine's incorporation of the portrait style of Trajan and Augustus, helped to embed a new situation in traditional notions. Similarly, the increased emphasis on the eyes in imperial portraiture adhered to long-existing physiognomic conventions. There was a range of expectations as to what an emperor could look like, how his portrait was linked to the person of the ruler and his character, and about what role imperial portraits played in society. Like we saw in the

---

[148] O. Hekster, 'Imperial Justice? The Absence of Images of Roman Emperors in a Legal Role', *Classical Quarterly* 69 (2020), 247–60; 250.

[149] Ando, *Imperial Ideology*, 251 with references.

[150] St. Basil, *De Spiritu Sancto* 18.45; Price, *Rituals and Power*, 203; J. A. Francis, 'Classical Conceptions of Visuality and Representation in John of Damascus' *Defense of Holy Images*', *Studies in Late Antiquity* 1 (2020), 284–308; 302–5. Cf. Athanasius, *Oratio III contra Arianos*, 5: 'The Shape and the Form of the King Are in the Image, and the Form in the Image is in the King'.

Figure 1.11 Emperor and senate: Marble frieze, Ara Pacis Augustae, south side (h. 1.60 m), from Rome, Campus Martius, 13–9 BC. The image of Augustus on the Ara Pacis firmly places him and his family in a senatorial context, emphasising the senate as a corporate body. But there are differences in the various togas, denoting difference in status
Source: Photo: Lien Foubert

development of the emperor's name, the range of options widened over time, but there was very little innovation that appeared out of the blue. If change was pushed too far, the emperor would no longer be recognisable.

Portraits of the emperor were always seen in their spatial setting, often with a name on the object or nearby. This helped people recognise the emperor and place him in context. Above all, imperial portraits were visible on coins, with a legend surrounding the emperor's head. Placing multiple heads alongside each other on a single coin, or placing the head of one ruler on a coin that was minted in an area where another ruler was in control, became an easy way of indicating joint rule.[151] Importantly, also, images of the emperor on monumental reliefs indicated the emperor's status and role through different architectural settings. Augustus' image on the Ara Pacis, surrounded by magistrates, senators and members of the imperial family (Figure 1.11), suggested a much more 'senatorial' emperor than the image of Septimius Severus (193–211) on the superb *quadrifons*

---

[151] M. Horster, 'The Emperor's Family on Coins (Third Century). Ideology of Stability in Times of Unrest (291–310)', in: O. Hekster/ G. de Kleijn/ D. Slootjes (eds), *Crises and the Roman Empire* (Leiden – Boston 2007), 291–307; 296–303.

arch in Lepcis Magna, which shows the emperor shaking hands with his sons Caracalla and Geta, observed by the empress Julia Domna and surrounded by divinities and personifications.[152] A famous funerary relief, possibly the base of a monumental column, showing Hadrian sitting opposite a personification of the *Campus Martius* while watching his deceased wife Sabina being carried to the heavens by a personification of *Aeternitas* gives yet another image of imperial roles.[153]

Perhaps the best-known examples of monumental reliefs are the narrative images on the columns in Rome of Trajan and Marcus Aurelius, and the friezes on victory arches such as those of Titus, Septimius Severus and Constantine. These showed the emperor too, of course, but they also formed hyper-elaborate bases for the imperial statuary that was placed on top of them: colossal statues of the emperor on the columns, and the emperor in a chariot on the arches. Archaeologists and art historians have fiercely discussed whether these narrative reliefs provided a historical report or a more generalised image showing exemplary values and behaviour. They probably did both.[154] The 184 scenes in the spiralling sculpted frieze on Trajan's column (Figure 0.1, above), for instance, show over 1,000 figures and many moments from Trajan's conquest of Dacia. Many of these have been retraced to specific moments in the campaign. But the overarching image is one of conquest, led by the emperor. The emperor had embodied the ideal virtues during his campaigns, and these were monumentalised in stone, as an example to his subjects and successors. In that sense, it did not matter that it would have been extremely hard (if at all possible) to 'read' the spiralling story in detail. It showed the victorious and dominant emperor in action, articulating the deeds of the figure who was represented on top of the column with a colossal statue.[155] The extended narrative friezes placed the

---

[152] B. Bergmann, *Der Kranz des Kaisers: Genese und Bedeutunge inerrömischen Insignie* (Berlin 2010), 22–33; A. Russell, 'Inventing the Imperial Senate', in: J. Osgood/ K. Morrell/ K. Welch (eds.), *The Alternative Augustan Age* (Oxford 2019), 325–41; V. M. Strocka, 'Beobachtungen an den Attikareliefs des severischen Quadrifons von Lepcis Magna', *Antiquités Africaines* 6 (1972), 147–72.

[153] On the different imperial roles, see below, pp. 106–182.

[154] T. Hölscher, 'The concept of roles and the malaise of 'identity': ancient Rome and the modern world', in: Bell/ Hansen, *Role Models*, 41–56; 45–46.

[155] S. Settis, 'La Colonne trajane. Invention, composition, disposition', *Annales* 40 (1985), 1165–94; P. Veyne, 'Conduct without Belief and Works of Art without Viewers', *Diogenes* 36 (1988), 1–22; 11: 'Everyone felt that space was occupied by a strong power using a language that was not heard but passed, like the wind, over one's head'.

emperor's image in specific contexts, and so helped to construct, reconstruct and redefine emperorship.[156]

Sculptural portraits were also regularly placed into context by incorporating them into a complete statue, often with a statue base that named the emperor. Statues could be placed together as a group, with other statues added later, creating a dynamic interplay between various emperors, members of the imperial households, and even dynasties that had no direct links.[157] These Roman imperial statue groups originated as dynastic monuments from the Hellenistic age, and became a standard way to celebrate some sort of extended imperial household.[158] Individual statues also transmitted messages. Whether a portrait was placed on a statue dressed in a toga, in a toga with the head covered, wearing a cuirass or depicted in the heroic nude made a massive difference as to how people would perceive their ruler – and that choice was inevitably a local one, even if the emperor or those directly surrounding him distributed prototypes of the imperial facial features.

Placing an emperor on horseback instantly emphasised his military qualities. The most famous of these equestrian statues in Roman times was probably the colossal sculpture of Trajan (*Equus Traiani*) that held a central place in Trajan's Forum. When Constantius II (337–61) visited Rome, Ammianus Marcellinus recounts how the emperor noted that he could never construct something as splendid as that forum, and would be happy to 'copy Trajan's steed alone', only to receive the reply that one needed better stables for a horse like that than the emperor possessed.[159] There are many more examples of splendid imperial equestrian statues, with the bronze statue of Marcus Aurelius surviving through the ages, becoming the centrepiece of Michelangelo's Capitoline Square.[160] Yet this type of sculpture was not unique to emperors, and did not by definition identify someone as such. The two famous equestrian statues of Nonnius Balbus maior and minor in Herculaneum are illustrative. Nor did

---

[156] On the importance of these monuments in the construction of the past and 'prospective memory' see above, p. 19 and below, p. 121.

[157] S. Heijnen, 'Statues in Dialogue: Visual Similarities in "Grown" Roman Imperial Statue Groups from the Greek East', *Ancient Society* 51 (2021), 123–156.

[158] B. Hintzen-Bohlen, 'Die Familiengruppe – ein Mittel zur Selbstdarstellung Hellenistischer Herrscher', *JDAI* 105 (1990), 129–54; 131–4; 138–40; C. B. Rose, *Dynastic Commemoration and Imperial Portraiture in the Julio-Claudian Period* (Cambridge 1997).

[159] Amm. Marc. 16.10. 15–16, with P. de Jonge, *Philological and Historical Commentary on Ammianus Marcellinus XVI* (Leiden – Boston 1972), ad loc.; C. Koldt, *Bescheidene Größe. Die Herrschergestalt, der Kaiserpalast und die Stadt Rom: Literarischen Reflexionen monarchischer Selbstdarstellung* (Göttingen 2001), 63–96.

[160] C. Vout, *The Hills of Rome: Signature of an Eternal City* (Cambridge 2012), 157.

equestrian statues ever become an imperial prerogative. Of the known examples set up after 284, the most of them were for emperors or members of the imperial household, but a substantial subset was for military commanders or high-ranking (local) magistrates.[161] Such non-imperial statues could even be constructed in central locations, like the fifth-century equestrian statue of the military commander Flavius Ardabur Aspar, who was commemorated in the Forum of Theodosius at Constantinople.[162]

Still, there could be marked differences between statues of private honorands and those of emperors – differences that seem to have become more demarcated over time. Statuary at Aphrodisias from the later fourth to early sixth century indicates that in terms of dress and hairstyle there was an increased gulf between depictions of private individuals and imperial statues.[163] Perhaps the most indicative way of showing the power of an emperor was to show him enthroned.[164] Again there is substantial cultural continuity. Julius Caesar already displayed his superiority by not standing up when members of the senate came to bring him honours, something for which he was reproached.[165] Showing such superiority was apparently no longer a problem for Augustus, who at least in a private context could be displayed as the only seated figure before barbarians and even gods (Figure 1.12, also Figure 1.21). Having a man sit while gods were standing was all the more striking since images of seated figures were associated with gods. The link between superiority and being seated was so strong that under the Julio-Claudians, only emperors could be depicted in Rome as seated togate statues.[166] But even seated representations were not unique to emperors. There is a range of depictions of seated magistrates, often but not exclusively in

---

[161] The Last Statues of Antiquity (LSA) database, which brings together evidence for statuary set-up after 284, lists thirty-three references to equestrian statues: 21 are for emperors, 3 for an emperor's father, 1 for an imperial cousin, 2 for king Theodoric (whose status was at least close to that of an emperor) and 6 for individuals without any monarchical links (search for 'equestrian' on http://laststatues.classics.ox.ac.uk/).

[162] *LSA* 353, erected between 242–471. There are a great many depictions of non-imperial figures on horseback on sarcophagi (e.g. the Mattei Lion Hunt Sarcophagus; the Lion hunt sarcophagus at the Louvre; the Ludovisi sarcophagus). They are also common in mosaics (e.g. the Mosaico della grande caccia from Pizza Armerina; the mosaic of the Greek charioteers from Carthage; the charioteer mosaic from Mérida) and can be found on ceramic lamps and plates.

[163] Smith, 'Late Antique Portraits', 160–1.

[164] Kiilerich, 'The image of Anicia Juliana', 177, with further references. The image of an enthroned Christ, such as on the late-fourth-century sarcophagus of Junius Bassus (now in the Museo Storico del Tesoro della Basilica di San Pietro), seems to have been a further development of this specific iconography. See also above, p. 29.

[165] Suet. *Caesar*, 78.1; Plut. *Caes.* 60.

[166] Rose, *Dynastic Commemoration*, 37–9; Kuttner, *Dynasty and Empire*, 37–44. There was a strong link between seated statues of the emperor and seated statues of Jupiter, see below, p. 94–5.

Figure 1.12 The seated ruler: Silver cup, (h. 10 cm, diam. 20 cm), from Boscoreale (Italy), c. 8/7 BC (original c. 27 BC), Louvre, Salle Henri II, Room 33, 1895. Augustus is shown enthroned, the only seated figure before barbarians and even gods. He may be seated in a magisterial curule chair and wear a toga, but the image is very imperial, highlighting the emperor's superior position
Source: CKD – Radboud University Nijmegen

funerary art, where they were no longer in competition with the ruler.[167] Living magistrates were represented seated as well. Far into the fifth century, an ivory diptych for the non-imperial Manlius Boethius shows him seated and holding an eagle-tipped sceptre; a private memento of his role as consul, with a splendid inscription identifying the man and his office.[168]

It was important that an imperial portrait was recognisable, because of its perceived bond with the person of the emperor. Not only did the presence of imperial standards legitimise legal proceedings, but portraits could also function as a stand-in for the actual emperor to sanctify diplomatic agreements or receive cult acts. In the Christian empire, the border between such 'normal' veneration of the imperial portrait and idolatry was not easily defined.[169] Although context will often have made clear when the

---

[167] T. Schäfer, *Imperii Insignia. Sella Curulis und Fasces. Zur Repräsentation römischer Magistrate* (Mainz, 1989), 135–41; H. Gabelmann, *Antike Audienz- und Tribunalszenen* (Darmstadt 1984), 189–95, nos. 89–93.

[168] A. Cameron, 'The Origin, Context and Function of Consular Diptychs', *JRS* 103 (2013), 174–207; 185, 190. On the diptychs, see below, p. 105.

[169] Ando, *Imperial Ideology*, 231–2.

emperor was portrayed, for a long time there was no visual vocabulary that unequivocally defined the emperor, apart perhaps from the size of statuary. Unlike the name Augustus, which was unique to rulers, private portraits could resemble imperial imagery closely. Indeed, sometimes the hairstyle and physiognomy of private portraiture were made so similar to portraits of particular emperors that there is continuing discussion about whether these are private or imperial portraits.[170] Adding the emperor's name to a portrait was an often-used way of removing any doubt as to who was represented.[171] Alternatively, including attributes that were specific to emperors made clear whose portrait was on show. From Constantine onwards, emperors were depicted wearing a diadem, which was a much clearer indication of supreme power than the laurel wreath which adorned many earlier imperial images. Diadems were not the only powerful props that could unambiguously define an emperor. When Gregory of Nazianzus blames the emperor Julian for demanding idolatry of his portraits, he lists the other ways in which emperors could be honoured. According to Gregory 'neither the crowns, nor the diadems, neither the brilliance of their purple robes, nor the numbered bodyguard' sufficed for Julian.[172] These, apparently, were the attributes that according to Gregory most clearly set a Roman emperor apart. Like the emperor's name and his portrait, the use and acceptance of such attributes shifted over time, once more showing how the image of Roman emperors developed through the centuries.

Denoting The Emperor (1): The Power of Dress

In 44 BC, just before he was assassinated, Caesar attended the Lupercalia festival wearing the toga *purpurea*, a purple-dyed toga that was associated

---

[170] W. Trillmich, 'Hispanien und Rom aus der Sicht Roms und Hispaniens', in: Idem/ H. Schubert (eds.), *Hispania Antiqua* (Mainz 1993), 41–70; 57–8. Note how foreign kings, too, could have their portraits constructed under the obvious influence of imperial sculpture: K. Fittschen, 'Juba II und seine Residenz Jol/ Caesarea', in: H. G. Horn/ C. B. Rügen (eds.), *Die Numider. Reiter und Könige nördlich der Sahara* (Cologne 1979), 227–42; Rose, *Dynastic Commemoration*, 53.

[171] A wonderful example is a bust of Caracalla in military armor from Skikda (North Africa), the identity of which was simply changed by inscribing the pedestal with the name of Constantine; M. Dondin-Payre, 'Annexe: le buste de Caracalla/Constantin de Philippeville (Rusicade), Algérie', in: S. Benoist/ A. Daguet-Gagey (eds.), *Un Discours en images de la condamnation de mémoire* (Metz 2008), 40–2.

[172] Gregory Naz. *Or.* 4.80.

with the Roman kings of old and the luxury of eastern courts. He also wore the red shoes of the ancient kings of Alba and a laurel crown. The senate had given him permission to wear these trappings of power, but the message of supremacy will have been clear. In this context, Antony thrice offered Caesar the diadem, only to be refused.[173] Still, the claim of kingship was too close for comfort and Caesar was killed. Rome clearly knew the marks that denoted supreme power, but openly wearing them carried great risks. Senatorial dress included purple stripes on the toga, so a balance between senatorial and regal dress was possible. Augustus' later biographer explicitly mentions how the purple stripe on his togas was 'neither too narrow nor too broad'.[174] Over time, certain symbols became normalised and allowed emperors to be instantly recognised. The highly ornamental representations of late antique emperors, diademed and dressed in purple, surrounded by guards and courtiers, is far removed from Augustus' alleged simplicity. The development of these trappings of power as acceptable symbols of the imperial role shows the same tensions between innovation and tradition as we have seen for the imperial name and portrait. New realities were anchored by using known symbols, reconciling the new with the old. In doing so these known symbols could change meaning and gain new associations.

How such a process of shifting meanings could work becomes clear when looking at the toga. Augustus and his direct successors are mostly shown in a 'magisterial' role, often wearing togas, avoiding too monarchical an image. But these were restyled togas, given shape under Augustan rule, double-layered like priestly garments. It was a new style of dress that was strongly embedded in traditional clothing. On the Ara Pacis relief (Figure 1.11, above) Augustus and his family are dressed in the new toga with rich drapery, whereas non-imperial figures wear the simpler old toga.[175] So though the imperial family is presented as traditionally Roman, it is a new kind of traditionally Roman. Moreover, the very fact that the Julio-Claudian emperors were so often depicted togate created associations between this new toga and emperorship – ultimately making it a symbol of monarchy.[176]

---

[173] Cic. *Phil.* 2.85 explicitly links purple robe, golden chair and crown with kingly power; Dio 43.43 notes how the colour of Caesar's toga followed 'the style of the kings who had once reigned in Alba'. Cf. Dio, 44.6.1 (describing a gilded crown); U. Rothe, *The Toga and Roman Identity* (London – New York 2020), 107–8; C. Brøns/ A. Skovmøller/ J. Gisler, 'Colour-Coding the Roman Toga: The Materiality of Textiles Represented in Ancient Sculpture', *Antike Kunst* 60 (2017), 55–79; 57–8.

[174] Suet. Aug. 73.1.

[175] Rothe, *The Toga and Roman Identity*, 110–11; Zanker, *Power of Images*, 162–6.

[176] Rothe, *The Toga and Roman Identity*, 114.

Whether, where, and accompanied by whom an emperor wore the toga became an indication of his style of rule, hence the comments in our ancient authors that Nero received senators in a 'short, flowered tunic', 'transgressing custom' in the process. Domitian was overly fond of showing his status and not only gained the right of wearing 'triumphal garb whenever he entered the senate house' but did so accompanied by twenty-four lictors.[177] During the civil war that followed Nero's reign, the emperor Vitellius (69) apparently had to be dissuaded from 'entering Rome as if it were a captured city' and changed from his general's cloak and arms into 'a senator's toga'.[178] The toga clearly indicated the magisterial role of the emperor. It would continue to do so for centuries to come. The emperor Julian is still praised for walking to the senate house 'clad in the toga *praetexta*, in the kind and colour of his own dress not much different from his magistrates'.[179] Yet, that very *praetexta* was purple-bordered, incorporating a colour that was increasingly linked to imperial power. There was, of course, a difference with the toga *purpurea* that Caesar had worn, which was wholly dyed, or with the toga *picta*, which was purple with decorative embroidery.

Depicting a togate emperor could indicate his regal status alongside his magisterial role. On an over life-size statue of Caligula, now in the Virginia Museum of Fine Arts, traces of purple are found in the fragments of ancient colouration that can be seen through microscopic examination (Figure 1.13).[180] Caligula showed his colours on permanent display. This fits well with a story that the emperor had king Ptolemy of Mauretania (20–40), who was the grandson of Mark Antony and thus Caligula's second cousin, killed because people at Rome paid too much attention to his 'purple cloak'. Local princes could wear the toga, but no longer apparently wear regal colours in Rome, for this suggested competition.[181]

---

[177] Dio, 62.13.3; 67.4.3. Suet. *Dom*, 14.3 states that the emperor was preceded by Roman knights clad in the *trabea*, the purple-striped toga of the early kings and consuls.

[178] Tac. *Hist.* 2.89; Rothe, *The Toga and Roman Identity*, 116. Whether Vitellius' coinage is, as Rothe argues, 'conspicuous in its frequent depiction' of the emperor togate and seated is a matter of discussion. Only 6 out of 110 coin types minted at Rome depict him in this way (*RIC* I, *Vit.* 94–7, 134–5) and none of the coins minted in Spain or Gaul. Cf. Suet. *Galba* 11.

[179] Pan. Lat. II.29.5. Cf. A. Alföldi, *Die monarchische Repräsentation im römischen Kaiserreich* (Darmstadt 1970), 126–8.

[180] Richmond, Virginia Museum of Fine Arts, Inv. 71.20; M. Abbe, 'The Togatus Statue of Caligula in the Virginia Museum of Fine Arts: An Archaeological Description', in: *The Digital Sculpture Project*, accessed 15 August 2020 (www.digitalsculpture.org/papers/abbe/abbe_paper.html).

[181] Suet. *Cal.* 35.1; A. A. Barrett, *Caligula. The Abuse of Power* (London – New York 2015), 159–60.

Figure 1.13 Caligula in purple: 3D-Reconstruction of marble statue (h. 203 cm), from Bovillae (Italy), 37–41, Richmond, Virginia Museum of Fine Arts, Inv. 71.20. Traces of purple can be traced on this monumental statue of Caligula. Whether he was shown with the *toga purpurea* or *toga picta* (as in this reconstruction) is unknown. That the statue showed a very dominant image of the emperor is clear
Source: Direct Dimensions and the Virtual World Heritage Laboratory, University of Virginia, www.digitalsculpture.org/papers/abbe/abbe_paper.html, accessed 3 September 2021

Such shifts were neither instantaneous nor absolute. Microscopy of a life-size marble statue of a certain Gaius Fundilius from the first half of the first century shows that he was portrayed in the toga *praetexta* at the sanctuary of Diana Nemorensis; a public location about 20 km northeast of Rome.[182] Wearing the toga never became a unique imperial prerogative – it was rather a symbol of Roman citizenship. But certainly in the Greek east, it also became linked to emperorship. The first portraits of togate individuals in the east, especially with the toga covering the head (*capite velato*) in a sign of piety, were erected during the time of Augustus. These were portraits of the emperor and was a new kind of imagery in the Greek east, coinciding with the introduction of sole rule.[183] Inevitably, this linked the symbolic meaning of the toga to the new political situation.

Around the beginning of the third century, a new toga was introduced (the so-called stacked toga) probably to distinguish between high-ranking magistrates and the increasing number of Roman citizens who could wear the toga. In the very late fourth century, yet a new shape of toga was developed to set apart members of a re-defined elite from other toga-wearers.[184] High-ranking magistrates, priests or those singled out for special honours would also continue to be shown in purple-bordered togas throughout Roman history.[185] This shows that although the use of the colour purple was of great importance for recognition of the emperor, this did not rapidly lead to an imperial monopoly of the colour. Private individuals, too, continued to wear purple, if they could afford it and did not mind the smell because Tyrian-dyed purple was made from shellfish. The poet Martial (38/41–101/104) could joke that a certain Philaenis stank so much that she wore 'garments dipped in every kind of purple' to drown out her own smell.[186] Yet even if private

---

[182] Ny Carlsberg Glyptotek, inv. 707; A. Skovmøller, 'Where Marble Meets Colour: Surface Texturing of Hair, Skin and Dress on Roman Marble Portraits as Support for Painted Polychromy', in: M. Harlow/ M.-L. Nosch (eds.), *Greek and Roman Textiles and Dress: An Interdisciplinary Anthology* (Oxford – Philadelphia 2014), 279–97; 288–93; P. Liverani, 'Per una "storia del colore". La scultura policroma romana, un bilancio e qualche prospettiva', in: P. Liverani/ U. Santamaria (eds.), *Diversimente bianco. La policromia della scultura romana* (Rome 2014), 9–32; 20–6. The statue is even more extraordinary, as Fundilius seems to have been a freedman.

[183] F. Havé-Nikolaus, *Untersuchungen zu den kaiserzeitlichen Toga statuen griechischer Provenienz. Kaiserliche und private Togati der Provinzen Achaia, Creta (et Cyrene) und Teilen der Provinz Macedonia* (Mainz 1998), 21–7, 52; Heijnen, *Portraying Change*, 115–19.

[184] Fejfer, *Roman Portraits*, 188–93; U. Gehn, 'Late Antique *Togati* and Related Inscriptions – A Thumbnail Sketch', in: K. Bolle/ C. Machado/ C. Witschel (eds.), *The Epigraphic Cultures of Late Antiquity* (Stuttgart 2017), 363–405.

[185] Bradley, *Colour and Meaning*, 197–201; M. G. Parani, 'Defining Personal Space: Dress and Accessories in Late Antiquity', in: L. Lavan/ E. Swift/ T. Putzeys (eds.), *Objects in Context. Objects in Use. Material Spatiality in Late Antiquity* (Leiden – Boston 2008), 495–529; 507–9.

[186] Mart. *Epig.* 9.62. Mart. *Epigr.* 2.16.3 mentions bedclothes 'dyed in smelly Sidonian'; M. Harlow, 'Satirically Sartorial. Colours and Togas in Roman Satire', in: M. García Sánchez/ M. Gleba (eds.), *Vetus Textrinum: Textiles in the Ancient World. Studies in Honour of Carmen Alfaro Giner* (Barcelona 2018), 185–95; 186–8.

individuals could wear purple, only few if any Romans are likely to have had a slave for purple garments like the empress Livia.[187] Later, in the second century, Suetonius writes how Nero forbade the use of Tyrian-purple dye, and stripped a matron in the audience who wore purple all the same at one of his recitals 'not only of her garments, but also of her property'.[188] The story may well be apocryphal, but it shows a strong perceived link between purple and imperial power.

Increasingly, there seems to have been the expectation that the emperor dressed in purple, according to his rank, to set him apart from the rest of society. Marcus Aurelius may have privately remarked that his 'father', Antoninus Pius did not care about the 'colour of his clothes', but his tutor and friend Fronto still wrote that Marcus and his father were 'bound to wear purple and crimson'.[189] In the sculptural reliefs on Trajan's Column in Rome, the emperor was highlighted for the viewers, who had to recognise him from a distance, by using purple paint.[190] When, almost a century later, a more ornamental imperial dress code was formalised under Diocletian, the new praxis of placing precious stones on dress and shoes and wearing a gold-brocaded robe was contrasted to an earlier time in which 'the emperor's insignia comprised only the purple robe' (*in chlamyde purpurea*).[191]

The complaint shows how strongly purple had become associated with imperial power – as we already saw in the use of porphyry for imperial statues and monuments.[192] It also shows how the notion of a modest emperor retained its attraction. The new situation under Diocletian was contrasted with an idealised past. This went against historical reality. Emperors had worn and been depicted in sumptuous clothing long before Diocletian. Caligula is said to have worn 'embroidered cloaks covered with precious stones', Nero wore 'white clothes woven with gold' (and was buried in them), Commodus 'silk woven with gold thread' and 'the toga and arms of a gladiator finished in gold and jewels', and Elagabalus is said to have alternatively worn 'a tunic made wholly of cloth of gold, one made

---

[187] *CIL* 6.4016; K. Olson, 'Dress, Adornment and Self-Presentation', in: B. Kelly/ A. Hug (eds.), *The Roman Emperor and His Court, ca. 30 BC–ca. AD 300 Volume 1: Historical Essays* (Cambridge 2022), 461–478; 473.
[188] Suet. *Nero*, 32.3.
[189] M. Aur. *Med.* 1.17.3; Fronto *Ad M. Caes.* 1.8.3 (Haines 1.121); Olson, 'Dress', 467.
[190] M. Bradley, 'The Importance of Colour on Ancient Marble Sculpture', *Art History* 32 (2009), 427–57; 436; M. del Monte/ P. Ausset/ R. A. Lefèvre 'Traces of ancient colours on Trajan's column', *Archaeometry* 40 (1998), 403–12; 410.
[191] Eutr. 9.26. Cf. Aur. Vict. *Caes.* 39.2–3. On the ceremonial reforms of Diocletian see also S. MacCormack, *Art and Ceremony in the Late Antiquity* (Berkeley 1981), 106–7, 116.
[192] Above, p. 59.

of purple, and a Persian one studded with jewels'. Gallienus allegedly appeared in 'a purple cloak with jewelled and golden clasps' and 'wore a man's tunic of purple and gold'.[193] These are moralising stories by later authors about emperors who transgressed senatorial norms.[194] But they indicate how extravagant dressing had been a way to show superiority well before Diocletian, even if it was negatively commented upon at the time.

The above-mentioned emperors chose to show themselves in a way that differed from the established (senatorial) norm. That was commented upon and their individual reputation suffered. But in doing so, these emperors influenced popular perceptions of possible imperial dress. After Caligula's heavily embroidered cloaks with gems, clothing that was 'merely' embroidered would have appeared much less extravagant than before Caligula. In this way, imperial dress that contravened conventions changed the possibilities that later emperors had. Luxurious clothing became more normalised every time an emperor chose to show himself dressed in silk, gems or purple and gold embroidery.[195] Moreover, Roman private dress grew increasingly elaborate and it is no surprise that imperial dress changed with it.[196] It was apparently unproblematic for Marcus Aurelius' wife Faustina to own 'silken gold-embroidered robes'.[197] On the so-called Severan Tondo, a small wooden panel painting now in Berlin, Septimius Severus and his family are shown in luxurious garments of gold and precious stones (Figure 1.14).[198]

---

[193] Suet. *Cal.* 52. Cf. Sen. *Ben.* 2.12.1 mentioning a 'golden slipper studded with pearls'; Suet. *Nero*, 50; HA, *Pertinax* 8.2–3; HA, *Elag.* 23.3; HA. *Gall.* 16.4, M. Zimmermann, 'Die Repräsentation des kaiserlichen Ranges', in: Winterling, *Zwischen Strukturgeschichte und Biographie*, 181–205; 193–5.

[194] M. Harlow, 'Dress in Historical Narrative: The Case of the Historia Augusta', in: L. Cleland/ M. Harlow/ L. J. Llewellyn-Jones (eds.), *The Clothed Body in Ancient World* (Oxford 2005), 143–53; 144–5, 152. It is noticeable how the unknown author of the *Historia Augusta* claims that before Gallienus' time 'the emperors always appeared in the toga' at Rome, which had not been true for a long time, if ever.

[195] This process of widening the range of imperial options, even after apparent failures of representation is already set out in O. Hekster, 'Provincial Emperors AD 98 –235', in: D. Potter/ N. Lenski/ N. Rosenstein (eds.), *The Oxford History of the Roman World* (Oxford forthcoming).

[196] See also R. MacMullen, 'Some Pictures in Ammianus Marcellinus', *Art Bulletin* 46 (1964), 435–55; 445–51.

[197] HA. *Marcus* 17.4, noting how these robes were sold at an auction to raise money for a military campaign.

[198] Antikensammlung Berlin 31329. The original shape of the *tondo* was a square: T. F. Mathews, *The Dawn of Christian Art in Panel Paintings and Icons* (Los Angeles: J. Paul Getty Museum 2016), 74–83, with n. 191. Such painted portraits on wood and other objects must have been common: R. Grigg, 'Portrait-Bearing Codicils in the Illustrations of the *Notitia Dignitata*', *JRS* 68 (1979), 107–24; 107 with n. 1.

Figure 1.14 Opulent emperorship: Wooden tondo (diam. 30.5 cm; originally a square), from Egypt, early-Severan age, Staatliche Museen, Antikensammlung Berlin, Schloß Charlottenburg. Inv. no. 31329. The emperor Septimius Severus, his wife Julia Domna and their eldest son Caracalla are shown in luxurious gold-hemmed costume, with jewelled diadem, and sceptre. Domna also wears pearls. This strongly anticipates Diocletian's ornamental imperial dresscode. On the left, the portrait of Severus' younger son Geta is removed

Source: CKD – Radboud University Nijmegen

Over time, depicting the emperor in sumptuous clothing shifted from a challenge to convention to an acceptable choice of representation. This shows how the range of imperial representation changed over time, even if emperors could still be attacked on an alleged fondness for luxury.

Diocletian's reforms, it seems, validated a practice that had been long foreshadowed. That did not make it meaningless. From the fourth century onwards, specific attire was increasingly used to differentiate between on the one hand emperor and dignitaries, and on the other the rest of the population. Certain items of dress were even used in legal text as synonyms for the rank they indicated, such as the *laticlavum* as shorthand for senators.[199] Such formalisation also applied to imperial dress. Imperial robes were more closely defined and could only be worn by the emperor. Purple became an imperial prerogative, possibly linked with the boom of porphyry for imperial portraits, sarcophagi and palace architecture.[200] The right purple attire defined the emperor, as an anecdote from Ammianus Marcellinus about the fourth-century usurper Procopius (365–6) shows: 'because a purple robe could nowhere be found, he was dressed in a gold-embroidered tunic, like an attendant at court, but from foot to waist he looked like a page in the service of the palace; he wore purple shoes on his feet, and bore a lance, and a small piece of purple cloth in his left hand'.[201] Procopius did not recover from such an inauspicious start. The passage shows both how important specific imperial dress had become, and the intrinsic link between emperorship and purple. This becomes clear, once more, in a decree of Theodosius from January 424, included in the Justinian Code, which explicitly states that all people 'shall abstain from the possession of that kind of material which is dedicated only to the Emperor and his household'.[202]

Apparently, the imperial household included officials whose type of dress often included purple elements. They, like the late antique emperor, are often portrayed in a *chlamys*, an ankle-length cloak fastened with a brooch. The imperial *chlamys* was purple and gold, with a bejewelled brooch; officials had a white *chlamys* with purple panels and a so-called crossbow brooch. The similarity of dress denotes the dignitaries as dependent on the emperor for their office.[203] On the so-called *missorium* of Theodosius, a massive commemorative silver plate from 388, this is illustrated by showing the emperor giving documents to a kneeling official, both in similar clothing (Figure 1.15). There is no mistaking who was emperor. Theodosius

---

[199] Cod. Theod. 6.4.17, 370; R. Delmaire, 'Le Vêtement dans les sources juridiques du Bas-Empire', *Antiquité Tardive* 12 (2004), 195–202; 197.

[200] M. Reinhold, *History of Purple as Status Symbol in Antiquity* (Brussels 1970), 60–4. See also Canepa, *Two Eyes of the Earth*, 192, rightly emphasising that not only Roman precedent, but also increasing contact with the Sasanid empire influenced imperial outfits (Cf. above, p. 56).

[201] Amm. Marc. 26.6.15. The story echoes a passage in Herodian (2.8.6), forecasting the failure of Pescennius Niger's (193–4) claims to the throne by describing the amateur way in which he was proclaimed emperor.

[202] Cod. Theod. 10.21.3; Cod. Just. 11.9(8).4.   [203] Parani, 'Defining Personal Space', 500–2.

Figure 1.15 Emperor and dignitary: Ceremonial silver dish (diam. 74 cm, c. 15 kg), from Constantinople?, 388, found in Almendralejo (Spain), Madrid, Real Academia de la Historia. This *Missorium* shows Theodosius I seated, flanked by his co-rulers Valentinian II and Arcadius. All hold sceptre, globe and diadem and all are shown with a nimbus or halo. Theodosius hands a document to a much smaller official, dressed similarly as the emperor. Soldiers on the side represent the imperial bodyguard. Only Theodosius is named in the text on the rim
Source: CKD – Radboud University Nijmegen

is enthroned, flanked by his co-rulers Valentinian II (375–92) and Arcadius (395–408), and wears a diadem of pearls. He is substantially larger than anyone else, and an inscription on the plate reads 'Our Lord (*Dominus Noster*) Theodosius, emperor forever (*Perpetuus Augustus*)'.[204]

---

[204] Real Academia de la Historia, Madrid; Parani, 'Defining Personal Space', 501; MacCormack, *Art and Ceremony*, 220. On the missorium and its context: R. E. Leader-Newby, *Silver and Society in Late Antiquity: Functions and Meanings of Silver Plate in the Fourth to Seventh Centuries* (Aldershot: Ashgate 2003), 11–60; Kolb, *Herrscherideologie*, 220–5.

Figure 1.16 King David as Roman emperor: Illuminated Greek Gospel book, purple-dyed vellum (h. c. 30 cm, w. c. 25 cm), from Syria?, sixth century, Paris, BN, suppl. Gr. 1286, folio 29r. Christian imagery appropriated imperial costume to show the majesty of biblical figures. On one folio of the *Sinope Gospels*, the clothing of King David (bottom left in the image) is very similar to that of late antique emperors
Source: CKD – Radboud University Nijmegen

Likewise, the officials standing next to the emperor Justinian on a famous mosaic in the San Vitale at Ravenna (ca. 544–8) (Figure 5.1) are dressed like the emperor, though in a white and purple *chlamys* whereas the emperor wears purple and gold. Justinian is instantly recognisable through his clothing, crown, centrality, and the halo surrounding his head. The official nearest the emperor is probably his great general Belisarius – the commander responsible for the reconquest of Italy in Justinian's campaign to reunite the Roman east and west (535–54) (Map 2.1). On the other side stands Bishop Maximian of Ravenna (499–556), richly dressed but not competing with the emperor in attire.[205] Christian imagery, however, had no difficulty with appropriating imperial dress: a fifth-century mosaic in Santa Maria Maggiore in Rome shows king David depicted diademed and dressed in a purple chlamys, just like he is illustrated in the sixth-century *Sinope Gospels* manuscript from Syria (Figure 1.16).[206] Christian martyrs,

---

[205] I. Andreescu-Treadgold, / W. Treadgold, 'Procopius and the Imperial Panels of S. Vitale', *The Art Bulletin*, 79 (1997), 708–23; 716–20, also noting the Maximian stands slightly in front of the emperor. On the relation between Justinian and Belisarius, see H. Börm, 'Justinians Triumph und Belisars Erniedrigung. Überlegungen zum Verhältnis zwischen Kaiser und Militär im späten Römischen Reich', *Chiron* 43 (2013), 63–91.

[206] A. Steinberg, *Weaving in Stones: Garments and Their Accessories in the Mosaic Art of Eretz Israel in Late Antiquity* (Oxford: Archaeopress 2020), 126–30, with references.

too, are often portrayed in a chlamys with a crossbow brooch, though this echoes the image of members of the earthly imperial court rather than that of the emperor, perhaps signposting the position they would hold in heaven.[207]

Like we saw with the toga, the associations that the *chlamys* held changed over time, becoming intrinsically linked to imperial power. In doing so, the chlamys lost some of the military connotations that it had previously held. In 382, senators were still legally forbidden to wear 'the awe-inspiring military cloak (*chlamydis terrore*)', within the walls of Constantinople, and obliged to instead wear 'sober robes', or a toga at public occasions.[208] This recalls Tacitus' above-cited anecdote about Vitellius changing from a general's cloak (*paludamentum*) into toga before entering Rome.[209] In fact, in his mid-sixth-century *On the Magistracies of the Roman Constitution*, John the Lydian notes the similarities between the *chlamys* and the *paludamentum*, which was worn by senior officials and army generals. Many Greek-writing authors in antiquity simply used *chlamys* as the straight translation of *paludamentum*.[210] This is yet another example of how apparent changes, like the formalisation of the purple *chlamys* as imperial dress, were embedded in much earlier modes of representation. The *paludamentum* had been linked to imperial power for a long time and the purple (or white) general's cloak, interwoven with gold, had become the exclusive indication of an emperor on military service already in the early empire.[211]

After all, if it was important to recognise the emperor in a civilian setting, it was all the more so in a military context. On the battlefield, one needed to know who the emperor was without any hesitation. There, emperors dressed to impress, as a contemporary account of a campaign by the emperor Aurelian (270–75) in the turbulent third century shows:

> Aurelian ... drew his army up in full battle order to intimidate the enemy. When he found the units arranged to his satisfaction, mounting a high speaker's platform, and donning a purple robe he arranged the entire force around him in a crescent. He also placed beside himself any officers who had been placed in any command, all of them on horseback.

---

[207] Parani, 'Defining Personal Space', 502.   [208] *Cod. Theod.* 14.10.1.
[209] Tac. *Hist.* 2.89; above, p. 71. Cf. Plin. *Pan.* 56.4.
[210] Johannes Lydus, *De Mag.* 1.17.1; M. Harlow, 'Clothes Maketh Man: Power Dressing and Elite Male in the Late Roman World,' in: L. Brubaker/ J. M. H. Smith (eds), *Gender in the Early Medieval World* (Cambridge 2004), 44–69; 59–60.
[211] K. Olson, *Masculinity and Dress in Roman Antiquity* (London – New York 2017), 77; M. Zimmermann, 'Die Darstellung des kaiserlichen Status und seines Prestiges', in: A. Kuhn, *Social Status and Prestige in the Graeco-Roman World* (Stuttgart 2015), 189–203; 194.

Behind the emperor were the standards of the elite units – golden eagles, images of the emperor, and plaques showing the names of the units picked out in gold letters – all held aloft and displayed on poles sheathed in silver. With everything so arranged he ordered the Juthungi to enter. The ambassadors, when they beheld this spectacle, were struck dumb with astonishment.[212]

But being so visible on the battlefield could be problematic, as an anecdote about Septimius Severus during the intermittent civil wars at the beginning of his reign (193–7) makes clear. In the fight against his ultimate rival Clodius Albinus, Severus is said to have 'slipped from his horse and fled, managing to escape by throwing off the imperial cloak (χλαμύδα τὴν βασιλικὴν)'.[213] Occasionally, it was better for an emperor not to be recognised.

Denoting the Emperor (2): The Importance of the Crown

In 44 BC, Antony's offer of a diadem to Caesar was highly problematic. By the time of Constantine, diadems were included on imperial portraits as a matter of course, with Gregory of Nazianzus mentioning 'crown and diadems' as obvious attributes of imperial power.[214] Of course, crowns had been indicative of power throughout the Mediterranean world and beyond well before Roman times. Depicting rulers with a crown or diadem was a traditional way of depicting monarchs that most Romans will have been aware of – even if monarchy had not been easily acceptable at the time of Caesar.[215] In that sense, the inclusion of a diadem to manifest Roman emperorship simply showed that emperorship itself had become unproblematic. Even so, Constantine's continuous use of the diadem could still be criticised, although implicitly.[216] The shift towards this general acceptance

---

[212] *Brill's New Jacoby* 100 F6= G. Martin, *Dexipp von Athen. Edition, Übersetzung und begleitende Studien* (Tübingen 2006), F 28.

[213] Herodian, 3.7.3. Cf. Dio 76 [75], 6 who argues that Severus took off the imperial cloak to rally his soldiers by showing that he was one of them and shaming them into action. Fake news already existed in antiquity.

[214] Above, p. 69.

[215] Smith, *Hellenistic Royal Portraits*, 34–8; M. García Sánchez/ M. Albaladejo Vivero, 'Diademas, tiaras y coronas de la antigua Persia: formas de representación y de adopción en el mundo clásico', in: C. Alfaro Giner/ J. Ortiz García/ M. Antón Peset (eds.), *Tiarae, Diadems and Headdresses in the Ancient Mediterranean Cultures: Symbolism and Technology* (Valencia 2014), 79–94; MacCormack, *Art and Ceremony*, 159–266.

[216] *Epit. de Caes.* 41.14.

once again illustrates the importance of recognisable symbols to express a new situation, the shift in the meanings of these symbols over time, and the importance of precedent in the way these meanings shifted.

The first major shift in the meaning of the crown in the Roman world preceded emperorship. Pliny the Elder (23/24–79) clearly states that 'in ancient times crowns were presented to none but a divinity'. Later, those involved in sacrifice 'began to wear them', followed by those 'employed in the sacred games', 'warriors when about to enjoy a triumph ... after which it became the custom to present them at our games'.[217] The historical accuracy of the passage is not terribly important. What matters is that in the early principate there was still a strong perceived link between the crown and divinities, and the awareness that there was a range of occasions at which people could wear various crowns, if only temporarily. Consequently, there was a wide variety of crowns, which created sufficient ambiguity for early emperors to be depicted with a crown but still claim to stick to tradition.

This, in fact, seems to be what Caesar tried to do when he gained the right to wear at all times the laurel wreath for triumphal generals (*corona triumphalis*) (Figure 1.2, above).[218] Laurel wreaths had connotations beyond the military – they were linked to Apollo and the Pythian Games – and indicated gallantry as well as victory.[219] It may have seemed a safe symbol. Augustus also used headgear with traditional Roman connotations, and effectively appropriated the civic crown (*corona civica*). This was a wreath made of oak leaves that was reserved for a Roman citizen who had saved the life of a fellow citizen by killing an enemy who had captured that fellow citizen. After the civil wars in which Augustus came to power it was argued that the new ruler had saved all fellow-citizens, and was therefore allowed to hang a *corona civica* above the door of his house.[220] This made him clearly superior to anyone else in Rome, but through traditional, and therefore acceptable, symbolism. As with the toga, adoption of the oak-and-laurel wreath by the emperors influenced how these wreaths were perceived and linked them to imperial power. For the *corona triumphalis* this became somewhat formalised, since already in the early

---

[217] Plin. *HN* 16.4. See also Aulus Gellius, 5.6 on the origins of the corona. Gellius also notes (2.11.1–2) how already in the fifth century BC. L. Sicinus Dentatus received 26 wreaths.
[218] Suet. *Caes.* 45.2, with Koortbojian *The Divinization of Caesar and Augustus*, 119.
[219] F. K. Yegül, 'A Victor's Message: The Talking Column of the Temple of Artemis at Sardis', *Journal of the Society of Architectural Historians* 73 (2014), 204–25; 208.
[220] *RGDA* 34.2; Dio, 53.16.4; Bergmann, *Der Kranz des Kaisers*, 135–83, esp. 146–54. The crown would ultimately also be shown above the door of Augustus' mausoleum.

principate holding a triumph became a privilege of the imperial family. Yet there were other variants of the laurel wreath (especially the *corona laurea*) which continued to be worn by soldiers and magistrates during rituals, or were given to victors at games. They could even be included on the funerary images of private individuals, such as the Egyptian Fayum portraits of local members of the elite.[221]

There is an apparent contradiction in arguing that specific symbolism became closely linked to the emperor, while noting that non-imperial individuals continued to be shown with the same symbols. What this suggests, however, are two linked trajectories. The first is that imperial associations functioned like fashion. Because the imperial family was depicted in a certain way, it became attractive to be similarly shown. This pattern has been firmly established for hairstyle, clothing and jewellery, with elite men and women following innovative imperial grooming.[222] Emperors, it seems, were looking for an acceptable visual vocabulary to distinguish them, but in doing so, they made it attractive for others to be similarly attired. This may lie behind the introduction of new styles of togas under Augustus and at the beginning of the third century: earlier variants were no longer sufficient to set the emperor apart.

The second trajectory is one in which emperor and empire became increasingly linked. The toga and laurel wreath gained imperial connotations but also retained a connection to being a Roman citizen. This was during a period in which the Roman empire kept expanding. New territory was added until well into the second century. More and more subjects gained citizenship, up to the universal grant of citizenship to all free inhabitants of the empire in 212 (the so-called *Constitutio Antoniniana*).[223] Being a Roman citizen was increasingly near-synonymous with being a subject of the Roman emperor. Consequently, the lines between symbols for Rome and symbols for the emperor became blurred, certainly in the provinces or for

---

[221] Alföldi, *Die monarchische Repräsentation*, 137–8; Bergmann, *Der Kranz des Kaisers*, 40–4, 92–4. Examples of Fayum portraits: Allard Pierson Museum, inv. no. 724; Metropolitan Museum of Art, acc. no. 09.181.6; The Art Institute of Chicago, Cat. 156 (1922.4799).

[222] A. Wallace-Hadrill, 'The Imperial Court', in: A. K. Bowman/ E. Champlin/ A. Lintott (eds.) *The Cambridge Ancient History: The Augustan Empire, 43 BC–AD 69*, revised edition, vol. X (Cambridge: Cambridge University Press 1996), 283–308; 292; K. Fittschen, 'Courtly Portraits of Women in the Era of the Adoptive Emperors (98–180) and Their Reception in Roman Society', in: D. E. E. Kleiner / S. B. Matheson (eds.), *I Claudia. Women in Ancient Rome* (New Haven 1996), 42–52; 42.

[223] Hekster, *Rome and its Empire*, 45–55. See further Imrie, *The Antonine Constitution*.

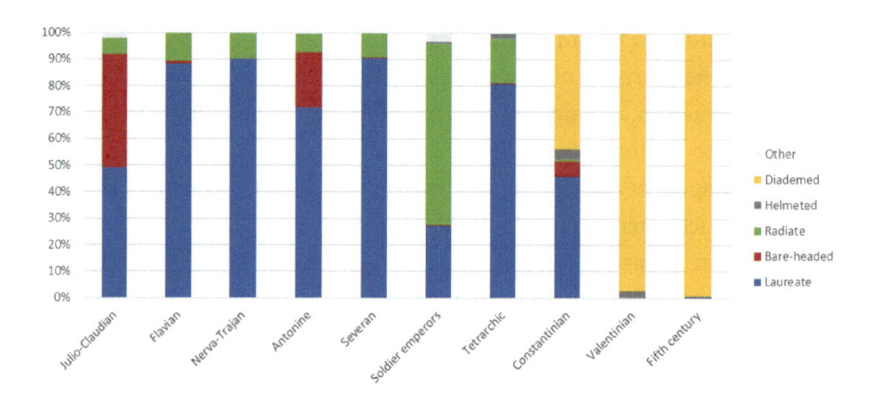

Graph 1.2 Imperial headgear on central coinage

those who had only recently gained citizenship.[224] And because the very symbols that were chosen to denote emperorship were embedded in Roman traditions, it was often difficult to separate the two.

An analysis of the headgear with which Roman emperors are represented on coins shows just how dominant the image of a wreathed ruler was on Roman central coinage (Graph 1.2). A couple of points stand out. First, on coins emperors were usually depicted with a laureate crown. Up to the reign of Septimius Severus, oak wreaths were occasionally included on the reverse of coins, with a legend in or surrounding the wreath, but only coins of Augustus and Galba show the emperor wearing an oak wreath.[225] Instead, the standard way of showing the emperor numismatically was laurel-wreathed. How rapidly the association was established even in the further reaches of the empire becomes clear from a change in the portraits of Nabatean kings. Already in the Augustan age, these started to be shown with laurel wreaths instead of the traditional diadem, as a sign of obedience or an attempt to link themselves to Augustan authority. In either case, it shows that the laurel wreath had become the established headgear of

---

[224] Ando, *Imperial Ideology* makes a powerful argument for seeing the emperor as the binding symbol of the empire. Cf. H. Gozalbes García, 'La corona cívica en la moneda provincial de la Hispania romana', *Espacio Tiempoy Forma. Serie II, Historia Antigua* 28 (2016), 75–96 for an exploration of how that trajectory influenced local depictions of the *corona cívica*.

[225] For references: http://numismatics.org/ocre/, search term: 'oak-wreathed' (total 50 references) and 'oak wreath' (total 310 references, of which 18 show an emperor with a wreath rather than a separate wreath). Note that *RIC* is not entirely systematic in differentiating oak- and laurel-wreaths, but the basic premise holds.

imperial power.[226] This is substantially different from what can be seen on statues. Out of the 277 surviving emperor portraits with some sort of headgear that have recently been assembled in the *RIPD*, 115 show the oak wreath (*corona civica*). These are portraits of almost all Roman emperors from Augustus to Severus Alexander, and also of Constantine, Theodosius, and some third- and fourth-century rulers who cannot be identified with certainty.[227] The emperor was depicted differently in the various types of sources available, as we already saw with the imperial name and portrait. Again, it is likely that local commissioners of statues were crucial in deciding how exactly the emperor was portrayed, rather than that one standardised image was simply reciprocated throughout the realm. Local interests and conventions played their roles. Possibly, the prominence of the *corona civica* in statuary can be also explained by its abundance. The oak-leaved wreath, especially with an incorporated medallion (*corona etrusca*: Figure 1.17) set the emperor apart from private laurel-wreathed individuals.[228] On central coins this was not necessary, as only members of the imperial family would have their heads on coins.

A second point that stands out when looking at imperial headgear on coins is the prominence, especially during the third century, of the so-called radiate crown: a spoked band, tied at the back. Such a crown, with its obvious solar imagery, carried divine connotations. The image of a monarch with rays extending from his head was used by Hellenistic kings to associate them with the sun god.[229] In coins from the Roman republic, only Sol wore a radiate crown. Yet, an alternative variant was introduced on imperial Roman coinage as a new attribute for the deified Augustus. That made it an accessory for a god (*Divus Augustus*) who had closely associated himself with the sun god Apollo when he had still been a living man. The radiate crown, in fact became a mark of deified emperors.[230]

---

[226] A. J. M. Kropp, 'Kings without Diadems – How the Laurel Wreath Became the Insignia of Nabataean Kings', *Archäologischer Anzeiger* (2013), 21–41.

[227] Heijnen, *Portraying Change*, 204–7, with fig. 64. It is, of course, possible that some of the bareheaded marble portraits originally included ornamental headgear made of different materials.

[228] B. Bergmann, 'Die Lorbeeren des Caesar' Oder: Wie erkennt man einen römischen Kaiser? in: D. Boschung/ F. Queyrel (eds.), *Porträt und soziale Distinktion* (Paderborn 2020) 205–58.

[229] N. Wright, 'Seleucid Royal Cult, Indigenous Religious Traditions, and Radiate Crowns: The Numismatic Evidence', *Mediterranean Archaeology* 18 (2005), 67–82; M. Bergmann, *Die Strahlen der Herrscher: theomorphes Herrscherbild und politische Symbolik im Hellenismus und in der römischen Kaiserzeit* (Mainz 1998), 58–84.

[230] This applied to historical reliefs as well as coinage, as can be seen on the so-called Ravenna relief: Rose, *Dynastic Commemoration*, 100–1. Note *RRC* 494/5 for an exceptional coin from 42 BC which shows a winged figure with a radiate crown on the reverse.

Figure 1.17 A very imperial image of Hadrian. Marble statue (h. 2.54), from Hierapitna (Crete), between 117–38, Istanbul, Archaeological Museum inv. 50. The size of the statue and his heroic victorious pose set this statue immediately apart as one of the emperor, dressed in a cuirass and a *paludamentum*. The wreath that he wears, probably the *corona etrusca*, further emphasises his superior status
Source: CKD – Radboud University Nijmegen

Because it was so clearly depicted tied at the back, the Roman radiate crown looked somewhat similar to the laurel and oak wreaths with which living emperors were portrayed on coins. This made the new radiate crown a sort of hybrid between a divine attribute and an honorific crown.[231] That, in turn, made it an interesting symbol for emperors who wanted to more openly show their superiority. The radiate crown oscillated between a divine and an honorific object, and had been worn by emperors – even if only deified ones. It was therefore an attractive attribute to depict Nero, especially since that emperor strongly associated himself with Apollo.[232] Possibly, the comparatively conventional numismatic image of an emperor with a radiate crown crossed over into more extravagant Neronian monuments showing the emperor with a solar crown.[233] Once it was worn by a living emperor, it became less problematic for later emperors to be shown with a radiate crown. Even changes in imperial imagery that may have drawn criticism at the time normalised that imagery – especially if later emperors refrained from the more excessive Neronian solar imagery. Vespasianic coinage displayed the radiate crown without apparent controversy.

Acceptance may have been boosted by linking the message to the medium. From Nero onwards, the image of an emperor wearing a radiate crown became the standard way to denote double value of coins. The *dupondius* (double the value of the *as*), the *antoninianus* (introduced at the value of two silver *denarii* under Caracalla), and the experimental double *sestertius* introduced by Trajan Decius (AD 249–51) all showed the radiated imperial portrait to indicate the double denomination (Figure 2.1, below).[234] With the radiate crown technically indicating the value of a coin, it became entirely straightforward for the ruler to be so depicted. The increase of radiated portraiture during the third century to a large extent follows the increased usage of the *antoninianus*. That did not wholly take the symbolism away. The larger number of images of emperors

---

[231] Bergmann, *Strahlen der Herrscher*, 112–20.
[232] Bergmann, *Strahlen der Herrscher*, 134–46, 172–80; J. Pollini, *From Republic to Empire: Rhetoric, Religion, and Power in the Visual Culture of Ancient Rome* (Norman 2012), 150–4; E. Varner, 'Incarnating the Aurea Aetas: Theomorphic Rhetoric and the Portraits of Nero' in: S. Blakely / E. Olin (eds.), *Gods, Objects, and Ritual Practice in Ancient Mediterranean Religions* (Atlanta 2017) 75–115; 103–6.
[233] Varner, 'Incarnating the Aurea Aetas', 106–8; Bergmann, *Strahlen der Herrscher*, 189–201. But note the cautionary comments by R. R. R. Smith, 'Nero and the Sun-god: Divine Accessories and Political Symbols in Roman Imperial Images', *JRA* 13 (2000), 532–42; 536–8.
[234] C. Howgego, *Ancient History from Coins* (London – New York 1995), 79; D. R. Sear, *Roman Coins and Their Values. Volume 5* (London 2014), 20–2.

Figure 1.18 Constantine's radiate crown, 326, Antioch. Gold medallion, 1.5 solidi (6.59 g.): Portrait of Constantine with radiate crown. The emperor is draped and cuirassed, and holds the globe. The legend reads: D N CONSTANTINVS MAX AVG/ Laureate portraits of Constantine II and Constantius II, each holding an eagle-tipped sceptre and globe. RIC 7, 70
Source: Numisbids, 29–30 May 2017, lot 637

with radiate crowns coincides with greater prominence of the cult of the sun god Sol Invictus, and more inscriptions in which emperors are addressed as *invictus*.[235] People systematically saw their emperor shown similar to Sol and that had consequences.

The third noticeable point when looking at the development of headgear on coins is the sudden shift towards diadems under Constantine. He is still occasionally portrayed with a radiate crown on his coins and medallions until well into his reign (Figure 1.18). This may be unsurprising considering the close association between Constantine and Sol, which precedes the emperor's emphasis on Christ as his preferred deity.[236] The emperor was probably also depicted with a radiate crown on a porphyry column in the centre of Constantinople. But the new numismatic image became that of the emperor wearing a diadem; an image that was not seen on coins before and would be wholly dominant in the later-fourth and fifth century. From Constantine

---

[235] S. E. Heijmans, 'Temples and Priests of Sol in the City of Rome', *Mouseion* 10 (2010), 381–427; 381–2. For the inscriptions, see Bönisch-Meyer, *Dialogangebote*, 222–5.

[236] *RIC* 7, 70; E. Marlowe, 'Framing the Sun: The Arch of Constantine and the Roman Cityscape', *The Art Bulletin* 88 (2006), 223–42. Double denominations also continued to exist after Diocletian's monetary reforms, making the inclusion of radiate crowns a logical consequence: R. Abdy, 'Tetrarchy and the House of Constantine', in: W. E. Metcalf (ed.), *The Oxford Handbook of Greek and Roman Coinage* (Oxford – New York 2012), 584–600; 585. On the disappearance of the radiate crown: Kolb, *Herrscherideologie*, 73–5.

onwards, the diadem became a clear addition to the imperial image – and one that was unique to emperors. The image was not instantly established. First depictions of Constantine's diadem are much less ornamental than the final version, which was heavily decorated with jewels. Especially these first versions are often compared to diadems of Hellenistic kings.[237] It is, however, worth noting that the simple band also has clear similarities to the laurel wreath, and that depictions of the final version of the Constantinian diadem are not miles apart from sculptural depictions of elaborate oak wreaths (Figure 1.17, above). Moreover, there had been earlier Roman rulers who wore diadems (aside from Caesar, who had refused one) as surviving portraits of Nerva, Septimius Severus, Caracalla, Elagabalus and Valerian show without any doubt (Figure 1.14, above).[238] Titus, Elagabalus, Gallienus, Diocletian and Maximian are alleged to have worn diadems by ancient literary sources, all of which criticise them for doing so.[239]

Empresses, too, had been presented wearing the diadem (or *stephane*) well before Constantine, even on coins and medallions from at least the second century onwards.[240] Images of the diadems on coins for the *Augustae* Helena (Constantine's mother) and Fausta (Constantine's second wife) are very similar to those of earlier empresses. Instead, the diadem of Aelia Flaccilla (379–386), the first wife of Theodosius, is a carbon copy of that of her husband. On these coins, Flaccilla is also depicted wearing the *paludamentum* (or *chlamys*). It seems that these attributes had by this time come to denote emperorship in such an abstract sense that empresses, too, could be associated with power in this fashion. Cloak and diadem became standard elements in the coinage of later *Augustae*, indicating the authority of the imperial household.[241]

---

[237] A. Alföldi, 'Insignien und Tracht der römischen Kaiser', *MDAIRA* 49 (1934), 1–177; 149–50; Canepa, *Two Eyes of the Earth*, 199.

[238] *RIPD*, nos. 689, 1742, 1745, 1862, 1945. The vast majority of diademed sculptural portraits postdates Constantine, with approximately 40 per cent of post-Constantinian imperial portraits wearing a diadem: Heijnen, *Portraying Change*, 208.

[239] A. M. Stout, 'Jewelry as a Symbol of Status in the Roman Empire', in: J. L. Sebesta/ L. Bonfante (eds.), *The World of Roman Costume* (Madison 1994), 77–100; 82–3 with references.

[240] *RIC* 3 (2nd ed.) Hadrian, nos. 2450, 2457–63 for Diva Matidia; nos.2472–523, 2538, 2543–5, 2548–9, 2554, 2562–9, 2575–83 for Sabina; *RIC* 3 Antoninus Pius, nos. 506c, 507b, 512B, 517B, 1107c, 1146Ac-d, 1173d, 1378C, 1386B, 1401C, 1404C for Faustina the Younger. *RIC* 2.1 (2nd ed.) Titus, nos. 405–8, 424–9: Livia as Justitia wearing a *stephane*. Sculptural display of empresses with diadem started earlier, as testified by the extravagant hairband on a posthumous marble portrait of Livia (Museo Capitolino, Stanza degli Imperatori 9. Inv. 144). Cf. Rose, *Dynastic Commemoration* 1997, 76–7.

[241] D. Angelova, 'The Ivories of Ariadne and Ideas about Female Imperial Authority in Rome and Early Byzantium', *Gesta* 43 (2004), 1–15; 3–4 with references. See below, p. 240.

The shift from laurel wreath to diadem was a substantial innovation. It may well have been influenced by eastern images of rulership – especially those of the Sasanian court – with which inhabitants of the eastern part of the Roman empire were increasingly confronted, and may possible even have made people think of Alexander the Great.[242] It certainly created, for the first time, an unequivocal point of reference to distinguish the imperial family from everyone else. But it was still a symbol that developed from established practice – not just local eastern notions of rulership, but also the longstanding habit of depicting Roman emperors with some sort of ornamental band around their heads. The adoption of the diadem by Constantine and his successors shows that it had become unproblematic to depict absolute rule. Yet the meaning of the diadem had shifted substantially from the time when Caesar refused one. It is likely that for many fourth-century viewers, the diadem was now associated with Roman rule, more than with Hellenistic monarchy.

Denoting the Emperor (3): The Sceptre

Imperial names, portraiture, clothes and crown all developed over time as symbols of imperial power. They helped to set the emperor apart from others in his empire and to make him recognisably the emperor. An attribute not mentioned by Gregory of Nazianzus but also strongly linked to emperorship was the sceptre. Analysing the appearance of this attribute in both imperial and non-imperial imagery suggests again how Roman emperorship was given visual shape by the use of traditional objects and concepts and how this continued to blur the lines between imperial and non-imperial imagery throughout Roman history. It also shows how the connotations of traditional attributes changed through imperial use, and how emperorship changed by the use of accessories with strong historical and religious connotations.

For the Romans the sceptre was strongly linked to supreme power. It was a relic of the royal age, and primarily an attribute of the gods. Like many powerful props, it made people think of Hellenistic kingship. When Cicero, in the late republic, tried to sketch a stereotypically negative image of the Egyptian king Ptolemy XII Auletes, he described him as 'sitting on his throne, with his purple and sceptre and all the other ensigns of royal

---

[242] Canepa, *Two Eyes of the Earth*, 199–200.

authority'.²⁴³ The dominant association, however, will have been with the gods. Only divinities, most dominantly Jupiter, are depicted with sceptres on Republican statuary and Roman coins up to 44 BC. When Caesar's head appeared on Roman denarii, a sceptre was included, but on the reverse, held by Venus.²⁴⁴ Perhaps unsurprisingly, in real life priests held sceptres, too, as did consuls (the ivory staff or *scipio eburneus*) and triumphing generals, indicating that their authority was divinely sanctioned.²⁴⁵

This made the sceptre an obvious symbol of Roman power in more generic terms. Foreign kings whose position was sanctioned by Rome were often given a consular ivory sceptre, something which was a sufficient source of pride to depict it on local coinage. Under the emperors the praxis of giving staffs to foreign rulers continued well into the sixth century, with late antique authors describing both staffs of silver and the consular staff.²⁴⁶ Through the Roman sceptre, local kings showed how the greater power of Rome endorsed their position. From Augustus onwards, the emperor embodied that greater power, something which was made visually clear by having an imperial portrait as sceptre-head, on the sceptres of friendly kings, but also on sceptres that were held by priests throughout the empire.²⁴⁷

The sceptre as a symbol of (peaceful) transference of power was recognised throughout the wider ancient world. There is a range of classical texts that were also referred to by Roman authors describing how divine or regal succession was indicated by handing over the sceptre.²⁴⁸ The precise

---

[243] Cic. *Sest.* 26.57; V. K. Khrustalev, 'The Image of the Egyptian King Ptolemy XII Auletes in Cicero's Speeches', *Journal of Ancient History* (Вестник древнейистории) 77 (2017), 91–105.

[244] http://numismatics.org/crro/, search term 'sceptre'. The Caesarian coins are *RRC* 480/4–5, 7b–14, 480/17–18. Coins minted in Hispania from 46–5 BC show Pompey the Great on the obverse and Córdoba or Pietas holding a sceptre on the reverse (*RRC* 470/1a–d, 477/1–3).

[245] J. W. Salomonson, *Chair, Sceptre and Wreath. Historical Aspects of their Representations on Some Roman Sepulchral Monuments* (PhD Amsterdam 1956), 53–64; M. Ricci/ G. Pardini/ C. Panella, 'Galleria di immagini', in: C. Panella (ed.), *I segni del potere. Realtà e immaginario della sovranità nella Roma imperial* (Bari 2011), 250–77; 250–8. Cf. *RRC* 494/1 for Lepidus (42 BC) with the Vestal Aemilia holding sceptre and simpulum on the reverse.

[246] Literary references to foreign kings receiving an ivory sceptre: Polybius 32.1.2–3; Liv, 27.4; 30.15; 30.17; 31.11; 42.14; Tac. *Ann.* 4.26.4. Servius, *ad Aen.* 4.242, 30.15.11; Procop. *Bell. Vand.* I [III], 25.1–9; Malalas, *Chron.* 17.9. Local coins: *RPC* I, 717; III, 917 (Bosporus); IV 3993–4004, 8963–5, 8967–8, 8970–8, 9130, 9587–91, 9744–50, 9921, 10775–7, 10795, 10797, 10800, 10975; IX, 185, 187, 193 (Bosporus).

[247] A. Esposito, *Performing the Sacra: Priestly Roles and their Organisation in Roman Britain* (Oxford 2019), 42–4.

[248] Quint. 9.3.57 and 11.3.158 explicitly refer to Homer. Cf. 9.4.140; Verg. *Aen.* 1.653, 7.247 and 7.252 also give Trojan connotations, though Vergil also links the sceptre to Etruscan kingship, especially in 8.507 and 10.852. For the role of the sceptre in theogonic poems, see: M. A. Santamaría Álvarez, 'The Sceptre and the Sickle. The Transmission of Divine Power in the

connotations of the object may have been different for people from different parts of the empire, but the link to the transfer of power would have been obvious to all. This meant that sceptres also remained a powerful symbol for taking up major magistracies. Consuls continued to carry sceptres, mostly the traditional Republican eagle-tipped variant (with strong connotations to Jupiter) but also sceptres crowned by one or more imperial portraits – probably to render tribute to the emperor who had effectively appointed them.[249]

Like other apparent imperial insignia – such as the wreath or purple robe – sceptres were not unique to the emperor, nor were emperors consistently depicted with a sceptre. But emperors were already portrayed holding a sceptre in the early empire. Between 19–4 BC Augustus is shown with a sceptre on central coinage, as is Tiberius on coins from 13–14 AD. Both images are in the clear context of a triumphal procession, an occasion at which sceptres were traditional. Yet, living triumphators had not before been placed on coins. Similarly, a coin from 22–3 AD of a togate Tiberius, seated on the magisterial curule chair and holding a sceptre depicts the emperor as a consul, who had the formal right to hold the sceptre. But it is clearly visually linked to a coin type minted in the same year that shows the deified Augustus seated in front of an altar, wearing a radiate crown and holding the sceptre (Figures 1.19–1.20). It also strongly recalls Republican coin types of Jupiter holding the sceptre.[250]

Even if it is possible to argue that the living emperor was only holding the sceptre in a traditional context, the overbearing image is one of absolute authority, establishing a direct link between the ruler, his deified father, and the supreme god of Rome. This same message, even more direct, can be found on a number of imperial gems. The famous Gemma Augustea (Figure 1.21) and Grand Camée de France leave little doubt that the emperor is depicted in the guise of Jupiter. There is debate about the exact date of the two gems, and they were hardly as public as central coins. These massive gems were so expensive that they will only have been displayed in very elite settings, by people close to the imperial family – if

---

Orphic Rhapsodies', in: A. Marmodoro/ I. F. Viltanioti (eds.), *Divine Powers in Late Antiquity* (Oxford 2017), 108–24.

[249] C. Olovsdotter, 'Representing Consulship. On the Concept and Meanings of the Consular Diptychs', *Opuscula* 4 (2011), 99–123; 104.

[250] *RIC* 1 (2nd ed.), Augustus, nos. 221–4, 280–4, 301, 311. Cf. *RIC* 1 (2nd ed.) Tiberius, nos. 1–4, 48–9; RRC 449/1c; G. Pardini, '*Signa* et *insignia* nell'iconografia numismatica', in: Panella, *I segni del potere*, 77–122; 82–5, 102–13.

Denoting the Emperor (3): Sceptre 93

Figures 1.19–1.20 Magisterial or imperial sceptre? Tiberius is shown on coins with the consular sceptre, dressed in a toga and seated on the curule chair. The coin was issued simultaneously with a visually similar one, showing the radiate and deified Augustus sitting in front of an altar and holding the sceptre. In parallel, the coins show the sceptre linked to emperorship
(Figure 1.19) 22, Rome. Bronze sestertius (27.52 g.): CIVITATIBVS ASIAE RESTITVTIS/ TI CAESAR DIVI AVG F AVGVST PM TR POT XXIIII, surrounding large S C. *RIC* I (2nd ed.) Tiberius 48
Source: ANS 1935.117.358, American Numismatic Society
(Figure 1.20) 22, Rome. Bronze sestertius (26.2 g.): DIVVS AVGVSTVS PATER/ TI CAESAR DIVI AVG F AVGVST P M TR POT XXIIII, surrounding large S C. *RIC* I (2nd ed.) Tiberius 49
Source: ANS 1944.100.39213, American Numismatic Society

Figure 1.21 Augustus as Jupiter: Sardonyx cameo (23 × 19 × 1.4–3.5 cm), found in Toulouse, 12?, Kunsthistorisches Museum, Vienna, Antikensammlung und Ephesosmuseum, inv. no. IX a 79. Augustus is depicted enthroned among the gods, in a pose reminiscent of Jupiter, and with the supreme god's eagle at his feet. He is physically separated from the toiling soldiers and captives below, emphasising his divine status
Source: CKD – Radboud University Nijmegen

not part of it.[251] Such limited accessibly means that these gems (like other high-value objects, such as the above-mentioned ivory diptychs) will have had little impact upon a wide audience. Still, they form (once again) evidence for the inclusion of monarchical or even divine notions in the repertoire of imperial imagery from the very beginning onwards.

Emperors would continue to be portrayed in their triumphal role throughout Roman history. Persisting to depict the emperor holding a sceptre in one role normalised the inclusion of the sceptre in other situations. Likewise, showing deified emperors with (or near) regal attributes or like Jupiter as a matter of course made it easier for living emperors to be

---

[251] E. Zwierlein-Diehl, *Antike Gemmen und ihr Nachleben* (Berlin – New York 2007), 149–54, 160–6. See the comparable imagery on the Boscoreale Cups, p. 68.

similarly portrayed. This will have increased the associations between the emperor and the supreme god. Only statues of emperors closely resembled those of Jupiter, enthroned or as a standing nude figure with a hip-mantle and holding the sceptre.[252] This was one way in which emperors could be distinguished from anyone else. Only they were depicted on statues or coins holding a triumph or in the guise of Jupiter.

This link between ruler and god became yet another mode to express supremacy. Our ancient literary evidence suggests that it was used by rulers who ignored senatorial norms, especially Nero, Domitian and Commodus. All of them used Jovian imagery. There are statues of Nero that visually melded the emperor with the god, including a full-length statue of Nero as Jupiter. Domitian's dining hall on the Palatine was known as the banqueting hall of Jupiter, and the court-flatterer Martial described a cult statue of Jupiter that took its likeness from the emperor. Martial may have been exaggerating, but under Commodus coins and medallions of Jupiter *Iuvenis* show a god whose eyes and beard closely resembled those of the emperor.[253]

But these 'bad' emperors were not the only ones to be somehow linked to the supreme god. Ovid already equated the house of Augustus with that of Jupiter, and the loyalty of the emperor's subject with human devotion to Jupiter.[254] This is poetic flattery, but a series of *denarii* that were struck just before the battle of Actium (31 BC) includes a pair which assimilates (the then still) Octavian with Jupiter. One obverse shows the head of the young ruler with the reverse a herm of Jupiter, with thunderbolt, and the legend IMP CAESAR. The other obverse shows the head of that herm, again with thunderbolt, but clearly with Octavian's features. The reverse shows Octavian on the *sella curulis*, holding a Victoriola.[255] Under the emperor Claudius, the

---

[252] C. H. Hallett, *The Roman Nude. Heroic Portrait Statuary 200 B.C.–A.D. 300* (Oxford 2005), 167–70, 182, 259; C. Maderna, *Iuppiter, Diomedes und Mercur als Vorbilder für römische Bildnisstatuen. Untersuchungen zum römischen statuarischen Idealporträt* (Heidelberg 1988), 18–55.

[253] Museo Nationale, inv. 3553; Salone, inv. 39 (original head was Neronian) *RIC* 3, Commodus, nos. 173, 187, 499, 542; Martial, *Ep.* 9.24.2–3; Stat. *Silv.*, 1.6.25–28; 4.3.128–9; Varner, 'Incarnating the Aurea Aetas', 82–4; Alföldi, *Die monarchische Repräsentation*, 222; J. R. Fears, 'The Cult of Jupiter and Roman Imperial Ideology', *ANRW* II.17.1 (1981), 3–141; 75–9; Bergmann, *Strahlen der Herrscher*, 265; Fig. 51.5–6 ; O. Hekster, *Commodus. An Emperor at the Crossroads* (Amsterdam 2002), 100–1; Mols/ Moormann/ Hekster, 'From Phidias to Constantine', 50–1.

[254] Ovid, *Trist.* 3.1.31–42; *Met.* 1.202; J.-M. Claassen, 'Seizing the Zeitgeist: Ovid in Exile and Augustan Political Discourse', *Acta Classica* 59 (2016): 52–79; 69–71; C. Segal, 'Jupiter in Ovid's *Metamorphoses*', *Arion* 9.1 (2001), 78–99; 89, 92, 94 with further references.

[255] *RIC* 1 (2nd ed.), 270; Rowan, *From Caesar to Augustus*, 118–20; Zanker, *Power of Images*, 55–6, figs.44 a–d; M. Koortbojian, 'The Bringer of Victory: Imagery and Institutions at the Advent of Empire', in: S. Dillon/ K. E. Welch (eds.), *Representations of War in Ancient Rome* (Cambridge 2006), 184–217.

recognisably older face of the emperor was placed on a semi-nude body holding a sceptre. In his other hand Claudius holds a libation dish rather than a thunderbolt, but the presence of an eagle, sacred to Jupiter, removes any doubt that this is the emperor in a Jovian form. A contemporary cameo shows a similar image, but now the emperor holds a thunderbolt (Figure 1.22).[256] Such an association between the most powerful man on earth and the supreme god was obvious throughout the empire, and several Greek inscriptions describe Augustus, Tiberius, Claudius and Domitian as Ζεύς. There is a boost in the number of inscriptions connecting emperor and god under Hadrian, who travelled extensively in the Greek world, and is frequently named Ὀλύμπιος in local inscriptions, occasionally even in Latin texts.[257]

For Hadrian's predecessor Trajan, the link was established in a different way in two much-discussed relief panels on the Arch at Benevento (about 50 km northeast of Naples). One shows Jupiter holding out a thunderbolt, the other Trajan accepting it.[258] This stops well short of equating emperor and god, but sends the message that Jupiter supports Trajan's reign – a notion that Pliny also put forward in his *Panegyric*.[259] People in Rome and in the provinces increasingly referred to the emperor as supported or even elected by the gods, especially from the late-first century onwards, when there was a long period of so-called adoptive emperors, whose dynastic claims were more difficult to express.[260] The strongest expression of such divine support was formulated during the Tetrarchy, in which the rulers took on the *signa* Jovius and Herculius – a sort of nickname through which they claimed personal association with the god, or declared their loyalty to him.[261]

---

[256] Vatican, Sala Rotonda, 243; Art Institute Chicago: 1991.375. Cf. a statue of Claudius as Zeus/Jupiter from Olympia, Archaeological Museum, inv. no. L.125; Mols/ Moormann/ Hekster, 'From Phidias to Constantine', 36–8.

[257] Bönisch, *Dialogangebote*, 142–55, 458–73, see above, p. 37. Bönisch notes how 37 per cent of all Greek epithets link the emperor with the divine, whereas the percentage is much lower in Latin inscriptions.

[258] K. Fittschen, 'Das Bildprogramm des Trajansbogen zu Benevent', *ArchäologischerAnzeiger* 87 (1972), 742–88. Cf. *RIC* 2, Trajan 549–50 for coins showing Trajan holding a thunderbolt, an image that was taken up again under Marcus Aurelius: *RIC* 3, Marcus Aurelius, 264–6.

[259] D. N. Schowalter, *The Emperor and the Gods. Images from the Time of Trajan* (Minneapolis 1993), 52–80.

[260] J. R. Fears, Princeps a diis electus. *The Divine Election of the Emperor as a Political Concept at Rome* (Rome 1977), 222–52, 258–64. On the expression of dynastic claims by adoptive emperors, Hekster, *Emperors and Ancestors*, 78–95.

[261] R. Rees, 'The Emperors' New Names: Diocletian Jovius and Maximian Herculius', in: H. Bowden / L. Rawlings (eds.), *Herakles and Hercules. Exploring a Graeco-Roman Divinity* (Swansea 2005), 223–39. On *signa* as a Late-Roman practice, see B. Salway, 'What's in a Name? A Survey of Roman Onomastic Practice from c. 700 BC to AD 700', *JRS* 84 (1994), 124–45; 136–7. See below, p. 144.

Figure 1.22 Claudius as Jupiter: Sardonyx cameo (7.6 × 5.7 × 0.8 cm), Italy, 41–54, Art Institute Chicago: Gift of Marilynn B. Alsdorf, inv. 1991.375. Claudius is shown with his own portrait and laurel wreath, but the much more muscular body of Jupiter. He is naked apart from Jupiter's aegis, and holds thunderbolt and sceptre. Jupiter's eagle looks at the emperor in Jovian guise. The link between the emperor and supreme god was apparently unproblematic
Source: The Art Institute of Chicago.

The Jovian aspect of the emperor, then, seems to have somewhat increased over time, although it had been present from the very beginning. None of this made the sceptre into a very specific imperial attribute. Approximately 15 per cent of all coin types minted with the emperor on the obverse show a sceptre, but if one looks at who holds the sceptre, there is no real discernible pattern over time (Graph 1.3). Up to the Christianisation of the empire, there are personifications, deities, emperors, and members of the imperial family holding the sceptre; after Constantine the deities disappear.[262] The implication of many of the coins is that the divinities or personifications support the emperor (whose face is on the obverse of the coin) with their divine power, or even transfer it to him. Actual images of the sceptre being handed over to an emperor are rare. They only really developed in the third century, when imperial legitimation became a real issue because of the many military, economic and political difficulties. Divine support for the emperor became increasingly important, and the handover of the sceptre by a god a powerful way to visualise that message on coins.[263]

Alternatively, the globe was used as a symbol to make the same point. There are also depictions of sceptres topped by orbs, which seem to be held only by gods and members of the imperial family.[264] Possibly, sceptres topped with busts (of emperors and gods) were reserved for consuls and praetors with responsibility for the games, but they were also held by personifications of the Genius Senatus. The eagle-tipped sceptre continued to be held by both emperors and consuls. Ultimately, attempts to classify sceptres into specific categories are complicated, especially on coins where it is occasionally even difficult to see if someone holds a long sceptre or a spear. In statuary, the hand-held objects are often lost.[265] Nor is there a very systematic differentiation of types of sceptres in Roman literature. Still, Isidore of Seville (c. 560–636) specifically records the eagle-tipped sceptre when describing the Roman triumph in his late-antique encyclopaedic *Origines*.[266] There was, at least, some continuous awareness of the backgrounds of different sceptres, though it is unlikely to have been widespread, nor did it stop consuls from being depicted both with eagle-tipped and with bust-topped sceptres.

---

[262] The category 'held by other', which is substantial for Julio-Claudian coinage, consists mainly of unidentified (female) figures, most probably personifications, though some of them may indicate Livia. Unlike later imperial coinage, the types do not include an explanatory legend.
[263] De Blois, *Image and Reality*, 242–6.
[264] P. Arnaud, 'L'Image du globe dans le monde romain: science, iconographie, symbolique', *MEFRA* 96 (1984), 53–116; 102–12; P. Bastien, *Le Buste monétaire des empereurs romains* (Wetteren, 1992), II, 498–9. A more extreme variant was the emperor enthroned on a globe: MacCormack, *Art and Ceremony*, 127–9.
[265] Pardini, 'Signa et insignia nell'iconografia numismatica', 77–122 gives an extremely useful overview of the different sceptres and lances and attempts to trace a development over time.
[266] Isid. *Orig.* 18.2.5.

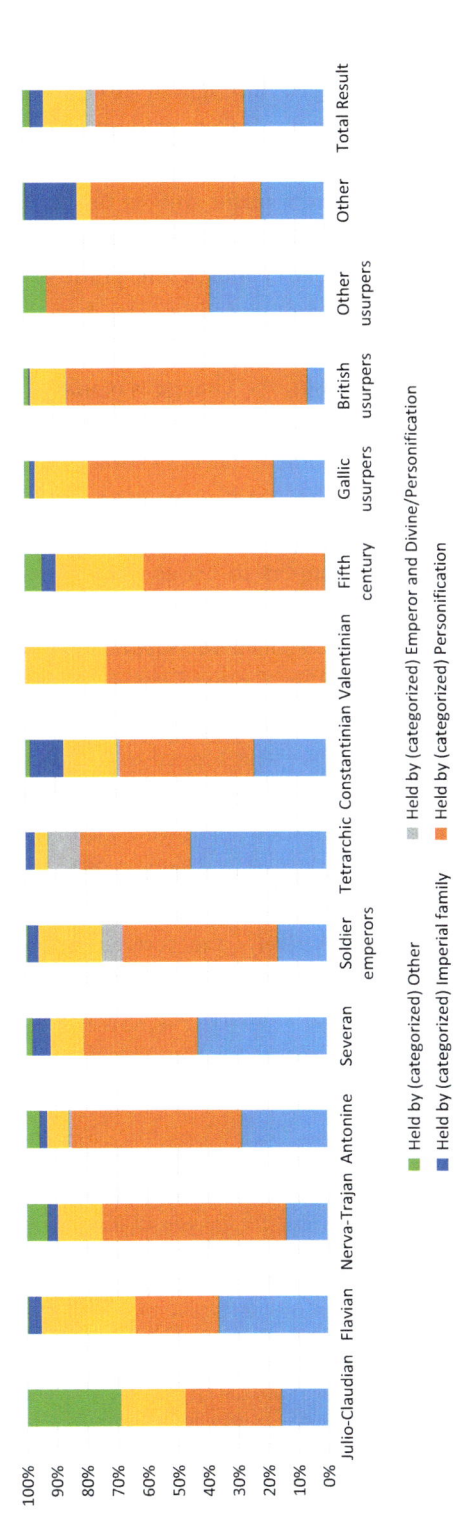

Graph 1.3 Sceptres on central coinage

It seems that the primary meaning of a sceptre as a token of (divine) power remained unchanged throughout Roman history. More specific connotations with consulship, Hellenistic kingship, triumphs and processions did not disappear altogether, but seem to have become of lesser importance. This facilitated a major shift in the depiction of sceptres after Constantine, in the Christian empire. Effectively, the sceptre became a cross. Pope Leo the Great (440–61) makes the point explicitly in one of his surviving sermons: 'the Lord carried the wood of the cross which should turn for Him into the sceptre of power'.[267] As the sceptre had always been about transference of power, the change was one of shape rather than of meaning. The construction of the so-called *labarum* will have helped the change. The *labarum* commemorated Constantine's vision of the sign of the cross the night before he won his important battle at the Milvian Bridge against his opponent Maxentius (306–12). It showed how Constantine was protected by Christian support in his attempt to gain sole control of the empire after the Tetrarchic experiment had effectively failed. Constantine's contemporary Eusebius described the *labarum* as 'a long spear, overlaid with gold [which] formed the figure of the cross by means of a transverse bar laid over it'.[268] The iconographic similarities between a standard topped with a cross, and the long sceptres topped with globes, portraits or an eagle are apparent. Fourth-century images on coins of emperors holding this cross-tipped standard often show them with Victory on a globe in the other hand, strengthening the association (Figure 1.23).[269]

Over time, the imagery shifted to emperors holding a long cross or cruciform sceptre. Alternatively, the reverse of coins showed Victoria holding a long cross, or a cross on a globe.[270] A regularly issued reverse type of a cross in a wreath similarly suggested that Christian piety sanctioned imperial power. Crosses became extremely common on imperial

---

[267] Leo, *Sermon* 59.8.4 ('Christ bearing His own cross is an eternal lesson to the Church').

[268] Euseb.*Constant.* 28–32; H. Singor, 'The Labarum, Shield Blazons, and Constantine's *Caeleste Signum*', in: L. de Blois et al. (eds.), *The Representation and Perception of Roman Imperial Power* (Amsterdam 2003), 481–500. M. Squire, 'How to Read a Roman Portrait? Optatian Porfyry, Constantine and the 'Vvltus Avgvsti', *PBSR* 84 (2016): 179–366; 219–21.On Maxentius, and the influence of his emperorship on Constantinian imagery: S. Betjes/ S. Heijnen, 'The Usurping Princeps. Maxentius' Image and its Constantinian Legacy', *JAHA* 5 (2018), 5–23. On the vision, see below, p. 140.

[269] Bastien, *Buste monetaire*, II, 428–32, 527, III, pl. 222–4. The first numismatic representations of the *labarum* are from 326: R. Leeb, *Konstantin und Christus. Die Verchristlichung der imperialen Repräsentation unter Konstantin dem Grossen als Spiegel seiner Kirchenpolitik und seines Selbstverständnisses als christlicher Kaiser* (Berlin 1992), 43–8.

[270] http://numismatics.org/ocre/, search terms 'Victoria cross'; 'Victoria long cross'.

Figure 1.23 Victory of the cross. 364, Antioch. Gold solidus (4.52 g.): the reverse of this coin shows Valens in imperial regalia, holding victory on a globe in one hand, and a cross-tipped standard in the other, similar to the iconography of the emperor holding a sceptre. The legend RESTITVTOR – REIPVBLICAE and depiction of a cross emphasise how the Christian emperor guaranteed the continuity of the realm. Obverse: portrait of the emperor, shown with diadem and cuirass: D N VALENTINI-ANVS P F AVG. *RIC* IX Antioch, 2b I (2nd ed.)
Source: ANS 1948.19.822, American Numismatic Society

coinage, as symbols on emperors' helmets or clothing, hand-held objects, or simply added to the figure of an emperor or empress on obverses.[271] Like earlier images of sceptres, they were never uniquely tied to emperorship, but continued to express divine support. In an analogous way, the image of the triumphing emperor in a *quadriga* was Christianised by adding a 'hand of god' to the iconography, reaching down from heaven to show how the Christian god guaranteed imperial triumph. The same hand of god is seen on fifth-century coins crowning various empresses, with the cross within a wreath or Victoria holding a long cross on the reverse (Figure 1.24).[272] Existing imagery was adapted and appropriated to transmit a message that was in practice a conventional one of divine election, although the god who did the electing had changed.

---

[271] I. Garipzanov, *Graphic Signs of Authority in Late Antiquity and the Early Middle Ages, 300–900* (Oxford 2018), 89–91; P. Guest, *The Transition to Late Antiquity on the Lower Danube. Excavations and Survey at Dichin, a Late Roman to early Byzantine Fort and a Roman aqueduct* (Oxford 2019), 240.

[272] http://numismatics.org/ocre/, search terms 'Hand of God'; J. D. MacIsaac, 'The Hand of God. A Numismatic Study', *Traditio* 31 (1975), 322–8.

Figure 1.24 Crowned by the Hand of God: 402–3, Constantinople. Gold solidus (4.457 g.): Empress Aelia Eudoxia, wife to Arcadius, is shown with jewels and diadem, crowned by the hand of God. The legend AEL EODOXIA AVG shows that she holds the rank of Augusta. The image of Victory inscribing the Chi-Ro sign on her shield, and the legend SALVS REIPVBLICAE indicates how the Christian god protected emperor and empire. RIC X, Arcadius 28
Source: ANS 1967.153.185, American Numismatic Society

The Creation of an Imperial Image?

At the end of the fifth century, the *magister militum* (the highest military commander) of the western Roman empire, the Germanic general Ricimer, effectively ruled the west (461–72). He did not claim imperial power, but controlled a series of puppet emperors.[273] One of these was Libius Severus, also known as Severus III (461–5), who was not recognised as emperor by the eastern emperor Leo I. Yet looking at coins struck for this ruler in the west, his relative impotence and contested status were invisible (Figure 1.25). On the obverse, we see the emperor with cloak and jewelled diadem. The accompanying legend names him D(OMINUS) N(OSTER) and AUG(USTUS). On the reverse, he stands holding a long cross in one hand and a Victoriola on a globe in the other. Severus III may not have had much power, but he was portrayed as emperors had come to be, with the relevant name and trappings of power. At first sight, the contrast to the early image of the emperor Augustus is pronounced. That, after all, was a ruler who had full control of the empire, but was usually depicted bare-headed or

---

[273] F. Anders, *Flavius Ricimer. Macht und Ohnmacht des weströmischen Heermeisters in der zweiten Hälfte des 5. Jahrhunderts* (Frankfurt a. M. 2010).

Figure 1.25 An impressive puppet emperor: 461–5, Ravenna, Gold solidus (4.45 g.): nothing on this coin shows Libius Severus' impotence. He is shown with jewelled diadem and draped cuirass, identified as D N LIBVS SEVERVS P F AVG/ VICTOR-IA AVGGG indicates his imperial victories, in contrast to historical reality. Likewise his pose, in military dress, holding a cross-tipped sceptre and victory on the globe depicts him in the now-standardised image of Roman emperorship. *RIC* X Libius Severus 2702; BM B.11208
Source: © The Trustees of the British Museum

wearing a simple oak- or laurel wreath. Statues and reliefs mainly show him in a magisterial toga, and he only holds a sceptre on coins depicting him in a specific triumphal setting. It seems, then, that a clear image of emperorship developed in late antiquity, which was far removed from the 'Republican' imagery of the early empire. Yet that is only part of the story.

For almost all elements that are included in the coinage of Severus III, or in very similar images of fifth- and sixth-century usurpers and established emperors, were already part of the (visual) vocabulary of the early empire. Clearly, use of these elements became less contested in the course of time, mainly through repeated exposure. Elite authors had criticised emperors like Caligula and Gallienus for their use of precious stones and purple and gold clothing but are silent about Justinian's ornamental dress. The diadem which Cicero had associated with the Alban kings and eastern monarchs had become a sign of Roman rule. After all, when subjects had sufficiently often seen radiate crowns linked to deified rulers, it became easier to accept these for living emperors. And even if that drew criticism, as Nero experienced, it still linked ruler with attribute and in doing so normalised use. The individual ruler may have faced disapproval, but the image still circulated throughout Roman territory – and not all in the empire will have disliked what they saw, or have known that others (for instance the senatorial elite) disliked it. In that sense, there were only temporary failures in centuries of experimenting in how to make the Roman emperor instantly recognisable. These were often problematic for individual rulers, but allowed emperorship to develop further. Moreover, there were enormous variations in imperial imagery from the very beginning. Local traditions and medial conventions influenced how emperors were depicted. In various contexts even the Julio-Claudian emperors could be described or depicted in a much more monarchical way without difficulties, as large imperial gems or portraits from Roman Egypt abundantly show.[274] The enormous variation of imperial nomenclature in which names and titles were abandoned in one context but continued in another also shows the inherent risk in looking for an official imperial image, let alone a uniform one.

Some developments can still be traced. The increase of 'Republican' titles when Vespasian founded a new dynasty, the surge of military images and names in the so-called crisis of the third century, the sudden appearance of the diadem during Constantine's reign, or the appearance of the cross and hand of god, alongside the title of *Dominus Noster* in the Christianised empire show how certain images and ideas were promulgated and adapted to make political and religious change comprehensible to Roman subjects. Similarly, the way in which certain symbols for Rome and its rulers became linked shows how images and concepts expressed an increased equation between emperor and empire. Neither promulgation nor equation were strictly top-down processes, nor linear ones. And these shifts in the imperial image inevitably made use of pre-existent notions and expectations, whether by adhering to 'physiognomic consciousness' (or even Hellenistic notions of royal appearance) or by adding symbols to well-known iconography. This did not 'overwrite' earlier meanings but added a layer. As Ovid aptly phrased it: 'everything changes, nothing perishes'.[275] The monarchic or divine connotations that many attributes of power held in the Mediterranean world did not disappear by their incorporation in imperial imagery. Emperors could continuously be characterised positively or negatively by referring to these meanings of accessories. Thus, Constantine's choice of 'adorning his head with a diadem at all times' was frowned upon, whereas Julian was praised for wearing an almost magistrate-like toga in contemporary panegyric.[276]

In many ways, the development of the image of Roman emperors was a search for a way to make the supreme position of the emperor recognisable

---

[274] For images on imperial gems, see above, p. 92–3. For imperial portraits in Egypt: S. Pfeiffer, *Der römische Kaiser und das Land am Nil. Kaiserverehrung und Kaiserkult in Alexandria und Ägypten von Augustus bis Caracalla (30 v. Chr.–217 n. Chr.)* (Stuttgart 2010), 53, 55–7, 124–33.
[275] Ovid. *Met.* 15.165.
[276] For criticism on Constantine, see above, p. 81, for praise of Julian, see above, p. 71.

The Creation of an Imperial Image? 105

in an acceptable way, through tools that were already available in one form or another. It cannot be sufficiently emphasised that emperorship as such was never unambiguously defined, other than by the name Augustus. Over time, the range of options which emperors and the inhabitants of the empire had to portray the ruler extended as previously less acceptable modes of representation became normalised. At the same time, there was some sort of congruence in what were typical imperial attributes. The much-discussed ceremonial reforms of Diocletian were a confirmation of practice, rather than a watershed. They did not end the variety of imagery. Honorius could still be flattered by naming him *princeps*, when *dominus noster* had become the norm. The philosopher and bishop Synesius of Cyrene (c. 370–c. 413) still credited unceremonious emperorship instead of the contemporary practice of wearing sumptuous clothing and celebrating major ceremonial occasions.[277] Expectations of how emperors ought to be described and portrayed continued to differ regionally, medially and between social groups, even when typically imperial modes of representation, with diadem, purple cloak and standardised facial features solidified. Very few typically imperial features, the diadem excepted, were unique to the emperor. One reason why imperial images – such as the *imagines clipeata* (portraits on shield-like frames) or the ruler's image on a toga or sceptre – may have been added to consular diptychs is to make sure that people did not mistake the highly decorated seated figure holding a sceptre for the emperor.[278] For many people, the Roman emperor would always remain a distant figure, far removed from their daily life. Synesius suggests that there were people in Ptolemais (a city in the northeast of modern Libya) 'who suppose that Agamemnon, the son of Atreus, is still king, the great king who went against Troy'.[279] Even if this story is unlikely, it shows how widely different the perceptions of emperorship in the Roman empire could be. No image would encapsulate the many different views and expectations of rule. Trying to trace the development of this image over time shows how various views were continuously embedded in existing symbolism. It also shows a tension between attempts to formulate and visualise emperorship in one identifiable way, and the widely differing expectations of what an emperor should look like and be.

---

[277] Syn. *On imperial rule*, 11.4–5; M. Icks, 'Keeping Up Appearances. Evaluations of Imperial (In)visibility in Late Antiquity', in: E. Manders/ D. Slootjes (eds.), *Leadership, Ideology and Crowds in the Roman Empire of the Fourth Century* AD (Stuttgart 2020), 163–79; 169–70.
[278] On imperial attributes on diptychs, see Olovsdotter, 'Representing Consulship, 104–5.
[279] Syn. *Letters* 148.16.

2 | Playing Imperial Roles

The best way of successfully acting a part is to be it*

Emperors and the Codification of Imperial Roles

Looking at the image of the Roman emperor over several centuries showed how certain modes of representation became linked to the figure of the emperor. Through an increasingly standardised use of specific images, emperors and the various groups in the empire could communicate, even if variation always remained possible. To an extent, the same applied to depictions of typically imperial roles.[1] There was some level of standardisation of ways in which types of imperial behaviour were depicted.[2] This was not just about imagery, but also about the expectations people had of what an emperor should actually do. Inevitably, considering the size of the empire, these expectations differed in the various provinces and among different social groups. We will return to these different perspectives in Chapter 4, in which perceptions of the emperor in Rome and Constantinople are placed alongside those in other parts of the empire. This chapter instead traces the development of the main roles that emperors were expected to play.

These core imperial roles were clear from the early empire onwards. He was supreme commander of the armies, intermediary between the Roman empire and its gods – as became clear from his priestly position – and magistrate, which included his role as ultimate source of law and justice.[3] Those roles go further back than the Augustan reign, and follow Republican prototypes. Well before there was one supreme ruler, Romans had been able to come to prominence through exploits in the field, senate

---

* Arthur Conan Doyle, 'The Adventure of the Dying Detective', *The Strand Magazine* 46 (1913).
[1] Parts of this chapter expand upon O. Hekster, 'Les Contraintes posées par la tradition dans la création de l'image impériale', in: P. Ledoze (ed.), *Le Costume de Prince. Regards sur une figure politique de la Rome antique d'Auguste à Constantin* (Rome 2021), 87–112.
[2] Hölscher, 'Historical Representations of the Roman Republic', 25–6; Trimble, 'Communicating with Images', 113; Seelentag, 'Antoninus Pius und die Herrschaftsdarstellung', 19–30.
[3] See p. 23 above for literature on these imperial roles.

house or courtroom (mainly through oratory), and by wielding influence on society as a priest. Moreover, these are standard roles for almost all monarchs in the ancient world, although the emphasis between roles may change.[4] It is, then, unsurprising that the ultimate Roman leader would need to stand out at all of these fields, or at least appear to do so. Perhaps more surprising is that there was hardly any precedent in the late Republic for a single individual excelling in all fronts. The great conqueror and administrator Pompey (106-48 BC), who famously cleared the Mediterranean of pirates in under three months (67 BC) had no legal mind and had only a moderate talent for oratory (*eloquentia medius*). Silver-tongued Cicero (106-43 BC) was hardly a military genius.[5]

The two Republican men who did stand out at all three levels also aimed at sole rule. Lucius Cornelius Sulla (138-78 BC) was an accomplished general, known as *Felix* ('fortunate') for his highly individual 'divine luck'. Sulla was also a proficient orator, as opposed to his opponent Gaius Marius (157-86 BC).[6] He is best known for his infamous march on Rome (88 BC), which was the first (but not the last) time that a Roman general assaulted his own capital. Ultimately, he became *dictator* (a formal role for periods of exceptional difficulties) without an established time limit, the first sole ruler of Rome since the kings.[7] The other example of a Roman statesman who shone as conqueror, religious leader and orator was of course Julius Caesar, who, like Sulla, would become dictator. Caesar, more than Sulla, became the ideal of a successful ruler – certainly in retrospect. He was Pontifex Maximus, and quite possibly divinely honoured while he lived.[8]

---

[4] A good overview is provided by the various contributions to S. Rebenich (ed.), *Monarchische Herrschaft im Altertum* (Berlin – Boston 2017), with an overview of various roles in S. Rebenich/ J. Wienand, 'Monarchische Herrschaft im Altertum. Zugänge und Perspektiven', in: Rebenich, *Monarchische Herrschaft im Altertum*, 1–41; 3–19. See J. P. Roth, 'Jews and the Roman Army', in: L. de Blois/ E. LoCascio (eds.), *The Impact of the Roman Army (200 BC–AD 476)* (Amsterdam 2007), 409–20; 411 on the Jewish king as commander-in-chief.

[5] Vel. Pat. 2.29.3–4, with H. van der Blom, 'Pompey in the Contio', *CQ* 61 (2011), 553–73. Cicero's military command: T. Wiedemann, *Cicero and the End of the Roman Republic* (London 1994), 60–1.

[6] On Sulla and the construction and perception of his divine luck, see A. Eckert, *Lucius Cornelius Sulla in der antiken Erinnerung. Jener Mörder, der sich Felix nannte* (Berlin – Boston 2016). 43–85. On Sulla's oratory skills: C. Steel. 'Sulla the Orator', in: A. Eckert /A. Thein (eds.), *Sulla. Politics and Reception* (Berlin 2020), 19–32. On Marius' lack or oratorical skills, see R. J. Evans, *Gaius Marius: A Political Biography* (Pretoria 1994), 85.

[7] F. J. Vervaet, 'The *Lex Valeria* and Sulla's Empowerment as Dictator (82–79 BCE)', *Cahiers du Centre Gustave Glotz* 15 (2004), 37–84. On the dictatorship see above, p. 3.

[8] On Caesar's divine honours, see Gradel, *Emperor Worship*, 54–72; Koortbojian, *The Divinization of Caesar and Augustus*, 32–9; G. McIntyre, *A Family of Gods. The Worship of the Imperial Family in the Latin West* (Ann Arbor 2016), 16–26.

He was, moreover, an immensely successful general and an orator who could inspire crowds.

Caesar and (to a lesser extent) Sulla were the immediate role models to whom Augustus had to relate when he had gained sole control of the empire. If nothing else, they provided situations to avoid. Sulla's reputation was ambivalent at best. And even if the new ruler distanced himself from his adoptive father Caesar in many ways, he still had to live up to the example that had been set. This is one reason why Augustus' qualities as a general are stressed by ancient authors and on coins and historical reliefs – although most evidence suggests that these qualities were mediocre at best. In reality, Augustus' right-hand man Marcus Vipsanius Agrippa (63–12 BC) was the superior strategist, who guaranteed the victories which Augustus then celebrated.[9] Still, the continuously repeated message that Augustus was a great general, through coins linking him to Victory, arches in Rome commemorating Actium and the Parthian settlement, poets praising his accomplishments and reliefs throughout the empire linking the emperor with military success, resounded. Augustus also seems to have taken great pains to emphasise his qualities as a general in his autobiography (*De Vita Sua*) written during the 20s BC.[10] In combination with real expansion of the empire, most importantly by the incorporation of Egypt and territory as far as the Danube in the east, the reputation of Augustus as a conquering ruler was guaranteed.

Caesar and Augustus were the main models of early Roman emperorship, and would remain exemplary for a long time.[11] The combination of qualities for which they had become well known – all of which had already been important indicators of esteem in Republican times – needed to be matched by later emperors. Roman subjects, as we will see throughout this chapter, expected their emperor to outshine the enemy, guarantee the *pax deorum* and still retain the qualities of 'civil' magistrates. These expectations would remain surprisingly stable over the centuries, and severely restrained emperors' freedom to create a unique imperial 'persona'.

---

[9] J.-M. Roddaz, *Marcus Agrippa* (Rome 1984), esp. 139–94.

[10] There are ninety-five coin types at http://numismatics.org/ocre/ with key word Victory for the reign of Augustus. On the arches, see J. W. Rich, 'Augustus's Parthian Honours, the Temple of Mars Ultor and the Arch in the Forum Romanum', *PBSR* 66 (1998), 71–128 and below, p. 116. Military conquest is emphasised in poems of Ovid, Propertius, and of course in Vergil, and in various reliefs of the Sebasteion at Aphrodisias. On the autobiography and its impact see A. Powell, 'Augustus' Age of Apology: An Analysis of the Memoirs – and an Argument for Two Further Fragments', in: C. Smith/ A. Powell (eds.), *The Lost Memories of Augustus and the Development of Roman Autobiography* (Swansea 2009), 173–94.

[11] Hekster, *Emperors and Ancestors*, 162–76.

The Emperor and His Military Role

As the emphasis on Augustus' perceived military qualities made clear, Roman rulers had to be successful in war, if not in reality, certainly in the public perception.[12] The notion that any Roman leader was above all a military leader is clear from the famous phrase 'If you are in good health, it is well. I and my army are in good health'.[13] As a starting phrase of Augustan letters to the senate, it is a chilling reminder of the military possibilities which a Roman emperor had at his disposal. But it had already been a stock phrase in the Roman republic, so well known that Cicero could abbreviate it in his letters.[14] The Civil Wars of the late Republic led to a centralisation of power that was new, and allowed Sulla and Caesar to become sole ruler – even if only for a brief period of time. Where before various military leaders had divided the loyalty of troops, or indeed competed for it, from the reign of Augustus onwards the armies, in general, served their emperor – and him alone. The emperor was the supreme military leader. Legionary commanders owed him their *imperium*; their victories were his to celebrate.[15] It is not coincidental that in the *Res Gestae Divi Augusti* (the accomplishments of the deified Augustus), the emperor emphasised how military actions were taken 'under my auspices'.[16] Decisions on whether to wage war or not were variously ascribed to imperial whim. Augustus was even described as 'lord of war and peace'.[17]

This military expectation was no problem for Augustus' immediate successor Tiberius, who was in his fifties when he came to the throne. He was an experienced general with major victories to his name (which had boosted Augustus' military reputation). But in the next three decades, none of the incumbents of the imperial throne had any military successes to speak of at the outset. Gaius (Caligula), Claudius and Nero could not refer

---

[12] Y. le Bohec, 'L'Empereur et l' armée sous le Principat', in: Ledoze, *Le Costume de Prince*, 437-74; O. Hekster, 'The Army and Imperial Propaganda', in: P. P. M. Erdkamp (ed.), *The Blackwell Companion to the Roman Army* (Oxford: Blackwell 2007), 339-58. Campbell, *The Emperor and the Roman Army* remains fundamental.

[13] Above, p. 11, with references.

[14] Cicero, *Ad. Fam.* 5.21 (*Si tu exercitusque valetis, bene est*); 5.7.1 (S. T. E. Q. V. B. E.).

[15] Vegetius, *De Re Military*, 2.5 transmits the military oath sworn by soldiers to the emperor. On the primacy of Augustus in victory-matters: J. W. Rich, *Augustus and the* spolia opima, *Chiron* 26 (1996), 85-127.

[16] *RGDA*, 4.2; 26.5; 30.2.

[17] Strabo 17.3.25 [840]. Cf. Florus, 2.30; Dio, 53.17.6, 53.22.5. For further discussion see J. B. Campbell, *Warfare and Society in Imperial Rome, 31 B.C.-A.D. 280* (London - New York 2002), 5. Cf. Campbell, *The Emperor and the Roman Army*, 152.

to previous conquests or victories. Even two of the men aiming for the throne in the Year of the Four Emperors (68–9) following the death of Nero had no military successes to boost. Yet this did not change the notion that an emperor needed to be a conquering hero. That was so firmly settled through Republican precedent and the examples of (Sulla), Caesar and Augustus that it survived notwithstanding the number of non-military rulers who could come to power. Instead, rulers without an obvious military portfolio had to fulfil their expected role. One way of doing so was by actual military conquest. Claudius, for instance, boosted his reputation by conquering Britain. This victory was crucial for stabilising his fragile position on the throne. He even had to bring senators with him to the north, so that they would not be able to damage his position in Rome, but left them at the French coast so that they would not be able to share in his victory.[18] This may be linked to a decree that Claudius is alleged to have passed which 'forbade soldiers to enter the houses of senators to pay their respects'. Soldiers could not be clients of anyone but the *princeps* himself.[19]

Starting a reign with a military campaign, however, carried risks. What if the emperor were to lose? An alternative to a real victory was the semblance of one. As so often, Augustus set the template. In 53 BC, the Parthians had resoundingly defeated the Roman armies of Marcus Licinius Crassus (c. 115–53 BC) at Carrhae, capturing several legionary standards in the process. Caesar had planned to punish the Parthians for this, but was assassinated before he could set off. Mark Antony did campaign against them several times between 40 and 36 BC, but without success. Expectations were high that Augustus would right that wrong, as poems proclaiming imminent victory make clear.[20] But the new emperor recognised the risks of failure, and instead managed to regain standards and prisoners through negotiation in 20 BC. That feat of diplomacy, however, was presented to the Roman people as a glorious success, through coins, reliefs, architecture, statues and texts that celebrated Augustus' triumphant retrieval of the standards.[21]

---

[18] Suet. *Claud.* 17; Dio, 60.21. Note especially Suet. *Galba*, 7.1, pointing out how Claudius delayed departing for Britain till Galba had recovered from (real or feigned) illness.

[19] Suetonius, *Div. Claud.* 25.1; C. Thomas, 'Claudius and the Roman Army Reforms', *Historia* 53 (2004), 424–52; 428.

[20] S. P. Mattern-Parkes, 'The Defeat of Crassus and the Just War', *Classical World* 96 (2003), 387–96.

[21] Rich, 'Augustus's Parthian Honours'; M. Koortbojian, *Crossing the Pomerium. The Boundaries of Political, Religious and Military Institutions from Caesar to Constantine* (Princeton – Oxford 2020), 37–9.

The Emperor and his Military Role 111

Figure 2.1 Proclaiming peace: 244–6, Antioch. Silver Antonianus (4.86 g). Coins proclaimed military accomplishments, even if reality in the field was very different. Philip Arabs, in military gear, and with radiate crown, also to indicate the double value of the Antoninianus: IMP C M IVL PHILIPPVS P F AVG P M/ The personification of Pax, holding the sceptre, emphasises how PAX FVNDATA CVM PERSIS. The implication is one of a dominant Rome establishing peace, whereas in practice Rome had been heavily defeated. RIC IV Philip I 69.
Source: ANS 1944.100.18347, American Numismatic Society

Later emperors would do the same, and present negotiated peace treaties as military successes. Commodus, for instance, celebrated a triumph for a peace settlement with the Marcomanni and the Quadi, against whom his father had fought fierce battles. He retained the Danube as the frontier of the Roman empire, but presented it as a military accomplishment.[22] Commodus' peace settlement was positive for Rome and long lasting. Moreover, peace as a result of negotiation was acceptable for most Romans, as long as Rome was negotiating from strength. So guaranteeing peace through proper negotiation could be presented as a victory.[23] But even near-defeats were presented in positive terms. When the emperor Philip Arabs was forced to buy off invading Sasanians (the successors of the Parthians as Rome's eastern enemies) in AD 244 after a failed battle in which his predecessor Gordian III (238–44) was wounded or possibly even killed, his coins presented this as the establishment of proper peace: PAX FUNDATA CUM PERSIS (Figure 2.1), this notwithstanding a settlement in which the Romans had to pay 500,000 *aurei* ransom for

---

[22] *AE* 1953.79; *ILS* 1327; *CIL* 14.2922 (= *ILS* 1420); HA, *Marc.* 22.10–1; *Comm.* 3.6; M. P. Speidel, 'Commodus and the King of the Quadi', *Germania* 78 (2000), 193–7; Hekster, *Commodus*, 40–9.
[23] H. Cornwell, Pax *and the Politics of Peace. Republic to Principate* (Oxford 2017), 29–32, 197–200.

Roman soldiers and accept Sasanian supremacy in Armenia and Mesopotamia.[24] The Sasanian king Shapur I (240-70) renamed the town Misiche, where the battle had taken place, to Peroz-Shapur ('Shapur is Victorious') and propagated his victory and Philip's loss through texts and monuments, listing Rome as 'tributary and subject'.[25] None of this stopped Philip from emphasising his military qualities and accomplishments in Rome. Likewise, the first non-senatorial emperor, Macrinus, boldly advertised his military qualities through coins proclaiming victory over the Parthians, although he lost a major battle at Nisibis, surrendered all prisoners and paid the Parthians large sums of money.[26]

More general images of the emperor in a military context were a third way of showing military qualities, as well as real victories or exaggerated settlements. It is no coincidence that the military notions of *virtus* and, to a lesser extent, *providentia* encompassed 25 per cent of all the imperial virtues that were displayed on *denarii* between AD 69-238. During the third century, in which the empire faced real military difficulties, the role of *virtus* on coinage rose even significantly above that, becoming strongly linked to individual emperors.[27] Similarly, a recent analysis of some 7,000 gold coins shows 'security', 'stability', 'support of the armies' and 'the emperor as victorious general' as dominant reverse types for Claudius, Otho, Vitellius, Titus, Nerva and Trajan, while 'relationship with armies' is the dominant theme on gold coins under the third-century rulers Geta, Caracalla, Macrinus, Elagabalus and Alexander Severus.[28] On many coins, the emperor was depicted wearing a cuirass and Neronian coins for the first time showed a draped cuirass. Under Hadrian, there is an adapted variant of a cuirassed portrait with a *paludamentum*, (cf. Figure 1.17, above) while an undraped variant is first used under Antoninus Pius (138-61). Such military portraiture on coins became increasingly dominant in the third to fifth centuries.[29]

---

[24] *RIC* 4.2, Philip I, 69; De Blois, *Image and Reality*, 63.
[25] *Res Gestae Divi Saporis*, 3-4; 5.3, 8.3; and M. P. Canepa, *The Iranian Expanse. Transforming Royal Identity Through Architecture, Landscape, and the Built Environment, 550 BCE-642 CE* (Oakland 2018), 132; 142; 260-1; Canepa, *Two Eyes of the Earth*, 108-11.
[26] *RIC* 4.2, Macrinus, 96-8; De Blois, *Image and Reality*, 49-50.
[27] Noreña, *Imperial Ideals*, 156; E. Manders, *Coining Images of Power: Patterns in the Representation of Roman Emperors on Imperial Coinage, A.D. 193-284* (Leiden – Boston 2012), 169-77. Coins with *Providentia* holding globe and sceptre show the link to peace and stability of the empire.
[28] C. Ellithorpe, *Circulating Imperial Ideology: Coins as Propaganda in the Roman World* (PhD University of North Carolina 2017), 174 fig. 13. Ellithorpe also notes (pp. 165-6) that the vast majority of military-themed coinage is found on denarii.
[29] C. King, 'Roman Portraiture: Images of Power', in: G. Paul / M. Ierardi (eds.), *Roman Coins and Public Life under the Empire. E. Togo Salmon Papers II* (Ann Arbor 1999), 123-36; 131, 134; Bastien, *Buste monetaire* 248-57.

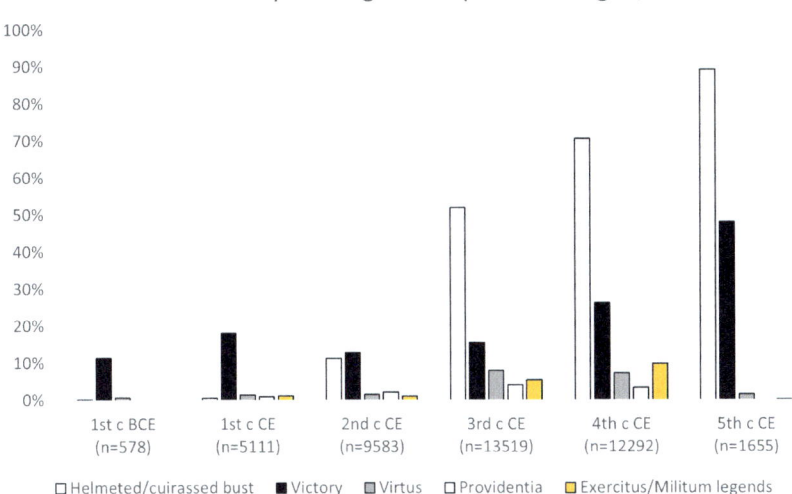

Military messages in imperial coinage

Graph 2.1 Military messages on central coinage

Analysing these different modes of military representation on central coinage (Graph 2.1) shows that presenting emperors as military leaders did not end when they stopped personally commanding armies in late antiquity.[30] Instead, the percentage of helmeted or cuirassed busts increased, as did the frequency with which Victory was depicted on reverses. In the fifth century, Victory's images on coins changed from holding a wreath and palm to holding a cross or *labarum*.[31] From the reign of Constantine onwards, the number of coin types showing the emperor holding a Victoriola increased, at the cost of depictions of Jupiter or other deities holding her. This was an inevitable consequence of the disappearance of pagan gods from Roman coinage, but also linked Victory more directly to the person of the emperor.[32] Under Justin I (518–27), this personal bond was explicitly linked to the Christian God. A male figure holding a long cross and a cross-topped globe was accompanied by the text VICTORIA AUGGG. The female personification of victory had turned into a male angel

---

[30] On the way military commands were organised in the fifth–century eastern Empire, see D. Lee, 'Theodosius and his generals', in: C. Kelly (ed.), *Theodosius II. Rethinking the Roman Empire in Late Antiquity* (Cambridge 2013), 90–108; 102–3. On the continuing expectation that emperors would lead their troops, see below, p. 128–129.

[31] The first Christian attribute was a cross on a globe, depicted at the end of the fourth century: *RIC* 9, Mediolanum 11A–C, 23A–C, 37A–C; Constantinople 75A–B. See above, p. 100.

[32] Betjes, *The Mind of the Mint*, 257–83, 404 graph. 4.8.

Figure 2.2 From Victory to angel: 519–27, Constantinople. Gold solidus (4.40 g): The emperor Justinus, recognisable through the legend D N IVSTINVS PP AVG wears a traditional cuirass and diadem with pearls. An angel, rather than the traditional personification of Victoria, holds a jewelled cross and a globe with cross on top, proclaiming VICTORI-A AVGGG I. Emperors gained their victories through the Christian God. Sear, *Byzantine Coins and Their Values* no. 56.
Source: Emporium Hamburg Numismatics, 2-9-2021, Lot 9870149

who guaranteed that the Christian emperor would conquer (Figure 2.2). Statuary also showed the emperor as a conqueror, either by depicting him in a cuirass, or as a heroic nude. Out of 198 surviving imperial statues as assembled by Heijnen, 150 show him in those two outfits. None of these statues was erected after Constantine, though that partly reflects the date range of surviving statues. Busts that show the emperor in a cuirass also rarely postdate Constantine, which suggests that there was a real change in the military presentation of emperors in statuary after Constantine's reign.[33] This is in contrast to the image on coins, once again showing a variation of messages between different media.

An extreme variant of presenting non-existent military accomplishments that emperors had at their disposal was holding a triumph for a 'fake' victory. Several such events are discussed with much glee in ancient literary sources. The first is about Caligula who put all logistics in place to conquer Britain (making it much easier for his successor Claudius to do so at the beginning of his reign), only to change his mind at the last moment.

[33] Betjes, *The Mind of the Mint*, 250–7; Heijnen, *Portraying Change*, 109, fig. 31, 132, 398–402, tables IV–VI. Including busts of emperors, the numbers rise to 415 (244 cuirass and 171 heroic nude) out of 521.

He instead instructed his soldiers to collect shells, which he is said to have called 'spoils from the Ocean, due to the Capitol and Palatine'.[34] This so-called victory over the Ocean was celebrated at Rome on a grand scale. There is much discussion on whether Caligula feared defeat, faced mutinous soldiers, or compensated his soldiers for the non-event that invading Britain had proved to be by allowing them to pick up oyster and mussel shells, which produced pearls. Possibly, he aimed for a symbolic victory over the gods, like when Alexander the Great is said to have sailed beyond the mouth of the Indus, to 'be able to say that he had navigated the great outer sea of India'.[35] Whatever the true background (and different factors may well have played a role), Caligula presented this as a victory. At some places, it seems also to have been recognised as such, as a relief from Koula (in Lydia) depicting Caligula overcoming Germania suggests.[36] Similarly, Nero would celebrate a much maligned triumph to celebrate his exploits in the east. The last Julio-Claudian emperor had managed to compete in the major Greek festivals as a poet, musician and charioteer, postponing the Olympic Games to be able to do so (perhaps because nobody dared to seriously oppose him).[37] On his return to the Italian peninsula, he allegedly celebrated these feats through a ceremony closely resembling a military triumph:

> in Rome, however, he made use of the very chariot in which Augustus had once conducted his triumphs; wearing a purple robe, picked out with stars of gold, a Greek cloak, and, on his head, the Olympic crown, his right hand holding the Pythian, he was preceded by a procession displaying his other crowns, labelled to indicate whom he had defeated and which songs or dramas. Following his chariot came the applauders shouting rhythmic praise and proclaiming that they were the Augustiani and the soldiers of his triumph.[38]

Ancient authors mocked Nero, like they had ridiculed Caligula. Yet it is possible that the two young rulers tried to live up to the idea of a

---

[34] Suet. *Cal.* 46-7; Dio 59.21; Aur. Vict. *Caes.* 3.11-12.
[35] Arrianus, Anabasis, 6.19.5; S. J. V. Malloch, 'Gaius on the Channel Coast', *Classical Quarterly* 51 (2001), 551-6; J. G. F. Hind: 'Caligula and the Spoils of Ocean: A Rush for Riches in the Far North-West?', *Britannia* 34 (2003), 272-4.
[36] Museo d'Antichità, Trieste, inv. 2228; below, p. 294.
[37] S. E. Alcock, 'Nero at Play? The Emperor's Grecian Odyssey', in: J. Elsner/ J. Masters (eds.), *Reflections of Nero: Culture, History, and Representation* (Chapel Hill - London 1994), 98-112; 98-100, 104-5.
[38] Suet. *Nero* 25 (translation C. Edwards); Dio, 63.20.1-6; C. Edwards, 'Beware of Imitations: Theatre and the Subversion of Imperial Identity', in: Elsner/ Masters, *Reflections of Nero*, 83-97; 90; E. Champlin, *Nero* (Cambridge [Mass.] - London 2003), 229-34.

triumphant emperor without the risk of defeat. Commodus may also have tried to establish his military qualities when publicly fighting as a gladiator. It may not be coincidental that the unknown author of the *Historia Augusta* notices how the emperor 'accepted the names usually given to gladiators with as much pleasure as if he had been granted triumphal decorations'.[39]

A slightly different variant of the 'fake' triumph was an exaggerated one. In 89, Domitian celebrated a double triumph over the Chatti and the Dacians, having already celebrated victories in 83 and 86. The victories were far from conclusive, and ancient authors are quick to criticise the emperor for overstating his case. Tacitus calls it a mock triumph, and claims that the emperor 'purchased from traders people whose dress and hair might be made to resemble those of captives'.[40] Juvenal is even more scathing, like Tacitus only after the emperor's death. His fourth satire is a 'mock epic' in which Domitian's generals and council of state debate the best way to prepare a turbot which is so large that it cannot be cooked conventionally. The fish, it is argued by sycophantic councillors, is an omen of future victory.[41] Other emperors seem to have anticipated criticism on whether or not their victory was worthy of a triumph. Augustus refused the small triumph (*ovatio*) that the senate proposed to celebrate his 'victory' over the Parthians in 20 BC, although he did allow the event to be commemorated by a monumental arch in the Forum.[42] Similarly, Septimius Severus refused the offer to celebrate his victories against the Parthians in 195 and 197 with a triumph, since they coincided with the civil wars in which he came to power, something which should not be formally celebrated. But he did accept a triumphal arch on which his victories and a procession were depicted.[43] Similarly, the Arch of Constantine (315) shows the ceremonial entry of the

---

[39] HA, *Comm.* 11.10–11; Hekster, *Commodus*, 156–8.
[40] Tacitus, *Agricola* 39.1–2; Dio 67, 7.2–4; Suet. *Dom.* 6.   [41] Juv. *Sat.* 4.57–74, 102–96.
[42] A. Russell, 'The Augustan Senate and the Reconfiguration of Time on the Fasti Capitolini', in: I. Gildenhard/ U. Gotter/ W. Havener/ L. Hodgson (eds.), *Augustus and the Destruction of History: The Politics of the Past in Early Imperial Rome* (Oxford 2019), 157–88; 163–5. Possibly, rather than erecting a new arch, the victory arch of 31 BC was adapted: Rich, 'Augustus's Parthian Honours'.
[43] A. R. Birley, *Septimius Severus. The African Emperor* (London 1988²), 116, 155; M. L. Popkin, *The Architecture of the Roman Triumph. Monuments, Memory and Identity* (Cambridge 2016), 144–51. Note the contrast with his son Caracalla, who proclaimed victory over 'the entire east', after which the senators voted him 'full triumphal honours out of fear and flattery' although they realised his victory was built on treachery (Herodian 4.11.9). On the prohibition of celebrating civil war victories with a triumph: Val. Max. 2.8; W. Havener, 'A Ritual against the Rule? The Representation of Civil War Victory in the Late Republican Triumph', in: C. Lange/ F. J. Vervaet (eds), *The Roman Republican Triumph. Beyond the Spectacle* (Rome 2014), 165–80.

Figure 2.3 To triumph or not? Marble frieze, Arch of Constantine, east side, from Rome, 315. The historical friezes going round the Arch of Constantine show his victory over Maxentius and entry into Rome. The image is clearly triumphal in tone, but elements from an 'official' triumph were omitted.
Source: CKD – Radboud University Nijmegen

emperor into Rome, although he had accomplished it by marching on Rome. Yet the emperor rides a *carucca* (the imperial travelling coach) instead of the triumphal *quadriga* (Figure 2.3). Moreover, a much-discussed inscription formulated that the arch was 'devoted' to Constantine as 'a monument renowned for triumphs', leaving open the question of whether Constantine had held an actual triumph for his victory in the Civil War. Possibly, the relief was originally made to display Diocletian's *adventus* into Rome in 303 and reworked to fit Constantine's purposes, which creates yet more fuzziness of interpretation.[44] Technically, it might have all been in order. Later viewers doubtlessly assumed that the arch celebrated a triumphant emperor. Whether this was finding the right balance or shamelessly manipulating memory is in the eye of the beholder.

Clearer cases of fake news in this context are the various victory titles and enumerated victories on the coins of Gallienus, including fictional victories, probably to compensate for real military success in difficult circumstances.[45] This particular practice was not adopted, but it always remained possible to declare victory after minor successes, or to exaggerate the original threat. How later historians reacted to such claims very much depended on the opinion they had of the emperor in the first place. As Mary Beard succinctly put it: 'In its simplest terms, "good emperors" held

---

[44] Koortbojian, *Crossing the Pomerium*, 134–40. The Latin of the inscription reads *arcus triumphis insignem dicavit*. See C. B. Rose, 'Reconsidering the Frieze on the Arch of Constantine', *JRA* 19 (2021), 1–36, 21–2 for the notion that the frieze originally showed Diocletian.

[45] *RIC* 5 Gallienus 75, 83–6, 129–30, 295, 304–6, 396–9, 410, 434–5, 519, 521–2, 524–8, with Manders, *Coining Images* (2012), 277–8. On Gallienus' military difficulties, see p. 54 above. Alternatively, these coins were minted on 'auto-pilot', in which case they show the expectation of continuous victory more than imperial attempts to mislead.

proper triumphs for proper victories, while "bad emperors" held sham ceremonies for empty victories'.[46]

Triumphs were not the only military ceremonies at which emperors manifested themselves. There were also the formal departure (*profectio*) and safe return (*adventus*) to and from a military campaign. The adventus as a formal return into the city after military activity was easily associated with the triumph, which was the celebration of a victory in such a campaign. They inevitably (and increasingly) shared some characteristics. In that sense, any safe return from fighting could be celebrated in a triumphal way (even if not as a formal triumph).[47] When, in the third century, wars were waged almost continuously, the number of coins depicting the *adventus* increased. Interestingly, the *profectio* was much more rarely depicted. Possibly, there was too much ad hoc fighting, often amongst generals competing for emperorship, to emphasise formal departures. Emperor and usurpers travelled from one battle to the next. Returning back to Rome with military support meant that one person had taken supreme power, and that was worth celebrating on coins and reliefs.[48]

As a consequence, it became easier to present civil war victories in triumphal tones – up to the point that the head of a defeated Roman opponent could be displayed in the capital. In many ways, victories over barbarians and opposing compatriots became difficult to differentiate.[49] This was not entirely new. Augustus's victories against Sextus Pompey at Naulochus and Mark Antony at Actium had already been celebrated through triumphal imagery, but some ambivalence remained. Although Augustus emphasised that he had ended civil war, he also pointed to an

---

[46] M. Beard, *The Roman Triumph* (Cambridge [Mass.] – London 2007), 271. Cf. M. Icks, 'Turning Victory into Defeat. Negative Assessments of Imperial Triumphs in Greco-Roman Literature', in: F. Goldbeck / J. Wienand (eds.), *Der römische Triumph in Prinzipat und Spätantike. The Roman Triumphal Procession in the Principate and Late Antiquity* (Berlin – Boston 2017), 317-34.

[47] J. Wienand/ F. Goldbeck/ H. Börm, 'Der römische Triumph in Prinzipat und Spätantike. Probleme – Paradigmen – Perspektiven', in: Goldbeck / Wienand, *Der römische Triumph*, 1-26; 16; MacCormack, *Art and Ceremony*, 30, 34-5. Cf. S. Benoist, *Rome, le prince et la cité. Pouvoir impérial et cérémonies publiques (Ier siècle av.–début du IVe siècle ap. J.–C.)* (Paris 2005), 25-101.

[48] Manders, *Coining Images*, 85-8; Benoist, *Rome, le prince et la cité*, 79-91; T. Hölscher, Victoria Romana. *Archäologische Untersuchungen zur Geschichte und Wesenart der römische Siegesgöttin von den Anfangen bis zum Ende des 3. Jhs. n. Chr.* (Mainz 1967), 61-2.

[49] M. McCormick, *Eternal Victory* (Cambridge 1986), 80-3; Wienand/ Goldbeck/ Börm, 'Der römischeTriumph', 16-17; M. Haake, 'Trophäen, die nicht vom äußeren Feinde gewonnen wurden, Triumphe, die der Ruhm mit Blut befleckt davontrug ... "Der Sieg im imperialen Bürgerkrieg im langen dritten Jahrhundert" als ambivalentes Ereignis', in: H. Börm/ M. Mattheis/ J. Wienand (eds) *Civil War in Ancient Greece and Rome* (Stuttgart 2016), 237-301; 271-4, with references.

external victory over Egypt and Cleopatra VII.[50] Unambiguously celebrating victories over competitors and usurpers was a later practice, becoming normal in the third and fourth centuries, probably because there was so much competition for the throne. Defeating Romans in battle in order to become or remain emperor increasingly became a normal practice.[51]

How closely being in power became linked to winning battles is clear from the celebration of Gallienus' ten years of imperial rule (*decennalia*) in 262, which had decidedly triumphal characteristics. By this stage, Gallienus had defeated enemies at the Danube and Rhine, and had brought the empire through the events of 260 in which his father Valerian had been captured by Shapur.[52] Coins issued for the *decennalia* emphasised the peace and security that the emperor had brought about. They also showed how Gallienus was supported by a range of deities to whom he sacrificed piously, and the loyalty of the soldiers.[53] Different literary accounts emphasise how he celebrated some sort of triumphal ceremony on the occasion. This was not an official triumph, nor an *adventus*, but military successes were emphasised all the same. They were ridiculed by the surviving literary sources, who single out the 'absurdity' of 'a band of 'Persians', supposed to be captives', that were included in the procession.[54] These are much later comments, doubtlessly playing into Gallienus' negative reputation, but it is clear that Gallienus saw the festivities of 262 as a possibility to emphasise his military accomplishments at Rome. Equally clearly, he was ultimately criticised for it – at least by some members of the elite, who created a discourse that was continued by later authors. The criticism recalls reactions to Domitian's triumph. It can also be contrasted to an apparently more positive response to Septimius Severus' decennalia celebrations, which were

---

[50] F. Vervaet/ C. Dart, 'Last of the Naval Triumphs: Revisiting Some Key Actian Honours', *JRA* 29 (2016), 389–410. The so-called Medinaceli reliefs celebrating the victory at Actium effectively form the first Roman monument to Romans killing Romans: T. Schäfer, 'Ciclo di rilievi Medinaceli', in: E. LaRocca et al. (eds), *Augusto* (Rome 2014), 321–3.

[51] M. Humphries, 'Emperors, Usurpers and the City of Rome. Performing Power and Contesting Monarchy from Diocletian to Theodosius', in: J. Wienand (ed.), *Contested Monarchy: Integrating the Roman Empire in the Fourth Century* AD (New York 2015), 151–68; 156.

[52] Above, p. 54.

[53] W. Kuhoff, *Herrschertum und Reichskrise. Die Regierungszeit der römischen Kaiser Valerianus und Gallienus (253–268 n. Chr.)* (Bochum 1979), 52; Manders, *Coining Images*, 291; L. de Blois, 'Two Third-Century Triumphal Decennalia (AD 202 and 262)', in: Goldbeck /Wienand, *Der römische Triumph*, 337–56; 350–1.

[54] Aur. Vict. *Caes.* 33.15; HA, *Gall.* 7.4–9.7 (the 'Persians' are mentioned in 9.5–7); De Blois, 'Two Third-Century Triumphal Decennalia', 347–9.

as martial as those of Gallienus.[55] Gallienus' (and Domitian's) perceived character influenced the way in which his actions were described by later authors. The actions of 'bad' rulers must have been wrong, even if highlighting military qualities at every opportunity was something that all Roman emperors from Augustus onwards had in common.

The image of the victorious emperor was pervasive, not only in Rome but throughout the empire. Through his victories, the emperor did not only protect the power of Rome, but also the safety of his subjects. The concepts of conquest and security went hand in hand. Arches and monumental buildings, decorated with narrative reliefs, transmitted the message of Rome's conquests, led by the emperor. These conquests were frequently represented as victories of Romans over barbarians.[56] Emperors claimed individual glory by adding victory titles, such as Germanicus or Parthicus to their name. This was a practice which Domitian started and clearly had contemporary resonance, as its prominence in Martial's *Epigrams* shows. Adding victory titles to the imperial name systematically took off under Trajan (Figure 2.7). Coins, moreover, showed how the emperor had placed friendly kings in new territories.[57] In doing so, emperors kept barbarians at bay. An altar from Gressenich (near Aachen) from 238 was dedicated 'for the safety of the empire (*pro salute imperi*)'.[58] If military accomplishments of the emperor fell short, the whole empire was potentially under threat. Images of belligerent emperors not only followed up on expectations that went back to the great men of the Roman republic, but also related to the need to keep the Roman empire safe. Monuments from Germania Superior linking imperial victory to the good health of the emperor (*Salus Augusta*)

---

[55] Domitian: above, p. 116; Septimius Severus: De Blois, 'Two Third-Century Triumphal Decennalia', 339–43 with references.

[56] I. Ferris, 'The Hanged Men Dance: Barbarians in Trajanic Art', in: S. Scott/ J. Webster (eds.), *Roman Imperialism and Provincial Art* (New York 2003), 53–68; S. Dillon, 'Women on the Columns of Trajan and Marcus Aurelius and the Visual Language of Roman Victory', in: Dillon/ Welch, *Representations of War*, 244–71;

[57] Mart. Ep. 2.2.3–4; 5.2.7; 5.3.1; 5.19.17; 8.4.3; 8.26.3; 8.39.3; 8.55 [53].15; 8.65.11; 13.4.1; M. Vitale, *Das Imperium in Wort und Bild. Römische Darstellungsformen beherrschter Gebiete in Inschriftenmonumenten, Münzprägungen und Literatur* (Stuttgart 2017), 144, 330; P. Kneissl, *Die Siegestitulatur der römischen Kaiser. Untersuchungen zu den Siegerbeinamen des ersten und zweiten Jahrhunderts* (Göttingen 1969), 84–9.

[58] CIL 13.7844. Cf. CIL 3.10994, 13.7778; AE 2017.1604; W. Eck, 'Krise oder Nichtkrise – das ist hier die Frage. Köln und sein Territorium in der 2. Hälfte des 3. Jahrhunderts', in: O. Hekster/ G. de Kleijn/ D. Slootjes (eds.), *Crises and the Roman Empire* (Leiden – Boston 2007), 23–43; 33–4.

illustrate the connection between emperor, conquest, and the continuity of a cultivated way of life.[59]

This barrage of imagery to a large extent defined the way in which people remembered the events and emperors that were so celebrated. Recent scholarship, making use of cognitive research on how humans remember, has indicated the importance of external stimuli to form individual and collective memories.[60] The images on coins and on the monuments formed such stimuli. The military emperor was paramount while walking around the empire's cityscapes and handling coins. In that sense, for an emperor's later reputation actually holding a triumph was less important than commemorating one. It is even likely that historical descriptions of war could be influenced by the images with which ancient authors were bombarded.[61]

People in the empire, and in the city of Rome, continuously encountered images of the victorious emperor. These images did not only influence memory, but also formed a kind of 'blueprint' for what was expected of Roman emperors as as if they were 'masters of the universe'. In this sense, they created a prospective memory to which any ruler had to live up.[62] Considering the massive numbers of monuments and speeches celebrating military accomplishment (exaggerated or not) by emperors from Caesar onwards, it was more or less inevitable that new emperors were expected to follow in their predecessors' footsteps. The many inscriptions describing the emperor as 'Lord over land and sea' (γῆς καί θαλάσσης δεσπότην; *ges kai thalasses despoten*) or as victorious ruler, erected by people who were unlikely to ever personally see the emperor in action, show how the military role resonated among provincial peoples as well as members of the Roman elite.[63] That the Roman elite expected their emperor to lead militarily becomes clear from speeches of praise emphasising the emperors' martial qualities, even when they were conspicuously absent. The emperor Tacitus was possibly even depicted in a single painting in five different ways: wearing a toga, a military cloak, armour, a Greek mantle and the garb of

---

[59] Badisches Landesmuseum C 4868–70; R. Kousser, 'Conquest and Desire: Roman *Victoria* in Public and Provincial Sculpture', in: Dillon/ Welch, *Representations of War*, 218–43; 235–9.

[60] Hölscher, *Visual Power*, 112–14; Popkin, *The Architecture of the Roman Triumph* 14–5, 80–1. Note her wonderful phrasing (p. 77): 'memory is not set in stone, but stones can affect how we remember'.

[61] Z. Rubin, 'Dio, Herodian, and Severus' Second Parthian War', *Chiron* 5 (1975), 419–44 argues that Herodian's description of Severus' Parthian wars follows what he saw on the triple arch in the Roman Forum.

[62] Popkin, *The Architecture of the Roman Triumph*, 84–5. See also below, p. 293–308 on provincial perspectives on the military role of the emperor.

[63] Bönisch, *Dialogangebote*, 222–7, 234–45. Above, p. 37.

the hunter. In reaction, a writer of epigrams is said to have responded critically: 'I do not recognise the old man in the armour, I do not recognise the man in the military cloak ... but I do recognise the man in the toga'.[64] Deviating from the military norm would become increasingly difficult, as the notion of a victorious ruler was confirmed again and again in text and image.[65]

There are only a very few examples of emperors acting against these expectations. Hadrian, immediately after taking office, gave up Mesopotamia, Assyria and large parts of Armenia (117). These were territories that his predecessor Trajan had conquered.[66] He did not try to present this as a victory, but is said to have cited a statement of Cato from 167 BC, who argued that there was no use subduing the Macedonians if they could not be held as subjects. By quoting precedent, even if remote, the emperor aimed to shift expectations.[67] Noticeably, Hadrian compensated for this decision by systematically visiting the various legions in the empire, making speeches about military discipline in the camps, and travelling in a tough military way. Cassius Dio notes how the emperor '

> either walked or rode a horse on all occasions, and never set foot in a chariot or a four-wheeled vehicle in this time. He did not cover his head in hot weather nor cold, but walked with his head bare, even in German snow or under scorching Egyptian suns. By his example and principles he trained and disciplined the entire military force throughout the whole empire in such a way that even today the methods which he then introduced are still the soldiers' rules for campaigning.[68]

There was also a substantial increase in military-style images that starts under Hadrian, who is almost exclusively depicted in a military mode (Figure 2.4). Out of the fifty-three portraits of the emperor that can be directly linked to a full statue, forty-six emphasise the emperor in his military role.[69] Moreover, as noted above, under Hadrian a new way of

---

[64] HA, *Tac.*16.2–3; K. Fittschen, 'Siebenmal Maximinus Thrax', *Archäologischer Anzeiger* (1977), 319–26. See below, p. 128 on the military expectations in speeches for Gratian and Honorius.

[65] S. Rutledge, *Ancient Rome as a Museum: Power, Identity, and the Culture of Collecting* (Oxford 2012), 123, 144–5.

[66] A. R. Birley, *Hadrian. The Restless Emperor* (London – New York 1997), 78–88; O. Hekster, 'Hadrian and the Limits of Power', in: C. Gazdac (ed.), *Group and Individual Tragedies in Roman Europe. The Evidence of Hoards, Epigraphic and Literary Sources* (Cluj-Napoca 2020), 277–87; 281–2.

[67] HA, *Hadrian*, 5.3 with Livy 45.17–18; Pricianus, *Gramm*.2.88.9. Above, p. 4 on the importance ancestral custom.

[68] Dio, 69.9.3–4. Hadrian addressing the troops: *CIL* 3.3676 (= *ILS* 2558); *CIL* 8.2532 and 18042 (= *ILS* 2487 and 9133–5).

[69] *RIC* II, p. 267 nos. 322–3; Heijnen, 'Living up to Expectations'.

Figure 2.4 Military Hadrian. Marble bust (h. 62.5 cm), from Italy, 127. Museo Archeologico Nazionale, Naples, inv. no. 6075. The most discussed aspect of Hadrian's portraiture is his beard. But the agelessness of his portrait, and the near systematic emphasis on his military role in which cuirass and military cloak (*paludamentum*) were combined is equally striking.
Source: CKD – Radboud University Nijmegen

combining the cuirassed bust with a *paludamentum* was introduced in numismatic portraiture. Hadrian appears in cuirass on the obverse of approximately 500 coins in the so-called Reka Devnia hoard, with a substantial number of reverse types showing warlike themes, such as a cuirassed Roma or Hercules seated on a cuirass.[70] It is unlikely that Hadrian's image

---

[70] https://chre.ashmus.ox.ac.uk/hoard/3406. Hadrian is depicted togate on only 60 reverse types in the RekaDevnia hoard. On the portrait type, above, p. 112 and Bastien, *buste monétaire*, I, 248, 257, figs. 28–9.

as a victorious general in statues and on coins was linked to the suppression of the Jewish Bar Kokhba revolt (132–6), which was the main military event of his reign. That had been such a dramatic event, with extreme Roman military loss, that it was not commemorated at Rome, although an arch was placed in Tel Shalem (near Bet Sche'an).[71] Rather, it seems that through his military imagery Hadrian compensated for giving up territory, perhaps protesting too much.

The monumental images that surrounded everyone in the Roman empire, and the expectations they created, influenced imperial actions. They also had an impact on the shape of specific events. This process becomes clear from a much-discussed visit of Constantius II to Rome on 28 April 357. It was a momentous occasion. No emperor had visited Rome for a generation, after Constantius' father Constantine had established Constantinople as the new imperial capital. The last imperial visit had been by Constantine in 326, and that had been an awkward affair.[72] Constantius II entered Rome more than three decades later, coinciding with his *vicennalia* (celebrations of twenty-year rule) and four years after he had defeated the usurper Magnentius, who had, in turn, defeated Constantius' brother Constans. These, then, were troubled times full of unrest. It is therefore unsurprising that the reigning emperor wanted to demonstrate his military accomplishments when entering the ancient capital. But how would such a demonstration be formulated? Was it an *adventus*, a triumph or a celebration of *vicennalia*? And how did these differ?

There is an extensive (and critical) description by Ammianus Marcellinus of the imperial visit, which notes how Constantius tried to overawe the inhabitants of Rome through the splendour of his military imagery, sitting 'alone upon a golden car in the resplendent blaze of shimmering precious stones', and 'surrounded by purple banners woven in the form of dragons and attached to the tops of gilded and jewelled spears'. Ammianus complains that Constantius celebrated 'a triumph over Roman blood'. Yet many earlier emperors had done the same.[73] It seems

---

[71] W. Eck/ G. Foster, 'Ein Triumphbogen für Hadrian im Tal von Beth Shean bei Tel Shalem', *JRA* 12 (1999), 294–313. See below, p. 295–8 for a possible local reaction to Hadrian's suppression of an earlier revolt.

[72] Constantine visited Rome in 326 after he defeated his last opponent Licinius, but seems to have been unhappy about his reception. A possible visit by his son Constans in 340 is much disputed. For dates and evidence: T. D. Barnes, *The New Empire Of Diocletian and Constantine* (Cambridge [Mass.] 1982), 73–7, 79–80; T. D. Barnes, *Athanasius and Constantius: Theology and Politics in the Constantinian Empire* (Cambridge [Mass.] 1993), 224–6.

[73] Ammianus Marcellinus, 16.10.1–17. Also above, p. 66. Ammianus' description may have been influenced by the visit of Theodosius to Rome in AD 389. Within the text, the visit is contrasted

that Constantius took these earlier festivities, or more precisely, the images and texts describing them, as an example in shaping his own entry into Rome. There are striking parallels between the description of events by Ammianus and the images on the arches of Septimius Severus and Constantine. Moreover, Ammianus stresses the immobility of the emperor, and notes how the armoured men accompanying him are similar to statues.[74] There are also obvious similarities to surviving passages in which the third-century historian Dexippos described the emperor Aurelian (270–5) intimidating the enemy in the field.[75] Finally, a gold solidus, struck in 346, well before Constantius' entry into Rome, portrays a very similar image as the one described by Ammianus, as does a fourth-century silver bowl now in the Hermitage, probably a diplomatic gift from the emperor to the Bosporus (Figure 2.5).[76] This, probably, was what Constantius imagined a victorious emperor to look like. It suggests that it was not merely Ammianus' description that was influenced by the depictions of earlier entries into Rome, but that the actual event was also shaped by the images that surrounded emperor and subjects. Of course the living experience of how imperial ritual was conducted will have mattered, and there may have been protocols of some sort. But there had not been an imperial entry into Rome for over thirty years, and the memory of earlier events would have been (re)shaped by how these events had been monumentalised. In this way, the many historical reliefs, sculptural *quadriga*, victory coins and historical texts that inundated the inhabitants of the Roman empire defined what a triumphal entry into Rome needed to be.

These images were, however, not homogenous. Over time, Christian images of pilgrimage became intertwined with images of the imperial entry. Scenes of Christ riding into Jerusalem on a donkey were portrayed on sarcophagi and discussed in texts. Standardised routes of pilgrimage began to appear in Rome, similar to previous triumphal routes. This created another layer of expectations, in which there was some friction between

---

to the entry into Paris of Julian the Apostate (361–3). On the description of Constantius as a critique: R. Flower, '*Tamquam figmentum hominis*: Ammianus, Constantius II and the portrayal of imperial ritual', *CQ* 65 (2015), 822–35. On celebrations of civil war: M. Humphries, 'Emperors, Usurpers, and the City of Rome: Performing Power from Diocletian to Theodosius', in: Wienand, *Contested Monarchy*, 151–68; 156–61.

[74] V. Neri, 'The Emperor as Living Image in Late Antique Authors', *RIHA Journal* 0223, 30 September 2019: www.riha-journal.org/articles/2019/0222-0229-special-issue-paradigms-of-corporeal-iconicity/0223-neri.

[75] Above, p. 80–1.

[76] *RIC* 8, Antioch 78; Hermitage, inv. 1820–79; J. Wienand, 'The Empire's Golden Shade. Icons of Sovereignty in an Age of Transition', in: Wienand, *Contested Monarchy*, 423–52; 423–6.

Figure 2.5 The victorious ruler: Gilded and nielloed bowl (diam. 24.9 cm; h. 3.9 cm), found Near Kerch (Bosporan Necropolis), fourth century. Hermitage, St Petersburg, inv. no. 1820–79. Images of Constantius as a triumphant ruler, sitting on a horse or chariot like a statue in ornamental clothing closely resemble descriptions of his triumphal entry into Rome.
Source: CKD – Radboud University Nijmegen

the superhuman status of the military victor and the simple piety of the Christian pilgrim.[77] Still, these images, too, portrayed a superior ruler entering a city on horse back. Even if Christians, and possibly

---

[77] P. Liverani, 'Victors and Pilgrims in Late Antiquity and the Early Middle Ages', *Fragmenta* 1 (2007) 83–102; P. Liverani, 'Dal trionfo pagano all'adventus cristiano: percorsi della Roma imperiale', *Anales de arqueología cordobesa* 18 (2007) 385–400; MacCormack, *Art and Ceremony*, 65–6. On emperors and Christian piety, and the impact of Christianity on the emperors' behaviour in Rome and Constantinople see M. McEvoy, 'Rome and the Transformation of the Imperial Office in the late-Fourth–Mid-Fifth Centuries AD', *PBSR* 78 (2010), 151–92; 163–70, 185–9; S. Diefenbach, 'Frömmigkeit und Kaiserakzeptanz im frühen Byzanz', *Saeculum* 47 (1996), 35–66.

Constantius himself, tried to phrase the visit as some sort of pilgrimage to Rome, the associations with previous military entries into the city must have been strong. The sound and smell of many horses would have further reminded people of the sculpted and painted images of horses visible throughout the city, almost always in a military context.

In this way, literary discourse, architectural setting and the images on coins and monuments forced emperors into a specific role. The notion that the emperor had to be a military man, and memories of ways in which victories had been celebrated over the centuries (set in metal, stone or stories, including ones that have not survived) were difficult to simply set aside. Of course, expectations may have differed from one group or individual to the other. The affairs of 238 make this clear. This was a year of six different emperors. Maximinus Thrax, the first non-senatorial emperor, had been elected by his troops in 235 because of his military accomplishments. In 238, landowners in Africa proclaimed their local governor Gordian and his son emperor – probably to help them with local administrative problems. Senators in Rome, who had objected to Maximinus' lack of senatorial status, switched allegiance to the two Gordians, who were however rapidly defeated by the governor of Numidia. Consequently, senators elected the elderly Pupienus and Balbinus, because of their experience and senatorial perspective. People in Rome objected so fiercely that the young Gordian III was given power. Apparently dynastic considerations outweighed senatorial status for the Roman plebs. Maximinus faced so many military difficulties that his soldier grew discontent and killed him. Still, unrest remained, and Pupienus and Balbinus are said to have planned major military campaigns against the Sasanians and the Carpians, once again showing the importance of military prestige to secure the throne. Before they could organise matters properly, however, the Praetorians killed them, making Gordian III sole ruler (238–44). Notably, the first coin types of his reign showed the emperor in a cuirass, with reverses proclaiming VICTORIA AVG(VSTI), VIRTVS AVG(VSTI), PAX AVG(VSTI) and FIDES MILITVM.[78]

Senators in Rome wanted different things from their ruler than local elites or the populace in Rome, or later Constantinople. The expectations of pagans and Christians may have differed too. Emperors had their own expectations. But the essential notion that the emperor was personally

---

[78] *RIC* 4, Gordian III, 1, 3, 5–7, 9–14. On the events of 238 see K. Haegemans, *Imperial Authority and Dissent: The Roman Empire in AD 235–238* (Leuven 2010).

responsible for the safety of the empire and had to demonstrably show his military qualities seems to have been remarkably stable over the course of the centuries.[79] Emperors were expected to fight and to win. Not coincidentally, in emperor Julian the Apostate's (360–3) *The Caesars* – a satirical competition for 'best emperor' with the gods as judges – three of the main competitors were selected because they were the greatest warriors (ὡς πολεμικωτάτους; *hos polemikotatous*).[80] Emperors could delegate military affairs to capable generals, as Augustus and Nero had done, but they had to make sure that military successes were attributed to them. In the tumultuous third century, moreover, emperors had to be seen to personally command the troops. This created a potential problem from the second half of the fourth century onwards. For about a century, the emperors who came to power were so young that they could not realistically fight a war. Gratian (367–83) was appointed by his father Valentinian I (364–75) at the age of eight. After the latter's death, Valentinian II (375–92) was proclaimed emperor when he was four by military men and imperial administrators. Honorius (395–423) ruled the western empire from his tenth birthday onwards, and Valentinian III (425–55) came to power at the age of six. A similar situation arose in the eastern empire with Arcadius (383–408) elevated at the age of six, and Theodosius II (402–50) when still a baby.[81] This phenomenon of so-called child emperors has been splendidly analysed by Meaghan McEvoy, who argues that the result was a differentiation of imperial roles. Important generals, many of Germanic descent, took control of the troops in the Roman west in their role of *magister militum*, whereas ceremonial and religious roles remained with the emperor.[82] The best known of these fourth- and fifth-century generalissimos was probably Stilicho (c. 359–408). Although he was half Vandal, he still ended up as regent for Honorius and married the niece of Theodosius I. Flavius Aetius (c. 391–454) similarly managed to be the western empire's most influential man for decades, acting as 'protector' for Valentinian III and his mother Galla Placidia.[83]

These great western generals had their work cut out for them. The pressure on the Roman frontiers, and regular attempts by usurpers to

---

[79] See now also F. K. Maier, *Palastrevolution. Der Weg zum hauptstädtischen Kaisertum im Römischen Reich des vierten Jahrhunderts* (Paderborn 2019), 1–67, noting how the image of the emperor as a victorious ruler influenced military activity.

[80] Julian, *Caesars* 317b.

[81] M. Kulikowski, *The Tragedy of Empire. From Constantine to the Destruction of Roman Italy* (Cambridge [Mass.] 2019), 67, 70–1, 11, 118–19, 135–6, 193–5.

[82] McEvoy, *Child Emperor Rule*, 322–4.   [83] McEvoy, *Child Emperor Rule*, 153–86, 251–72.

obtain the throne had guaranteed that third- and fourth-century emperors routinely marched with their troops. Attempts by eastern emperors to influence who ruled the west made matters even more complicated. Aetius, for instance, first fought on behalf of Honorius' locally chosen successor Joannes (423–5), who was not, however, accepted by the eastern emperor Theodosius II. He sent his cousin Valentinian III to the west, on behalf of whom Aetius ended up fighting. Aetius faced Theodoric I and other threats to the integrity of the western Roman empire. He was also involved in various power struggles against other Roman generals. In 451, Aetius convinced Theodoric to join him in the battle against Attila the Hun and fought side-by-side with his erstwhile enemy. Subsequently, Aetius managed to betrothe his son to Valentinian's daughter. This was perceived as an attempt to gain the throne himself, and Valentinian had him assassinated, only for the emperor to be murdered half a year later.[84]

The generalissimos fought amongst themselves and against external enemies. The young emperors, instead, became more or less passive figureheads. This was the practical upshot of the situation, and may have been in the best interest of general, emperor and even the state at large, since it created some sort of stability. But the reality of these affairs did not take away the expectation that emperors were military leaders. Speeches held before the young emperors still praised their martial qualities. Symmachus told the nine-year old Gratianus how 'as a boy you fight for old men', compared him with the likes of Hercules and Alexander the Great, who accomplished great deeds when young, and generally described him as the 'longed-for hope of a new age'.[85] Claudian, court poet to Honorius and Stilicho exhorts to the eleven-year-old emperor how 'as a child you crawled over shields, the fresh-won spoils of kings were your toys'. Coins, as also discussed above, continued to express imperial victory.[86] It was impossible to simply ignore the emperor's traditional military role.

The expectation of a victorious emperor created difficulties when child emperors grew up. It proved almost impossible to have *de facto* military

---

[84] Kulikowski, *The Tragedy of Empire*, 193–201, 207–8, 212–13; McEvoy, *Child Emperor Rule*, 291–2.

[85] Symmachus, *Oration* III, 2–3, 6; D. Jussen, 'Enduring the Dust of Mars: The Expectation of Military Leadership in Panegyric to the Child-Emperor Gratian', *Arethusa* 52 (2019), 253–73; 257–61. McEvoy, *Child Emperor Rule*, 109–113 notes the tensions between image and reality.

[86] Claudian, *Panegyric on the Third Consulate of Honorius*, 22–3; Jussen, 'Enduring the Dust of Mars', 270; M. Icks/ D. Jussen/ E. Manders, 'Generaals in de groei: De militaire representatie van de kindkeizers Gratianus en Honorius op munten en in lofdichten', *Tijdschrift voor Geschiedenis* 132 (2020), 541–58, especially 547 figs. 2–3, 550 fig. 5, 552 fig. 6 and 555–6 figs. 7–9 for the military aspects of coinage under Gratian and Honorius.

regents when emperors came of age. Emperors needed to take control themselves, with dire consequences when they failed to live up to the standards previously set by their generals or lost the power struggle with their generals. Gratian was deserted by his troops after he failed to defeat the usurper Magnus Maximus (383–8), Valentinian II had to formally dismiss his general Arbogast when the latter forbade him leading the troops. The emperor was found hanged shortly afterwards (392). Valentinian III only survived the removal of Aetius in 454 by half a year.[87] The failure of these emperors to take military control shows how complicated the situation in the (western) empire had become. That they tried to take control all the same shows how dominant the notion of the military emperor remained. Likewise, the lack of emperors personally fighting campaigns in the eastern empire from the death of Theodosius II (379–95) to Justin II (565–78), did not stop the emperor from being the ultimate figure of military authority. He was still expected to organise and direct his troops, even if he did not fight himself.[88] The damning criticism by the fifth-century diplomat and historian Priscus of Panium on Theodosius II is telling. Theodosius succeeded to the throne, 'although he was unwarlike and spent his life in cowardice. He won peace with money, not with arms'. Priscus had accompanied a Roman embassy to Attila the Hun, and recounts how that leader was celebrated through songs 'celebrating his victories and deeds of valour in war'.[89] The contrast between the two leaders is pronounced, and it is clear that the Roman emperor did not live up to his subjects' expectations.

Expectations and reality could differ radically. The notion that emperors controlled the army ran contrary to the available evidence. Individuals behind the throne took on many of the responsibilities that belonged to the emperor, exercising power on his behalf. In the west, prominent generals became the emperors' main partners. In the east, the situation seems to have been somewhat different. Whereas there were two posts of *magister militum* in the west, from the reign of Theodosius I onwards there were five major commands in the east, making it more difficult for one man

---

[87] Kulikowski, *The Tragedy of Empire*, 94–5, 119, 213; McEvoy, *Child Emperor Rule*, 317–18. See below, p. 224–225.

[88] F. R. Trombley/ S. Tougher, 'The Emperor at war', in: S. Tougher (ed.), *The Emperor in the Byzantine World* (London – New York: Routledge 2019), 179–95; 179–80, 190.

[89] Priscus, fr. 52; fr. 8.160. Translation from J. Given, *The Fragmentary History of Priscus: Attila, the Huns and the Roman Empire, AD 430–476* (Merchantville [NJ] 2014), 22, 73.

to take control.[90] Consequently, though there is much talk of high-ranking civilians, palace eunuchs or the emperors' wives taking control, there were no great generals effectively running the empire, as seems to have been the case in the west.[91]

Stories about people running the emperor precede late antiquity. Dominating mothers, wives, freedmen and generals are recurring figures in ancient literature. They formed a possible explanation for 'wrong' behaviour by good emperors, while selecting the wrong favourites was typical behaviour of 'bad' emperors. This mechanism is not unique to Rome; the idea that life would be better 'if only Stalin knew what really happened' is as common as rulers being blamed for all sorts of events that were clearly beyond their control.[92] There was also ample precedent for emperors who had difficulties in personally controlling their troops. Famous generals like Corbulo under Nero or Agricola under Domitian had to be removed or they would have become a threat to the throne.[93] During the so-called crisis of the third century, any victorious general became a serious claimant for emperorship, whoever was officially in charge. Still, inhabitants of the empire expected the emperor to control their men. When during the chaotic reign of Gordian III – yet another child-emperor, who became sole ruler at the age of thirteen – Roman troops confiscated goods and demanded accommodation in the town of Skaptopara (modern Bulgaria), the townspeople petitioned the emperor to end this situation.[94] They must have been disappointed with the imperial reaction, as the emperor sent them back to the governor. The reality was that he dare not get involved. But that did not stop his subjects from expecting that he would. Throughout Roman history, there had been occasions in which emperors had to depend on others to control the armies. They still claimed all military glory and were expected to do so.

---

[90] Lee, 'Theodosius and his Generals', 93, 102, following Jones, *The Later Roman Empire*, I, 174–5, 178. Cf. Maier, *Palastrevolution*, 339–47.

[91] On the role of palace eunuchs, see below, p. 213–7 and on imperial wives see below, p. 227–243. Even the eastern general Flavius Aspar (c. 400 –71), who played an important part in imperial politics for decades, never gained the prominence of Stilicho or Aetius: M. McEvoy, 'Becoming Roman?: The Not-So-Curious case of Aspar and the Ardaburii', *Journal of Late Antiquity* 9 (2016), 483–511; 484–92.

[92] L. Zoja, *Paranoia. The Madness that Makes History* (London – New York 2017), 196. See below, p. 142–3.

[93] R. Ash, 'Following in the Footsteps of Lucullus? Tacitus' Characterisation of Corbulo', *Arethusa* 39 (2006), 355–75; 374–5.

[94] *CIL* 3.12336 (20 December 238); T. Hauken, *Petition and Response. An Epigraphic Study of Petitions to Roman Emperors 181–249* (Bergen 1998), 98, 117.

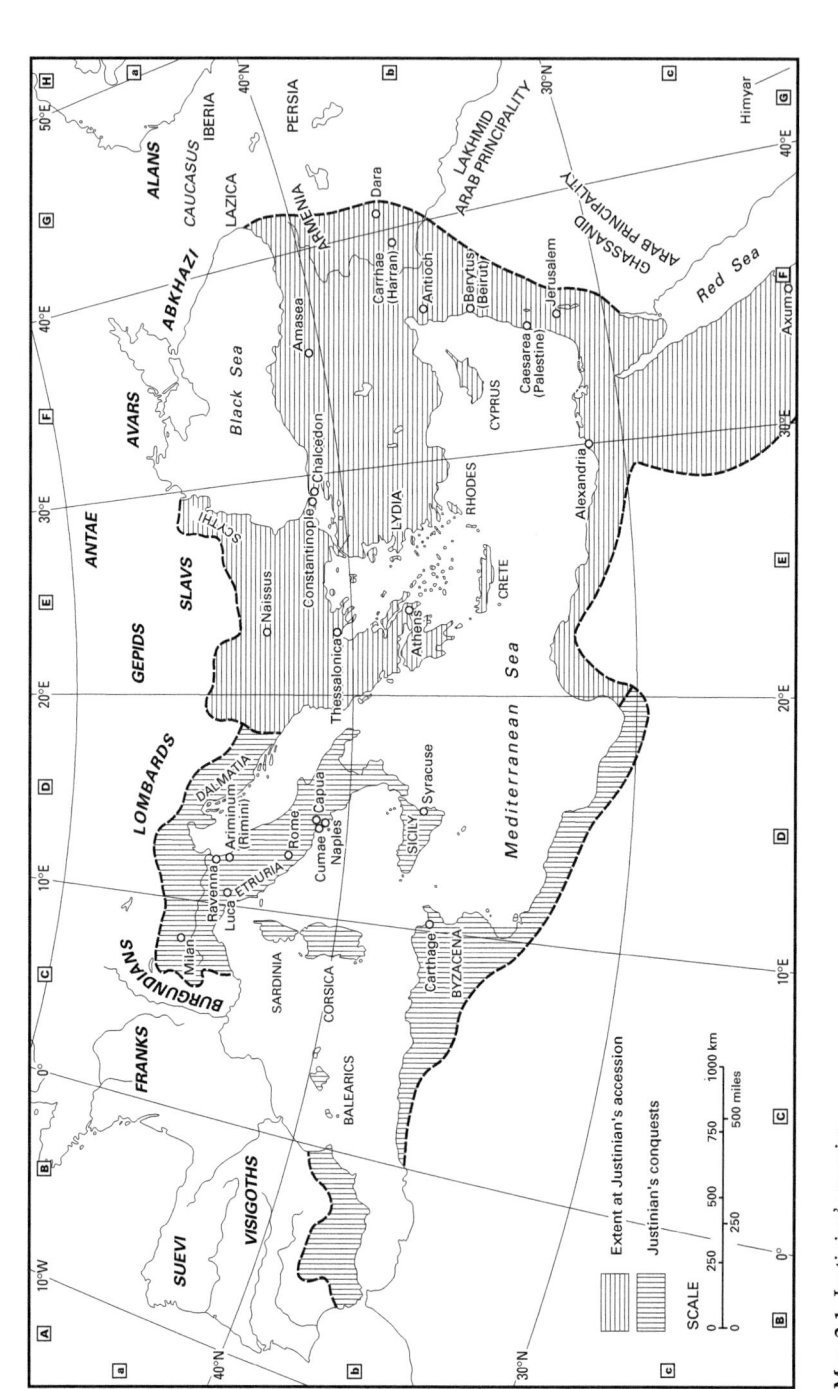

Map 2.1 Justinian's empire

In 533, Justinian launched an expedition against the Vandal kingdom in North Africa, led by his general Belisarius. This began what ended up being the last attempt to unify the Roman empire under sole control of one ruler. Decades of war against the Visigoths in Hispania and especially the Ostrogoths in the Italian peninsula ensued (Map 2.1).[95] Belisarius led the troops, but Justinian celebrated the victories and claimed the glory. Importantly, the immediate cause for the attack on the Vandals seems to have been the need for a legitimising victory to bolster a regime that was close to collapse.[96] These are contexts and circumstances that can be applied to a great many earlier Roman rulers. The military organisation of the sixth-century Roman empire was manifestly different from that of the early principate. Ways in which victories were celebrated and monumentalised had shifted in shape. But the core notion of the emperor's military role had remained remarkably stable over the centuries. It was difficult to escape the expectations of so many people, shaped over so much time, and confirmed again and again by the texts and images surrounding them.

The Emperor and His Religious Role

Military qualities were a necessity to be considered a good ruler, but so was divine support.[97] How that support was expressed was, at least in the late Republic, fairly flexible. There were very specific cases, like Sulla's highly individual 'divine luck', but also a more general sense that 'the gods' needed to be behind any action for it to be successful. Caesar's fellow consul Marcus Calpurnius Bibulus (c. 102–48 BC), for instance, attempted to block some of Caesar's more far-reaching legislation by watching for omens. This was neither ridiculous nor unfounded.[98] If the gods did not agree, surely they would make this clear. Bibulus' apparent popularity suggests that many Romans agreed that Caesar threatened the balance

---

[95] P. Heather, *Rome Resurgent: War and Empire in the Age of Justinian* (Oxford – New York 2018), 123–79.
[96] Heather, *Rome Resurgent*, 114.
[97] Parts of this section were already explored in O. Hekster, 'Ruling through Religion? Innovation and Tradition in Roman Imperial Representation', in: R. Dijkstra (ed.), *The Early Reception and Appropriation of the Apostle Peter (60–800): The Anchors of the Fisherman* (Leiden – Boston 2020), 26–40, from which a number of ideas and formulations are taken.
[98] See above, p. 107 on Sulla; L. de Libero, *Obstruktion: Politische Praktiken im Senat und in der Volksversammlung der ausgehenden römischen Republik (70–49 v. Chr.)* (Stuttgart 1992), 53–68 on Bibulus and other notions of 'sacred' obstruction in the Roman Republic.

between men and gods, the important notion of *pax deorum* ('peace of/ with the gods').[99]

To rule in Rome, one needed the gods on one's side. There is even an argument to be made that ruling implied some sort of divine status. Worship, after all, was a way of asking favours of beings with immense power. The worshipper offered, and in return hoped to receive benefits, illustrated by the Latin notion of *do ut des* ('I give, so that you give').[100] Whether people appealed to an immortal god, a local hero, or a supreme ruler was not a categorical difference. Divinity, in this sense, was relative. In a polytheistic society, there were enormous differences between the various superhuman beings. Jupiter was a stronger divinity than a local river god, but the river god was divine all the same.[101] Even immortality was not a clinching argument. There were gods like Hercules, who had only gained immortality after his death, or Castor and Pollux, who were immortal for half of the year, but forced to stay in the underworld for the other half. A Roman deity was anyone who could solve problems in a way that a human could not, take vengeance accordingly when due respect was not given, answered prayers and wanted devotion. Much of this was automatically the case for the man who ruled the world.[102]

Throughout much of the ancient Mediterranean world, there were forms of ruler cult. This included parts of the world with which Rome had interacted. Rome's expanding empire guaranteed that Romans encountered Hellenistic kings, Parthian 'Kings of Kings' (or 'Great Kings') and Egyptian pharaohs, all of whom were worshipped by their subjects. Indeed, people in the Greek east had paid divine honours to Roman generals, perhaps most famously to T. Quinctius Flamininus whose 'liberation' of Greece in 196 earned him so much adulation that he was voted divine honours in Chalcis and Geithion (in Laconia). He was also the first Roman to have his portrait on a coin issued by a Greek city.[103] But in Rome, worshipping living

---

[99] J. Scheid, *Religion et pieté à Rome* (Paris 2001), 25–6.
[100] J. Rüpke, *The Religions of Rome* (Cambridge – Malden [Mass.] 2007), 149.
[101] I. Gradel, *Emperor Worship and Roman Religion* (Oxford 2002), esp. 26 and 72. D. S. Levene, 'Defining the Divine in Rome', *TAPA* 142 (2012), 41–81, 73 instead argues that there were lines between who was and was not divine, but that these were fuzzy.
[102] Levene, 'Defining the Divine', 53–8; C. W. King, *The Ancient Roman Afterlife: Di Manes, Belief, and the Cult of the Dead* (Austin 2020), 6–13. See M. Lipka, *Roman Gods. A Conceptual Approach* (Leiden – Boston 2009), 1–8 for an overview of the historiography on Roman conceptions of divinity.
[103] Plut. *Flam.* 16.3–17.1; *SEG* IX. 923, lines 11–12; *RRC* 548/1a–b. See further the various articles in N. Brisch, (ed.) *Religion and Power: Divine Kingship in the Ancient World and Beyond* (Chicago 2012), esp. G. Woolf, 'Divinity and Power in Ancient Rome', 235–51, 236–7 on Rome's encountering different forms of ruler cult.

men did not start before Caesar's dictatorship. After his victory in the Civil War, Caesar had gained a uniquely prominent position in the Roman state. Consequently, he received exceptional honours, such as a priest (*flamen*), temples and possibly even the name Divus Julius.[104] There is debate about whether that made him a god in an absolute sense, but it certainly put his power in a superhuman perspective. There is no doubt that he was formally recognised as a god after his death. Many emperors would likewise become 'official' gods (*divi*) after they died. Some of them explicitly claimed divine status while alive. All of them played a major role in the organisation of Roman religion, and in doing so guaranteed that the Roman state was supported by the gods.

Emperors, then, were priests who intervened between Rome's subjects and its gods and interpreted the gods' wishes, leaders who guaranteed the goodwill of these same gods, and rulers who held some sort of superhuman status.[105] All of these aspects would remain important in the emperors' religious role throughout the centuries. For their position as intermediary the position of Pontifex Maximus was probably the most important. This priest was the elected leader of the *pontifices*, who formally supervised the religious life of the Roman state, which included everything that was not specifically assigned to other priesthoods. The Pontifex Maximus was also elected for life. This made him the most powerful Roman priest.[106] It is hardly surprising that Caesar made sure to obtain the position and that Augustus, too, took over the role when it became vacant.[107] Before he became Pontifex Maximus, Augustus had already ensured positions within the four major priestly colleges at Rome, and advertised this inclusion through his coinage.[108] That made him the prime figure in Rome to interact with the gods.

Because of the importance of the priestly role, but also because Caesar and Augustus had both prominently advertised their position as Pontifex Maximus, it was logical that later rulers would follow in their footsteps.

---

[104] Cic. *Phil* 2.110; Suet. *Div. Iul.* 76.1; App. BC 2.106; Dio 43.14.6; 42.3–45.2; *AE* 1952, 169; *ILS* 72–3. See p. 107 n. 8 above for modern historiography.

[105] P. Rietbergen, 'Not of This World ...? Religious Power and Imperial Rule in Eurasia, ca. Thirteenth–ca. Eighteenth Century', in: M. van Berkel/ J. Duindam (eds.), *Prince, Pen, and Sword: Eurasian Perspectives* (Leiden – Boston 2018), 129–296; 134–41 places these various religious roles of Roman rulers in a comparative Eurasian perspective.

[106] Festus 198, 29–200, 4; Gellius, *NA* 10,15,21; Servius. *Aen.* 2,2; M. Beard/ J. North/ S. Price, *Religions of Rome* (Cambridge 1998), I, 55–9.

[107] Suet. *Div. Iul.* 13; *Augustus*, 31.3; *RGDA* 20.4. After Caesar's death, the position went to Lepidus, who only died in 12 BC. Up to that time, Augustus had to wait; R. T. Ridley, 'The Absent *Pontifex Maximus*', *Historia* 54 (2005), 275–300.

[108] *RIC I*^{2} *Augustus* 69 (no. 367) (16 BC); 73 (no. 410) (13 BC); already *RSC* no. 91 (37 BC).

Tiberius, Gaius, Claudius and Nero were all given the post. This made the link between Pontifex Maximus and emperor unavoidable.[109] Until the accession of Nerva in 96 AD, new emperors waited until the official election of the Pontifex Maximus in March to take up the role. From 96 onwards, the supreme pontificate had become so much part and parcel of the imperial office that the emperor took up the role on accession to the throne. The title and role were systematically emphasised in imperial statuary, inscriptions and coins.[110] It was deemed so important, that the emperors Pupienus and Balbinus, who briefly ruled jointly in AD 238, both became Pontifex Maximus. This was technically impossible, but apparently an ideological necessity.[111] This close link between emperorship and the title of *Pontifex Maximus* influenced people's associations. Where in Caesar's and Augustus' time, the ruler had derived authority from the title, and used the priesthood to position imperial religious actions in Republican precedent, by the third century the title would make people think of Roman emperors in general, and of Augustus in particular.[112]

Notwithstanding these strong associations, the title disappeared from coin legends from the mid-third century onwards. This coincided with a decline of coin types depicting the emperor making a sacrifice, dressed as a priest and with priestly attributes. There are also no surviving sculptural portraits that show the emperor with the typically priestly gear of a toga covering his head (*capite velato*) after the beginning of the third century (Figure 2.6).[113] Instead of the emperor's priestly role, his personal divine

---

[109] D. Musiał, 'The Princeps as *Pontifex Maximus*: The Case of Tiberius', *Electrum* 21 (2014), 99–106.

[110] See above p. 32, 36; R. Stepper, *Augustus et Sacerdos. Untersuchungenzumrömischen Kaiser als Priester* (Stuttgart 2003), 50; A. Cameron, '*Pontifex Maximus*: From Augustus to Gratian – and Beyond', in: M. Kahlos (ed.), *Emperors and the Divine – Rome and its Influence* (Helsinki 2016), 139–59; 140; Manders, *Coining Images of Power*, 133–54.

[111] Cameron, *Pontifex Maximus*, 141. The emphasis on religious equality between the two emperors even led to the erection of statues of both of them in the guise of Jupiter in Piraeus: Piraeus, Archaeological Museum, inv. 125; inv. 278; Maderna, *Iuppiter, Diomedes und Merkur*, 55, 196, nos. JV 3–4. This presumed equality was not an issue when Marcus Aurelius and Lucius Verus (and subsequently Marcus and Commodus) shared rule, when Marcus was the sole Pontifex Maximus.

[112] S. Benoist, 'Du *Pontifex maximus* à l'élu de dieu: l'empereur et les sacra (Ier s. av. n.e.–Ve s. de n.e.)', in: O. Hekster/ S. Schmidt-Hofner/ C. Witschel (eds.), *Ritual Dynamics and Religious Change in the Roman Empire* (Leiden – Boston 2009), 33–51; 43–7; F. van Haeperen, 'Des Pontifes païens aux pontifes chrétiens. Transformations d'un titre: entre pouvoirs et représentations', *RBPh* 81 (2003): 137–59.

[113] E. Manders/ O. Hekster, 'Identities of Emperor and Empire in the Third Century AD', in: S. Benoist/ Chr. Hoët-van Cauwenberghe (eds.), *Figures d'empire, fragments de mémoire*.

Figure 2.6 Caracalla as a priest. Marble portrait (h. 49 cm), from Pergamon, c. 214., Bergama, Archaeological Museum, inv. 163. The last surviving portrait of an emperor *capite velato* comes from the beginning of the third century. That did not mean he stopped being Pontifex Maximus.
Source: C. Vermeule, Roman Imperial Art in Greece and Asia Minor, Cambridge 1968, p. 306, fig.161 of 31 b

Pouvoirs (pratiques et discours, images et représentations) et identités (sociales et religieuses) dans le monde romain impérial (Ier s. av. J.-C.-Ve s. ap. J.-C.) (Villeneuve-d'Ascq 2011), 153–62; 160–1, fig. 2; Stepper, *Augustus et Sacerdos*, 9; J. Rüpke, *Fasti Scerdotum. Die Mitglieder der Priesterschaften und das sakrale Funktionspersonal römischer, griechischer, orientalischer und jüdisch-christlicher Kulte in der Stadt Rom von 300 v. Chr. bis 499 n. Chr.* (Stuttgart 2005), III, 1605–15.

luck was advertised on later coinage, through the legend *Pius Felix* and by linking the emperor to specific divinities.[114] This did not stop the emperor from making sacrifices to other gods or interpreting their will and nor did it indicate a lessening of the emperor's religious authority. Rather, at about this time he started to more openly legislate about universal religious matters, most noticeably about persecution and toleration of cults. Decius issued an edict of universal sacrifice; Valerian ordered the persecution of Christians, ended by Gallienus' edict of tolerance, followed in turn by the many religious edicts of the Tetrarchs. These edicts, furthermore, were promulgated by being publicly read out when they arrived in cities. Consequently, many Romans will have experienced an intensification of the emperor's role as arbiter of religion in a way that had never been the case before.[115] So, although the priestly role of the emperor almost disappeared from coins and statues, it was still prominently visible in other media, also after the second half of the third century. Inscriptions of the Tetrarchs and Constantine still regularly include the title *Pontifex Maximus*, and link it uniquely to the *Augusti*, illustrating the continuous importance of the role. Constantius II appointed men to vacant positions in the traditional priestly colleges when he visited Rome in 357. The emperor Julian is even said to have appreciated the title of 'priest' as much as that of emperor.[116] Julian (also known as the Apostate) was fiercely anti-Christian and his enthusiasm for the pagan priesthood may not have been a surprise. But many Christian emperors continued to be Pontifex Maximus.

It is often maintained that Christianity and imperial priesthoods were mutually exclusive. Magnus Felix Ennodius (473/4–521), the bishop of Pavia, complains that earlier emperors had been called 'gods and priests', whereas Pope Gelasius (492–6) claimed that only pagan emperors had

---

[114] Manders/Hekster, 'Identities of Emperor and Empire', 161 fig. 2. See above, p. 32, 35 on Pius Felix.

[115] J. Rives, 'The Decree of Decius and the Religion of the Empire', *JRS* 89 (1999), 135–54; F.M. Ausbüttel, 'Die Tolerierung der Christen in der Zeit von Gallienus bis zur sogenannten Constantinischen Wende (260–313)', *Millennium* 12 (2015), 41–74. On the importance of emperors at sacrifice: R. L. Gordon, 'The Veil of Power. Emperors, Sacrificers and Benefactors' in: M. Beard / J. North (eds.), *Pagan Priests. Religion and Power in the Ancient World* (London 1990) 199–231. On the reading out of imperial edicts and letters by intermediaries: J. Matthews, *Laying Down the Law: A Study of the Theodosian Code* (New Haven 2000), 187–8.

[116] Symmachus, *Relatio* 3.7; Libanius, *Oratio* 12.80: χαίρει καλούμενος ἱερεὺς οὐχ ἧττον ἢ βασιλεύς; Cameron, 'Pontifex Maximus', 142–4.

taken the title *Pontifex Maximus*, induced to do so by the devil.[117] The early sixth-century Zosimus claimed that the emperor Gratian (367–83) point blank refused to be named *Pontifex Maximus*, since that was 'impious for a Christian'. Inscriptions, however, show that the title was included in the imperial formula well into the fifth century. Ultimately, there was a shift from the title *Pontifex Maximus* to *Pontifex Inclitus* (Honourable Pontiff), suggesting that the original (pagan) role had become problematic.[118] But abandoning a title that had been continuously linked to Roman rule from Caesar onwards was not easy. Abandoning the expectations that went with the title proved impossible.

Instead, the meaning of the word *pontifex* may have changed over time. Rather than solely denoting an important pagan priestly college, it also became the word for Christian bishops.[119] Any title that described the emperor as supreme *pontifex* also placed him above the bishops and gave him an important role in interpreting God's will. At the same time the position of the bishop of Rome in the church hierarchy increased. His rising profile became reflected in the name *Summus Pontifex* (Highest Pontiff), creating tension between the authority of the emperor and that of the bishops. Gelasius explicitly wrote to the emperor Anastasius in 494 that 'There are two, august emperor, by which this world is chiefly ruled, namely the sacred authority (*auctoritas sacrata*) of the priests and the royal power (*regalis potestas*) ... You are also aware, most clement son, that ... in divine matters you bend your neck devotedly to the bishops'.[120] The emperor did not necessarily agree. He, too, was expected to play an important role in the communication between humans and the divine. This expectation was embedded in centuries of Roman rule. When Constantine embraced Christianity, he had to transfer this role as divine mediator onto a very different kind of religion. Increasingly prominent bishops (and especially the bishops of Rome) had different views from the emperor on

---

[117] Ennodius, *Pan. Theoder.* 17 (81); Gelasius *Tract.* 4.11 (*Epist. Rom. Pont*; ed. A. Thiel, 1868, I, 557–8); A. Cameron, 'The Imperial Pontifex', *HSCP* 103 (2007): 341–84; 263; Van Haeperen, 'Des Pontifes païens', 152–3.

[118] Zos. *Hist. Nova*, 4.36; Cameron, 'The Imperial Pontifex',343–8, 355–6; R. Dijkstra/ D. van Espelo, 'Anchoring Pontifical Authority: A Reconsideration of the Papal Employment of the Title *Pontifex Maximus*', *JRH* 41 (2017), 312–25; 315–18, with references.

[119] Van Haeperen, 'Des Pontifes païens', 159.

[120] Gelasius, *Epist. Rom. Pont.* (Thiel), I, 349–58 no.12; Dijkstra/ Van Espelo, 'Anchoring Pontifical Authority', 318; J. Curran, 'From Petrus to *Pontifex Maximus*', in: Dijkstra, *The Early Reception and Appropriation of the Apostle Peter*, 43–57; 54–5. See below, p. 195–207 on the relationship between emperor and bishops, also in Constantinople.

who was in control of defining the divine will.[121] The emperor continued to fulfil priestly functions, but as paganism disappeared his role changed too. It is probably not coincidental that an early-eighth-century document describes only those emperors who had presided over ecumenical councils as 'emperors and priests'.[122] Imperial priesthood was now formulated within the confines of Christian doctrine.

The focal point for this reformulation was the reign of Constantine. Looking both at Constantine's actions and at the Christian historiography describing these actions suggests debate about what role the first Christian emperor could play in a religious system that was still in development. Constantine's vision, on the verge of his battle with Maxentius, was one point of contention. The almost certain later constructed story tells of an imperial vision in 312, either on the night before the battle against Maxentius, or sometime earlier. Constantine allegedly saw 'a cross-shaped trophy formed from light, and a text attached to it which said, Ἐν Τούτῳ Νίκα' ('By this, conquer'). The vision was followed by a dream in which Christ appeared and told Constantine to use the sign against his enemies.[123] The story suggests a direct personal relationship between God and the emperor to whom he spoke. But Constantine's Christian biographer Eusebius insisted instead that the emperor could only understand the meaning of this vision through the interpretation of bishops.[124] This was not the only discussion surrounding Constantine's superior links to God. The emperor also attempted to become, as it were, a thirteenth apostle. A prime example of this was the construction of the Church of the Holy Apostles (the *Apostoleion*) just outside of the city centre of

---

[121] H. A. Drake, *Constantine and the Bishops. The Politics of Intolerance* (Baltimore – London 2000), 389–90 on this process. D. Benétos, 'From *Divus Augustus* to *Vicarius Christi*: Examples of Self-Presentation in a Period of Transition', in: A. Gavrielatos (ed.), *Self-Presentation and Identity in the Roman World* (Cambridge 2017), 208–39; 229–32 shows how important the title *Pontifex Maximus* still was for Constantine. Ongoing tension about divine support for bishops or emperors is expressed in Socrates, *Ecclesial History*, 6. pro. (307) [*Patrologia Graeca* 67, 660]. The discussion on who could claim to be the intermediary of God would last a long time: P. Raedts/ M. Derks, 'Introduction', in: J. W. Buisman/ M. Derks/ P. Raedts (eds.), *Episcopacy, Authority, and Gender. Aspects of Religious Leadership in Europe, 1100-2000* (Leiden – Boston 2015), 1–8; 2.

[122] G. Dagron, *Emperor and Priest. The Imperial Office in Byzantium* (Cambridge 2003), 159–64 with further references.

[123] Eusebius, *Vit. Const.* 1.28–9. See for a variant account Lactantius, *De Mortibus Persecutorum*. There is no reference to the vision in the contemporary speech celebrating Constantine's victory: *Panegyrici Latini* 12(9), with the comments by C. E. V. Nixon/ B. Saylor Rodgers, *In Praise of Later Roman Emperors: The Panegyrici Latini*. (Berkeley 1994), 292–3.

[124] Eusebius. *Vit. Const.* 1.32, with Drake, *Constantine and the Bishops*, 391–2. On the vision and the consequent construction of the *labarum* see above, p. 100.

Constantinople (Map 4.2). The church, as the name indicates, was dedicated to the twelve Apostles. Constantine intended to be buried between the symbolic references to the Apostles, linking his posthumous status to theirs.[125] The notion would not hold. Later Christian authors disputed the emperor's elevated role. As Ambrose of Milan (c. 340–97) stated, the emperor was 'in the church and not above the church'. The *Apostoleion* was also completely redone in the decades after Constantine's death, which suggests that his successors did not wish to make the same bold claims as Constantine had made. As a compromise between the apparent importance of Constantine as first Christian emperor and the need of bishops to retain authority over the church, Constantine posthumously became the reference point for later Byzantine leaders, and obtained personal sainthood.[126]

Constantine's vision of 312 indicates how thin the line could be between communicating with the gods, obtaining their good will, and being under their protection. The vision advised the emperor how to defeat his opponent. That victory guaranteed consequent peace for the Roman state. These events also showed how the new emperor was under the protection of the Christian God. The adapted standards (showing the so-called *labarum*) displayed the special relationship between the conquering emperor and the god who supported him. All of this behaviour was perfectly in line with centuries of precedent. Already in the civil wars of 44–31 BC, which would lead to Augustus' supremacy, the different combatants claimed and advertised divine support.[127] The notion that gods singled out specific individuals went back much further, as Cicero pointed out: 'the care and providence of the immortal gods is not only given to the human race as a whole, but also tends to be extended to individuals ... It was this reason which drove the poets, and especially Homer to attach to their chief

---

[125] Eusebius, *Vit. Const.* 4.61–75, esp. 4.64; C. Mango, 'Constantine's Mausoleum and the Translation of Relics', *BZ* 83 (1990), 51–62; K. Dark/ F. Ozgumuş, 'New Evidence for the Byzantine Church of the Holy Apostles from Fatih Camii, Istanbul', *Oxford Journal of Archaeology* 21 (2002), 393–413. Only a minor part of the Church was constructed under Constantine, but enough to testify to Constantine's intention to be remembered as thirteenth apostle.

[126] Ambrose, *Ad Auxentium* 36, as noted by Dagron, *Emperor and Priest*, 148 n. 78. On pp. 127–57 Dagron sets out the debate surrounding Constantine's posthumous status. The reconstruction of the Apostoleion is set out by M. Johnson, *The Roman Imperial Mausoleum in Late Antiquity* (Cambridge 2009), 124–9.

[127] Zanker, *Power of Images*, 44–53; Mark Antony: Plutarch, *Life of Antony*, 4.1–3, 60.3, with U. Huttner, 'Marcus Antonius und Herakles', in: C. Schubert/ K. Brodersen (eds.), *Rom und der Griechische Osten. Festschrift für Hatto H. Schmitt zum 65. Geburtstag* (Stuttgart 1995), 103–12 ; 104 n.7. Lepidus: Livy, *Periochae* 63.4; Dio, 87.3; *RRC* 502–11; Sextus Pompeii: Dio, 48.19.2; 38.31.5.

heroes ... certain gods as companions'.[128] This was the cultural framework in which Augustus presented Apollo as some sort of divine protector. Even some of the apparently more innovative ways of stressing that relationship, such as the establishment of a temple to his patron god next to his house on the Palatine, drew on established practices – although adapted to his own purposes.[129] Through the support of Apollo, Augustus would guarantee peace, harbouring a new Golden Age. Divine support for a leader encompassed benefits for the state as a whole.

Emperors ruled through support of the gods, and in doing so, guaranteed peace and prosperity. It was perfectly fitting for an emperor to show closeness to one particular god. The emperor Galba, for instance, favoured Fortuna, as ancient authors and coins with the legend FORTUNA AUG(USTI) illustrate.[130] Fortune was explicitly stated to support the emperor's position. No ancient author seems to have found this remarkable. There are, on the other hand, many negative stories surrounding the way Nero linked himself to Apollo, Domitian to Minerva, Commodus to Hercules, or Elagabalus to his eponymous Sun god. Partly, these negative stories were the result of the extreme attention given to those gods by the emperors, at times even extending into some sort of assimilation with the gods. Commodus, for instance, started with Hercules as divine protector, but ultimately put forward the claim that he was an actual incarnation of the god, and would personally bring about a prosperous new Golden Age. That was something quite different from the traditional notion of being under a god's protection.[131] Partly, however, the negative stories surrounding the attitudes of these rulers to their supporting gods seem to be there because these emperors were portrayed as bad emperors anyhow. Consequently, all their actions could (or even needed to) be portrayed negatively. Nero's links to Apollo, for example, were not that far removed from Augustus'

---

[128] Cicero, *Nature of the gods*, 2.164–6.
[129] E. Bertrand-Ecanvil, 'Présages et propagande idéologique. A propos d'une liste concernant Octavien Auguste', *MEFRA* 106 (1994), 487–531; R. A. Gurval, *Actium and Augustus. The Politics and Emotions of Civil War* (Ann Arbor 1995), 91–113 rightly argues that evidence for the association is almost entirely from the period after 36 BC. On the temple: O. Hekster/ J. W. Rich, 'Octavian and the Thunderbolt: The Temple of Apollo Palatinus and the Roman Tradition of Temple Building', *CQ* 56 (2006), 149–68.
[130] Suet. *Gal.* 4.3; Dio, 64.1.2; *RIC* I², Galba, 238–9, nos. 127–8.
[131] Nero: Champlin, *Nero*, 112–44; Domitian: Hekster, *Emperor and Ancestors*, 253–5; Commodus: Hekster, *Commodus*, 104–11, 165–6; Elagabalus: M. Icks, *The Crimes of Elagabalus: The Life and Legacy of Rome's Decadent Boy Emperor* (London 2011), 72–91. Still fundamental on the relation between emperors and their divine protectors: A. D. Nock, 'The Emperors' Divine *Comes*', *JRS* 37 (1947), 102–16.

links to that same god, but are still described as outlandish. Importantly, the notion that an emperor was supported by a specific god, and that this guaranteed the stability of his rule and the wellbeing of the Roman state was hardly ever placed in doubt. There are several anecdotes about gods appearing before their favoured emperors in a dream or vision in order to warn them that they withdrew support, anticipating these emperors' fall from power. This suggests that an emperor needed to be seen to lose the support of a god with whom he had publicly advertised links, before that emperor could be safely disposed of.[132]

There was nothing remarkable about a god protecting a specific emperor. Moreover, if the Roman state gods were meant to protect the empire, it is unsurprising that people expected them to safeguard the emperor too. Famously, Vergil's *Aeneas* has Jupiter predict Rome's bright future, explicitly linked to the actions of Aeneas' descendants (Caesar and Augustus).[133] From Nero's reign onwards, coins were issued depicting Jupiter CUSTOS (the guardian) and CONSERVATOR (the preserver), and then Jupiter as CONSERVATOR AUGUSTI in the third century.[134] These are relatively rare coin types, but they confirm the common expectation that the supreme god of the Roman pantheon would defend the safety of the Roman emperor. In some cases, this was made even more obvious, as when Domitian allegedly dedicated a temple to Jupiter *Custos* 'with his own effigy in the lap of the god', celebrating a narrow escape he had during the Civil War in which his father Vespasian came to power.[135] Similarly, coins were struck under Commodus for Jupiter DEFENSOR SALUTIS AUGUSTI (protector of the welfare of the Emperor) and Jupiter OPTIMUS MAXIMUS SPONSOR SECURITATIS AUGUSTI (bondsman for the security of the emperor), possibly in reaction to a failed plot against him.[136]

Roman emperors were also seen to be chosen by Jupiter and to act on his behalf, as a sort of earthly counterpart. This, in a sense, was indicated when the emperor was portrayed holding a sceptre or thunderbolt. It was made

---

[132] O. Hekster, 'Reversed Epiphanies: Roman Emperors Deserted by Gods', *Mnemosyne* 63 (2010), 601–15.
[133] Virg. *Aen.* 1,257–96.
[134] Jupiter CUSTOS: *RIC* 1 (2nd ed.), Nero, 52–3, 63–4, 69; Civil Wars, 61, 78; Vespasian, 850, 863, 874, Domitian, 466, 635. Jupiter CONSERVATOR: RIC 1 (2nd ed), Civil Wars, 40, 60; Domitian, 143–4; *RIC* 3, Commodus, 304, 308Ca–d, 328a–b. Jupiter CONSERVATOR AUGUSTI: *RIC* 4, Elagabalus, 61d, 62–3; Uranius Antoninus, 1–2; *RIC* 5, Galienus, 172; Aurelian, 358; Tacitus, 111, 134, Florian, 17–18, 114–5; Carus, 373; Diocletian, 259–65, 356, 577–82. See p. 94–7 above on depictions of the emperor in the guise of Jupiter.
[135] Tac. *Hist.* 3.74. Cf. Suet. *Dom.* 5; Mart. *Ep.* 6.10.
[136] *RIC* 3, Commodus 596–7; Hekster, *Commodus*, 102–3.

very explicit in Pliny's panegyric to Trajan: 'Now he (Jupiter) is rid of this part of his duties, free to devote himself to the concerns of heaven, because he has given you to us to fill his role with regard to the whole human race'. This echoes an earlier passage by Seneca, in which Nero is stated to 'have been chosen and thought fit to perform the office of a god upon earth'.[137] Such a notion of divine election, like that of divine protection, went back to earlier times. Cicero already defended the appointment of Pompey the Great to a major military command in 66 BC by referring to divine Providence and the good Fortune of Rome, and described Pompey as 'this great blessing which the immortal gods have given to you'.[138]

Emperors held a more prominent position than had been possible during the Roman republic. It is unsurprising that this position was given a divine underpinning. Certainly by the time of Pliny, it was recognised that the emperor was viceregent of Jupiter, and that Jupiter was (therefore) the protector of the emperor.[139] This notion was strongly put into play from a central perspective during the Tetrarchy. After decades of civil war, a new system of collegiate rule was created, which attempted to put the emperorship out of reach of a military usurper. The new rulers Diocletian and Maximian as *Augusti*, later joined by the *Caesares* Galerius and Constantius, made much use of the idea of divine election.[140] The emperors and Caesars were given the *signa* (a semi-official nickname) *Jovius* and *Herculius*. Literary texts, coinage and especially epigraphic evidence show how these names were used throughout the empire, and emphasised the message that Jupiter and Hercules had elected and protected the four rulers of the empire.[141] A five-column monument in the Forum Romanum in Rome displayed the four Tetrarchs and Jupiter, indicating the strong links between the imperial college and the supreme god. An imperial cult chamber in a famous Tetrarchic complex at Luxor similarly shows the Tetrarchs with an image of Jupiter and an eagle holding a crown.[142] Jupiter and Hercules were

---

[137] Pliny, *Pan.* 80.5. See also 1.4–6; 5.3–4; 6.I–3; 8.1–4; 56.3; 94.I; Seneca, *Clem.* 1.2, with J. R. Fears, 'Nero as the Vicegerent of the Gods in Seneca's de Clementia', *Hermes* 103 (1975), 486–96. See p. 96–7 above on the emperor holding sceptre and in the guise of Jupiter.
[138] Cicero, *Pro Man.*14 (42), 15 (45), 16 (49), with Fears, 'Nero as the Vicegerent', 495 for further ancient references to the notion of divine election.
[139] J. R. Fears, 'The Cult of Jupiter and Roman Imperial Ideology', *ANRW* II.17.1 (1981), 3–141; 69–76, especially 71.
[140] See p. 96 above.
[141] Rees, 'The Emperors' New Names', 225; F. Kolb, *Herrscherideologie in der Spätantike* (Berlin 2001), 145–6; Hekster, *Emperors and Ancestors*, 297–300, with further references.
[142] Forum Romanum: G. Kalas, *The Restoration of the Roman Forum in Late Antiquity. Transforming Public Space* (Austin 2015), 35–40. Luxor complex: S. McFadden, 'The Luxor

presented as the divine companions and electors of the Tetrarchs. None of this was new (Figures 1.21 and 1.22). The Tetrarchs followed in their predecessors' footsteps, although they did so in a very emphatic way. Diocletian, it seems, had fully understood the power of divine consent or, better even, a divine mandate to legitimise his rule.[143]

When Constantine and his Christian successors were presented as elected by the Christian God, with texts and images referring to the cross as a symbol of authority, or showing the hand of god bestowing legitimacy (Figure 1.24), this was wholly in line with already existing explanations about divine election of emperors. The practice continued. As formulated by Justinian in the preface to the Digest (530): 'By the grace of God governing Our empire, which was entrusted to us by heavenly majesty, We both felicitously conclude wars, adorn peace, and uphold the condition of the State'.[144] A clearer indication of the continuous notion of divine election and support to fulfil traditional imperial roles is difficult to find.

Roman emperors, then, were thought to act on behalf of the gods, and to be protected and elected by the gods. After their deaths, they could even become part of the group of gods who supported the state. Several emperors and members of their family were posthumously recognised as *divi* or *divae*. Throughout Roman culture, the dead had always held some sort of elevated status, and comparisons between deceased individuals and gods on for instance sarcophagi were not at all uncommon. These were 'private apotheoses', through which the qualities of late loved ones were equated to those of a divinity.[145] Actual apotheosis also had its precedents in Roman history, although one needed to return to mythological times for that. Romulus had become a god after his death. Ovid, in his *Metamorphoses*, described the mythological events in which 'the omnipotent one . . . veiling the sky with dark clouds, terrified men on earth with thunder and lightning'. Romulus, 'dealing royal justice to his people',

---

Temple Paintings in Context. Roman Visual Culture in Late Antiquity', in: M. Jones/ S. McFadden (eds.), *Art of Empire. The Roman Frescoes and Imperial Cult Chamber in Luxor Temple* (New Haven 2015) 105–33; 126–33.

[143] F. Kolb, *Diokletian und die erste Tetrarchie. Improvisation oder Experiment in der Organisation monarchischer Herrschaft* (Berlin 1987), 89–91.

[144] *Codex Justinianus* 1.17,1 (=Digest, praef. 1). Translation: B. W. Frier et al., *The Codex of Justinian. Based on a Translation by Justice Fred H. Blume* (Cambridge 2016), 267–9. See also Socrates, *Ecclesial History*, 6.6.1, with T. Gelzer, 'Das Gebet des Kaisers Theodosius in der Schlacht am Frigidus (Socr. h. e. 5, 25)', in: E. Campi/ L. Grane/ A. M. Ritter (eds.), *Oratio. Das Gebet in patristischer und reformatorischer Sicht* (Göttingen 1999), 53–72; 68.

[145] Gradel, *Emperor Worship*, 264; H. Wrede, *Consecratio in Formam Deorum. Vergöttlichte Privatpersonen in der römischen Kaiserzeit* (Mainz 1981), 28, 180.

was collected by Mars, his 'mortal body dissolved in the clear atmosphere'. Instead, he became the god Quirinus, placed at 'the sacred high seats of the gods'.[146] Debate about divine honours was stronger in the late Republic than it had been before, and it is possible that Romulus' deification was only properly formulated at that time, to function as a parallel for contemporary discussions.[147] Caesar's divine honours were an important reason to trigger these.

Caesar, after all, claimed some sort of divine status during his life. Positioning a statue with the inscription *Deo Invicto* in the temple of Quirinus was only one way in which Caesar signposted how he expected to follow in Romulus' footsteps.[148] There was much debate about Caesar's supposed divinity when he was alive. His posthumous deification was less problematic. A comet sighted in 44 BC during Caesar's funerary games confirmed the popular notion that the late dictator was a divinity, and it is probably true that he was 'numbered among the gods, not only by a decree, but also by the belief of the people'.[149] The deification of Caesar was of great interest to his adopted nephew and heir, because it allowed Octavian to become son of a god (*divi filius*), something that was advertised widely, alongside the many references to the comet or Star of Caesar (*Sidus Iulium*) on central coins and in poetry.[150] The deified Caesar had become his heir's divine protector alongside Apollo.

When Augustus died, he had ruled for more than forty years, and his extraordinary status after his death was beyond doubt (Figure 1.20). His funeral was a momentous affair leading to an inevitable apotheosis. An eagle was released to bear Augustus to the gods, and witnesses went on record to state that they saw Augustus ascend as Romulus had done.[151] Not all future emperors would turn into posthumous gods. Of the first dynasty,

---

[146] Ovid. *Met.* 14.816–28.
[147] Cic. *Rep.* 2.20; S. Cole, *Cicero and the Rise of Deification at Rome* (Cambridge 2013), 88–105.
[148] Koortbojian, *The Divinization of Caesar and Augustus*, 85–91 and p. 107 n. 8 above for further references.
[149] Suet. *Div. Jul.* 88; Plin, *HN* 2.23.94; Dio 45.6.4–7.2; N. B. Pandey, *The Poetics of Power in Augustan Rome: Latin Poetic Responses to Early Imperial Iconography* (Cambridge 2018), 35–6, 39–40.
[150] Pandey, *Poetics of Power*, 43–80.
[151] Suet. *Aug.* 100.2–4; Tac. *Ann.* 1.8.3–6, Dio, 56.34–42. See W. Kierdorf, '"Funus» und «consecration". Zu Terminologie und Ablauf der römischen Kaiserapotheose', *Chiron* 16 (1986), 43–69, esp. 62–9; S. R. F. Price, 'From Noble Funerals to Divine Cult: The Consecration of Roman Emperors', in: D. Cannadine/ S. Price (eds.), *Rituals of Royalty. Power and Ceremonial in Traditional Societies* (Cambridge – New York – Melbourne 1987), 56–105; 72–7 (about links to Caesar's comet); Gradel, *Emperor Worship*, 271–96; P. Zanker, *Die Apotheose der römischen Kaiser* (Munich 2004).

only Claudius would be deified, showing some flexibility in these early stages of Roman imperial rule.[152] From Vespasian onwards, however, it became the norm for emperors and a number of other members of the imperial family, such as mothers, cousins or sisters, to be turned into *divi* after their death. Excluding an emperor from this expanding group was a statement on his perceived inaptness. It also (and perhaps more importantly) signalled that a successor wanted to distance himself from his predecessor.[153] Suitability was important, because the *divi* as a group protected the reigning emperor and by extension the Roman state. This is shown, for instance, by the Acts of the Arval Brethren. These reflect centuries of dedications by a group of priests who originally made sacrifices for good harvests. In imperial times, these acts were mainly dedications to the good fortune of the emperor, often referring to sacrifices to the *divi* to ensure the current emperor's safety. The surviving remains of monuments to the *divi*, such as the impressive temple to Divus Antoninus and Diva Faustina in the Forum Romanum, further show how much weight was given to the cult of the deified rulers.[154]

The importance of the *divi* seems to have suffered in the second half of the third century. One reason may have been the many military changes of power. These meant that emperors often did not want their predecessor to be deified. When someone came to power because his predecessor failed to maintain the loyalty of the troops, it was difficult to still boost that predecessor's reputation by deifying him. Consequently, new *divi* became rare. Another reason for the diminished importance of deified emperors might have been the religious shifts at the time, with increased interest for so-called mystery cults, and upcoming Christianity. At the beginning of the third century, there is still evidence that the *divi* fulfilled their traditional role. The Arval Acts document worship of twenty different *divi* in 224. A religious calendar from the reign of Severus Alexander (222–35), the so-called *Feriale Duranum* from the eastern frontier town of Dura Europos, similarly shows frequent sacrifices for the divine emperors and empresses.[155] The emperor Decius (249–51)

---

[152] O. Hekster, 'Honouring Ancestors: The Dynamic of Deification', in: O. Hekster/ S. Schmidt-Hofner/ C. Witschel (eds.), *Ritual Dynamics and Religious Change in the Roman Empire* (Leiden – Boston 2009), 95–110; 102.
[153] Gradel, *Emperor Worship*, 336–49; Woolf, 'Divinity and Power', 242–3.
[154] J. Scheid, *Commentarii Fratrvm Arvalivm Qui Svpersvnt. Les copies épigraphiques des protocols annuels de la confrérie Arvale (21 av. – 304 ap. J.C.)* (Rome 1998); Gradel, *Emperor Worship*, 262, 344 fig. 12.10.
[155] Gradel, *Emperor Worship*, 355–6; Hekster, *Rome and its Empire*, 66, 127–9.

issued a remarkable series of coins commemorating eleven deified emperors, clearly expecting this to reflect positively upon his reign, and he was followed in this by his successor Trebonianus Gallus (251–3).[156] But the third-century historian Herodian describes how Maximinus Thrax (235–8) 'handed over to the mints the dedications to the temples, the statues of the gods, the honours of *divi*, and decorations on public buildings or the city adornments, in short, any material suitable to make into coins'.[157] This is a general diatribe against an unpopular ruler, but it is noticeable that the *divi* are singled out. It seems that the honours which they lost were the temple funds, and that the cult as a whole was discontinued. The emperor Tacitus (275–6) is stated to have 'ordered that a temple was built to the deified emperors, in which should be the statues of the good *principes*', which suggests that previous temples had closed at an earlier stage, although the passage is from a fourth-century source and may not be trustworthy.[158]

Even if the influence of the *divi* diminished, that did not signal the end of imperial deification. As late as 317/8, well into Constantine's rule, Claudius Gothicus (268–70), Constantius Chlorus (305–6) and Maximian (285–310) were still recognised as *divi* on coins.[159] Posthumous coins issued between 337 and 340 even used the legend DIVO CONSTANTINO ('for the deified Constantine').[160] Up to Theodosius I, who in 380 made Christianity the state religion, consecration is attested in literary texts, with several references to dead emperors as *divus*. Nor did it end even then. The poet Claudian could refer to Theodosius himself as 'best of all the gods' in a panegyric for the emperor Honorius held in 404. An anonymous epigram argued that Theodosius II 'had died as a man, but lives as a god'. In the middle of the fifth century, the poet and bishop Sidonius still designated dead emperors as *divi*, as did the sixth-century poet Corippus, writing

---

[156] *RIC* 4.3, Trajan Decius, 77–98; E. Manders, 'Communicating Messages through Coins: A New Approach to the Emperor Decius', *Jaarboek voor Munt- en Penningkunde* 98 (2011), 17–38; S. Dmitriev, '"Good Emperors" and the Emperors of the Third Century', *Hermes* 132 (2004) 211–24; 218–19; J. Blay Detrell, '"Divi Series", una emisión conmemorativa de antoninianos de restitución del siglo III d.C.', *Gaceta Numismática* 165 (2007), 69–82.

[157] Herodian, 7.3.5. [158] HA, *Tacitus*, 9.5; Gradel, *Emperor Worship*, 357, 363.

[159] *RIC* 7, Treveri, 201–7, Arelate, 173–8, Rome, 104–28, Aquileia, 21–6, Siscia, 41–6, Thessalonica, 24–6. Claudius Gothicus was presented as Constantine's ancestor, Constantius was his father, and Maximian his father-in-law: Hekster, *Emperors and Ancestors*, 226–9, figs. 81–3.

[160] *RIC* 7 Lugdunum, 2–3, 12, 17; Arelate, 17, 32, 40–2.

under Justinian.[161] People continued to expect their good emperors to become gods after their death.

This seems to have created some problems in Christian Constantinople. These can be illustrated by the aftermath of the death of Constantine. Pagan deification was not an option. Instead, a range of more or less traditional elements came together that would ultimately lead to the bestowal of personal sainthood on the late emperor (celebrated on 21 May). There was a procession led by the new emperor Constantius II, with a funerary mass. Constantine was interred in the Church of the Holy Apostles, but attempts to present him as ἰσαπόστολος (equal to the Apostles) or even as Christ-like would not be taken up. The emperor's holiness, on the other hand, was not in doubt, and the Christian church historian Philostorgius (368–439) complains how Christians sacrificed to 'the image of Constantine set up upon the porphyry column, paying homage to it with lamp-lighting and incense, or praying to it, as to a god'.[162] In the fourth and fifth centuries a process of 'posthumous sanctification' took place, in which Constantine's life was continuously rewritten to make it more fitting for a Christian saint. From the early fifth century onwards, Constantine figured in liturgical celebrations and became systematically referred to as St Constantine.[163] By the early sixth century, a canonical story existed, which gave space to the expectation that someone as important as Constantine would still have the divine power to protect his people after his death.

In a Christian empire, sainthood was the only role in which past emperors could still be seen to protect the state. Imperial sainthood, however, was not unproblematic and would never become as normal as

---

[161] Claudian, *Panegyric on Honorius' Sixth Consulship*, 55–6; *Ant. Graec.*1,105; Sidonius, *Carmina* 2,210; 2.318; Corippus, *Laus Iustini* 3,127; C. O. Tommasi Moreschini, 'Coping with Ancient Gods, Celebrating Christian Emperors, Proclaiming Roman Eternity: Rhetoric and Religion in Late Antique Latin Panegyrics', in: Kahlos, *Emperors and the Divine*, 177–209; 190; M. Meier, 'Der Monarch auf der Suche nach seinem Platz. Kaiserherrschaft im frühen Byzanz (5. bis 7. Jahrhundert n. Chr.)', in: Rebenich, *Monarchische Herrschaft im Altertum*, 509–44; 509–10.

[162] Philostorgius, *Historia Ecclesiastica* 2.17, translation R. Amidon, *Philostorgius: Church History* (Atlanta: Society of Biblicals Studies 2007), with 35 n. 49; L. Pitsakis, 'Sainteté et empire. À propos de la sainteté impériale: formes de sainteté "d'office" et de sainteté collective dans l'Empire d'Orient?', *Bizantinistica* 3 (2011), 155–227; 200; G. Bonamente, 'Dall'imperatore divinizzato all' imperatore santo', in: P. Brown/ T. Lizzi Testa (eds.), *Pagans and Christians in the Roman Empire: The Breaking of a Dialogue, IVth–VIth Century* A.D. (Münster 2011), 339–70. See also p. 141 above.

[163] Dagron, *Emperor and Priest*, 143–8; L. M. Ciolfi, 'Not Another Constantine. Rethinking Imperial Sainthood through the Case of John III Vatatzes', in: I. Vainovski-Mihai (ed.), *New Europe College. Yearbook 2015–2016* (Bucharest 2018), 23–52; 26–8.

deification had been before. Instead, it focused on the exemplary figure of Constantine. His holiness was detached from his role as emperor, so that successors could not claim it. Yet most subsequent rulers were still included in Constantinople's *Synaxarium* – a liturgical compilation of hagiographies – on the day of their burial.[164] Even though this did not bestow formal sanctity upon them, it shows the continuous expectations that emperors had a special connection to the divine, even after their death. How important that link was and how universally it was acknowledged had changed dramatically between the reigns of Constantine and Justinian. In a religious system with one supreme god, the posthumous divinity of Roman emperors suffered.

The divine status of a living emperor was even more problematic for Christians than that of a dead one. Roman emperors, however, were perceived as superhuman beings. Whether they were worshipped as actual gods while alive remains a matter of debate, but that they were worshipped is clear. Temples and cults for the living emperor existed from the reign of Augustus onwards. They can be found in the east where there was a long-lasting tradition of worshipping kings, but also in the west, including the Italian peninsula and Rome. The forms in which emperors were worshipped differed from region to region, and there was no centrally controlled imperial cult. But there were imperial cults throughout the Roman empire from the very beginning of emperorship, and these included imperial priests, festivities, altars and temples.[165] The emperor's role in the religious domain was important to all inhabitants of the Roman empire. The emperor rose so far above his subjects that for many his status could only be conceived of in divine terms. There is an exemplary letter written in 41 by the emperor Claudius to the inhabitants of Alexandria. In it, the emperor accepts many of the honours which the city has proposed to give him, but he refuses 'the appointment of a high priest' and 'the building of temples', because these were 'granted to the gods alone'. The preface to this letter by the prefect of Egypt explains that he 'deemed it necessary to display the letter publicly in order that reading it one by one you may wonder at the majesty of our god Caesar'.[166] There was no escaping the

---

[164] A. Luzzi, 'Per l'identificazione degli imperatori bizantini comme morati nel Sinassario di Costantinopoli', *Rivista di Studi Bizantini e Neoellenici* 33 (1996), 45–66; 47–51; Ciolfi, 'Not Another Constantine', 28–30.

[165] The bibliography is immense. For an insightful recent overview: G. McIntyre, *Imperial Cult* (Leiden – Boston 2019) (= *Ancient History* 2.1 [2019]), 7–14, 42–70.

[166] P. London 1912, 7–9; 49–51. Fishwick, *The Imperial Cult in the Latin West* II.1, 424 notes how Claudius was addressed as *dues noster Caesar* or *divini principis* with some regularity.

perception that the emperor was divine if even a refusal of priests and temples emphasised the divine majesty of the emperor.

How pervasive this divine status of emperors was also becomes clear from worship of members of the imperial family. From the early empire onwards, there are references to the divine household (*domus divina*). They range from literary texts, such as the first-century fabulist Phaedrus, to inscriptions in honour of the *domus divina*.[167] Under Domitian there were inscriptions 'for the health of the emperor and the whole divine household' (*imperatoris totiusque domus divinae*) and in the second and third century the abbreviation *in h.d.d.* (*in honorem domus divinae*: 'in honour of the divine household') became common. If something can be abbreviated, it must be standard language, testifying to an all-encompassing perception that the emperor's divine status reflected upon his family too.[168] Members of the imperial family, like the emperor, also received their own priests and priestesses. This practice continued even when Christianity had become the state cult. A certain Astius Mustelus from Ammaedara (in Tunisia) was commemorated after his death in 526 as a Christian and *flamen perpetuus* – responsible for the worship of the imperial family.[169] There can be little doubt that throughout the history of the empire many people thought of the emperor as a divine being.

Romans commonly perceived their emperor in superhuman terms, but there remained tensions surrounding claims of imperial divinity. First, the divine status of the emperor was unproblematic for the vast majority of people, including soldiers, in Italy and the provinces, but there was some resentment among the senatorial elite. Divine status, after all, placed emperors far above all other members of the elite. This came close to the semblance of monarchy which Augustus and many of his successors had tried to avoid. The notion of divine election already threatened the idea

---

[167] *CIL*, 13.4635; *AE*, 1978, 295; *I.Ephesos*, 18; Phaedrus, 5.7.38; Fishwick, *Imperial Cult*, II.1, 423–9; M. Corbier, 'Maiestas Domus Augustae', in: G. A. Bertinelli and A. Donati (eds), *Varia epigraphica. Atti del colloquio internazionale di epigrafia Bertinoro* (Faenza 2001), 155–99; 166–78; Chastagnol, 'L'Expression épigraphique du culte imperial dans les provinces gauloises', *REA* 97 (1995), 593–614.

[168] M.-T. Raepsaet-Charlier, 'La Datation des inscriptions latines dans les provinces occidentales de l'empire romain d'après les formules "IN H(ONOREM) D(OMUS) D(IVINAE)" et "DEA DEAE"', *ANRW* II(3) (1975), 232–82; D. Fishwick, 'Numinibus Domus Divinae', *ZPE* 159 (2007), 293–6; 296; Hekster, *Emperors and Ancestors*, 182 with full references.

[169] *CIL* 8.10516, 11528; McIntyre, *Family of Gods*, 135–4. For the continuation of imperial cult practices in the third and fourth century: F. R. Trombley, 'The Imperial Cult in Late Roman Religion (ca. A.D. 244–395): Observations on the Epigraphy', in: J. Hahn (ed). *Spätantiker Staat und religöser Konflikt. Imperiale und lokale Verwaltung und die Gewalt gegen Heiligtümer* (Berlin 2011), 19–54.

that senators had a claim in deciding who the next emperor was going to be. An emperor whose status derived from his personal divinity was even more threatening.[170] For people who only meant to serve, the emperor's superhuman status was straightforward – obliging a divinity was normal practice. For those who claimed to work with the emperor, advise him and in many ways be on a par with him, divine status was not so clear-cut. Unsurprisingly, most criticism of emperors emphasising their divinity can be found in texts written by the senatorial elite.

Second, there seems to have been the perception, outside as well as inside senatorial circles, that real honour could not be taken, but had to be given. Paying honour to someone was normal practice in the Roman world, but demanding that honour was not publicly acceptable. That had too many associations with the relation between master and slave, or king and subject.[171] Much of the criticism against emperors who presented themselves too openly as divine has to do with the fact that they themselves claimed their divinity. Caligula, for instance, is said to have been

> demanding that he was to be regarded as more than a human being, and he used to claim that he had intercourse with the Moon, that Victory put a crown upon him, and to pretend that he was Jupiter ... he would pose as Neptune ... impersonated Hercules, Bacchus, Apollo, and all the other divinities ... Indeed, to match the change of name he would assume all the rest of the attributes that belonged to the various gods, so that he might seem to really resemble them.[172]

A very hostile eyewitness account by the Jewish author Philo of Alexandria (c. 15–50), who participated in a diplomatic mission to Caligula, notes how the same emperor received him with the words: 'Are you the god-haters who do not believe me to be a god; a god acknowledged among all the other nations but not to be named by you?'[173] Of course, honouring an emperor as a god was an idea that was anathema to the Jews. That made Caligula's actions more offensive to Philo than to other contemporaries. Yet there seems little doubt that the emperor actively claimed divine honours. Several authors claim that he placed his own portraits on the statues of divinities and that he ordered people to worship his personal cult statues. Some claims, like the notion that Caligula linked the temple of

---

[170] P. Veyne, *Le Pain et le cirque. Sociologie historique d'un pluralisme politique* (Paris 1976), 540–89, esp. 542, 553–60, 565, 575–80.
[171] J. E. Lendon, *Empire of Honour. The Art of Government in the Roman World* (Oxford 1997), 23–4. See p. 23.
[172] Dio, 59.26.5–6. [173] Philo, *Embassy to Gaius*, 353.

Castor and Pollux to the palace complex, or that he gave excessive divine attention to his sisters, are supported by archaeological evidence.[174]

There had been images of Augustus and Tiberius assimilating them to gods, temples to Augustus and Rome while the emperor was alive, and previous divine worship of members of the imperial family.[175] Many of the presumed claims of Caligula resembled honours that had already been given to his predecessors. But by demanding these divine honours, rather than reluctantly accepting them, the emperor crossed a boundary. It is possible that he tried to become a Hellenistic king like Alexander the Great. He may simply have been insane. In any case, he put forward one systematic image of supreme and divine rule – ignoring the need to formulate Roman emperorship in a way that allowed for the various expectations of what an emperor should be. Complaints about the divine claims of other 'mad' emperors like Nero, Domitian, Commodus or Elagabalus are very similar. There are descriptions of their cruelty and perversity, pushed to absurdity, but the real problem was their attempt to seek self-deification and demand that others honour them. Roman emperorship was shaped through parallel images and narratives. Different notions, names and images existed alongside one another.[176] A divine emperor who stressed his own supremacy ignored this flexibility, which created antagonism among the groups whose expectations of emperorship were thwarted. This antagonism made it more likely that these emperors came to a violent end, and all but guaranteed a negative reputation in ancient historiography.

Attempts by emperors to push for personal divinity led to their unpopularity with (at least) the senatorial elite. There are, however, signs of continued popularity among the military, the lower classes and even some members of the elite in Rome and the provinces for emperors such as Nero and Commodus.[177] The emperors' 'unacceptable' behaviour still normalised the notion of an openly divine emperor. Those who had already thought that the emperor was sacred were confirmed in their expectations. For those who had previously objected, there was now a precedent against

---

[174] Suet. *Cal.* 21–2; Dio, 59.26.5–8, 59.28.2–5; C. J. Simpson, 'Caligula's Cult. Immolation, Immortality, Intent', in: A. Small (ed.), *Subject and Ruler. The Cult of the Ruling Power in Classical Antiquity* (Ann Arbor 1996), 63–71; 69–71; A. Carandini (ed.), *The Atlas of Ancient Rome. Biography and Portraits of the City* (Princeton – Oxford 2017), I, 172.
[175] A. A. Antoniou, 'Cassius Dio (51.20.6–8) and the Worship of the Living Emperor in Italy', *Mnemosyne* 72 (2019), 930–48, with references.
[176] Cf. Hekster, 'Imagining Power'.
[177] Camplin, *Nero*, 11–12, 28–34; Hekster, *Commodus*, 163–86.

which to compare an emperor who claimed divinity. Caracalla (198–217) bombarded his subjects with divine images on central coinage. Diocletian formalised rituals and the ceremonial role of the ruler. Yet both emperors presented themselves as less extravagantly divine than, for instance, Commodus had done with his claims to be the new incarnation of Hercules.[178] Consequently, there was less criticism. For some groups, the emperor had been divine from Augustus onwards. As time progressed, openly divine emperorship became acceptable to ever more people.

By the time that Christianity established itself as the dominant religion of the empire, the expectation that emperors displayed superhuman status was firmly embedded. This again created some difficulties in a system with one god, though it is worth remembering that Christianity was to a large extent shaped in the context of the Roman world in general and specifically the imperial cult. There are, for instance, obvious links between Christ as the Son of God and the emperor as a *divi filius*. It has been argued that in the *Gospel of Mark*, Christ's baptism can be seen as a form of adoption into a divine family, and that the dove is presented as a counter-symbol to the emperor's eagle. Christians, too, lived in a Roman world and could only understand new concepts through the adaptation of existing language and symbols.[179] Still, in the Christian empire, absolute imperial divinity was no longer an option. That did not mean the superhuman status of the emperor was diminished. Personal divinity might have been complicated, but the rituals through which the emperor manifested himself grew increasingly religious in tone.[180] The elevated status of the emperor could also be expressed by presenting him with a halo or a nimbus, as visible on the Missorium of Theodosius or on Justinian's mosaic in Ravenna (Figures 1.15 and 2.5 and 5.1). This placed them visually in line with saints and prophets.[181] Justinian, moreover, made use of the emerging notion of the holy man; someone whose extreme piety made him a conduit through whom God could be reached, filling the footsteps of the 'divine men' of

---

[178] Caracalla: Manders, *Coining Images of Power*, 229–42 with fig. 33–4; C. Rowan, *Under Divine Auspices. Divine Ideology and the Visualisation of Imperial Power in the Severan Period* (Cambridge 2012), 111–12. Diocletian, see above, p. 74.

[179] M. Peppard, *The Son of God in the Roman World. Divine Sonship in its Social and Political Context* (Oxford 2011), 86–131, with the notion of Jesus as 'a counter-emperor' set out on p. 87; I. E. Rock, *Paul's Letter to the Romans and Roman Imperialism: An Ideological Analysis of the Exordium (Romans 1:1–17)* (Cambridge 2017), 159–60.

[180] A. Cameron, 'Images of Authority: Elites and Icons in Late Sixth-Century Byzantium', *Past & Present* 84 (1979), 3–35; 4. Cf. MacCormack, *Art and Ceremony*, 58.

[181] J. Elsner, *The Art of the Roman Empire AD 100–450* (Oxford – New York 2018²), 77–80.

Greek and Roman myth. The emperor could play the same role, and become himself a *vir sanctus* who achieved miracles.[182]

Though the specifics of the emperor's perceived divine status shifted over time, emperors continued to be flattered in divine language. In 389, the Gallic panegyrist Pacatus praised Theodosius as 'a god whom we can actually see'.[183] Over a century later, Ennodius still referred to the Ostrogothic king Theoderic's 'divine rule', even if in the rest of the speech he firmly placed the king in a Biblical context.[184] How difficult it was to properly flatter a Christian emperor without referring to his divine majesty follows from a speech of praise to Anastasius (491–518) by the rhetorician Priscian. He starts by proclaiming that 'the poet who grants divine attributes to mortal men is condemned in the judgement of all wise men'. Later, he mentions the 'sacred palace' and describes the emperor as 'a reflection of the heavenly judge' who gives 'holy oracles to the people'.[185]

In the minds of those praising the emperor, the expectation of divine support and status remained important. How it was expressed shifted over time. Different groups or regions may have placed more emphasis on the ways in which emperors interacted with (or even incorporated) the divine. Emperors who expressed personal divinity and ordered emperor worship, rather than accepting what was given, were harshly criticised in later writing, but even that behaviour seems to have been acceptable to many layers of Roman society. Like the core ideas about the emperor's military role, notions of the emperor's relationship with the divine stayed surprisingly stable over the years, notwithstanding the major religious shifts. No emperor could rule without the gods. Again, the expectations of what an emperor needed to do and be strongly limited the leeway he had in defining his own image.[186]

---

[182] Coripp. *Laud. Just* I, 175. Cf. Coripp. *Laud. Just.* II, 129, II, 428: 'The earthly king is the image of the omnipotent'; M. Meier, *Das andere Zeitalter Justinians. Kontingenzerfahrung und Kontingenzbewältigung im 6. Jahrhundert n. Chr.* (Göttingen 2003), 619–20, 641. On the holy men, see: P. Brown, 'The Rise and Function of the Holy Man in Late Antiquity', *JRS* 61 (1971), 80–101.

[183] *Pan.Lat.* II (12), 4.5. Also II (12), 472; Nixon/Rodger, *In Praise*, 453 n. 17; Tommasi Moreschini, 'Coping with Ancient Gods', 192–3.

[184] Ennodius, *Pan. Theoder.*, 1(4); C. Rohr, *Der Theodorich-Panegyricus des Ennodius* (Hanover 1995), 42–6. The Biblical context is set out in Tommasi Moreschini, 'Coping with Ancient Gods', 196.

[185] Prisc. *Laud Anast.* Pref., 119; 193 (translation: P. Coyne 1991).

[186] See also p. 315 below on the continuous role of the emperor in religious legislation, and p. 272, 283 on the expectation that the emperor constructed churches.

The Emperor and His Civic Role

All Roman emperors needed to show military qualities and stress their relationship to the divine. A less straightforward aspect of Roman emperorship was the expected role of the emperor as a 'civic' ruler. The way Roman emperorship was shaped under Augustus made it appear non-monarchical while showing absolute rule. Republican traditions, and the expectations that these created, formed a framework within which rule was shaped. Augustus' position of sole rule was formulated over decades. In that period, various honours and powers were accumulated step-by-step. It was important in this process that the emperor did not seem to acquire these powers actively (to avoid appearing monarchical) but that they were bestowed upon him by existing (Republican) institutions.[187] That is clear from the different claims to formal power put forward by Augustus over time, as famously formulated in the *Res Gestae Divi Augusti*, inscribed throughout the empire after the *princeps*' death. In one of the most-often cited passages it states:

> In my sixth and seventh consulships [28 and 27 BC], after I had put an end to civil wars, although by everyone's agreement I had power over everything (*potens rerum omnium*), I transferred the state from my power into the control of the Roman senate and people. For this service, I was named Augustus by senatorial decree ... After this time I excelled everyone in influence (*auctoritas*), but I had no more power (*potestas*) than the others who were my colleagues in each magistracy.[188]

Much attention has been paid to the emphasis on *auctoritas* in this passage, and on the construction of a 'Republican façade' behind which an autocratic construction lay hidden.[189] Yet as the opening sentence of the passage makes clear, the emphasis is on how the new sole ruler was able to replace and rephrase his power at the end of the civil wars into an acceptable traditional structure.[190] The extraordinary position held by

---

[187] See p. 24–5 above; L. Hodgson, *Res Publica and the Roman Republic: 'Without Body or Form'* (Oxford 2016), 264–5.
[188] *RGDA* 34 (translation Cooley).
[189] See especially Rowe, 'Reconsidering the Auctoritas of Augustus', on the problems of interpreting the passage as a programmatic statement. The tension between *potestas* versus *auctoritas* is well contextualised in G. Agamben, *State of Exception* (Chicago – London 2005), 80–4.
[190] Cooley, *Res Gestae*, 257–8; P. Botteri, 'L'integrazione Mommseniana a *Res Gestae divi Augusti* 34.1 "*potitus rerum omnium*"', ZPE 144 (2003), 261–7; F. Constabile, 'RG 34.1: [POT]*I*ENS RE [RU]M OM[N]IUM e l'Edictum de reddenda re publica', in: G. Purpura (ed.), *Revisione ed*

Augustus was based on senatorial acclamation. He was 'simply' a more prominent member of the elite. At the same time, as we have seen, he was a military conqueror and a superhuman being – for some even a god.

The emperor's superior status was apparent to most (or even all) inhabitants of the Roman empire. But following Augustus' precedent, emperors also had to portray themselves as a leader who behaved in a citizen-like manner; the so-called *civilis princeps*.[191] The continuous attention to the emperor as a superior senator furthered expectations and created the framework within which successive rulers had to formulate their position. This is a reason for the emphasis in our sources on how well emperors performed in the traditional Republican qualities of elite men. Authors such as Suetonius and Tacitus at least partly measured an emperor's worth by his success or failure as an orator. The rumours that Nero had not written his own funeral oration for his adopted father Claudius were meant to show how he was unsuitable for the job. Perhaps the emperor's later commitment to perform before crowds, and his attempts to improve his voice, such as lying down with a leaden plate on his chest to strengthen his diaphragm, were a reaction to this criticism. An emperor, like a senator of old, needed to be a 'good man, skilled in speaking' (*vir bonus, dicendi peritus*).[192]

In an important letter to Marcus Aurelius, Fronto makes the same point when he sets out the emperor's responsibilities:

> For the duties of the emperor are: to urge necessary steps in the senate; to address the people on very many matters in public meetings; to correct the injustices of the law; to send letters to all parts of the globe; to bring compulsion to bear on kings of foreign nations; to repress by their edicts the faults of the provincials, give praise to good actions, quell the seditious and terrify the fierce ones. All these are assuredly things to be achieved by words and letters.[193]

---

integrazione dei Fontes Iuris Romani Anteiustiniani (FIRA). Studi prepratori I. Leges (Turin 2012), 255–94.

[191] A. Wallace-Hadrill, 'Civilis Princeps: Between Citizen and King', *JRS* 72 (1982), 32–48. See Millar, 'State and Subject' on public perception of the emperor's superior status.

[192] Tac. *Ann.* 13.3; Suet. *Nero.* 20.1, 25.3; Plin. *NH.* 19.108; Cato, *Frag.* 1; T. Habinek, *Ancient Rhetoric and Oratory* (Malden [Mass.] – Oxford 2008), 35–6; G. S. Aldrete, *Gestures and Acclamations in Ancient Rome* (Baltimore 1999), 87–9.

[193] Fronto, *Ad. M. Antoninus de eloquentia* 2.7 (= *Amic.* 141.22); Millar, *Emperor*, 203. On Fronto and the status of his letters: C. Davenport/ J. Manley, *Fronto. Selected Letters* (London 2014), 1–3, 6–7.

This is a remarkably one-sided definition of imperial duties. Fronto makes only minimal reference to the emperor's military tasks and omits his religious role altogether. Fronto's framing of the emperor's role and the emphasis on 'words and letters' is undoubtedly shaped by the fact that he was tutor in Latin rhetoric to Marcus Aurelius and Lucius Verus. This was a way of emphasising his own role in the education and success of his imperial pupils. All the same, Fronto must have thought that this was a convincing argument, and in that sense the letter shows how pervasive the idea of the civic emperor was, at least for some members of the senatorial elite in Rome, and for the emperor himself. The letter does not hide imperial authority, but formulates it through a very senatorial set of actions. Members of the elite continued to judge emperors on how well they were equipped for these tasks. In the third century, Herodian points out with disdain that Maximinus Thrax needed 'some of his friends' to write his speeches. The soldierly Maximian (286–305, 306–8), selected as co-ruler by Diocletian for his military acumen, is praised in a speech from 289 by a certain Mamertinus because he manages 'to observe which governors emulate your justice, which commanders maintain the glory of your courage, to receive countless messengers from every quarter and to send out just as many dispatches'. In the rest of the speech, the author of this panegyric emphasises the military qualities and divine support of the emperor much more than Fronto had done, but it remains noticeable how civic duties were stressed. Later still, Eusebius emphasised that Constantine wrote his own letters and speeches, although he had his Latin text translated into Greek by interpreters. Emperors' letters, speeches and edicts, and their ability to write these themselves, remained important for at least some sections of society.[194]

Senators paid most attention to this aspect of the emperor's role. They were not the only people to do so. Roman emperors continued to address their populace in person, noticeably when they took their oath as consul. In this way they showed that they were still traditional office holders, who abided by the law, something that Pliny also emphasised in his panegyric to Trajan.[195] Public performances before the people were, however, not

---

[194] Herodian, 7.8.3; *Pan. Lat.* XI (X), 3.3–4; Eusebius, *Life of Constantine*, 4.32; Millar, *Emperor*, 205–6, with further references. Note how in reality there were many administrators who wrote the emperors' edicts, letters and speeches: C. Davenport, 'Giving Voice to the Late Roman Emperor: Eumenius', *For the Restoration of the Schools (Pan. Lat. 9[4]) in context*', *Journal of Late Antiquity* 14 (2021), 9–28.

[195] Dio 59.13.1; 60.10.1; HA. *Sev. Alex.* 25.11; Plin. *Pan.* 65; F. Pina Polo, 'Public Speaking in Rome: A Question of Auctoritas', in: M. Peachin (ed.), *The Oxford Handbook of Social Relations in the Roman World* (Oxford 2011), 286–303; 295.

Figure 2.7 Trajan as an orator: 103, Rome. Bronze sestertius (26.76 g): The laureate portrait of Trajan was surrounded by IMP CAES NERVAE TRAIANO AVG GER DAC P M TR P COS V P P, combining the emperor's ancestry, victory titles, and traditional Republican offices. Trajan is shown in a toga in a rare example of a coin showing the emperor speaking to his people, with the legend explicitly addressing the senate and people of Rome: S P Q R OPTIMO PRINCIPI S C. *RIC* 2, Trajan, 553.
Source: ANS 1964.183.1, American Numismatic Society

widely advertised beyond the city of Rome. There were regular coin issues that showed the speeches which emperors held before the soldiers (*adlocutio*), but up to the reign of Trajan there was no civic equivalent. Scenes showing the emperor distributing grain or *congiaria* come close, as they usually show the emperor seated on a so-called curule chair (a prerogative of magistrates in the Republic, and an expression of their civil role) among the people who are to receive his gifts.[196] But the focus of the coins is on the emperor bestowing gifts to his subjects rather than on him addressing them. Between 103 and 111, however, a series of coins showed a togate Trajan standing on a tribunal, his hand raised in an oratorical gesture towards a group of toga-wearing Romans (Figure 2.7). Hadrianic coins from 125–8 show a similar scene, though here the emperor stands in front of a temple. But the number of coins showing emperors addressing their troops far outnumber these civic images.[197] A famous surviving set of

---

[196] On the curule chair see: T. Schäfer, *Imperii Insignia. Sella Curulis und Fasces. Zur Repräsentation römischer Magistrate* (Mainz 1989), 50–5, 63–9. The emperor distributing gifts, see p. 167 below.

[197] *RIC* 2, Trajan, 553–4; *RIC* 2.3 (2nd ed.) Hadrian, 826–827; Pina Polo, 'Public Speaking in Rome', 296.

reliefs from either the reign of Trajan or Hadrian, the so-called Anaglypha Traiani, also shows the togate emperor in front of his people. Details on the reliefs make clear that the scene is explicitly set in the Roman Forum. A near-contemporary relief on the so-called Arco di Portogallo shows Hadrian on the rostrum in the Roman Forum, holding a scroll and speaking to two men and a child.[198] It is no coincidence that both reliefs are explicitly set at the centre of Roman political life. The image of the civic emperor, speaking to the assembled people, was more important in Rome than in the further regions of the empire.

The descriptions of imperial duties by Fronto and Mamertinus were right in the sense that substantial parts of an emperor's day were filled with receiving dispatches and sending out letters and edicts in response. The literary, epigraphic and papyrological evidence for this is overwhelming and brought together in Fergus Millar's unsurpassed *The Emperor in the Roman World*, which famously stated: 'the emperor was what the emperor did'. Emperors were expected to react to their people's demands, often by taking the final decisions in disputes.[199] Many ancient authors assess their emperor on how well they performed in this task. Marcus Aurelius, for instance, is said on one occasion to have spent five days with 'the examination of law cases', in contrast to Lucius Verus who was 'either banqueting or preparing banquets' at the time. Trajan is praised by Dio for his attention to civil administration and the dispensing of justice. How much of a commonplace the judging ruler was is clear from a statement in Menander Rhetor's third-century guide about how to flatter rulers. It highlights how an emperor's humanity towards petitioners was a good way to praise him.[200] But this was only part of the story. For large parts of the empire, the civil emperor was invisible, outshone by the divine and victorious monarch.

The emperor who obediently served his people was a powerful narrative. It is famously expressed in a much-cited passage about Hadrian: '... once, when a woman made a request of him as he passed by on a journey, he at first said to her, "I haven't time", but afterwards, when she cried out, "Stop,

---

[198] Carandini, *Atlas of Ancient Rome*, I, figs 39–40, 175–6, 484–5, II, tab. 202a; N. Brown, 'The Living and the Monumental on the Anaglypha Traiani', *American Journal of Archaeology*, 124 (2020), 607–30; 608–10.

[199] Millar, *Emperor*, esp. 465–77 on access to the emperor and 537–49 on petition and response, with K. Tuori, 'Greek Tyrants and Severan Emperors: Comparing the Image', *BICS* 55 (2012), 111–19; 113–14. See p. 17 above.

[200] Herodian, 1.11.5; HA, *Verus*, 8.9; Dio, 68.10; Menander Rhetor, 2.375; Hekster, 'Imperial Justice?', 247–60, which already set out some of the arguments and formulations of the following paragraphs.

then, being emperor", he turned about and granted her a hearing'.[201] The number of people who could actually approach the emperor in this way was limited. They were mostly people from the upper echelons of society. Among the petitioners to whom imperial responses to specific requests or demands (known as rescripts) are addressed there are some who are from the lower social classes, but these people could only petition the emperor when he was nearby.[202] It is not a coincidence that the story of Hadrian takes place during one of the emperor's journeys. People without sufficient status and wealth could only approach the emperor in places which he visited: of 770 published petitions from Egypt (30 BC to AD 284) only four were to emperors. The province was rarely visited by emperors.[203] People who could either travel themselves or send envoys had a better chance of petitioning the emperor. Those who did so successfully had a clear incentive to make the imperial decision permanently and publicly visible by inscribing it at important locations. This means that such imperial reactions may be overrepresented in the epigraphic record.[204] The many prominently visible inscriptions will have boosted the narrative of the responding emperor, at least among those who could read. Even at the frontiers of the empire, people could see inscriptions mentioning imperial responses to local problems. But these responses often applied to elite affairs.

The emperor as someone who understood administrative and legal disputes was important for the elites, both in Rome and the provinces. Less so for others. As noted above, emperors speaking in front of civilians were only rarely depicted on coins and public monuments. The same applies to the emperor-at-law. In monumental art and on central and provincial coinage there is remarkably little attention to imperial justice. When it does feature,

---

[201] Dio, 69.6.3. The story is not unique to Rome. Similar stories are told about the Hellenistic kings Philip II (382–336 BC) and Demetrius Poliorcetes (336–283 BC); Plut. *Mor.* 179 c–d, *Dem.* 42.3–4; Millar, *Emperor*, 3–4.

[202] B. Kelly, *Petitions, Litigation, and Social Control* (Oxford, 2011), 150–9, 167–8; S. Connolly, *Lives Behind the Laws. The World of the Codex Hermogenianus* (Bloomington – Indianapolis 2010), xiii–xv, 67–80; L. Huchthausen, 'Herkunft und ökonomische Stellung weiblicher Adressaten von Reskripten *des Codex* Iustinianus (2. und 3. Jh. u. Z.)', *Klio* 54 (1974), 199–228.

[203] *P.Coll.Youtie* 2.66; *P.Oxy.* 4.705.15–53, 4.705.65–90; *SB* 16.12509. This information was kindly supplied to me by Ben Kelly on the basis of his database of petitions on papyri. It is probably no accident that the large collection of imperial rescripts from Egypt (the so-called *apokrimata*) come from the time of Septimius Severus' visit: *P.Col.* 123; W. Turpin, 'Imperial Subscriptions and the Administration of Justice', *JRS* 81 (1991), 101–18; 106–7; R. Haensch, 'Apokrimata und Authentica. Dokumente römischer Herrschaft in der Sicht der Untertanen', in: R. Haensch and J. Heinrichs (eds.), *Herrschen und Verwalten. Der Alltag der Administration des Römischen Reiches in der Kaiserzeit* (Vienna 2007), 213–33.

[204] Noreña, *Imperial Ideals*, 157.

it is almost inevitably in the form of the emperor dispensing justice over conquered people, not showing justice towards his subjects. Certainly outside of the city of Rome, the image of the victorious ruler was much more prominent than that of the judicial one. There are no depictions of subjects presenting petitions to emperors in person, even though this happened and would have been easy to depict.[205] Of course, there was less need to put images on coins and monuments that reflected notions which were especially important to senators. They could see their emperor on a regular basis. Instead, coins and monuments put forward messages that were of interest to a much larger and more remote audience.[206]

Looking at depictions of imperial justice over a longer a stretch of time shows one period in which the emperor-at-law was more frequently visible in media that were at central disposal. During the reign of Hadrian (117–38) the numbers of coins showing justice or a related theme rise remarkably; almost 75 per cent of such coin types issued in the first three centuries of the empire were struck under Hadrian. The only images of a togate emperor seated on a curule chair on provincial coins likewise depict Hadrian. A colossal porphyry statue of a seated and togate Hadrian from Caesarea Maritima may be linked to this set of images, although there are similar statues from the Tetrarchic period.[207] It is tempting to associate this rise of monumental images to Hadrian's many travels. During these, he became visible to a larger group of subjects, and was more approachable to give judgement than more stationary emperors had been and would be. Hadrian also played an important role in the harmonisation of Roman law, and through his visits and many letters intervened directly in legal affairs throughout the empire.[208]

---

[205] Hekster, 'Imperial Justice?' gives a more extensive argument, with full references.

[206] N. Elkins, *The Image of Political Power in the Reign of Nerva, AD 96–98* (Oxford 2017), 93. Cf. R. Wolters/ M. Ziegert, 'Umbrüche – Die Reichsprägung Neros und Domitians im Vergleich', in: S. Bönisch et al. (eds.), *Nero und Domitian. Mediale Diskurse der Herrscherrepräsentation im Vergleich* (Tübingen 2014), 43–80; 64–6, with further references on the different groups being addressed by imperial coinage.

[207] Central coinage can be traced through queries in the *OCRE* website (http://numismatics.org/ocre/). An analysis of bronze coins from hoards shows a similar percentage, with 99 out of 140 coins minted under Hadrian: Noreña, *Imperial Ideals*, 349. The provincial coins are *RPC* 3, nos. 5167 and 5260. The colossal statue: H. R. Goette, *Studien zu römischen Togadarstellungen* (Mainz 1989), 45–9, 155, no. M 31, Plate 66.2. Cf. 132, nos. Bb 35–42, reworked in the sixth century: *LSA* no. 1026. The Tetrarchic statues are *LSA* nos.455, 1003. Cf. *LSA* 2712.

[208] J. M. Cortés-Copete, 'Governing by Dispatching Letters. The Hadrianic Chancellery', C. Rosillo-López (ed.), *Political Communication in the Roman World* (Boston – Leiden 2017), 107–36; Honoré, *Emperors and Lawyers*, 12–16. Hadrian was named *nomothetes* on public monuments of Cyrene (*SEG* 17.809) and Megara (*IC* VII.70-2); M. T. Boatwright, *Hadrian and the Cities of the Roman Empire* (Princeton 2003), 91–2.

It is possible that Hadrian tried to emphasise this aspect of emperorship more widely. If so, it did not fundamentally change the expectations which people had of later emperors. There was no continuation of the images of imperial justice after Hadrian's reign. The emperor-at-law remained only really interesting for a relatively small subset of Roman subjects. Even an emperor like Septimius Severus, whose interest in legal matters is often cited in ancient literary sources, was not depicted in a legal role on imperial imagery. Severus' reign in many ways coincided with the great age of Roman jurists, with famous legal authors such as Papinianus, Paul, Messius, Ulpian and Modestinus reaching important administrative positions.[209] That did not make the legal emperor an important image to transmit. Apparently, other imperial roles remained more prominent for the populace at large. After all, even Hadrian's military qualities were stressed much more frequently than his legal importance.[210]

The role of the emperor as a dispenser of justice was an important one that will have taken up much of his time. It also dominated different types of literary narratives, and was included in philosophical treatises, martyr acts and hagiographies, showing that the conception of the emperor as a law giver was important beyond senatorial circles.[211] But in the eyes of the vast majority of his people, it never held the same importance as his military and religious tasks. Because textual evidence still strongly influences modern ideas about the Roman world, the prejudices of the literary sources have strongly shaped modern ideas about emperorship. The emperor may well have spent most of his time on administrative affairs (and in that sense the emperor was what he did), but most of his subjects expected him to be doing something different. That, too, was an expectation that emperors had to live up to.

It is tempting to assume that the legal role of the emperor increased in importance in late antiquity. The great legal compendia assembled under Theodosius and Justinian (promulgated respectively in 437 and 529) suggest

---

[209] Dio, 75(76), 73, Herodian 2.9.4–7; HA, *Caracalla* 8.2; *Septimius Severus* 3.2; 18.6; *Clodius Albinus*, 7 .1; E. S. Daalder, 'The *Decreta* and *Imperiales Sententiae* of Julius Paulus: Law and Justice in the Judicial Decisions of Septimius Severus', in: O. Hekster/ K. Verboven (eds.) *The Impact of Justice on the Roman Empire* (Boston – Leiden 2019), 49–67; 62–6; L. de Blois, 'Roman Jurists and the Crisis of the Third Century AD in the Roman Empire', in: L. de Blois (ed.), *Administration, Prosopography and Appointment Policies in the Roman Empire* (Amsterdam 2001), 136–53; 138–40.

[210] See p. 122–3 above.

[211] C. Davenport, 'Dying for Justice: Narratives of Roman Judicial Authority in the High Empire', in: A. König/ R. Langlands/ J. Uden (eds.), *Literature and Culture of the Roman Empire 69–235* (Cambridge 2020), 269–87, with full references.

that law was a matter of urgency for at least these two emperors. There were increased possibilities to draw on other models of rule, such as that of the Sasanians or Old Testament kingship, in which the monarch was more established as a law giver than he was in Roman conceptions of rule.[212] The position of the emperor as someone who was both bound by the law but in some ways superseded it were of the utmost importance for the running of governance. There was even an explicit link between the legitimacy of an emperor and his capacity to issue general law. Several rulers explicitly nullified the enactments of predecessors whom they considered usurpers to illustrate that they had not been proper emperors. Similarly, it has been argued that an important reason for the compilation of the Theodosian Code was to establish authority of the emperor in Constantinople over the western parts of the empire. The code was explicitly accepted in a senate meeting in Rome, effectively showing deference to eastern authority.[213] The introduction to Justinian's code also emphasises how Justinian had done what earlier emperors deemed urgently necessary but dared not do. This, the text states, was one reason why the emperor decided to arrange for 'this codex to be called by our own auspicious name', showing the link between the person of the emperor and his legal code.[214] Yet even in late antiquity the importance of the emperor as a lawgiver seems to have been limited to high politics. The image of the emperor-at-law was not visually disseminated at a large scale. Law was important to show imperial supremacy, and with the division between the eastern and western empire notions of sovereignty became involved. But none of this had as directly an impact on people as the emperor's military or religious role. For most people, the emperor was the law, but the relevance of this for their daily life was very limited.[215]

Still, the emperor was expected to play a less stringently defined civil role. The idea of the emperor as a magistrate, rather than a ruler, can be traced throughout Roman history. This was the emperor in a toga, modestly walking to the senate house.[216] This, also, was the emperor surrounded by his councillors. Roman Emperors participated in a range of more or less

---

[212] Dagron, *Emperor and Priest*, 163–6; Canepa, *Two Eyes of the Earth*, 151 on Roman use of Biblical and Sasanian models of kingship.

[213] F. Bono, 'The Value of the Stability of the Law. A Perspective on the Role of the Emperor in Political Crises', in: Hekster/ Verboven, *The Impact of Justice*, 68–85; B. Salway, 'The Publication and Application of the Theodosian Code. NTh. 1, the *Gesta Senatus*, and the *Constitutionarii*', *MEFRA* 125 (2013), 327–54; 348–9.

[214] Cod. Just. Pr. 1, 3.

[215] B. Stolte, 'Law is the King of All Things? The Emperor and the Law', in: Tougher, *The Emperor in the Byzantine World*, 171–8; 177: 'for practical purposes the *basileus* was the *nomos*'.

[216] See p. 71 above.

formalised meetings, regularly consulting with his advisors. The form of meetings inevitably made clear that the emperor held the highest social prestige, yet the very fact that the meetings were held showed that the ruler was still abiding by the convention to listen to his advisors.[217] This concept of the Roman emperor as a sort of superior servant, who was present for his advisors and had to listen to his subjects was incorporated into the image that emperors had of their role. The famous *Meditations* of Marcus Aurelius include a number of passages in which the emperor reminds himself not to aim for too exalted a status, to 'take care that you are not made into a Caesar, that you are not dyed with this dye; for such things happen' (6.30), to 'speak both in the senate and to every man, whoever he may be, appropriately' (8.30) and to 'stop and take the best advisers [...] if you do not see clear' (10.12). Marcus, it seems, had taken Fronto's earlier-cited advice to heart. Two centuries later, the notion of the modest civil emperor was still at the core of Julian's *Caesars*.[218] The work is ironical about much, but takes its ultimate winner Marcus Aurelius very seriously. His temperance and philosophical way of life are praised. Julian also praises the very pro-senatorial Nerva (96–8): 'Very mild were his manners, most just his dealings' (311g). Augustus is praised, among other qualities, for the way he let himself be advised to administer an empire (325c–d).

These are again (extreme) elite points of view, but the more abstractly 'civil' emperor was depicted on coins and monuments much more frequently than the legal emperor, or the emperor holding speeches. Reliefs include the Ara Pacis (Figure 1.11), but are found in later times too. A Severan relief from the Palazzo Sacchetti at Rome shows Septimius Severus dressed in a toga, seated on a platform, presenting his two sons to assembled senators. The Arch of Constantine shows the emperor seated on a curule chair, dressed in a toga, displaying his generosity to assembled people (Figure 2.8). This specific relief was probably a reworked panel from the time of Marcus Aurelius, but that does not diminish the continuous relevance of the image of the civil emperor in the early fourth century.[219] Coins with a togate emperor seated on a platform either receiving tributes

---

[217] O. Hekster, 'Emperors and Councillors: Imperial Representation between Republic and Empire', in: H. Kaal/ D. Slootjes (eds.), *New Perspectives on Power and Political Representation from Ancient History to the Present Day: Repertoires of Representation* (Leiden – Boston 2019), 11–25 and below p. 187–8.

[218] Fronto: see p. 157–8 above; Julian, *Caesares*, 311g, 324c–d.

[219] Carandini, *Atlas of Ancient Rome*, II, tab. 152; N. Hannestad, *Roman Art and Imperial Policy* (Aarhus 1986), 268–9. See p. 160 above and p. 41–2.

Figure 2.8 Constantine as *civilis princeps*. Marble Attic frieze, Arch of Constantine, north side, from Rome, 315, reworked from monument to Marcus Aurelius (176). The image of a 'senatorial' Constantine was prominent on his victory arch in the centre of Rome. The reworked image of Marcus Aurelius shows the emperor seated on a curule chair and surrounded by togate Romans.
Source: CKD – Radboud University Nijmegen

or handing out goods to citizens appear from the Augustan age until the reign of Gordian III (238–44). Under Hadrian, these 'platform' scenes are particularly common on bronze coins, with almost 89 per cent of the coins that emphasise the emperor's generosity showing the emperor seated in front of his people. Gold coins show the same message through a personification of *Liberalitas*.[220] Apparently the emperor's role as benefactor to his people was made more explicit to the lower classes, suggesting that it was more important to them than to the more solvent higher echelons of society. Similarly, a coin of Caligula, who is not known for his senatorial appeasement, shows the emperor seated on the magisterial curule chair, dressed in a toga, with the surrounding legend proclaiming 'agreement of the senate, the order of knights, and the Roman people'. It is a bronze coin, so the upper classes are unlikely to have been the targeted audience of this coin type. Local inscriptions proclaiming emperors to be 'indulgentissimus et celementissimus' (kindest and mildest), likewise suggest that the more general image of the civil emperor – as opposed to the specific image of the legal emperor – appealed to a larger group of Roman subjects.[221] This appeal seems to have been long lasting. Constantine was still depicted in a similar way. The relief on his arch (Figure 2.8), aside, several of his coins show a togate emperor in a curule chair, by now holding globe and sceptre. The legend refers to the emperor's power of the tribune (*tribunicia potestas*) and to his role as proconsul, emphasising the magisterial aspect of his emperorship.[222] A bronze coin minted in 328–9 to advertise Constantine II as imperial successor shows the same image with the legend advertising the young man as *princeps iuventutis* and consul, again harking back to terms with Republican associations that had lost much of their original meaning, but would make people think of the emperor's civil roles.[223]

---

[220] http://numismatics.org/ocre/, search term 'togate' and 'platform'. The Augustan coins are *RIC* 1 (2nd ed.), Augustus 201a–b, 350. The coins from Gordian are *RIC* 4, Gordian III, 275, 275a, 317. The percentages and analyses of Hadrian's coins: Ellithorpe, *Circulating Imperial Ideology*, 159–64, with figures 6a–b.

[221] *RIC* 1 (2nd ed.), Caligula 56: CONSENSV SENAT ET EQ ORD P Q R. This is a commemorative type celebrating Divus Augustus, who features on the obverse, and is probably connected to Caligula's acceptance of the title *pater patriae*, following Augustus' precedent: Davenport, *A History of the Roman Equestrian Order*, 374. That does not diminish the image of the civil emperor. For local inscriptions: Bönisch, *Dialogangebote*, 252–6. See p. 44 above.

[222] *RIC* 6, Treveri, 795, *RIC* 7, Treveri, 19–21; 242–4, Arelate, 48, 69, Ticinum 30, 38. Other coins show Constantine's deified ancestors in their civil role: *RIC* 7, Treveri, 200–7, Arelate, 173–8, Aquileia, 21–6, Siscia, 41–6, Thessalonica, 24–6.

[223] *RIC* 7, Treveri, 517.

There was a change in the course of the fourth century. As we saw in the previous chapter, emperors were increasingly depicted in ornamental clothing and with imperial insignia. This was specific to them, as other members of the elite in the period between 284 and 550 continued to be predominantly shown in the toga.[224] The ornamental imperial clothing was not an innovation as such, but the increasing number of depictions of the emperor in his 'monarchical' appearance went at the cost of images of the 'civil' emperor. In the same period, court ceremony shifted towards more open obedience to the emperor. This has often been seen as an 'orientalising' of the Roman court under the influence of Sasanian court culture. To a large extent, such a view follows the presuppositions of Greek and Roman authors, who used 'Persian' as a shorthand to describe everything they did not like. Many of the changes in late-antique court ceremony instead developed from existent Roman practices. For instance, the often-discussed practice of kneeling before the emperor (*proskynesis*) had a long history in the Roman world before it was formalised as a practice under Diocletian.[225] Still, from the early-fourth century onwards, what seems to have previously been an optional manner of greeting the emperor became an obligatory one, highlighting imperial superiority over civil emperorship. The notion of a modest and civil emperor did not disappear. But it was, as it were, relegated to the speeches, letters and treatises of the Roman elite. In this, the civil role differed from the religious and military role of the emperor, which continued to be shown in all types of source material.

It is tempting to connect this shift to the move away from Rome as imperial residence. The *civilis princeps* was strongly related to a traditional notion of the Roman republic, and to the Roman Forum with its rostra and curia. Many elements that had defined the city of Rome were incorporated into the physical and institutional layout of Constantinople (and to a lesser extent into the later western capital Ravenna), including an eastern senate.[226] But the move away from the ancient capital created leeway.

---

[224] E. Wueste, 'The Costumes of Late Antique Honorific Monuments: Conformity and Divergence within the Public and Political Sphere', in: M. Cifarelli/ L. Gawlinski (eds.), *What Shall I Say of Clothes? Theoretical and Methodological Approaches to the Study of Dress in Antiquity* (Boston 2017), 179–201; 182–4, fig. 2, table 1.

[225] A. Alföldi 'Die Ausgestaltung des monarchischen Zeremoniells am römischen Kaiserhofe', *MDAIR* 49 (1934) 1–118; 1–25; 46–72; A. Hunnell Chen, *From the Seed of the Gods: Art, Ideology and Cultural Exchange with the Persian Court under the Roman Tetrarchs, 284–324 CE* (PhD Columbia 2014), 389–90.

[226] On the role of Ravenna as imperial capital, see p. 191–2 below. On the way the monumental landscape of Rome and Constantinople influenced imperial behaviour and people's perceptions of emperorship, see pp. 269–276, 283 below.

Moreover, there was more interaction between court ceremony in Constantinople and that of its Sasanian neighbours than had been the case when the court resided at Rome. This was not a one-way trajectory. Prostration before the emperor, for instance, may well have been a Roman practice picked up by the Sasanians rather than the other way around. But being in the vicinity of, and regularly having to deal with, the openly monarchical Sasanian court must have influenced Roman practices.[227] By the time of Justinian, kneeling before the emperor had given way to kissing the purple of the emperor's boots, even by those of senatorial rank. The emperor's supremacy was evident.[228] Even then, some traces of the civil ruler remained. That, at least, is the easiest explanation for the absence of images of Romans prostrating themselves before their ruler. There are plentiful representations of conquered people kneeling before the Roman emperors, but no equivalent of Roman subjects doing so in visual culture. By the time of Justinian, Roman emperors dressed and behaved more openly supreme than before emperors had left Rome, but apparently they could not ignore the idea of a civil emperor altogether. Roman emperors continued to be constrained, at least in their representations, by the expectations that centuries of rule had shaped.

Combining Imperial Roles: Exemplary Emperors

Roman society was heavily influenced by precedent. Behaviour and actions of noteworthy men became examples for other men to imitate, and norms by which other men were judged. These exemplary historical figures were so important in Rome that there was continuous emphasis on the ancestral customs (*mos maiorum*). Changes could be blocked by referring to their innovative nature.[229] Inevitably, these social constraints played a role in the arrival of emperorship in the political landscape. This new power structure, like all changes in society, needed to be formulated within existing worldviews, not only for rulers to legitimate themselves, but also for subjects to

---

[227] Canepa, *Two Eyes of the Earth*, 151.
[228] E. Herrmann-Otto, 'Der Kaiser und die Gesellschaft des spätrömischen Reiches im Spiegel des Zeremoniells', in: P. Kneissl/ V. Losemann (eds.), *Imperium Romanum. Studien zu Geschichte und Rezeption. Festschrift für Karl Christ zum 75. Geburtstag* (Stuttgart 1998), 346–69; 355–6; Canepa, *Two Eyes of the Earth*, 150.
[229] Roller, *Models from the Past*, 8; A. Wallace-Hadrill, *Rome's Cultural Revolution* (Cambridge 2008), 213–58, with R. Osborne/ C. Vout, 'A Revolution in Roman History?', *JRS* 100 (2010), 233–45.

be able to understand the world they were living in. New ideas and notions needed to be connected to what people expected, valued and understood. Traditional terminology aided the conceptualisation and communication of these new ideas and notions. Both ruler and subjects had an interest in formulating a new situation as part of a traditional framework. In that way, the new situation could be much more easily understood. Both parties, therefore, had an interest in continuing to use traditional notions, even when the actual situations described through these notions had moved away from any original meanings.

This is an important factor behind the surprising continuity of the roles that emperors were expected to play.[230] Of course, expectations differed between different regions and between different social groups. The expected religious role of emperors was different in Egypt, with centuries of Pharaonic rule, than it was at Rome. The belligerent imperial role was emphasised more emphatically in images that were likely to reach soldiers than senators; the emperor-at-law was transmitted predominantly in literary sources and inscriptions set up by the imperial elite and almost invisible in sources aimed at a wider audience. But no role was exclusively reserved for one audience. The roles themselves, moreover, remained fairly static, notwithstanding all the changes that took place through centuries of Roman society. What about the relative importance of the three main roles? Was one of the three main roles substantially more important in one period of Roman rule than the others? If so, was there a continuous development, or were there ad hoc reasons for one role to be more important than the others?

Probably the best way of tracing the roles that the centre emphasised, is through an analysis of messages on coins. Looking at the way imperial roles are referred to on the reverses of all coin types from Augustus to Zeno under different dynasties allows for some sort of overview (Graph 2.2a).[231] Especially noticeable is the increase of military images from the fourth century onwards, mostly at the cost of emphasis on the emperor's civil duties, but also eating into references to the religious role of the emperor. Taking a reign-by-reign approach (Graph 2.2b), shows more variation in which aspects of imperial rule received most attention, especially in the

---

[230] Zimmermann, 'Repräsentation des kaiserlichen Ranges', 205.
[231] This graph was kindly provided to me by Sven Betjes. 'Cult and Devotion' consists of gods, temples and the emperor at sacrifice (including vota-messages); 'military and triumph' includes Victoria, virtus, chained or kneeling barbarians, trophies and triumphs; 'civil duties and benefits of empire' are coins with the emperor as consul, personifications of Pax, Felicitas and Securitas, and images of imperial buildings.

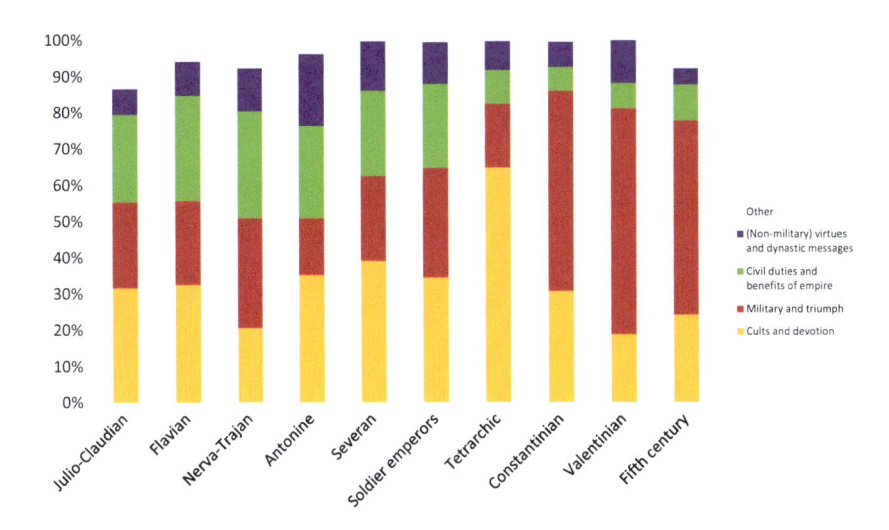

Graph 2.2a Reverse themes on central coinage (per dynasty)

early empire. There are massive differences, for instance, between the messages on the coins of Caligula (predominantly dynastic) and on those of his successor Claudius (predominantly civil). Apparently emperors could highlight certain aspects of rule, even if they could not ignore the other imperial roles altogether. Even so, real aberrations to the trend are rare. The emphasis on the religious role of the emperor under, for instance, Domitian betrays an attempt by that emperor to place emperorship on a more religious basis, which was noted and negatively commented upon. The increased emphasis on civil duties under his successor Nerva might well have been a reaction to this.[232] Yet even when looking at individual rules, the sudden shift on coinage after Constantine's rule towards military messages and away from the civil role of the emperor remains clear.

It needs to be emphasised that this is only a very rough indication. References to 'peace' and 'security', which are categorised here as 'civil duties and benefits of empire', might with some justification be seen as references to the military role of the emperor. Looking only at reverse types also excludes the images of the emperor on the obverse, which from Antoninus Pius up to the Valentinian dynasty onwards predominantly showed the emperor in military gear, highlighting his role as victorious general even if the reverse

---

[232] See now the various articles in Raimondi Cominesi et al, *God on Earth*, especially F. G. Naerebout, 'Domitian and religion', 147–51; D. A. Conlin, 'Master and God: Domitian's Art and Architecture in Rome', 153–8 and A. Augoustakis/ E. Buckley, 'Man and God: Literature', 159–65. For the precise make up and relative frequency of Nerva's coins: Elkins, *The Image of Political Power*, 155–71.

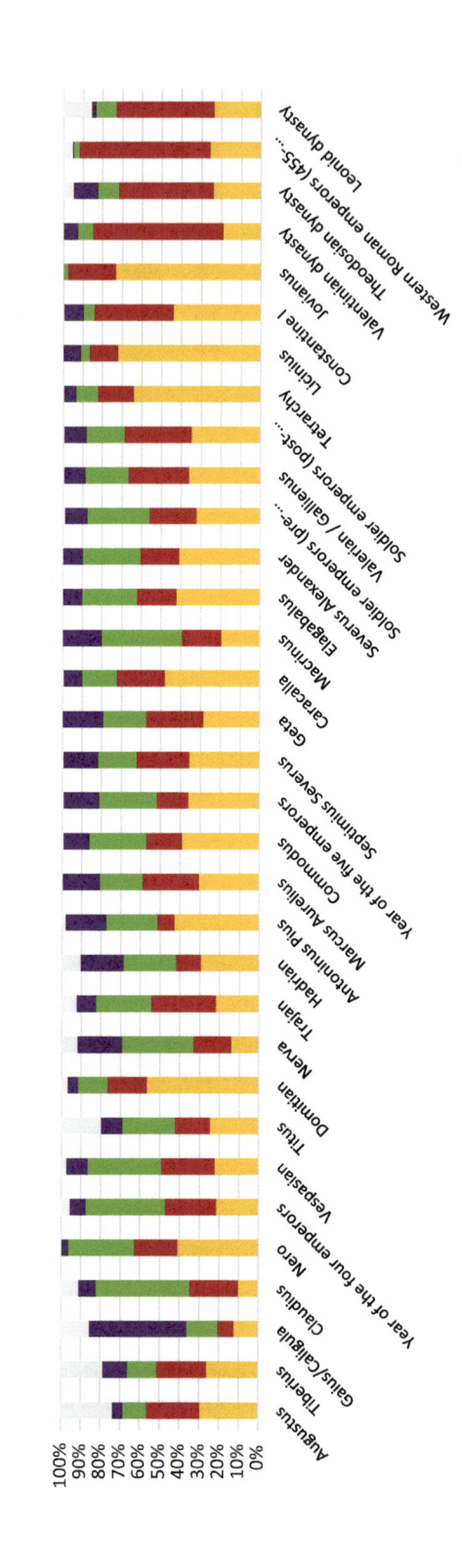

Graph 2.2b Reverse themes on central coinage (reign-by-reign)

Figure 2.9 Different roles on one coin: 337–40 Rome, Bronze medallion (38.42 g). An obverse with Constantius II in consular robes, holding an eagle-topped sceptre, surrounded by a legend naming him D(OMINVS) N(OSTER) and P(IVS) F(ELIX) is combined with a reverse in which the emperor is shown in a military role, on horseback, riding down one enemy and striking another with his spear. The legend identifies him as a DEBELLATOR GENT[T](IVM) BARBAR[R](VM), conqueror of barbarian people. *RIC* 8, Rome 345.
Source: bpk / Münzkabinett, SMB / Lutz-Jürgen Lübke (Lübke und Wiedemann)

types did not indicate that aspect of rule. Late third-century coin portraiture, for instance, increasingly showed the emperor helmeted and in military garb, which must have boosted the sense of a military emperor, even if reverse themes stressed other aspects of imperial rule. The opposite could also be the case. There are a few post-Constantinian coins and medallions that show emperors wearing consular robes on the obverse, whereas the reverse is military (Figure 2.9).[233] Looking only at reverses also ignores the imperial roles that were named in the obverse legends, although there, too, references to 'Republican' offices and powers decreased over time.[234]

A recent analysis of nearly 7,000 gold coins minted between the reigns of Augustus and Alexander Severus has traced dominant themes for the different reigns on the reverses of these *aurei* in more detail (Graph 2.3).[235] It shows how the messages on these much more valuable

---

[233] *RIC* 8, Treveri 274–5, *RIC* 8, Arelate 226, 228, *RIC* 8, Rome 345, 349, *RIC* 10, Theodosius II (east), 221. Cf. *RIC* 6, Rome 261, 270; British Museum 1928,0208.1.
[234] See pp. 32–4 above.
[235] This is an adapted version of Ellithorpe, *Circulating Imperial Ideology*, 176 fig. 14. I am very grateful to Corey Ellithorpe for providing me with this much more detailed overview, and for kindly answering numerous questions.

and therefore less common coins occasionally differed from the general pattern sketched above, and again shows how there were noticeable shifts in between reigns. The religious role of the emperor, through emphasising divine protection, depicting a favourite god, showing temples or highlighting sanction of the gods for a specific reign, was the main message on the gold coins of Nero (73 per cent, mostly references to Jupiter Custos) and Domitian (59 per cent, overwhelmingly Minerva), but also of Pertinax (93 per cent). Explicitly military themes such as emphasis on the emperor as a victorious general or the relationship with armies was the most common central message on the gold coins of Trajan (27.5 per cent), Severus (37 per cent), Geta (82 per cent, with large part referring to harmony with the troops), Caracalla (40 per cent), Macrinus (50 per cent), Elagabalus (53 per cent) and Alexander Severus (40 per cent), and also on the gold coins of Nerva (63,5 per cent), whereas the latter's message on coins of all denomination had stressed civil duties. Gold coins were an important means of paying the armies, which might explain the military emphasis.[236]

An unambiguously civil role was only dominant on the gold coins of Hadrian, whose *aurei* emphasise imperial beneficence (18 per cent) and praise the Roman state and populace (10 per cent), with an additional 4 per cent of coins listing the emperor's virtues and 2.5 per cent commemorating his deeds in service of the empire.[237] But religious and military aspects of rule are also very visible, through the notion of a victorious emperor (16 per cent), the depiction of specific divinities (15.5 per cent) and a large number of founding mythologies (12.5 per cent); a category which is almost absent on the coins of other emperors, again suggesting the importance of the relation between emperor and empire under Hadrian. There was also a civil aspect in coins stressing the virtues of the emperor, which is the dominant theme under Claudius (37 per cent) and Marcus Aurelius (32.5 per cent). Under both emperors, the notions of a civil emperor was also highlighted through other categories. Claudius' coins commemorated his deeds in service of the empire (13.5 per cent) and Marcus' his imperial beneficence (9 per cent). Yet again, the military role also featured on these emperors' coins, although the religious role received less attention (Claudius: 11 per cent military; 6 per cent religious; Marcus: 26 per cent military; 7 per cent religious).

---

[236] Campbell, *The Emperor and the Roman Army*, 167.
[237] Coins depicting buildings are excluded from this analysis. On the emperor as a builder and the importance of the built environment on the development of emperorship, see p. 270–2 below.

Combining Imperial Roles: Exemplary Emperors 175

Main themes on imperial coinage (Augustus to Severus Alexander (n=6678))

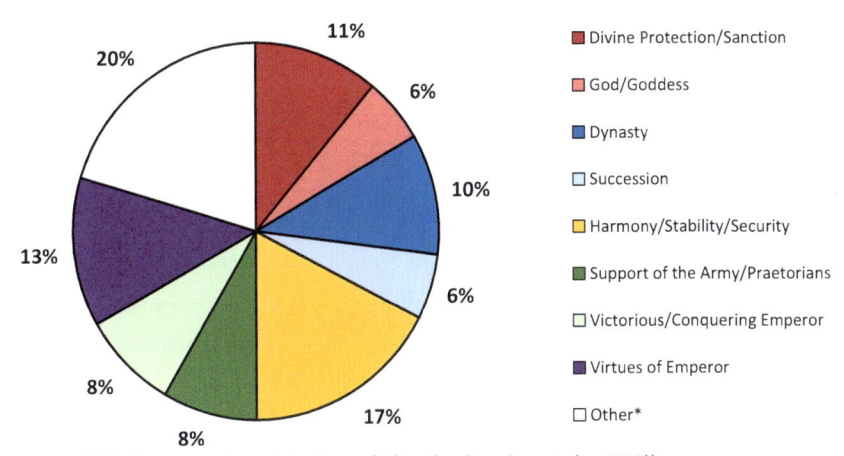

- Divine Protection/Sanction — 11%
- God/Goddess — 6%
- Dynasty — 10%
- Succession — 6%
- Harmony/Stability/Security — 17%
- Support of the Army/Praetorians — 8%
- Victorious/Conquering Emperor — 8%
- Virtues of Emperor — 13%
- Other* — 20%

Main themes on imperial coinage (Julio-Claudian dynasty (n=2428))

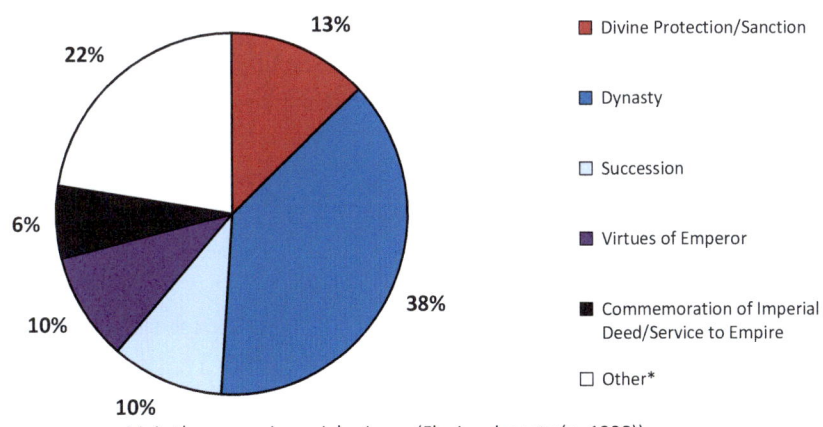

- Divine Protection/Sanction — 13%
- Dynasty — 38%
- Succession — 10%
- Virtues of Emperor — 10%
- Commemoration of Imperial Deed/Service to Empire — 6%
- Other* — 22%

Main themes on imperial coinage (Flavian dynasty (n=1938))

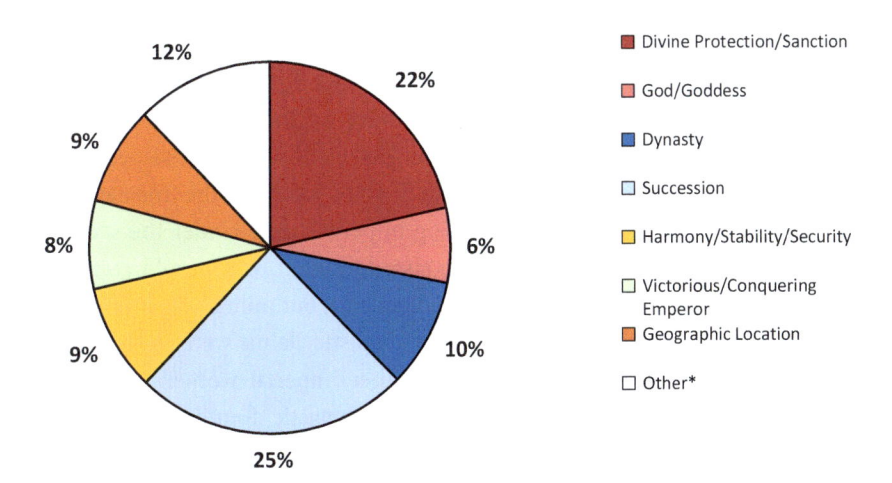

- Divine Protection/Sanction — 22%
- God/Goddess — 6%
- Dynasty — 10%
- Succession — 25%
- Harmony/Stability/Security — 9%
- Victorious/Conquering Emperor — 8%
- Geographic Location — 9%
- Other* — 12%

Graph 2.3 Reverse themes on *aurei*

176 *Playing Imperial Roles*

Main themes on imperial coinage (Nerva-Antonine dynasty (n=1938))

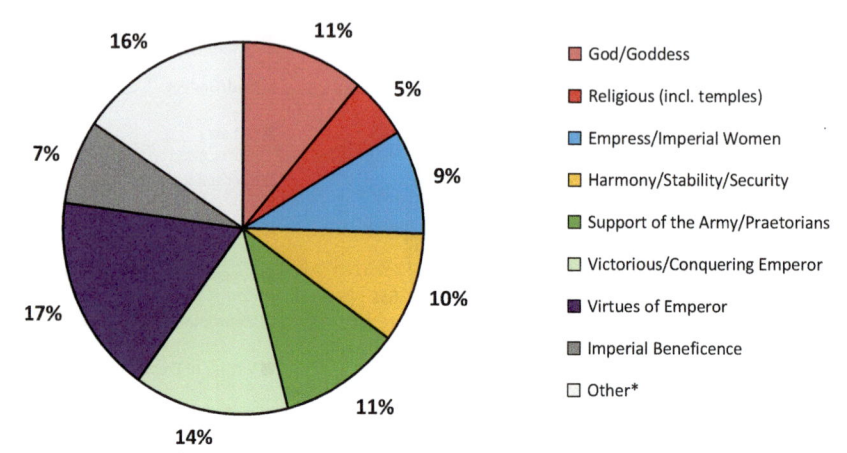

- God/Goddess — 11%
- Religious (incl. temples) — 5%
- Empress/Imperial Women — 9%
- Harmony/Stability/Security — 10%
- Support of the Army/Praetorians — 11%
- Victorious/Conquering Emperor — 14%
- Virtues of Emperor — 17%
- Imperial Beneficence — 7%
- Other* — 16%

Main themes on imperial coinage (Severan dynasty (n=239))

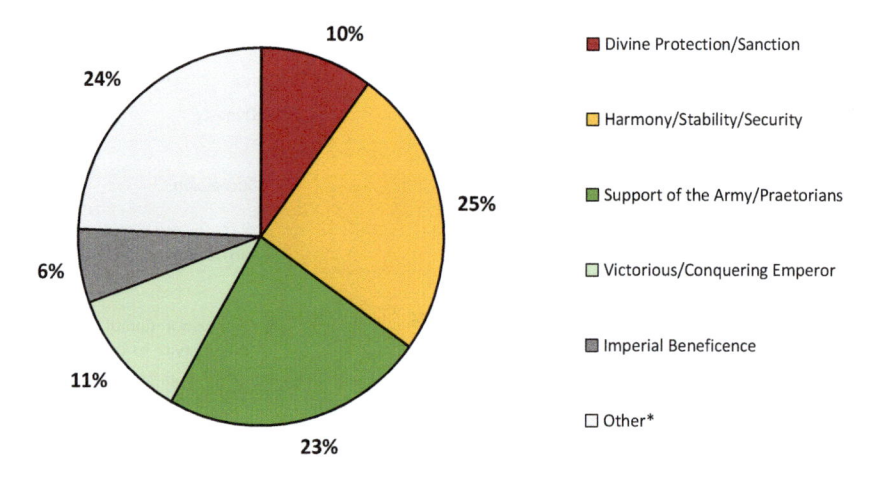

- Divine Protection/Sanction — 10%
- Harmony/Stability/Security — 25%
- Support of the Army/Praetorians — 23%
- Victorious/Conquering Emperor — 11%
- Imperial Beneficence — 6%
- Other* — 24%

Graph 2.3 (*cont.*)

During several reigns, notions of dynasty and legitimacy were stressed on gold coins. This was extreme at the very beginning of the imperial period, under Augustus (41 per cent) but especially Tiberius (94 per cent) and Caligula (89 per cent). Their gold coins stressed the message of dynastic continuity rather than defining imperial roles. Under the second dynasty, succession and dynasty were also dominant on the gold coins of Vespasian (49 per cent) and Titus (51.5 per cent), but military and religious aspects were also visible. Antoninus Pius' dynastic claims were put forward through emphasis on the empress and other imperial women (37.5 per cent), as was the case under yet another dynastic founder, Septimius Severus (16 per cent imperial women and 11 per cent succession).

There is no obvious pattern, other than that during civil wars and times of military unrest the armies received most attention.[238] If the other themes on these gold coins are taken into account, the limited range of themes becomes clear. At the very beginning of the principate, the dynastic notion was stressed at the cost of anything else. From then on, there were different emphases on specific imperial roles within certain reigns. Coins of individual emperors could highlight specific messages, but they would still include references to the three main roles that had become linked to emperorship, often through text and images that had already been used by predecessors. References to military aspects of rule were only absent from the gold coins of the emperors Nero, Domitian and Commodus – who were ridiculed for their fake triumphs or fights in the arena.[239] This suggests, once again, that a fixed set of expectations surrounding emperorship had developed remarkably rapidly. Within two or three generations, there seems to have been a well-established notion of the various roles emperors had to play, leading to an almost prescriptive mode of imperial behaviour. Ignoring one of these roles came at a cost.

Looking at coinage gives a good overview of the imperial roles that were broadcast by the imperial centre, with differences between the pattern of messages on gold coins and on those on coins of different denominations indicating some sort of audience targeting. A very different way of tracing the balance between the different imperial roles over time is analysing the popularity of individual emperors. More precisely, by looking at which emperors were used as exemplary rulers, it is possible to see what aspects of rule were deemed most important at a given time by people beyond the court, though this perspective is still mostly limited to the writing elite of the empire. The importance of exemplarity in Roman society meant that emperors could increasingly be judged against their predecessors. Earlier emperors, alongside other historical figures, became the cornerstones against which current emperors were measured. Which earlier emperors – and which actions or character traits of these emperors – were highlighted gives some indication about which imperial roles were more or less important at a given time. This is illustrated by a famous passage of the

---

[238] Ellithorpe, *Circulating Imperial Ideology*, 105–11 notes how coins emphasising Concordia or Fides were almost exclusively minted during civil wars. See already F. Kemmers, *Coins for a Legion: An Analysis of the Coin Finds from the Augustan Legionary Fortress and Flavian canabae legionis at Nijmegen* (Mainz 2006), 219–44.

[239] See p. 114–6 above.

fourth-century historian Eutropius, who wrote a popular *Short History of the Roman Empire*:

> So much respect has been paid to his [Trajan's] memory that right up to our age the emperors are still acclaimed in the senate as 'More fortunate than Augustus, better than Trajan' (*Felicior Augusto, melior Traiano*). To such an extent has the reputation of his goodness lasted that it provides those who either (wish to) flatter or to praise sincerely with the opportunity to use him as the most outstanding model.[240]

According to Eutropius, Augustus and Trajan were *the* exemplary rulers.

These two emperors are often named in surviving panegyrical texts, alongside Caesar, Antoninus Pius and Marcus Aurelius. Other historical figures feature as well, with Alexander the Great dominating the field. These are not random individuals. Writers of laudatory speeches are known to have carefully selected their exempla to fit contemporary times and circumstances.[241] The choice of specific rulers is telling. Nor were there only positive examples. Someone like the Persian king Xerxes (486–465 BC) epitomised tyrannical rule and could be used as a telling parallel for the unwanted behaviour of the likes of Caligula and Nero.[242] In turn, Nero himself became byword for tyrannical behaviour, explicitly used as a negative example in various orations of the late-fourth century statesman and orator Themistius (317–c. 90).[243]

The rulers who were used as positive exempla changed over time. Trajan had become the best illustration of good governance by the time of Eutropius, but he had not always been the first positive point of comparison.[244] Earlier authors were more ambivalent. Fronto, whose advice to Marcus Aurelius about good emperorship was cited above, finds that Trajan was not 'equally cleared in the eyes of all' when justice or clemency were concerned. Moreover, Fronto noted that Trajan's 'own glory was likely to have been dearer than the blood of his soldiers'.[245] Fronto wanted to

---

[240] Eutr. *Brev.* 8.5.3.
[241] C. Chiavia, 'Presente e passato nei Panegyrici Latini: personaggi storici a confronto', in: P. Desideri/ S. Roda/ A. M. Biraschi (eds.), *Costruzione e uso del passato storico nella cultura antica* (Alessandria 2007), 523–43.
[242] Sen. *Ira*, 3.16.3–17.1; 3.18.3–19.5; *Brev*, 18.5; Pausanias, 10.7.1; Philost. *Apoll.* 5.7; E. Bridges, *Imagining Xerxes: Ancient Perspectives on a Persian King* (London 2014), 170–2; 181.
[243] Them. *Or.* 3.45a; 6.72d; 6.74c; 8.110c;13.173b; 16.210ab; 18.219a; 19.226b; 19.229c. These references were kindly provided by Dennis Jussen.
[244] See more extensively O. Hekster/ S. Betjes/ S. Heijnen/ K. Iannantuono/ D. Jussen/ E. Manders/ D. Syrbe, 'The Fame of Trajan: A Late-Antique Invention', *Klio* 104 (2022), forthcoming, from which the following paragraph takes references and formulations.
[245] Fronto, *Princ. Hist.* 14–15; N. Méthy, 'Une Critique de l'optimus princeps: Trajan dans les "Principia historiae" de Fronton', *Museum Helveticum* 60 (2003), 105–23.

glorify Verus' achievements in the Parthian War by praising him in comparison with his predecessors, but Trajan also appears far from universally positive in the second-century historiographical accounts of Tacitus, Cassius Dio and Herodian. Herodian only mentions the emperor twice. For him, instead, Marcus Aurelius was the exemplary ruler par excellence.[246]

Even in the fourth century, Augustus was still used as point of comparison more frequently than Trajan. The latter is almost always paired with Antoninus Pius and Marcus Aurelius and used as an example of a ruler who promoted philosophy, or initiated debt remissions. In brief, as a civil ruler.[247] Trajan's belligerent character, for which Fronto still somewhat blamed him, was praised for the first time in a speech for Theodosius in 389. There, the author Pacatus has the Roman *res publica* herself speak to the emperor, comparing his reign positively to 'when gentle Nerva, Titus, the darling of the human race, and Antoninus, memorable for his piety, were in charge of me, when Augustus was adorning me with walls, Hadrian instructing me in the law, and Trajan extending my frontiers'.[248] Historiographical sources had already stressed Trajan's military reputation before, so the absence of military references in previous panegyrics must have been a conscious choice to highlight Trajan's civil role rather than his military one.[249] The shift towards a more military emperor on coins seems to be reflected in the increased popularity of Trajan as an exemplary conqueror in late-fourth century panegyric.

The emperor Theodosius may well have played a role in the increased popularity of Trajan. He claimed Trajanic descent, possibly because both emperors were born in Spain. His new Forum in Constantinople was modelled on Trajan's Forum in Rome and suggested that the emperor was a new Trajan.[250] This was picked up by the public speakers in their

---

[246] Tacitus: V. Schultz, *Deconstructing Imperial Representation: Tacitus, Cassius Dio, and Suetonius on Nero and Domitian* (Leiden – Boston 2019), 148 n. 80 with further references. Herodian: A. Kemezis, *Greek Narratives of the Roman Empire under the Severans. Cassius Dio, Philostratus and Herodian* (Cambridge 2014), 234. The two references are *Roman History*, 1.7.4, 6.2.4. Dio: G. Seelentag, *Taten und Tugenden Traians: Herrschaftsdarstellung im Principat* (Stuttgart 2004), 488–92, with references.

[247] Them. *Or.* 5.63d; *Or.* 8.115c; 11.145b; 13.166b; 13.173c; 17.215a; 19.229c; Aus. *Grat. Act.* 16.73; *Pan. Lat.* II (12).11.6.

[248] *Pan. Lat.* II(12), 11.6.

[249] Fest. *Brev.* 8.2, 14.3, 20.2-3; Eutr. 8.4.1; Aur. Vict. *Caes.* 13.2-3; Amm. Marc. 16.1.4 ; 25.8.5 ; E. Thienes, *Remembering Trajan in Fourth-Century Rome: Memory and Identity in Spatial, Artistic, and Textual Narratives* (PhD University of Missouri 2015), 110 with further references.

[250] *Epit. Caes.* 48.1; 48.8-9; Claudian, *IV Cos. Hon.* 20-4; *Pan. Lat.* 2(12).4.23-5; Thienes, *Remembering Trajan*, 99–100, 139, 148-9.

Figure 2.10 Trajan among the gods. Marble relief, *pronaos* of the so-called Temple of Hadrian, south-eastern side (h. c. 60 cm; w. c. 203 cm), from Ephesus, 114–18 CE. The figure at the centre of the relief is probably the emperor Trajan represented as *divus* and accompanied by Artemis' sacred deer. Active preservation and monumentalising of this site during Theodosius' reign can be related to attempts to link Theodosius' dynasty and Trajan.
Source: Selçuk, Efes Müzesi, inv. n. 716. Photo: Ketty Iannantuono. Adaptation: CKD

praise of Theodosius. It was also picked up elsewhere, as suggested by the transformation of the so-called temple of Hadrian at Ephesus. There, statues of Theodosius and members of his family were placed next to a conserved relief of (probably) Trajan, with typical attributes of Artemis (Figure 2.10).[251] At about the same time, also, Trajan was 'cleared' of persecuting Christians. Eusebius was still critical of the emperor's behaviour against Christians, but in the work of the historian and theologian Orosius (c. 375–after 418) the narrative is much more friendly, with Trajan seeing the error of his ways and consequently changing his behaviour.[252] In the late fourth century, then, Trajan became a victorious Christian emperor. In that role, he was a good example for Theodosius to follow.

---

[251] K. Iannantuono, 'A Christian Emperor between Pagan Gods: Accommodating Imperial Representation and Religious Change in Late Antique Ephesus', *Journal of Applied History* 3 (2021), 3–46; K. Iannantuono, 'Artemis, the Divus Trajan and the Demos. Reinterpreting the Frieze at the So-Called "Temple of Hadrian" at Ephesus', *Jahreshefte des Österreichischen Archäologischen Institutes in Wien* 90 (2022), forthcoming.

[252] Eusebius, *Eccl. Hist.* 3.33; Oros. 7.13. Orosius also reformulated Augustus in Christian terms: M. C. Sloan, 'Augustus, the Harbinger of Peace. Orosius' Reception of Augustus in *Historiae Adversus Paganos*', in: P. Goodman (ed.), *Afterlives of Augustus, AD 14–2014* (Cambridge 2018), 103–21.

When the latter, in turn, became an exemplary ruler for fifth- and sixth-century emperors, it was because of his piety and military qualities.[253] Religious and military imperial roles continued to be exemplary, but the civil role of the emperor had apparently lost much of its importance.

The emphasis of Hadrian as an emperor-at-law in Pacatus' speech to Theodosius coheres with the above-average attention paid to that role during Hadrian's rule. It is tempting to link the reference to 'gentle Nerva' in the same speech to the many coins highlighting the emperor's civil duties that were issued during Nerva's reign. This suggests that it was possible for emperors to shape their image by stressing one particular role over another – as long as they remained within the confines of expectations. Speeches of praise and historical treatises putting forward Constantine's exemplary status often take his religious role as their starting point.[254] Yet the shift of Trajan from an exemplary ruler because he had promoted philosophy towards an exemplary military man in the fourth and fifth centuries shows that what an emperor was celebrated for was very much in the eye of the beholder. Stressing one role much more than previous emperors had done also brought reputational risks with it, as Nero's negative exemplarity makes clear.

Speeches of praise, as well as so-called mirrors of princes, were written by the imperial elite. They therefore stress aspects of imperial rule that cohere to elite expectations and wishes. Unsurprisingly, then, the civil role of the emperor received much attention, although there were major differences between the expectations of members of the Roman aristocracy and those of Greek and eastern elites. The latter continued to use the vocabulary of kingship found in authors such as Homer and Plato, and examples from Greek history, whereas the former continued to return to examples of the Roman republic. Throughout the empire, however, the tension between the emperor as a *civilis princeps* and as an absolute military leader needed to be more explicitly addressed as time went on.[255] As a trend, then, there was a similar shift over time in coinage and in speeches of praise towards emphasis on the emperor's military role at the cost of attention to his civil role.

---

[253] M. Rodríguez Gervás, 'Teodosio, construcción de una vida y muerte ejemplares', *História* 39 (2020) https://doi.org/10.1590/1980-4369e2020052.
[254] On Constantine's posthumous reputation, see pp. 141, 149 above.
[255] A. Gangloff, *Pouvoir imperial et vertus philosophiques: l'évolution de la figure du bon prince sous le Haut-Empire* (Leiden – Boston: Brill 2019), 397–456; D. Jussen, 'Leading by Example: Historical Exemplarity in Fourth-Century Imperial Panegyric', *Talanta* 54 (2022).

Imperial behaviour, much like the emperor's name and image, was multi-faceted, with different people expecting different things at different times. But the variation was limited. A defined set of imperial roles – military, religious, and civil – was established remarkably rapidly and remained important throughout Roman history. Although there was variation of the balance between these different roles, it was difficult, perhaps even impossible, for any emperor to wholly ignore any of them. Emperors could not simply present themselves as they saw fit. In that sense, Roman emperorship shows striking continuity. Continuity is not stagnation. The empire developed, and emperorship developed with it. Some of these shifts took place within traditional patterns. Christianity reformulated the emperor's religious role, but did not redefine it. Child emperors were still expected to be military leaders. The move away from Rome as the emperors' residence, however, seems to have had a different kind of impact, diminishing the importance of some of the more 'Republican' expectations with which Roman emperors had to cope up to then.[256] Yet for a Roman emperor to become exemplary, he had to satisfy different demands, even after Constantinople became the emperor's capital. The emperor Julian seems to have recognised this when he describes Augustus as 'changing colour continually, like a chameleon, turning now pale, now red'. The first emperor's adaptability is stressed, with emphasis on the various aspects of Augustus character: in Julian's text he was a military man, close to his favourite god Apollo, with concern for civil government. Much later, the chronicler John Malalas (c. 491–578), parallels Justinian with the by then Christianised Augustus, again through the various imperial roles. Justinian himself makes much the same point when he opens his Digest by stressing how he fights wars and maintains the edifice of the state, by the grace of God.[257] Playing the right roles for the relevant people was the best way to become the perfect emperor.

---

[256] Yet there was much continuity, too, with the urban topography of Constantinople following that of Rome (see p. 279 below). Moreover, the other 'imperial cities' in which Roman emperors resided continued to be home to consular inaugurations, for instance.

[257] Julian, *Caes.* 309A–B; *Codex Justinianus* 1.17,1 (=*Digest*, praef. 1); S. Tougher, 'Julian Augustus on Augustus: Octavian in the Caesars', in: Goodman, *Afterlives of Augustus*, 87–102; 91–5; K. Simić, 'The Byzantine Augustus', in: Goodman, *Afterlives of Augustus*, 122–37; 128–30.

3 | Being around the Emperor

Roman emperors were defined by their name and image, and by the different roles they were expected to play. They were also defined by the people who surrounded them. All rulers need an entourage, consisting of those who support their pomp and splendour, guarantee succession, undertake administrative and military roles, or simply encourage and advise. The composition of this supporting cast can vary wildly between systems of government. On one end of the spectrum are rulers who surround themselves with people who wholly belong to the monarch and depend on his whims for their position. On the other side of that spectrum are monarchs interacting with an institutionally based group of advisors. Those councillors hold their position independently through long-established patterns. Examples abound throughout history of both weak rulers effectively outranked by powerful aristocratic courtiers and of strongmen supported by yes men.[1]

Roman emperors cannot easily be placed in this range of possibilities. There certainly was the expectation that rulers incorporated members of the elite in the system of government as advisors, governors, and generals. Yet members of that elite were dependent on the emperor for those positions, and often even for their place within the elite. There is a strong narrative tradition which praises emperors who abide by senatorial wishes and blames rulers who heed the advice of freedmen and women, or indeed anyone outside the 'accepted' inner circle. There were, however, no institutional constraints on the people with whom Roman emperors wanted to surround themselves. This did not mean an emperor could do as he pleased.

---

[1] See already Hekster, 'Emperors and Councillors', which forms the starting point for some of the observations in this section and from which various arguments and formulations are taken. On the ruler-elite relation: J. Duindam, 'Rulers and Elites in Global History: Introductory Observations', in: Van Berkel/ Duindam, *Prince, Pen, and Sword*, 1–31. The career bureaucrats in Han China are clear example of a strong counterforce to sole rule: H. van Ess, 'Konzeptionen monarchischer Herrschaft im frühen China', in: Rebenich, *Monarchische Herrschaft im Altertum*, 401–12; 410–11. A much-used example of absolute rule supported by dependents is that of Haile Selassie, described in a wonderful anecdote by Kapuscinski, *The Emperor*, yet there are examples from the ancient world, too, such as the rule of the Cypriot city kingdoms in the fifth and fourth centuries BC: C. Körner, 'Monarchie auf Zypern im 5. und 4. Jahrhundert v. Chr.: Herrschaft von König und Polis?', in: Rebenich. *Monarchische Herrschaft im Altertum*, 217–44.

As so often, expectations were important in shaping Roman emperorship. These applied both to the more or less 'official' advisors with a magisterial role and to the part played by the emperor's family and the people at the court.[2] As we have seen throughout this book, expectations differed between groups and areas. There were also shifts over time, and the emperors' entourage included many different types of people. Yet, looking at the groups who were most important in terms of numbers, influence, or prominence, there was remarkable continuity, even after the emperor's move away from Rome in the later empire.

Institutional Entourage: Senators and Bishops

Roman emperorship did not formally exist, at least not at the beginning of the principate. This made it difficult to name and depict the emperor. It also meant that there were no official assistants or advisors.[3] There was no system in place to appoint people to the various tasks that needed to be done to govern the empire. Consequently, the way in which these positions had been filled during the Republic remained important. That had been a system in which senators took on the most important positions. These same senators had been instrumental in the process through which Augustus had acquired his powers, not by taking them but by having them bestowed upon him. Senators, then, were a strongly institutionally embedded group, who had played a major part in the construction of the principate. Not coincidentally, the *Res Gestae* emphasised the importance of senatorial support, a message which was also inscribed on a golden shield in the senate house (Figure 3.1). Importantly, also, Augustus only accepted the honorific title of *pater patriae* after senators had confirmed the offer by a delegation of the *plebs*.[4]

This made Roman emperorship a system in which, at least in the eyes of certain groups, power was derived from and supported by the traditional

---

[2] There is a difference between imperial entourage and court, but it is subtle. Who belonged to the 'court' is often determined by their proximity to the emperor. This chapter does not discuss the court as a physical location, nor court ceremony, but there is substantial overlap between the people at court and the notion of court: A. Winterling, *Aula Caesaris: Studien zur Institutionalisierung des römischen Kaiserhofes in der Zeit von Augustus bis Commodus (31 v. Chr.–192 n. Chr.)* (Munich 1999), 2; B. Kelly, 'Introduction', in: Kelly/ Hug, *The Roman Emperor and His Court*, 1–15; 7.
[3] Millar, *Emperor*, 59–60.
[4] RGDA 35; Suet. *Aug.* 58.1; Russell, 'Inventing the Imperial Senate', 327–8. See also above 156.

Figure 3.1 The emperor's virtues. Marble copy (h. 110 cm; w. 91.5 cm) of the golden *Clipeus Virtutis* awarded to Augustus in 26 BC, from Arles. Musée départemental Arles Antique. inv. no. CRY 510095. The word SENATVS is prominently on display on this shield, which further stresses typically 'Republican' imperial virtues
Source: CKD – Radboud University Nijmegen

Republican elite, shaped as it was in traditional Republican magistracies. Emperors could execute and exile individual senators and magistrates but they would then need to be replaced by other, similar councillors.[5] The emperor needed to publicly interact with the traditional elite, and show them due deference. Inevitably, this gave that elite an enormous status, and encouraged emperors to be judged on Republican criteria, making it more difficult to place their superior power in open view.[6] Illustrative of this is a famous remark that Trajan is alleged to have made to his praetorian prefect Sextus Attius Suburanus: 'take this sword and use it for me if I rule well, and against me if I rule badly'. Emperors were continuously assessed by people surrounding them, and senatorial authors such as Pliny and Cassius

---

[5] A.-C. Michel, *La Cour sous l'empereur Claude: les enjeux d'un lieu de pouvoir* (Rennes 2015), 195–232.
[6] Wallace-Hadrill, 'Civilis Princeps', 36: 'pose of denial'.

Dio found it both laudable and normal that those people could challenge the emperor if he fell short of their expectations.[7] These and other elite authors also described emperors who claimed to rule with senators positively, whereas they portrayed those who explicitly ruled over senators in negative terms. They only did so after the emperor's death. Challenging a reigning emperor carried enormous risks. Not only senatorial authors used the relationship between the ruler and his councillors as a benchmark for good rule. Other authors, too, saw 'aristocratic rule' as the best way to guarantee successful emperorship.[8]

At the same time, the role of senators changed drastically during the principate. Any decisions of real importance came into the hands of the emperor. Though senators remained important in the administration and organisation of the empire (as governors, priests, holders of various Roman magistracies, and generals), they did so under the direct command of the emperor, exemplified through the emperors' inclusion in all major priesthoods and, especially, the development of extraordinary *imperium* for emperors and selected members of their family.[9] Before there was an emperor, senatorial considerations carried much authority. If senators reached consensus, their advice was invariably followed by the people's assemblies who technically passed laws. After the reign of Augustus, senatorial decrees formally took on legal status, but this boost of their formal powers was only minor compensation for the loss of informal authority.[10] The senate still represented an institution of great power, yet it had become rapidly clear that senators could no longer rule without an emperor – as early as the death of Caligula, it was clear that the question was not if but by whom the late emperor would be replaced. Still, for a long time only senators could become emperor, showing their continued position at the top of the political elite.[11]

---

[7] Dio, 68.16.1^2; Plin. *Pan.* 67.8; J. F. Drinkwater, 'The Principate – Lifebelt or Millstone around the Neck of the Empire', in: O. Hekster/ G. de Kleijn/ D. Slootjes (eds.), *Crises and the Roman Empire* (Leiden – Boston 2007), 67–74; 68–9.

[8] Herodian, 2.3.10, 8.7.5; B. Kuhn-Chen, *Geschichtskonzeptionen griechischer Historiker im 2. und 3.Jahrhundert n. Chr.* (Frankfurt am M. 2002), 303–5.

[9] On the development of this system of *imperium*, see now P. Sawiński, *Holders of Extraordinary Imperium under Augustus and Tiberius: A Study into the Beginnings of the Principate* (Abingdon – New York 2021), with references to earlier historiography.

[10] Talbert, *The Senate*, 324–37; I. Rollé Ditzler, *Der Senat und seine Kaiser im spätantiken Rom. Eine kulturhistorische Annäherung* (Wiesbaden 2019), 87–91.

[11] Th. Wiedemann, 'Tiberius to Nero', in: A. Bowman/ E. Champlin/ A. Lintott (eds.), *CAH.*, Vol. 10 (Cambridge 1996^2), 198–255; 198–209. Macrinus was the first non-senator to take the throne in 217, see p. 189 below.

One consequence was a shift in which the senate developed a new corporate identity.[12] During the Republic, individual senators had competed fiercely for important positions. After Augustus had come to power, the senate instead presented itself with a new cohesion (although in reality competition within the senate remained, now centred on gaining the emperor's favour). As a group, they represented a traditional elite whose position had come under threat by the arrival of a monarch. The senators accompanying the imperial family on the friezes of the Ara Pacis (Figure 1.11) demonstrate this process. They form a recognisable unity, and show how the emperor had to include members of the senate into his surroundings. The same notion was put forward by inscribing the names of important senators from the past on public monuments as a group (the so-called *Fasti Consulares* and *Triumphales*), emphasising the traditional importance of senators. Coins with the letter S(ENATUS) C(ONSULTUM) – 'by order of the senate' – on them, or the arrival of an iconographical personification of the Genius of the Senate further showed how the senate as a whole was given prominence although the power of its individual members decreased (Figure 2.7). This was both an advantage to senators, who could continue to make sense of their public importance, and to the emperor, who could boost his legitimacy through the support of the traditional elite.

This notion of the senate as an integral part of Roman rule would continue for centuries, and even survive the transfer to Constantinople as imperial capital. Both Rome and Constantinople would hold an important senate.[13] In practice, however, non-senators rapidly replaced senators in important aspects of the imperial entourage. For example, from the early empire onwards, emperors made use of a so-called *consilium principis*, a 'council of the *princeps*'. This resembled the family councils which had been normal in the Republic, and the Republican practice by senior magistrates to ask advice on judicial questions from a *consilium*.[14] At the beginning of imperial rule the council consisted of senators drawn by lot, but appointments to this council by the emperor rapidly established itself

---

[12] This paragraph closely follows the insightful analyses of A. Russell, 'Inventing the Imperial Senate' and A. Russell, 'The Augustan Senate and the Reconfiguration of Time on the Fasti Capitolini', in: I. Gildenhard et al. (eds.), *Augustus and the Destruction of History: The Politics of the Past in Early Imperial Rome* (Cambridge 2019), 157–86.

[13] L. Grig/ G. Kelly, 'Introduction: From Rome to Constantinople', in: L. Grig/ G. Kelly (eds.), *Two Romes. Rome and Constantinople in Late Antiquity* (Oxford – New York 2012), 3–30; 12, 14–16 and see p. 193–4 below.

[14] Aulus Gellius, *NA* 17.21; Valerius Maximus. 5.9.1; Seneca, *Clem*. 1.15; Cicero, *Att*. 4.2.5.

as the norm. Rather than being a permanent body, the council could be called together by the emperor on a case-by-case basis. Membership could shift from one council to the next, depending on specific expertise. Already during the reign of Tiberius, non-senators were asked to be part of an imperial *consilium*. This was a problem for senators, who lost easy access to the emperor. Increasingly, discussing matters in the *consilium principis* came to represent the way in which emperors could show that they listened to their councillors, effectively sidestepping the senate as an advisory body. The expectation that emperors would include senators in the group to which he listened remained. 'Good' emperors still filled their councils with senior senators and high-ranking other members of the elite. Nothing, however, formally stopped an emperor from excluding senators from his advisory board.[15] But those emperors who omitted senators from their group of councillors gained negative reputations, probably because of a senatorial bias in our source material. The importance of notional senatorial influence continued for a long time. After Constantine moved to his new capital, the council was renamed as *consistorium*. Its procedures became formalised as was, to an extent, its membership. There were now *ex officio* members, but that only marginally hid the fact that the emperor could (and did) still co-opt anyone he wanted, and could of course decide to simply not convene his councillors.[16] Almost anyone could advise the emperor, but senators still held enormous status.

Senators were also replaced in other positions of imperial support. Equestrians took on important positions in the organisation of the military and administration of the state from the beginning of the principate onwards, through institutionalised magistracies (such as the prefect of Egypt) and important 'secretarial' positions. There were also other people at the court who were integral to the imperial entourage.[17] Yet none of this

---

[15] W. Eck, 'Der Kaiser, die Führungsschichten, und die Administration des Reiches', in: W. Eck (ed.), *Die Verwaltung des römischen Reiches in der hohen Kaiserzeit*, vol. 2 (Basel 1997), 3–145; 7–8, 13; W. Eck, 'The Emperor and His Advisers', *CAH* 10, 195–213; J. Crook, *Consilium Principis. Imperial Councils and Councillors from Augustus to Diocletian* (Cambridge 1955), 26, 105.

[16] Ammianus Marcellinus, 15.5, 16.7–8, 30.6.2, with J. den Boeft / J. W. Drijvers/ D. den Hengst/ H. Teitler, *Philological and Historical Commentary on Ammianus Marcellinus XXX* (Leiden – Boston 2015), 140–1; *Codex Justinianus* 1.14.8; J. Harries, 'Men without Women: Theodosius' Consistory and the Business of Government', in: Kelly, *Theodosius II*, 67–89; 87.

[17] Millar, *Emperor*, 83–110, 122–31; W. Eck, 'Imperial Administration and Epigraphy: In Defence of Prosopography', in: A. K. Bowman/ H. M. Cotton/ M. Goodman/ S. Price (eds.), *Representations of Empire. Rome and the Mediterranean World* (Oxford 2002), 131–52; 143–5 and p. 209–226 below.

diminished the idea of senators as the most important advisors to the emperor. They remained relevant players in the political landscape. The inclusion of non-senators in the government of the empire was a way of keeping potential rivals away from positions of power. There are prohibitions by Marcus Aurelius against people governing their province of origin and by Gallienus against any senator governing a province. These were understandable actions, considering the historical precedents of senators revolting because of the strength of their provincial positions. From 260 onwards senators were no longer given legionary commands.[18] These measures show how well into the third century, high-ranking senators were conceived as candidates for supreme power. The idea of a non-senator becoming emperor was still absurd. When Macrinus (217–18) became the first equestrian to obtain the purple, Cassius Dio explicitly stated that he ought to have given up his claim for someone of senatorial status.[19] Roman emperors were also expected to come to Rome to be acclaimed by senators.

Certainly in the city of Rome, the senate was perceived as a crucial factor in giving the emperor legitimacy, and occasionally even as an actual counterbalance to imperial power. Senators distinguished themselves from other members of the imperial entourage in that they held status independent of the emperor. This was especially noticeable during an emperor's absence from Rome. At the beginning of the principate, when Tiberius spent years away from Rome but still lived in the Italian peninsula, senators struggled with their relative position of power. And after his successor Caligula was assassinated, they were unable to put forward their own candidate to the throne.[20] Yet the expectation that they held some sort of control remained, as is clear from the proclamation to the throne of senatorial favourites Nerva (96–8), and Pupienus and Balbinus (238) in periods of dynastic uncertainty.[21] Senatorial influence in the Italian

---

[18] C. Davenport, *A History of the Roman Equestrian Order* (Cambridge 2019), 534–45; I. Mennen, *Power and Status in the Roman Empire, AD 193–284* (Leiden – Boston 2011), 143–4, also noting the continuing dominance of the urban elite in holding traditional magistracies (91–134).

[19] *PIR*² O 108; Dio 79 (78), 11.1, 41.2–3, with A. G. Scott, *Emperors and Usurpers. An Historical Commentary on Cassius Dio's Roman History* (Oxford – New York 2018), 48–9 and ad loc 41.2–3. G. Andrews, *Rethinking the Third Century CE: Contemporary Historiography and Political Narrative* (PhD Cambridge 2018), 58–9 notes the emphasis in Dio's unabbreviated text on Macrinus' equestrian status.

[20] F. Hurlet, 'Les Sénateurs dans l'entourage d'Auguste et de Tibère: un complément à plusieurs synthèses récentes sur la cour impériale', *RPh* 74 (2000), 123–50.

[21] A. W. Collins, 'The Palace Revolution: The Assassination of Domitian and the Accession of Nerva', *Phoenix* 63 (2009), 73–106; C. Davenport/ C. Mallan, 'Herodian and the Crisis of Emperorship, 235–8 AD', *Mnemosyne* 73 (2020), 419–40.

peninsula increased when emperors were more systematically absent, through the creation of new senatorial posts and the role of high-ranking senators replacing the emperors on legal matters, as *iudices vice Caesaris*.[22] There was also a loss of influence, however, as the urban-based elite had fewer possibilities to (regularly) meet with the absent emperor, losing the advantages of immediate imperial vicinity.[23] With the more structural disappearance of the emperor from Rome, it became more difficult for senators to influence relations between the distant emperors and the city of Rome. It did not stop them from trying. The fourth and the fifth centuries saw regular attempts by senators to bring emperors back to Rome, with much more success than often assumed. When emperors (and later king Theoderic) arrived in Rome, they were inevitably met by a senatorial delegation, visited the Forum and gave a speech in the senate house.[24]

In the city itself, the relationship between (absent) emperors and senators was emphasised through the erection by senators of monuments that stressed the emperor's importance, many of them in the area around the senate building. These showed the continuous link between emperor and senate (Figure 3.2).[25] From the fourth century onwards, furthermore, a practice developed in which senatorial statues stood next to imperial monuments. Base inscriptions described how senators had honoured the emperor, or had been allowed to be honoured themselves by the emperor. This illustrated the superior position of the emperor, whose status had risen far above that of Roman senators. It was a major change from the early empire, when it was proclaimed that emperors ruled courtesy of the senate. The senate had instead become a monarchical aristocracy, bound to

---

[22] C. Bruun, 'Roman Government and Administration', in: C. Bruun/ J. C. Edmondson (eds.), *The Oxford Handbook of Roman Epigraphy* (Oxford 2015), 274–98; 282; M. Peachin, *Iudex Vice Caesaris. Deputy Emperors and the Administration of Justice during the Principate* (Stuttgart 1996), 112–14, 123–32.

[23] B. Salway, 'Equestrian Prefects and the Award of Senatorial Honours from the Severans to Constantine', in: A. Kolb (ed.), *Herrschaftsstrukturen und Herrschaftspraxis. Konzepte, Prinzipien und Strategien der Administration im römischen Kaiserreich* (Berlin – New York 2006), 115–35. On the relation between access and influence, though for a later period, see: D. Raeymakers/ S. Derks (eds.), *The Key to Power? The Culture of Access in Princely Courts, 1400–1750* (Leiden – Boston 2016).

[24] MacCormack, *Art and Ceremony*, 17–61; M. Humphries, 'Roman Senators and Absent Emperors in Late Antiquity', *Acta ad archaeologiam et atrium historiam pertinentia*, 17 (2003), 27–46; 31–2; C. Machado, *Urban Space and Aristocratic Power in Late Antique Rome: AD 270–535* (Oxford 2019), 110–13, 118–19, 121.

[25] J. Weisweiler, 'From Equality to Asymmetry: Honorific Statues, Imperial Power, and Senatorial Identity in Late-Antique Rome', *JRA* 25 (2012), 319–50; 332–5.

Figure 3.2 The absent emperor in Rome. Marble statue base, Roman Forum, 352–3. Monumental praise to the emperor remained important in the fourth century. Constantius II was honoured with an equestrian statue, the pedestal of which names him 'restorer of the city of Rome and of the world ... victor and triumphator, forever Augustus'. The statue was erected by the city prefect Naeratius Cerealis. *CIL* 6.1158= *ILS* 731
Source: CKD – Radboud University Nijmegen, photo Diane Kuster

the emperor.[26] But apparently it was still important to both emperors and senators to visually present a continuous link between emperor and senators. They may have become junior partners in government, but were still undeniably part of that government, the 'best part of the human race' to whom emperors had to relate.[27]

Even, after the division of the empire in 395, when western emperors started to mainly reside first in Milan and from 408 onwards in Ravenna, the Roman senate retained its status. Nor were Milan and Ravenna ever exclusive residences of emperors. Honorius (393–424) and Valentinian III (425–50) still regularly stayed in Rome. Between 450 and 476, five out of ten emperors were raised in Rome, and out of the four who were raised at

---

[26] Weisweiler, 'From Equality to Asymmetry', 336–48; J. Weisweiler, 'Domesticating the Senatorial Elite: Universal Monarchy and Transregional Aristocracy in the Fourth Century AD', in: Wienand, *Contested Monarchy*, 17–41; 34–5.
[27] Symm., *Ep.* 1. 52: *pars melior humani generis*.

Ravenna, two afterwards transferred to Rome. Proximity to senators was an important reason to be in the capital. The senatorial elite remained rich and politically relevant through its wealth, prestige and connections.[28] Two Roman senators, Petronius Maximus (455) and Anicius Olybrius (472) were even elevated to the throne, although their reigns were only brief. Major restoration works on important senatorial buildings that were damaged during the sack of 410 show the priority given by members of the Roman aristocracy to their 'own' monuments. This went at the cost of imperial monuments. A monument to Gratian, Valentinian II and Theodosius was even despoiled to aid the restoration of the Curia and its annexes. There are no surviving statue bases from the Roman Forum dedicated to an emperor between 410 and 608, although there are many from the fourth century.[29] Apparently Roman senatorial self-awareness boomed in the fifth century. John Malalas' *Chronicle* of the fifth-century west assumes that all successors to Honorius were either Roman senators or appointments by eastern emperors, locked in a continuous power struggle with senators.[30] Malalas was factually wrong, but his descriptions show how long the expectation survived that the senate formed a counterbalance to imperial power.

After Odoacer had deposed Romulus Augustulus (476), Ravenna became the capital of the west, but it was still compared to Rome, with Rome being more important in terms of wealth and population.[31] The number of senators had decreased enormously by that stage, with only about 100 active members remaining. These hardly held positions of real power (in contrast to Malalas' assumptions), but were still employed at the court of Theoderic, and used as intermediaries with the eastern emperor. The emphasis on traditional discourse and notions of shared *romanitas* between senators and Theoderic in, for instance, Cassiodorus' *Variae* shows the importance of claims of continuity, notwithstanding (or because of) major changes in society.[32] At the same time, Theoderic seems to have kept the most prominent members of the

---

[28] A. Gillet, 'Rome, Ravenna and the Last Western Emperors', *PBSR* 69 (2001), 131–67; 137–57, 162–3; A. Chastagnol, *Le Sénat romain sous le règne d'Odoacre* (Bonn 1966), 44–5; M. Humphries, 'Valentinian III and the City of Rome (425–55): Patronage, Politics, Power', in: Grigg/ Kelly, *Two Romes,* 161–82; 162, 174–9.

[29] Machado, *Urban Space and Aristocratic Power,* 118–19.

[30] Malalas, *Chron.* 13, 49–50; 14.7; Gillet, 'Rome, Ravenna and the Last Western Emperors', 159.

[31] Tacoma, *Roman Political Culture,* 212.

[32] Tacoma, *Roman Political Culture,* 212–13, 224; C. Radtki, 'The Senate at Rome in Ostrogothic Italy', in: J. Arnold/ M. S. Bjornlie/ K. Sessa (eds.), *A Companion to Ostrogothic Italy* (Leiden – Boston 2016), 121–46; 123, 126, 128; M. S. Bjornlie, *Politics and Tradition between Rome, Ravenna and Constantinople: A Study of Cassiodorus and the* Variae, *527–554* (Cambridge – New York 2013), 49–50, 251–3.

senatorial elite away from crucial positions. These were instead given to senators with lesser social prestige.[33] Perhaps the king wanted to avoid the contrast at court between senators who could boast of their traditional heritage and the newly established Ostrogothic king. Clearly, as embodiments of Rome's glorious past, senators remained a relevant though sometimes problematic group to put forward representative claims.

In many ways, then, Roman senators constituted a core group of imperial support. Senators formed a link to the past, and their visible vicinity to the emperor expressed continuity of rule. They were needed as a symbol. The senate functioned as some sort of visible counterbalance to the emperor's supreme power, even if individual senators were wholly dependent on the emperor for their careers and even their lives, and even after senators had lost many of their actual positions of power. The idea of such a counterbalance was more important than its practical application. Senators rarely exercised independent power, and certainly could not nullify an imperial decision (at least not as long as that emperor was in power). Yet emperors were supposed to listen to senatorial advice and take it seriously. 'Good' emperors were supposed to abide to senatorial norms, and in that sense senators really did form a check on unlimited power. This need for the senate in a representative role goes some way in explaining why Constantine needed senators in Constantinople. He may even have instituted a new senate, although it is possible that the formalisation of such a second senate in Constantinople only took place under Constantius II. Expectations, in any case, necessitated some sort of senatorial support and proximity.[34] When in 355 the orator and philosopher Themistius was adlected to the senate of Constantinople, Constantius II explicitly mentioned that Themistius was a resident of that city.[35] Senators in Constantinople were even more dependent on the emperor than their

---

[33] P. Eich, 'Quod Prosperum Nobis Utile Rei Publicae Sit. Senatorische Macht und Ressourcenkontrolle im Italien Theoderichs', in: H.-U. Wiemer (ed.), *Theoderich der Große und das gotische Königreich in Italien* (Berlin – Boston 2020), 193–22.

[34] R. Pfeilschifter, *Der Kaiser und Konstantinopel. Kommunikation und Konfliktaustrag in einer spätantiken Metropole* (Berlin – New York 2013), 453–549; M. Moser, *Emperors and Senators in the Reign of Constantius II. Maintaining Imperial Ruler between Rome and Constantinople in the Fourth Century AD* (Cambridge 2018), 57–77, with 214–76 for the argument that the second senate was only established under Constantius II. M. Bodnaruk, 'Administering the Empire. The Unmaking of an Equestrian Elite in the 4th Century CE', in: R. Varga/ V. Rusu-Bolindet, *Official Power and Local Elites in the Roman Provinces* (London – New York 2017), 145–67; 156–7.

[35] *Dem. Const.* 21b, 22d; P. Heather/ D. Moncur, *Politics, Philosophy and Empire in the Fourth Century. Select Orations of Themistius* (Liverpool 2001), 43–4, 112. On senatorial residences in Constantinople, see Moser, *Emperors and Senators*, 253.

Roman counterparts had been. The number of senators in Constantinople was increased enormously, rising from about 600 to, ultimately, some 2,000. This probably reduced the entry threshold to the senate in terms of both cash and status. Moreover, senatorial status was now granted to high-ranking equestrians, and lower equestrian officeholders were subsequently elevated. Still, the status of the new senate echoed that of Rome. Almost the entirety of book six of the *Theodosian Code* and much of book twelve of the *Justinian Code* deal with senatorial matters.[36] Becoming a senator was, more than before, an imperial gift, and the emperor controlled how senators should behave. It may be more than coincidental that the sole surviving letter of Constantine to the senate addressed it as 'his own senate (*senatui suo*)'. The possessive pronoun is telling.[37] Yet none of that diminished the need to have a prominent senate in the new capital, representing an age-old balance of power – even if only a fictitious one.

A final indication of how strongly such symbolic links to the past remained a factor in thinking about imperial rule is the long-lasting importance of the consulate. In 537, Justinian ordered that dating ought to be according to imperial regnal years, instead of using consular years. Consuls were, however, still included in dating formulae. The law explicitly mentioned that this was not abolished, perhaps anticipating protest. It also argued that Roman history had always been dominated by monarchs, from Aeneas, Romulus and Numa to Caesar and Augustus, so that first naming the emperor fitted precedent.[38] Four years later, the office was abolished altogether, ending a millennium-old tradition. The reaction was widespread and negative. The emperor was blamed for personal greed and immorality. The language is similar to that which described anti-senatorial emperors in the earlier empire.[39] When Justin II (565–78) succeeded his uncle, a poem of praise celebrating his accession put the claim into the emperor's mouth that he would restore the consulship.[40] He never did. That even after Justianian's death people pushed for the reinstatement of the consulate shows the strength of the opposition to its abolition. But apparently, Justinian thought that the disturbance caused by the continuity of the office was greater than the unrest caused by its end. The emperor's

---

[36] C. Begass, *Die Senatsaristokratie des oströmischen Reiches, ca. 457–518. Prosopographische und sozialgeschichtliche Untersuchungen* (Munich 2018), 35–57.
[37] *CIL* 6.40776; Millar, *Emperor*, 354 n. 94. Cf. *CIL* 6.1873.   [38] Justinian, *Novella*, 47.
[39] M. Kruse, *The Politics of Roman Memory. From the Fall of the Western Empire to the Age of Justinian* (Philadelphia 2020), 116–45 with references and further discussion.
[40] Corippus, *In laudem Iustini Augusti Minoris* 2.351–3.

motivation cannot be retraced with certainty. It may have been to emphatically show that he held supreme authority, or an attempt to thwart attempts by former consuls to rebel against his regime (such as his popular general Belisarius). Alternatively, he may have intended to diminish the status of the powerful western generals who held the position.[41] What is clear, however, both from the emperor's actions and the various reactions, is that the Roman past remained important in sixth-century Constantinople. Traditional magistracies bestowed status, even if their practical importance had diminished. Emperors could disrupt tradition, as Justinian showed. But their reputation suffered. Roman rulers were expected to continue existing practices.

The relationship between emperors and senators shows at least a semblance of continuity over the centuries. Senatorial involvement in governing the empire suggested a check on supreme rule. The senate personified the ancient *res publica*, a concept that retained its importance throughout Roman history, even if its meaning shifted significantly, ranging from a political structure to a semi-synonym for the Roman state.[42] Over time, another apparent check on supreme rule developed, with the arrival of a group of people whose position was, like that of senators, separate from the emperor. Christian bishops would come to collaborate strongly with the emperor and were an inevitable part of his entourage from at least the late-fourth century onwards. In many ways, they were to take a similar position to senators in their interactions with the emperor. As was the case for senators, the bishops' hierarchical position preceded these imperial interactions. The senate had been important before there were emperors. Bishops had gained their position of power well before emperors embraced Christianity. Ultimately, like senators, bishops could put pressure on the emperor and (as a corporate group) could not be simply set aside. That would leave the emperor open to accusations of arrogance and abuse of power.

The role of bishops was different from that of senators in two important ways. First, bishops did not on the whole reside in Rome (or later Constantinople), as senators did. Consequently, many bishops did not have the geographic proximity to emperors that (most) senators had.

---

[41] Kruse, *The Politics of Roman Memory*, 146.
[42] On the changing meaning of *Res Publica* in the transition to the principate: C. Moatti, *Res publica. Histoire romaine de la chose publique* (Paris 2018). On the continuation of the notion of *Res Publica* into the Byzantine era: A. Kaldellis, *The Byzantine Republic. People and Power in New Rome* (Cambridge [Mass.] – London 2015).

That was of course different for those bishops whose sees were in capital cities, or for someone like Ossius of Corduba (d. 357/8) who became an important religious advisor of Constantine.[43] A subset of bishops, then, was close to the emperor. A second difference between senators and bishops was that the bishops' role related especially to the emperor's religious activities. Bishops increasingly took over the position that members of the ancient pagan priestly colleges had held. Tertullian appears to be our earliest indication of the notion of bishops as such. This equation was especially championed by the bishops of Rome, where senatorial priests had been most influential. Damasus pushed the notion in the fourth century, Leo in the fifth, and Hormisdas in the sixth. It was never formalised, but shows how at least some bishops were interested in being considered as alternatives to senators.[44] Christian bishops might have been a new group in late antiquity, but in their relation to the emperor, they fitted into a long-established pattern of balancing power. To an extent, this image may be the result of Christian sources trying to strengthen bishops' profiles. But surviving letters from the court and legal evidence show how intensively emperors and at least the more prominent bishops interacted.[45] In doing so, they cohered to existing expectations about the relationship between emperors and an institutionalised elite. The institution was different, but the pattern was the same.

Numbers were similar, too. Recent calculations of the number of bishops around 400 estimate that there was a maximum of 900–1,000 bishops in the eastern empire, with the number most likely lower, and about 1,000 bishops in the western empire, with about 800 of them in North Africa.[46]

---

[43] Socrates, *HE* 1.7.1; S. Fernández, 'Who Convened the First Council of Nicaea: Constantine or Ossius?', *Journal of Theological Studies* 71 (2020), 196–211.

[44] Van Haeperen, 'Des Pontifes païens aux pontifes chrétiens', 159; A. Evers, 'Someone Else's Robe? Emperor Gratian's Refutation of the Imperial Title Pontifex Maximus', forthcoming, both with full references. On the clergy's positioning in power disputes: P. Brown, *Augustine of Hippo. A Biography* (London 2000²), 18. On the relative absence of members of the senatorial elite among fourth-century bishops: F. D. Gilliard, 'Senatorial Bishops in the Fourth Century', *Harvard Theological Review* 77 (1984), 153–75.

[45] The letters of Gelasius or Hormisdas I are clear examples, as is the assembled material in the *Collectio Avellana*: A. Evers (ed.), *Religion, Power, and Politics in Late Antiquity: Bishops, Emperors, and Senators in the Collectio Avellana, AD 367-553* (Leuven forthcoming); B. Neil / P. Allen, *The Letters of Gelasius I (492-496): Pastor and Micromanager of the Church of Rome* (Turnhout 2014). Cf. P. Allen/ B. Neil, *Greek and Latin Letters in Late Antiquity: The Christianisation of a Literary Form* (Cambridge 2020).

[46] R. Van Dam, 'Bishops and Clerics during the Fourth Century: Numbers and Their Implications', in: J. Leemans/ P. Van Nuffelen/ S. W. J. Keough/ C. Nicolaye (eds.), *Episcopal Elections in Late Antiquity* (Berlin – Boston 2011), 217–42; 220–5.

This is comparable in scope to the number of senators. The regional distribution between bishops and senators within the empire was very different, even taking into consideration former senatorial officials who returned to their provincial place of origin, where they could form a link between local elites in the imperial centre. This gave bishops a stronger local base than most senators, although of course it also meant that the vast majority of them had no regular access to the emperor.[47] Yet a fictitious discussion (*On Political Science*) between two officials at the court of Justinian by an unknown author from the first half of the sixth century explicitly incorporates bishops into the political hierarchy of late antiquity, directly after discussing senators: 'A second law will deal with the senate ... and also, in the way we've said, the political order. The third law will govern the selection of high priests [bishops] – to take place with the greatest respect and fear of the divine ...'.[48] Moreover, bishops could claim competing authority derived from the power of a supreme god which senators could not. Christianity ultimately made it impossible for emperors to claim absolute divinity themselves, and although they retained some of their superhuman status, it was firmly derived from the same supreme god with whom the bishops claimed to communicate. The balance between imperial power and the bishops' authority was explicitly addressed by Justinian in 535:

> There are two greatest gifts which God, in his love for man, has granted from On-high: the priesthood and the imperial dignity. The former serves divine things, while the latter directs and administers human affairs; both, however, proceed from the same origin and adorn the life of mankind. Hence, nothing should be such a source of care to the emperors as the dignity of the priests, since it is for their (imperial) welfare that they constantly implore God. For if the priesthood is in every way free from blame and possesses access to God, and if the emperors administer equitably and judiciously the state entrusted to their care, general harmony will result and whatever is beneficial will be bestowed upon the human race.[49]

---

[47] P. Brown, *Through the Eye of a Needle: Wealth, the Fall of Rome, and the Making of Christianity in the West, 350–550 AD* (Princeton 2012), 21–30; P. Norton, *Episcopal Elections 250–600. Hierarchy and Popular Will in Late Antiquity* (Oxford 2007), 57.

[48] *Dialogus Scientiae politicae*, 5.18–5.19; P. N. Bell, *Three Political Voices from the Age of Justinian* (Liverpool 2009), 9–13, 149.

[49] Justinian, *Novella*, 6, pref., with F. Dvornik, *Early Christian and Byzantine Political Philosophy. Origins and Background*, Dumbarton Oaks Studies, IX, 2 (Washington, DC 1966), 815–19.

Justinian, at the end of the period with which this book deals, formulates the joint dependence on a supreme god by emperors and bishops in positive terms. Yet from Constantine's conversion onwards, there had also been clear competition as to who perceived most clearly the divine will of that superior being.[50] Furthermore, when emperors had embraced Christianity, the imperial cult had suffered. Traces of it remained in many parts of the empire up to the sixth century, but the emperor was no longer universally present as an object of cult throughout the empire.[51]

Christian leaders could become locally more visible than the emperor, and their opinion could decide religious policy. Bishops, with some regularity, actively disturbed and demolished local pagan centres of cult, sometimes against the emperors' inclinations. At Gaza, for instance, the famous temple of Zeus Marneion was demolished by St Porphyry (c.347–420), the local bishop, although emperor Arcadius had originally argued against closure of local shrines and temples: 'I know full well that this city is dedicated to idolatry; nonetheless, it loyally fulfils its tax duties and brings in high income'. But the bishop, probably with the support of Empress Eudoxia (married to Arcadius from 395 to her death in 404), changed the emperor's mind and managed to put forward his own religious policy. Likewise, the destruction of the ancient Serapeion of Alexandria was initiated by the local bishop Theophilus, without an imperial edict backing up these momentous anti-pagan actions. This was an important affair that reverberated through the empire.[52] By claiming divine inspiration and authority, bishops could become much more activistic than the emperor, and remove themselves from imperial control.

This relative autonomy also applied to a bishop's legal authority. With the rise of Christianity, the bishop was increasingly approached as a legal authority. This placed them well beyond the position that local community leaders had previously held, but encroached on the monopoly of state officials. Constantine officially recognised this status, allowing the so-called *audienta episcopalis*, which further boosted the number of people who approached bishops as judges. This position of power was codified in

---

[50] Drake, *Constantine and the Bishops*, 389–90. See p. 140 above.
[51] J. Hahn, 'The Challenge of Religious Violence: Imperial Ideology and Policy in the Fourth Century', in: Wienand, *Contested Monarchy*, 379–404; 403–4.
[52] Sozom. *Hist. eccl.* 7.15.13; Hahn, 'The Challenge of Religious Violence', 390, 392; J. Bremmer, 'Priestesses, Pogroms and Persecutions: Religious Violence in Antiquity in a Diachronic Perspective', in: J. Dijkstra/ C. Raschle (eds.), *Religious Violence in the Ancient World: From Classical Athens to Late Antiquity* (Cambridge 2020), 46–68; 46, 62–6. On the role of empresses in Christian policy, see p. 231–3 below.

law. Bishops were even attributed higher moral authority than other judges, certainly by fellow Christians.[53]

Like senators, bishops could not be simply ignored. There were of course different categories of bishops. Bishops in small communities on the periphery of the empire were vastly outranked by metropolitans – holding the see of a provincial capital. The former were much less likely to be regularly in touch with the emperor. The same differentiation of status, however, would apply within the group of senators, especially from the third century onwards.[54] Emperors could ignore bishops (and senators) individually, but not as a group. That did not make bishops and senators exactly the same in their relation to the emperor. Senators formed a fairly homogenous group in the capital whereas bishops were much more geographically dispersed. Bishops, however, did increasingly form a recognisable category; one to which the emperor had to relate. The actual interaction was between the emperor and the most prominent bishops, but emperors could not easily exclude those bishops from their proximity.

None of this granted individual bishops protection against imperial power. Emperors could certainly dispose of bishops and exile them. The important fifth-century theologian Theodoret (c. 393–c. 458/66) who was bishop of Cyrrhus (in modern Syria) blames various emperors for not listening to bishops before they banished them, but never denies the emperor's authority to take these actions. Constantine banished the important bishop John Archaph against the wishes of the Synod of Tyre (335), which the emperor himself had convened.[55] The power of the emperor to do so was never challenged. Ultimately, no bishop could openly go against imperial wishes without consequences. Macedonius, who held the episcopal see of Constantinople from 342 to 360 (with an interruption between 346 and 351), managed for a long time to influence religious policy more

---

[53] CTh.1.27.1 (318); CJ 1.4.7 (398) restricted in CTh 16.11.1 (399) but confirmed in CTh 1.27.2 (408); R. Haensch, 'Die Rolle der Bischöfe im 4. Jahrhundert: Neue Anforderungen und neue Antworten', Chiron 37 (2007), 153–81; 162–3; A. J. B. Sirks, 'The Episcopalis Audientia in Late Antiquity', Droit et cultures, 65 (2013), 79–88. J. Corke-Webster, 'Emperors, Bishops, Art and Jurisprudence: The Transformation of Law in Eusebius of Caesarea', Early Medieval Europe 27 (2019) 12–34 on the conscious attempts by bishops to gain authority through a claim on legal (and literary) expertise.

[54] C. Davenport, 'Inscribing Senatorial Status and Identity, AD 200–300', in: Kuhn, Social Status and Prestige, 269–89; 270–3.

[55] H. Leppin, Von Constantin dem Großen zu Theodosius II. Das christliche Kaisertum bei den Kirchenhistorikern Socrates, Sozomenus und Theodoret (Göttingen 1996), 181–2, 185, with references.

strongly than the emperor Constantius II. Yet, when Macedonius removed the coffin of Constantius' father Constantine from his mausoleum in the Church of the Holy Apostles, the emperor immediately removed Macedonius from his post. The bishop may have tried to cut down the developing cult of Constantine and strengthen the pre-eminence of the Christian church. But he had failed to consult the emperor, who did not respond well to such an intervention in imperial prerogatives.[56]

Similarly, John Chrysostom (c. 347–407) was deposed from the episcopal see in Constantinople after he openly disapproved of the erection of a statue of Eudoxia near the Hagia Sophia, and seems to have insulted the empress in the process. He was also suspected of sympathising with Arianism, against imperial wishes. Consequently, John was expelled from his position, confined to his house and then exiled. Armed soldiers entered churches, taking Chrysostom's supporters to prison. They apparently forced some of the faithful to flee naked from the baptisteries where they were about to be baptised. Protests by Chrysostom's friends, the bishop of Rome and even the emperor's brother Honorius, emperor of the west, were of no effect. Honorius did exchange letters with his brother, but a mission to Arcadius failed miserably after being faced with ill-treatment, attempted bribery and the actual theft of some of the mission's documents. Chrysostom remained banished and ultimately died in 407 on his way from one place of exile to the next.[57] In the struggle for power between emperor and bishops, might remained with the emperor.

Still, there was a major difference between the power that emperors held over senators and over bishops. Senators were, with some regularity, forced to commit suicide or simply executed. There are few, if any, examples of emperors killing bishops after Constantine's conversion. Quite possibly, Constantius II played a part in the murder of Paul of Constantinople, who was installed and deposed three times from his see, before he was strangled in Cappadocia (c. 350). Constantius' role is not explicitly mentioned in the sources, and the case is extraordinary as it also involves a struggle for

---

[56] E. Manders, 'Macedonius, Constantius and the Changing Dynamics of Power', in: C. A. Cvetković / P. Gemeinhardt (eds.), *Episcopal Networks in Late Antiquity* (Berlin – Boston 2020), 249–66. On the developing cult of Constantine, see p. 149 above. On Constantius' tendency to banish bishops: W. Stevenson, 'Exiling Bishops: The Policy of Constantius II', *Dumbarton Oaks Papers* 68 (2014), 7–27.

[57] *Collectio Avellana*, 38; J. Torres, 'Concerning John Chrysostom: *Collectio Avellana* 38 and his Controversy in the West', in: Evers, *Religion, Power, and Politics in Late Antiquity*, forthcoming; K. C. Choda, 'Losing the Empress's Favour: On the Margins of John Chrysostom's Homily 48 on Matthew', in: Choda/ de Leeuw/ Schulz, *Gaining and Losing Imperial Favour*, 125–50.

authority between Constantius and his brother Constans, the western emperor.[58] On the whole, emperors were not involved in the deaths of bishops.

One reason may be that senators, unlike bishops, were potential competitors to the throne. Equally importantly, bishops had much more potential to rapidly mobilise people over a wide area than senators ever had.[59] Several violent conflicts in the fourth and fifth century between Christians and pagans, and often also between different groups of Christians, made clear how volatile the local populace could become when religiously motivated.[60] Emperors needed to take care that such violence would not turn on them, especially when it involved affairs in the capital. This is even mentioned explicitly in an extraordinary case during the reign of Valens (364–78). Discussion about the succession of Eudoxius as bishop of Constantinople (360–70) grew so fierce that the emperor sent in troops to end 'popular tumult' in the capital. Certain church leaders complained about 'the ill-usage to which they had been subjected', to the annoyance of the emperor, who gave his prefect a secret order to put these men to death. The prefect 'fearing that he should excite the populace to a seditious movement' pretended to exile them, but had their ship set on fire in the middle of the Astacian Gulf, burning the persons on board alive.[61] The veracity of the story is less important than the fear of popular uprising following the execution of Christian leaders that seems to be a given. It was much safer to depose bishops than to kill them.

Emperors could not only depose and banish bishops. They could also play a major part in their appointment. Inevitably, this applied much more to the main dioceses than to lesser sees. Imperial activity was, moreover, most noticeable when there was dispute about a bishop's legitimacy. The events after the death of Rome's bishop Zosimus in 418 are exemplary. Two different successors, Eulalius and Boniface were anointed (by two

---

[58] Soz., *Church History*, 3.7.7; 3.9; 4.2.2; Socr. Schol., *Church History* 2.13, 2.15.1, 2.16; 2.18.1; 2.20.1–2; 2.22.4; 2.26.6; 5.9.1; Manders, 'Macedonius, Constantius and the Changing Dynamics', 252–6.

[59] E. Fournier, 'Exiled Bishops in the Christian Empire: Victims of Imperial Violence?', in: H. A. Drake (ed.), *Violence in Late Antiquity. Perceptions and Practices* (London – New York 2006), 157–66; 162.

[60] B. D. Shaw, *Sacred Violence: African Christians and Sectarian Hatred in the Age of Augustine* (Cambridge 2011), 224; J. C. Magalhães de Oliveira, 'Late Antiquity: The Age of Crowds?', *Past & Present*, 249 (2020), 3–52; 6–7, 14–15, 28–30, 40–2, placing 'religious' violence in a wider social context.

[61] Socr. Schol. *Church History* 4.15–16.

different groups and in two different churches), after which Emperor Honorius was approached for a solution. He first ordered Boniface to be banished, but after violence in Rome and a new petition, Honorius reconsidered and called both would-be-bishops to him. The emperor ordered all parties to stay out of Rome and sent private letters of consultation to influential bishops such as Augustine and Paulinus of Nola. Ultimately, the emperor decided that Boniface was the rightful successor and had Eulalius arrested and removed from the city.[62] The potential of violence surrounding bishops is clear in this narrative, as is the undoubted supremacy of the emperor. Prominent bishops such as Augustine might have expected to be consulted in these matters, but accepted the emperor as arbiter. That the emperor had to be consulted in the first case was because of the enormous potential for conflict on how bishops were elected. Occasionally, recommendation by a predecessor was the crucial factor, but acclamation by the local populace, or popularity among fellow bishops could also be decisive. Even miraculous appointments could be seen as legitimate.[63] This gave the emperor quite a lot of leeway in whom to appoint. Imperial interests focused on a relatively small number of positions. The sees of the bishops of the important cities Alexandria, Antioch, Aquileia, Arles, Carthage, Constantinople, Jerusalem, Milan, Ravenna and Rome saw regular interventions from the eastern court and the Latin successor kingdoms. The other episcopal sees did not. On the whole, bishops in the majority of local sees were elected by the local population and the clergy, making it 'a form of democratic activity'. Disapproval of a candidate could lead to outbreaks of mob violence, once again showing the popular support that bishops could have at their disposal.[64]

The relationship between emperor and bishops in the late empire was in many ways analogous to that of emperor and senators in the earlier empire. Again, this did not mean that all bishops were expected to have access to the emperor, but the more prominent bishops held their positions as representatives of a well-established category of people. Bishops, moreover, seem to have held a dominance over the emperor that senators never did. No senator ever forbade an emperor anything. Bishops occasionally could.

---

[62] *Collectio Avellana*, 14-37, with D. Liebs, 'From the Archives of the City Prefecture in Rome: *Collectio Avellana* 1-40 (AD 367-420)', in: Evers, *Religion, Power, and Politics*, forthcoming.

[63] Leppin, *Von Constantin dem Großen zu Theodosius II*, 185. Cf. Jones, *Later Roman Empire*, II, 887 on the 'woeful lack of rules'. But note how there were necessary preconditions for an episcopal election to be valid: A. Evers, *Church, Cities and People. A Study of the Plebs in the Church and Cities of Roman Africa* (Leuven 2010), 97-110.

[64] Norton, *Episcopal Elections*, 7, 68-78, 82-111.

Probably the most famous example of this took place in 390, when St Ambrose, the bishop of Milan (c. 340–97) prohibited Theodosius from entering the basilica in Milan and literally brought the emperor to his knees in an act of penance.[65] This event, however, took place in volatile circumstances and was not as much of an imperial loss of face as is often maintained. Theodosius had just defeated the usurper Magnus Maximus (383–8), who had made the western emperor Valentinian II (375–92) flee to Theodosius' court. Theodosius consequently became *de facto* ruler over the whole of the empire, celebrated by a triumphal entry into Rome in 389. Formally, though, he reinstated Valentinian in the west.[66] Civil war inevitably causes upheaval, and this one was no exception. Infamously, in the spring of 390, the inhabitants of Thessalonica complained about the presence of a local garrison, and were massacred without trial.[67] Ambrose consequently refused the emperor entry into the Milan basilica until he had repented. When the emperor duly obliged, he could consign these events to history and added 'a new role to the imperial repertoire', that of the repentant Christian. It raised Ambrose's status enormously, but did not make his position unassailable. Equally important, it allowed Theodosius to dispel accusations of tyranny that would usually be associated with the slaughter of innocents by imperial command.[68] In some ways, the religious acceptance by Ambrose can be compared to a senatorial acclamation; a process that implied the right of senators *not* to acclaim the emperor.

Senatorial acclamation was a confirmation of the emperor's status as ruler. Ambrose did not accept the emperor as head of the church. Yet bishops did seemingly accept that role for the emperor whenever they assembled at an imperially led synod. It was the emperor who convened the various councils, from the first ecumenical church council at Nicaea (325) convened by Constantine to the second council at Constantinople in 553, convoked by Justinian. Bishops deliberated among themselves as well,

---

[65] N. McLynn, *Ambrose of Milan: Church and Court in a Christian Capital* (Berkeley – Los Angeles – London 1994), 298–330, with references; Brown, *Through the Eye of a Needle*, 120–47; G. Bowersock, 'From Emperor to Bishop: The Self-Conscious Transformation of Political Power in the Fourth Century AD', *Classical Philology* 81 (1986), 298–307; 306.

[66] J. F. Matthews, *Western Aristocracies and the Imperial Court* (Oxford 1975), 224–5. See p. 62 above.

[67] Theodor. *Church History* 5.17 mentions 7,000 victims. See D. Washburn, 'The Thessalonian Affair in the Fifth-Century Histories', in: Drake, *Violence in Late Antiquity*, 215–24 for full discussion of the massacre and the reliability of the relevant historical sources.

[68] McLynn, *Ambrose of Milan*, 323–30; McEvoy, *Child Emperor Rule*, 42–3; C. Kelly, 'Stooping to Conquer. The Power of Imperial Humility', in: Kelly, *Theodosius II*, 221–43, 237 notes how 'a momentary suspension of superiority ... demonstrated his fitness to rule'.

and had their own motives for wanting to participate in synods, but only the emperor could call all church leaders together. The imperial supremacy was visualised through showing the emperor in a central position, dominant over the bishops (Figure 3.3). In his shining purple robes, the emperor became an *episcopus maximus* among the bishops. Imperial officials, moreover, were tasked with controlling the council's proceedings, and carry out its decisions. Ecclesiastical authorities obviously influenced what happened at the synods, but the decisions held a firm stamp of imperial authority.[69]

The leading role of the emperor in religious matters also becomes clear in the great religious debates of the fourth to sixth century, most notably the struggle between Arianism and Donatism, and the Nestorian schism.[70] Whatever the specific religious issues were, it was crucial to have the emperor on one's side to emerge victorious. Bishops and other members of the clergy, but also local dignitaries, continuously attempted to convince the emperor that they were right and their rivals wrong. As St Augustine noted: 'They annoyed the emperor with daily appeals'.[71] The anti-Donatist 'Edict of Unity' was put forth on February 12, 405 by the emperors Honorius, Arcadius and Theodosius II in separate laws, simultaneously issued. Bishops certainly had their say in religious disputes, but ultimately, the emperor decided.[72]

---

[69] J. B. Torres, 'Purple and the Depiction of Constantine in Eusebius and other Contemporary Panegyrical Works', in: M. P. García Ruiz/ A. J. Quiroga Puertas (eds.), *Emperors and Emperorship in Late Antiquity. Images and Narratives* (Leiden – Boston 2021), 76–92; 83–5; H. Amirav, *Authority and Performance. Sociological Perspectives on the Council of Chalcedon (AD 451)* (Göttingen 2015), 97–8. On the interactions between emperor and bishops before and during council meeting: D. Slootjes 'Dynamics of Power at the Imperial Court: Theodosius II, Pulcheria, Nestorius, Cyril and the Council of Ephesus of 431', in: C. Davenport/ M. McEvoy (eds.), *The Roman Imperial Court. Pathways from the Principate to Late Antiquity* (Oxford, forthcoming).

[70] The literature on the subject is immense. Possibly the best and most accessible starting point on Donatism is R. Miles (ed.), *The Donatist Schism. Controversy and Contexts* (Liverpool 2016). Still seminal: W. H. C. Frend, *The Donatist Church: A Movement of Protest in Roman North Africa* (Oxford 1952). On Nestorianism and further Christological debate, see now: S. Leuenberger-Wenger, *Das Konzil von Chalcedon und die Kirche. Konflikte und Normierungsprozesse im 5. und 6. Jahrhundert* (Leiden – Boston 2019).

[71] Augustine, *Ep.* 105.8; C. R. Calvão-Sibrinho, *Doctrine and Power. Theological Controversy and Christian Leadership in the Later Roman Empire* (Berkeley – Los Angeles – London 2013), 78–93.

[72] *CTh* 16.5.38, 16.6.3–5. Cf. Augustine, *Ep.* 105.3: 'you are being forced into unity by the orders of the emperor ... you have forced the emperor to issue these orders against you'. See M. V. Escribano Paño, 'Bishops, Judges and Emperors: CTh 16.2.31/ CTh. 16.5.46/ Sirm. 14(409)', in: A. Fear/ J. Fernández Urbiña/ M. Marcos (eds.), *The Role of the Bishop: Conflict and Compromise* (London – New York 2013), 105–26 on the interaction between bishops and emperors about issuing law during religious conflicts.

Figure 3.3 Constantine at Nicaea. Compendium of canon law, drawing on vellum, from Northern Italy, c. 825, Vercelli, Archivio Capitolare Eusebiano, MS CLXV. Constantine's superior position at the council of Nicaea, where Arianism was condemned (*heretici Arriani damnati*), was clearly presented on imagery. The earliest surviving representation is this ninth-century drawing. It explicitly mentions Constantine as *im(perator)*, among the 318 (*CCCXVIII*) holy fathers. The image shows soldiers although Eusebius argues that they were not present
Source: CKD – Radboud University Nijmegen

Military might was an important reason for the emperor's supremacy. During the Second Council of Ephesus (449), the emperor's might was even expressed through armed soldiers in the church (Figure 3.3). Bishop Theodoret, who was excluded from the council by the court and subsequently excommunicated, describes the reaction of his supporters: 'We were threatened with deposition. We were threatened with exile. Soldiers with clubs and swords stood by, and we took fright at the clubs and swords. We were intimidated into signing'. Theorodet may have exaggerated, but there is no doubt that the emperor could employ the threat of violence to push matters forward. This had been the case for Constantine at Nicaea and still applied at the Council of Chalcedon in 451, called by Marcian (450–7), to set aside the decisions of the Ephesian Synod of 449.[73] Roman emperors had systematically informed senators that they and the armies were well, emphasising the potential for imperial violence.[74] Bringing soldiers into the church very much sent home the same message to bishops, with a very similar result.

A second reason for the acceptance by bishops of the emperor's supremacy was discord between the bishops. As there had been competition between senators about gaining privileges, so bishops competed for prominence.[75] Imperial support was instrumental, not only for individual clergymen to become bishops, but also in disputing which bishopric stood at the apex of the hierarchy. This was a continuous discussion between the different sees. Rome and Constantinople were obvious candidates for supremacy, but Antioch too claimed importance, as did Caesarea, Alexandria and Carthage, closely following imperial infrastructure. The absence of Jerusalem as an important episcopal see is noticeable.[76] Rome's supreme position over its eastern competitors was not a given. In the fifth century, it was no longer the imperial capital, and the sack of the city in 410 further diminished confidence in Rome's institutions. But it retained historical status. Rome was steeped in sacred history, with the notion of St Peter as Rome's first bishop perhaps the most important one in a Christian empire. Attempts to compare the sack of Rome to that of Troy or Jerusalem were used to further raise the city's spiritual status in order to

---

[73] Theodoret, *Church History* I.54; Amirav, *Authority and Performance*, 122–3.
[74] See p. 11 above.   [75] See p. 201–2 above.
[76] E. Albu, 'The Battle of the Maps in a Christian Empire', in: C. Rapp/ H. A. Drake (eds.), *The City in the Classical and Post-Classical World* (Cambridge – 2014), 202–16; 210–11 on Christian maps placing Jerusalem in a central position.

compensate for loss of political prominence.[77] The bishop of Rome made use of Rome's historical status to claim and retain supremacy in the Christian empire. The bishop of Constantinople, on the other hand, could boost immediate political relevance, and had easy access to the emperor. Again, prominent bishops turned to the emperor to settle matters. Rome remained at the episcopal summit, but the bishop of Constantinople managed to rise in seniority through the help of Theodosius, who at the Council of Constantinople of 381 promoted his see to second in status.[78] Grumbling about the relative positions of the bishoprics remained, however, and the issue was raised again explicitly in 451 at the Council of Chalcedon, when under the auspices of Marcian (450–7), Anatolius of Constantinople was confirmed as second in the hierarchy of Roman bishops, before the bishops of Alexandria and Antioch. Importantly, the status of both Rome and Constantinople was explicitly linked to the emperor:

> The Fathers fittingly bestowed seniority on the see of Elder Rome (πρεσβυτέρας Ῥώμης; *presbuteras Romēs*) on account of the exercise of imperial power in that city, and, with the same aim, the 150 most god-loving bishops [at Constantinople] undertook to apportion the same seniority to the most holy see of New Rome (νέας Ῥώμης; *neas Romēs*), reasonably judging that the city should be exalted in ecclesiastical affairs like [Elder Rome] and have authority in second place after it, because [New Rome] was honoured by the imperial office and a senate, and because it enjoyed equal seniority to Elder imperial Rome (πρεσβυτέρᾳ βασιλίδι Ῥώμῃ; *persbuterai basilidi Romē*).[79]

The reference to both imperial power and the senate is striking, showing the continuous role of senatorial status in mid-fifth-century Constantinople. The comparison between senators and bishops is also noticeable. After Chalcedon, bishops of Rome regularly tried to assert their authority over matters of church hierarchy. In doing so, they not only faced imperial resistance, but also continuous discord with other bishops, not helped by the major doctrinal debates that characterised fourth- and fifth-century Christianity.

---

[77] L. Grig, 'Deconstructing the Symbolic City: Jerome as Guide to Late Antique Rome', *PBSR* 80 (2012), 125–43; 142. See R. Dijkstra, 'Peter, Popes, Politics and More: The Apostle as Anchor', in: Dijkstra, *The Early Reception and Appropriation of the Apostle Peter*, 3–25 for discussion and bibliography of the Petrine tradition at Rome.

[78] Kruse, *The Politics of Roman Memory*, 186.

[79] *Acts of Chalcedon*, 28; The Latin translation uses *nova Roma* and *senior Roma*; Kruse, *The Politics of Roman Memory*, 189–91.

Military and economic might on the part of the emperor, and discord amongst bishops assured imperial supremacy. Justinian expressed his authority in church matters explicitly in 545, when he published *Novel* 131. Though the text recognises that he places into law 'ecclesiastical rules which were adopted and confirmed by the four Holy Councils', it is the emperor issuing the law. It reconfirms that 'the most blessed archbishop of Constantinople, New Rome, should hold the second place after the most holy apostolic see of Elder Rome, but that [he] precedes all others in honour'.[80] Alexandria and Antioch fell under the aegis of the bishop of Constantinople. Through this law, Justinian asserted imperial control over the organisation of the Church, not even a decade after he had abolished the consulate to show his dominance in matters of state.

In a society in which imperial appointments and administrative reorganisations had been the norm for centuries, it was unsurprising that the emperor decided on which see should become dominant. This fitted historical precedent perfectly. Emperors had been crucial in inter-city competition from the very beginning of the principate. As early as 31 BC, Octavian responded to an embassy of the Asian city of Rhosus which offered him honours and a gold crown with the statement: 'When I come to those parts I will do my best to be of service to you and preserve the privileges of the city'.[81] Such confirmation of privileges was important, especially in the Greek east, since any rights of cities were likely to be challenged by neighbouring cities. This competition between cities was notorious, famously expressed by Herodian who noted how 'this continuous inter-city struggle and the desire to ruin a rival who seems to have grown too powerful is a long-standing weakness of the Greeks'.[82] Confirmation of status was prominently displayed to raise a city's status, while negative imperial answers to requests were publicly displayed in competing cities. The emperor was the inevitable arbiter in this competition, and communication between various cities and the emperor can be traced with remarkable continuity over the centuries.[83] Cities consequently tried to flatter emperors into boosting their rights, recording verbatim the ever-more extensive acclamations on public inscriptions, milestones and even the reverses of coins. Emperors appreciated these tokens of allegiance

---

[80] Justinian, *Novella* 131.1–2; Kruse, *The Politics of Roman Memory*, 187.
[81] *IGLS* 3.718; Millar, *The Emperor*, 410–11.   [82] Herodian, 3.2.8.
[83] Millar, *The Emperor*, 410–20.

and responded by, for instance, allowing a city to build a temple to the imperial cult (*neokoros*), the number of which raised a city's status.[84]

Imperial intervention was not only positive. Getting it wrong, for instance by acclaiming the wrong contender during civil war, could mean loss of status. Marcus Aurelius forbade the city of Antioch to organise any 'spectacles, public meetings, and assemblies of any kind' because they had supported a rebellion against the emperor. His successor Septimius Severus deprived Nicaea of the title of 'first city' after it had sided with Pescennius Niger in the civil war, to the great joy of nearby rival Nicomedia.[85] Imperial involvement in deciding which see held supremacy fitted these precedents perfectly. Emperors had decided on the relative status of cities for centuries, including at a religious level through allowing the construction of temples to the imperial cult. It was not only the emperor's capacity for violence that made bishops turn to him to decide on internal rivalry. The emperor was the obvious person to turn to, because he was the figure to whom people had always turned in similar situations. The notion of being surrounded and advised by individuals who held independent status, like senators and bishops (even if only a subset of them would actually advise him), constrained the emperor. But the notion that the emperor was the ultimate arbitrator constrained senators and bishops. Emperors presented themselves as 'special senators' or 'special bishops' to live up to expectations, but these very expectations also allowed emperors to remain on top and keep the institutionally based group of people who surrounded them in check.[86]

Closeness to Rule: The Emperor's Men at Court

Throughout Roman imperial history, emperors were expected to collaborate with institutional elites. Individual members of that elite might have been dependent on the emperor, but their status derived at least as much from a shared corporate identity as from imperial support. For a substantial number of people directly surrounding the Roman emperor, the

---

[84] C. Roueché, 'Acclamations in the Later Roman Empire: New Evidence from Aphrodisias', *JRS* 74 (1984), 181–99; 185–6; S. J. Friesen, *Twice Neokoros. Ephesus, Asia and the Cult of the Flavian Imperial Family* (Leiden – Boston 1993); Hekster, *Rome and Its Empire*, 62–3.

[85] HA, *Marcus*, 25.8–26; Malalas, *Chron.* 12.3; L. Robert, 'La Titulature de Nicée et de Nicomédie: la gloire et la haine', *HSCP* 81 (1977), 1–39; Lendon, *Empire of Honour*, 140–1; Hekster, *Commodus*, 37–8.

[86] Wallace-Hadrill. 'Civilis Princeps', 47. On the emperor as special bishop, see p. 139–40 above and p. 204.

situation was different. Their position and status was wholly dependent on imperial favour. The Roman empire is fairly exceptional in comparison to other monarchical societies in that no court aristocracy, whose positions (and wealth) relied on court offices ever developed. There were no clearly defined 'official' roles for higher echelons of society at the court, which indicated and raised someone's hierarchical position within the elite.[87] Possibly, the continuous expectation that senators and later bishops were to be institutionally involved by the emperor blocked the development of such formal court roles. Alternatively, a formalised court structure would have come too close to Hellenistic court life, and be interpreted as a sign of open monarchy. Although certain elements of the Hellenistic court were taken over, its formal organisation was not.[88] Consequently, rather than a visible 'court aristocracy' with a defined internal hierarchy, the direct favour of the emperor defined an individual's position. This meant that a whole range of persons who might never have risen through the ranks of hierarchical offices could gain enormous influence over the emperor – and fall from grace spectacularly when the emperor dismissed them. Among the best-known cases are the praetorian prefects Sejanus (20 BC–AD 31) under Tiberius, and Plautianus (c. 150–205) under Septimius Severus, or the Grand Chamberlain Eutropius (d. 399) under Arcadius. All of them gained power above their normal station, publicly recognised by the erection of bronze and marble statues, monumental reliefs, and painted portraits, sometimes explicitly linked to images of the emperor. These were erected in various towns of the empire, by a range of different groups, from local elites to senators. When their closeness to the emperor ended, their images were publicly destroyed.[89] Consequently, all sorts of rumours abound who was in favour at a given moment, and how to attract imperial goodwill abounded.

There was clear tension between, on the one hand, senators and bishops as institutionalised groups expected to hold power and, on the other, men (and women) wielding enormous influence simply by being close to the emperor. That tension increased when, as was often the case, individuals of

---

[87] R. Wei/ B. Kelly, 'The Roman Aristocracy at Court', in: Kelly/ Hug, *The Roman Emperor and His Court* I, 85–114.

[88] R. Strootman, 'Hellenstic Influences on Roman Court Culture', in: Kelly/Hug, *The Roman Emperor and His Court* I, 16–34; 29–33.

[89] Tac. *Ann.* 3.72.3; Dio, 58.2.7, 58.4.4, 58.11.3, 76(75).14.6–7, 76(75).16.5; Juv. 10.58.64; *CTh.* 9.40.17; Davenport, *Roman Equestrian Order*, 345–6; Wei/ Kelly, 'The Roman Aristocracy at Court', 90–2; B. Kelly, 'Court Politics and Imperial Imagery in the Roman Principate', in: Russell/ Hellström, *Social Dynamics*, 128–58; 146–7. On Eutropius see p. 217 below.

low civic status held sway. Many imperial domestic servants did hold clearly delineated roles. How otherwise could logistics for the enormous number of people at court be properly organised? Staff were needed to provide what was expected of the emperor: dinners, the *salutatio*, and a well-run court. A papyrus from 129 provides a sense of scale. It lists the supplies that were necessary to provide for Hadrian and his entourage while he travelled in Egypt, indicating that the travelling court consisted of about 5,000 people. How logistics were organised becomes clear from more than 4,000 surviving epitaphs of imperial slaves and freedmen.[90] These allow for a taxonomy of posts, showing well-known important positions for freedmen, such as the *a rationibus* (in charge of the imperial finances), the *a libellis* (processing petitions to the emperor) and *ab epistulis* (imperial correspondence), but also positions which inevitably meant closeness to the emperor, such as the *a cubiculo* (chamberlain) or the *ab admissionibus*, who controlled access to the emperor.[91]

These must have been coveted positions, and from the later second century onwards the positions of *a rationibus*, *a libellius* and *ab epistulis* were taken up by equestrians rather than freedmen.[92] This somewhat diminished the status gap, but it remained the case that access to the emperor through a privileged position was more systematically available to people of lower social status. Possibly, this changed under the Tetrarchy and Constantine, when the main imperial secretaries became addressed as *magister*. They seem now to have been drawn from the richer echelons of society, though mainly from provincial cities. That, at least, is indicated by passages from the *Codex Theodosianus* and *Codex Justinianus* which state that after these secretaries retired, they (and their children and grandchildren) were to be exempt from city offices or obligations – tasks that rich men in the provincial cities would normally have to take up.[93] The increased presence of members of provincial cities near the emperor in the period in which Rome's status as imperial capital became disputed suggests that moving away from Rome loosened some constraints on the emperor.

---

[90] *SB* 6.9617; H. Halfmann, *Itinera Principum: Geschichte und Typologie der Kaiserreisen im Römischen Reich* (Stuttgart 1986), 84, 110; Wallace-Hadrill, 'The Imperial Court', 297; Winterling, Aula Caesaris, 83–160.

[91] J. Edmondson, 'Domestic Servants in the Imperial Court', in: Kelly/ Hug, *The Roman Emperor and His Court* I, 168–203; 29–33; Millar, *Emperor*, 69–83.

[92] C. Davenport/ B. Kelly, 'Administration, Finances, and the Court', in: Kelly/ Hug, *The Roman Emperor and His Court* I, 115–45–117, 124, 127; Millar, *Emperor*, 101–6.

[93] *CTh.* 6.35.3; *CJ.* 12.28.2; Millar, *Emperor*, 108–9. Cf. B. Sirks, 'Status and Rank in the Theodosian Code', in: Kuhn, *Social Status and Prestige*, 291–302 on the development of a systems of honorifics marking attachments to the imperial system.

He was apparently no longer expected to (only) give important secretarial positions to men who had risen through equestrian careers. The provincial elite whom the emperor met outside of Rome increased their influence – once again showing the importance of imperial proximity. This was, however, more a change in personnel than a fundamental shift in imperial entourage. No senators, let alone bishops, are known to have filled these imperial offices. There remained a clear divide between different types of imperial closeness.

The 'lesser' domestic posts, moreover, remained firmly tied to lower-status individuals throughout Roman history. No one other than slaves and freedmen was expected to dress the emperor, serve and taste his food, or carry his wine. They were unavoidably close to the emperor, regularly leading to a more intimate relationship. Trajan's manumitted slave Phaedimus, for example, rose from being the emperor's 'cup-bearer' to having responsibility for the wine cellar. His next post was steward of the dining room, and he ultimately became 'secretary of the grants of imperial favours' (*a commentariis beneficiorum*). He was explicitly named as closest attendant when Trajan was moving around in public (*lictor proximus*). His influence was entirely dependent on the emperor's trust. Perhaps to keep a close eye on whom the emperor was close with, he seems to have ensured that his own former slave Valens was 'in charge of the emperor's private wardrobe'.[94] There is more attention in ancient (and modern) literature for so-called bad emperors who became infatuated with freedmen and allowed them to wield influence, but the case of Phaedimus is illustrative for the importance that those close to the emperor held in any reign. Literary sources, mostly written by elite men, are extremely dismissive of emperors who followed the advice of the 'wrong' sort of people over the ideas of the traditional elite. This is a narrative that recurs throughout Roman imperial history, showing continuing unease by the institutional elite with the power that intimacy with the emperor granted those of much lower status. How unsuitable these low-status friends of the emperor were in elite eyes is often expressed through extreme stories, regularly emphasising sexual perversities. Other evidence, much of it epigraphic, shows that many in the empire simply accepted the

---

[94] *CIL* 6.1884, 8550 (= *ILS* 1792, 1756); M.-L. Constant, 'Commentaires et conjectures sur la carrière et la mort d'un affranchi de Trajan: Marcus Ulpius Phaedimus', *BCEA* 37 (2001), 65–74; Edmondson, 'Domestic Servants', 178. The evidence for Valens' position as *a veste* postdates Phaedimus' death, so Valens might have obtained the position in his own right.

influence of such men, and approached them with requests for the emperor.[95] Apparently, elevating people in his direct vicinity to positions of power was perfectly normal behaviour for an emperor, even if senators did not agree.

One advantage for the ruler of low-status people who were wholly dependent on him was that they could not be a threat to his position in their own right. Alienating them could still be dangerous, as the stories of imperial assassinations involving former favourites make clear.[96] But they could not claim the throne themselves. This dependence on the emperor applied even more strongly to eunuchs. These were far more prominent in the early Roman empire than is often assumed, with the notion of castrated men already part of Roman society by at least the second century BC. They were visible at the imperial court from the early empire onwards, as they were in the households of elite Roman society.[97] Eunuchs are already mentioned in relation to the imperial family in the reign of Tiberius, with the emperor's son Drusus attracted by the eunuch Lygdus' 'years and looks', so that he came to hold 'a prominent place among his attendants'. Pliny mentions how during the reign of Claudius, an unnamed Thessalian eunuch 'from motives of ambition had enrolled himself as one of the freedmen of the emperor'.[98] That eunuchs could rise through the ranks in the early empire is indicated through Claudius' food taster Halotus. Both Tacitus and Suetonius involve him in the death of the emperor, only to then serve under Nero and Galba, the latter of whom supposedly even gave him 'a very important stewardship'. Whether these stories are true is less important than that they were deemed possible. Eunuchs were part of the emperor's surroundings and so close to him that they were useful allies in conspiracies.[99] They were thought of as young and beautiful beings, the ownership of whom showed wealth and status. The imperial household

---

[95] H. Mouritsen, *The Freedman in the Roman World* (Cambridge 2011), 93–109, also pointing out how the discourse about powerful freedmen emerged in the late Republic; A. Hug/ N. Bernstein/ B. Kelly, 'Court Relationships', in: B. Kelly/ A. Hug, *The Roman Emperor and His Court, ca. 30 BC–ca. AD 300 Volume 2: A Sourcebook* (Cambridge 2022), 79–131; 79–80.

[96] For example, Suet. *Dom.* 17.1–2; Herodian, 1.17.4–11, echoing Dio 67.15.1–5; Dio 73(72).22.

[97] S. Tougher, *The Roman Castrati. Eunuchs in the Roman Empire* (London – New York 2020), 27–31, 51–3; P. Guyot, *Eunuchen als Sklaven und Freigelassene in der griechisch-römischen Antike* (Stuttgart 1980), 121–9.

[98] Tac. *Ann.* 4.10.2; Pliny, *NH* 12.5.

[99] Tac. *Ann.* 12.66.2, Suet. *Claud.* 44.2; Suet. *Galba* 15.2; Tougher, *Roman Castrati*, 52. Note the emphasis in these stories about eunuchs and assassinations on poison, which was a typically 'female' weapon in Roman discourse: N. Purcell, 'Livia and the Womanhood of Rome', *PCPS* 32 (1986), 78–105; 95.

rose above all others in status and power, and should therefore include these exotic beings.[100]

The normality of eunuchs at the court, and their low social status, is described in a passage from Tacitus that describes how Vitellius marched on Rome during the civil war of 69: 'The closer Vitellius' march drew (to Rome), the more corrupt it became, with actors, mobs of eunuchs, and everything else typical of the Neronian court being mingled in'. The senatorial historian displays his disdain. The unwillingness to accept that people of low civic status, let alone societal outcasts, could form an integral part of the court is clear. Yet it may well have been their very position of outcasts, and therefore fully dependent on the emperor, that made these men interesting to the emperor as important allies.[101] Eunuchs often combined physical closeness to the emperor with a dependence upon him, inevitably giving rise to a whole series of stories about sexual depravity. The continuity of these stories, however, suggests that it was not exceptional for eunuchs to be in a position of proximity to the emperor in the first two centuries of the principate. The many narratives surrounding the well-known eunuchs Sporus and Earinus, who held privileged positions during the reign of Nero and Domitian, highlight how they held sexual power over the emperors as a way to explain their closeness to the emperor. Envy is sometimes apparent, as when Statius writes 'boy dear to the gods, who is chosen to taste the revered nectar before anyone else and so often to hold the mighty hand that the Getae seek to know and the Persians, Armenians and Indians to touch'. Parallels are drawn with Jupiter and Ganymede, perhaps partly to normalise the relations by drawing on divine precedent, making the eunuchs less of a political threat in the process. After all, Ganymede did not dictate whom Jupiter favoured.[102] But the eunuchs' exalted position in the reigns of Nero and Domitian was real.

---

[100] L. Foubert, 'The Lure of an Exotic Destination: The Politics of Women's Travels in the Early Roman Empire', *Hermes* 144 (2016), 462-87; 471-3; P. Christoforou, *Living in an Age of Gold: Being Subject of the Roman Emperor* (PhD Oxford 2016) emphasises how emperors' appropriation of the exotic emphasised their dominion over the entire Roman world. Cf. N. Lindberg, 'The Emperor and His Animals: The Acquisition of Exotic Beasts for Imperial Venationes', *Greece and Rome* 66 (2019), 251-63.

[101] Tac. *Hist.* 2.71.1. Cf. Tac. *Ann.* 15.34.2 on the jester Vatinius who, notwithstanding 'his twisted body' became extremely powerful because of his favour with Nero; B. Kelly, 'Conceptualising the Roman Court', in: Kelly/ Hug, *The Roman Emperor and His Court*, II, 10-31; 18-9 no1.8d-e.

[102] Statius, Silv., 3.4.60-3. On Sporus and Earinus: Tougher, *Roman Castrati*, 33-51, and C. Vout, *Power and Eroticism in Imperial Rome* (Cambridge 2007), 136-212, both with further references. The comparison to Ganymede is in Martial, 9.11, 9.16, 9.36. On the relation between stories about an emperor's sex life and the understanding of imperial power: Vout, *Power and Eroticism*, 5.

Other eunuchs held similar positions, and may even have used their closeness to the emperor to wield political influence. Under Caracalla (198–217), Sempronius Rufus managed the access to the emperor, leading the contemporary senatorial historian Cassius Dio to note: 'what was finally disgraceful and unworthy of the senate and of the Roman people – we had a eunuch to domineer over us'.[103] The tension between institutional advisors and personal favouritism is noticeable. The late-fourth century *Historia Augusta* explicitly contrasts the 'bad' emperor Elagabalus with his 'good' successor Severus Alexander in the power they gave to eunuchs:

> [Severus Alexander] never had eunuchs in his councils or in official positions; these creatures alone cause the downfall of emperors, because they wish them to live like foreign people or as the kings of the Persians, and keep them well removed from the people and from their friends, and they are go-betweens, often delivering other messages than the emperor's reply, hedging him about, and aiming above all to keep knowledge from him.[104]

It is possible that the passage says more about fourth-century perceptions than early-third century practices, yet the idea that eunuchs had already been influential members of the court in the period of the Severans was not outrageous, and apparently believable to a fourth-century audience.

By the time that the *Historia Augusta* was written, the structural position of eunuchs as a relevant factor in palace politics was beyond doubt. This position of eunuchs as an established group holding power is often taken as a key distinction between the courts of the so-called high empire and late antiquity.[105] Both classical and modern historians describe this as an innovation by Diocletian. Frequently, it is linked to the Diocletian's elaboration of court ritual and the imperial costume, possibly influenced by Galerius' (293–311) capture of the Persian harem in 298.[106] An influence from eastern court life would not be surprising, as interchange between the Roman and Persian court can also be recognised at a ceremonial and architectural level, especially after the construction of new imperial

---

[103] Dio, 78 (77), 17.2; A. G. Scott, 'Cassius Dio, Caracalla, and the Senate', *Klio* 97 (2015), 157–75; 165–6 interprets the passage to mean that Rufus managed imperial access.
[104] HA, *Alex. Sev.* 66.3. Cf. 23.4–6; 34.3; 45.4–5.
[105] Most recently, Hug/ Bernstein/ Kelly, 'Court Relationships', 118.
[106] Lactantius, *Death of the Persecutors*, 15, 21; Hopkins, *Conquerors and Slaves*, 172–96, 192–3; C. Mango / R. Scott, *The Chronicle of Theophanes Confessor: Byzantine and Near Eastern History AD 284–813* (Oxford 1997). 13 n. 4. See p. 74 above on the changes in court ritual and imperial clothing.

residences during the Tetrarchy and the reign of Constantine. Eastern monarchies, moreover, had been known for their employment of eunuchs in important positions for a long time.[107] Imperial use of eunuchs in the fourth century, however, also fitted Roman precedent. Neither a transformation under Diocletian nor eastern impact is necessary to understand the position of eunuchs in the late-Roman court. Sporus, Earinus and Sempronius Rufus had held as much influence as their Persian or late-Roman equals, or had at least been believed to hold such influence. Roman authors regularly blamed 'the east' for anything that was not to their liking, and privileged positions for eunuchs did not fit elite expectations of good emperorship. Yet even if the eastern connection was only perceived by these Roman authors rather than the real explanation for the practice, the fact that the emperors persisted despite it is interesting. Ultimately, eunuchs can be placed in a long-established pattern in which Roman emperors limited the power of the institutional elite by placing low-status individuals in positions of power.[108]

None of this is to deny the more systematic influence of eunuchs from the fourth century onwards. Two points stand out. First, eunuchs are increasingly recognised as an influential group in brokering imperial power. Second, the most powerful eunuch came to hold the office of Grand Chamberlain, literally the 'provost of the sacred bedchamber' (*praepositus sacri cubiculi*). He controlled the imperial household and was directly subordinated to the emperor. The chamberlain wielded real political influence and the position was coveted. Already in the late-fourth century it was among the most important offices in the empire. Being chamberlain not only brought power but also gave elevated status. It brought the rank of *illustris* with it, which was reserved for the highest echelons of society – outranking many senators. The high rank of the Grand Chamberlain was set down in law, and other documents make clear that in the late fourth and early fifth centuries the office was fourth in hierarchy of imperial posts in the east and fifth in the west, only outranked by the Praetorian and City prefects, and by the highest military

---

[107] A. Hunnell Chen, 'Rival Powers, Rival Images: Diocletian's Palace at Split in Light of Sasanian Palace Design', in: M. Peachin/ D. Slootjes (eds.), *Rome and the World Beyond Its Frontiers* (Leiden – Boston 2016), 213–42; R. Strootman, 'Eunuchs, Renegades and Concubines: The "Paradox of Power" and the Promotion of Favorites in the Hellenistic Empires', in: A. Erskine/ L. Llewellyn-Jones/ S. Wallace (eds.), *The Hellenistic Court: Monarchic Power and Elite Society from Alexander to Cleopatra* (Swansea 2017), 121–42.

[108] Tougher, *Roman Castrati*, 91; Hopkins, *Conquerors and Slaves*, 188–9. Vout, *Power and Eroticism*, 211 n. 106 explicitly describes Earinus as a prototype for Byzantine court eunuchs.

positions.[109] Like previous prominent eunuchs, the incumbents of the position of Grand Chamberlain were close to the emperor, and their tenure continued only as long as the emperor wanted. Yet, unlike their predecessors, they derived prestige from a defined office, the status of which no longer wholly depended on imperial favouritism, nor on the character of the individual holding the post. Some Grand Chamberlains gained exceptional influence, like Eusebius who occupied the office for all of Constantius' II reign, or Eutropius, who is presented as a leading power under much of Arcadius's reign. Eutropius was even made consul in 399, although he dramatically fell from favour immediately afterwards. Not all Grand Chamberlains wielded as much power, but all of them were central to court politics, as literary and documentary sources indicate clearly.[110] They were imperial favourites, but in a much more institutionalised way than Sporus or Earinus had been.

The establishment of the Grand Chamberlain, supported in his tasks by eunuch officials such as the 'superintendent of the sacred bedchamber' (*primicerius sacri cubiculi*) or the 'steward of the sacred palace' (*castrensis sacri palatii*) showed how eunuchs as a group had taken over some of the roles that freedmen and equites had held before. It also shows a systemisation of court positions, which were emphatically kept out of the hands of members of the traditional elite. The emperor elevated the rank of an office which was only held by people who would be considered social outcasts by most. This undermined the position of the institutional elite. Awarding Eutropius the consulate in 399 must have hammered the message home. It is possible that such structuring of court life, and the increased visibility of eunuchs as a group, was influenced by interactions with the Persian court. It certainly fitted the more monarchical and ornate image and ceremony of the later Roman empire. Still, the tension between an institutional elite and imperial dependents had been a continuous factor in Roman emperorship from the very beginning. Chamberlains and domestic servants who used and abused their power to control access to the emperor feature in almost all stories surrounding 'bad' emperors. Underlying structures of Roman emperorship seem to have changed remarkably little over the centuries, giving rise to a limited set of narratives that described interactions between the emperor and his entourage.

---

[109] *CTh* 7.8.3, 6.8.1, 11.18.1; *CJ* 3.24.3, 12.5.5; *Notitia Dignitatum* Or. 1, Occ. 1; Hopkins, *Conquerors and Slaves*, 174–5.
[110] Tougher, *Roman Castrati*, 82–95, with full references for Eusebius (83–9) and Eutropius (89–95).

Imperial secretaries and domestic servants, and increasingly various eunuchs, all held a defined role at the court. These roles, their titles and the social standing that people could derive from them may have shifted over time, but closeness to the emperor started from a specific task that placed them in imperial vicinity. Another group of people who was expected to form part of the emperor's surrounding often held no defined position at all. Emperors needed to relate to intellectuals such as philosophers, orators, seers and later different kinds of 'holy men', some of them (temporarily) linked to the court, some of them meeting the emperor during his travels. These various individuals could become part of the imperial entourage because of their relationship with the emperor, but also because they had become so well-known in their own right that they inevitably entered into the imperial orbit. Imperial tutors held influence over the emperor through their relationship with the monarch before he had come to power. Emperors were expected to take their opinion into consideration. This was visible from the very beginning of the principate. When in 30 BC Octavian conquered Alexandria, which had been the centre of activities for Cleopatra and Mark Antony, he publicly announced that he would spare the city as a favour to his tutor, the Alexandrian philosopher Areus.[111] Famous examples of influential tutors are Seneca and Fronto, whose correspondence to Marcus Aurelius is sometimes close to a declaration of love. That such an affinity for former tutors remained standard is clear from the fondness with which Julian writes about his childhood teacher, the Gothic eunuch Mardonius, whom he still regularly consulted when emperor. Similarly, Gratian honoured his tutor, the poet Ausonius, and his family when he became emperor, even making Ausonius consul in 379.[112]

Other 'intellectuals' came to the court to become part of the emperor's circle through their reputation. Exemplary are some second- and early-third century men who became prominent in the intellectual circles of the Greek provinces and were called to the emperor because of their local status, such as Hadrian of Tyre (c. 11–193). He was a pupil of the sophist and statesman Herodes Atticus (101–77) in Athens, where he was appointed to the chair of rhetoric. Hadrian of Tyre's repute was such that when Marcus Aurelius visited the city, the emperor wanted to hear him speak. This was apparently impressive. The emperor 'exalted him to the

---

[111] Plut. *Ant.* 80.1–3; *Moralia* 207 B, 814D; Millar, *Emperor*, 9, 85.
[112] Julian, Misopogon, 352–3; A. Richlin, *Marcus Aurelius in Love. The Letters of Marcus and Fronto* (Chicago 2006); Brown, *Through the Eye of a Needle*, 188–9.

skies by grants and gifts', and he was promoted to the chair of rhetoric at Rome. In his later life his reputation grew even further, up to the point that it is alleged that 'even the members of the Senate would rise from their seats, and the members of the equestrian order would rise' when he was about to proclaim. The emperor Commodus reportedly even nominated the octogenarian Hadrian as his *ab epistulis Graecis* – showing how high he had risen in the emperor's esteem from outside a normal position at the court. Similar trajectories are described for Alexander, the 'Clay-Plato' from Seleucia, and Aelius Antipater, who studied under Hadrian of Tyre and is called 'my friend and teacher' by the emperor Caracalla.[113] Similarly, in the fourth and fifth centuries, there were many men of letters from the provinces, often occupying a local oratorical chair, who spoke before the emperor, or corresponded intensely with him, and so gained his appreciation, confident in the expectation that the emperor would appreciate their intellectual skill.[114]

Not all those who surrounded the emperor only praised him. There are many stories about intellectuals criticising emperors. In particular individuals who came to the court through an established reputation of their own could be expected to occasionally contradict the emperor. This was never without risks. The statement by the second-century rhetorician and philosopher Favorinus after a dispute with Hadrian, that the 'most learned man is the one who has thirty legions' was not without grounds. Favorinus, a hermaphrodite from Arles, was apparently so dramatic a speaker that he gained the emperor Hadrian's interest and friendship. He also, famously, disagreed with the emperor. People expected him to consequently fall from favour. Athenian magistrates are said to have run 'to throw down Favorinus' bronze statue as if the man were the Emperor's bitterest enemy'. People in Corinth seem to have done the same, leading Favorinus to react how 'honour, like a dream, taking to the sky flies away'. Philostratus, through whose *Lives of the Sophists* most stories about Favorinus are transmitted, explicitly praises Hadrian for not killing him on the spot. Favorinus was instead exiled to Chios when he lost the emperor's

---

[113] Phil. VS 2.10; 2.5; 2.24; [Galen] *On Theriac to Piso*, 2 (= ed. Leigh 2016, 72); Millar, *Emperor*, 91–3.

[114] Millar, *Emperor*, 98–101; B. Marien, 'Symmachus' Epistolary Influence: The Rehabilitation of Nicomachus Flavianus through Recommendation Letters', in: Choda/ de Leeuw/ Schultz, *Gaining and Losing Imperial Favour*, 105–24.

support.[115] How an emperor reacted to criticism was a powerful narrative about his suitability to rule. Not killing the culprit was a relatively positive reaction. Laughing criticism away was even better. Having people around who dared contradict the ruler gave emperors the possibility to show their benevolence. Sometimes individuals went too far and were exiled or even killed. But throughout Roman history there are stories about individuals disputing with the emperor – almost always people who had become close to the emperor as a result of personal intellectual or religious status.

After the advent of Christianity, the role of the second- and third-century sophists was taken up by holy men. Although they, like bishops, derived their status from religiosity, it was through a non-institutionalised variant. The hagiographic stories surrounding these men form a new and very specific genre of literature, filled with feats of endurance, miracles and demons. But they still included interactions between holy men and the emperor as a matter of course. Perhaps the most extraordinary case is that of the Syrian monk Barsauma (c. 384–c.456).[116] His extensive hagiography, written in Syriac, describes how he was ordained as a deacon (§12.3) but became known because of the various miracles he performed, and through the destruction of pagan temples and idols. Such was his fame that the empress Eudoxia, who was visiting Jerusalem 'sent him a great quantity of gold. He refused the gift. She then sent him a long letter, requesting an interview; so he came to see her and he spoke with her at length. Afterwards, she prostrated herself at his feet' (§83.1–3). He then travelled to Constantinople, where he met with emperor Theodosius (§104–105), who already knew him by reputation (§89.1, 96.12) and had wanted to see him for a long time (§104.1). Barsauma refused the emperor's gifts, and spoke to the emperor 'about the true Faith and a god-fearing way of life' (§104.1). Theodosius was so impressed that he deemed him one of the apostles, and urged him to become archbishop of Antioch and 'father of all the bishops', which Barsauma again refused (§105.1–3). Consequently, the emperor gave him his ring: 'in all simplicity of heart, Barsauma accepted

---

[115] HA, Hadr. 15.13; Phil. VS 2.8. T. S. Barton, *Power and Knowledge. Astrology, Physiognomics, and Medicine under the Roman Empire* (Ann Arbor 1994), 117–8. On the removal of the statue in Corinth and Favorinus' reaction: C. W. Concannon, 'Honor Flits Away as though It Were a Dream. Statues, Honor, and Favorinus' Corinthian Oration', *Classical Philology* 116 (2021), 61–75.

[116] J. Hahn/ V. Menze, *The Wanderings of the Holy Man. The Life of Barsauma, Christian Asceticism, and Religious Conflict in Late Antique Palestine* (Oakland 2020), including a translation by A. N. Palmer (pp. 187–271), also available as A. N. Palmer, *The Life of the Syrian Saint Barsauma. Eulogy of a Hero of the Resistance to the Council of Chalcedon* (Oakland 2020), from which the citations below are taken.

the ring. The emperor did not explain that by giving it to him he was investing him with his own authority' (§105.4). According to the *Life*, Barsauma was then given a crucial role at the council of Ephesus (§106–7). Strikingly, the monk's presence at the synod is confirmed through the *Acts of Chalcedon*, which includes proceedings from the Ephesus council and mentions that 'it has seemed good to our Divinity that the most god-fearing priest and archimandrite Barsauma, renowned for purity of life ... is to sit down with ... all the most holy fathers'. Barsauma was the last person to sign the Acts, showing he held real status there.[117] The claims in his hagiography are doubtlessly exaggerated, but the personal holiness of Barsauma had emphatically brought him into imperial circles. It did not end well. The *Life* (§121–8) has the holy man arrested in the aftermath of the Council of Chalcedon. As the *Acts of Chalcedon* testify, the monk dramatically refused to acknowledge that council's decisions.[118] The *Life* lays blame squarely with Theodosius' successor Marcian and his wife Pulcheria, who 'leaned towards an evil way of thinking' (§116.1). Barsauma curses Pulcheria, and she dies in agony (§128.5). Even the emperor Valentinian III is named, (§120.3, 121.2–3), with the suggestion that Barsauma was on his way to the west to lend him his support against Marcian. Barsauma leaves Constantinople, first for Nicomedia and then, on imperial orders, back to his monastery (§129.1). Numerous miracles follow, as does jealousy from bishops in the area of the monastery, who even write to the emperor to have him arrested again (§152.1–7). Barsauma then makes a glorious statement that through his faith in Christ 'Marcian's authority will never be imposed on me' (§153.1) and he dies amidst various signs (§157). Marcian's death follows soon afterwards (§159.2).[119] These are exalted circles, and it was Barsauma's reputation for personal piety that brought him there. That also gave him the right to criticise emperors, much like sophists had before him. Roman emperors were expected to interact with individuals wielding non-worldly power. How they reacted to these people was a telling indicator of how they used their imperial might.[120]

---

[117] Acts of Chalcedon: I, 47, 109, 1066; S. Corcoran, 'Barsauma and the Emperors', in: Hahn/Menze, *The Wanderings of the Holy Man*, 25–49; 32–4.
[118] Acts of Chalcedon: IV, 77–81, 95; Leuenberger-Wenger, *Das Konzil von Chalcedon*, 278–81, 496.
[119] Corcoran, 'Barsauma and the Emperors', 42–4, 46–9.
[120] Similarly, reactions to astrologers are taken as indications of imperial behaviour, but astrologers did not become members of the court systematically. Tiberius' friend Thrasyllus of Mendes was an exception: Suet. Tib, 14,4, Tac. Ann. 6.20–2; Dio, 55.11.2–3, 58.27.1–2, 58.28.1; Barton, *Power and Knowledge*, 58–62.

An emperor's might was clearly expressed through the soldiers and bodyguards who systematically surrounded him (Figures 1.15 and 3.3). The Roman notion of *potestas* (power) was closely linked with the capacity to unleash violence, which is why in the Republic magistrates and priests, and often also senators and ambassadors, were accompanied by lictors carrying *fasces* which held axes.[121] Emperors inevitably obtained similar rights. More lictors meant more power. Domitian's alleged insistence on employing twenty-four lictors whenever he entered the senate was a clear way of showing his dominance.[122] The emperors' military escort, much like the rest of their entourage, included both 'institutional' members and 'outsiders' appointed directly by the ruler. On the one hand there were Roman soldiers, especially the Praetorian Guard, who for a long time were led by members of the institutional elite. Up to the end of the third century, praetorian prefects tended to be equites, and from the middle of the fourth century senators.[123] Praetorians escorted the emperor and members of his family. Having them assigned to your person was a clear indication of imperial power. When Caracalla was killed, his mother Julia Domna is said to have taken great solace when 'no change was made in her royal retinue or in the praetorian guards in attendance upon her'.[124] On the other hand there were privately owned or recruited 'barbarian' bodyguards. Their role in protecting the emperor went back to the very beginning of the principate. Caesar had already employed German cavalry in Gaul and Spanish guards in Rome. The German bodyguards were inherited by Augustus. Famously, they reacted aggressively to the assassination of the emperor Caligula, slaying some of the conspirators on the spot. This may have been because of devotion to the emperor, but was also a fitting response from people who had been wholly dependent on the man that was just slain. The *Germani* are well attested up to their dismissal by Galba in 69. This did not end the practice of 'barbarian' bodyguards. The *Historia Augusta* refers to the German guards of the 'good' emperors Pupienus and Balbinus as a matter

---

[121] Cic. *QFr.* 1.1.13; F. K. Drogula, 'Imperium, Potestas, and the Pomerium in the Roman Republic', *Historia* 56 (2007), 419–52; 432–4 with further references.

[122] Dio 67.4.3; Suet. *Dom* 14, see p. 71 above.

[123] M. Absil, *Les Préfets du prétoire d'Auguste à Commode. 2 avant Jésus-Christ–192 après Jésus-Christ* (Paris 1997); J. Migl, *Die Ordnung der Ämter. Pratorianerprafektur und Vikariat in der Regionalverwaltung des Romischen Reiches von Konstantin bis zur Valentinianischen Dynastie* (Frankfurt am M. 1994).

[124] Dio 79 (78), 23.2. See p. 227–243 below on imperial wives and mothers as members of the emperor's entourage.

of public knowledge.[125] Most of the fourth-century palace guards, the so-called *Scholae Palatinae*, were represented in typically Germanic dress and recruited from 'barbarian' tribes, most prominently Germans from the Rhine area.[126] In the later empire, Leo I (457–74) founded the Excubitors as an imperial guard. These consisted of Isaurians and would play an important role in imperial politics for the next centuries. Tarasicodissa, better known as the emperor Zeno (474–91), Justin I (518–27), Tiberius II Constantine (574–82) and Maurice (582–602) all rose to the throne from their rank as officer or commander (*comes*) of the Excubitors.[127] A much later example from the eastern empire of private imperial bodyguards who were recruited from outsiders is the so-called Varangian Guard, which consisted of Norsemen.[128]

A successor to the German bodyguard, more institutionalised than the likes of the Varangian Guard, were the so-called *equites singulares Augusti*. These cavalry men were individually selected from non-Roman soldiers along the Rhine and Danube, and were often nicknamed the *Batavi* as they were so similar to the earlier German bodyguard, functioning as the emperor's bodyguard in the city as well as soldiers in the field.[129] Their closeness to the emperor reached its zenith under the reign of Maxentius (306–12), resulting in the actual disbanding of the troops by his opponent Constantine. Apparently the *equites singulares* had been among the first to proclaim Maxentius, and may well have been the last to stop defending him. They may even be depicted on the relief on the arch of Constantine which shows Maxentius' rout. Constantine afterwards clearly felt that the *equites singulares* needed to be punished for this support. He built the Lateran Basilica on the remains of their camp, and the basilica of

---

[125] Caes. *BG.* 7.13.1; Appian, *BC* 2, 109; HA, *Max. et Balb.* 14.2, 14.8; Josephus, *Jew. Ant.* 19.1.15; Suet. *Galba*, 12.2; Millar, *Emperor*, 61–4.

[126] R. I. Frank, *Scholae Palatinae. The Palace Guards of the Later Roman Empire* (Rome 1969), 58–72 with references.

[127] Frank, *Scholae Palatinae*, 204–5, 211–13; B. Croke, 'Leo I and the Palace Guard', *Byzantion* 75 (2005), 117–51. But note how an overview of the 772 men documented as having served in the armies AD 518–610 suggests that there were proportionally more Romans than non-Romans among imperial bodyguards: D. A. Parnell, *Justinian's Men. Careers and Relationships of Byzantine Army Officers, 518–610* (London 2017), 56–7, figs. 3.1–2, 59.

[128] R. D'Amato, *The Varangian Guard 988–1453* (Oxford 2020). The guard was active from the tenth to the fifteenth century.

[129] Herodian 1.8.6, with A. Galimberti, *Erodiano e Commodo. Traduzione e commento storico al primo libro della Storia dell'Impero dopo Marco* (Göttingen 2014), 89; Millar, *Emperor*, 63; C. J. Fuhrmann, *Policing the Roman Empire: Soldiers, Administration, and Public Order* (New York 2012), 128–9.

Marcellinus and Peter, and his own mausoleum, in their cemetery, using their own gravestones.[130] Constantine's removal of a group of soldiers that had become a factor in acclaiming the emperor recalls Galba's dismissal of the German bodyguard. It did not mean an eradication of imperial bodyguards. When Constantine took his seat at the assembly of Nicaea, the absence of the bodyguards 'who usually accompanied him' was noticeable (Figure 3.3) and in contrast to the celebrations of his twenty-year rule, when 'detachments of the bodyguard and other troops surrounded the entrance of the palace with drawn swords'.[131] Emperors were expected to be surrounded by military men who were directly loyal to him. Marcus Aurelius' statement that Antoninus had taught him that it was 'possible to live in a palace and yet not need a bodyguard' shows that this was the exception, not the rule.[132] And such bodyguards needed to be replaced when they had been too close to an opponent, even if that meant disbanding a unit that had long been part of the emperor's entourage.

Throughout Roman history, the emperor was surrounded by men whose status depended on him, either because he had given them official posts or assigned them to duties linked to his personal comfort or safety. Yet the court was also filled with men whose intellectual or religious renown had made them unavoidable, and with senators (and later bishops) whose social status was such that they at least needed to be included as representatives of their group. Both the 'emperor's men' and members of the 'status group' held important military and administrative positions. When the great command and governorships were taken away from senators in the course of the third century, other positions, such as that of praetorian prefectures, came in their place. And throughout Roman imperial history, the emperor had the practical power to appoint whomever he chose in whatever position he felt necessary.[133] Even the power of the great fourth- and fifth-century generals who acted as 'protectors' for child emperors remained at some risk of imperial involvement. Flavius Aetius effectively managed the western empire for over two decades, but was still disposed and killed by Valentinian III (454), although this was a short-lived success for the

---

[130] *Pan. Lat*, 12 (9), 17.1; Zosimus 2.16; M. Speidel, 'Maxentius and His *Equites Singulares* in the Battle at the Milvian Bridge', *Classical Antiquity* 5 (2) (1986), 253–62; 257–9, 260–2 pl.1–3; P. Liverani 'Introduzione topografica', in: ibid. (ed.), *Laterano 1. Scavi sotto la basilica di S. Giovanni in Laterano. I materiali* (Rome 1998), 7–16; 15.
[131] Eusebius, *Life of Constantine*, 3.10.2; 3.15.2; Millar, *Emperor*, 66.
[132] Marc. Aur. *Med*. 1.17. Herodian 1.4.4 attributes a similar sentiment to Marcus.
[133] Parnell, *Justinian's Men*, 77–93 highlights how Justinian systematically appointed people close to him, such as family members and members of his personal guard, to senior generalships.

emperor, whose death followed within half a year.[134] Valentinian II had been less successful in dismissing Arbogast in 392, who is said to have taken up his command without proper imperial appointment and to have claimed 'You neither gave me the command, nor can deprive me of it', when the emperor handed him his dismissal from the imperial throne.[135] The emperor's death shortly afterwards and his replacement by Arbogast's puppet Eugenius suggest that Arbogast was right, but it is important to remember that the only way in which Arbogast could continue after his imperial dismissal was by removing the emperor. Simply ignoring him was not an option.

The combination of people at the court who had access to the emperor, from palace staff to generals, continuously influenced the emperor. An important analysis of the reign of Nero has recently drawn attention to the way in which these various individuals could band together and function as an 'establishment team', dampening the impact of individual imperial wishes. In this way, the excesses of malfunctioning emperors could be avoided.[136] Such systematic collaboration between members of various power groups runs counter to most of our literary narratives. These emphasise competition between the disparate groups, with ad hoc alliances made and broken continuously.[137] Yet, friends and advisors – official and unofficial – did have a shared interest in keeping the imperial system going and may well have cooperated under various emperors. Often, they must have been able to modify some of the emperor's ideas which they did not agree with. Doubtlessly, also, much of the daily affairs of court life, and (minor) requests coming the emperor's way, would have been dealt with by the emperor's entourage without direct imperial involvement – although the Roman emperor was expected to react to requests in person more than was the case in other monarchical systems.[138]

Whether the influence of such 'establishment teams' changed over time is difficult to say. On the one hand, monarchical power was more openly expressed from the fourth century onwards (although alternatives continued to circulate). On the other, there is the assumption that the imperial system of the later period – the more formalised administrative and court structures especially of the eastern part of the empire and the court at

---

[134] See p. 130 above. [135] Zosimus, 4.53.2-3; Kulikowski, *The Tragedy of Empire*, 119.
[136] J. F. Drinkwater, *Nero: Emperor and Court* (Cambridge 2019), 56–65, 81–2.
[137] Hug/ Bernstein/ Kelly, 'Court Relationships', 79. Cf. J. Duindam, *Dynasties: A Global History of Power, 1300–1800* (Cambridge 2016), 291.
[138] This is one of key notions of Millar, *Emperor*. See also p. 160–1 above.

Constantinople – could more robustly resist imperial interventions.[139] There are fewer stories about 'mad' emperors from the early fourth century onwards, although the narratives surrounding the reigns of Zeno (474–91) and his opponent Basilicus (475–6) are similar in hostility to those of the likes of Domitian and Caracalla, including derision of their physical appearance.[140] No establishment team seems to have been able to curb the extremes of Justin II's foreign affairs. He was, however, fairly rapidly replaced by Tiberius II (574–82) after he went openly insane sometime after 572.[141] Whether that rapid replacement is taken as sign of a more robust imperial system, or the lack of intervention in foreign affairs as a sign that individual imperial decisions remained difficult to curb is a matter of perspective. Throughout the centuries of Roman imperial rule, there are stories of servants ruling as powers behind the throne and of emperors on the loose whose erratic behaviour cannot be contained by their advisors. There was not only tension within the imperial entourage between members of the institutionalised elite and those whose influence depended on their closeness to the emperor, but often also between the emperor himself and the people who surrounded him.

The Imperial Family

Closeness to the emperor was a competitive commodity. This put members of the emperor's family in a prominent position. Roman expectations about family relationships were such that most relatives were assumed to have easy access to their relative. Many of them did. Immediate and more distant relatives, from uncles and aunts to sisters and sons, could become powerbrokers at the court or in Roman society at large, receiving requests, dispensing patronage, and being flattered with honours.[142] The position of

---

[139] M. Kulikowski, 'How to End a Dynasty. Rehabilitating Nero', *London Review of Books* 42.6 (2020).

[140] A. Laniado, 'Some Problems in the Sources for the Reign of the Emperor Zeno', *Byzantine and Modern Greek Studies* 15 (1991), 147–74; Baldwin, 'Physical Descriptions of Byzantine Emperors', 15–16.

[141] Jones, *Later Roman Empire* I, 306; J. Kroll/ B. Bachrach, 'Justin's Madness: Weak-Mindedness or Organic Psychosis?', *Journal of the History of Medicine and Allied Sciences* 48 (1993), 40–67; 40–4.

[142] A. Hug, 'The Imperial Family', in: Kelly/ Hug, *The Roman Emperor and His Court*, I, 60–84; J. Paterson, 'Friends in High Places: The Creation of the Court of the Roman Emperor', in: A. J. S. Spawforth (ed.), *The Court and Court Society in Ancient Monarchies* (Cambridge – New York 2007), 121–56; 141.

very close relatives, especially brothers and sons, was both stronger, and fraught with more risk than that of more remote members of the family. Brothers and sons were, after all, from the very beginning of the empire the obvious candidates for co-rulership and potential rivals. But all male members of the family, including sons-in-law, could become emperors in their own right. Consequently, they tended to be either trusted allies taking on important positions, or removed because they posed a threat. Women could not rule on their own in Rome, but they played a prominent role in dynastic considerations, something which was well advertised and recognised throughout the empire.[143] Female members of the imperial family could supply legitimacy to imperial claims of their men (husbands, sons or even grandsons). These could become a threat to the emperor, the women themselves a powerful voice in the emperor's ear. The influence of sisters, daughters, mothers and wives (and mistresses) on the emperor features continuously in ancient narratives. Many of the stories are negative and hyperbolic. Elite authors found it already problematic that lower-status individuals could influence imperial decisions. Having women meddle in politics was even more troubling.[144]

At the same time, inhabitants of the empire found it unproblematic to petition an emperor's wife, and expected that request to be taken seriously. When sometime before 19 BC, Augustus' wife Livia tried to obtain freedom of taxation for the people of Samos, the emperor felt forced to publicly explain why he turned her down:

> You yourselves are able to see that I have awarded the privilege of freedom to no people except the Aphrodisians, who were on my side in the war and were made captives because of their goodwill towards us. Indeed, it is not right that the greatest privilege of all should be granted indiscriminately and without cause. I am sympathetic to you and I wish I could oblige my wife, who is active on your behalf, but not to the extent that I abandon my usual practice.[145]

Even more public was the recognition of Livia's position in the so-called *Senatus consultum de Cn. Pisone patre* (SCPP), a senatorial decree put up throughout the empire in AD 20, which explicitly stated that Livia was 'most worthy of the state not only because she gave birth to our emperor [Tiberius] but also because of her many and not insignificant favours

---

[143] Hekster, *Emperors and Ancestors*, 111–59.
[144] See especially N. Purcell, 'Livia and the Womanhood of Rome', PCPS 212 (1986), 78–105.
[145] Reynolds, *Aphrodisias and Rome*, no. 13; Hug/ Bernstein/ Kelly, 'Court Relationships', 104 no. 3.27; 105–6 no. 3.29. See p. 234–5 below.

towards men of each order – although she, by right and by merit ought to possess the greatest influence in the things which she asked of the Senate, she made very sparing use of it'.[146] The passage recognises the empress's influence and praises her for not using it too often. By this stage, of course, Livia had changed from emperor's wife to imperial mother, another much-discussed role in imperial historiography.

The involvement of Livia, both as a wife and mother, in imperial decisions is in striking contrast to the narratives surrounding Caesar's mother Aurelia, or his wives Pompeia and Calpurnia. They are mainly mentioned in the context of private affairs, although Pompeia's presumed affair with Clodius had political consequences. Precedent for Livia's position is found with Mark Antony's wife Fulvia (at the time Caesar's mother-in-law), whose influence was presumed to be such that contemporary sources blame her for conducting state business. Her likeness may well have been depicted on coins, and her name was engraved on graffiti on sling bullets used during the War of Perusia (41–40 BC). Perhaps inevitably, her posthumous reputation suffered.[147] From the reign of Augustus onwards, however, female members of the imperial household are said to have intervened in public affairs as a matter of course, and documentary evidence shows that they regularly did. Looking at the involvement of mothers, wives, mistresses and other female members of the imperial family over several centuries shows noticeable continuity in the expectation that various people had of the behaviour of these women, and of the emperor's reactions to them, although there seems to have been a shift after the Roman empire became Christian.

There are, as so often when looking at Roman emperorship, different narratives in different media that continuously recur. Many of these are morally laden. One set of stories is about women, in particular mothers and wives, who are too dominant and ambitious. These almost inevitably include references to sexual licentiousness, including incest, and also to scheming and poisoning opponents so as to better their own position or that of their relatives or lovers. The best-known examples are probably those surrounding Agrippina Minor (15–59). They include her lack of boundaries by convening senators on the Palatine so that she could

---

[146] *SCPP* 119–20; C. Kunst, *Livia. Macht und Intrigen am Hof des Augustus* (Stuttgart 2008), 76–7.
[147] Cic. *Phil.* 2.95; 3.4; 3.10; 5.11; 5.22; *Att.* 14.12.1; Martial 11.20; *CIL* 11.6721.3–5, 6721.14; *RRC* 489/5, 489/6, 494/40, 514/1; *RPC* I, Eumenea, 3139. Cf. Dio 48.4.1 R. A. Fischer, *Fulvia und Octavia: Die beiden Ehefrauen des Marcus Antonius in den politischen Kämpfen der Umbruchszeit zwischen Republik und Principat* (Berlin 1999), 48, 160; L. Foubert, 'Crowded and Emptied Houses as Status Markers of Aristocratic Women in Rome: The Literary Commonplace of the *Domus Frequentata*', *EuGeStA* 6 (2016), 129–50, 312–38.

Figure 3.4 Agrippina and Nero 54, Rome, Aureus (7.59 g): Nero and his mother are looking at each other on the obverse of this coin, and her name AGRIPP AVG DIVI CL AVD NERONIS CAES MATER is in the surrounding legend, making her the dominant figure; the emperor's name and titles NERONI CLAVD DIVI F CAES AVG GERM IMP TR P are relegated to the reverse of the coin, surrounding an oak wreath and the letters EX SC. *RIC* 1 (2nd ed.), Nero, 1

Source: ANS 1905.57.291, American Numismatic Society

overhear what was said and intervene, the strong suggestion that she poisoned her husband Claudius to boost her son Nero's chances to the throne, and stories alleging that she first seduced her uncle Claudius, and then had incestuous relations with her son after he had gained the throne.[148]

Agrippina clearly did have a prominent position at the court, perhaps indicated most clearly by the presence of her portrait alongside that of the emperor on coins from the beginning of Nero's reign (Figure 3.4). The position was widely recognised, as her visibility in statue groups, monumental art and provincial coinage makes clear.[149] Similar stories exist surrounding other influential empresses throughout the ages, such as Julia Domna (c. 160–217), whose public status is clear from coins, inscriptions and monuments, and who is accused of incest with Caracalla and

---

[148] [Ps] –Seneca, *Octavia*, 31, 44, 102, 164–5; Pliny *N.H.* 22.92; Juv. *Sat.* 5.147, 6.620–1; Martial 1.20.4; Tac. *Ann.* 12.66; 12.67.1; 13.5; 14.2; Suet. *Claud.* 44.2, *Nero* 28.2; Dio 61.34.1–4; J. Aveline, 'The Death of Claudius', *Historia* 53 (2004), 453–75; J. Ginsburg, *Representing Agrippina: Constructions of Female Power in the Early Roman Empire* (Oxford – New York 2006), 9–54, 107–12; 120–32.

[149] Hekster, *Emperors and Ancestors*, 129–34 with references.

rising above her station.[150] Likewise, the prominence of Eudoxia is beyond doubt, as is that of Theodora (c. 500–48), who was even explicitly included in the oath that governors took when they acceded to office. The extremely negative assessment of the empress in the *Historia Arcana* of the contemporary historian Procopius (c. 500–after 565) includes capricious and transgressive behaviour, manipulation and the use of magic (no poison this time). There are no allegations of incest and adultery, but much emphasis on sexual depravity before she married Justinian, including having abortions and killing an embarrassing son.[151] The continuity of the literary commonplaces with which these imperial women were diminished is striking, and shows how the notion of a powerful woman influencing the emperor was a continuous problem for male elite authors.[152]

The continuity of stories also suggests that such powerful women were a regular occurrence. Negative narratives not only aimed to reduce their reputation, but often also that of the emperor who allowed them such prominence. This could be by describing the emperors as equally debauched, like the stories accusing Caligula and Domitian of incest with their sister and niece, or Nero and Caracalla with their mothers.[153] More commonly, however, the stories of dominant women aimed to emasculate the emperor. Claudius is a famous example of such criticism in the earlier principate, but very similar comments are found regarding Constantius II. The latter is said to have been 'too trusting of his friends and companions and subsequently, too, excessively influenced by his wives' by Eutropius (c. 320–c. 390) and 'to an excessive degree under the influence of his wives, and the shrill-voiced eunuchs' by Ammianus Marcellinus.[154] Alternatively,

---

[150] Herodian 4.9.3; HA, *Caracalla*, 10.4, 11.5; C. Davenport, 'The Sexual Habits of Caracalla: Rumour, Gossip, and Historiography', *Histos* 11 (2017), 75–100; Hekster, *Emperors and Ancestors*, 143–53.

[151] Justinian, *Novella* 8, oath; Procopius, 9.19; 13.19; 17.17.2; 22.27–8; E. A. Fischer, 'Theodora and Antonina in the Historia Arcana: History and/or Fiction?', *Arethusa* 11 (1978), 252–79; 266–7, 270–2. On Eudoxia, see p. 200, 220 above.

[152] M. Icks, 'Agrippina, Theodora and Fredegund as Evil Empresses in the Historiographic Tradition', in: S. A. Samoilenko/ M. Icks/ J. Keohane/ E. Shiraev (eds.), *Routledge Handbook of Character Assassination and Reputation Management* (New York 2019), 183–95; L. Foubert, 'Literary Constructions of Female Identities. The Parallel Lives of Julio-Claudian Women in Tacitus' *Annals*', in: C. Deroux (ed.), *Studies in Latin Literature and Roman History*. Vol. 15 (Brussels 2010), 344–65; 345–9.

[153] Suet. *Cal.* 24.1; Dio 59.11.1; Suet. *Dom.* 22; Dio 67.3.2; Pliny min., *Ep.* 4.11.6–7; Herodian 4.9.3; HA, *Sev.* 20.2; 21.7; *Carac.* 10.1–4; Victor, *Caes.* 21.2–3; *Epit. de Caes.* 21.5; Eutrop. 8.20; Orosius. 7.18.2; Davenport, 'The Sexual Habits of Caracalla', 77–9, 84–90.

[154] Eutr. 10.15; Amm. Marc. 21.16.16; S. Tougher, 'Eusebia and Eusebius: The Roles and Significance of Constantinian Imperial Women and Court Eunuchs', in: N. Baker-Brian/ S. Tougher (eds.), *The Sons of Constantine, AD 337–361* (Cham 2020), 185–220; 185–6;

'good' emperors could face this criticism, although in these cases blame falls more heavily on the dominant woman than on the emperor. As formulated in Herodian's death notice of Severus Alexander '[his reign] might have won renown for its perfection had not his mother's petty avarice brought disgrace upon him'.[155]

There were, then, regularly recurring negative narratives about women and their undue influence on emperors, who by implication had been too weak to resist this female cunning. Yet there was also a different set of much more positive stories. These consisted of a narrative tradition which was effectively the inversion of the negative stories, describing women who closely stuck to the social conventions of Roman *matronae*, such as Octavia the Younger or the elder Faustina.[156] But there are also positive stories about strong women working with their emperor. Surprisingly, Suetonius and especially Cassius Dio are fairly positive about Vespasian's mistress Caenis (d. 74), even though she was a freedwoman. Dio notes how 'she was exceedingly faithful and was gifted with a most excellent memory'. Moreover, ancient authors emphasise how Vespasian treats her like his lawful wife. There is criticism, especially when Dio notes how 'she received vast sums from many sources, sometimes selling governorships, sometimes procuratorships, generalships and priesthoods, and in some instance even imperial decisions'. This does not, however, lead to a final negative judgement of Caenis. Indeed, some of the blame is taken away from the mistress and placed on the emperor: 'while it was Caenis who received the money, people suspected that Vespasian willingly allowed her to do as she did'.[157] Nor are all the stories about Livia and Julia Domna negative ones.

In the later empire, empresses who intervened with their husband or sons on behalf of Christians could even be praised for their involvement in imperial decision making. Constantine's mother Helena (c. 246–c. 330) springs to mind, whose influence on her son, alongside the legend that she brought

---

A. Wieber, 'Eine Kaiserin von Gewicht? Julians Rede auf Eusebia zwischen Geschlechtsspezifik, höfischer Repräsentation und Matronage', in: A. Kolb (ed.). *Augustae. Machtbewusste Frauen am römischen Kaiserhof? Herrschaftsstrukturen und Herrschaftspraxis II* (Berlin 2010), 253–75.

[155] Herodian 6.9.8; K. Laporte/ O. Hekster, 'Herodian, Memory and judgement: Emperors and their Death', in: A. Galimberti (ed.), *Herodian's World: Empire and Emperors in the Third Century* (Leiden – Boston 2022), 88–109.

[156] E. Hemelrijk, 'Octavian and the Introduction of Public Statues for Women', *Athenaeum* 93 (2005), 309–17; Roller, *Models from the Past*, 197–232.

[157] Dio, 65.14.1–4; Suet. *Vesp.* 3.3; M. B. Charles/ E. Anagnostou-Laoutides, 'Vespasian, Caenis and Suetonius', in: C. Deroux (ed.), *Studies in Latin Literature and Roman History* 16 (2012), 530–47; A. Tatarkiewicz, 'Caenis. Augusta in All but Name', *Classica Cracoviensia* 15 (2012), 223–9.

the True Cross to Rome, has made her an important figure in Christian historiography. Bishop Paulinus of Nola (c. 354–431) even claimed that Helena was the emperor's co-ruler, and that her faith, alongside that of her son allowed the emperor to rule.[158] In the first half of the fifth century, Aelia Pulcheria (398/9–453) is perhaps the most extraordinary example of a powerful woman with a positive reputation. She was an important influence on her young brother Theodosius II, taking so much responsibility that she became known as the emperor's guardian. In this role, she made sure he was properly trained in Christian doctrine. Strikingly, she 'devoted her virginity to god', and forced her sisters to do the same, in order 'to remove any opportunity for the plots of ambitious men', according to the extremely positive description by Sozimus.[159] Pulcheria's role increased even further after Theodosius' death in 450. For a month, she seems to have been in sole control, then took Marcian (450-7) as her husband, whom she is said to have crowned herself and who accepted his wife's vow of virginity. Remaining unmarried and at the head of the empire was apparently not an option, but there was little doubt who was in control. Correspondence between Pulcheria and the Roman pontiff Leo shows her dominance in imperial religious policy of the time. This was further confirmed when, at the Council of Chalcedon, Pulcheria was acclaimed in equally laudatory terms as her husband. She is explicitly praised because she 'drove out the heretics' and is hailed as the new Helena. Marcian, accordingly, was named the new Constantine.[160] This is a striking example of an influential empress who was positively acclaimed, even gaining a posthumous sainthood, without negative reflections on her husband. In the west, Galla Placidia (388/9 or 392/3–450) played a similar role, although stories of incest with her brother

---

[158] Paulinus of Nola, *Epistolae*, 31.4; D. Angelova, 'The Ivories of Ariadne and Ideas about Female Imperial Authority in Rome and Early Byzantium', *Gesta* 43 (2004), 1-15; 3; J. W. Drijvers, *Helena Augusta. The Mother of Constantine the Great and the Legend of Her Finding of the True Cross* (Leiden – Boston 1992), with 39–54 on her role at Constantine's court; L. Brubaker, 'Memories of Helena: Patterns of Imperial Female Matronage in the Fourth and Fifth Centuries', in: K. James (ed.), *Women, Men and Eunuchs: Gender in Byzantium* (London 1997), 52–75.

[159] Soz. 9.1.2–4; 9.1.8; Joh. Chrys. *De inani gloria*, 78, 83; K. G. Holum, *Theodosian Empresses: Women and Imperial Dominion in Late Antiquity* (Berkeley – Los Angeles 1982), 79–111; A. Busch, *Die Frauen der Theodosianischen Dynastie. Macht und Repräsentation kaiserlicher Frauen im 5. Jahrhundert* (Stuttgart 2015), 110–25.

[160] Zon. 13.24; Malalas 14.3–4, 14.27–8; Leo, *Letters* 30–1, 45, 60, 70, 77, 79, 84, 95, 105, 115; *Acts of Chalcedon* 6.11, 6.13, 6.15, 6.20; R. Price/ M. Gaddis, *The Acts of the Council of Chalcedon*. Vol. 1 (Liverpool 2005), 39, 88–9; Holum, *Theodosian Empresses*, 208–16; Busch, *Die Frauen der Theodosianischen Dynastie*, 125–35. Note the negative image on Pulcheria in the *Life of Barsauma*, which did not agree with the Council of Chalcedon, see p. 221 above.

Honorius indicate a more traditional discontent with her powerful position from the side of elite authors.[161]

There are more positive narratives about powerful empresses in the period after Constantine than before. That suggests some sort of shift in the fourth century towards a greater acceptance among the elite of the influence that these imperial consorts wielded. It coincided with greater acceptance of an openly monarchical imagery of the emperor, and with increased recognition of eunuchs as group of imperial powerbrokers. Equally importantly, it matched a period of systematic dynastic succession. Continuous dynastic rule had similarly raised the profile of the Antonine and Severan women. In the second and third centuries, however, imperial women had mainly been presented in relation to matters connected to family life, the continuity of the dynasty, and relating to the private sphere. Even a title such as *Mater Castrorum* (mother of the military camps), with clear military connotations, emphasised the motherly role. After the imperial conversion to Christianity, a new role for empresses developed which fell somewhere between the public and private domain. They could become pious and outspoken Christians. In that capacity, they could impinge on roles that had been out of bounds before.[162] Theodosius' II military successes against the Persians in 421 were explicitly linked to the piety of his sisters, as fragments of an inscription on the base for a (lost) monumental statue of the emperor at Constantinople make clear: 'Victor, through the vows of his sisters' (Figure 3.5). The reverse of solidi struck for Pulcheria between 450 and 453 show the goddess Victoria with the legend VICTORIA AVGGG (victory of the Augusti). It is tempting to suggest that GGG stands for three Augusti, which then must be Marcian, Valentinian III and Pulcheria, although it must be emphasised that fifth-century coins were far from systematic in matching GG or GGG (occasionally even GGGG) with the number of Augusti. There had been earlier examples of empresses who were linked to Victoria, but never with such explicit reference to victory through specific actions.[163]

---

[161] Busch, *Die Frauen der Theodosianischen Dynastie*, 86–109 with references.
[162] S. Joska, "Show Them that You Are Marcus's Daughter' The Public Role of Imperial Daughters in Second- and Third-Century CE Rome', in: J. Rantala (ed.), *Gender, Memory, and Identity in the Roman World* (Amsterdam 2019), 105–30; L. Foubert, 'Men and Women Tourists' Desire to See the World: "Curiosity" and "a Longing to Learn" as (self-) Fashioning Motifs (First–Fifth Centuries C.E.)', *Journal of Tourism History* 10 (2018), 5–20; 13–16; Hekster, *Emperor and Ancestors*, 144–6, 196.
[163] *LSA* 31; Dumbarton Oaks, Byzantine Collection, 48.17.1183; Angelova, 'The Ivories of Ariadne', 9, with fig. 11; Grierson/ Mays, *Catalogue of Late Roman Coins*, 85–6. On earlier empresses and Victory: T. Mikocki, *Sub specie deae. Les impératrices et princesses romaines assimilées à des déesses: étude iconologique* (Rome 1995), 115–16.

Figure 3.5 Victory through vow. Inscribed proconnesian marble fragment from a monumental column of Theodosius II, found at Bakirköy; from the Hebdomon, Constantinople. Gardens of Hagia Sophia (Istanbul). Original column shaft h. 11.25 m; diam. 1.50 m.
The reconstructed inscription shows the religiosity of Pulcheria and her sisters as intrinsic part of Theodosius' military successes:
LSA 31

> *Domino nostro Theodosius pius felix Augustus/* Our Lord, pious and fortunate Theodosius Augustus
> *Imperator et fortissimus triumphator/* Commander-in-chief, mightiest, triumphant
> *gentium barbararum, perennis et ubique/* Over barbarian nations, always and everywhere
> *victor, pro votis sororum pacato/* Victor, through the vows of his sisters, having pacified
> *orbe romano celsus exultat/* The Roman world, rejoices on high

Source: David Hendrix/The Byzantine Legacy ©

Literary portrayals of imperial women form highly biased evidence for imperial women's positions and for the acceptance of those positions. The texts, after all, show a male elite perspective. For many Romans, the prominent status of the emperor's wife and mother (and of his sisters and aunts too) was expected and apparently unproblematic, as is indicated by other types of ancient sources. Livia's intercession on behalf of the people of Samos is only one example of an established pattern of inscriptions which indicates that towns or individuals asked and received favours of imperial women. This is, perhaps, unsurprising considering their influence with the emperor and their individual wealth.[164] Many towns, moreover, struck local coins with the portraits of imperial wives, mothers and sisters on them, often in combination with locally relevant goddesses, or erected statues for the empresses, as part of a statue group or as sole recipient. The aim was to flatter these imperial women and establish links to them, in the expectation that this would boost a town's status – if not with the empresses themselves then with the neighbouring towns.[165] None of these actions make much sense if the position of the imperial women was as contested at the local level as it was by the writing elites of Rome, and to a lesser extent Constantinople.

That the empresses' importance was deemed acceptable by large numbers of people well before the fourth century is also clear from their prominence in centrally broadcast imperial images. Coins were struck on behalf of empresses and other female members of the imperial family, especially but by no means exclusively during the Antonine and Severan dynasty, and again in the fifth century (Graph 3.1a). These were coins that showed the empress' portrait on the obverse, issued in her name.[166] Strikingly, the messages on the reverses of these coins were not for the most part dynastic (Graph 3.1b). Images of the empresses' cult and devotion dominate for most of the period, to be replaced by military messages in the fourth- and fifth century, mainly through the image of the goddess Victoria, but also through the legends SALUS REI PUBLICA (Safety of the state), CONCORDIA MILITUM (unity of the soldiers) and, to a lesser extent, FIDES MILITUM (loyalty of the soldiers). Before the fourth century, imperial women were mostly linked to goddesses like Ceres, Venus, Juno, and Vesta, adhering to female virtues such as beauty, fecundity and fidelity. Yet empresses were also compared to Concordia, Felicitas, Pax, Pietas, Salus,

---

[164] *AE* 1891.20; *ILS* 7784, ll. 1–17; *CIL* 14.3579; *AE* 1920.53, ll. 21–3; Joseph. *AJ* 18.164–7; Fronto *Ad Ant. Imp.* 2.1; Hug, 'The Imperial Family', 70–1.

[165] E. Hemelrijk, *Hidden Lives, Public Personae. Women and Civic Life in the Roman West* (Oxford – New York 2015), 150–2, 169, 296, 308; Hekster, *Emperors and Ancestors*, 129–31, 138–9, 148–50, 159.

[166] C. Rowan, 'The Public Image of the Severan Women', *PBSR* 79 (2011), 241–73; 271–2 suggests a special *officina* (workshop) that produced coin types for the Severan imperial women. Taking the important Reka Devnia hoard as basis, rather than the type selection of RIC, only increases the dominance of coins showing imperial women. For both the Antonine and Severan dynasties, 14 per cent of RIC coin types show a member of the imperial family who is not the emperor or his heir. In the Reka Devnia hoard this becomes 31 per cent (Antonine) and 21 per cent (Severan), mainly through coins showing the deified Faustina Maior, Faustina Minor and Julia Domna. I owe this point to Sven Betjes.

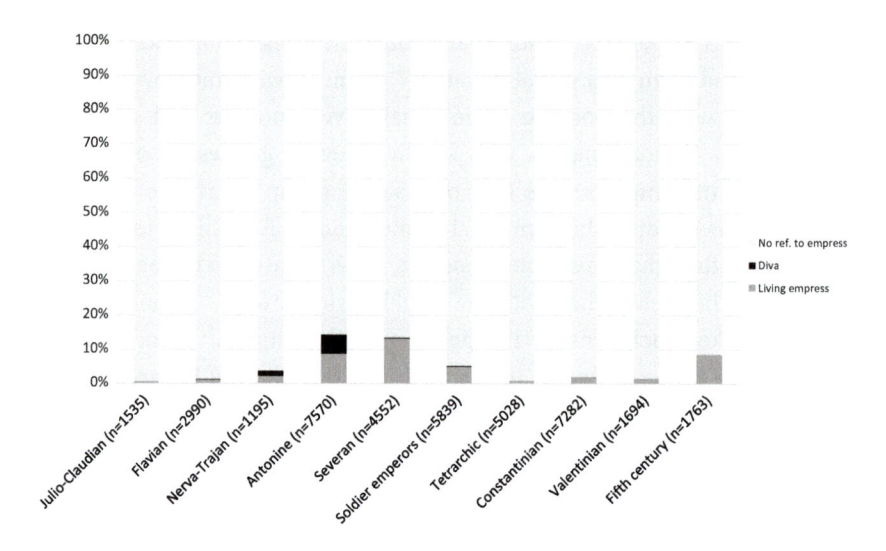

Graph 3.1a Number of coins struck for empresses

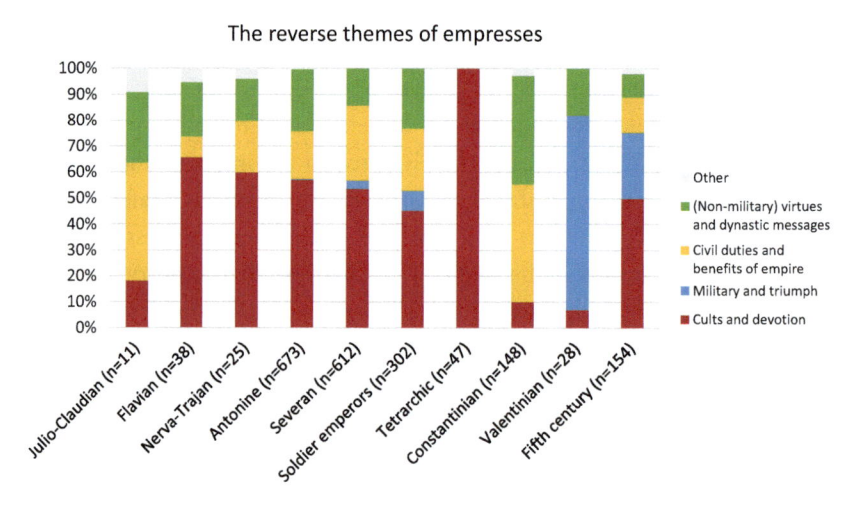

Graph 3.1b Messages on coins struck for empresses

Securitas and Victoria well before the fourth century – not only on central coins but also through gems, statuary and provincial coinage.[167] Clearly, distributing images of empresses as a dominant force beyond their dynastic role was deemed unproblematic.

[167] Mikocki, *Sub specie deae*, 94–5, 98, 107–8, 110–12, 115–16.

The numbers rise further if coins are included that show imperial women on the reverse as well – suggesting closeness to the emperor rather than a position in their own right.[168] The first living woman to appear on coinage was Augustus' daughter Julia, who figured on the reverse of silver denarii accompanied by her sons Gaius and Lucius. The image was accepted without much criticism as a portrayal of dynastic continuity. The next numismatic depiction of imperial women was much more contested. In AD 37, sesterces depicted Caligula's three sisters identified by name in the legend, which contributed to rumours about the emperor's unnatural closeness to them.[169] Still, portraying imperial women on coins rapidly became normal practice, certainly in the eastern provinces. Only the appearance of Agrippina alongside her son on the obverse of *aurei* in AD 54 provoked discussion (Figure 3.4).[170] Even such a combination of an emperor and empress on the obverse normalised in the course of time, as did images of the emperor with his (grand)mother. Jugate portraits of, for example, Julia Domna with Septimius Severus or Caracalla, Julia Maesa with Severus Alexander, or Tranquillina with Gordian III appear on provincial coinage and glass intaglios (Figure 3.6). Central coins show Gallienus (260–8) alongside his wife Salonina.[171]

Regular sculptural depictions of empresses, in buildings, as part of statue groups or in historical reliefs further illustrate the often-uncontested expectation that imperial women played an important role in the emperor's entourage.[172] Even in Rome, Augustus found it unproblematic to construct the so-called porticus Octaviae, named after his sister (and Antony's ex-wife) as early as 27 BC.[173] Various buildings named after imperial

---

[168] Hekster, *Emperors and Ancestors*, 112, table 2.

[169] *RIC* 1², Caligula 33, 41; Augustus 404–5.

[170] Hekster, *Emperors and Ancestors*, 124–5 with references. The Agrippina coin was anticipated by a less frequently discussed *cistophorus* from Ephese (50/51) showing Claudius and Agrippina on the obverse: *RIC* 1², Claudius 119.

[171] I. Varbanov, *Greek Imperial Coins and Their Values* (Bourgas 2005–7), 852, 1029, 1049, 1629, 2048; British Museum 1923,0401.818; *RIC* 5, Gallienus and Salonina (2) 1, 3; L. Yarrow, 'Markers of Identity for Non-Elite Romans: A Prolegomenon to the Study of Glass Paste Intaglios', *Journal of Ancient History and Archaeology* 5 (2018), 35–54; 41; C. Hotalen, *Embodying the Empire: Imperial Women and the Evolution of Succession Ideologies in the Third Century* (PhD University of South Florida 2020), 142–3.

[172] K. Fittschen, 'Courtly Portraits of Women in the Era of the Adoptive Emperors (98–180) and Their Reception in Roman Society', in: D. E. E. Kleiner/ S. Matheson (eds.), *I, Claudia: Women in Ancient Rome* (New Haven 1996), 42–52; M. T. Boatwright, 'Just Window Dressing? Imperial Women as Architectural Sculpture', in: D. E. E. Kleiner/ S. Matheson (eds.), *I, Claudia II: Women in Roman Art and Society* (Austin 2000), 61–75.

[173] A. Viscogliosi, 'Porticus Octaviae', *LTUR* 4, 141–5.

Figure 3.6 The Emperor and empress together. Marcianopolis AD 210–211, bronze Pentassarion (12.81 g). Septimius Severus and Julia Domna are shown facing each other, identified by the legend ΑΥ Λ ϹΕΠ ϹΕΩΗΡΟϹ ΙΟΥΛΙΑ-ΔΟΜΝΑ-ϹΕ/ The unity of Marcianopolis is shown through the figure of Homonoia, addressed by name, ΥΦΛ ΟΥΛΠΙΑΝΟΥ ΜΑΡΚΙΑΝΟΠΟΛΙΤΩΝ, holding cornucopiae and patera. I. Varbanov, *Greek Imperial Coins And Their Values*, no. 861
Source: Numisbids, 6 February 2020, lot 646

women would follow. Many of these buildings and other monuments emphasised the role of women as part of the ruling imperial family. This made the position of imperial women different from that of individuals whose influence depended solely on their closeness to the emperor. Female members of the imperial family, unlike these other individuals, could ensure continuity of the dynasty. That made them a potential powerbase in their own right, which could not be easily ignored. This is an important aspect underlying the stories of promiscuity, which showed the risks of men gaining status by sleeping with imperial women, and attacked the legitimacy of these women's children. The vow of virginity by Pulcheria and her sisters was a rather extreme action to prevent such stories. It ensured that no other men would be able to threaten the position of her brother Theodosius, since it took away the possibility for members of elite families to marry into the imperial household. But the vows of chastity also gravely endangered the continuity of the Theodosian family when Theodosius died childless, and were not to be repeated.[174]

---

[174] M. McEvoy, 'Celibacy and Survival in Court Politics in the Fifth Century AD', in: Tougher, *The Emperor in the Byzantine World*, 115–34. Cf. A. Hunnell Chen, 'Omitted Empresses: The (Non)role of Imperial Women in Tetrarchic Propaganda', *Journal of Late Antiquity* 11 (2018), 42–82; 57–69 on the inclusion of empresses in dynastic and non-dynastic ideology in the first three centuries AD, and their absence in Tetrarch imagery.

The position of imperial women was similar to that of other favourites in that it was never institutionalised. The first time the *cognomen* Augusta was given was by the senate to Livia after her husband's death, as part of the stipulations of his will. Caligula bestowed it upon his grandmother Antonia the Younger at the beginning of his reign. Agrippina received it a year after she married Claudius, when the latter adopted Nero as his son and heir. Poppaea Sabina, Nero's wife, became Augusta when their daughter Claudia – who received the name Augusta at birth – was born in AD 63. Unlike the bestowal of the name Augustus, it was never settled on who, or when someone, became Augusta. Under some emperors only wives received the name, often (but not always) after the birth of their first child. Under other emperors (grand)mothers, sisters and nieces were honoured in this way, and sometimes there was no Augusta at all. During the so-called Gallic Roman empire (AD 260–74), only Victoria, the mother of Emperor Victorinus (AD 269–70) seems to have received the *cognomen*. Matters did not clarify in the fourth and fifth century. Effectively, the ruling emperor decided, although people must have increasingly expected imperial wives to be named Augusta at some stage of their lives.[175]

Other titles and honorifics for empresses remained similarly undefined. Like the name and image of the emperor, there was some inflation and increased ostentation over time, but also clear differentiation between different groups, media, and areas. Livia, for instance, was explicitly named MATER PATRIAE (Mother of the Fatherland) on coins from Lepcis Magna, an honorific which the emperor Tiberius is said to have refused her at Rome.[176] In the late second and third centuries, only Faustina the Younger, Julia Domna and Julia Mamaea were named *Mater Castrorum* (Mother of the Camps) through coins or inscriptions that were clearly sanctioned from the centre. But local coins and inscriptions through which subjects appealed to the empresses' good will awarded the title to a further ten empresses. Similar differences can be found for the honorifics *Mater Senatus* or *Mater populi Romani*.[177] These

---

[175] A. Kolb, '*Augustae* – Zielsetzung, Definition, prosopographischer Überblick', in: Kolb, *Augustae*, 11–35; 14–17. She supplies a complete overview of all Augustae up to 548, and the moment they received the name, with full references (23–35); Kienast/ Eck/ Heil, *Römische Kaisertabelle*, 47–50.
[176] RPC I, nos. 849–50; Tac. *Ann.* 1.14. 1–4; Dio 57, 12.4–6.
[177] Hotalen, *Embodying the Empire*, 31, 43, 47, 156–8; Hug, 'The Imperial Family', 69; Underlying data can be found at: http://hennarot.forest.usf.edu/main/other/severan/. See also J. Langford/ C. Hotalen, 'Mater Castrorum: A History of Imperial Women and Succession Ideology', in: L. L. Brice / E. M. Greene (eds.), *Women and the Roman Army* (Cambridge, forthcoming).

types of honorifics became more common in the third century. They were not new. Even the grandiose title *Mater universi generis humani* (mother of the entire human race) that can be found on a statue base honouring Julia Mamaea from New Carthage (Spain) was anticipated in earlier times. Livia was already addressed as 'originator of the world' by coins from Romula and an inscription from Anticaria (both in Spain).[178] In the fourth and fifth century, the depiction of empresses with diadems and *paludamenta* on central coinage suggests some sort of official confirmation of the status of imperial women. The same is indicated by the depiction of Theodora in the San Vitale mosaic in a purple robe, wearing a diadem of precious stones, or by early-sixth century ivories showing empresses as authoritative figures in their own right.[179] It had been unacceptable for the Roman elite when Agrippina had worn a *chlamys* and had 'sat in state before the Roman standards'.[180] By the sixth century that had changed. Empresses could now be depicted as co-rulers without much apparent debate. But whether they obtained that position was never systematised.

An important reason for empresses to be publicly presented as a figure of power was when they formed a dynastic lynchpin. The various monuments, inscriptions and coins for the different imperial women who linked the adoptive emperors of the second century, such as the elder and younger Matidia, illustrate that.[181] The most spectacular example is probably the empress Ariadne (c. 450–513/515), daughter of Emperor Leo I (457–74) and Aelia Verina (d. 484), who was the sister of Emperor Basiliscus (475–6). When Leo fell ill, he made Ariadne's son Leo II co-ruler at the age of six. A few months later, in January 474, Leo I died and his grandson became sole ruler. Ariadne's husband, the Isaurian Zeno, was made co-emperor shortly afterwards, to rule on his own after Leo II's death in February of the same year. It was a troubled reign, interrupted by a revolt led by Ariadne's mother Verina and her uncle Basiliscus. After that was put down, Zeno remained in control till his death in 491. He was succeeded by Ariadne's new husband, the palace administrator Anastasius I (491–518), then in his sixties, who was chosen over Zeno's brother Longinus. The important point is that the legitimacy of Leo II, as a very young grandson, Zeno, as a foreigner and Anastasius, chosen in preference to the former emperor's brother, wholly

---

[178] *CIL* 2.3413; *CIL* 2.2038; *RPC* I, no. 73.
[179] Angelova, *Ivories of Ariadne*, 2–4, with full references; K. Schade, *Frauen in der Spätantike – Status und Repräsentation. Eine Untersuchung zur römischen und frühbyzantinischen Bildniskunst* (Mainz 2003), 108–11.
[180] Tac. *Ann.* 12.37.4; 12.56. See p. 228–9 above.
[181] C. Bruun, 'Matidia die Jüngere – Gesellschaftlicher Einfluss und dynastische Rolle', in: Kolb, *Augustae*, 211–33; Hekster, *Emperors and Ancestors*, 139–43.

Figure 3.7 The hierarchical place of the empress. Constantinople, 517, Diptych leaf, ivory (h. 36.2.cm, w. 12.7.cm), V&A 368-1871.
Anastasius, identified as V(ir) INL(ustris) and CONS(ul) ORD(inarius) is shown with the consular sceptre and ceremonial robes. Over his head are (from left to right) the busts of his fellow-consul Pompeius, the emperor Anastasius and Ariadne. On the throne are images of gorgons and personifications of Rome and Constantinople. The consul is flanked by small victories on a globe
Source: © Victoria and Albert Museum, London

depended on their link to Ariadne.[182] Consequently, Ariadne's image was widely promulgated, and her surviving visual representations, on coins and ivory, show her authority. On ivory diptychs from 517, which celebrate the consulate of Anastasius, the emperor's eponymous great-nephew, three clipeate portraits are shown above the enthroned consul (Figure 3.7). The emperor is at the centre, but Ariadne's posthumous portrait is on his right, making hers the second-most important image, outranking that of the second consul Pompeius on the left. It indicates how Anastasius' throne still depended on his late wife's birthright.[183] Ariadne was also widely represented through marble and bronze statues and busts when she was still alive. These were found in Constantinople, for instance on pedestals near the Chalke Gate, but also elsewhere. Surviving busts from Rome and Niš (Serbia) testify the distribution of her image in east and west.[184]

Elite narratives and local and central imagery suggest a greater acceptance of powerful empresses from the fourth century onwards.[185] It seems that in a Christian empire, women of the imperial family could gain influence through the traditional female virtue of piety. Yet, as we have seen throughout this book, much of what became normalised in the later period of Roman imperial rule was foreshadowed in earlier times. Moreover, different narratives continued to exist alongside one another. The negative stories surrounding Eudoxia and Theodora are remarkably similar to those critiquing Livia or Julia Domna, even if it had become unexceptional to depict empresses with diadems and in purple robes. What was deemed normal may have shifted over time, but how to condemn women who transgressed that normality had not. Finally, the position of Roman imperial women shows once more how difficult it is to place Roman emperorship in the bandwidth of rulers surrounded by hangers-on who are wholly dependent on them and monarchs interacting with an institutionally based entourage. Female relatives of the emperor could be said to be neither, which may

---

[182] A. McClanan, *Representations of Early Byzantine Empresses: Image and Empire* (New York 2002), 66–8; M. McEvoy, 'Leo II, Zeno, and the Transfer of Roman Imperial Rule from a Son to His Father in 474 CE', in: J. W. Drijvers/ N. Lenski, *The Fifth Century: Age of Transformation* (Bari 2019), 197–208; 204–7. On Zeno, see p. 223 above. On the practice of making young heirs co-emperor, see p. 249–50 below.

[183] Victoria and Albert Museum, London, inv: 368–1871; McClanan, *Representations of Early Byzantine Empresses*, 74–7; M. Meier, 'Ariadne – Der "Rote Faden" des Kaisertums', in: Kolb, Augustae 277–91; 287–90.

[184] LSA, nos. 109, 496, 755–7, 2750; D. Stutzinger, 'Das Bronzbildnis einer spatantiken Kaiserin aus Balajnac im Museum von Nis', *Jahrbuch für Antike und Christentum* 29 (1986), 146–65; McClanan, *Representations of Early Byzantine Empresses*, 83–9.

[185] Schade, *Frauen in der Spätantike*, 156–7.

explain some of the variations of the stories surrounding them. Dynastic considerations were of the utmost importance for their position. Many women became Augusta after giving birth. But this was never formalised, as the virgin empress Pulcheria shows. Whether wives, mothers or even sisters were dominant – and how dominant they could be – depended on their character and on the specific context of a reign.

The position of Roman imperial women at the court became normalised but never formalised. A similar lack of structure surrounded the appointment of imperial heirs. In practice, Roman emperorship was dynastic from the very beginning. Octavian's claims to power rested on being Caesar's adopted son and heir, and his own successors were for generations drawn from the Julio-Claudian household. Throughout Roman imperial history, only violent succession could bring people who were not members of a dynasty to power, and even they often claimed to be related to successful predecessors. How closely someone was related to a reigning emperor was a factor. Sons could not be ignored, but when they were not around (which was often) adopting a more remote male member of the family was always a possibility.[186] The importance of dynastic succession notwithstanding, there was no formal way in which succession was organised. Considering the lack of a clear definition of Roman emperorship, this is hardly a surprise. The result was that the status of a presumed heir, and the expectations of the role he played, remained similarly undefined. There were, of course, shifts over time, but as we have seen throughout this book, these were often a normalisation of earlier practices. Different narratives and practices, moreover, continued to exist alongside one another.

Male members of the imperial family, including sons-in-law, or sons of empresses by previous husbands, could be presented as hope for the future and guarantors of continuity, but they were also possible loci of unrest. The many stories surrounding empresses' infidelities are directly linked to this. Any man with a direct link to the ruling family could be perceived as a candidate for the throne. Brothers were particularly difficult, especially for rulers who inherited the throne young. It is hardly surprising that neither Britannicus (41–55) nor Geta (189–211) survived their brother's accession to the throne for long. Famously, Tacitus describes the execution of Agrippa Postumus (12 BC–AD 14), just after Augustus died, as 'the first crime of the new regime'.[187]

---

[186] O. Hekster, 'All in the Family. The Appointment of Emperors Designate in the Second Century A.D.', in: L. de Blois (ed.), *Administration, Prosopography and Appointment Policies in the Roman Empire* (Amsterdam 2001), 35–49.

[187] Tac. *Ann.* 1.6.1.

Men with a more distant link to an emperor could also be a threat. Commodus, Septimius Severus and Caracalla killed off all men whose lineage could be traced back (through marriage or direct descent) to the families of Marcus Aurelius or Lucius Verus, when they showed even the merest hint of political ambition.[188] Rome never developed a systematic way to deal with these threats, unlike, for instance, the fourteenth-century kingdom of Ethiopia, where all male members of the royal family, except those who received specific dispensation, were sent to the 'Mountain of the Kings'. There they and their descendants lived under armed guard. Equally rigorous is the so-called *Zanan-nameh* issued by the Ottoman Mehmed II (1451–81), who claimed the title *Qayser-i Rûm* (Caesar of Rome). It stated: 'The majority of legists have declared that those of my illustrious children and grandchildren who shall ascend the throne shall have the right to execute their brothers, in order to ensure the peace of the world.' This remained Ottoman practice until the early seventeenth century.[189] Nothing similar exists for Rome. Many male members of the family met an untimely end, but no emperor could simply execute his siblings without pretext and the risk of serious loss of reputation.

Deciding who was the presumed heir was equally undefined. Sons were always expected to follow in their father's footsteps, but more often than not Roman emperors died without a son. Child mortality was one reason for this. The absence of ways of (almost) guaranteeing an heir was another. Roman emperors, like all elite Roman men, practised serial monogamy. For obvious reasons, this limited the numbers of legitimate heirs. The Roman empire was an exception in this respect: most non-Christian pre-modern societies allowed multiple wives for one man (polygyny). In dynastic settings, polygyny was even more common, even when that went against wider societal norms. The need to guarantee an heir and peaceful transition of power overruled sexual standards. Roman emperors must have been well aware of this practice, considering Roman contacts for example with Macedonia, Egypt and Persia. Yet it never became acceptable for Roman emperors to keep various mistresses alongside a wife – let alone institute a harem.[190]

---

[188] H. G. Pflaum, 'Les gendres de Marc-Aurèle', *JS* 1 (1961), 28–41; Hekster, *Commodus*, 26–7.

[189] F. A. Dombrovski, 'Internment of Members of the Royal Family in Ethiopia, Turkey, and India', *Rassegna di Studi Etiopici* 31 (1988), 45–57; 46–7; 55–6 and J. Duindam, *Dynasties: A Global History of Power, 1300–1800* (Cambridge 2016), 132–6, both with further references.

[190] W. Scheidel, 'Sex and Empire: A Darwinian Perspective', in: I. Morris/W. Scheidel (eds.), *The Dynamics of Ancient Empires: State Power from Assyria to Byzantium* (Oxford 2009), 255–324; 282; Duindam, *Dynasties*, 110–13; 119–21; E. D. Chrol/ S. Blake, 'Sexuality and the Court', in: Kelly/ Hug, *The Roman Emperor and His Court*, I, 349–70; 350–4.

The Roman way to guarantee imperial heirs was by giving noticeable honours to, and ultimately adopting, more remote male family members. Consequently, there was much anticipation about who would be the presumed heir in the absence of natural sons. Augustus' long-lasting reign, with prominent positions for the emperor's nephew Marcellus, his son-in-law Agrippa, his wife's son (and son-in-law after the death of Agrippa) Tiberius, and his grandsons Gaius and Lucius set the tone. The harsh banishment of Augustus' daughter Julia in 2 BC, after accusations of adultery and without any trial, suggests that men linked to imperial daughters gained instant importance in matters relating to succession.[191] Still, some patterns and expectations about who was to be the emperor's heir were rapidly established. Intended successors received special honours when they were still very young, such as an early consulate, portraits on coins, or the honorific *princeps iuventutis* (Figure 1.4). Triumphal arches, altars, temples and other public buildings erected throughout the empire indicated both central promotion of young princes and local expectations about how to honour them. From the reign of Vespasian onwards, a practice developed in which the ruling emperor indicated his heirs by bestowing the name Caesar on them.[192]

It could, however, long remain unclear who was going to be the ultimate successor – especially since brothers were often both publicly promoted. Such images may have meant to broadcast the general message that the imperial family was flourishing and that there were candidates for succession in the family, guaranteeing a smooth transfer of power in due course. They also led to fierce speculation about who was the favourite heir. Local honours for various men of the imperial household show who people in the different areas of the empire thought to be the main candidates for the throne. Attempts to eradicate names and tear down statues of the men who fell out of favour at the earliest opportunity show how closely succession was watched. The eradication of images of those who had fallen from grace was noticeable, and involved systematic iconoclasm, often leaving bare places in texts or monuments (Figure 1.14).[193] Occasionally news seems to have spread rather slowly all the same. People at Amisus (Pontus) still

---

[191] E. Fantham, *Julia Augusti: The Emperor's Daughter* (London – New York 2006), 85–91; 138–46.

[192] Zanker, *Power of Images*, 221; M. Hammond, 'The Transmission of the Powers of the Roman Emperor from the Death of Nero in A.D. 68 to that of Alexander Severus in A.D. 235', *Memoirs of the American Academy in Rome* 24 (1956), 63–33; 78–95.

[193] E. R. Varner, *Mutilation and Transformation. Damnatio Memoriae and Roman Imperial Portraiture* (Leiden – Boston 2004), with a full overview into the fourth century.

included Britannicus in an imperial statue group sometime between AD 63 and 65, apparently not aware of (the rumours of) Nero's involvement in his brother's death.[194]

The best way to remove doubt was by elevating someone to co-Augustus and have him reign jointly with the current emperor to ease the transition of power. Even then, a frontrunner for succession could die prematurely, throwing everything into chaos. Cabals and unrest at the court were rife. This was an important reason why emperors publicly promoted clear heirs. In that way, they could simultaneously broadcast the status of their prospective heirs and stress the stability that dynastic continuity would bring.[195] The latter certainly becomes clear from Vespasian's coins, almost 40 per cent of which show his sons Titus and Domitian as successors, ensuring a peaceful transition of power, in contrast to the civil war that followed the end of the Julio-Claudian dynasty. Septimius Severus, after yet another civil war, placed similar emphasis on his two sons Caracalla and Geta, emphasising the benefits of a guaranteed 'prospective' lineage. Even in times of peace the safety that undisputed heirs provided was a message worth putting forward. Under Antoninus Pius, large numbers of *aurei* show a personification of Pietas holding the globe, standing between two children. The suggestion is that the emperor will do his duty by leaving his dominion over the world to his heirs, the young (adopted) Marcus Aurelius and Lucius Verus. It is tempting to link this emphasis on Antoninus' coins to the chaotic situation in the last years of Hadrian, when his intended Caesar and heir, Lucius Ceionius Commodus (102–38), died when the emperor was already ill, and to the previous chaotic succession of Trajan by Hadrian, whose ultimate claim to succession was a doubtful adoption document, signed by Trajan's wife Plotina.[196]

Heirs could greatly benefit from experience in the roles that they were to take on as emperor. The bestowal of military commands, important priesthoods, or major administrative roles could indicate who was considered a candidate for succession. Titus' and Caracalla's positions as frontrunners

---

[194] SEG 16 (1959), no. 748; Hekster, *Emperors and Ancestors*, 133.

[195] A. Mlasowsky, '*Nomini ac fortunae caesarum proximi*. Die Sukzessionspropaganda der römischen Kaiser von Augustus bis Nero im Spiegel der Reichsprägung und der archäologischen Quellen', *JDAI* 111 (1996), 249–388; Hekster, *Emperors and Ancestors*, 117–18, 127–30, 144.

[196] Hekster, *Emperors and Ancestors*, xxix, 86, 90–1, 149–52; C. Rowan, 'Imaging the Golden Age. The Coinage of Antoninus Pius', *PBSR* 82 (2013), 211–46; A. R. Birley, *Hadrian: The Restless Emperor* (London – New York 1997), 289–90; Y. Roman/ B. Rémy/ L. Riccardi, 'Les Intrigues de Plotine et la succession de Trajan. À propos d'un aureus au nom d'Hadrien César', *REA* 111 (2009), 508–17.

were made clear in this way, at the cost of their younger brothers Domitian and Geta. The latter, for instance, was only made co-Augustus in 209, more than a decade after his brother, who was only a year older.[197] Giving such a position to an heir was a good way to prepare him for emperorship. The imperial family also took a monopoly in holding triumphs and (from Domitian onwards) in organising spectacles in Rome, to make sure that only the emperor and his household could gain popular support in this way.[198] These honours and important positions were kept in the family to avoid outside threats to the throne, although it created the possibility for inside threats. Emperors had to trust the male members of the family with whom they surrounded themselves. Their dependence on these men could lead to purges, when emperors perceived their position to become threatened. Septimius Severus, and Gordian III had to deal with an extremely powerful son-in-law or father-in-law, whom they had made their praetorian prefect, and who ended up being too powerful for safety. They were consequently killed and their loss of position and life advertised to the empire at large. Occasionally emperors acted too late. Numerian's (283–4) father-in-law and prefect Aper is said to have killed his son-in-law.[199]

In the troubled third century, with regular rebellions, it was important to have a dependable praetorian prefect, and emperors sought safety in family. Pupienus and Albinus are claimed to have appointed Pupienus' older relative Pinarius Valens, Tacitus (275–6) his maternal half-brother Florianus.[200] The importance of a trustworthy praetorian prefect is best exemplified by Vespasian, who appointed Titus to the post. In the aftermath of civil war, when the Flavian claim to the throne was not yet firmly established, Vespasian's eldest son and main heir was the most suitable person to entrust his safety to. How closely Vespasian and Titus worked together is also clear

---

[197] *CIL* 8.2465 (= 17953); *AE* 1995.1165; *IAM* 2.350; *AE* 1930.111; *RMD* 3.191; Hug, 'The Imperial Family', 62–3; F. Kemmers, 'Out of the Shadow: Geta and Caracalla reconsidered', in: S. Faust/ F. Leitmeir (eds.), *Repräsentationsformen in severischer Zeit* (Berlin 2011), 270–90. Note the dominance of military themes on the reverses of *princeps iuventutis* coins: Ellithorpe, *Circulating Imperial Ideology*, 167.

[198] M. Beard, *The Roman Triumph* (Cambridge [Mass.] 2007), 297–302, H. Flower, 'Augustus, Tiberius, and the End of the Roman Triumph', *Classical Antiquity* 39 (2020), 1–28, arguing that Augustus wanted to abolish the triumph altogether; T. Wiedemann, *Emperors and Gladiators* (London – New York 1995), 8.

[199] Herodian, 3.11–12; Dio 78 (77). 1–6; HA, *Gordiani* 23.6, 27.2; Aur. Vict. *Caes.* 38.6–8; Eutr. 9.18.2; *Epit. de Caes.* 38.4–5. Hug, 'The Imperial Family', 63–4. See p. 210 above on Plautianus and Sejanus and p. 222 on praetorian prefects.

[200] HA, *Maximus and Balbinus*, 4.4, 5.5; Zonaras, 12.29. Julius Julianus was the father-in-law of Constantine's half-brother Julius Constantius, but served as praetorian prefect under Constantine's opponent Licinius.

from their seven joint consulates and a joint position as censor (73–4). Having to settle the empire after the civil war did not benefit Titus' reputation, but it did make clear to everyone that he was the intended heir.[201]

Imperial sons had little to gain from their father's death. Their position depended on dynastic claims. They had more to gain from smooth succession than from an abrupt death of their father. That may have been slightly different when there were younger brothers around, whose status could in time outgrow theirs. Even then, risks outweighed possible benefits. There are rumours surrounding the death of Claudius at a time when the adopted Nero was clearly more senior than the emperor's natural son Britannicus (although Agrippina rather than Nero is blamed for this), or about the death of Septimius Severus, which at that time benefited Caracalla more than Geta. But such stories are rare, and inevitably part of conspiracy narratives aimed to blacken the reputation of emperors who went against senatorial expectations, such as the claim of Cassius Dio that Marcus Aurelius died 'by the act of his physicians, as I have been plainly told, who wished to do Commodus a favour'. Not even other authors who are negative about Commodus echo the story.[202] Possibly, Constantine's eldest son might have been part of a conspiracy against his father. That, at least, is one explanation for his unexpected execution in 326, followed shortly afterwards by the death of his stepmother Fausta. It is also possible that he was instead the victim of machinations by Fausta, who tried to boost the chances of succession for her own three children. The situation remains unclear and exceptional. Smooth succession was the ideal, but throughout Roman history, inter-family killing was an often resorted-to method to guarantee an uncontested transfer of power.[203]

On the whole, bestowing major offices and responsibilities on sons was a good way to show stability of rule. It made clear to everyone who the presumed heir was, and allowed that heir to gain a reputation in the roles on which he was going to be judged as an emperor. It is small wonder then that emperors involved their sons at the earliest opportunity. How young that was shifted over time. Augustus had been eighteen when Caesar died. Nero was seventeen when he became Augustus, but he had been admitted into the major priestly colleges when he was fourteen. Commodus was thirteen when

---

[201] Levick, *Vespasian*, 202–5 with full references.
[202] Dio, 72 (71), 33.4²; Herodian 3.15.2; Laporte/ Hekster, 'Herodian, Memory and Judgement', 95–8. See p. 229 above for accusations against Agrippina.
[203] T. D. Barnes, *Constantine: Dynasty, Religion and Power in the Later Roman Empire* (Hoboken 2011), 144–9; Varner, *Mutilation and Transformation*, 221–2.

he was admitted into these priestly colleges, even before he received the toga of manhood (*toga virilis*). He was made co-Augustus at the age of sixteen. Caracalla was made Caesar and perceived as *particeps imperii* (partner in rule) before he was eleven, or even nine (his date of birth is unsure), and elevated to Augustus a year later. Severus Alexander was made Caesar and heir at thirteen, at the same time as he was adopted by Elagabalus and received his *toga virilis*. Macrinus (217–18) made his son Diadumenianus Caesar when he was eight, and Philippus, son of Philip Arabs (244–9) was proclaimed Caesar when he was either six or seven, and Augustus at nine or ten. Licinius junior, the son of Constantine's opponent Licinius, was even proclaimed Caesar at the age of two. These could be seen as more than mere token appointments. Dio criticises the emperor Macrinus, of whom he was a contemporary, for omitting his son's name in a letter to the senate, although he had 'named him Caesar and emperor'.[204]

It is possible that the dynastic instability of much of the third century made it important for emperors to stake dynastic claims as soon as possible. Yet, whatever the reason, by the fourth century appointing sons as heirs or even co-rulers at a young age had become a matter of routine, and people throughout the empire expected these boys to be presented as such, as inscriptions honouring young princes make clear. Nobody will have thought that a two-year-old waged war or dictated policy, but real positions – even if possibly only honorary ones – were given to teenage heirs without discussion.

When, in 367, Valentinian I proclaimed his son Gratian co-emperor at the age of eight, he was following precedent and expectation. There was an element of innovation involved: Ammianus Marcellinus protested that Valentinian overstepped the traditional order in making Gratian co-Augustus, rather than Caesar.[205] Also, from the Valentinian dynasty onwards, Caesars disappear from central coinage, although junior Augusti are still included. But the actual elevation of Gratian seems to have been unproblematic. Valentinian was ill when he appointed his son, and there was discussion at court about who would replace him. Experienced military men were rumoured to be frontrunners, perhaps indicating that Gratian

---

[204] Kienast/ Eck/ Heil, *Römische Kaisertabelle*, 53, 88, 140, 157, 163, 165, 170, 192. Caracalla as *particeps imperii*: *CIL* 8.1211 = 22851. Criticism on Macrinus: Dio 79 (78).37.6–38.2. The age of Saloninus (son of Gallienus) and Tetricus II (son of Tetricus I) is not known, but they too seem to have been proclaimed Caesar and Augustus in childhood. Cf. McEvoy, *Child Emperors*, 3–4.

[205] Amm. Marc. 27.6.16, McEvoy, *Child Emperor Rule*, 49.

was too young to be taken seriously by at least some factions at the court. Still, Valentinian

> purposed to bestow the imperial insignia upon his son Gratian, who had by this time nearly reached the age of puberty. And when everything was ready, when the soldiers had been won over to accept this with willing minds, and Gratian had appeared, the emperor advanced into the plain and mounted the tribunal; then, surrounded by a brilliant assemblage of men of high rank, he took the boy by the hand, led him into their midst, and commended the future emperor to the army.[206]

Apparently it had not been difficult to convince relevant groups of Gratian's new role. Nor was this mere lip-service to a dying monarch. Gratian would survive his father's death, and rule in his own name, although greatly influenced by his *magister militum* Merobaudes and his tutor Ausonius. Gratian's survival on the throne may have set the precedent for the so-called child emperors of the fourth- and fifth-century Roman west, although at sixteen he was not much younger than Nero had been when becoming sole emperor. His appointment as heir, moreover, fitted existing patterns of behaviour. The systematic way in which young emperors like Honorius II or Valentinian II and III afterwards came to play a ceremonial role, 'supervised' by their great generals, was new, although people continued to expect emperors to take up their traditional roles.[207] The appointment of young sons as heir and co-regents became fully normalised, and as close to a formal procedure as any aspect of Roman emperorship ever became. This may be one reason for the relative absence, from the Theodosian age onwards, of imperial family group imagery that includes women among the emperors and their heirs. Statues, busts and coins still depict empresses, but the dynastic message on these coins became less pronounced, and they were rarely included in images of emperors and their sons.[208] Perhaps it had become so self-evident how succession worked that it was no longer necessary to portray imperial women in their motherly role.

When the position of the heir was contested, and depended strongly on the status of his mother, women were still brought into family compositions. An exceptional and important example of this is the Stilicho diptych,

---

[206] Amm. Marc. 27.6.4; Zos. 4.12.1; McEvoy, *Child Emperor Rule*, 48–50; D. Potter, *The Roman Empire at Bay. AD 180–395* (London – New York 2004), 540–1.
[207] See p. 129–30 above.
[208] N. Kampen, *Family Fictions in Roman Art* (Cambridge – New York 2009), 133.

Figure 3.8 Stilicho's family: 396, Ivory diptych (h. 32.2 cm, w. 16.2 cm), Monza, S. Giovanni Battista, Duomo Treasury.
The two panels of the diptych show on one panel (originally the left) a military man with a spear and shield, and on the other a high-ranking woman and a small boy, holding the codicils of office. The only figures who could be depicted are Stilicho with his wife Serena and their son Eucherius. The inclusion of Serena shows her importance for the position of Stilicho and especially Eucherius
Source: CKD – Radboud University Nijmegen

a late-antique ivory family scene now in the Treasury of the cathedral of Monza (Figure 3.8). It shows the *magister militum* Stilicho, his wife Serena, who was the niece and possibly adopted daughter of Theododius I, and their son Eucherius. Their daughters Maria and Thermantia, respectively first and second wife of Honorius, are not included in the scene. It was through Serena that Eucherius could be presented as a grandson of Theodosius, 'born to rule', a candidate to marry Theodosius' daughter Galla Placidia. These notions were explicitly put forward by the poet

Claudian in his panegyrics to the general.[209] The diptych sent out the same message, portraying Eucherius as possible heir to the throne of the western empire. This did not meet normal expectations, and the inclusion of Serena aimed to bring imperial status to Stilicho's household.

Similarly, the dominant presence of the Ostrogothic queen Amalasuntha (526–35) on the so-called Orestes diptych from 530 results from the precarious position of her son Athalaric (526–34). On the diptych, Amalasuntha's clipeate portrait occupies the top right position, which indicates higher authority than the portrait of Athalaric on the left (cf. Figure 3.7).[210] She was the daughter of Theodoric and acted as queen regent for Athalaric, who was ten years old when his grandfather passed away, four years after the death of Eutharic, Athalaric's father. Eutharic had been the obvious heir to Theodoric, and the accession of Athalaric brought tensions to the fore between Amalasuntha who wanted to raise her son in Roman traditions, and members of the Gothic elite who pursued a more Gothic military training for their king. Amalasuntha's portrayal as superior queen, similar in attire to Byzantine empresses like Ariadne, was part of a power struggle in which Athalaric was an important pawn. In such a contested context, the young heir was visually accompanied by his mother.[211] After Athalaric died, he was succeeded by his mother's cousin Theodahad (534–6), showing how the rules of succession remained fluid even in late antiquity, at least in the western kingdoms. The political instability that followed was one excuse for Justinian and Belisarius to intervene and start the last attempt to unify the eastern and western Roman empire.[212]

For the whole period under discussion in this book, the position of imperial heirs was dependent on the reigning emperor while he was alive. A reigning emperor's son could never be ignored, but his status was strengthened by honours which his father could bestow upon him from a young age onwards. When there was no son, any man related to the imperial family was a possible heir, and the emperor decided whom to

---

[209] Claudian, *Cons. Stil. iii*, 176–81, *Cons. Stil ii*. 339–61; Zos. 5.32.1; A. Cameron, 'The Status of Serena and the Stilicho Diptych', *JRA* 29 (2016), 509–516; 511–12; Kampen, *Family Fictions*, 123–6.

[210] Diptych of Orestes, Victoria and Albert Museum, London, inv. 139–1866.

[211] McClanan, *Representation of Early Byzantine Empresses*, 79–81. Cassiodorus positively contrasts Amalasuntha with Gallia Placidia, unsurprising considering his adherence to Theoderic: Cassiod. *Variae*, 11.1.9–11; Busch, *Die Frauen der Theodosianischen Dynastie*, 103. See p. 42 above on Theodoric.

[212] Heather, *Rome Resurgent*, 150–3.

honour, elevate or execute. The combination of a dynastic principle and lack of a clear hierarchy of succession within the dynasty made discussions about who would be heir a continuous potential source of unrest. The many stories about cliques at court supporting one candidate over the other, and the recurring accusations of conspiracies and adultery are a reflection of an atmosphere in which succession was of the utmost importance, but difficult to properly anticipate when there was either no son, or more than one. After an emperor's death, women of the imperial family played an important role in boosting the status of an emperor who had just inherited the throne, or of a candidate for the throne when there was no uncontested heir. Images showing a man alongside the emperor's widow, daughter or sister almost inevitably formed part of a debate about proper succession.

Within the spectrum of institutionalised and dependent members of the imperial entourage, which has been an important theme of this chapter, clear heirs cannot be properly positioned on either side. They should rather be seen as extensions of the emperor, given positions of trust that could not be given to any other man who could conceivably make a bid for the throne. The situation was different for the group of male family members from whom an heir would be chosen in the absence of a son. They were part of an elite group with an expected position in governing the empire, but the entire power of that group rested on the continuity of the dynasty, which could only be guaranteed through a ruling emperor. Women of the imperial family could not rule themselves, but still played an important part as representatives of the ruling dynasty. They were expected to have the emperor's ear and could become important powerbrokers in their own right. Especially after the conversion of the Roman empire to Christianity, dominant female members of the ruling dynasty could become involved in imperial policy, especially in debates about the Christian faith. For members of the imperial family, then, the dichotomy between institutional status and a position dependent on the emperor does not seem to apply. All living members of the imperial family were expected to be closely linked to the emperor – an expectation that was shared throughout the empire and by different groups in the empire. But even living male members of a dynasty that was no longer in power retained dynastic status. They were always a potential threat, and tended to be executed whenever they attracted too much attention.

Centuries of Roman rule created certain expectations about who would inherit the throne, with eldest sons and the husbands of widows as clear frontrunners. But the lack of a formalised system was a continuous source of unrest. Diocletian's attempts to systematise succession through the

Tetrarchy failed, probably because its exclusion of emperors' sons from rule went against centuries of expectations.[213] Even the shift to Christianity, and the notion of an emperor appointed by God, did not ease these problems. There was expectation and anticipation about which family members were in the emperor's favour at any given time, and therefore likely to succeed. But there were always competing interests, and varying contexts. As we have seen throughout this book, precedent and expectations strongly influenced imperial behaviour, but not through linear developments. Rather, there was a limited group of men who could be heir, and there were different ways in which they and other members of the imperial family could behave. Deciding whom to promote and honour was a delicate process. The emperor needed his family to rule and guarantee the continuity of the dynasty, but that did not always make them easy people to surround himself with.

Emperors and Entourage

There are very different ways in which rulers can interact with their entourage. The contrast between different historical monarchies is pronounced, and structures have fluctuated enormously, even between different dynasties within one territory. The Chinese Qin dynasty (221–206 BC), for instance, markedly weakened the role of the hereditary nobility in the circle of imperial helpers, only for the succeeding Han dynasty (202 BC–AD 220) to substantially compromise with regional families.[214] When considering the relation between rulers and the people who were regularly in their proximity as a spectrum between weak rulers dominated by an (institutional) entourage and strong rulers dominating their surroundings, it is difficult to properly position Roman emperorship. Perhaps this is unsurprising when analysing a system of government over 600 years. The position of an adult emperor after a military victory was very different from that of a young heir

---

[213] Hekster, *Emperors and Ancestors*, 287–96; S. Betjes/ S. Heijnen, 'The Usurping Princeps: Maxentius' Image and Its Constantinian Legacy', *JAHA*, vol. 5.3 (2018), 5–23; 5–14.

[214] Burbank/ Cooper, *Empires in World History*, 43; Z. Wang, *World Views and Military Policies in the Early Roman and Western Han Empires* (PhD Leiden 2015), 167–8; Van Ess, 'Konzeptionen monarchischer Herrschaft im frühen China', 408, 410–11. See now G. Vankeerberghen, 'Of Gold and Purple: Nobles in Western Han China and Republican Rome', in: H. Beck/ G. Vankeerberghen (eds.), *Rulers and Ruled in Ancient Greece, Rome, and China* (Cambridge 2021), 15–68; 16–17, 30–3 for a comparison of the social position of early Chinese and Republican Roman elites.

after a contested succession. Noticeably, however, there does not seem to have been a clear development of the way in which interactions between an emperor and those who surrounded him were formulated in Roman history from one dynasty to the next. Rather, a limited range of types of relationships between emperors and the men and women who surrounded him recurred throughout Roman imperial history.[215]

When looking for developments over time, then, there was much continuity in whom emperors surrounded themselves with and whom they favoured. From the early empire onwards, there was a finite range of possibilities: high status men (mostly, but not always, from an institutionalised group), low-status favourites and members of the family. Specific circumstances and the character of the emperor and the individuals surrounding him determined what the balance between these groups was in the imperial entourage, and who gained dominance. The reactions to these often ad hoc constellations of power were very different in (male elite) literary narratives from what can be traced through the material culture from the centre and from the provinces. At local level, it seems to have been accepted from the very beginning of the principate that there were individuals close to the emperor, that it was worth approaching them with requests, and that the status of these individuals could vary wildly. Locally based senators or bishops were employed by localities in order to reach the emperor's ear, but so were (local) intellectuals, members of the emperor's family, or any well-known favourite with whom connections could be made. The construction of statues or other monumental honours to people close to the emperor, and their rapid destruction when these individuals fell from grace, shows permanent attention at the local level to those members of the imperial entourage who could help gain access to the emperor. In various regions of the empire, this would have been a continuation of earlier practices. There had been interactions with influential favourites of Hellenistic kings in areas that had only recently been included into the Roman empire at the onset of the principate. But even in the west, where the notion of imperial favourites must have been new, the practical issue of how to reach the emperor, and how to placate the people who could be instrumental in this, seems to have been much more prominent than who would be the appropriate people to play this role.

More 'imperial' imagery, such as central coins and monuments in Rome and Constantinople also honoured imperial favourites, but other factors

---

[215] O. Hekster, 'Epilogue: Continuity and Change at the Roman Imperial Court', in: Kelly/Hug, *The Roman Emperor and His Court*, I, 479–97; 483–8.

were in play as well. Senators, and the senate as a corporate body, remained on display, even when the influence of individual members of the senate was occasionally minimal. There were some shifts, with explicit numismatic references to senators disappearing from central coinage from the third century onwards. But small togate figures were still shown alongside the emperor on coins from 367–75, illustrating a continued role of the senate in legitimising imperial rule (Figure 3.9).[216] Their position was markedly inferior to that of the emperor, but senators were still included in central representations of the emperor's entourage. Likewise, members of the imperial family were visually included on central imagery throughout Roman imperial history. There were shifts as to which members of the family received most attention, with sons, mothers and wives often vying for attention. This reflected the different makeup of the various imperial families, rather than showing a (linear) development over time. Instead, the influence that individual members of the family managed to obtain decided who was most prominently depicted. Context and character determined which family member stood out, but the expectation that family members held a prominent position in the emperor's vicinity was a constant in six centuries of Roman imperial rule. Low-status favourites, on the contrary, might receive statues, and were often publicly praised through poems and poetry, but they did not feature on coins or monumental reliefs. Apparently there were still limits on how permanently their position could be displayed. Elite friends and advisors, and members of the imperial family were less problematic to honour than personal favourites of low status, even in the late empire.

The tension between 'acceptable' members of the emperor's entourage, and 'unsuitable' favourites is most pronounced in literary narratives. Emperors paying too much attention to their wives, lovers, or personal favourites from outside elite circles are often heavily criticised, whereas those rulers who gave 'proper' attention to the senatorial elite, and later to bishops, were praised. These literary accounts most clearly show the tension between the two poles that made up Roman emperorship: the emperor had to show 'Republican' modesty, but he was also a conquering and divinely sanctioned ruler. Notwithstanding greater acceptance of ostentatious supremacy in the later empire, the notion of civil emperorship

---

[216] *RIC* IV, Caracalla no. 234; *RIC* 7, Antioch, nos. 39–41; *RIC* 9, Antioch, nos. 20a–f; Hekster, 'Emperors and Councillors', 23. The north-eastern side of the base of Theodosius' Obelisk at Rome also seems to include senators among represented members of the imperial court.

Figure 3.9 The continued role of the senate: 367, Antioch, gold solidus (4.43 g). The reverse of this coin shows the emperors Valens and Valentinian II, seated and with full imperial regalia. In between them is a much smaller togate figure, holding an inscribed shield proclaiming 'vows on the fifth anniversary, more of this hoped for on the tenth anniversary': Vo(TIS) V (=5) M(ULTIS) X (=10). The legend also indicates that the emperors should provide hope for the state: SPES R(EI)P(VBLICE). *RIC* 9, Antioch 20b
Source: ANS 1944.100.25920, American Numismatic Society

remained an issue. Literary accounts of life at the imperial court describe how the dynamics between these two apparently opposing principles played out – with most authors firmly supporting a civil emperor advised by the traditional elite.[217]

There does seem to be an easier acceptance of the role of powerful women in the later empire – partly because they could be involved in religious policy through Christian piety – and some systemisation of the role of certain court officials, such as the Grand Chamberlain. This increased acceptance, however, was not so much an innovation as a normalisation of long-existent practices that had been frowned upon before. Eunuchs, for example, had played an important part in the entourage of various emperors before they became a 'normal' part of the imperial court. Regular precedent often normalised behaviour that was seen as unsuited the first time, changing what was deemed 'acceptable' and with

---

[217] P. F. Bang, 'Court and State in the Roman Empire – Domestication and Tradition in Comparative Perspective', in: J. Duindam/ T. Artan/ M. Kunt (eds.), *Royal Courts in Dynastic States and Empires. A Global Perspective* (Leiden – Boston 2011), 103–28; 127. Cf. C. Bruun, 'Der Kaiser, die republikanischen Institutionen und die kaiserliche Verwaltung', in: Winterling, *Zwischen Strukturgeschichte und Biographie*, 161–79; 179.

it the expectations of what was likely to take place. The likes of Agrippina and Sporus may have moved too far away from traditional conceptions of proper behaviour. But their behaviour, however abhorred at the time, still changed expectations about the reasonable limits of the influence of imperial women and eunuchs. In this sense, Agrippina or Sporus can be seen as trailblazers who broke conventions. Having done so, they could function as a negative example (later imperial women could be presented as at least not as bad as Agrippina).[218] Alternatively, people simply grew used to a new normal. After the influence at court of the eunuchs Lygdus, Halotus, Sporus, Earinus and Sempronius Rufus, the role of someone like Eutropius no longer seemed exceptional.

Such normalisation did not take away preconceptions. Pliny still praised Trajan's wife Plotina 'as a supreme model of the ancient virtues … unswerving in her devotion not to your power but to yourself'. He also notes how 'many distinguished men have been dishonoured by an ill-considered choice of a wife or weakness in not getting rid of her'.[219] Moreover, the negative stories surrounding many late-antique imperial women or low-status favourites are strikingly similar to those about their counterparts in the earlier empire. It always remained possible to criticise an emperor for his dependence on women and lower-status individuals. No literary text criticises a Roman emperor for being overly dependent on senators, nor on the bishops who in many ways would take over the senators' role as an institutionalised elite advising the emperor. Indeed, the notion that senators had to play a role in imperial circles remained, even at the times of the western kingdoms, when they came to represent Rome's glorious past. There were, then, not only tensions between the notion of civil and authoritative rule, but also between an increasing acceptance among the writing elite of the influence of women and 'the emperor's men' and the continuing notion among members of that same elite that there was a proper 'traditional' way of ruling the empire.

There were changes over time in the Roman imperial entourage. Certain roles became more defined over time, and certain types of behaviour less contested. It is doubtful whether we should see this as an 'institutionalisation' of the Roman court. It is true that the beginning of the principate saw the establishments of certain patterns in the relation between the emperor and those who surrounded him. But the specific set-up could

---

[218] See p. 17–22 above on how members of the imperial family could be remembered in the Roman world, even long after their deaths.
[219] Plin. *Pan.* 83.

change substantially from one emperor to the next. And whether a presumed shift towards a system that was less dependent on imperial whims took place at the end of the second or the end of the third century is much debated.[220] This suggests that the entourage of Roman emperors never quite grew into a stable structure. Even the composition of the supposedly formalised administration of the late-Roman eastern empire could fluctuate heavily from one reign to the next – and who wielded most influence depended at least as much on the character of the individual as on the structure in which they functioned. Over time, a wider range of types of behaviour became acceptable. Most of these were already tried out at the very beginning of Roman rule, and became acknowledged as (more or less) acceptable modes of conduct over time. This was less an institutionalisation of the circles surrounding the emperor than a widening of scope, though never leading to endless fluidity. Changes in society also altered the composition of the people who had the emperor's ear, and the power they could wield. The increased militarisation of Roman society in the third century, and the emperor's absence from Rome, had an impact on the emperor's entourage. Even more noticeable was the way imperial women could wield independent power in a Christianised empire. The move away from Rome as unchallenged imperial capital changed the position of senators at court, though they retained importance. When comparing the composition and behaviour of people who were regularly in the emperor's proximity at the beginning of the principate and in the middle of the sixth century, there were substantial differences. Moreover, the distance between the emperor and his entourage had increased – and ceremonies emphasised the difference between the emperor and those he ruled.[221] Expectations had clearly shifted over time, but this had not been a linear process, and many traces of earlier discourse remained.

---

[220] Winterling, *Aula Caesaris*; B. Schöpe, *Der römische Kaiserhof in severischer Zeit (193-235 n. Chr.)* (Stuttgart 2014), 359.
[221] MacCormack, *Art and Ceremony*, 17–61, 161–21; C. Davenport, 'The Court and Ceremonial', 288–317; 317.

4 | The Emperor in the Capital and Provinces

The Roman emperor ruled one of the largest empires in world history. It consisted of different peoples living in wildly different contexts. They had different expectations of who the emperor was and how he should behave, although the range of those expectations was limited. This book so far has focused on developments over time, but views of emperorship were also locally dependent. The image of the emperor was not the same throughout the empire, and was often closely bound to his visibility in and his relationship with a specific region. How emperors were represented through statues, historical reliefs, victory arches, temples and other monuments, and through the ceremonies that surrounded emperorship, had an enormous impact on how the people who encountered these monuments or participated in these ceremonies perceived their emperors. As the number of monuments accumulated over time, they created an increasingly stable local 'memoryscape'. Existing imagery influenced both the creation of new local images and the expectations of imperial behaviour.[1] This process can perhaps be best traced at Rome and Constantinople, but it equally influenced expectations of emperors in different areas of the empire. People continuously lived surrounded by past emperors.

Often, pre-imperial monuments, images and rituals mattered as well. In Rome, emperors acted in a monumental landscape that celebrated consuls and heroes of old. The shift to Constantinople seems to have allowed emperors some leeway in moving away from 'Republican' expectations. At the same time, the division into an eastern and western empire had an impact upon the image of the emperor as ruler of a unified realm. Perceptions and expectations in either capital could be very different from those in more remote areas of the empire. The earlier-cited comment of Synesius about people in Ptolemais who still thought that Agamemnon ruled is illustrative, if unlikely to be true.[2] Differences between (and sometimes also within) various regions were substantial, not least in the established modes of rule prior to the coming of Rome. These were often

---

[1] Weisweiler, 'Making Masters, Makings Subjects', 67–75, see p. 19 above.
[2] Syn. *Letters* 148.16. See p. 105 above.

commemorated through local monuments but also transmitted through stories and texts. All of these influenced the expectations that people had of rulership. Egypt with its pharaonic tradition is probably the best-known example, but people in other Roman regions were equally influenced by their historical modes of rule. A chronological analysis of honorific statues in the Athenian agora shows how Athenian citizens were first commemorated there, to be replaced by statues of Hellenistic kings, Roman magistrates and then Roman emperors and their relatives. The imperial statues stood alongside earlier Athenian reactions to rule and this must have influenced how those statues were perceived.[3] The east/west divide was important in that respect, with Greek and Hellenistic traditions of kingship more dominant in the Greek-speaking world. Even in the fourth and fifth centuries, panegyrical speeches in Greek made much more use of Greek historical examples and references to earlier Greek modes of rulership than Latin ones, which continued to refer to Republican exemplarity.[4]

Emperors also had to build relationships with many of the people living in the provinces of the empire. The individuals in the emperor's immediate vicinity (institutional or not) had an impact on his rule, but so did groups who were scattered across the empire, especially soldiers and provincial elites. They, too, played a crucial role in governing the empire, and in the perception of what a Roman emperor should be and do. From the reign of Domitian onwards, most emperors spent time touring the provinces, allowing members of the elites from the cities which the emperor visited increased access to him. These elites subsequently advertised their relationship with the emperor, for instance through inscriptions proclaiming themselves 'guest friends' of the emperor, or merely noting that they had welcomed and hosted the emperor in their city.[5] A major aspect of imperial travelling was also that it built personal bonds between the emperor and

---

[3] S. Leone, *Polis, Platz und Porträt die Bildnisstatuen auf der Agora von Athen im Späthellenismus und in der Kaiserzeit (86 v. Chr.–267 n. Chr.)* (Berlin – Boston 2020), 40–6, 83–93, 109–23. On the development of the Agora: C. P. Dickenson, *On the Agora. The Evolution of a Public Space in Hellenistic and Roman Greece (c. 326 BC–267 AD)* (Leiden – Boston 2017). On the notion that Egypt was not so different from other provinces as ancient and modern authors presume: N. Lewis, 'The Romanity of Roman Egypt: A Growing Consensus', in: *Atti del XVII Congresso Internazionale di Papirologia* (Naples 1984), 1077–84; 1084; A. K. Bowman, *Egypt after the Pharaohs, 332 BC–AD 642: From Alexander to the Arab Conquest* (London 1986), 160–1.

[4] Jussen, 'Leading by Example'; D. Burgersdijk, 'Neoplatonic Philosophy in Tetrarchic and Constantinian Panegyric', in: A. J. Ross/ A. Omissi (eds.), *Imperial Panegyric from Diocletian to Theodosius* (Liverpool 2020), 167–89.

[5] *Illion* 83; *IGR* 4.136; Halfmann, *Itinera Principum*, 35–56; 113–36, with further references; H. Halfmann, 'Imperial Journeys', in: Kelly/ Hug, *The Roman Emperor and His Court*, 267–87; 275–7.

the legions which he visited. Hadrian's surviving speeches (about military discipline, and highlighting his own tough military way of travelling) from the many legionary camps at which he spent time are illustrative, as is the famous epitaph of the Batavian Soranus:

> I am the man who, once very well known to the ranks in Pannonia, brave and foremost among one thousand Batavians, was able, with Hadrian as judge, to swim the wide waters of the deep Danube in full battle kit. From my bow, I shot an arrow, and while it hung still in the air and was falling back, with a second arrow I hit and broke it.

The archery is impressive, but it became worthwhile because the emperor was watching.[6]

Imperial interactions with people in the provinces and with the crowds in Rome and Constantinople were of major importance in the construction of emperorship, though the relative importance of different groups shifted over time. And how people understood those interactions to work could differ markedly from the reality. Sometime in the fifth century, Shenoute of Atripe, the renowned abbot of the White Monastery near Sohag (Egypt), who is said to have lived an amazingly long life (348–465), described the power of the emperor:

> When the emperor issues an edict or publishes decisions, so that everyone in his empire will heed and obey them, then this happens with great command and authority: to all countries of the empire, to all cities and villages, whether near or far. And then there is great dread in his whole empire that everyone also executes with great care what the ruler has ordered – from the prefects and generals, from the *comites* and provincial governors to the tribunes and *protoi* and the soldiers ... Because the emperor spares neither the prefect nor the general nor the provincial governor, and not tribunes either, or soldiers, or civilians – whatever kind of people, be they bishop or priest or monk.[7]

By this stage, imperial power was disputed in different parts of the empire. It was partly taken over by the great generals in the west. The city of Rome itself had been ransacked in 410, leading Jerome to proclaim 'the brightest

---

[6] *CIL* 3.3676 (= *ILS* 2558); *CIL* 8.2532 and 18042 (= *ILS* 2487 and 9133–5); Dio 69.9.1–4. See p. 122 above.

[7] É Amélineau (ed.), *Oeuvres de Schenoudi, texte copte et traduction française. Tome II, fasc. 3* (Paris 1914); 523, 7–22. Translation adapted from: J. Hahn, 'Schenute von Atripe, die kaiserliche Religionspolitik und der Kampf gegen das Heidentum in Oberägypten', in: F. Feder/ A. Lohwasser (eds.), *Ägypten und sein Umfeld in der Spätantike: vom Regierungsantritt Diokletians 284/285 bis zur arabischen Eroberung des Vorderen Orients um 635-646* (Wiesbaden 2013), 81–108; 83. I owe the reference to Johannes Hahn.

light of the whole world is extinguished. Indeed, the head has been cut off from the Roman empire'. Two decades later, the Vandals had conquered Carthage. There were disputes between bishops and emperors about religious dominance, with some bishops destroying pagan cult centres against imperial wishes.[8] Still, the concept of a dominant emperor who was fully in control of his empire had not disappeared. This, after all, was the notion that was repeated again and again, through coins, inscriptions, statues and monumental buildings, dominating the landscapes of the Roman empire. In the mind of Shenoute, the emperor's dominance was closely associated with his relationship with provincial governors, local elites and soldiers. People had great expectations of imperial power, and these retained their importance for a very long time.

Emperors in Their Capitals

The dominant image of Roman emperorship in much of the source material is that of the emperor in his capital. This is, as so often, partly due to the bias of the senatorial elite (and later of the bishops of Rome and Constantinople), but it also indicates the strong interconnection between the emperors and the cities in which they spent most of their time. Looking at the whole period from Caesar to Justinian, emperors who were systematically away from the main imperial residence are much rarer than ones spending most of their time there.[9] For the first centuries of imperial rule, emperors were expected to reside in Rome. When they were more regularly absent from the capital later, the link between emperor and city was expressed through the much-cited notion that 'Rome is where the emperors is'.[10] Emperor and capital were closely connected in the eyes of his subjects. After all, both emperor and the city of Rome were key symbols of the empire. Their importance is transmitted in Justinian's *Digest*, citing a passage by the third-century jurist Callistratus: 'A relegated person cannot remain in Rome, even if this is not included in his

---

[8] Jerome, *In Ezek.* I, praef.; *In Ezek.* II, praef.; B. Ward-Perkins, *The Fall of Rome and the End of Civilization* (Oxford 2006), 13–17, 28–9 with references; M. Meier/ S. Patzold, *August 410 – Ein Kampf um Rom* (Stuttgart 2010). See also p. 128–9, p. 140–1 and p. 198.

[9] On imperial travels from Augustus to Carinus, see also Halfmann, Itinera Principum, 157–242, with 243–4 with literature on the period 285–395; Millar, *Emperor*, 28–40. On the continuing presence of emperor in Rome in the fifth century, see p. 191–2 above and on the impact of the move to Constantinople for the itinerant emperor see p. 284 below.

[10] Herodian 1.6.5, more often quoted through its echo in *Pan.Lat.* 11 (3). 12.2 'the seat of imperial power could then appear to be the place to which each emperor had come'.

sentence, because it is the common *patria*, nor in a *civitas* in which the emperor is staying or through which he is passing; for only persons who can enter Rome are permitted to look on the emperor, since the emperor is the *pater patriae*'.[11] Each city that the emperor visited effectively became the centre of the 'common patria'. One way of expressing that notion was by calling these cities 'Rome'. From the fourth century onwards, eastern emperors were expected to be in Constantinople, but the regular references to Constantinople as 'New Rome' and explicit comparisons to 'Old Rome' after it became imperial residence show the continued importance of the old capital.[12] The emperor could move away from Rome, but not from the notion that he somehow needed to be in Rome – at least in a new or temporary Rome.

The strong bond between emperor, empire and the city of Rome is clear from the many references to Rome in text and image. Noticeably, up to the fourth century, coin legends and inscriptions refer to *Roma* rather than *Romani* (the Romans), whereas for conquered territories both the place and its inhabitants are used (e.g. *Germania* and *Germani*). These territories, and indeed the whole world, were said to be 'made subject to the rule of the Roman people'.[13] The goddess Rome and her eponymous city were named to personify the Roman empire. In the fourth and fifth centuries, instead, coins with the legends Gavdivm Romanorvm (joy of the Romans) and especially Gloria Romanorvm (glory of the Romans) were among the most frequently used types. This increased emphasis on 'the Romans' did not mean that 'Rome' disappeared from view. Depictions of Roma on the reverses of coins were more frequent under the Valentinian dynasty than before.[14] The situation in the east, however, was somewhat different. After the death of Theodosius I Rome is almost-absent from eastern coinage. In the west, she continued to be shown on coins well into the sixth century. This suggests that in the east the shift to Constantinople as eastern capital loosened the ties between Roman emperors (and perhaps even the idea of being Roman) and the old city of Rome, although that notion remained strong in the west.

---

[11] *Dig.* 48.22.18(19) (translation Watson); Millar, *Emperor*, 39.

[12] For the continuing importance of fifth- and sixth-century Rome in the western empire, see p. 191–2. On the comparison of 'Old Rome' and 'New Rome', p. 207.

[13] RGDA, heading; M. Vitale, *Das Imperium in Wort und Bild. Römische Darstellungsformen beherrschter Gebiete in Inschriftenmonumenten, Münzprägungen und Literatur* (Stuttgart 2017), 60, 64.

[14] The distribution of Romanorvm coins, and reverses with Roma can be traced through the OCRE website (http://numismatics.org/ocre/). The pattern for the first three centuries is confirmed in the Reka Devnia hoard: https://chre.ashmus.ox.ac.uk/hoard/3406.

In a more ceremonial way, the notion that the emperor belonged in his capital was expressed though the acts of *profectio*, when emperors departed from Rome, and *adventus* when he returned. The absence of the emperor from his capital, in other words, was an aberration that needed to be ritually addressed. Emperors should be safe and sound in Rome, to show that they were in power. This is one reason why cities in which the emperor stayed for a prolonged period of time were transformed into temporary capitals, as implicated in the text from Callistratus cited above.[15] Over time, there were many changes in the precise set-up of especially the *adventus*. It increasingly emphasised the relation of the emperor with the divine, and in terms of location shifted from taking place at the city walls to happening in the palace.[16] Moreover, with emperors more rarely leading the armies in person in the fifth and sixth centuries, *adventus* ceremonies became less about the emperor (victoriously) returning to his city and more an occasion at which the emperor emphasised his relation to the inhabitants of the city.[17] In Constantinople, the *adventus principis* became an integral part of the coronation ceremony. The emperor progressed slowly through the city, praying at each of the great protective walls, and moving towards the palace. In the process, the emperor changed dress, and with it his role. Starting in a military outfit and on a warhorse, he ended by walking in consular dress, surrounded by his subjects, and even removing his crown, which was then given back to him by the patriarch. Ultimately, proclamation of the emperor would take place in Constantinople's Hippodrome, with the adventus leading from the palace to the Hagia Sophia, but the notion of an emperor who through a procession in the capital took up his rightful place at the heart of the empire remained.[18] Notwithstanding these various shifts, the adventus remained the same in its essentials. It was a celebration of the emperor returning to his eternal city – first Rome, later Constantinople – and interacting with the inhabitants of that city. In doing so, the emperor showed his hold over the capital, the empire, and its inhabitants.

---

[15] Halfmann, 'Imperial Journeys', 273–5. On the relation between *profectio* and *adventus*: J. Lehnen, *Adventus Principis. Untersuchungen zu Sinngehalt und Zeremoniell der Kaiserankunft in den Städten des Imperium Romanum* (Frankfurt a. M. 1997), 97–103. See also p. 118 above.

[16] MacCormack, *Art and Ceremony*, 22–33, 44–5; C. Badel, 'Adventus et salutatio', in: A. Bérenger/ É. Perrin-Saminadayar (eds.), *Les Entrées royales et impériales: histoire, représentation et diffusion d'une cérémonie publique, de l'Orient ancien à Byzance. de l'archéologie à l'histoire* (Paris 2009), 157–75.

[17] MacCormack, *Art and Ceremony*, 59–60. On emperors no longer leading the troops (but still being expected to be victorious), see p. 130 above.

[18] Dagron, *Emperor and Priest*, 64–9. On the emperor walking into the city, and exchanging his military gear for a toga, see p. 71 above.

The interaction with his people was an essential part of what was expected of Roman emperors, and the people in the capital took pride of place. Not only during the adventus, but at various rituals the inhabitants of the capital were part of ceremonies which expressed *consensus universorum* (universal harmony). The procession at imperial funerals in Rome is illustrative. It included representatives of the different Roman orders, but also of the wider Roman world (local elites, foreign kings) in the pomp. This expressed the communal loyalty to the emperor. It also showed social and political order and Rome's primacy. Senators before knights before the rest of the inhabitants of the city, and those living in the capital before people from outside Rome.[19] A similar order can be traced in the imperial funerals at Constantinople, although senators had lost some of their prestige. According to Eusebius, at the funeral of Constantine:

> The commanders of the whole army, the *comites* and all the ruling class, who were bound by law to pay homage to the emperor first, making no change in their usual routine, filed past at the required times and saluted the emperor on the bier with genuflections after his death in the same way as when he was alive. After these chief persons the members of the Senate and all those of official rank came and did the same, and after them crowds of people of all classes with their wives and children came to look'.

Later imperial burials at Constantinople seem to have followed the same pattern, although with an increased role for the clergy, who saluted their deceased emperor alongside men of senatorial rank.[20]

Such assemblies confirmed the notion of the emperor as the centre of the world, based in his capital. The interaction between the emperor and his people was also visible during the games. In Rome, the spectators in the Colosseum regularly petitioned the emperor, and expected him to be present and to listen. Through a hierarchy of seating, social order was confirmed. This behaviour was copied in provincial cities, where local magistrates and members of the elite could show their power and status by organising major games. But emperors, on the whole, only provided games for Rome or for the cities where they were residing for a prolonged period of time.[21]

Famously, communication between the emperor and his people continued in the Hippodrome of Constantinople. Already in Rome, the Circus

---

[19] P. Zanker, *Die Apotheose der römischen Kaiser* (Munich 2004), 20–34, 40.

[20] Eus. *Vita Constantini* 4.67.1 (translation Cameron and Hall, *Life of Constantine*, 179–80); C. Rapp, 'Death at the Byzantine Court: The Emperor and his Family', in: K-H. Spieß/ I. Warntjes (eds.), *Death at Court* (Wiesbaden 2012), 267–86; 268–75.

[21] Wiedemann, *Emperors and Gladiators*, 166–77. Cf. A. Bérenger, 'L' adventus des gouverneurs de province', in: Bérenger/ Perrin-Saminadayar, Les entrées royales et impériales, 125–38 on the way gubernatorial entrances into provincial cities echoed imperial actions in Rome.

Maximus had been an important venue for people to express their support or discontent with emperors. In 190, crowds in the Circus rose up against Commodus' unpopular freedman Cleander, leading to his fall from power. Three years later, inhabitants of the city who were discontented with the appointment of Didius Julianus as their emperor are said to have 'seized arms and rushed together into the Circus, and there spent the night and the following day without food or drink, shouting and calling upon the remainder of the soldiers, especially Pescennius Niger and his followers in Syria, to come to their aid'. More examples could be easily added.[22] The Circus Maximus, like the Colosseum, was a locus for public acclamation. This made it an important element of communication between the emperor and his people. It is no coincidence that when the Tetrarchs constructed subsidiary capitals (so that none of them could claim supremacy by being based in Rome), all of these included a palace which, like the Palatine complex, was linked to a hippodrome where the emperor could be present among the inhabitants of his capital.[23]

Yet it was in Constantinople's Hippodrome that the most dramatic scenes played out, especially after it was incorporated into the imperial coronation ceremony. Being acclaimed by the united people of the capital was an established element in the accession of a Roman emperor. On the whole, this was a mere formality. But a combination of the role of the so-called 'circus factions' (groups of organised spectators, named Reds, Whites, Blues and Greens after the colours of their teams) and the lack of clear successors to the eastern throne for much of the period 450–610 created political tensions that were regularly played out through the masses at the Hippodrome.[24] This was evident at the accession of Justin I (518–27). Apparently a tribune named John was supported by the *excubitors*, but the Blues protested vehemently against his appointment and even 'pelted him with stones'. One alternative, the general Patricius,

---

[22] Dio, 73(74).13.2–5; 72 (73).13.3. Herodian, 1.12.5, 2.7.3–6; Hekster, *Commodus*, 72–4; J. Sünskes Thompson, *Demonstrative Legitimation der Kaiserherrschaft im Epochenvergleich: zur politischen Macht des stadtrömischen Volkes* (Stuttgart 1993), 39–40. On popular unrest in Rome in connection with the relation between emperor and *plebs* see Kröss, *Die politische Rolle der stadtrömischen Plebs*, 175–268.

[23] P. Magdalino, 'Court and Capital in Byzantium', in: Duindam/ Artan/ Kunt, *Royal Courts in Dynastic States*, 131–44; 132; J. H. Humphrey, *Roman Circuses. Arenas for Chariot Racing* (London 1986), 582–602, 636–7; C. Heucke, *Circus und Hippodr om als politischer Raum* (Hildesheim 1994), 319–99; V. Jaeschke, 'Architecture and Power. Defining Tetrarchic Imperial Residences', in: E. Manders/ D. Slootjes (eds.), *Leadership, Ideology and Crowds in the Roman Empire of the Fourth Century* (Stuttgart 2020), 19–33; 27–8.

[24] G. Dagron, *L'Hippodrome de Constantinople: Jeux, Peuple, et Politique* (Paris 2011), 29–51; J. H. W. G. Liebeschuetz, *Decline and Fall of the Roman City* (Oxford 2001), 211–12.

was not acceptable to the *excubitors*. Consequently, the elderly commander of the *excubitors*, Justin, was elected instead. After his election, he sent a letter to Pope Hormisdas, emphasising how he was chosen by 'the most noble men of our sacred consistory, and the most sacred senate, and certainly also the most steadfast army'. No emperor came to power without military support, but the importance of popular acclamation was not to be underestimated.[25] To gain such public popular support, the (would-be) emperor needed to be in the capital. One reason for the election of Leo I in 457 after the death of Marcian, rather than the latter's son-in-law Anthemius, who had probably been the intended successor, was that Anthemius was absent from Constantinople at the relevant moment.[26]

The best-known example of the power of the people in the capital, and of its limits, is the Nika revolt of 532. A combination of unrest over taxes, over Justinian's attempts to curb the power of the circus factions (which may have been one reason why he chose to have his crowning ceremony in the palace, rather than in the Circus) and over lack of successes at the front, transformed into uproar when Justinian refused to pardon two arrested rioters. Masses at the races chanted 'Nika' (Victory), acclaimed first Probus and later Hypatius (both nephews of former emperor Anastasius) as emperors instead of Justinian, and even assaulted the palace. A substantial number of buildings in the capital were burnt down. Ultimately Justinian, according to our literary sources spurred on by Theodora, decided to set soldiers on the spectators in the Hippodrome, reportedly killing 30,000 rioters.[27] Military might remained the cornerstone of imperial control, but the importance of public support in the capital had been made abundantly clear to the emperor. Justinian first issued harsh measures against the senators and circus factions who had been involved

---

[25] *Book of Ceremonies* I. 93; A. Moffatt/ M. Tall, *Constantine Porphyrogennetos: The Book of Ceremonies* (Leiden – Boston 2012), 426–30; *Collectio Avellana* 141 (1 August 518): 'Amplissimi proceres sacri nostri palatii, sanctissimus senatus, firmissimus exercitus'; M. McEvoy, 'Dynastic Dreams and Visions of Early Byzantine Emperors (ca. 518–565 AD)', in: B. Neil/ E. Anagnostou-Laoutides (eds.), *Dreams, Memory and Imagination in Byzantium* (Leiden – Boston 2018), 99–117; 103–4. See J. J. Ayaita, *Justinian und das Volk im Nikaaufstand* (PhD Heidelberg 2015), 23–76 on the increasing power of the people in imperial acclamations. On the *excubitors*, see p. 223 above.

[26] R. Pfeilschifter, *Der Kaiser und Konstantinopel: Kommunikation und Konfliktaustrag in einer spätantiken Metropole* (Berlin 2013), 147–8; B. Croke, 'Dynasty and Ethnicity: Emperor Leo I and the Eclipse of Aspar', *Chiron* 35 (2005), 147–203; 149–50.

[27] Ayaita, *Justinian und das Volk*, 158–99, with full references and detailed analysis of the various groups participating in the revolt; Pfeilschifter, *Der Kaiser und Konstantinopel*, 178–210.

in the revolt, but he rapidly struck a much more conciliatory tone. Yet only the great successes of Belisarius in the west salvaged Justinian's reputation.[28]

The persistence of the various consensus rituals and public acclamations in Rome and Constantinople showed the continued importance of the capital's inhabitants to the emperor's position. The involvement of crowds in the struggles between competitors for the Roman bishopric, closely observed by the emperors, can be seen in a similar context.[29] The populace of the capitals of course consisted of different groups, each with their own expectations of what their leader needed to do. Emperors had to take care not to alienate the *plebs*, but inhabitants of the capital also included knights, senators and later members of the clergy, and of course soldiers through the praetorians, *equites singulares* and imperial bodyguards. Only with support of these different groups could emperors claim the universal rule which they were meant to personify. This has been described as a model of acceptance: imperial legitimacy depended on support from the different groups that constituted the Roman people, with the plebs and elite of Rome, and later Constantinople, important participants. Gaining and holding on to imperial power was an exercise in political communication.[30] Consequently, emperors had to live up to the expectations of those various groups.

These different expectations are closely linked to the emperor's image, his various roles and his entourage, as discussed in the earlier chapters of this book. They were also visible in the very fabric of the city of Rome, further embedding the relation between the emperor and his capital. Centuries of building activities produced monuments for the various emperors and dynasties. Imperial fora showed the emperor in his main roles. The Forum of Caesar set the tone, with its dominant temple to Venus (his mythical ancestor) celebrating his divine lineage. The construction of the temple was said to be a fulfilment of a vow which Caesar made on the eve of the battle of Pharsalus (48 BC), in which he decisively defeated Pompey. But the complex also emphasised the civil role

---

[28] Ayaita, *Justinian und das Volk*, 200–14. On Belisarius' campaign as a reaction to the near collapse of Justinian's regime, see p. 133 above.

[29] The best-known example is probably that of Damasus and Ursinus in 366: M. Sághy, 'Damasus and the Charioteers. Crowds, Media and Leadership in Late Antique Rome', in: Manders/Slootjes, *Leadership, Ideology and Crowds*, 117–33. See p. 201–2 above on Eulalius and Boniface

[30] Fundamental to this notion of 'Akzeptanzmonarchie' is E. Flaig, *Den Kaiser herausfordern. Die Usurpation im Römischen Reich* (Frankfurt a. M. 2019²), with 39–197 on the (refined) model and the relation between the emperor and his constituent groups. See also F. Hurlet, 'Le Consensus et la concordia en Occident (Ier-IIIe siècles ap. J.-C.). Réflexions sur la diffusion de l'idéologie impériale', in: H. Inglebert (ed.), *Idéologies et valeurs civiques dans le monde romain. Hommage à Claude Lepelley* (Paris 2002), 163–78 on the importance of provincial elites, and Pfeilschifter, *Der Kaiser und Konstantinopel*, 355–451 on the role of the Constantinian clergy.

of the ruler, through its major porticoes which linked it to the *Atrium libertatis* (which housed lists of Roman citizens and maps of public land) and the senate house.[31] Many subsequent emperors followed Caesar's example. Their building activities are still visible through the remains of the great imperial Fora of Augustus, Vespasian, Domitian/Nerva and Trajan (Map 4.1). The Forum of Trajan is probably the most magnificent example. It included a massive basilica, two libraries (probably holding state archives), the column showing Trajan's military successes (Figure 0.1), the famous equestrian statue of the emperor, and many sculptural decorations, which included the imperial family and his conquests.[32] Hadrian's temple of Venus and Rome with its surrounding colonnades, and Maxentius' massive basilica (the Basilica Nova) alongside the Via Sacra were in many ways continuations of those imperial fora.[33] These great complexes, much like the victory arches or the temples to deified emperors and empresses, did not only commemorate individual rulers but also communicated what people could expect of an emperor.

Existing imperial buildings raised expectations about future buildings. Consequently, new constructions were either larger or more ornamental than existing ones. Such 'monumental inflation' is visible in the fora and also when looking at the various bathhouses that were constructed in Rome under imperial auspices over the centuries. The first complex, built in the name of Augustus' right-hand man Agrippa in 25 BC (completed in 19 BC) was an impressive innovation, but subsequent bathhouses were increasingly impressive, leading to the magnificently decorated bathhouse of Diocletian (AD 306), which measured 316 by 356 metres, accommodating approximately 3,000 people.[34] These bathhouses, like aqueducts or

---

[31] Carandini, *Atlas of Ancient Rome* I, 167–8, 207–8, II, table 28–31. Cf. Hölscher, *Visual Power*, 123–32 on the commemoration of the regal past in Rome.

[32] Carandini, *Atlas of Ancient Rome* I, 208–14, table 38–9, 51–4, 99. E. Packer, *The Forum of Trajan in Rome. A Study of the Monuments* (Berkeley 1997) provides a magisterial overview of Trajan's forum. On the equestrian statue, see p. 66.

[33] Carandini, *Atlas of Ancient Rome* I, 295–6, 298–9, II tab. 102; S. T. A. M. Mols. 'The Cult of Roma Aeterna in Hadrian's Politics', in L. de Blois et al. (eds.), *The Representation and Perception of Roman Imperial Power* (Amsterdam 2003), 458–65; Hekster, 'The City of Rome in Late Imperial Ideology', 724–7.

[34] G. Ghini, 'Thermae Agrippae', in: *LTUR* 5, 40–2; G. Ghini, 'Thermae Neronianae/ Alexandrinae', in: *LTUR* 5, 60–3; G. Caruso, 'Thermae Titi/ Titianae', in: *LTUR* 5, 66–7; G. Caruso/ R. Volpe, 'Thermae Traiani', in: *LTUR* 5, 68–9; M. Piranomonte, 'Thermae Antoninianae', in: *LTUR* 5, 42–28; L. LaFollette, 'Thermae Decianae', in: *LTUR* 5, 51–3; D. Palombi, 'Thermae Aurelianae', in: *LTUR* 5, 48–9; D. Candilio, 'Thermae Diocletiani', in: *LTUR* 5, 53–8. Cf. J. Delaine, 'Building the Eternal City: The Building Industry of Imperial Rome', in: J. Coulston / H. Dodge (eds.), *Ancient Rome: The Archaeology of the Eternal City* (Oxford 2000), 119–41 and O. Hekster, 'Imagining Power', 119 on monumental inflation.

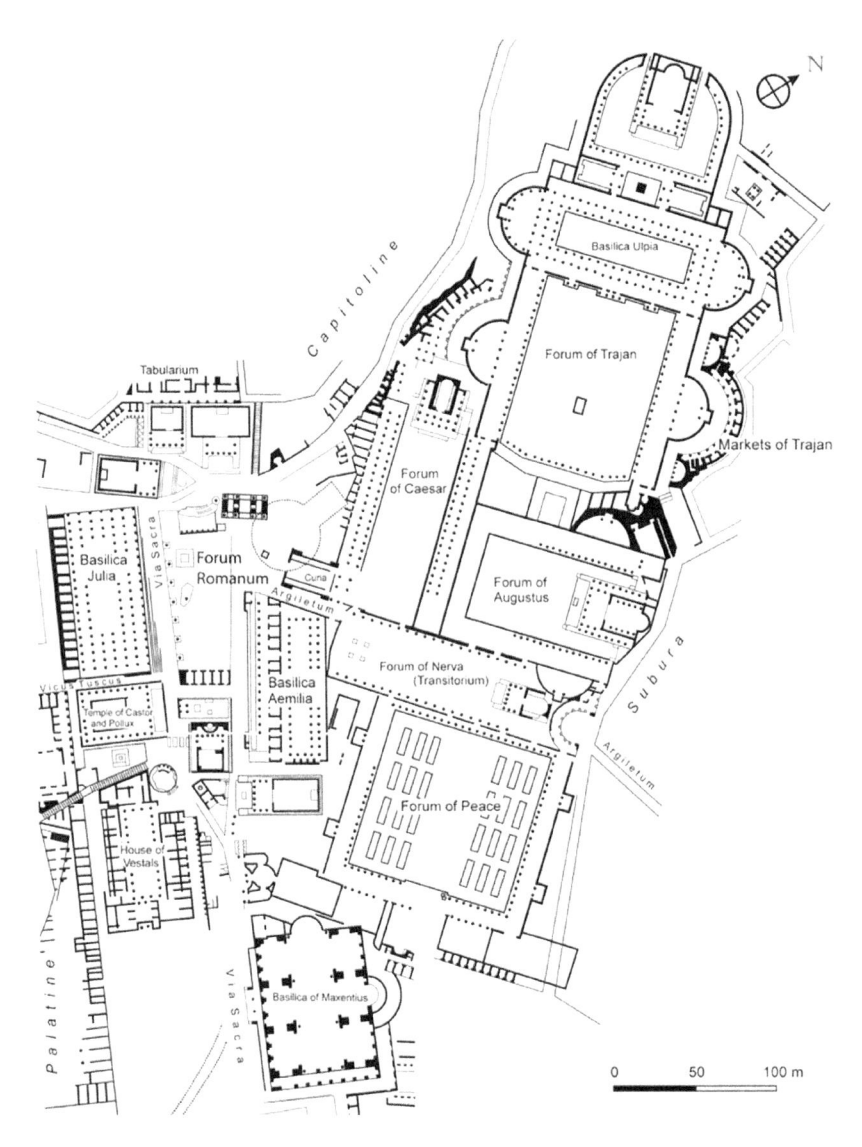

Map 4.1 Rome's imperial fora: A map of Rome's imperial fora shows both how the different complexes were dominated by a temple and porticoes, and how the fora increased dramatically in size over time, with each successive emperor needing to outdo his predecessor
Source: CKD – Radboud University Nijmegen

buildings for entertainment such as (amphi)theatres and circus complexes, were evidence of the emperor's care for his people. Their construction can be seen as part of the emperor's civil role. The same applies to imperial basilicas, with emphasis on the emperor's role as a magistrate.[35] Yet it would be misleading to argue that the very act of building was part of the emperor's civic persona. That depended greatly on what was being built. Victory arches celebrated the emperors' victories, temples and later churches their piety and relation to the divine. Through the construction of different types of buildings emperors could emphasise specific aspects of emperorship.

Emperors were not wholly free in their choice of what to build. People in Rome expected their emperors to live up to standards set previously, exemplified through both the many imperial and the earlier Republican monuments. In that sense, the existing built environment of Rome became somewhat proscriptive for new construction activities and imperial behaviour in general.[36] The capital's cityscape shaped expectations. An emperor who would only build victory arches – satisfying the wishes of those who preferred a military leader over anything else – neglected the expectations of those who wanted a civil ruler, and saw how previous emperors had emphasised that role through the many basilicas and bathhouses named after emperors. Something like this may lie behind a passage in Suetonius' *Life of Domitian*, which states that 'He erected so many and such huge vaulted passage-ways and arches in the various regions of the city, adorned with chariots and triumphal emblems, that on one of them someone wrote in Greek: "It is enough (*arci*)"'.[37] Emperors at least partly constructed buildings in order to live up to their subjects' expectations, and in doing so further strengthened those expectations for later generations that saw specific imperial roles expressed in the capital's built environment. Similarly, locations such as the Forum Romanum where people had assembled and communicated with their Republican leaders for centuries, continuously recalled that the *Res Publica* went back further than the time of Caesar.

The importance of acceptance by the plebs and elite from Rome for imperial legitimacy guaranteed strong ties between the emperor and his capital. The cityscape of that capital further shaped what was expected of

---

[35] On the civil role of the basilica: F. de Angelis, '*Ius* and Space: An Introduction', in: *Spaces of Justice in the Roman World* (Leiden – Boston 2010), 1–27; R. Färber, *Römische Gerichtsorte. Räumliche Dynamiken von Jurisdiktion im Imperium Romanum* (Munich 2014), 118–19.

[36] Cf. M. J. Versluys, 'Object-Scapes. Towards a Material Constitution of Romaness?', in: A. van Oyen/ M. Pitts (eds.), *Materialising Roman Histories* (Oxford 2017), 191–9; 197 and p. 19 above.

[37] Suet. *Dom.* 13.2. 'Arci' is a transliteration of the Greek ἀρκεῖ.

the emperor by the inhabitants of the city. This applied even more strongly to the imperial residence on the Palatine. Augustus had combined a series of rich aristocratic houses into a complex which was less modest than often assumed, but nowhere near as elaborate as contemporary Hellenistic palatial structures.[38] Over time, it was transformed into a real palace. Under Augustus' immediate successors, the complex was extended on the Palatine and linked to the Forum Romanum. In Domitianic times it came to include one of the largest rooms in antiquity, the so-called Aula Regia, which measured over 1,000 m^2. During the reign of Trajan it was visually and functionally linked to the Circus Maximus. By the end of the Severan reign, it included high substructures on all four sides.[39] Throughout, the Palatine complex consistently continued to make references to the emperor's civil role. It incorporated rooms that accommodated traditional aristocratic interactions such as the *salutatio*, and places where the emperor took on his magisterial role. Yet it also showed his supreme status and his relation to the divine. It included architectural references to aristocratic houses, luxurious villas, public structures such as the basilica, and temples. Many of these were built to a scale that underscored the emperor's position as the head of state.[40] The Palatine complex, then, evolved over time, ultimately visualising a much more monarchical ruler than had been possible under Augustus – although Augustus' residence had already flirted with the idea of a palace, through

---

[38] For a splendid recent and comprehensive overview of Augustus' residence: T. P. Wiseman, *The House of Augustus: A Historical Detective Story* (Princeton – Oxford 2019). On the luxury of the so-called modest house: A. Raimondi Cominesi, 'Augustus in the Making: A Reappraisal of the Ideology behind Octavian's Palatine Residence through Its Interior Decoration and Topographical Context', *Latomus* 77 (2018), 704–35.

[39] For the development of the palace, see, M. Royo *Domus imperatoriae: Topographie, formation et imaginaire des palais impériaux du Palatin (IIe siècle av. J.-C.–Ier siècle apr. J.-C.)* (Rome 1999), 119–301; Winterling, Aula Caesaris, 47–8; R. Mar, *El Palatí: la formació dels palaus imperials a Roma* (Tarragona 2005), 339–52; M. A. Tomei, 'Le residenze sul Palatino dall'età repubblicana all'età antonina', in: N. Sojc/ A. Winterling/ U. Wulf-Rheidt (eds.), *Palast und Stadt im severischen Rom* (Stuttgart 2013), 61–83; J. Pflug, 'Die bauliche Entwicklung der Domus Augustana im Kontext des südöstlichen Palatin bis in severische Zeit', in: Sojc/ Winterling/ Wulf-Rheidt, *Palast und Stadt*, 181–212; 185–93, 197–204; J. Pflug/ U. Wulf-Rheidt, 'The Imperial Palaces on the Palatine Hill: Architecture as a Reflection of Social Practices and Imperial Authority', in: Kelly/ Hug, 204–238. On the link to the circus: E. Bukowiecki/ U. Wulf-Rheidt, 'I bolli laterizi delle residenze imperiali sul Palatino a Roma', *MDAI(R)* 121 (2015), 311–482; 372. On the extensions under the Julio Claudians: M. A. Tomei/ M. G. Filetici, *Domus Tiberiana: scavi e restauri 1990–2011* (Milan 2011), 118–23.

[40] Pflug/ Wulf-Rheidt, 'The Imperial Palaces on the Palatine Hill', 219–20.

its links to the Palatine temple of Apollo with its gilded temple capitals, architraves and cornices.[41] Importantly, however, the complex changed through continuous adaptations rather than major breakthroughs. Over the centuries, it adhered to a fundamental palace model that dated from the beginning of the principate.

The longer emperorship had been centred on the Palatine complex, the more difficult it became to fundamentally change the palace according to the wishes of individual rulers.[42] Moreover, much like the monuments in the city influenced expectations of imperial behaviour, the Palatine palace not only represented Roman emperorship but also forced emperors to imitate (or otherwise confront) certain traditions. This may explain Nero's construction of his *Domus Aurea* (Golden House).[43] Only by leaving the Palatine could Nero fundamentally shift notions of emperorship. Even Nero did not abandon the Palatine altogether. Rather, he linked existing buildings to the gardens of Maecenas on the Esquiline, creating a massive residence in the area between the Palatine, Caelian and Oppian hills, dwarfing earlier structures. Ultimately, Nero's attempt to relocate and redefine emperorship failed and drew massive criticism, certainly in retrospect.[44]

Later emperors returned to the Palatine but this did not mean that they spent all their time there. Vespasian informally received visitors in the imperial gardens, as did many third-century rulers. Septimius Severus is said to have 'spent most of his time in the imperial villas

---

[41] S. Zink/ H. Piening, 'Haec Aurea Templa: the Palatine Temple of Apollo and Its Polychromy', JRA 22 (2009), 109– 22; 109–16, 122; A. Claridge, 'Reconstructing the Temple of Apollo on the Palatine Hill in Rome', in: C. Haeuber/ G. M. Winder/ F.-X. Schütz (eds.), *Reconstruction and the Historic City: Rome and Abroad – an Interdisciplinary Approach* (Munich 2004), 128–52, but note S. Zink, 'Old and New Evidence for the Plan of the Palatine Temple of Apollo', JRA 25 (2012), 388–402.

[42] M. Beard, 'Imaginary *Horti*; or Up the Garden Path', in: E. La Rocca/ M. Cima (eds.), *Horti Romani* (Rome 1998), 23–32; 32.

[43] On the Domus Aurea, see P. Meyboom/ E. M. Moormann, *Le decorazioni dipinte e marmoree della Domus Aurea di Nerone a Roma* I–II (Leuven 2013); E. M. Moormann, *Nerone, Roma e la Domus Aurea* (Rome 2020); M. A. Tomei, 'Nerone sul Palatino', in: M. A. Tomei/ R. Rea (eds.), *Nerone: Catalogo della Mostra (Roma, 13 Aprile–18 Settembre 2011)* (Milan 2011), 118–35; 123–33; H.-J. Beste, 'Domus Aurea, il padiglione dell'Oppio', in: Tomei/ Rea, *Nerone*, 170–5.

[44] Suet. *Nero*, 38.2; Tac. *Ann.* 15.40; Plin. *NH*, 36.24.111; Mart. *Lib. Spec.* 2; Seneca, *Letters*, 90.43; Seneca, *Thyestes*, 455–65, 641–9. But note how these negative reactions to the Palatine need not reflect contemporary opinions: J. Elsner, 'Constructing Decadence: The Reputation of Nero as an Imperial Builder', in: Elsner/ Masters, *Reflections of Nero*, 112–30; 123; D. B. Unruh, 'The Predatory Palace: Seneca's Thyestes and the Architecture of Tyranny', in: A. M. Kemezis (ed.), *Urban Dreams and Realities in Antiquity: Remains and Representations of the Ancient City* (Leiden 2015), 246–72, 258–68; Mar, *El Palatí*, 121–3.

outside Rome and on the coast of Campania, giving judgement and seeing to political affairs'. Severus Alexander allegedly even built a *palatium cum stagno* ('palace with a lake') at Baiae, probably referring to additions to a villa complex that was visited by most emperors from the early empire up to late antiquity.[45] The best-known example of an emperor spending most of his time away from Rome is probably Hadrian, not only during his travels, but also at his Villa at Tivoli. That may well have been an attempt to replace the Palatine as the main imperial residence. It was built to the emperor's preferences, and placed Rome – quite literally – in the background. Yet even that monumental villa was no complete alternative to the Palatine, with many courtiers still left in Rome.[46] Away from the Palatine, it was easier to accommodate individual imperial preferences, but emperors could not wholly escape their links to the imperial palace.

Even when emperors left Rome for shorter or longer periods of time, the Palatine palace remained paramount. It had become a symbol for Roman emperorship. Claudian, in his panegyric for the sixth consulship of Honorius (404) has the goddess Roma lament: 'Why do my Palaces, which gave their name to all the others, lie desolate in neglect?'[47] At least in some literary discourses, emperors were still expected to live in Rome. The Palatine pull remained. Even in the fifth century, emperors did not wholly abandon Rome as the imperial residence.[48] And in many ways the new eastern capital of Constantinople would parallel Roman structures, becoming a New Rome in more than just a name.

It is tempting to interpret the transformation of Constantinople into a new imperial capital as an attempt to escape the constraints of Rome. In a new capital emperors would no longer be confronted with testimonies of

---

[45] Dio Cass. 65(66).10.4–5; Hdn. 3.13.1; Dio Cass. 80.5.2; HA *Alex.Sev.*26.9; Hekster, 'Epilogue: Continuity and Change', 482; M. Cima, 'Gli *Horti Liciniani*: una residenza imperiale della tarda antichità', in: Cima/La Rocca, *Horti Romani*, 425–52; A. Grüner, 'Die kaiserlichen Villen in severischer Zeit: Eine Bestandsaufnahme', in: Sojc/ Winterling/ Wulf-Rheidt, *Palast und Stadt*, 231–86; 235; A. Raimondi Cominesi, 'From Villa to Palace: The Creation of a Palatial Culture in Rome under the Severans', forthcoming. For the Baiae villa: F. Maniscalco, *Ninfei ed edifice marittimi severiani del Palatium imperial di Baia* (Naples 1997).

[46] M. George, 'Imperial Villas', in: Kelly/ Hug, *The Roman Emperor and His Court*, 239–66; 249–59. On the villa: J. Charles-Gaffiot/ H. Lavagne, *Hadrien. Trésors d'une villa imperial* (Milan 1999); P. Gros, 'Hadrien architecte. Bilan des recherches', in: M. Mosser/ H. Lavagne (eds.), *Hadrien empereur et architecte. La Villa d'Hadrien: tradition et modernité d'un paysage culturel* (Geneva 2002), 33–53.

[47] Claud. *VI Cons. Hon.*, 409–11.

[48] Gillet, 'Rome, Ravenna and the Last Western Emperors', 137–57 and p. 191–2 above.

past behaviour that created political, religious and military expectations. Rome was not so easily abandoned. The Tetrarchs founded different capitals, partly because in a system of joint rule one ruler could not be living in Rome (although military and logistical reasons were also of the utmost importance). Any emperor based in Rome would be perceived as more important than the rest. Yet the absence of emperors from Rome allowed Maxentius (306–12) to make a prolonged bid for the throne, focusing on the capital's traditions and revitalising the notion of a *princeps* based in Rome.[49] Moreover, the urban layout of the various Tetrarchic capitals systematically followed a template set by Rome.[50] It is possible that the polis of Byzantium on the Golden Horn was one of those capitals, the residence of Constantine' last remaining rival Licinius. The first refurbishing of Byzantium by Constantine, beginning the transformation of the town into a (Christian) capital city, might well have been an attempt by Constantine to appropriate his opponent's main city, turning it into some sort of victory monument.[51] Perhaps Constantinople was not originally intended to be Rome's rival and successor city. Constantine and his sons continued to move between the various Tetrarchic capitals of Thessalonica, Nikomedia, Nicaea and Antioch. The unknown late-antique author known as the *Anonymus post Dionem* even reported that Constantine stated that Serdica (modern Sofia) was his Rome.[52] Though this is unlikely to be a true story, it shows that in the early fourth century Constantinople was considered as one of the new imperial residences, rather than a permanent alternative to Rome.

On the other hand, there is also some evidence from the early fourth century that Constantinople, dedicated as Nova Roma on 11 May 330, was intended to replace Rome as a capital from the beginning. A series of bronze and gold coins from 324–31 shows personifications of respectively Vrbs Roma and Constantinopolis (Figures 4.1 and 4.2). Constantinople holds the imperial sceptre and is laureated and helmeted, whereas Rome only wears the helmet.[53] This seems to symbolise a shift in status from the old

---

[49] S. Betjes/ S. Heijnen, 'The Usurping Princeps. Maxentius' Image and Its Constantinian Legacy', *JAHA* 5.3 (2018), 5–23; Hekster, 'The City of Rome in Late Imperial Ideology'.

[50] U. Wulf-Rheidt, 'Die Bedeutung der severischen Paläste für spätere Residenzbauten', in: Sojc/ Winterling/ Wulf-Rheidt, *Palast und Stadt*, 287–306 and p. 267 above.

[51] P. Stephenson, *Constantine: Unconquered Emperor, Christian Victor* (London 2009), 193.

[52] *Anon. post Dio.* fr. 15.1 (130); G. Dagron, *Naissance d'une capitale: Constantinople et ses institutions de 330 à 451* (Paris 1974), 25–9; J. Vanderspoel, 'A Tale of Two Cities. Themistius on Rome and Constantinople', in: Grig/ Kelly, *Two Romes*, 223–40; 224 n. 5.

[53] *RIC* 7, Rome, 295, 297, 300–1, 303–5, 307, 315–17, 331–4, 338; Lugdunum, 241–2, 246–7; Treveri, 522–3, 629–30; Arelate, 343–4, 351–2, 356–7. The series continues in later years.

Figures 4.1 and 4.2 Rome and New Rome: two bronze coins show the images of Rome and Constantinople, very similar in their design, but Constantinople is shown with the imperial sceptre and a wreath over her helmet, whereas Rome is not. This suggests that Constantinople is more closely linked to imperial rule.

(Figure 4.1) AD 331–32, Rome. Constantian bronze (2.47 g.): CONSTANTI-NOPOLIS on either side of a personification of Constantinople holding a sceptre and with a wreath over her helmet / Victory standing left on the prow, holding spear and shield. *RIC* VIII Rome 339

Source: ANS 1944.100.7404, American Numismatic Society

(Figure 4.2) AD 330, Rome. Constantian bronze (2.48 g.): VRBS – ROMA on either side of the goddess Rome, with helmet but without wreath or sceptre. The she-wolf is suckling twins, two stars above. *RIC* VIII Rome 331

Source: ANS 1944.100.7382, American Numismatic Society

Rome to the new one. A Constantinian law of 334 is issued 'for the advantage of the city which we have endowed with the name Eternal', and already in 326, Optatian called Constantinople 'Altera Roma'.[54] Ultimately, it is difficult to know what Constantine's intentions were and impossible to draw a single conclusion about the various reactions to the foundation of the new city. Quite possibly, complimentary (or even contradictory) motives dictated his actions. Yet even if Constantinople was originally intended as only one of the alternative imperial residences, it would ultimately become *the* new Rome.

Was the move to Constantinople meant to create a new Christian capital for the converted emperor? Eusebius certainly said so. In his *Life of Constantine*, he emphasised how the Christian emperor annihilated paganism in the city that bore his name:

> he embellished it with very many places of worship, very large martyr-shrines, and splendid houses ... By these he at the same time honoured the tombs of the martyrs and consecrated the city to the martyrs' God ... he saw fit to purge it of all idol-worship, so that nowhere in it appeared those images of the supposed gods which are worshipped in temples, nor altars foul with bloody slaughter, nor sacrifice offered as holocaust in fire, nor feasts of demons, nor any of the other customs of the superstitious.

Yet even Eusebius could not deny that Constantine filled the city with antique 'objects of skilled artwork' from throughout the empire. His argument that in doing so the emperor made these pagan monuments into 'toys for the laughter and amusement of the spectators' rings hollow. The passages suggest that the city was embellished by traditional methods, but that Constantine's actions were reformulated post hoc by Christian authors to put a Christian spin on them.[55] The discourse is comparable to that which we have seen at various point in this book surrounding 'good' and 'bad' emperors: the reputation of an emperor decided whether specific imperial behaviour was interpreted positively or negatively. Similarly, Constantine's actions were positively described as properly Christian, because the emperor was a Christian.

---

[54] *CTh.* 13.5.7.1; Opt. *Carm.* 4.6; Grig/ Kelly, 'From Rome to Constantinople', 11.

[55] Eus. *VC.* 3.48.1–2; 3.54.3 (translation Cameron). Several *Epigrams* of Palladas also discuss pagan statuary imported into Constantinople through a Christian lens. These are now redated to the foundational years of Constantinople: K. W. Wilkinson, 'Palladas and the Foundation of Constantinople', *JRS* 100 (2010), 179–94; 192–4. Eusebius' notion of Constantine as Christian foundation is accepted by Barnes, *Constantine*, 111.

Looking at the emperor's actions rather than at Christian interpretations of them indicates that the refoundation of the city was an imperial statement rather than a specifically Christian one. Alongside pagan statuary, Constantine also incorporated temples to Rhea/ Cybele and the *Tyche* (fortune) of Constantinople into his major renovation of the city.[56] Of course Constantine also embellished the urban landscape of his eponymous city with churches, yet this can be easily interpreted (at least in the early part of his reign) as showing obedience to the god in whose name he had conquered – a traditional way for emperors to show their relationship with the divine.[57] That very traditionality is worth emphasising. Much like the Tetrarchic capitals, Constantine's 'new Rome' was firmly modelled on the old one. All the elements that had defined (and perhaps constrained) emperorship in Rome were emulated in the new city. The imperial palace was constructed in close vicinity to the Hippodrome, where the populace could acclaim their ruler, and to the monumental baths, much like the ones in Rome. Constructions also included a monumental imperial forum with a senate building and a Capitolion, dedicated to the Capitoline triad. All of these emphasised the links to the traditional institutions and traditions of ancient Rome (Map 4.2).[58]

Moreover, much as had been the case for emperors throughout Roman history, the imperial family was made visible in the public space. Constantine's colossal bronze statue wearing a radiate crown, standing on top of a monumental porphyry column, is only the best known of a large number of statues depicting the emperor and his family.[59] Outside Rome, Constantine could make his dynastic mark without real competition from the past. There were no paradigmatic Byzantine figures or strong historical associations to compete with Constantine's dominance in the fourth-century city. Consequently, Constantine came to be associated with his city

---

[56] Zosimus, 2.31.2–3, with N. Lenski, 'Constantine and the Tyche of Constantinople', in: Wienand, *Contested Monarchy*, 330–9; 347; J. Elsner, 'Perspectives in Art', in: N. Lenski, *The Cambridge Companion to the Age of Constantine* (Cambridge 2006), 185–220; 209; R. Stephens Falcasantos, *Constantinople: Ritual, Violence, and Memory in the Making of a Christian Imperial Capital* (Oakland 2020), 49–51.

[57] Dagron, *Naissance d'une capital*, 388–400. See Hekster, 'The City of Rome in Late Imperial Ideology', 742 for similar Constantinian behaviour at Rome.

[58] S. Basset, *The Urban Image of Late Antique Constantinople* (Cambridge 2004), 23–32; Stephens Falcasantos, *Constantinople*, 49–50; A. Kaldellis, 'The Forum of Constantine in Constantinople: What Do We Know about Its Original Architecture and Decorations', *GRBS* 56 (2016), 714–39.

[59] Hallett, *The Roman Nude*, 265–8; J. Bardill, *Constantine, Divine Emperor of the Christian Golden Age* (Cambridge 2012), 104–9; Kaldellis, 'The Forum of Constantine', 731–5.

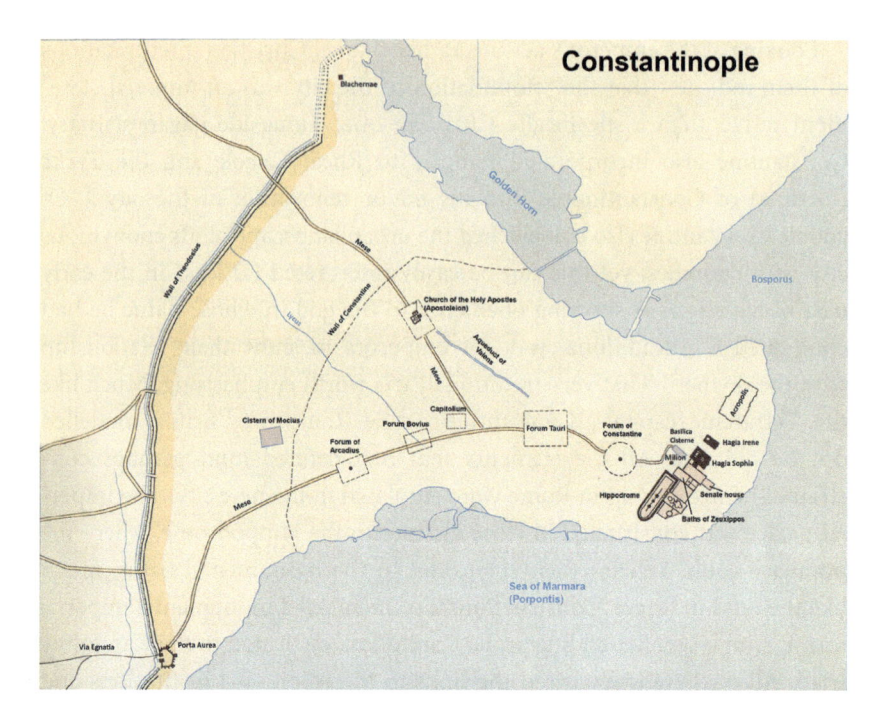

Map 4.2 The traditional topography of Constantinople: comparing the urban centre of Constantine's new city with that of Rome, the similarities are noticeable. New Rome reflected the old capital in its urban landscape
Source: CKD – Radboud University Nijmegen

more than any earlier emperor had been with Rome. This is clear from contemporary and later images showing Constantine as a founder (Figure 4.3). It is also clear from textual references. Illustrative is the early-eighth century Παραστάσεις σύντομοι χρονικαί (*Parastaseis suntomoi chronikai*; 'Brief historical notes'), an overview of statues and monuments in Constantinople. The text refers to Constantine as a semi-legendary figure, highly present in the cityscape. The *Notes* name approximately 200 statues or statue groups by name, forty of which are deemed to have depicted Constantine, with twelve statues of the emperor in the forum alone.[60]

---

[60] *Parastaseis*, § 7, 43–4a, 36, 68, 68a. Cf. § 10, 23, 38, 56, with A. Cameron/ J. Herrin, *Constantinople in the Early Eighth Century: The* Parastaseis Syntomoi Chronikai. *Introduction, Translation, and Commentary* (Leiden – Boston 1984). This point is made more extensively in Hekster, 'Ruling through Religion', 35–7, from which I have taken references and some formulations. The dominance of Constantine's image in the city is such that it has been argued that the emperor originally intended the city to be a dynastic city, rather than an eastern capital: J. Vanderspoel, *Themistius and the Imperial Court. Oratory, Civic Duty, and* Paideia *from Constantius to Theodosius* (Ann Arbor 1995), 51–61.

Figure 4.3 Constantine as founder: fourth-century sardonyx cameo (h 18.5cm, w 12.2 cm), reworked in the nineteenth century. Hermitage, St Petersburg, inv. ГР-12534. Constantine was commemorated as the undoubted founder of his eponymous city. On this roughly contemporary gemstone, he is crowned by the Tyche of Constantinople
Source: CKD – Radboud University Nijmegen

Later emperors could not outshine Constantine, but not for lack of trying. Much like had been the case in Rome, there was monumental inflation in Constantinople. Competition, however, was not just with existing buildings in Constantinople's city scape, but also with the glamour of Rome. The great Forum of Theodosius (effectively a reconstruction in AD 393 of Constantine's Forum Tauri) and the Forum of Arcadius (constructed in AD 403) echoed Constantine's Forum and that of Trajan. Both included marble columns, and the column of Arcadius appears to have been somewhat higher than its Roman counterparts.[61] Another column, in the *Augusteum*, was topped by an equestrian statue of Theodosius – reminiscent of the famous equestrian statue in Trajan's Forum. It was replaced by an even more monumental variant in 543 when Justinian reconstructed the area after the destructions during the Nika riots. Justinian's new column would be the tallest freestanding column erected in the premodern world, topped by the largest bronze equestrian statue constructed before the end of the seventeenth century (probably an appropriation of an existing equestrian statue).[62] The erection of obelisks in Constantinople was another way through which emperors could make their mark on the capital and try to compete with Rome's status. Several obelisks were imported from Egypt, including one of Egyptian porphyry, tailor-made for the eastern capital. Rome, however, had too much of a head start. In obelisks and in other secular monuments Constantinople never quite matched 'Old Rome'.[63]

Constantinople did, however, come close to Rome, and perhaps even overtake it, in the construction of buildings that illustrated two important imperial roles: the civil role of the emperor through aqueducts and cisterns, and the military role through monumental walls. The often-explicit comparisons to Rome in ancient descriptions of the construction and maintenance of these buildings is striking, as is the way in which they reflect traditional imperial roles.[64] The emperor's religious role was also firmly expressed. The much referred to development of Constantinople as a Christian capital can be seen as a form of competition with Rome and its religious tradition. After all, Rome was the final resting place of Paul and especially Peter – something that was near-impossible for Constantinople

---

[61] B. Ward-Perkins, 'Old and New Rome Compared: The Rise of Constantinople', in: Grig/ Kelly, *Two Romes*, 53–80; 57–8.
[62] E. Boeck, *The Bronze Horseman of Justinian in Constantinople: The Cross-Cultural Biography of a Mediterranean Monument* (Cambridge 2021), 53–71.
[63] Ward-Perkins, 'Old and New Rome Compared', 59–61.
[64] Ibid., 63–6 with further references.

to match.[65] The construction of impressive churches, Justinian's rebuilt *Hagia Sophia* the most important of them, was one way to compensate for Rome's religious primacy and to promote the emperor as a religious leader. By building 'the Church of Constantinople (which men are accustomed to call the Great Church)' as the largest church in the world with enormously rich decoration, Justinian both emphasised his religiosity and the supreme status of his capital.[66] The emperor did not only compete with Rome. He is often cited as having declared 'Solomon, I have surpassed you' at the opening ceremony of the church. The quotation is from the *Account of the Construction of Hagia Sophia* (known as the Διήγησις), which is a ninth-century account of dubious reliability, but there is little doubt that Justinian's great building was meant to emulate not only the churches of Rome but also the Biblical temple of Solomon.[67] The religious role of the emperor may not have changed massively over time, but by the mid-sixth century the past and tradition of Rome were no longer the only ones which were taken into account.

The lack of earlier monuments and a remarkable past was a disadvantage for Constantinople in its direct competition for status with Rome. But it allowed emperors more leeway in the new capital than they had in the old one. Notwithstanding the traditional (Roman) template used for the embellishment of the new capital, there were no places or monuments that recalled a Republican past. Even if the new Great Palace was linked to the Hippodrome and the public acclamation took place there, much like the Palatine had been linked to the Circus Maximus, the Constantinople residence did not have previous associations with 'traditional Roman-ness'. Moreover, the emperor residing in the Greek east, and being near the frontier of the new Persian empire, had an impact upon perceptions of rule and allowed for more monarchical forms of imperial representation, although these did not replace traditional expectations.[68]

---

[65] M. Humphries, 'Romulus and Peter: Remembering and Reconfiguring Rome's Foundation in Late Antiquity', in: Dijkstra, *The Early Reception and Appropriation of the Apostle Peter*, 172–87; 179–85. Cf. J. Dresken-Weiland, 'The Role of Peter in Early Christian art: Images from the 4th to the 6th Century', in: Dijkstra, *The Early Reception and Appropriation of the Apostle Peter*, 115–34.

[66] Procopius, *Buildings*, 1.1.66.

[67] *Diegesis*, ch. 27; G. Dagron, *Constantinople imaginaire. Études sur le recueil des Patria* (Paris 1984), 265–72. An English translation of the Διήγησις (alongside the Greek) is included in A. Berger, *Accounts of Medieval Constantinople. The Patria* (Cambridge [Mass.] – London 2013), 266–7.

[68] On cultural exchange between the two courts and a more monarchical form of representation, see pp. 90 and 168–9 above.

In this way, the development of Constantinople as imperial residence widened the range of imperial behaviour.

One change of behaviour that is often associated with the move to Constantinople as the imperial residence was a change towards a more stationary emperorship, from the itinerant emperorship of the earlier period.[69] That process was not linear, nor was there ever an absolute differentiation between the itinerant emperors in the early empire and palace monarchs in late antiquity. As we have seen throughout this book, there was continuity between emperorship in Rome and in Constantinople, and there are examples of non-travelling emperors well before late antiquity. Antoninus Pius rarely left Rome during his reign, and never the Italian peninsula. That did not stop him from being described as 'one man present in everything and overseeing everything, provinces, cities, armies, the commanders themselves'.[70] Even in the tumultuous third century, Elagabalus and Severus Alexander spent almost their whole reign in Rome. Nor did emperors cease to be itinerant when Constantinople became the main imperial residence. Valens (364–78), for instance, was almost continuously on the move. And at the very end of the fourth and beginning of the fifth century, Arcadius and his son Theodosius II still left Constantinople on several occasions; yet most of the times they only travelled to the Propontis shoreline, or to cities in western Asia Minor. Theodosius II seems to have intended to travel to the western empire in order to install Valentinian III, only to return to the capital because of problems with his health. His journeys also included pilgrimage, which would become a new form of imperial travel – though no emperor ever visited the Holy Land.[71]

Fifth- and sixth-century eastern emperors seem to have been more systematically present in or very near their capital than earlier rulers. Theodosius' successors rarely travelled outside of the Bosporus area,

---

[69] Maier, *Palastrevolution*, 451–62.
[70] Aristides, *To Rome*, 88, with C. P. Jones, 'Elio Aristide e i primi Anni di Antonino Pio', in: P. Desideri/ F. Fontanella (eds.), *Elio Aristide e la legittimazione greca dell'impero di Roma* (Bologna 2013), 39–67. On Antoninus' 'static' rule: C. Michels, *Antoninus Pius und die Rollenbilder des römischen Princeps. Herrscherliches Handeln und seine Repräsentation in der hohen Kaiserzeit* (Berlin – Boston 2018), 112–13.
[71] Socrates 7.24.4; S. Destephen, 'Mobile Center to Constantinople. The Birth of Byzantine Imperial Government', *Dumbarton Oaks Papers* 73 (2019), 9–24; 12–13, 17–20; S. Destephen, 'Le Prince chrétien en pèlerinage', in: S. Destephen/ B. Dumézil/ H. Inglebert (eds.), *Le Prince chrétien de Constantin aux royautés barbares (IVe–VIIIe siècle)* (Paris 2018), 270–313, 311–13; B. Ward-Perkins, 'A Most Unusual Empire: Rome in the Fourth Century', in: Rapp/ Drake, *The City in the Classical and Post Classical World*, 109–29, 117, 122–3.

perhaps partly because various summer palaces were constructed in the vicinity of the capital, enabling the imperial family to travel locally and easily.[72] Justinian did not leave his capital to lead his campaigns, nor did he visit his troops. More strikingly, he did not visit his conquered territories. The size of an expanding court is often mentioned as a reason for this decreased mobility, but that seems unlikely. Malalas may have noted how Theodora travelled through Bithynia in 529 'accompanied by 4,000 people', but that is similar in size to Hadrian's retinue in Egypt exactly four centuries earlier.[73] Perhaps the new Constantinian palace had by now become so strongly linked to emperorship that it led people to expect that the emperor was present in his palace, creating new constraints on imperial behaviour. The highly elaborate 'campaign palaces' – the imperial entourage and tents, including objects that were closely connected to imperial power and the Great Palace – in which the emperor stayed during campaign from at least the ninth century onwards suggest an ever-closer connection between the emperor and the spaces in which he resided and received guests.[74] The very fact that these mobile palaces were necessary shows that eastern emperors never became fully stationary. Even when Constantinople had become a fixed imperial capital focused on the palace, emperors still needed to be on the move. Emperors were presumed to be in their capital, but also to visit their people. As so often, different people expected different actions from their ruler.

Expectations of a Civic Ruler

Sometime in the 360s, the governor of Caria (western Anatolia) rebuilt the so-called *Tetrastoon* in front of the theatre at Aphrodisias. It was necessary to create a new honorific gallery for prestigious statues, since the *scaena* and the inside of the theatre were filled to the brim with them. For much of Aphrodisias' history, statues had been erected of emperors, office holders, local men and women, athletes and gods. Statues continued to be erected in late antiquity, but at a much lower rate, and with a shifting emphasis of

---

[72] H. Hellenkemper, 'Anatolische Riviera: Byzantinische Kaiserpaläste in Bithynien', in: E. Winter/ K. Zimmermann (eds.), *Neue Funde und Forschungen in Bithynien* (Bonn 2013), 61–81; Destephen, 'Mobile Center', 21.
[73] Malalas 18.25; Destephen, 'Mobile Center', 22. The size of Hadrian's travelling court, see p. 211 above.
[74] On 'campaign palaces': L. Jones, 'Taking It on the Road. The Palace on the Move', in: S. Tougher, *The Emperor in the Byzantine World*, 322–40; 323–35.

honorands. From the fourth century onwards, imperial office holders were much more likely to be honoured with a public statue at Aphrodisias, whereas local men received far fewer public statues. Women were no longer given public statues at all. Honorific statues for emperors continued to be constructed at about the same rate as in the earlier periods. Noticeably, in many of the public spaces at Aphrodisias (such as the *Tetrastoon*), emperors were depicted alongside their various subjects, all wearing togas, though the emperor was clearly recognisable.[75]

It is hardly surprising that members of the local elite often chose to depict their emperor and the governors who personified Roman power in a toga. They wanted to emphasise the civic, magisterial, role of the emperor. In that context he was responsible for urban status and administration, areas in which the local elites were themselves involved.[76] By honouring the emperor, members of the local elite aimed to guarantee his good will. By honouring him in a role that they themselves found particularly appealing, these local elites also tried to convince the powers that be of the importance of that role. This was a dynamic and reciprocal process, aimed to reinforce the relation between emperors and the leading members of provincial cities. Emperors could interact directly with cities throughout the empire. They could elevate the status of towns, grant them privileges or remove them. Emperors were also with some regularity involved in major building schemes, and were expected to help any region in which calamity struck. Some emperors were more active in this respect than others, with the much travelled Hadrian apparently interacting with more than 130 cities. Yet all emperors were expected to involve themselves in the wellbeing of their cities.[77]

Imperial administrative interventions were important for towns, and were commemorated publicly. The theatre of Aphrodisias included a so-called 'archive wall', which publicly displayed positive imperial responses to

---

[75] R. R. R. Smith, 'Aphrodisias', in: R. R. R. Smith/ B. Ward-Perkins (eds.), *The Last Statues of Antiquity* (Oxford 2016), 145–59; 146–9 with figs. 12.2, 155–6; R. R. R. Smith, 'Late Antique Portraits in a Public Context: Honorific Statuary at Aphrodisias in Caria, AD 300–600', *JRS* 89 (1999), 155–89 describes how changes in dedicatory practice reflect a changed political culture.

[76] On the relationship between emperors, officials and local elites, see fundamentally Millar, *Emperor*, 363–463.

[77] M. T. Boatwright, *Hadrian and the Cities of the Roman Empire* (Princeton 2003), 15 notes the number of 130 cities. T. E. Fraser, *Hadrian as Builder and Benefactor in the Western Provinces* (Oxford 2006), 35–8, 54–8, 61–2, 72–8, 97–103, 116–23, 235–45 similarly shows that Hadrian's civic building works exceed those of his predecessors and successors in many of the provinces. Note, however, that patterns of interaction with cities are very similar for other emperors, even if the frequency of interaction is lower. See, for instance, R. Bertolazzi, *Septimius Severus and the Cities of the Empire* (Faenza 2020).

requests made by the city, and negative reactions by competing cities.[78] Its nearby competitor city Ephesus explicitly thanked Hadrian because 'he provided shipments of grain from Egypt, rendered the harbour navigable, and diverted the river Caÿster, which had been harming the harbours'.[79] Such major infrastructural projects emphasised Roman power and prowess. Frontinus (c. 40–103) compares the 'array of indispensable structures carrying so many waters' positively with 'the idle pyramids or the useless, though famous, works of the Greeks' echoing Dionysius of Halicarnassus (60 BC–AD 7), who proclaimed that 'the three most magnificent works of Rome, in which the greatness of her empire is best seen, are the aqueducts, the paved roads and the construction of the sewers'.[80] The costs of such projects were so high that imperial support was extremely important. The aqueduct at Alexandria Troas, for instance, was sponsored for 3 million drachmae (12 million sesterces) by Hadrian at the request of Herodes Atticus. The costs skyrocketed to 7 million drachmae, and procurators in Asia complained to the emperor, who made Herodes responsible for the surplus costs.[81] Hadrian is known to have sponsored at least eight newly constructed aqueducts, the restoration or extension of four more and work on the harbours of yet another four cities. Dio argues that Hadrian aided almost all the cities which he visited 'giving to some a water supply, to other harbours, food, public works, money and various honours'. He seems not to have exaggerated.[82] Hadrian might have been exceptional in his involvement with the cities of the Roman empire, but other emperors, too, were heavily involved in the financing and organisation of major engineering projects in the provinces.[83] Showing munificence was an important virtue for Roman aristocrats, as it had been for Hellenistic kings, and the major works in which emperors were involved showed them to be the ultimate benefactor.[84]

---

[78] J. Reynolds, *Aphrodisias and Rome. Documents from the Excavation of the Theatre at Aphrodisias Conducted by Professor Kenan T. Erim Together with Some Related Texts* (London 1982), esp. 33–7.
[79] SIG 839, ll. 12–16, quoted by Ando, *Imperial Ideology*, 323.
[80] Frontinus, *Aq.* 1.16; Dion. Hal. 3.67.5.
[81] Phil. VS. 548–9; S. Mitchell, 'Imperial Building in the Eastern Roman Provinces', *Harvard Studies in Classical Philology* 91 (1987), 333–65; 346–7.
[82] Dio, 69.5.1; HA, *Hadr.* 20.5. New aqueducts: Alexandria Troas, Syrian Antioch, Argos, Athens, Corinth, Coronea, Dyrrachium, Sarmizegetusa. Restoration and extension: Caesarea (Judaea), Cingulum, Gabii, Italica. Harbour works: Ephesus, Lupiae, Puteoli, Trapezus. See Boatwright, *Hadrian and the Cities*, 109 table 6.1, 112, with full references.
[83] Mitchell, 'Imperial Building', 352–3.
[84] P. Veyne, Le *Pain et le cirque. Sociologie historique d'un pluralisme politique* (Paris 1976), 278–9; A. Zuiderhoek, *The Politics of Munificence in the Early Roman Empire* (Cambridge 2009), 110–12.

The role of the emperor as key benefactor was even more important when disaster struck. Roman emperors were expected to rapidly supply help in times of need. When earthquakes or floods occurred, emperors intervened upon request or even proactively, often with spectacular measures.[85] In doing so emperors followed precedents set by Hellenistic kings. When, for instance, the island of Rhodes was struck by an earthquake in 227 BC, damaging its famous Colossus, the Rhodians sent embassies to Hellenistic kings, who were so keen to show their munificence that the island was rapidly restored to its former splendour.[86] Greek cities came to expect such a reaction, and it seems that by the late Republic, wealthy Roman individuals had become systematically involved in disaster recovery, even if there appears to have been no centrally coordinated disaster relief on the part of the Romans until the reign of Augustus.[87] From then onwards, it became a standard and well-advertised aspect of Roman imperial behaviour. The appendix to Augustus' *Res Gestae* explicitly mentions that the first emperor lavishly compensated 'towns destroyed by earthquake and fire'. When in AD 17, a massive earthquake demolished so many cities in Asia Minor that it became known as the 'Twelve City Quake', Tiberius responded to this 'most powerful earthquake in living memory' by giving money to the cities, tax relief, and the sending a senator to assess the damage and liaise with the emperor. Later emperors would react in similar ways.[88] Tiberius' measures were advertised through a series of sesterces minted in 22–3 that showed the emperor in toga on a curule chair, with the legend CIVITATIBUS ASIAE RESTITUTIS ('the cities of Asia re-established', Figure 1.19).[89] Disaster relief might have ultimately followed Hellenistic precedent, but it was firmly formulated in the visual language of a *civilis princeps*.

In some cases when cities petitioned the emperor for disaster relief, emphasis was placed on the special relationship between ruler and town.

---

[85] H. Sonnabend, *Naturkatastrophen in der Antike: Wahrnehmung – Deutung – Management* (Stuttgart – Weimar 1999), 215–29; M. Meier, 'Roman Emperors and "Natural Disasters" in the First Century AD', in: A. Janku/ G. Schenk/ F. Mauelshagen (eds.), *Historical Disasters in Context: Science, Religion, and Politics* (London – New York 2011), 15–30; 15.

[86] Polybios 5.88–90; M. T. McCoy, *The Responses of the Roman Imperial Government to Natural Disasters 29 BCE–180 CE* (PhD University of Arkansas 2014), 32, 63–8.

[87] McCoy, *Responses*, 68–9; P. Garnsey, *Famine and Food Supply in the Graeco-Roman World* (Cambridge – New York 1988), 84–5; Sonnabend, *Naturkatastrophen*, 210–15.

[88] RGDA, appendix 4; Plin. NH. 2.200; Tac. Ann. 2.47; Velleius Paterculus 2, 126; Meier, 'Roman Emperors', 18–20, 26–7 nn. 31–2 with further references; Mitchell, 'Imperial Building', 350–2; Millar, *Emperor*, 423–4.

[89] RIC 1 (2nd ed.), Tiberius, 48. It is possible that these coins refer to restorations after a more minor earthquake in 23, but the point remains the same.

Aelius Aristides, for instance, wrote to Marcus Aurelius when an earthquake struck Smyrna in AD 177 or 178, to petition the emperor for help. He recalled Marcus' recent visit to the city in AD 176, and the past fidelity of Smyrna to Rome. Moreover, Aristides emphasised that the damage was so extensive that only the emperor had the means to pay for its restoration. Only if the emperor desired it, Smyrna would be restored. Hence Aristides' personal (and somewhat hyperbolic) appeal to Marcus.[90] It seems likely that disaster relief grew more important over time, as the changing climate made natural disasters more likely after about the second half of the second century. Before then, the Roman empire had been fortunate with surprisingly moist and warm weather. This co-called 'Roman Climate Optimum' ended in the AD 150s with more disasters, including the outbreak of a pandemic as consequence.[91] Global environmental history, it appears, created problems which could not be (financially) solved by local elites, increasing the importance of the emperor as a benefactor. Closer personal ties meant more imperial involvement. This did not only apply to disaster relief, but also to the maintenance or improvement of civic amenities. The embellishment of Italica and Lepcis Magna, as the cities of birth of Hadrian and Septimius Severus respectively, form somewhat extreme examples of this.[92] The unknown Gallic orator who in AD 310 invited Constantine to come to Autun was explicit in his expectation that a visit from the emperor would lead to the restoration of the city: 'you will grant favours, and establish privileges, and at last restore my native place … The ancient nobility of this city … awaits the assistance of your majesty'. Nor was Autun disappointed, as a visit by Constantine in 311 led to major tax remissions.[93] It was small wonder, then, that cities tried to establish positive relationships with the ruling emperor. To ensure his favour, they sent embassies to express joy at his accession, or to ask the emperor to accept local honours that had been voted to him – in the process emphasising how much the city wanted to honour the emperor.[94]

---

[90] Arist, *Or.* 19; McCoy, *Responses*, 82–95; Millar, *Emperor*, 424.
[91] K. Harper, *The Fate of Rome: Climate, Disease and the End of an Empire* (Princeton 2017), 12–19, 65–137.
[92] Boatwright, *Hadrian and the Cities*, 162–7; Fraser, *Hadrian as Builder*, 111, 117–8; Bertolazzi, *Septimius Severus and the Cities*, 197–202; J. B. Ward-Perkins, *The Severan Buildings of Lepcis Magna: An Architectural Survey* (London 1993).
[93] *Pan. Lat.* 7(6), 22.3–4; Nixon/ Saylor Rodgers, *In Praise of Later Roman Emperors*, 251–2; Millar, *Emperor*, 424–5.
[94] Millar, *Emperor*, 410–20.

Such honours were not, however, only meant to impress the emperor – important as that aspect was. Cities also emphasised their relationship to emperors to surpass neighbouring cities. The choice of Samos to commemorate Claudius as the 'new founder' because of his financial support following an earthquake in AD 47 was a proper way to express gratitude to the ruler, but also a way to afterwards show the island's superior imperial connections. The same applied to the establishment of temples for the imperial cult. There was fierce inter-city competition about the right to build a provincial temple to the Roman emperor and become 'temple warden' (*neokoros*).[95] Building such a temple, or at a lower level, dedicating a statue to the emperor or inscribing an emperor's favourable reaction to an embassy, honoured the emperor and simultaneously raised a city's status. Moreover, those who dedicated such a statue or temple, or were named in the inscription, boosted their status within a city. This is one reason why a disproportionate number of building inscriptions from Carthage and its hinterland refer to the involvement of local elites in the building of temples and arches for emperors. There was more value in commemorating the erection of these structures than other types of buildings.[96] In other words, ties to the emperor were important to gain status at local level, between cities and within them. In this way, the unchallenged position of the emperor as a central conferrer of gifts and honour helped to bind periphery and centre in a highly disparate empire.[97]

The emperor took a central position as benefactor in his empire, but in practical terms, many of actions attributed to him were carried out by others. Imperial officials played an important part in this. The increased emphasis on imperial office holders among the honorific statues at Aphrodisias from the fourth century onwards, at the cost of statues for

---

[95] *AE* (1912), 217. On temples for the imperial cult, see p. 209 above and p. 315 below. B. Burrell, *Neokoroi: Greek Cities and Roman Emperors* (Leiden – Boston 2004), 353–5; S. J. Friesen, *Twice Neokoros: Ephesus, Asia and the Cult of the Flavian Imperial Family* (Leiden – New York – Cologne 1993), 17–18, 21.

[96] M. Hellström, 'Epigraphy and Ambition: Building Inscriptions in the Hinterland of Carthage', *JRS* 110 (2020), 57–90; 61–2. But cf. J. Quinn/ A. Wilson, 'Capitolia', *JRS* 103 (2013), 117–73 who show an unusually large number of Capitolia in Africa, where building inscriptions suggest local initatives for local purposes, with emperors less emphatically present. They do note (p. 167) how 'a temple whose ideological significance expressed loyalty to Rome or the imperial house' was often placed in relation to the forum.

[97] Ando, *Imperial Ideology*, 132–5, 175–81. On the role of honour in this process: Lendon, *Empire of Honour*, 136–9, 140–1, 151–3. On the importance of local interests for the erection of imperial statues: M. Hellström, 'Local Aspirations and Statues of Emperors in Roman North Africa', in: Russell/ Hellström, *Social Dynamics*, 159–79.

local men (and especially women), suggests that people in the provinces recognised the increased involvement of central government in financing and organising local civic life, and attributed it more than before to high-ranking officers, especially governors. This understanding of an empire run by imperial decisions, which are faithfully carried out by underlings, comes close to the vision of Shenoute.[98] Imperial legates and procurators had always been the focus of local citizens. Already in the course of the first and second centuries, local individuals approached Rome directly, rather than local city magistrates or assemblies, often by petitioning the governor.[99] Major administrative reforms under the Tetrarchs systematised imperial administration and taxation, making governors directly responsible for tax collection in their provinces.[100] It was unsurprising, then, that governors were honoured in increasing numbers of statues and through increasingly elaborate phrases.[101]

Governors and other local imperial officers were in practice responsible for most of the imperial benefactions in the provinces. This was recognised by local subjects, who saw how directly the actions of these officials influenced their daily life. Yet ultimate agency was still attributed to the faraway emperor. This was apparently deemed important by emperors, as a law from AD 394 makes clear: 'if any of the governors should inscribe their own names, rather than the name of Our Eternity, on any completed public work, they shall be held guilty of high treason'.[102] That did not stop locals who benefited from these public works from acclaiming the officials who had brought the buildings about, but always with due regard to the emperor. Emperors also kept track of major infrastructural works, and legislated that no governor 'should begin any public work without consulting Our Piety', although this only applied to 'the most important and largest works, not in connection with every trivial work'.[103]

---

[98] See above 262.   [99] Eck, 'Provinicial Administration and Finance', 288–9.
[100] C. Kelly, *Ruling the Later Roman Empire* (Cambridge [Mass.] – London 2004), 110–11; D. Slootjes, *The Governor and his Subjects in the Later Roman Empire* (Leiden – Boston 2006), 34–9. See Jones. *The Later Roman Empire* 1964, 448–69, 727–31 on tax collection and distribution in the late-antique Roman world.
[101] M. Horster, 'Ehrungen Spätantiker Statthalter', *Antiquité Tardive* 6 (1998), 37–59; O. Salomies, 'Some Interesting Expressions Found in Late Antique Honorific Inscriptions', in: G. Paci (ed.), *Epigraphai. Miscellanea epigrafica in onore di Lidio Gasperini. Vol. 2* (Tivoli 2000), 931–42. See now S. Penders, *Empire of Virtue? Normative Language and the Legitimation of Power in the Roman North Africa* (PhD Leiden 2021).
[102] *Cod. Theod.* 15.1.31.
[103] *Cod. Theod.* 15.1.2, 15.1.37; Slootjes, *The Governor and His Subjects*, 80–5.

The expectation that emperors involved themselves in the wellbeing of their subjects existed throughout the empire, and continued for the whole period discussed in this book. The importance of this relationship was such that when weakening central control over the periphery of the empire made imperial patronage impossible at local level, as was the case in much of fourth- and fifth-century Gaul, others would take the emperor's place. These could be local leaders, borrowing the language of imperial authority or even aiming for the position of emperor themselves. Alternatively, there were groups rebelling against Rome, such as the enigmatic Bacaudae, which are described as peasants reacting against the oppressiveness of taxation without civic benefits.[104] An important role was also taken up by bishops and other local church leaders, who increasingly functioned as integrating figures in their own communities and in connecting different communities in Gaul and the wider world.[105] Yet all of this happened when central control was lacking. When there was a clear ruler, inhabitants of the Roman empire turned to him. Theodoric, for instance, was clearly expected to take his traditional role as benefactor in the early sixth century when marshes needed to be drained in Italian peninsula. A local senator ran the project (and received tax benefits in return) but the project was to a large extent ascribed to Theodoric.[106] Nor did the expectation of imperial involvement end with the reign of Justinian. When Gortyn (Crete) was struck by an earthquake in AD 618, the emperor Heraclius responded with major reconstructions.[107] It is, then, unsurprising that emperors continued to be honoured in their civil role till (at least) the end of the sixth century.

---

[104] D. Lambert, 'Salvian and the Bacaudae', in: S. Diefenbach/ G. M. Müller (eds.), *Gallien in Spätantike und Frühmittelalter: Kulturgeschichte einer Region* (Berlin – New York 2012), 255–78; 257–9; C. Wickham, *Framing the Early Middle Ages* (Oxford 2005), 527–33; J. F. Drinkwater, 'Patronage in Roman Gaul and the Problem of the Bacaudae', in: A. Wallace-Hadrill (ed.), *Patronage in Ancient Society* (London – New York 1989), 189–203; 198–200.

[105] P. Sarris, *Empires of Faith. The Fall of Rome to the Rise of Islam, 500–700* (Oxford 2011), 208–10; P. Eich, *Gregor der Große. Bischof von Rom zwischen Antike und Mittelalter* (Paderborn 2016), 150–8. Still seminal: M. Heinzelmann, *Bischofsherrschaft in Gallien. Zur Kontinuität römischer Führungsschichten vom 4. bis zum 7. Jahrhundert. Soziale, prosopographische und bildungsgeschichtliche Aspekte* (Zürich – Munich 1976).

[106] Tacoma, *Political Culture*, 196–203, 214–24. On the importance of imperial involvement in creating cultivated territory in marshy land in the later Roman Empire, see now: F. Bono, '*Adluvionum ea natura est, ut semper incerta possession sit*. Picturing and regulating alluvial lands in *Nov. Theod.* 20', in: M. Horster/ N. Hächler (eds.), *The Impact of the Roman Empire on Landscapes* (Leiden – Boston 2021), 206–22.

[107] Wickham, *Framing the Early Middle Ages*, 628; J. Francis/ G. W. M. Harrison, 'Gortyn: First City of Roman Crete', *AJA* 107 (2003), 487–92; 491.

Expectations of a Military Ruler

The emperor was not only honoured in his civil role. Often that role was intrinsically linked to other parts of imperial behaviour. The temples that were erected for the imperial cult celebrated the emperors' relation to the gods and his divine status. Many of the major building works in the provinces, especially the construction of canals and aqueducts, were carried out by soldiers.[108] It was not only the manpower for building work that the armies provided, but also technical expertise. In AD 152, for instance, Nonius Datus, the hydraulic engineer of the African Third Legion, needed to be sent to the city of Saldae (Mauretania) to help with various technical issues involved in the building of an aqueduct there, since

> they were despairing over the useless labour put into an underground passage, and had almost abandoned it, since the boring-work which had been done was greater than the distance across the mountain. It appeared that the tunnels had wandered away from their straight course, so that the higher tunnel had headed right and southwards, while the lower had also headed to its right, which is to say towards the north: so the two parts were wandering apart, having abandoned the straight course ... When I was assigning the work, I divided it between marines and Gaulish soldiers so that they would all know how to go about the boring process, and they agreed to carry out the joint tunnelling through the mountain in this way. So I had made the measurements, organised the digging of the conduit and undertaken that it should be done according to the plan which I had given to the Procurator Petronius Celer. The work was carried out, the water flowed and Varus Clemens the Procurator dedicated it.

The inscription that includes this anecdote makes clear that Nonius Datus was asked to come to Saldae various times over the course of over four years, showing how rare his skills were – and hence how important army involvement was in major building projects. It also makes clear how unsafe travelling in the provinces could be, as it explicitly mentions how Datus 'set

---

[108] See: R. MacMullen, 'Roman Imperial Building in the Provinces', *HSCP* 64 (1959), 207–35; 214–18. The extent of infrastructural impact of the legions in the Rhine and Danube area is set out in K. Strobel, 'Von marginalen Grenzraum zum Kernraum Europas. Das römische Heer als Motor der Neustrukturierung historischer Landschaften und Wirtschaftsräume', in: L. de Blois/ E. LoCascio (eds.), *The Impact of the Roman Army* (200 BC–AD 476) (Leiden – Boston 2007), 207–37.

out and encountered brigands on the roads; I and my companions escaped naked and injured'.[109]

Civic life could only flourish in peace, and keeping brigands at bay was an important task of imperial rule. Bandits were not the only problems. Soldiers who were meant to keep these bandits at bay could cause problems themselves. In the early- to mid-third century, inhabitants of the Lydian town of Ağa Bey Köyü requested imperial protection against agents of the military police who had taken nine inhabitants of the imperial estate hostage, and 'put them in chains . . . and after payment of a sum of money . . . they let one of the nine go, but held back the remainder in fetters'.[110] When faced with such problems, people in the provinces approached imperial representatives, and sometimes ultimately the emperor himself. Many of the petitions (*libelli*) from provincial civilians to the emperor deal with abuse by soldiers, or by the officials who were meant to keep them in check.[111] The importance that emperors attached to keeping peace in the provinces becomes clear from the high priority that a governor was supposed to give to ensure 'that the province he rules remains pacified and quiet'.[112] The impact of military unrest on daily life was immediate and often devastating. This applied to all regions of the empire, in the cities and on the countryside. Emperors were expected to keep such unrest at bay. When they failed to do that, their regime was in trouble.

Roman emperors, as we have seen, were expected to be successful in war. This was partly an ideological construct but partly also a real necessity for those whose whole livelihood depended on uninterrupted trade, untrampled lands and the absence of brigands or soldiers from their territory. Provincial images of a belligerent and victorious emperor expressed the importance of an emperor who was sufficiently powerful to protect them. Sometimes these images celebrated victories that were far removed from the location at which the emperor was praised for his military achievements. A relief from Koula (in Lydia) shows an armed horseman rising over a standing woman. An accompanying inscription identifies the figure on horseback as Caligula and the woman as Germania, making this one of the few positive representations of the much-maligned German campaign

---

[109] *CIL* 8.2728; Hekster, *Rome and Its Empire*, 17–17, 118 no. 16; MacMullen, 'Roman Imperial Building', 215–16.

[110] Hauken, *Petition and Response*, 36–57 (no. 3); Hekster, *Rome and Its Empire*, 18, 121–2 no. 17. See p. 131 above for a similar situation at Skaptopara.

[111] C. J. Fuhrmann, *Policing the Roman Empire: Soldiers, Administration and Public Order* (Oxford – New York 2012), 148–9. On petitioning the emperor and imperial response: Millar, *Emperor*, 240–52, 537–49.

[112] *Dig.* 1.18.13.pr (Ulpian); *Dig.* 1.18.3 (Paulus); Fuhrmann, *Policing the Roman Empire*, 150–1.

of Caligula in AD 39/40.[113] Similarly, reliefs on the famous *Sebasteion* at Aphrodisias, paid for by two wealthy local families, showed the emperor Claudius assaulting a personification of Britannia, and Nero mishandling a personification of Armenia (Figure 4.4).[114] Claudius' conquest of Britain was widely celebrated through coins and a triumphal arch at Rome. The Roman arch is echoed by a triumphal arch at Cyzicus (Asia), erected by local citizens. Nero's achievements in Armenia, however, were not widely disseminated.[115]

The monuments in Aphrodisias and Koula reflect local (artistic) choices, which differed from centrally disseminated messages. These choices were influenced by local traditions, drawing for instance on Hellenistic monarchic images. The main point seems to have been to honour the emperor for his role in personally extending the empire and making it safe through faraway victories. Sometimes the need for a belligerent emperor was much more immediate. Small terracotta figurines from Egypt, for instance, show a bearded military figure holding a barbarian by his hair and threatening him with a sword (Figure 4.5). Stylistically, the image mixes Egyptian and Graeco-Roman imagery. The figure depicted seems to have been Hadrian, who is only rarely centrally depicted suppressing enemies, although there are several statues showing Hadrian subjugating a barbarian in the eastern Mediterranean world.[116] In all likelihood, these statues and figurines were local reactions to Hadrian's suppression of the so-called 'Jewish Diaspora War' (AD 115–117), in which groups of Jews in Libya, Cyprus and Egypt rebelled. This uprising was a massive affair. Cassius Dio mentions 220,000 deaths in Cyrenaica, and 240,000 deaths in Cyprus. In Egypt, papyri stop indicating payment of temple tax from 18 May 116, onwards, dating the start of the uprising very precisely. One surviving papyrus account even states that the insurgents defeated a legion. 'Many tens of thousands of Jews' are said to have been killed in Egypt, with the need for a coordinated Roman reaction under the command of Lusius Quietus to ultimately contain the uprising. Inscriptions from the different regions make clear

---

[113] *ILS* 8791; Museo d'Antichità, Trieste, inv. 2228; Suet. *Cal.* 43–8; Dio, 59.21.2–23.6; C. Davenport, 'Roman Emperors, Conquest, and Violence', in: Russell/Hellström, *Social Dynamics*, 100–27; 103–5. On Caligula's 'fake triumph' after the campaign, see p. 115 above.
[114] R. R. R. Smith, 'The Imperial Reliefs from the Sebasteion at Aphrodisias', *JRS* 77 (1987), 88–138; 140–3, 145–7, Vout, *Power and Eroticism*, 25, 48.
[115] *CIL* 3.7061; *CIL* 6.40416; Davenport, 'Roman Emperors', 106–7.
[116] P. Karanastasi, 'Hadrian im Panzer. Kaiserstatuen zwischen Realpolitik und Philhellenismus', *JDAI* 127/128 (2012/2013), 323–91; 326–9, 350–4, 386–8; Davenport, 'Roman Emperors', 117–22. Note that the ruler as a subjugator was a consistent theme in Egyptian art.

Figure 4.4 Imperial might against the provinces: AD 43–60, Aphrodisias, marble relief (h. 1.68 m, w. 1.35 m, d. c. 0.45 m), Aphrodisias museum inv. no. 80–159. This scene is part of a series of reliefs showing Roman emperors with their conquests, placed alongside reliefs of mythological scenes. The emperors are portrayed in heroic nude. Showing maltreatment of Britannia was apparently not a problem in Asia Minor
Source: CKD – Radboud University Nijmegen

Expectations of a Military Ruler 297

Figure 4.5 A local image of the belligerent emperor: c. 118 (?), Egypt, terracotta figurine (h. 17.5 cm, w. 10.5 cm, d. 5 cm); British Museum, inv. 1983,0723.1. This small figure probably depicts Hadrian in cuirass, with an eagle on his shoulder, holding a kneeling captive by the hair and pointing a sword towards him. The emperor is shown actively subduing his enemies, probably in reaction to local upheavals
Source: © The Trustees of the British Museum

that the restoration of peace was frequently attributed to Hadrian.[117] The Egyptian statuettes may well reflect the same sentiment. In the various regions that were directly impacted by the Diaspora War, the emperor was explicitly depicted as a dominant warrior. People praised their ruler for the restoration of peace in an area that had been severely disturbed.[118]

There was a potential problem with creating images of the emperor as a belligerent figure in the provinces. The Roman empire, after all, had grown through conquest. Being subjugated by the Romans was a bloody affair. This may be one reason why locally instigated images of the emperor personally crushing enemies were near-absent from the Roman west in the early empire. Instead, there are images of violence performed by Roman officers.[119] Gaul was only brought under Roman dominion by Caesar, through major bloodshed, the scale of which has recently been made clear through archaeological research.[120] Images of a conquering emperor in its aftermath would have been too strong a reminder of the violence with which Gaul was added to the empire. Few people would like to commemorate a bloody defeat in which friends and family had been slaughtered. Showing the emperor killing your kin was a bad idea. Showing him killing other enemies of Rome was much less problematic, as the images of the emperor subjugating Britons in faraway Koula and Aphrodisias make clear. Such a differentiation will have been difficult in the immediate aftermath of conquest. It was much easier to celebrate the role of the emperor in guaranteeing the safety of the empire if one had not just lived through the wars that accompanied subjugation. Being reminded

---

[117] *Corpus Papyrorum Judaicarum* 438; Karanastasi, 'Hadrian im Panzer, 350–4; A. R. Birley, *Hadrian. The Restless Emperor* (London – New York 1997), 72–4, with 324 n. 20, 152; F. Ziosi, 'Sulle iscrizioni relative alla ricostruzione di Cirene dopo il 'tumultus Iudaicus', e sul loror contesto', *ZPE* 172 (2010), 239–48; Hekster, 'Hadrian and the Limits of Power', 281. Cf. G. Gambash, *Rome and Provincial Resistance* (New York – London 2015), 2015, 144–79.

[118] Similarly, Hadrian's suppression of the Bar Kochba revolt (132–6) may have been commemorated by a number of cuirass statues showing the emperor subjugating barbarians: B. Bergmann, 'Bar Kochba und das Panhellenion: Die Panzerstatue Hadrians aus Hierapytna/Kreta (Istanbul, Archäologisches Museum Inv. Nr. 50) und der Panzertorso Inv. Nr. 8097 im Piräusmuseum von Athen', *Istanbuler Mitteilungen*, 60 (2010), 203–89. On central military imagery of Hadrian, see p. 122–3 above.

[119] Z. Kiss, 'Représentations de barbares dans l'iconographie romaine impériale en Egypte', *Klio* 71 (1989), 127–37; 127–8; Davenport, 'Roman Emperors', 101. There do seem to be local commemorations in Gaul of Caesar's conquest from the Augustan era, but in newly established veteran colonies, recalling the soldiers' victories rather than local defeats: I. M. Ferris, *Enemies of Rome. Barbarians through Roman Eyes* (Thrupp – Stroud 2000), 22–4. See below p. 300–2.

[120] N. Roymans, 'Conquest, Mass Violence and Ethnic Stereotyping: Investigating Caesar's Actions in the Germanic Frontier Zone', *JRA* 32 (2019), 439–58.

of personal subjugation was never a good thing, hence the difference in the opening lines of the Latin version of Augustus' *Res Gestae* at Rome and its Greek translation in the provinces. The inscription in Rome opens: 'Below is a copy of the acts of the deified Augustus, by which he made the whole world subject to the rule of the Roman people, and of the expenses which he incurred for the state and the people of Rome, as inscribed upon two bronze columns which have been set up in Rome'. The Greek translation, for which there seems to have been no centrally issued template, leaves the world-conquest out, opening instead: 'Translated and inscribed below are the achievements and gifts of the god Augustus, which he left in Rome engraved on two bronze tablets'.[121]

After the horror of conquest became a remote memory, the emperor could be more easily depicted as a victor in the assimilated provinces, especially since the Roman empire was famously integrative with citizenship. This meant that substantial numbers of newly conquered Romans, especially members of the local elite, would become Roman citizens reasonably rapidly.[122] This changed perceptions of what defeating enemies of Rome would mean. People in the provinces could now identify with the conquering Romans, rather than the defeated 'foreigners'. Provincial elites even rose to become senators. In AD 48, Claudius convinced senators to include notables from Gallia Comata (the area conquered by Caesar) into their midst, creating a loyal group of senatorial supporters in the process.[123] It took longer before prominent eastern families were admitted to the senate, probably because of Roman prejudices against the Greeks. That changed under Vespasian, who had been proclaimed emperor by eastern troops, with a renewed influx under Trajan, probably linked to his wars in the east. Imperial vicinity offered local elites the opportunity to show their qualities directly to the emperor.[124] Such closeness was locally expressed. The so-called Parthian Monument at Ephesus, for instance, which included

---

[121] *RGDA*, pr. (translation Cooley); O. Hekster, 'Left behind in Translation? The Image of Augustus in Asia Minor', in: M. Derks/ R. Ensel/ M. Eickhoff/ F. Meens (eds.), *What's Left Behind, The Lieux de Memoires of Europe beyond Europe* (Nijmegen 2015), 176–82; 180–1. On local freedom of choice for the translation: P. Thonemann, 'A Copy of Augustus' *Res Gestae* at Sardis', *Historia* 61 (2012), 280–8.

[122] The seminal work remains A. N. Sherwin-White, *The Roman Citizenship* (Oxford 1979²).

[123] *CIL* 13.1668; Tac. *Ann.* 11.23–4. See p. 4 above. On the appropriation of a Roman 'identity' by these Gallic elites: G. Woolf, *Becoming Roman. The Origins of Provincial Civilization in Gaul* (Cambridge 1998).

[124] H. Halfmann, *Die Senatoren aus dem östlichen Teil des Imperium Romanum bis zum Ende des 2. Jahrhunderts n. Chr.* (Göttingen 1979), 71–9; Hekster, 'Hadrian and the Limits of Power', 280–1.

a narrative relief of about 70 metres, prominently showed Antoninus Pius, who had been proconsul of Asia in AD 135/6. Shortly after his tenure, the first Ephesian became a senator, so there were local reasons to celebrate the emperor. On a much-discussed image, the emperor is depicted wearing a toga, alongside his adopted dynasty: Hadrian, Marcus Aurelius and Lucius Verus. Most of the rest of the relief, however, shows belligerent images with the emperor in military dress, posing like Mars or riding the chariot like Homeric heroes of old. The style and imagery recalls Hellenistic royal monuments, such as the nearby Pergamum Altar. Images of conquered cities complement the notion of the emperor as a military victor.[125] Antoninus never left the Italian peninsula during his reign, but that did not stop prominent Ephesians depicting him in a military guise, in their own local style.

The above examples illustrate provincial images and local expectations of the emperor as a military leader. But in some cases the notion of a dominant and victorious ruler was emphasised in the provinces by the centre. The massive *Tropaeum Alpium* (7/6 BC) at La Turbie (France), for instance, explicitly commemorates subjugation of the local populace (Figure 4.6). It is also known as the *Tropaeum Augusti* and celebrates Augustus' victory over the tribes of the western Alps between 23–7 BC. It was placed at the highest point of the Via Julia Augusta, and the height of its cone-shaped roof rose to 49 metres, with an enormous statue of Augustus on top. The names of forty-nine Alpine tribes who had been conquered are inscribed on a colossal inscription which notes how 'all Alpine nations who live between the Upper Sea (Adriatic) to the Lower (Tyrrhenian), were submitted to the empire of the Roman people'. Representations of the subjugated tribes were visible on reliefs on either side of the inscription showing male prisoners, kneeling with their bound hands behind their backs, under a tree on which their armour is hung. A much less well-preserved trophy in Saint-Bernard-de-Comminges was erected on the border area between Gaul and Spain, of which about 150 sculptural and architectural fragments have survived. It similarly stood at the centre of a major road structure and included Gallic and Hispanic

---

[125] H. Halfmann, *Städtebau und Bauherren im römischen Kleinasien* (Tübingen 2001), 75; Elsner, *The Art of the Roman Empire*, 114–16; Hekster, *Emperors and Ancestors*, 90–2; S. Faust, *Schlachtenbilder der römischen Kaiserzeit. Erzählerische Darstellungskonzepte in der Reliefkunst von Traian bis Septimius Severus* (Rahden 2012), 149–60, which also convincingly dismisses the notion that this was a posthumous monument for Lucius Verus.

Figure 4.6 An emperor subjugating local tribes: 7/6 BC, La Turbie. Square base (w. 32.5 m) with a conic shaped roof on column-bases on top (h. 49 m). A colossal statue of Augustus will have stood on the roof. On the base, an inscription commemorates Augustus' victory over forty-nine Alpine tribes. Reliefs visualised the subjugated people. The monument was restored in modern times, with the fragments of the inscriptions re-inserted into the building
Source: CKD – Radboud University Nijmegen

trophies, flanking a larger naval trophy.[126] There is also a clustering of near-contemporary victory arches with martial imagery in southern Gaul. Noticeably, there mainly seem to be images of Gallic warriors on arches that can be linked to Roman veterans. Arches at Vienne, Carpentras and Saint-Rémy instead show figures that can be identified as Dalmatian or Parthian. An arch at Susa found yet a different way of adapting the message of Roman victory, this time without military imagery. Local elites responded to the Augustan commemoration of victory, but seem to have sought ways to avoid showing defeated Gauls in this context. Roman veterans had no such qualms.[127]

At Adamklissi (Romania), another monumental structure was erected; the co-called *Tropaeum Traiani* (109). Like the monuments at La Turbie, it would have been built on central orders and was meant to dominate its surroundings. The location of the monument is telling, far from any metropolitan centre but near a mausoleum and an altar commemorating the dead of Domitian's Dacian wars, which had been a problematic affair. This was a monument built to erase previous military setbacks.[128] Its shape was similar to the monument at La Turbie. A massive concrete circular drum held a conical roof, topped by a trophy over ten metres high: a stone tree trunk adorned with weapons and standards of the Dacians who had been conquered by Trajan between AD 102 and 106. Four sculpted figures of bound captives sat below the tree. The base of the monument was decorated with a band of fifty-four narrative friezes (metopes), of which forty-nine survive. These show the Roman victory through scenes of combat, pursuit of fugitives and review of the captive prisoners. Dying barbarians abound (Figure 4.7), with Trajan prominently on display receiving an offer of surrender (scene 10) and personally in pursuit of fugitives (scenes 36–38). The monument, like the *Tropaeum Alpium*, advertised the strength of Roman imperial power, led by its emperor. Other than at the La

---

[126] *CIL* 5.7817; Plin. *NH.* 3.20.136–8; Ferris, *Enemies of Rome*, 39–44. For a good overview with illustrations of the two monuments: S. Binninger, *Le Trophée d'Auguste à la Turbie* (Paris 2009); E. Boube, *Le Trophée augustéen. Collection du musée archéologique départemental de Saint-Bertrand-de-Comminges* 4 (Saint-Bertrand-de-Comminges 1996).

[127] Ferris, *Enemies of Rome*, 44–7 on the victory arches, with further references. On the Susa arch: K. Iannantuono, 'La monumentalizzazione del potere nelle Alpi Cozie all'indomani della conquista romana. Una "descrizione densa" dell'arco di Susa', *SEGUSIUM* 58 (2020), 11–48; H. Cornwell, 'The King Who Would be Prefect: Authority and identity in the Cottian Alps', *JRS* 105 (2015), 41–73.

[128] I. Ferris, 'The Hanged Men Dance: Barbarians in Trajanic art', in: S. Scott/ J. Webster (eds.), *Roman Imperialism and Provincial Art* (Cambridge 2003), 53–68; 62. See p. 116 above on Domitian's triumphal celebrations of the Dacian campaigns in Rome.

Figure 4.7 Roman victory, provincial style: 109, Adamklissi, lime sandstone metope (h. 150, w. 117,5). Muzeul Adamclisi (Adamklissi, Romania), inv. no 20. The massive monument at Adamklissi was adorned with reliefs showing victorious Romans and vanquished Dacians, depicted in a local style but with a clear imperial message
Source: CKD – Radboud University Nijmegen

Turbie monument, however, the style of the metopes took local beholders very much into account. The scenes in the friezes were depicted in a non-Roman way, probably carried out by Dacian carvers in a local visual vocabulary. That does not quite make it a local monument. The images expressed imperial rhetoric. Yet even when the brutality of conquest was purposefully emphasised, local traditions could be taken into account.[129]

The power of Rome and its emperors could be made explicit to people in the provinces, in a (visual) language that was understood by all. Monuments with a clear message of imperial dominance were mostly erected after difficult conquests, or suppressed uprisings.[130] Political and cultural contexts were essential for the way imperial power was represented in the provinces. Rather than looking for one persistent mode of representation of emperorship in the provinces, local contexts were important.[131] Central imagery, however, seems to show a development over time in the emergence and depictions of provincial personifications on coins and reliefs. Under Hadrian these were famously depicted in their own right rather than as conquered figures (Figure 4.8), but this was part of a longer trajectory of increased depictions of the unity of the empire that took off under the Flavians and flourished in the early Antonine period.[132] This shift towards 'peaceful' images of the provinces on central imagery was not entirely linear, as is clear from Trajanic coinage that showed personifications of a defeated Dacia through images that are iconographically (though not stylistically) similar to the scenes on the Adamklissi monument. Noticeably, the coins that depicted the Dacians through the most humiliating iconography were not circulated in Dacia itself. This suggests once more awareness that emphasising imperial brutality could be problematic.[133] After Hadrian's reign, territories inside the Roman empire were hardly ever shown as conquered peoples, partly, of course, because there was little further expansion of the empire. Moreover, from the second century onwards, coins struck by cities in the east increasingly depicted scenes from their own local myth and history, showing mythical city founders and famous citizens. From the early-third century onwards, such

---

[129] Elsner, *The Art of the Roman Empire*, 116–17; Ferris, 'The Hanged Men Dance', 65, 57; J.-R. Carbó García/ F. J. Rodríguez San Juan, 'STVDIA DACICA ET PARTHICA (II). El Tropaeum Traiani de Caracene. Expresiones del poder romano en los límites del Imperio', *Dialogues d' histoire ancienne* 38 (2012), 17–35. The difference in style and similarity in message to depictions of the same wars on the column of Trajan are noticeable.

[130] Illustrative is the victory arch set up in Jerusalem by Hadrian commemorating the suppression of the Bar Kokhba Revolt: W. Eck, 'The Bar Kokhba Revolt Roman Point of View', *JRS* 89 (1999), 76–89 with its monumental Latin inscription: Israel Museum, Jerusalem: inv. 1977-524/1-6.

[131] Vitale, *Das Imperium*, 47–8, 334.   [132] Vitale, *Das Imperium*, 99–101, 112–23.

[133] *RIC* 2, Trajan, nos. 98, 216–23, 324–5, 543–5; Ellithorpe, *Circulating Imperial Ideology*, 122–38; Vitale, *Das Imperium*, 104–12.

Figure 4.8 Provinces in their own right: AD 145, Rome, marble Attic relief from the Hadrianeum (h. 208, w. 1.90). Palazzo Massimo alle Terme (Rome), inv. no. 137. Under Hadrian, provinces were no longer represented as subdued, but presented in their own right. The contrast between this personification of Dacia and the defeated Dacians visible at Adamklissi or on some of Trajan's coinage is striking
Source: CKD – Radboud University Nijmegen

provincial coins also began to depict provinces in a personified form.[134] Rather than specific to the reign of Hadrian, then, this 'emancipation' of the provinces seems to have been a trend, although Hadrian's reign was remarkable for the attention to provinces. The so-called Reka Devnia hoard, which consists of over 100,000 denarii from Mark Antony to Trajan Decius, includes 819 denarii depicting individual provinces (or clearly linked toponyms like *Nilus*) on the reverse. Apart from fifty-one coins depicting Judea, issued under Vespasian, and two coins showing Hispania struck under Galba, all of them are struck in the second or third century, mostly under Hadrian (over 450), but with substantial numbers issued under Marcus Aurelius (about 220) and Septimius Severus (about 80).[135] The image of the emperor conquering provinces, then, tapered off after the reign of Hadrian, but more slowly in provincial than in central imagery. There were, apparently, differences between Roman and provincial perspectives of imperial rule.

The image of the emperor as a figure defeating outside enemies was less problematic than that of the ruler pacifying his provinces, especially in an ever more unified empire. It therefore continued to be used for much longer. After all, the violence that was involved in eradicating enemy populations made sure that inhabitants of the Roman empire lived peacefully.[136] This imperial role could be depicted through images of emperors trampling 'barbarian' enemies, as illustrated by central coins of Lucius Verus on a horse, mowing down kneeling Parthians. The image resembles scenes on contemporary battle sarcophagi, showing Roman military commanders and their soldiers trampling barbarian enemies. Other coins, issued under Caracalla and various fourth- and fifth-century emperors, depicted emperors (or Victoria) dragging captives by their hair. The message that emperors protected their empire and guaranteed peace was important throughout Roman imperial history.[137]

---

[134] V. Heuchert, 'The Chronological Development of Roman Provincial Coin Iconography', in: C. Howgego/ V. Heuchert/ A. Burnett (eds.), *Coinage and Identity in the Roman Provinces* (Oxford 2005), 29–56; 51–2; Vitale *Imperium in Wort und Bild*, 275–81.

[135] The references follow the Reka Devnia hoard as tabulated on https://chre.ashmus.ox.ac.uk/hoard/3406. This same point is made in Hekster, 'Provincial Emperors'.

[136] M. Lavan, 'Devastation: The Destruction of Populations and Human Landscapes and the Roman Imperial Project', in: Berthelot, *Reconsidering Roman Power*, 179–205 on the normality of violence in (mostly central) literary and visual representations of Roman imperial power.

[137] *RIC* 3, Marcus Aurelius, 543–5, 549, 567; *RIC* 4.1, Caracalla, 172; *RIC* 6, Rome, 269; Ferris, *Enemies of Rome*, 105–6; 125–6; C. W. Malone, 'Violence on Roman Imperial Coinage', *Journal of the Numismatic Association of Australia* 20 (2009), 58–72; 58–68. There are 209 fourth-century references in *RIC* to emperors dragging barbarians, mostly by their

When emperors could not provide such safety, their legitimacy to rule was in danger. The Gallic and Palmyrene 'counter empires' of the third century resulted from local figures guaranteeing safety better than the emperor could.[138] In the east, the Palmyrene Septimius Odaenathus helped Gallienus fight the new Persian ruler Shapur. In doing so, he gained so much status that in bilingual Greek and Palmyrene inscriptions he was hailed as 'prince of Palmyra' and 'restorer of the whole east'. He was also called 'king of kings'.[139] The titles seem to be expressions of gratitude to the man who kept the region safe. The vocabulary used makes sense in the local context, with 'king of kings' referring to the title of Shapur, whom Odaenathus had managed to stop in his tracks. Yet these kinds of honours made Odaenathus an alternative for, and hence a threat to, the power of the emperor. This became even more explicit when his wife Zenobia and his son Vaballathus inherited these titles.[140] In the west, the Roman commander Postumus similarly managed to defeat invaders and was hailed as *Germanicus Maximus*. He was proclaimed emperor shortly afterwards. Eutropius, much later, notices how 'almost the whole Roman empire had been lost, when Postumus ... restored the provinces which had been almost entirely consumed'.[141] Keeping territory safe was deemed a sufficient cause for being raised to (near)imperial status. The gratitude by people in areas that were defended by the likes of Odaenathus and Postumus was real, and to be expected. The consequences of warfare in areas that experienced it directly should not be underestimated. In the period between AD 254–61, Franks, Juthungi, Goths and Shapur's Sasanian troops ravaged Germania Inferior, Gaul, Spain, the Danube area, Asia Minor, and the eastern frontier of Rome's empire. The damage was enormous. It was small wonder that local leaders tried to rally troops to repel enemies. When they did so successfully, they had taken on one of the key roles of the emperor – making a small step towards personal bid for

---

hair: http://numismatics.org/ocre: 'dragging captive'. See also p. 130 above on the continuous importance of the emperor's military role.

[138] On the Gallic Empire: A. Luther, 'Das gallische Sonderreich', in: K.-P. Johne (ed.), *Die Zeit der Soldatenkaiser: Krise und Transformation des Römischen Reiches im 3. Jahrhundert n. Chr. (235–284)* (Berlin 2008), 325–41 and J. F. Drinkwater, *The Gallic Empire. Separatism and Continuity in the North-Western provinces of the Roman Empire AD 260–274* (Stuttgart 1987). On the Palmyrene Empire: U. Hartmann 'Das palmyrenische Teilreich', in: Johne, *Die Zeit der Soldatenkaiser*, 343–78.

[139] CIS 2.3956, 2.3971.

[140] De Blois, *Image and Reality*, 77, 80; Hartmann, 'Das palmyrenische Teilreich', 349–59.

[141] Eutropius, 9.9; *AE* 1993.1231; De Blois, *Image and Reality*, 79–83.

supreme power.[142] The same process applied in the fifth-century Roman west. Areas that saw prolonged warfare were hit especially hard, like northern and eastern Gaul, which was contested by Romans, *Bacaudae*, Britons, Saxons, Franks, Burgundians, Thuringians, Alamans, Alans, and Goths from 406 onwards, only to have some tranquillity restored by the foundation of the Frankish and Burgundian kingdoms. The Iberian peninsula was similarly disputed by various groups between AD 409 and the establishment of Visigothic control in the 470s.[143]

Two early-fifth century texts illustrate how dire the situation was perceived to be. The Gallic poet and bishop St Orientius described the situation after invasions in AD 407–409: 'Through villages and villas, through countryside and market-place/ Through all regions, on all roads, in this place and that/ There was death, misery, destruction, burning, and mourning/ The whole of Gaul smoked on a single funeral pyre'. More dramatic even were descriptions by Bishop Hydratius of Aqua Flaviae (modern Chaves, Portugal) (c. 400–c.469) describing his local situation in the same years:

> As the barbarians ran wild through Spain and the deadly pestilence continued on its savage course, the wealth and goods stored in the cities were plundered by the tyrannical tax-collector and consumed by the soldiers. A famine ran riot so dire that driven by hunger human beings devoured human flesh; mothers too feasted upon the bodies of their own children whom they had killed and cooked with their own hands.[144]

Clearly (and hopefully), there is poetic exaggeration here. Yet it is unsurprising that, in this context, people looked for whatever protection they could get, whether by priest or local warlord.

The rising prestige of priests and 'barbarian' kings at the cost of the status of the western emperor was a result of the latter's failure to keep his realm safe. Guaranteeing peace in the provinces was essentially bound to what people expected of Roman emperors. Moreover, images of the victorious emperors were all around. That made the contrast even more striking when emperors failed to fulfil that function. There had been

---

[142] Hekster, *Rome and Its Empire*, 20–1.
[143] Ward-Perkins, *The Fall of Rome*, 13–24, with full references.
[144] Orientius, *Commonitorium*, lines 179–84; R. Ellis (ed.), *Poetae Christiani Minores. Corpus Scriptorum Ecclesiasticorum Latinorum XVI* (Vienna: Österreichische Akademie 1888); Hydatius, *Chronicle*; 39 (47); R. W. Burgess, *The Chronicle of Hydatius and the Consularia Constantinopolitana: Two Contemporary Accounts of the Final Years of the Roman Empire* (Oxford 1993), 82–3; Ward-Perkins, *The Fall of Rome*, 16, 22–3.

military upheaval within the Roman frontiers well before the fifth and sixth centuries (like the Jewish Diaspora War or the third-century invasions) but in the late-antique Roman west, the unrest went on for a very long time and was not quelled by either the emperor or his generals. Consequently local substitutes to imperial rule developed. When emperors no longer lived up to expectations, people found attractive alternatives in holy men chasing away enemies through miracles, or Frankish and Visigothic kings keeping order – although their new status and position were often formulated in traditionally imperial language and imagery. The very different socio-political contexts in the eastern and western empire are important reasons for the difference in the relative status of emperorship in east and west in the fifth century. The expectations of emperorship were not significantly different, but reality in the west made it more difficult for emperors to live up to those expectations.

Expectations of a Religious Ruler

There were, then, local interpretations and visualisations of the civic and military roles of the emperor. These interpretations, furthermore, were continuously influenced by events (most strikingly disasters and warfare) and by social interactions. Emperors forged relations with local elites and soldiers. There was inter-city competition in which articulating imperial support was a valuable asset, and also competition within the city, in which building monuments for the emperor was a way of showing status. These monuments further shaped the local image of the emperor. The resulting expressions of imperial power varied, but the centrality of the emperor and his role in guaranteeing peace and prosperity was systematically put forward. There was, it seems, a limited vocabulary through which the emperor could be praised, but that vocabulary could be adapted to local needs. The same applies to the construction of dynastic imagery of the emperor, another acceptable way of depicting Roman rulers in the provinces. Who was included in dynastic messages and how these figures were depicted was heavily context dependent. But dynastic imagery was on display throughout the empire, often demonstrating (or creating) relations between the emperor and a specific city or individual.[145]

---

[145] Hekster, *Emperors and Ancestors*, 125–6, 158.

A much-discussed example of locally different reflections on an empire-wide understanding of emperorship was the way in which emperor worship was shaped. Modern scholarship has emphasised how important it is to talk of 'emperor worship' or 'imperial cults' rather than to assume some sort of monolithic imperial cult through which the emperor was worshipped.[146] There is indeed a difference between, for instance, Greek cities which integrated imperial priesthoods, festivals and altars and temples into existing civic cults, and the more self-sustained forms in which emperor worship took shape in the Latin west. Western worship may also have been more of a top-down process than the imperial cult in the east. Worship in Egypt was integrated in pharaonic traditions, which set it apart from the rest of the empire.[147] As we have seen throughout this chapter, specific local choices were dependent on existing traditions. Again, also, the choice of representing the emperor in this mode rather than one of the other available choices was closely related to the benefits it brought to the persons constructing a monument or initiating a cult. We have already discussed inter-city competition in Asia Minor as a factor in erecting temples to the Roman emperor. In the Near East, instead, client kings were the most important instigators for the spread of the imperial cult, with these kings themselves often functioning as the local chief priest. By emphasising the emperor's divine status, kings showed that they were sanctioned and supported by a higher power.[148] The importance for kings of such support becomes clear from Herod's institution of a festival tied to the imperial cult, and the foundation of several temples to Augustus and Roma. He even ensured that there were daily offerings for the wellbeing of the emperor in the Temple at Jerusalem, pushing the religious status of the emperor as far

---

[146] Beard/ North/ Price, *Religions of Rome*, 169, 206–10, 318, 360–2; McIntyre, *Imperial Cult*, 7–14, 42–70, with an overview of previous historiography. On the emperor's religious authority and his religious status see p. 138 above.

[147] Beard/ North/ Price, *Religions of Rome*, 354–7, 361. On emperor worship in the East, see: S. F. R. Price, *Rituals and Power: The Roman Imperial Cult in Asia Minor* (Cambridge 1984). For the West, the evidence is meticulously assembled and analysed by D. Fishwick, *The Imperial Cult in the Latin West. Studies in the Ruler Cult of the Western Provinces of the Roman Empire*. Vol. I.1–III.4 (Leiden – Boston 1987–2005), III.1, 219 arguing for local cult 'as an instrument of imperial policy'. On Egypt, see: S. Pfeiffer, 'The Imperial Cult in Egypt', in: C. Riggs (ed.), *The Oxford Handbook of Roman Egypt* (Oxford 2012), 83–100.

[148] H. Bru, *Le Pouvoir imperial dans les provinces syriennes. Représentations et celebrations d'Auguste à Constantin (31 av. J.-C.–337 ap. J.-C.)* (Leiden – Boston 2011), 287–93; J. Wilker, 'Modelling the Emperor. Representations of Power, Empire, and Dynasty among Eastern Client Kings', in: Russell/ Hellström, *Social Dynamics*, 52–75; 61–3; see p. 290 above.

as it was acceptable for the Jewish population of his kingdom.[149] Yet, the difference in agency should not be pushed too far. Though diffusion of the imperial cult in the Near East seems to have been slower in areas without client kings, analysis of the situation in the Decapolis cities and Palmyra shows many similarities to Asia Minor, with the elite using the imperial cult to establish and show their relationship with the emperor.[150]

In the Near East, as elsewhere in the empire, the presentation of the emperor in his religious role and as object of worship was integrated into a wide variety of local religious patterns. Dura Europos, on the very eastern frontier of the empire, provides illustrative examples. The archaeological evidence for Dura is extremely rich, making it an excellent location to analyse life at the furthest periphery of the Roman empire. The town also housed people from a variety of cultures, who envisaged the emperor in different ways.[151] For example, the emperor seems to have been incorporated into the imagery of the late second-century temple of Artemis Azzanathkona. It includes a dedication to Jupiter Optimus Maximus and other gods in honour of Septimius Severus. More importantly, a scene painted centrally in the temple depicts a sacrifice and shows a standing figure in the middle, placed on a pedestal, dressed in Roman military gear, holding sceptre and robe, and wearing a radiate crown (Figure 4.9). He is identified as the Palmyrene god Yarhibol. Yet, the figure's dress and attributes, and the iconography of the scene, which includes a flying Victory about to crown him on the right, and the word 'Conqueror' (ΝΕΙΚΑΤΩΡ), written on the left, recall that of the emperor, as do almost all representations of cuirassed Palmyrene gods. Further references to Antonine and Severan princes and emperors in the room strengthen the association.[152] Moreover, the *Feriale Duranum* was

---

[149] Jos. *BJ*, 1.404, 1.414, 2.198, 2.409, 2.415–16; A. Kropp, 'King – Caesar – God: Roman Imperial Cult Among Near Eastern "Client" Kings in the Julio-Claudian Period', in: M. Blömer/ M. Facella/ E. Winter (eds.), *Lokale Identität im römischen Nahen Osten: Kontexte und Perspektiven* (Stuttgart 2009), 99–150; 104–10.

[150] L. Dirven, 'The Imperial Cult in the Cities of the Decapolis, Caesarea Maritima and Palmyra. A Note on the Development of Imperial Cults in the Roman Near East', *ARAM* 23 (2011) 141–56. Slowness of distribution: M. Sartre, 'Les Manifestations du culte imperial dans les provinces syriennes et en Arabie', in: C. Evers (ed.), *Rome et ses provinces. Genèse et diffusion d'une image du pouvoir. Hommages à Jean-Charles Balty* (Brussels 2001), 167–86; 185.

[151] On the historiography of Dura-Europos, and its prominence in various archaeological debates: T. Kaizer, 'Introduction', in: D. Praet/ T. Kaizer/ A. Lannoy (eds.), *Franz Cumont: Doura-Europos. Bibliotheca Cumontiana. Series Minora VII* (Turnhout 2020), xi–xcviii; J. Elsner, '100 Years of Dura Europos', *JRA* 34 (2021), 764–84.

[152] C. M. Acqua, 'Imperial Representation at Dura-Europos: Suggestions for Urban Paths', in: T. Kaizer (ed.), *Religion, Society and Culture at Dura-Europos* (Cambridge 2016), 144–64; 148–9 with full references, though Acqua emphasises the similarities of the central figure to Sol

312 The Emperor in Capital and Provinces

Figure 4.9 The emperor and local gods: c. 256, Dura Europos, ink on gypsum scene in the temple of Artemis Azzanathkona (h. 38.5, w. 79 cm). Art Gallery, Yale: inv. 1932.1208. The central figure in this scene is identified as the Palmyrene god Yarhibol, but through the radiate crown, sceptre, clothing, and the crowning Victory, there is at least a conflation with imperial iconography
Photo credit: Yale University Art Gallery

found in this temple, listing the religious festivities that had to be observed throughout the year, with sacrifices to divine emperors and empresses numerically dominant among them.[153] The temple itself was included in the third-century *principia* complex, which housed the military standards that displayed images of the emperor. An important role of the complex as a whole was housing those standards and providing an environment in which they, and by inclusion the emperor, could be properly honoured.[154]

Possibly, the emperor was also honoured in other sanctuaries at Dura. A panel in the so-called 'temple of the Palmyrene gods' (also known as the

Invictus, a favourite imperial counterpart at the time. On the adaptation of the iconography of Palmyra's main gods towards that of Roman emperors: Dirven, 'The Imperial Cult', 154–5.

[153] On the Feriale Duranum, see R. O. Fink/ A. S. Hoey/ W. F. Snyder, 'The Feriale Duranum', *Yale Classical Studies* 7 (1940), 1–222; D. Fishwick, 'Dated Inscriptions and the Feriale Duranum, *Syria* 65 (1988), 349–61; M. B. Reeves, *The Feriale Duranum, Roman Military Religion, and Dura-Europos: A Reassessment* (PhD: Buffalo 2004). See p. 147 above.

[154] Acqua, 'Imperial Representation', 147–8; Reeves, *The Feriale Duranum*, 145.

Figure 4.10 Emperors or gods? AD 239, Dura Europos, paint on plaster, temple of the Palmyrene gods (h. 107 cm, w. 165 cm). Art Gallery, Yale: inv. 1931.386. The Roman tribune Terentius makes a sacrifice to either three Palmyrene gods or three emperors. The iconographical closeness of emperors and gods is noticeable. The emperor's standard is placed alongside the figures who receive worship
Photo credit: Yale University Art Gallery

'temple of Bel') shows the Roman tribune Julius Terentius making an offering to three haloed figures in military dress, holding sceptre-like objects, and to the personification of Dura and Palmyra (Figure 4.10). The three figures were first identified as the Palmyrene gods Yarhibol, Aglibol and Malakbel, but later as Roman emperors. Neither identification has gained unanimous support, but perhaps the ambiguity was intentional. In any case, the Roman imperial connotations of the panel are clear from the central position of the *vexillarius* holding the standard. He is placed on the left side of the altar, among the figures who are being worshipped, placing the emperor and his might in the context of the divine.[155] All of

---

[155] Acqua, 'Imperial Representation', 153–5; T. Pekáry, 'Das Opfer vor dem Kaiserbild', *BJ* 186 (1986), 91–103; O. Stoll, *Zwischen Integration und Abgrenzung: Die Religion des Römischen Heeres im Nahen Osten. Studien zum Verhältnis von Armee und Zivilbevölkerung im römischen Syrien und den Nachbargebieten* (St Katharinen 2001), 367–79; T. Kaizer, 'A Note on the Fresco of Iulius Terentius from Dura-Europos', in: R. Rollinger/ B. Truschnegg (eds.), *Altertum und Mittelmeerraum: Die antike Welt diesseits und jenseits der Levante* (Stuttgart 2006), 151–9, noting how Palmyrene soldiers at Dura-Europos worshipped the emperor.

this makes the prominence of emperor worship in Dura Europos clear, though sometimes visualised in a very local context. Nor was Dura Europos exceptional. Emperor worship was similarly incorporated into the provincial life of other areas of the Roman Near East. Even religious life at Palmyra, which remained surprisingly unaffected by its incorporation into the Roman empire (probably during the reign of Tiberius), adopted the imperial cult as a prominent institution. The chief priest of the Palmyrene's main local cult of Bel was simultaneously priest of the emperor, and most imperial statues at Palmyra were set up by priests of Bel. Statues of Tiberius, Drusus and Germanicus even seem to have been placed in the temenos of Bel's temple.[156]

The case of Dura Europos makes clear how important the military could be as agents for the distribution of religious representations of the emperor in the provinces. This applied throughout the empire. For obvious reasons, it was important for emperors to ensure the loyalty of soldiers to them, and religion was an important way of doing so. The imperial cult was strictly adhered to in all legionary camps and formed an essential (though not the only) part of Roman army religion.[157] The soldiers' oath of allegiance was a sacred rite, which was formally dissolved at the end of service.[158] Regular festivals in the emperor's honour further cemented the relation between emperor and his troops. These were attended by both soldiers and civilians. Pliny explicitly wrote to Trajan that he had 'administered the oath of allegiance to your fellow soldiers in the usual form, and found the provincials eager to take it, too, as proof of their loyalty'. The emperor responded that he 'was glad to hear ... of the rejoicing and devotion with which ... my fellow-soldiers and the provincials have celebrated the anniversary of my accession'. Joint celebrations, sacrifices and parades of soldiers and civilians are also testified elsewhere.[159] Clearly, then, the emperor played a central role in religious structures throughout the empire, notwithstanding

---

[156] T. Kaizer, *The Religious Life of Palmyra* (Stuttgart 2002), 148–51, 239; Dirven, 'The Imperial Cult', 153–6; J.-B. Yon, *Les Notables de Palmyre* (Beirut 2002), 42–3, 122–3.

[157] O. Stoll, 'The Religions of the Armies', in: Erdkamp, *A Companion to the Roman Army*, 451–76; 453–64; Stoll, *Zwischen Integration und Abgrenzung*, 176–209, 349–79; P. Herz, 'Das römische Heer und der Kaiserkult in Germanien', in: W. Spickermann/ H. Cancik/ J. Rüpke (eds.), *Religion in den germanischen Provinzen Roms* (Tübingen 2001), 91–116. Still seminal: E. Birley, 'The Religion of the Roman Army', *ANRW* II.16.2 (1978), 1506–41.

[158] Vegetius, 2.5; Herodian, 8.7.4; Dig. 49.18.2 (Ulpian); H. Cancik, 'Der Kaiser-Eid. Zur Praxis der römischen Herrscherverehrung', in: H. Cancik/ K. Hitzl (eds.), *Die Praxis der Herrscherverehrung in Rom und seinen Provinzen* (Tübingen 2003), 29–45.

[159] Plin. *Letters*, 10.52–3, 10.110–103; Stoll, 'The Religions of the Armies', 457. Cf. Tac. *Hist.* 2.80.3 noting the close interactions between soldiers and civilians.

local differences. He was worshipped in the furthest regions of the empire, portrayed along with the gods, or in the act of sacrifice. The numbers of altars and temples to the emperor were enormous. Local differentiation may have been pronounced, but within that variation the same message resonated again and again.

The religious representation of the emperor in the provinces changed after the Christianisation of the empire. The emperor could no longer be a universal object of cult.[160] Nor could emperors be easily paralleled to local gods and divinities when pagan cults where no longer allowed. But this did not mean that the emperor stopped being a religious or even sacred figure. The military oath continued to be taken, and important imperial events, like the accession, were still celebrated – if anything in a more sacralised form than in earlier times.[161] Moreover, changes in the religious status did not take place overnight. Constantine and Constantius II closed pagan temples and banned sacrifices, but still supported the imperial cult, as illustrated by their permission to found a temple and local priesthood to the imperial family (the *gens Flavia*) at Hispellum.[162] Fourth-century inscriptions from Oinoanda and Sagalassos, the first on the base of a statue for Constantius II, still emphasised the status of the city as *neokoros*, as did a fifth-century inscription from Sardis.[163] Temples to the imperial cult continued to be present in the landscape, and often were still in use. Although many pagan temples were converted into churches, there is no evidence for a temple to the imperial cult being converted for other use.[164] Notwithstanding the far-reaching Christianising laws of Theodosius, which included limits on 'the vainglorious heights of adoration' of imperial statues, at Ephesus statues of that very emperor and members of his family were integrated into a pagan cultic setting, which otherwise remained almost unchanged. People still requested asylum at these imperial statues, as passages in the *Legal Codes* of Theodosius and Justinian make clear. It is indeed possible that the later notion of church asylum was a modified continuation of this practice.[165] Moreover, there is substantial evidence for

---

[160] Hahn, 'The Challenge of Religious Violence', 403–4. See p. 198 above.
[161] MacCormack, *Art and Ceremony*, 161–266.
[162] *CTh.* 16.10.2, 16.10.4, 16.10.6; *CIL* 11.5265; *ILS* 705; *AE* 2002, 442; N. P. Milner, 'A New Statue-Base for Constantius II and the Fourth-Century Imperial cult at Oinoanda', *Anatolian Studies* 65 (2015), 181–203; 196.
[163] Milner, 'A New Statue-Base', 190; Burrell, *Neokoroi*, 113–14, 238, 303.
[164] Trombley, 'The Imperial Cult in Late Roman Religion', 31–2.
[165] *CTh* 9.44.1, 9.45.1, 15.4.1; *Dig.* 47.10.38; 48.19.28.7; Iannantuono, 'A Christian Emperor between Pagan Gods', forthcoming; C. R. Raschle, 'Bis wann bleibt der Kaiser "Kult"? Die Verehrung des Kaiserbildes als Akt der Zivilreligion in der Spätantike Giuliano', in: A. Kolb/ M. Vitale (eds.),

the continuing appointment of provincial and municipal priests to the emperor, well into the sixth century. There are especially many inscriptions referring to imperial priests from the African provinces. Strikingly, the Vandal invasions of the fifth century, which took much of North Africa out of imperial control, did not put an end to appointing a priest for the imperial cult.[166]

Christianisation changed aspects of the religious image of the emperor, but the prolonged continuation of practices related to the imperial cult in the provinces is noticeable. Christian authors were aware of this. That is one reason for the many discussions about, for instance, the exact status of the imperial portrait. Authors like Gregory of Nazianzus tried to formulate a way in which the worship of the imperial portrait could continue within a Christian context. Honouring the statue was allowed, but without cultic behaviour. Alternatively, it was argued that honouring statues of the emperor meant honouring the Roman state or office of emperorship, rather than the man. So, when the emperor Julian placed his own statue among those of pagan gods, Gregory blamed him for forcing military men and people in the provinces to worship pagan gods. Paying homage to the imperial statue was apparently unproblematic for Gregory.[167] The sixth-century dialogue *On Political Science* emphasises that the emperor needed to appear as a reflection or representation (μίμησις) of God to his subjects, and highlights the divine status of imperial portraits.[168] The dialogue, of course, discusses the role of the Christian emperor, ruling his empire by the grace of god, but the similarities to how pagan rulers were presented are striking. The religious differences between Christian and pagan modes of honouring emperors were of the utmost importance to elite Christian authors. But it is doubtful to what extent they were relevant to people in

---

Kaiserkult in den Provinzen des Römischen Reiches. Organisation, Kommunikation und Repräsentation (Berlin – Boston 2016), 477-96; 488-9.

[166] C. Leppeley, *Les Cités de l'Afrique romaine au Bas-Empire*. Vol. 1, *La Permanence d'une civilisation municipal* (Paris 1979), 362-9; Trombley, 'The Imperial Cult in Late Roman Religion', 38-9; McIntyre, *A Family of Gods*, 125-41; A. Filippini, 'Fossili e contraddizioni dell' "era costantiniana": i dignitari del culto imperiale nella tarda antichita e il loro ruolo nelle "riforme religiose" di Massimino Daia e Giuliano', in: Kolb/ Vitale, *Kaiserkult in den Provinzen*, 409-75.

[167] Gregory Naz. *Or.* 4.81; Raschle, 'Bis wann bleibt der Kaiser "Kult"?', 486, 489; Price, *Rituals and Powers*, 202-5.

[168] *Dialogus Scientiae politicae*, 5.1-9, 5.45, 5.122, 5.124; 5.130, 5.132, 5.134, 5.196-7; C. M. Mazzucchi, *Menae Patricii cum Thoma Referendario de Scientia Politico Dialogus* (Milan 1982); H. A. Drake, 'Topographies of Power in Late Antiquity and Neyond', in: Rapp/ Drake, *The City in the Classical and Post Classical World*, 217-39; 219; Raschle, 'Bis wann bleibt der Kaiser "Kult"?', 491.

the provinces, who continued to worship imperial statues, in a cityscape that still commemorated the appointment of priests to the imperial cult. Notwithstanding the real changes that Christianity brought, the traditional religious image of the emperor retained its prominence in the provinces.

Emperors in Their Provinces

There was, as we have seen throughout this chapter, variation in the way people formulated and visualised Rome and its emperors in different regions.[169] These local interpretations are important, but seem to have led to a different 'phrasing' of emperorship rather than to different ideas of what the emperor needed to be and do. In both the capitals and in the provinces, different people had different expectations of their emperors in different contexts. But these expectations seem to have been limited to a fairly static repertoire of roles. Still, modern scholarship has tried to locate more systematic local differences. Noticeably, differences between the Latin-speaking west and the Greek-speaking east have been highlighted. They were substantial, even before the division of the empire under Arcadius and Honorius in AD 395. The dominant language was probably the most important one, although we should not forget that the Roman empire was much more multilingual than a division between Latin and Greek suggests, and that speaking of 'the west' and 'the east' hides the differences within these massive regions from view.[170] The other most-mentioned difference, especially relevant when thinking about emperorship, is that of prior history of rule. After all, most of the eastern provinces had known monarchic rule before the coming of Rome, and had developed (visual) modes through which to interact with these rulers, whereas much of the western region of the empire had previously been organised according to tribes. In the east, moreover, many people continued to live in long-established cities, expressing a city identity which was much less

---

[169] On the ways in which Roman power was conceived and understood at local level, see Dench, *Empire and Political Cultures*, esp. 29–46 with an exemplary discussion of earlier debates.

[170] Fundamental: J. N. Adams, *Bilingualism and the Latin Language* (Cambridge 2003). Also W. Eck, 'Lateinisch, Griechisch, Germanisch ...? Wie sprach Rom mit seinen Untertanen?', in: L. de Ligt/ E. Hemelrijk/ H. W. Singor (eds.), *Roman Rule and Civic Life: Local and Regional Perspectives* (Amsterdam 2004), 3–19; Millar, *Roman Near East*, 232–4. Even in the Italian peninsula, Oscan was used deep into the first century, even if it was officially banned in 80 BC: A. Cooley, 'The Survival of Oscan in Roman Pompeii', in: A. Cooley (ed.), *Becoming Roman, Writing Latin? Literacy and Epigraphy in the Roman West* (Portsmouth, RI 2002), 77–86; 84.

developed in the western provinces.[171] As a result of these factors, it seems that eastern cities more explicitly placed images of Roman emperors in their own local contexts, whereas imperial images in the western provinces followed more closely the images presented by the centre.

The difference is perhaps best visible in the so-called provincial coinage. These are the coins that were issued by autonomous provincial or regional federations of cities (*koina*), individual cities, and coins of 'dependent kings', throughout the Roman world. In the west, those coins tended to look like Roman issues, using the same denominations used by central mints, and similar weight standards. The design on western provincial coins often followed closely Roman central examples – especially in its portrayal of emperors and members of the imperial family on the obverses.[172] Coins issued by eastern provincial cities, instead, continued to make use of pre-existing denominations and materials, with far fewer direct references to Roman politics. Instead, the coins often emphasised local aspirations (and especially how the issuing city was superior to its neighbour). The reverses of these coins depicted locally important divinities and their temples, and from the third century onwards local festivals through ever more varied iconographical types.[173] Formulated differently, local elites in the west issued provincial coins to show their loyalty to Rome and emphasise how Roman they had become, whereas the coins issued by eastern cities highlighted how closeness to the emperor benefited the specific city and its elite.[174]

---

[171] It is difficult to properly place Roman Africa into this divide. For the Romans, it seems to have been part of the west, as illustrated by its inclusion in the prefecture of Italy (alongside Italy and Illyricum) when the empire was split into a western an eastern zone in 364: J. W. Drijvers, 'The *divisio regni* of 364: The End of Unity?', in: R. Dijkstra/ S. van Poppel/ D. Slootjes (eds.), *East and West in the Roman Empire of the Fourth Century* (Leiden – Boston 2015), 82–96; 86–90. Yet there clearly were many cities in pre-Roman Africa and longstanding systems of monarchic rule: D. Stone, 'A Diachronic and Regional Approach to North African Urbanism', in: L. de Ligt/ J. Bintliff (eds.), *Regional Urban Systems in the Roman World, 150 BCE–250 CE* (Leiden – Boston 2020), 324–49. Binary opposites rarely work to explain divisions in complex societies.

[172] P. Ripollès, 'Coinage and Identity in the Roman Provinces: Spain', in: C. Howgego/ V. Heuchert/ A. Burnett (eds.), *Coinage and Identity in the Roman Provinces* (Oxford 2005), 79–93; 90–1; A. Burnett, 'The Roman West and the Roman East', in: Howgego/ Heuchert/ Burnett, *Coinage and Identity*, 171–80; 177–8.

[173] V. Heuchert, 'The Chronological Development of Roman Provincial Coin Iconography': in: Howgego/ Heuchert/ Burnett, *Coinage and Identity*, 29–56; Burnett, 'The Roman West and the Roman East', 178; N. Elkins, *Monuments in Miniature: Architecture on Roman Coinage* (New York: 2015), 146–61.

[174] Burnett, 'The Roman West and the Roman East', 178. See also G. Woolf, 'Becoming Roman, Staying Greek: Culture, Identity and the Civilising Process in the Roman East', *The Cambridge Classical Journal* 40 (1994), 116–43; 130–4 on interactions between roman emperors and greek

Figure 4.11 The Roman empire as a foreign country: AD 217–218, Anazarbus bronze (24.26). The obverse of this coin shows a laureate Macrinus, while the reverse depicts the city's *Tyche* handing him a crown. The legend mentions how the city was 'adorned with Roman trophies', implying that Rome is still seen as an external factor, although all the city's free inhabitants held Roman citizenship
Quotation from: *Sylloge nummorum Graecorum / Switzerland* 1, Suppl. 1 / Levante – Cilicia (1993), no. 1414.

This is an important reason why between the reigns of Tiberius and Claudius production of locally issued coins ended in Britain, Gaul, Spain, Sicily and Africa, whereas in the eastern provinces minting lasted till the end of the third century. In the west, the provincial coins did not differ sufficiently from central coins to make the continuation of local minting worthwhile. In the east local coins continued to express city identity for centuries.[175] The city of Anazarbus (Cilicia), for instance, struck coins that showed the emperor receiving a crown from the city's *Tyche*, with a reverse that explicitly stated how Anazarbus 'was adorned with Roman trophies' (ΡΩ[μαικοις] ΤΡΟ[παιοις] ΚΕ[κοσμημενη]; *RO[maikois] TRO[paiois] KE [kosmèmenè]*) (Figure 4.11), well into the third century.[176] This was after all free inhabitants of the empire had obtained citizenship through the Constitutio Antoniniana (AD 212), but Anazarbus still presented the emperor as some sort of outside power, mediating in inner-city affairs.

elites and Dench, *Empire and Political Cultures*, 9–16 on the historiography of local reactions to Rome.

[175] A. Burnett, 'Moneda foránea en el occidente y oriente romano', *X Congreso Nacional de Numismática. Actas* (Albacete 1998), 65–9.

[176] SNG Levante 1414; R. Ziegler, *Kaiser, Heer und Städtisches Geld. Untersuchungen zur Münzprägung von Anazarbos und anderer ostkilikischer Städte* (Vienna 1993), nos. 339–40, 444.

This notion should not be pushed too far. Not all eastern cities continued to produce local coinage. Cyprus ended its local production in the second century, and Lycia hardly took up minting at all. Almost all provincial coinage from Asia, moreover, portrayed the emperor on the obverse, indicating his central and unifying role in the empire. Yet, Syrian local coinage included members of the imperial family much more rarely.[177] Even individual choices could matter. Several coins from Smyrna that were explicitly struck under the auspices of the sophist Marcus Antonius Polemon (c. 90–144), whose name is on the reverse, placed a portrait of Hadrian's deified lover Antinous on the obverse. The iconography chosen for the reverse (bull and panther motives) was new for Smyrna, but was elsewhere used more often to associate Antinous to Hermes and especially Dionysus. This linked the coins back to Polemon in a different way, since he held an important priestly role in the local festival dedicated to Dionysus.[178] Polemon's coins, then, connected Antinous to the local Dionysus cult, and to Polemon's own religious office. These coins did not depict the emperor, but it is clear that closeness to the ruler was implied.

Differences within 'the east' could be as pronounced as differences between east and west. Nor did all reverse types of eastern provincial coins emphasise local issues. Coins issued by eastern client kings – whom we have already encountered as main instigators of the imperial cult in their kingdoms – sometimes followed central Roman issues very closely, although they also made much use of Hellenistic imagery. Rhoemetalces of Thrace (11 BC–AD 12) included Augustus' zodiacal sign of Capricorn on his coins, an image that linked him to the Roman emperor rather than Thracian traditions. Much further to the west, Juba II of Mauretania (25 BC–AD 23) did likewise.[179] Agrippa I of Judea (AD 41–44) imitated an (in)famous Caligulan coin type that depicted the emperor's sisters Julia,

---

[177] Burnett, 'The Roman West and the Roman East', 179–80; A. Burnett, 'Syrian Coinage and Romanisation from Pompey to Domitian', in: C. Augé/ F. Duyrat (eds.), *Les Monnayages syriens. Quel apport pour l'histoire du Proche-Orient hellénistique et romain?* (Beirut 2002), 115–22.

[178] RPC III, nos. 1975–1983; R. Bennett, *Local Elites and Local Coinage: Elite Self-Representation on the Provincial Coinage of Asia 31 BC–AD 275* (London 2004), 94–6, with plate 11, 144–6; Philost. *VS*, 531, 543; D. O. A. Klose, *Die Münzprägung von Smyrna in der römischen Kaiserzeit* (Berlin 1987), 250–4.

[179] Wilker, 'Modelling the Emperor', 54–6; A. Kropp, *Images and Monuments of Near Eastern Dynasts, 100 BC–AD 100* (Oxford 2013), 231–2.

Drusilla and Agrippina on the reverse.[180] Agrippa II (AD 49–c. 97) even went further than his predecessor in his association with Rome through his coin types, imitating Roman prototypes including Latin legends. He even adopted coin types that celebrated Rome's defeat of the Jewish revolt.[181] All these kings, then, minted coins that spoke of their close adherence to the emperor, as this strengthened their position in their kingdoms. Client kings had different purposes from civic elites in creating and distributing imperial images. The similarity of these kingly purposes apparently outweighed the regional differences between east and west.

In the Roman provinces, as at central level, there was not one image of Roman emperorship. Kings had different perspectives on how to relate to their ruler from civic elites. Nor was there one way in which all elites reacted. Context was crucial. Members of the local oligarchy in the Carthaginian hinterland, as we have seen, found it so important to show that they had raised arches and temples in honour of emperors that these buildings are disproportionately recorded in the surviving epigraphic record. No similar disbalance exists for the rest of Roman North Africa, which in its distribution of building inscriptions is much closer to that of Asia Minor than that of Carthage.[182] Apparently, it was more important to be seen to dedicate a monument for an emperor (or a god) to obtain a prestigious position in Carthage and its surroundings than it was in Mauretania. An altogether different perspective again emerges when looking at the representation of emperors in literary Jewish sources or the early-Christian *Alexandrian Acts*. There, Roman rulers often are regarded as suppressing tyrants.[183] This is a world away from Agrippa II's flattering images of Roman emperors, showing once more how pronounced the role of people creating an imperial image could be, and how different images existed within one region. The continuing expectation that emperors played important civic, military and religious roles, and were

---

[180] Y. Meshorer, *A Treasury of Jewish Coins: From the Persian Period to Bar Kokhba* (Nyack, NY 2001), no. 112; Kropp, *Images and Monuments*, 251. The Caligula coin: *RIC* 1², Caligula 33, 41 and see p. 237 above.

[181] Meshorer, *Treasury*, nos. 139, 141, 144, 147, 152, 154–5, 162; Kropp, *Images and Monuments*, 252.

[182] Hellström, 'Epigraphy and Ambition', 62–3; A. Zuiderhoek, 'Controlling Urban Public Space in Roman Asia Minor', in: T. Bekker-Nielsen (ed.), *Space, Place and Identity in Northern Anatolia* (Stuttgart 2014), 99–108; 102. See p. 290 above.

[183] The literature is immense. See: A. Harker, *Loyalty and Dissidence in Roman Egypt: The Case of the Acta Alexandrinorum* (Cambridge 2011), 32, 43, 91–2, 141–151, 176; C. Hayes, 'Roman Power through Rabbinic Eyes: Tragedy or Comedy', in: Berthelot, *Reconsidering Roman Power*, 443–71.

therefore represented as such, still left a wide range of possibilities for imperial representations – both positive and negative. Differences in ways of portraying the emperor within 'the east' could, then, be more pronounced than differences between east and west.

The construction of the imperial image in the provinces was a many-layered process. Different actors participated with different motives, and taking different local contexts into account, though in almost all cases individuals or groups used the image of the emperor to position themselves in relation to him, and so raise their own status. Going from one place to the next, there might be very diverse images of the emperors. This diversity becomes even more pronounced when perspectives from different types of sources are placed alongside each other – inscriptions honouring emperors for helping cities after natural disasters created a different image than reliefs showing them conquering enemies (or pacifying a province). The different images of the emperor were, however, complimentary ones. In almost all display contexts in which imperial statues were erected, for instance, images of emperors wearing togas, cuirasses or in the heroic nude stood alongside each other, in a fairly even distribution – though there are no surviving togate emperor statues from military contexts. There were, in other words, no clear preferences for a specific type of costume and the imperial roles which these indicated in particular settings.[184] All were reflections of accepted and expected roles of the emperor. The ruler was praised by emphasising these limited numbers of roles, in the provinces as much as in the centre. The plurality of provincial images of emperors suggests a surprisingly uniform range of expectations of imperial behaviour, and of ways of praising the emperor. Contradictory notions of emperors (such as the tyrannical ruler) are mainly found in literary texts that will not have had a direct impact on provincial subjects' direct surroundings.[185]

Different individuals and groups used different ways of portraying the emperor in different areas and contexts. But someone walking through cities in various parts of the empire would continuously be confronted with images of Roman rulers in a limited range of roles. It is likely that the generic notion of the emperor as a dominant figure, a military and religious leader who might help after disaster and with whom important members of local elite

---

[184] Heijnen, *Portraying Change*, 216–21 with figs. 67–9.
[185] Modern scholarship on subversive messages in ancient literature and how these reflect resistance to Rome is vast. A good starting point is T. Whitmarsh, 'Resistance Is Futile? Greek Literary Tactics in the Face of Rome', in: P. Schubert/ P. Ducrey/ P. Derron (eds.), *Les Grecs héritiers des Romains: huit exposés suivis de discussions* (Geneva 2013), 57–85.

could try to forge bonds, was the one which most non-elite provincial encountered on a daily basis. This image will have grown ever stronger as monuments and statues accumulated over time. Much like the imagery at Rome and Constantinople, the visual landscape in the provinces will have solidified expectations of what the Roman emperor should be and do. Statues in the theatres, temples and town squares, historical reliefs on major and minor monuments, military camps, standards and marching soldiers, governors and other officials making major decisions, local and central coinage depicting the emperor's centrality; the emperors' power and dominance was visible all around. Though individual portrayals of emperors differed, the range of images was limited. Shenoute's proclamation to his monks that everyone in the Roman empire heeded and obeyed the emperor will have been close to an image with which people in many of the provinces of the empire were confronted on a daily basis.[186] When the discrepancy between that image and reality grew too large, for instance when invasions indicated imperial impotence, the emperor's legitimacy was under serious threat.

Throughout Roman imperial history, there was tension between the existence of parallel images of emperorship, and the notion of the emperors as unifying figure in the empire. There may have been differences in emphasis over time. In AD 447, the eastern emperor Theodosius II sent an apology to his western co-emperor Valentinian III. Theodosius had issued new laws after the Theodosian Code had been compiled a decade earlier, but had not brought these to the attention of Valentinian or anyone else in the west. An important symbolic aspect of the Theodosian Code was that it included all current laws and so embodied the unity of the Roman empire. By failing to communicate eastern laws to the west, the difference between the eastern and western parts of the empire became clear which explains Theodosius' apologies. He sent the promulgated laws to Valentinian so that 'they may become formally known to Your subjects, provinces and peoples, and their tenor may begin to be observed in the western part of the empire also'. Glabrio Faustus, who was central to the dissemination of the law code in the west, was explicitly commemorated as a man who was 'elevated by the judgements of both authorities'. On the one hand, this shows how there was a real separation between the Latin western and Greek eastern empire, but on the other, the unity of the empire apparently remained a real concern for Theodosius II.[187]

---

[186] See p. 262 above.
[187] *Nov. Th.* 2; *ILS* 1283, 8–10; Millar, *A Greek Roman Empire*, 1–2; G. Traina, *428 dopo Cristo. Storia di un anno* (Rome 2007), 41–8; D. Potter, 'The Unity of the Roman Empire',

In the middle of the fifth century, the differences between east and west were perhaps more pronounced than ever before. They forced Priscus of Panium to explicitly differentiate between 'western Romans' and 'eastern Romans'.[188] Military upheaval and loss of territory in the west, and the firm establishment of Constantinople as the eastern capital had made a twinned empire, rather than a unified one, a geographical truth. This 'twinned empire' would not become a permanent reality. The removal of Romulus Augustulus in AD 476, followed by Justinian's conquests, would restore unity (Map 2.1), though at an increasingly smaller scale as Islamic conquests would further reduce Roman territory.[189] The fall of the western empire, and the long survival of the eastern empire makes it tempting to think of the late-antique west and east as separate entities. Yet if we look at Roman imperial history from Caesar to Justinian, the political division between the two parts of the empire occupied only two relatively brief periods; during the Tetrarchy, and from the establishment of Arcadius and Honorius in AD 395 to the deposition of Romulus Augustulus. The different military, political and socio-economic trajectories of (roughly speaking) the eastern and western provinces from the fourth century onwards have received much attention. But in many ways people within individual provinces continued to imagine and present their emperor much as they had done before.

There were developments over time, of course. The prohibition and consequent slow disappearance of pagan cults meant an end to the creation of images such as those of the local Palmyrene gods looking like Roman emperors. Similarly, with the end of provincial coinage sometime in the 260s and 270s (apart from Egypt, where it continued up to Diocletian's currency reforms), a further avenue of local formulations of the imperial image disappeared. Over time, too, there were fewer inscriptions and fewer statues as well.[190] Central portraiture, moreover, became more homogeneous,

---

in: S. McGill/ C. Sogno/ E. Watts (eds.), *From the Tetrarchs to the Theodosians. Later Roman History and Culture, 284–450 CE* (Cambridge – New York 2010), 13–32; 13.

[188] Priscus, fr. 2., 6.1, 8.45, 8.75, 8.152, 11; J. Given, *The Fragmentary History of Priscus*, 14, 42, 54, 58, 72, 75 Potter, 'The Unity of the Roman Empire', 13. On Priscus, see p. 131 above.

[189] Millar, *A Greek Roman Empire*, 3–4.

[190] On the end of Roman provincial coinage: K. Butcher, *Roman Provincial Coins: An Introduction to the Greek Imperials* (London 1988), 21. On the so-called epigraphic habit, see also the seminal article by R. MacMullen, 'The Epigraphic Habit in the Roman Empire', *The American Journal of Philology* 103 (1982), 233–46. On the 'statue habit', from the third century onwards, see R. R. R. Smith, 'Statue Practice in the Late Roman Empire: Numbers, Costumes and Styles', in: Smith/ Ward-Perkins, *The Last Statues of Antiquity*, 1–27; B. Ward-Perkins, 'The End of the Statue Habit, AD 284–620', in: Smith/ Ward-Perkins, *The Last Statues of Antiquity*, 295–307.

expressing general emperorship rather than individual rulers. This had repercussions for imperial portraits in the provinces, too, and limited the scope for regional variation even further.[191] The empire itself of course also grew smaller and the ultimate loss of the west meant that the remaining part of the empire was more culturally homogeneous. There were fewer new imperial images in the provinces in the fifth and sixth centuries, and what was still available (such as central coinage) is likely to have been more similar to central imagery than before. Many of the old statues still stood though, and existing reliefs, monuments and inscriptions could still be seen. These might even have become more important as emperors travelled less, further limiting direct interaction between them and their subjects, although emperors were still expected to visit the provinces, at least occasionally.

All of this must have had some impact on the notion of emperorship throughout the empire. Yet for most people living in the provinces, the emperor had always been a remote and superior figure – someone who could be appealed to and whose actions had serious consequences, but was ultimately unknowable. This would not have changed in the fifth and sixth centuries. The shifting imperial imagery of the later empire indicates changes in the relationship between the emperor and the (provincial) elites and officials. This, in turn, influenced the ways in which these individuals and groups in the provinces expressed their own status and aspirations. Whether it really changed the perception of what the emperor was and needed to do is doubtful. That, after all, was a multifaceted image that had been created over centuries, building on expectations that had been confirmed again and again. Emperors were what people expected them to be, everywhere in their empire.

---

[191] Smith, 'Late Antique Portraits', 182–3. See p. 56 above.

Conclusions

Emperors in a Changing World

The Roman emperor did not exist. Of course, for most of the time from about 50 BC to AD 1453 there was a man in Rome, and later Constantinople, who for all intents and purposes ruled the empire and was named Augustus. But the expectations of what that man should be and do differed wildly. Various people in various contexts at various times knew exactly what to expect of *their* emperor. Yet these people did not necessarily agree with one another. That there were such different expectations mattered. They influenced the way in which emperors were depicted and described, the way in which they were remembered, the people who surrounded them, and even how they acted. Throughout this book we have seen how context created emperorship. Different groups and individuals tried to understand and formulate the supreme position of the Roman emperor, and then adapt these formulations to changing contexts. They had to, as emperorship as such was never decidedly defined. Sole rulership was contested when Caesar came to power, and it was consequently formulated through experimenting, rather than clearly embedded in fixed structures. After Augustus' victory in the civil wars that followed Caesar's assassination there was no doubt that a single man was in charge of the empire. Yet what the position of this sole ruler had to entail remained a matter of perspective.

From Caesar's attempt at sole rule onwards, Roman emperorship was constructed and formulated in a permanent process of adaptation and negotiation. Some emperors crossed apparent lines, for instance by presenting themselves as more monarchical than certain groups found acceptable, and suffered consequences, from loss of reputation to loss of life (and sometimes the latter first, followed by the former). Yet in doing so, they set precedent. Later emperors could be less monarchical than their maligned predecessors, yet still more monarchical than before these maligned predecessors had changed expectations about the limits of acceptability. Placing his own portrait on coins had suggested Caesar's overbearing ambition to some of his contemporaries, but it became standard practice for his successors. In this way, the range of options to describe and understand emperorship extended as previously unacceptable modes of behaviour became normalised through precedent. But little, if any of this, was ever formalised, certainly not in an 'official' or legal sense. Under other emperors, positive patterns were established which were so successful that successors followed suit. This, too, widened the range of possible imperial behaviour. At the same time, there was also congruence in what was typical imperial behaviour and imagery. After Vespasian included the family name Caesar in the way in which he was addressed, it became a standard element of imperial titulature. After Constantine was systematically depicted with a diadem, it became a symbol of emperorship. Likewise, after several generations of emperors had emphasised their civil persona, it became near-impossible for successors to break that habit. The continuation of the role of *Pontifex Maximus* for Christian emperors, later reformulated as *Pontifex Inclitus*, fits the same trend.

Over time, more elaborate imperial dress and titles became more readily acceptable. But these can invariably be traced back to much earlier periods. Specific symbols, such as the sceptre, the radiate crown or laurel wreath, were appropriated for the emperor, not always only by the emperor himself. People needed cognitive footholds to come to terms with and adapt to new situations. In this process of 'anchoring' change, familiar terms, structures or visual language were a necessity to fit new structures and situations into established world views. People used existing concepts or images to understand emperorship. In using these concepts and images for an emperor, they changed meaning, and often became specific to the emperor, firmly entrenched in the public mind as defining elements.[1] This was regularly a development from a more private to a more public display of images or behaviour. So in earlier periods we can often find 'new' costumes or names on objects or in texts that were likely only to reach a more limited (and targeted) audience, or functioned in a very specific context. Early imperial cameos, for example, showed emperors in the guise of Jupiter well before Trajanic reliefs showed Jupiter holding out his thunderbolt and the emperor accepting it, which predate Tetrarchic coinage that assimilated emperors with the supreme god.

All of this means that even the ornate and ceremonial emperor of late antiquity was embedded in earlier emperorship. Ultimately, of course, there was a real difference between the public face of early- and late-Roman emperors. Comparing Justinian as he is depicted on the impressive mosaic

---

[1] On the concept of anchoring, see Sluiter, 'Anchoring Innovation'; O. Hekster, 'Religion and Tradition in the Roman Empire: Faces of Power and Anchoring Change', *Journal of Ancient Civilizations* 32 (2017), 13–34.

Figure 5.1 Late-antique splendour 547, Ravenna, San Vitale, north apse wall, mosaic (h. 2.64 m, w. 3.65 m). The emperor is highly recognisable as the central figure dressed in purple and gold clothing, and with a halo. He is placed among his advisors, among them his general Belisarius and Bishop Maximian of Ravenna. Soldiers hold a shield with the chi-rho symbol on it
Source: CKD – Radboud University Nijmegen, photo Mariëtte Verhoeven

in the Basilica of San Vitale in Ravenna (Figure 5.1) with Augustus on the Ara Pacis (Figure 1.11) shows a much more richly decorated ruler, standing out from the men who surround him. But there is continuity, too, in how both rulers are portrayed among their advisors – standing out but clearly part of the group. Continuity, also, in how both are presented in a religious context even if the religious system had changed. And Justinian is not depicted in a more elaborate way in San Vitale than Septimius Severus was on the Berlin tondo (Figure 1.14) nor more dominant in his position than Augustus on the Gemma Augustea (Figure 1.21). Nor was the Justinian depicted in the San Vitale the only Justinian. Indeed, the emperor never saw the way in which he was depicted in Ravenna and is very unlikely to have had anything do to with it. In Constantinople, he was most prominently commemorated through the great equestrian statue that echoed the one for Trajan in his Roman forum. Yet Justinian also had to react to public opinion in Constantinople after the Nika revolt with more modesty than many of his predecessors. He then had to show that he was a victorious conqueror to contain the damage that his harsh reaction to the revolt had caused. There were different imperial personae that were ascribed to the emperor and which Justinian had to embody, much as had been the case for all of his predecessors. Julian's description of Augustus 'changing colour continually, like a chameleon' is a sharp observation about what made a successful Roman emperor, from one of the limited group of people who had experienced this first hand.[2] Specific elements of emperorship, like the emperor's name and imperial attributes, visibly changed over six centuries. Yet Roman emperors continued to be different figures to different people. They differed in similar ways for a very long time.

Some shifts in imperial behaviour or appearance can be related, directly or indirectly, to developments in society. When the Roman empire was under military threat, the role of the emperor as a victorious warrior became more dominant, as increasingly military titulature suggests at those times. It also increased the importance of generals in the imperial entourage. The increasing importance of Christianity, instead, allowed bishops to become prominent in that entourage, and seems to have allowed more leeway for empresses to involve themselves in matters of state. It is indeed possible that more systematic interaction with Sasanian society changed what was acceptable in both the Roman and Sasanian courts. But these changes were neither linear nor abrupt. Bishops, for instance, in many ways took the position that senators had held. Christian symbols were added to existing iconographies. Discussions about which Christian city held religious supremacy were arbitrated by the emperor, in much the same way that emperors had settled previous intercity disputes. And Christian empresses who were perceived to hold too much power were still regularly held accountable to 'typically female' virtues and vices that went back centuries, as a comparison of the stories surrounding Theodora and Agrippina makes clear.

What we have seen throughout this book is the continued existence of different discourses. The perception and description of an emperor could differ radically in different sources, in different contexts or among different groups. These discourses did not necessarily change when society did. They also did not have to be consistent. Pulcheria could be praised for much the same political influence which Theodora was chastised for, simply by emphasising different elements of the empresses' behaviour. Augustus' infidelities were passed over 'as committed not from passion but from

---

[2] Julian, *Caes.* 309A–B, p. 182 above.

policy', whereas Nero's seduction of married women was placed in the same context as his 'abusing freeborn boys' and even a Vestal Virgin.[3] Often, in other words, actions were acceptable if committed by an emperor or empress whom an author deemed 'good' whereas the same behaviour was condemned for 'bad' emperors or empresses.

These negative and positive discourses form only limited reflections of how an emperor functioned and was perceived whilst alive and after his death. Of course all sources show only biased and partial reflections, as has long been recognised. That emperors regularly had to play different roles to satisfy the different groups who formed their constituents has likewise been emphasised, and lies at the heart of the much-discussed 'acceptance model'.[4] We should go further. Roman emperors always needed to be multifaceted and fulfil contradictory demands. They had little leeway to create their own imperial persona. They were constrained by their subjects' different expectations. The kaleidoscopic image of emperorship that our sources provide is therefore not a distortion but shows the multiple roles that every emperor continuously had to play. These roles cannot be closely tied to specific groups. One group, or even one individual, expected different things from the emperor in different contexts and highlighted different elements as the situation requested. Trying to establish official names and titles, a hierarchy of roles or images, or to tie specific roles to clearly defined groups is ultimately not that useful. We should not be looking for the 'real' Roman emperor. People approached their emperors in different ways at different times. This was accepted practice. In that sense, there was no such thing as *the* Roman emperor.

Notwithstanding all this variation, however, there was no endless repertoire of imperial roles and types of imperial behaviour. What people expected of their emperor was to a large extent the result of how earlier rulers had behaved and how they had been commemorated, shaped further by local traditions. Throughout the empire, imperial titles and images dominated the surroundings in which Roman subjects lived. Stories circulated discussing the behaviour of emperors, their families and their advisors. These images and stories shaped expectations, and these expectations influenced imperial behaviour which was, in turn, remembered

---

[3] Suet. *Aug.* 69.1; Suet. *Nero*, 28.1.
[4] On the sources as various reflections of the individual emperor, see especially Elsner/Masters, *Reflections of Nero*. On the acceptance model: Flaig, *Den Kaiser herausfordern* and see p. 269 n.30 above. The different roles are set out in Michels, *Antoninus Pius und die Rollenbilder* and pp. 107–8 above.

through stories and monuments. Most of these monuments and stories showed and discussed the emperor in his military, religious and civil roles. These remained the core functions of Roman emperors from Caesar to Justinian. In fact, they anticipated Caesar's rule and would remain important roles for Justinian's various successors in the west and east. Indeed, individuals who became pre-eminent in these roles, for instance by guaranteeing the safety of the empire when the reigning emperor did not, were often addressed in imperial language and became a threat to the throne. The balance between and formulation of these roles differed markedly between reigns and regions, but the roles remained, and show remarkable continuity. If anything, they became ever more ingrained in collective memory through their continuous repetition.

The memoryscape of the Roman empire also influenced imperial behaviour more directly. The many monuments and ceremonies in Rome that commemorated previous (Republican) practices, for instance, had an impact on how emperors were supposed to act and where they had to live. Different memoryscapes existed in the various provinces, which explains why emperorship was formulated differently there. Yet this was more a refined phrasing of emperorship than a different understanding of its substance. The core roles of the emperor allowed for a wide range of refractions. The emperor's civil, military and religious roles could always be presented in ways that suited the local circumstances. But emperors still had to live up to the expectations that these local formulations of their rule established. In this way, Roman emperors were effectively in continuous competition with their predecessors, or at least with the posthumous image of those predecessors. The late-antique senatorial acclamation 'More fortunate than Augustus, better than Trajan' was both encouraging and adhortative.[5] Behaving like Augustus and Trajan had come to mean acting like a civil ruler who paid much attention to senators. It was small wonder, then, that senators praised their emperors in this way. Provincial appellations to Septimius Severus as 'kindest and mildest prince, our lord' (*indulgentissimus et clementissimus princeps dominus noster*) function in much the same way, encouraging the emperor to act in a certain manner by expressing specific expectations.[6]

The relative fluidity of Roman emperorship was a result of the step-by-step process through which the position of sole ruler had taken shape. It allowed emperors to be men for all seasons. Yet there was no endless

---

[5] Eutr. *Brev.* 8.5.3, p. 178 above.   [6] *CIL* 10.7274, p. 44 above.

flexibility. Emperors had to respond to expectations created in the past. They could not simply present themselves as they saw fit – at least not without running the risk of character assassination or actual loss of life. Even in terms of representation, Roman emperors were mostly passive rulers, reacting to their subjects' wishes and expectations. But not always. Some emperors decided to do things differently. Often this led to conflicts with at least some important groups, but even that did not always cause serious repercussions. Augustus, Hadrian, Diocletian, Constantine and Justinian have regularly appeared in this book because of major shifts occurring during their reigns. All of them managed to reign for a long period of time and none of them died violently. Expectations could be adapted. Tellingly, all of them did so by adjusting existing concepts, implicitly and explicitly referring to earlier practices. It was also certainly possible to highlight one aspect of emperorship over another. Such adaptations were not easy. Caesar, Caligula and Elagabalus exemplify the risks that emperors ran when pushing through changes too rapidly. Perhaps the same applies to Zeno, although the latter reigned for a long time and seems to have died of an illness.[7]

Of course military events and socio-economic developments were enormously important for the success or failure of individual reigns and for the development of emperorship as a whole. The military crises of the third and fifth centuries made the military aspects of the emperors' role more important for a prolonged period, though not permanently. Here, too, communication and representation mattered, as is made clear by the way panegyric text and coin images predicted (mostly fictive) martial qualities of child emperors. Modern scholarship has often tried to model how such communication worked and what role (visual) sources played in these processes of communication and representation. Was communication about emperorship top-down? Or was it bottom-up? Did statues and narrative reliefs form a clear semantic system that many (or few) people would be able to 'read'? Were there clearly defined local and social dialects and discourses through which emperorship could be represented? The answer to all of the above notions is yes, which means that none of them explains the process properly. Different ways of formulating and reformulating Roman emperorship interacted all the time. There were attempts to propagate specific messages from the centre, as well as attempts by provincial towns – or even individual

---

[7] The story that Zeno was buried alive, crying and wailing from his sarcophagus which Ariadne refused to open because he was so hated, is almost certainly a later invention: Zonaras 14.2.31–5; Psellus, 68. It does show the negative posthumous reputation of the emperor.

people in those towns – to present the emperor in a specifically local context. People interpreted images in different ways, often even when they belonged to the same group. Messages and concepts telling how people understood a title or image changed over time. The formulation of Roman emperorship was as much a game of Chinese whispers as it was targeted propaganda. The Roman empire was a complex and geographically enormous area, consisting of many peoples, groups and individuals with ideas and purposes that occasionally overlapped and regularly clashed. Either/or questions cannot do it justice. Inconsistencies in behaviour and formulations were not just inevitable, but they were integral part of Roman emperorship.

This applies to the Roman world as much as to the modern one. Contemporary leaders, much like ancient Roman ones, have to live up to expectations and formulate changes in language and images that can be understood by a variety of audiences. Modern societies, like the Roman empire, include multiple groups with multiple patterns of expectations, often mutually contradictory. Mass media has made it more difficult to present parallel images to different groups. Any image is, after all, now likely to be seen by many groups and people (and probably many times). But people still often see what they want to see, and the very recent past has shown how it is still possible for leaders to simultaneously present apparently contradictory messages without difficulty. Even those leaders have to abide by expectations and traditions. The inauguration ceremony of American presidents is a case in point. There can be variation in the contents of the speech, and the number of attending subjects may vary (in which competition with past presidents plays a potentially powerful part) but on the whole the continuity of the event is key. An accumulation of past ceremonies has fixed certain elements firmly into place. Walking on Pennsylvania Avenue and standing on the Capitol steps are inescapable parts of the inauguration. But the constraints of expectations are not limited to behaviour at ritual events; presidents are expected to visit their troops and go to church, travel to disaster zones and supply help for victims. They are presented as military victors whenever there is cause (and occasionally when there is not) and live in the White House, which puts some constraints on who surrounds them. It is, perhaps, no coincidence that American presidents are so often compared to Roman emperors. Modern rulers, like Roman emperors, are shaped by the behaviour of their predecessors and the memoryscape through which this behaviour is remembered. The past influences the present. Leaders are constrained by the great expectations of their subjects.

Appendix

THE JULIO-CLAUDIANS

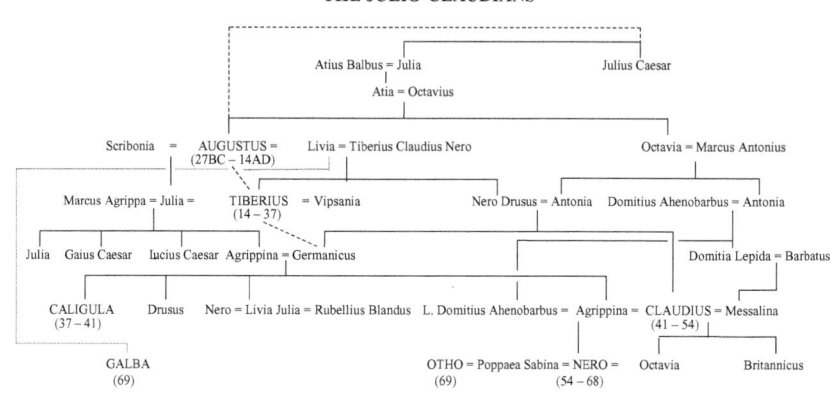

```
                            Atius Balbus = Julia                    Julius Caesar
                                    |
                              Atia = Octavius
```

Scribonia = AUGUSTUS = Livia = Tiberius Claudius Nero   Octavia = Marcus Antonius
           (27BC – 14AD)

Marcus Agrippa = Julia =   TIBERIUS = Vipsania   Nero Drusus = Antonia   Domitius Ahenobarbus = Antonia
                           (14 – 37)

Julia Gaius Caesar Lucius Caesar Agrippina = Germanicus   Domitia Lepida = Barbatus

CALIGULA   Drusus   Nero = Livia Julia = Rubellius Blandus   L. Domitius Ahenobarbus = Agrippina   CLAUDIUS = Messalina
(37 – 41)   (41 – 54)

      GALBA   OTHO = Poppaea Sabina = NERO =   Octavia   Britannicus
      (69)   (69)   (54 – 68)

THE FLAVIANS

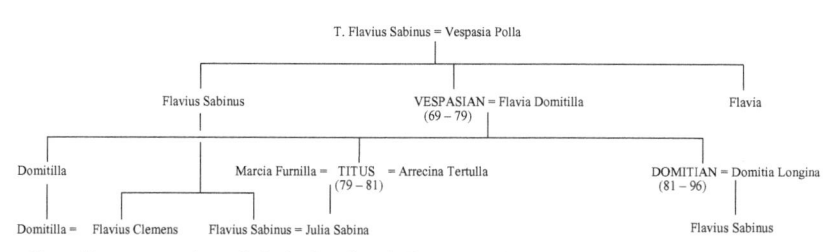

```
                    T. Flavius Sabinus = Vespasia Polla
```

Flavius Sabinus   VESPASIAN = Flavia Domitilla   Flavia
                              (69 – 79)

Domitilla   Marcia Furnilla = TITUS = Arrecina Tertulla   DOMITIAN = Domitia Longina
                                 (79 – 81)   (81 – 96)

Domitilla = Flavius Clemens   Flavius Sabinus = Julia Sabina   Flavius Sabinus

Notes: Emperors are in capitals; broken lines indicates adoption; dotted lines indicate fictive lineage

THE ADOPTIVE AND ANTONINE EMPERORS

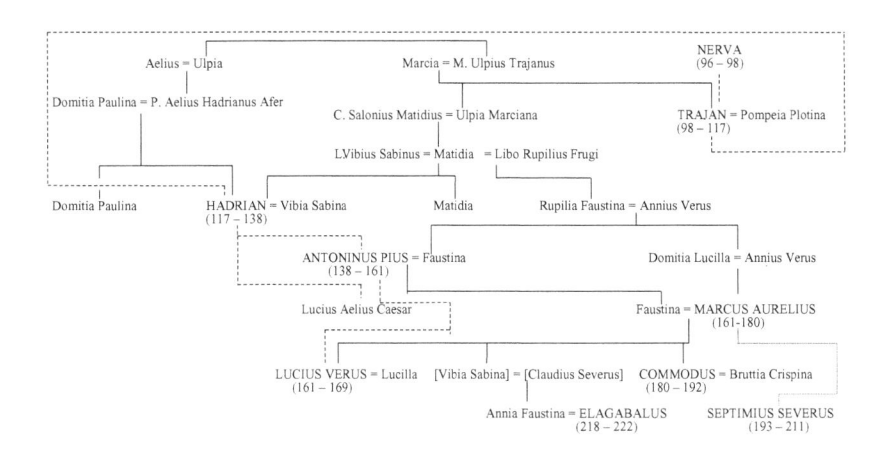

```
                    Aelius = Ulpia              Marcia = M. Ulpius Trajanus              NERVA
                                                                                        (96 – 98)
Domitia Paulina = P. Aelius Hadrianus Afer
                                        C. Salonius Matidius = Ulpia Marciana     TRAJAN = Pompeia Plotina
                                                                                  (98 – 117)
                                         L.Vibius Sabinus = Matidia = Libo Rupilius Frugi

Domitia Paulina    HADRIAN = Vibia Sabina       Matidia       Rupilia Faustina = Annius Verus
                   (117 – 138)
                           ANTONINUS PIUS = Faustina              Domitia Lucilla = Annius Verus
                           (138 – 161)
                              Lucius Aelius Caesar                Faustina = MARCUS AURELIUS
                                                                            (161-180)
                        LUCIUS VERUS = Lucilla   [Vibia Sabina] = [Claudius Severus]   COMMODUS = Bruttia Crispina
                        (161 – 169)                                                    (180 – 192)
                                       Annia Faustina = ELAGABALUS         SEPTIMIUS SEVERUS
                                                       (218 – 222)         (193 – 211)
```

THE SEVERI

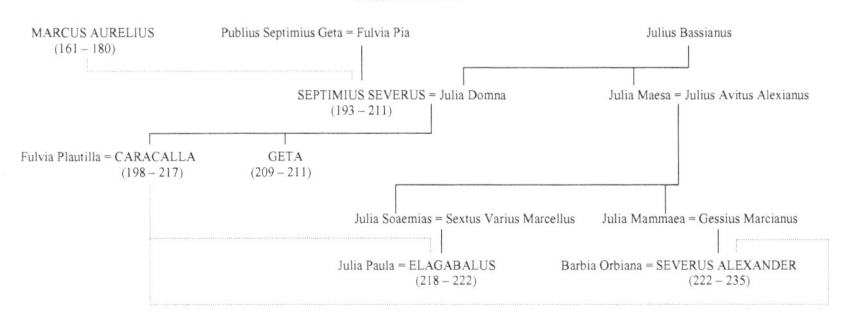

```
MARCUS AURELIUS       Publius Septimius Geta = Fulvia Pia                Julius Bassianus
(161 – 180)
                            SEPTIMIUS SEVERUS = Julia Domna     Julia Maesa = Julius Avitus Alexianus
                            (193 – 211)
Fulvia Plautilla = CARACALLA   GETA
                 (198 – 217)   (209 – 211)
                         Julia Soaemias = Sextus Varius Marcellus    Julia Mammaea = Gessius Marcianus
                                Julia Paula = ELAGABALUS         Barbia Orbiana = SEVERUS ALEXANDER
                                              (218 – 222)                         (222 – 235)
```

THE TETRARCHY

```
DIOCLETIAN = Prisca     MAXIMIAN = Eutropia = Afranius Hannibalianus     CLAUDIUS II GOTHICUS
(284 – 305)             (286– 310)                                       (268 – 270)
GALERIUS = Galeria Valeria
(293 – 311)                                    Theodora = CONSTANTIUS I = (?)Helena
                                                         (293 – 306)
Maximilia = MAXENTIUS              Fausta = CONSTANTINE
            (306 – 312)                     (337 – 337)
   Romulus
```

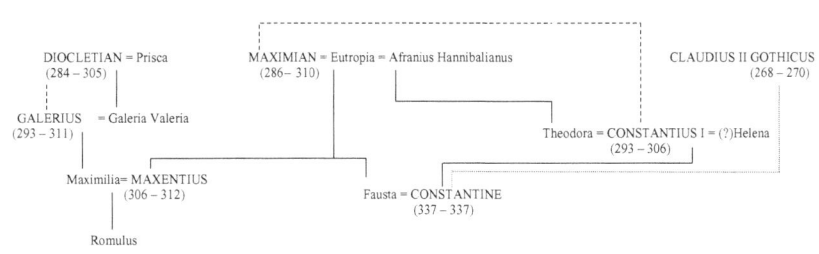

Notes: Emperors are in capitals; broken lines indicates adoption; dotted lines indicate fictive lineage

THE CONSTANTINIAN DYNASTY

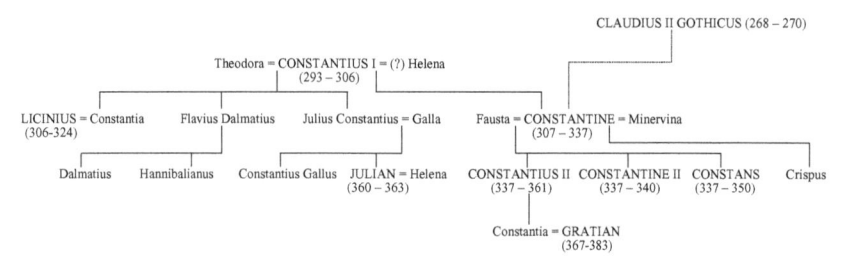

```
                                                                CLAUDIUS II GOTHICUS (268 – 270)
                    Theodora = CONSTANTIUS I = (?) Helena
                              (293 – 306)
   ┌──────────────┬──────────────────┬─────────────────┐        ┌──────────────────┐
LICINIUS = Constantia  Flavius Dalmatius  Julius Constantius = Galla   Fausta = CONSTANTINE = Minervina
(306-324)                                                              (307 – 337)
   ┌──────┐                    ┌──────────────┐              ┌──────────────┬──────────────┬─────────┐
Dalmatius Hannibalianus  Constantius Gallus  JULIAN = Helena  CONSTANTIUS II  CONSTANTINE II  CONSTANS  Crispus
                                             (360 – 363)     (337 – 361)     (337 – 340)    (337 – 350)
                                                  Constantia = GRATIAN
                                                             (367-383)
```

THE VALENTINIAN DYNASTY

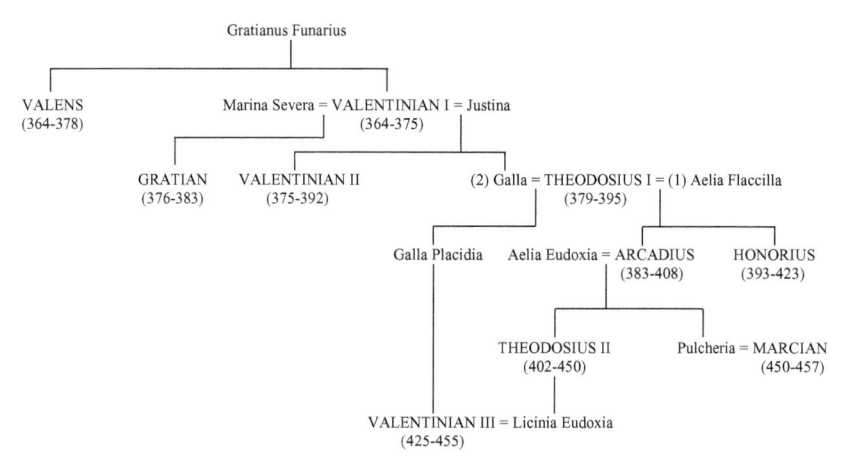

```
                         Gratianus Funarius
          ┌──────────────────────┴──────────────────┐
   VALENS               Marina Severa = VALENTINIAN I = Justina
  (364-378)                           (364-375)
                    ┌──────────────┬──────────────────────────────┐
                GRATIAN      VALENTINIAN II          (2) Galla = THEODOSIUS I = (1) Aelia Flaccilla
               (376-383)      (375-392)                         (379-395)
                                         ┌──────────────┬──────────────────────┐
                                     Galla Placidia  Aelia Eudoxia = ARCADIUS   HONORIUS
                                                                 (383-408)     (393-423)
                                                        ┌──────────────┬─────────────┐
                                                     THEODOSIUS II           Pulcheria = MARCIAN
                                                       (402-450)                       (450-457)
                               VALENTINIAN III = Licinia Eudoxia
                                  (425-455)
```

Notes: Emperors are in capitals; dotted lines indicate fictive lineage

Glossary

ab admissionibus	official in control of access to the emperor
ab epistulis	official responsible for imperial correspondence
a cubiculo	chamberlain
adlocutio	address of an army commander in the military
adventus	ceremonial arrival of the emperor to a city
a libellis	official responsible for processing petitions to the emperor
antoninianus	silver coin introduced under Caracalla of the value of two silver *denarii*, later almost entirely made of bronze
a rationibus	official in charge of imperial finances
as	bronze coin; later copper
aureus	gold coin; the most valuable Roman denomination
capite velato	with covered head (with the toga covering the head) for ritual practices
carucca	four-wheeled carriage for people of distinction
chlamys	ankle-length cloak fastened with a brooch (see *paludamentum*)
civilis princeps	emperor who behaved in a citizen-like manner
civitas	social body of the citizens, united by law
cognomen	third name of a Roman citizen; surname
comes (plurar *comites*)	companion
consilium principis	council of the *princeps*; ad hoc advisory body to the emperor
consistorium	the highest political council from Constantine onwards; replaced the *consilium principis*
Constitutio Antoniniana	universal grant of citizenship to all free inhabitants of the Roman Empire in AD 212
cursus honorum	career ladder of the Roman elite

damnatio memoriae	condemnation of the memory of a deceased person
decennalia	festival celebrating ten years of imperial rule
denarius	silver coin, worth ten *asses*
dictator	magistrate in sole control of the Roman state, appointed for a limited period of time during exceptional difficulties
diploma (military)	document certifying that a veteran had received Roman citizenship upon discharge
divi	deified emperors
divi filius	son of a god
domus divina	divine household; the imperial family
dupondius	bronze coin, worth two *asses*
equites singulares Augusti	imperial mounted guard, often nicknamed the Batavi
excubitors	Byzantine imperial guard
imperator	commander
imperium	power of a magistrate to command
iudex vice Caesaris	high-ranking senator deputising for emperors on legal matters
koinon (plural *koina*)	regional federations of cities
laticlavus	broad purple stripe indicating senatorial status
legatus	magistrate sent by the emperor to command a province
libelli	brief documents; petitions to the emperor
magister militum	'master of soldiers'; senior military officer
mos maiorum	ancestral custom; the way things were previously done
neokoros	city with a temple for the imperial cult
nomen (*gentilicium*)	middle name of a Roman citizen
ovatio	minor triumph
paludamentum	cloak worn by military commanders, later restricted to the emperor. Often used synonymously with *chlamys*
Panegyrici Latini	set of Latin panegyric orations
patria	homeland
pater patriae	father of his country (honorific title)
pax deorum	peaceful relationship between gods and men
pileus	cap indicating freedman status and through it liberty

Pontifex Maximus	chief priest of Rome; greatest pontiff
praefectus praetorio	prefect (commander) of the praetorian guard, the only armed troops in the Italian peninsula
praefectus urbi	prefect (commander) of the city of Rome, responsible for maintaining order in the city
praenomen	first name of a Roman citizen
princeps	'the first'; prominent mode of address for the emperor
princeps iuventutis	first of the youth
princeps senatus	leading member of the senate
profectio	ceremonial departure of generals and emperors from Rome
rex	king
salutatio	formal greeting
sella curulis	curule chair; seat for magistrates holding *imperium*
senatus consultum	decree of the senate
sestertius	large brass coin, worth two and a half *asses*
Sidus Iulium	Caesar's comet or star; sign of Caesar's deification
Tetrarchy	system of collegiate emperorship instituted by Diocletian, in which four men, two Augusti and two Caesares, ruled different parts of the empire
toga picta	purple toga with gold embroidery worn by victorious commanders and by emperors
toga praetexta	white toga with purple stripe
toga purpurea	purple-dyed toga, associated with the Roman kings
toga virilis	toga of manhood; plain white toga
tribunicia potestas	the power of the people's tribune
vexillarius	standard bearer in Roman legions
vicennalia	festival celebrating twenty years of imperial rule

Bibliography

Abbe, M. 2013. 'The Togatus Statue of Caligula in the Virginia Museum of Fine Arts: An Archaeological Description', *The Digital Sculpture Project*, accessed 15 August 2020 (www.digitalsculpture.org/papers/abbe/abbe_paper.html).

Abdy, R. 2012. 'Tetrarchy and the House of Constantine', in: W. E. Metcalf (ed.), *The Oxford Handbook of Greek and Roman Coinage*. Oxford; New York, 584–600.

Absil, M. 1997. *Les Préfets du prétoire d'Auguste à Commode. 2 avant Jésus-Christ – 192 après Jésus-Christ*. Paris.

Abu El-Enen, M. M., J. Lorenz and K. A. Ali. 2018. 'A New Look on Imperial Porphyry: A Famous Ancient Dimension Stone from the Eastern Desert of Egypt – Petrogenesis and Cultural Relevance', *International Journal of Earth Sciences* 107: 2393–408.

Acqua, C. M. 2016. 'Imperial Representation at Dura-Europos: Suggestions for Urban Paths', in: T. Kaizer (ed.), *Religion, Society and Culture at Dura-Europos*. Cambridge, 144–64.

Adams, J. N. 2003. *Bilingualism and the Latin Language*. Cambridge.

Adornato, G. 2018. 'The Dilemma of the Prima Porta Augustus: Polykleitos or Not Polykleitos?', in: G. Adornato, I. Bald Romano, G. Cirucci and A. Poggio (eds.), *Restaging Greek Artworks in Roman Times*. Milan, 245–74.

Agamben, G. 2005. *State of Exception*. Chicago; London.

Albornoz, L. (ed.). 2015. *Power, Media, Culture: A Critical View from the Political Economy of Communication*. London; New York.

Albu, E. 2014. 'The Battle of the Maps in a Christian Empire', in: C. Rapp and H. A. Drake (eds.), *The City in the Classical and Post-Classical World*. Cambridge, 202–16.

Alcock, S. E. 1994. 'Nero at Play? The Emperor's Grecian Odyssey', in: J. Elsner and J. Masters (eds.), *Reflections of Nero: Culture, History, and Representation*. Chapel Hill; London, 98–112.

Aldrete, G. S. 1999. *Gestures and Acclamations in Ancient Rome*. Baltimore.

Alföldi, A. 1934. 'Die Ausgestaltung des monarchischen Zeremoniells am römischen Kaiserhofe', *MDAIR* 49: 1–118.

    1934. 'Insignien und Tracht der römischen Kaiser', *MDAIRA* 49: 1–177.

    1970. *Die monarchische Repräsentation im römischen Kaiserreich*. Darmstadt.

Allen, P., and B. Neil. 2020. *Greek and Latin Letters in Late Antiquity: The Christianisation of a Literary Form*. Cambridge.

Amedick, R. 2010. 'Immortal Ambitions. Sarcophagi and Social Distinction in Roman Culture', in: O. Hekster and S. T. A. M. Mols (eds.), *Cultural Messages in the Greco-Roman World*. Leuven, 33–46.

Amélineau, É. (ed.). 1914. *Oeuvres de Schenoudi, texte copte et traduction française*. Tome II, fasc. 3. Paris.

Amidon, R. 2007. *Philostorgius: Church History*. Atlanta.

Amirav, H. 2015. *Authority and Performance: Sociological Perspectives on the Council of Chalcedon (AD 451)*. Göttingen.

Anders, F. 2010. *Flavius Ricimer: Macht und Ohnmacht des weströmischen Heermeisters in der zweiten Hälfte des 5. Jahrhunderts*. Frankfurt am Main.

Ando, C. 2000. *Imperial Ideology and Provincial Loyalty in the Roman Empire*. Berkeley; Los Angeles; London.

Andreescu-Treadgold, I., and W. Treadgold. 1997. 'Procopius and the Imperial Panels of San Vitale', *Art Bulletin* 79: 708–23.

Andrews, G. 2018. *Rethinking the Third Century CE: Contemporary Historiography and Political Narrative*. PhD Cambridge.

Angelova, D. 2004. 'The Ivories of Ariadne and Ideas about Female Imperial Authority in Rome and Early Byzantium', *Gesta* 43: 1–15.

Antoniou, A. A. 2019. 'Cassius Dio (51.20.6-8) and the Worship of the Living Emperor in Italy', *Mnemosyne* 72: 930–48.

Arnaud, P. 1984. 'L'Image du globe dans le monde romain: science, iconographie, symbolique', *MEFRA* 96: 53–116.

Ash, R. 2006. 'Following in the Footsteps of Lucullus? Tacitus' Characterisation of Corbulo', *Arethusa* 39: 355–75.

Assmann, J. 1997. *Moses the Egyptian: The Memory of Egypt in Western Monotheism*. Cambridge [Mass.].

Augoustakis, A., and E. Buckley. 2021. 'Domitian and Religion', in: A. Raimondi Cominesi, N. de Haan, E. M. Moormann and C. Stocks (eds.), *God on Earth: Emperor Domitian. The Re-invention of Rome at the End of the 1st Century AD*. Leiden, 155–71.

Ausbüttel, F. M. 2015. 'Die Tolerierung der Christen in der Zeit von Gallienus bis zur sogenannten Constantinischen Wende (260–313)', *Millennium* 12: 41–74.

Aveline, J. 2004. 'The Death of Claudius', *Historia* 53: 453–75.

Ayaita, J. J. 2015. *Justinian und das Volk im Nikaaufstand*. PhD Heidelberg.

Badel, C. 2009. 'Adventus et Salutatio', in: A. Bérenger and É. Perrin-Saminadayar (eds.), *Les Entrées royales et impériales: histoire, représentation et diffusion d'une cérémonie publique, de l'Orient ancien à Byzance. de l'archéologie à l'histoire*. Paris, 157–75.

Bagnall, R. S., and K. A. Worp. 2004². *Chronological Systems of Byzantine Egypt*. Leiden; Boston.

Baldwin, B. 1980. 'Tacitus, the *Panegyrici Latini*, and the *Historia Augusta*', *Eranos* 78: 175–8.

1981. 'Physical Descriptions of Byzantine Emperors', *Byzantion* 51: 8–21.

Bang, P. F. 2011. 'Court and State in the Roman Empire – Domestication and Tradition in Comparative Perspective', in: J. Duindam, T. Artan and M. Kunt (eds.), *Royal Courts in Dynastic States and Empires. A Global Perspective*. Leiden; Boston, 103–28.

Baraz, Y. 2018. 'Discourse of Kingship in Late Republican Invective', in: N. Panou and H. Schadee (eds.), *Evil Lords. Theories and Representations of Tyranny from Antiquity to the Renaissance*. Oxford, 43–60.

Bardill, J. 2012. *Constantine, Divine Emperor of the Christian Golden Age*. Cambridge.

Barnes, T. D. 1982. *The New Empire of Diocletian and Constantine*. Cambridge [Mass.].

1993. *Athanasius and Constantius: Theology and Politics in the Constantinian Empire*. Cambridge [Mass.].

2011. *Constantine: Dynasty, Religion and Power in the Later Roman Empire*. Hoboken.

Baroin, C. 2003. *Se souvenir à Rome: formes, representations et pratiques de la mémoire*. Paris.

Baroni, A. 2007. 'La titolatura della dittatura di Silla', *Athenaeum* 95: 775–92.

Barrett, A. 2015². *Caligula. The Abuse of Power*. London; New York.

Barton, T. S. 1994. *Power and Knowledge. Astrology, Physiognomics, and Medicine under the Roman Empire*. Ann Arbor.

Basset, S. 2004. *The Urban Image of Late Antique Constantinople*. Cambridge.

Bastien, P. 1992–1994. *Le Buste monétaire des empereurs romains*. 3 vols. Wetteren.

Beard, M. 1998. 'Imaginary *Horti*; or Up the Garden Path', in: E. La Rocca and M. Cima (eds.), *Horti Romani*. Rome, 23–32.

2007. *The Roman Triumph*. Cambridge [Mass.]; London.

Beard, M., J. North and S. Price. 1998. *Religions of Rome*. Cambridge.

Beetham, D. 2013². *The Legitimation of Power*. Basingstoke; New York.

Begass, C. 2018. *Die Senatsaristokratie des oströmischen Reiches, ca. 457–518. Prosopographische und sozialgeschichtliche Untersuchungen*. Munich.

Bell, P. N. 2009. *Three Political Voices from the Age of Justinian*. Liverpool.

Bell, S. 2008. 'Role Models in the Roman World', in: S. Bell and I. L. Hansen (eds.), *Role Models in the Roman World. Identity and Assimilation*. Ann Arbor, 1–39.

Benétos, D. 2017. 'From *divus Augustus* to *Vicarius Christi*: Examples of Self-presentation in a Period of Transition', in: A. Gavrielatos (ed.), *Self-Presentation and Identity in the Roman World*. Cambridge, 208–39.

Bennett, R. 2004. *Local Elites and Local Coinage: Elite Self-representation on the Provincial Coinage of Asia 31 BC– AD 275*. London.

Benoist, S. 2005 *Rome, le prince et la Cité. Pouvoir impérial et cérémonies publiques (Ier siècle av. – début du IVe siècle ap. J.-C.)*.

2009. 'Du *pontifex maximus* à l'élu de dieu: l'empereur et les sacra (Ier s. av. n.e.–Ve s. de n.e.)', in: O. Hekster, S. Schmidt-Hofner and C. Witschel (eds.),

Ritual Dynamics and Religious Change in the Roman Empire. Leiden; Boston, 33–51.

2018. 'Images, effigies et corps du prince à Rome: une mise en scène du discours impérial dans la cité', in: D. Carrangeot, B. Laurioux and V. Puech (eds.), *Rituels et cérémonies de cour de l'Empire romain à l'âge baroque*. Septentrion, 25–37.

Bérenger, A. 2009. 'L' adventus des gouverneurs de province', in: A. Bérenger and É. Perrin-Saminadayar (eds.), *Les Entrées royales et impériales: histoire, représentation et diffusion d'une cérémonie publique, de l'Orient ancien à Byzance. de l'archéologie à l'histoire*. Paris, 125–38

Berg, J. 2018. 'Lumping and Splitting', *Science* 359: 1309.

Berger, A. 2013. *Accounts of Medieval Constantinople. The Patria*. Cambridge [Mass.]; London.

Bergmann, B. 2010. 'Bar Kochba und das Panhellenion: Die Panzerstatue Hadrians aus Hierapytna/Kreta (Istanbul, Archäologisches Museum Inv. Nr. 50) und der Panzertorso Inv. Nr. 8097 im Piräusmuseum von Athen', *Istanbuler Mitteilungen*, 60: 203–89.

2010. *Der Kranz des Kaisers: Genese und Bedeutung einer römischen Insignie*. Berlin.

2020. 'Die Lorbeeren des Caesar' Oder: Wie erkennt man einen römischen Kaiser?' in: D. Boschung and F. Queyrel (eds.), *Porträt und soziale Distinktion*. Paderborn, 205–58.

Bergmann, M. 1977. *Studien zum römischen Porträt des 3. Jahrhunderts nach Christus*. Bonn.

1998. *Die Strahlen der Herrscher: theomorphes Herrscherbild und politische Symbolik im Hellenismus und in der römischen Kaiserzeit*. Mainz.

2007. 'Bildnisse der Tetrarchenzeit', in: A. Demandt and J. Engemann (eds.), *Imperator Caesar Flavius Constantinus. Konstantin der Grosse. Ausstellungskatalog*. Mainz, 58–73.

Bertolazzi, R. 2020. *Septimius Severus and the Cities of the Empire*. Faenza.

Bertrand-Ecanvil, E. 1994. 'Présages et propagande idéologique. A propos d'une liste concernant Octavien Auguste', *MEFRA* 106: 487–531.

Beste, H.-J. 2011. 'Domus Aurea, il padiglione dell'Oppio', in: M. A. Tomei and R. Rea (eds.), *Nerone: Catalogo della Mostra (Roma, 13 Aprile–18 Settembre 2011)*. Milan, 170–5.

Betjes, S. 2022. *The Mind of the Mint. Continuity and Change in Roman Imperial Coin Design from Augustus to Zeno (31 BCE–491 CE)*. PhD Nijmegen.

Forthcoming. 'Moneta, the Memory of Roman Coinage: The Storage of Dies (or Coins) at the Mint of Rome', *Journal of Archaeological Numismatics*.

Betjes, S., and S. Heijnen. 2018. 'The Usurping Princeps. Maxentius' Image and Its Constantinian Legacy', *JAHA* 5.3: 5–23.

Bingen, J. 2016. 'The Imperial Roman Site of the Mons Claudianus (Eastern Desert of Egypt)', *Diogenes* 61: 7–17.

Binninger, S. 2009. *Le Trophée d'Auguste à la Turbie*. Paris.
Birley, A. R. 1988². *Septimius Severus. The African Emperor*. London.
   1997. *Hadrian. The Restless Emperor*. London; New York.
Birley, E. 1978. 'The Religion of the Roman Army', *ANRW* II.16.2: 1506–41.
Bjornlie, M. S. 2013. *Politics and Tradition between Rome, Ravenna and Constantinople: A Study of Cassiodorus and the Variae, 527–554*. Cambridge; New York.
   2014. 'Audience and Rhetorical Presentation in the Variae of Cassiodorus', *Revue belge de philologie et d'histoire* 92: 187–207.
Blay Detrell, J. 2007. '"Divi Series", una emisión conmemorativa de antoninianos de restitución del siglo III d.C.', *Gaceta Numismática* 165: 69–82.
Boatwright, M. T. 2000. 'Just Window Dressing? Imperial Women as Architectural Sculpture', in: D. E. E. Kleiner and S. Matheson (eds.), *I, Claudia II: Women in Roman Art and Society*. Austin, 61–75.
   2003. *Hadrian and the Cities of the Roman Empire*. Princeton.
Bodnaruk, M. 2017. 'Administering the Empire. The Unmaking of an Equestrian Elite in the 4th Century CE', in: R. Varga and V. Rusu-Bolindet (eds.), *Official Power and Local Elites in the Roman Provinces*. London; New York, 145–67.
Boeck, E. 2021. *The Bronze Horseman of Justinian in Constantinople: The Cross-Cultural Biography of a Mediterranean Monument*. Cambridge.
Bolaño, C. 2015. 'Communication and Epistemological Struggle', in: L Albornoz (ed.), *Power, Media, Culture. A Critical View from the Political Economy of Communication*. London; New York, 189–99.
Bonamente, G. 2011. 'Dall'imperatore divinizzato all' imperatore santo', in: P. Brown and T. Lizzi Testa (eds.), *Pagans and Christians in the Roman Empire: The Breaking of a Dialogue, IVth–VIth Century A.D.* Munster, 339–70.
Bönisch-Meyer, S. 2021. *Dialogangebote. Die Anrede des Kaisers jenseits der offiziellen Titulatur*. Leiden; Boston.
Bono, F. 2019. 'The Value of the Stability of the Law. A Perspective on the Role of the Emperor in Political Crises', in: O. Hekster and K. Verboven (eds.) *The Impact of Justice on the Roman Empire*. Boston; Leiden, 68–85.
   2021. '*Adluvionum ea natura est, ut semper incerta possessio sit*. Picturing and regulating alluvial lands in *Nov. Theod.* 20', in: M. Horster and N. Hächler (eds.), *The Impact of the Roman Empire on Landscapes*. Leiden; Boston, 206–22.
Börm, H. 2013. 'Justinians Triumph und Belisars Erniedrigung. Überlegungen zum Verhältnis zwischen Kaiser und Militär im späten Römischen Reich', *Chiron* 43: 63–91.
   2015. 'Antimonarchic Discourse in Antiquity: A Very Short Introduction', in: H. Börm (ed.), *Antimonarchic Discourse in Antiquity*. Stuttgart, 9–24.
Boschung, D. 1993. *Die Bildnisse des Augustus, Das römische Herrscherbild*. Vol. 1 (2). Berlin.

Botteri, P. 2003. 'L'integrazione Mommseniana a *Res Gestae divi Augusti* 34.1 "*potitus rerum omnium*"', *ZPE* 144: 261–7.

Boube, E. 1996. *Le Trophée augustéen. Collection du musée archéologique départemental de Saint-Bertrand-de-Comminges 4*. Saint-Bertrand-de-Comminges.

Bowersock, G. 1986. 'From Emperor to Bishop: The Self-Conscious Transformation of Political Power in the Fourth Century AD', *Classical Philology* 81: 298–307.

Bowman, A. K. 1986. *Egypt after the Pharaohs, 332 BC–AD 642: From Alexander to the Arab Conquest*. London.

Bradley, M. 2009. 'The Importance of Colour on Ancient Marble Sculpture', *Art History* 32: 427–57.

  2009. *Colour and Meaning in Ancient Rome*. Cambridge.

Bradley, M., and E. Varner. 2014. 'Roman Noses', in: M. Bradley (ed.), *Smell and the Ancient Senses*. London; New York, 171–80.

Bremmer, J. 2020. 'Priestesses, Pogroms and Persecutions: Religious Violence in Antiquity in a Diachronic Perspective', in: J. Dijkstra and C. Raschle (eds.), *Religious Violence in the Ancient World: From Classical Athens to Late Antiquity*. Cambridge, 46–68.

Bridges, E. 2014. *Imagining Xerxes: Ancient Perspectives on a Persian King*. London.

Brisch, N. (ed.). 2012. *Religion and Power: Divine Kingship in the Ancient World and Beyond*. Chicago.

Brøns, C., A. Skovmøller and J. Gisler. 2017. 'Colour-Coding the Roman Toga: The Materiality of Textiles Represented in Ancient Sculpture', *Antike Kunst* 60: 55–79.

Brown, N. 2020. 'The Living and the Monumental on the Anaglypha Traiani', *American Journal of Archaeology* 124: 607–30.

Brown, P. 1971. 'The Rise and Function of the Holy Man in Late Antiquity', *JRS* 61: 80–101.

  2000². *Augustine of Hippo. A Biography*. London.

  2012. *Through the Eye of a Needle: Wealth, the Fall of Rome, and the Making of Christianity in the West, 350–550 AD*. Princeton.

Bru, H. 2011. *Le Pouvoir imperial dans les provinces syriennes. Représentations et celebrations d'Auguste à Constantin (31 av. J.-C.–337 ap. J.-C.)*. Leiden; Boston.

Brubaker, L. 1997. 'Memories of Helena: Patterns of Imperial Female Matronage in the Fourth and Fifth Centuries', in: K. James (ed.), *Women, Men and Eunuchs: Gender in Byzantium*. London, 52–75.

Brunt, P. A. 1977. 'Lex de Imperio Vespasiani', *JRS* 67: 95–111.

Bruun, C. 2003. 'Roman Emperors in Popular Jargon: Searching for Contemporary Nicknames (1)', in: L. de Blois et al. (eds.) *The Representation and Perception of Roman Imperial Power*. Amsterdam, 69–98.

  2010. 'Matidia die Jüngere–Gesellschaftlicher Einfluss und dynastische Rolle', in: A. Kolb (ed). *Augustae. Machtbewusste Frauen am römischen Kaiserhof? Herrschaftsstrukturen und Herrschaftspraxis II*. Berlin, 211–33.

2011. 'Der Kaiser, die republikanischen Institutionen und die kaiserliche Verwaltung', in: A. Winterling (ed.), *Zwischen Strukturgeschichte und Biographie. Probleme und Perspektiven einer römischen Kaisergeschichte (Augustus bis Commodus)*. Munich, 161–79.

2015. 'Roman Government and Administration', in: C. Bruun and J. C. Edmondson (eds.), *The Oxford Handbook of Roman Epigraphy*. Oxford, 274–98.

Bukowiecki, E., and U. Wulf-Rheidt. 2015. 'I bolli laterizi delle residenze imperiali sul Palatino a Roma', *MDAI(R)* 121: 311–482.

Buongiorno, P. 2017. *Claudio, il principe inatteso*. Palermo.

Burbank, J., and F. Cooper. 2010 *Empires in World History. Power and the Politics of Difference*. Princeton; Oxford.

Burgersdijk, D. W. P. 2020. 'Neoplatonic Philosophy in Tetrarchic and Constantinian Panegyric', in: A. J. Ross and A. Omissi (eds.), *Imperial Panegyric from Diocletian to Theodosius*. Liverpool, 167–89.

Burgersdijk, D. W. P., and A. J. Ross (eds.). 2018. *Imagining Emperors in the Later Roman Empire*. Leiden; Boston.

Burgess, R. W. 1993. *The Chronicle of Hydatius and the Consularia Constantinopolitana: Two Contemporary Accounts of the Final Years of the Roman Empire*. Oxford.

Burnett, A. 1998. 'Moneda foránea en el occidente y oriente romano', *X Congreso nacional de numismática. Actas*. Albacete, 65–9.

2002. 'Syrian Coinage and Romanisation from Pompey to Domitian', in: C. Augé and F. Duyrat (eds.), *Les Monnayages syriens. Quel apport pour l'histoire du Proche-Orient hellénistique et romain?* Beirut, 115–22.

2005. 'The Roman West and the Roman East', in: C. Howgego, V. Heuchert and A. Burnett (eds.), *Coinage and Identity in the Roman Provinces*. Oxford, 171–80.

2011. 'The Augustan Revolution Seen from the Mints of the Provinces', *JRS* 101: 1–30.

Burrell, B. 2004. *Neokoroi: Greek Cities and Roman Emperors*. Leiden; Boston.

Busch, A. W. 2015. *Die Frauen der Theodosianischen Dynastie. Macht und Repräsentation kaiserlicher Frauen im 5. Jahrhundert*. Stuttgart.

Busch, A. W., and M. J. Versluys. 2015. 'Indigenous Pasts and the Roman Present', in: D. Boschung, A. Busch and M. J. Versluys (eds.), *Reinventing the Invention of Tradition? Indigenous Pasts and the Roman Present*. Paderborn, 7–15.

Butcher, K. 1988. *Roman Provincial Coins: An Introduction to the Greek Imperials*. London.

Caballos Rufino, A. 2021. 'Un senadoconsulto del año 14 DC en un epígrafe bético', *ZPE* 219: 305–21.

Callu, J.-P. 2000. 'Pia Felix', *RN* 155: 189–207.

Calvão-Sibrinho, C. R. 2013. *Doctrine and Power. Theological Controversy and Christian Leadership in the Later Roman Empire*. Berkeley; Los Angeles; London.

Cameron, A. 2007. 'The Imperial Pontifex', *HSCP* 103: 341–84.
    2013. 'The Origin, Context and Function of Consular Diptychs', *JRS* 103: 174–207.
    2016. '*Pontifex Maximus*: From Augustus to Gratian – and Beyond' in: Maijastina Kahlos (ed.), *Emperors and the Divine – Rome and Its Influence*. Helsinki, 139–59.
    2016. 'The Status of Serena and the Stilicho Diptych', *JRA* 29: 509–16
Cameron, Av. 1979. 'Images of Authority: Elites and Icons in Late Sixth-Century Byzantium', *Past & Present* 84: 3–35.
Cameron, A., and J. Herrin. 1984. *Constantinople in the Early Eighth Century: The Parastaseis Syntomoi Chronikai. Introduction, Translation, and Commentary*. Leiden; Boston.
Campbell, J. B. 1984. *The Emperor and the Roman Army, 31 B.C.–A.D. 235*. Oxford.
    2002. *Warfare and Society in Imperial Rome, 31 B.C.–A.D. 280*. London; New York.
Cancik, H. 1990. 'Größe und Kolossalität als religiöse und aesthetische Kategorien. Versuch einer Begriffsbestimmung am Beispiel von Statius, Silvae I: Equus Maximus Domitiani Imperatoris', *Genres in Visual Representations; Visible Religion* 7: 51–65.
    2003. 'Der Kaiser-Eid. Zur Praxis der römischen Herrscherverehrung', in: H. Cancik and K. Hitzl (eds.), *Die Praxis der Herrscherverehrung in Rom und seinen Provinzen*. Tübingen, 29–45.
Candilio, D. 1999. 'Thermae Diocletiani', in: *LTUR* 5, 53–8.
Canepa, M. P. 2009. *The Two Eyes of the Earth. Art and Ritual between Rome and Sasanian Iran*. Berkeley; Los Angeles; London.
Canepa, M. P. 2018. *The Iranian Expanse. Transforming Royal Identity through Architecture, Landscape, and the Built Environment, 550 BCE – 642 CE*. Oakland.
Canter, H. V. 1928. 'Personal Appearance in the Biography of the Roman Emperors', *Studies in Philology*, 25: 385–99.
Carandini, A. (ed.). 2017. *The Atlas of Ancient Rome. Biography and Portraits of the City*. Princeton.
Carbó García, J.-R., and F. J. Rodríguez San Juan. 2012. 'STVDIA DACICA ET PARTHICA (II). El Tropaeum Traiani de Caracene. Expresiones del poder romano en los límites del Imperio', *Dialogues d' histoire ancienne* 38: 17–35.
Carey, J. W. 2009[2]. 'A Cultural Approach to Communication', in: J. W. Carey, *Communication as Culture: Essays on Media and Society*. New York; London, 11–28.
Caruso, G. 1999. 'Thermae Titi/Titianae', in: *LTUR* 5, 66–7.
Caruso, G., and R. Volp. 1999. 'Thermae Traiani', in: *LTUR* 5, 68–9.
Champlin, E. 2003. *Nero*. Cambridge [Mass.]; London.
Charles, M. B., and E. Anagnostou-Laoutides. 2012. 'Vespasian, Caenis and Suetonius', in: C. Deroux (ed.) *Studies in Latin Literature and Roman History 16*. Brussels, 530–47.

Charles-Gaffiot, J., and H. Lavagne. 1999. *Hadrien. Trésors d'une villa imperial.* Milan.

Chastagnol, A. 1966. *Le Sénat romain sous le règne d'Odoacre.* Bonn.

—— 1995. 'L'Expression épigraphique du culte imperial dans les provinces gauloises', *REA* 97: 593–614.

Cheung, A. 1998. 'The Political Significance of Roman Imperial Coin Types', *SchwMbll* 48: 53–61.

Chiai, G. F. 2019. 'Good Emperors, Bad Emperors: The Function of Physiognomic Representation in Suetonius' *De Vita Caesarum* and Common Sense Physiognomics', in: J. C. Johnson and A. Stavru (eds.), *Visualizing the Invisible with the Human Body. Physiognomy and Ekphrasis in the Ancient World.* Berlin; Boston, 203–26.

Chiavia, C. 2007. 'Presente e passato nei panegyrici latini: personaggi storici a confronto', in: P. Desideri, S. Roda and A. M. Biraschi (eds.), *Costruzione e uso del passato storico nella cultura antica.* Alessandria, 523–43.

Choda, K. C. 2019. 'Losing the Empress's Favour: On the Margins of John Chrysostom's *Homily* 48 on Matthew', in: K. C. Choda, M. S. de Leeuw and F. Schultz (eds.), *Gaining and Losing Imperial Favour in Late* Antiquity. Leiden; Boston, 125–50.

Choda, K. C., M. S. de Leeuw and F. Schultz (eds.). 2019. *Gaining and Losing Imperial Favour in Late* Antiquity. Leiden; Boston.

Christoforou, P. 2016. *Living in an Age of Gold: Being Subject of the Roman Emperor.* PhD Oxford.

Chrol, E. D., and S. Blake. 2022. 'Sexuality and the Court', in: B. Kelly and A. Hug (eds.), *The Roman Emperor and His Court, ca. 30 BC–ca. AD 300. Volume 1: Historical Essays.* Cambridge, 349–70.

Cima, M. 1998. 'Gli *Horti Liciniani*: una residenza imperiale della tarda antichità', in: E. La Rocca and M. Cima (eds.), *Horti Romani.* Rome, 425–52.

Ciolfi, L. M. 2018. 'Not Another Constantine. Rethinking Imperial Sainthood through the Case of John III Vatatzes', in: I. Vainovski-Mihai (ed.), *New Europe College. Yearbook 2015-2016.* Bucharest, 23–52.

Claassen, J.-M. 2016. 'Seizing the Zeitgeist: Ovid in Exile and Augustan Political Discourse', *Acta Classica* 59: 52–79.

Claes, L. M. G. F. E. 2014. 'A Note on the Coin Type Selection by the a Rationibus', *Latomus* 73: 163–73.

Claridge, A. 2004. 'Reconstructing the Temple of Apollo on the Palatine Hill in Rome', in: C. Haeuber, G. M. Winder and F.-X. Schütz (eds.), *Reconstruction and the Historic City: Rome and Abroad – an Interdisciplinary Approach.* Munich, 128–52.

Clarke, J. R. 2006. *Art in the Lives of Ordinary Romans. Visual Representation and Non-Elite Viewers in Italy, 100 BC–AD 315.* Berkeley; Los Angeles; London.

Cole, S. 2013. *Cicero and the Rise of Deification at Rome.* Cambridge.

Collins, A. W. 2009. 'The Palace Revolution: The Assassination of Domitian and the Accession of Nerva', *Phoenix* 63: 73–106.

Concannon, C. W. 2021. 'Honor Flits Away as Though It Were a Dream. Statues, Honor, and Favorinus' Corinthian Oration', *Classical Philology* 116: 61–75.

Conlin, D. A. 2021. 'Domitian and Religion', in: A. Raimondi Cominesi, N. de Haan, E. M. Moormann and C. Stocks (eds.), *God on Earth: Emperor Domitian. The Re-invention of Rome at the End of the 1st Century* AD. Leiden, 153–8.

Connolly, S. 2010. *Lives Behind the Laws. The World of the Codex Hermogenianus*. Bloomington; Indianapolis.

Constabile, F. 2012. 'RG 34.1: [POT]IENS RE[RU]M OM[N]IUM e l'Edictum de reddenda re publica', in: G. Purpura (ed.), *Revisione ed integrazione dei Fontes Iuris Romani Anteiustiniani (FIRA). Studi prepratori I. Leges*. Turin, 255–94.

Constant, M.-L. 2001. 'Commentaires et conjectures sur la carrière et la mort d'un affranchi de Trajan: Marcus Ulpius Phaedimus', *BCEA* 37: 65–74.

Cooley, A. 2002. 'The Survival of Oscan in Roman Pompeii', in: A. Cooley (ed.), *Becoming Roman, Writing Latin? Literacy and Epigraphy in the Roman West*. Portsmouth, RI, 77–86.

2009. *Res Gestae Divi Augusti. Text, Translation, and Commentary*. Cambridge.

Corbeill, A. 2004. *Nature Embodied: Gesture in Ancient Rome*. Princeton; Oxford.

Corbier, M. 2001. 'Maiestas Domus Augustae', in: G. A. Bertinelli and A. Donati (eds.), *Varia epigraphica. Atti del colloquio internazionale di epigrafia Bertinoro*. Faenza, 155–99.

Corcoran, S. 2020. 'Barsauma and the Emperors', in: J. Hahn and V. Menze (eds.), *The Wanderings of the Holy Man. The Life of Barsauma, Christian Asceticism, and Religious Conflict in Late Antique Palestine*. Oakland, 25–49.

Corke-Webster, J. 2019. 'Emperors, Bishops, Art and Jurisprudence: The Transformation of Law in Eusebius of Caesarea', *Early Medieval Europe* 27: 12–34.

Cornwell, H. 2015. 'The King Who Would Be Prefect: Authority and Identity in the Cottian Alps', *JRS* 105: 41–73.

2017. *Pax and the Politics of Peace. Republic to Principate*. Oxford.

Cortés-Copete, J. M. 2017. 'Governing by Dispatching Letters. The Hadrianic Chancellery', C. Rosillo-López (ed.), *Political Communication in the Roman World*. Boston; Leiden, 107–36.

Craig, R. T. 1999. 'Communication Theory as a Field', *Communication Theory* 9: 119–61.

Crawford, M. 1983. 'Roman Imperial Cointypes and the Formation of Public Opinion', in: C. Brooke, B. Stewart, J. Pollard and T. Volk (eds.), *Studies in Numismatic Method: Presented to Philip Grierson*. Cambridge, 54–5.

Croke, B. 2005. 'Dynasty and Ethnicity: Emperor Leo I and the Eclipse of Aspar', *Chiron* 35: 147–203.

2005. 'Leo I and the Palace Guard', *Byzantion* 75: 117–51.

Crone, P. 2003². *Pre-Industrial Societies: Anatomy of the Pre-Modern World*. Oxford.

Crook, J. 1955. *Consilium Principis. Imperial Councils and Councillors from Augustus to Diocletian*. Cambridge.

Curran, J. 2020. 'From Petrus to *Pontifex Maximus*', in: R. Dijkstra (ed.), *The Early Reception and Appropriation of the Apostle Peter (60–800): The Anchors of the Fisherman*. Leiden; Boston, 43–57.

d'Amato, R. 2020. *The Varangian Guard 988-1453*. Oxford.

Daalder, E. S. 2019. 'The *Decreta* and *Imperiales Sententiae* of Julius Paulus: Law and Justice in the Judicial Decisions of Septimius Severus', in: O. Hekster and K. Verboven (eds.), *The Impact of Justice on the Roman Empire*. Boston; Leiden, 49–67.

Dabrowa, E. 2004. 'Le Uexillum sur les monnaies coloniales (IIe–IIIe s. aprés J.-C.)', *Latomus* 63: 394–405.

Dagron, G. 1974. *Naissance d'une capitale: Constantinople et ses institutions de 330 à 451*. Paris.

1984. *Constantinople imaginaire. Études sur le recueil des Patria*. Paris.

2003. *Emperor and Priest. The Imperial Office in Byzantium*. Cambridge.

2011. *L'Hippodrome de Constantinople: Jeux, Peuple, et Politique*. Paris.

Dark, K., and F. Ozgumuş. 2002. 'New Evidence for the Byzantine Church of the Holy Apostles from Fatih Camii, Istanbul', *Oxford Journal of Archaeology* 21: 393–413.

Davenport, C. 2015. 'Inscribing Senatorial Status and Identity, AD 200–300', in: A. Kuhn (ed.), *Social Status and Prestige in the Graeco-Roman World*. Stuttgart, 269–89.

2017. 'The Sexual Habits of Caracalla: Rumour, Gossip, and Historiography', *Histos* 11: 75–100.

2019. *A History of the Roman Equestrian Order*. Cambridge.

2020. 'Dying for Justice: Narratives of Roman Judicial Authority in the High Empire', in: A. König, R. Langlands and J. Uden (eds.), *Literature and Culture of the Roman Empire 69–235*. Cambridge, 269–87.

2020. 'Roman Emperors, Conquest, and Violence', in: A. Russell and M. Hellström (eds.), *The Social Dynamics of Roman Imperial Imagery*. Cambridge, 100–27.

2021. 'Giving Voice to the late Roman Emperor: Eumenius' *For the Restoration of the Schools (Pan. Lat.* 9[4]) in context', *Journal of Late Antiquity* 14: 9–28.

Davenport, C., and B. Kelly. 2022 'Administration, Finances, and the Court', in: B. Kelly and A. Hug (eds.), *The Roman Emperor and His Court, ca. 30 BC–ca. AD 300. Volume 1: Historical Essays*. Cambridge, 115–45.

Davenport, C., and C. Mallan. 2020. 'Herodian and the Crisis of Emperorship, 235–238 AD', *Mnemosyne* 73: 419–40.

Davenport, C., and J. Manley. 2014. *Fronto. Selected Letters*. London.
de Angelis, F. 2010. 'Ius and Space: An Introduction', in: F. de Angelis (ed.), *Spaces of Justice in the Roman World*. Leiden; Boston, 1–27.
de Blois, L. 1976. *The Policy of Emperor Gallienus*. Leiden.
  2001. 'Roman Jurists and the Crisis of the Third Century AD in the Roman Empire', in: L. de Blois (ed.), *Administration, Prosopography and Appointment Policies in the Roman Empire*. Amsterdam, 136–53.
  2017. 'Two Third-Century Triumphal Decennalia (ad 202 and 262)', in: F. Goldbeck and J. Wienand (eds.), *Der römische Triumph in Prinzipat und Spätantike. The Roman Triumphal Procession in the Principate and Late Antiquity*. Berlin; Boston, 337–56.
  2019. *Image and Reality of Roman Imperial Power in the Third Century AD. The Impact of War*. Abingdon; New York.
de Jong, J. 2014. 'More than Words: Imperial Discourse in Greek Papyri', *Cahiers du Centre Gustave Glotz* 25: 243–61.
  2016. 'Emperor Meets Gods. Divine Discourse in Greek Papyri from Roman Egypt', in: M. Kahlos (ed.), *Emperors and the Divine – Rome and Its Influence*. Helsinki, 22–55.
  2019. 'Memoria, Morality, and Mnemonic Hegemony of Roman Emperors', *JAHA* 6: 17–26.
de Jonge, P. 1972. *Philological and Historical Commentary on Ammianus Marcellinus XVI*. Leiden; Boston.
de Libero, L. 1992. *Obstruktion: Politische Praktiken im Senat und in der Volksversammlung der ausgehenden römischen Republik (70–49 v. Chr.)*. Stuttgart.
Delaine, J. 2000. 'Building the Eternal City: The Building Industry of Imperial Rome', in: J. Coulston and H. Dodge (eds.), *Ancient Rome: The Archaeology of the Eternal City*. Oxford.
Delmaire, R. 2004. 'Le Vêtement dans les sources juridiques du Bas-Empire', *Antiquité Tardive* 12: 195–202.
del Monte, M., P. Ausse, and R. A. Lefèvre. 1998. 'Traces of Ancient Colours on Trajan's Column', *Archaeometry* 40: 403–12.
den Boeft, J., J. W. Drijvers, D. den Hengst and H. Teitler. 2015. *Philological and Historical Commentary on Ammianus Marcellinus XXX*. Leiden; Boston.
Dench, E. 2018. *Empire and Political Cultures in the Roman World*. Cambridge.
Destephen, S. 2018. 'Le Prince chrétien en pèlerinage', in: S. Destephen, B. Dumézil and H. Inglebert (eds.), *Le prince chrétien de Constantin aux royautés barbares (IVe–VIIIe siècle)*. Paris, 270–313.
  2019. 'Mobile Center to Constantinople. The Birth of Byzantine Imperial Government', *Dumbarton Oaks Papers* 73: 9–24.
Dickenson, C. P. 2017. *On the Agora. The Evolution of a Public Space in Hellenistic and Roman Greece (c. 326 BC–267 AD)*. Leiden; Boston.

Diefenbach, S. 1996. 'Frömmigkeit und Kaiserakzeptanz im frühen Byzanz', *Saeculum* 47: 35–66.

Dignas, B., and E. Winter. 2007. *Rome and Persia in Late Antiquity: Neighbours and Rivals*. Cambridge.

Dijkstra, R. 2020. 'Peter, Popes, Politics and More: The Apostle as Anchor', in: R. Dijkstra (ed.), *The Early Reception and Appropriation of the Apostle Peter (60-800): The Anchors of the Fisherman*. Leiden; Boston, 3–25.

Dijkstra, R., and D. van Espelo. 2017. 'Anchoring Pontifical Authority: A Reconsideration of the Papal Employment of the Title *Pontifex maximus*', *JRH* 41: 312–25.

Dillon, S. 2006. 'Women on the Columns of Trajan and Marcus Aurelius and the Visual Language of Roman Victory', in: S. Dillon and K. E. Welch (eds.), *Representations of War in Ancient Rome*. Cambridge, 244–71.

Dirven, L. 2011. 'The Imperial Cult in the Cities of the Decapolis, Caesarea Maritima and Palmyra. A Note on the Development of Imperial Cults in the Roman Near East', *ARAM* 23: 141–56.

Dmitriev, S. 2004. '"Good Emperors" and the Emperors of the Third Century', *Hermes* 132: 211–24.

Dombrovski, F. A. 1988. 'Internment of Members of the Royal Family in Ethiopia, Turkey, and India', *Rassegna di Studi Etiopici* 31: 45–57.

Dondin-Payre, M. 2008. 'Annexe: le buste de Caracalla/Constantin de Philippeville (Rusicade), Algérie', in: S. Benoist and A. Daguet-Gagey (eds.), *Un Discours en images de la condamnation de mémoire*. Metz, 40–2.

Drake, H. A. 2000. *Constantine and the Bishops. The Politics of Intolerance*. Baltimore; London.

— 2014. 'Topographies of Power in Late Antiquity and Beyond', in: C. Rapp and H. A. Drake (eds.), *The City in the Classical and Post-Classical World*. Cambridge, 217–39.

Dresken-Weiland, J. 2020. 'The Role of Peter in Early Christian Art: Images from the 4th to the 6th Century', in: R. Dijkstra (ed.), *The Early Reception and Appropriation of the Apostle Peter (60-800): The Anchors of the Fisherman*. Leiden; Boston, 115–34.

Drijvers, J. W. 1992. *Helena Augusta. The Mother of Constantine the Great and the Legend of Her Finding of the True Cross*. Leiden; Boston.

— 2015. 'The *Divisio Regni* of 364: The End of Unity?', in: R. Dijkstra, S. van Poppel and D. Slootjes (eds.), *East and West in the Roman Empire of the Fourth Century*. Leiden; Boston, 82–96.

Drijvers, J. W., and M. McEvoy. 2021. 'Introduction', in: J. W. Drijvers and M. McEvoy (eds.), *Envisioning the Roman Emperor in Speech and Word in Late Antiquity* (= *Journal of Late Antiquity* 14). Baltimore, 2–8.

Drinkwater, J. F. 1987. *The Gallic Empire. Separatism and Continuity in the North-Western Provinces of the Roman Empire AD 260–274*. Stuttgart.

1989. 'Patronage in Roman Gaul and the Problem of the Bacaudae', in: A. Wallace-Hadrill (ed.), *Patronage in Ancient Society*. London; New York, 189–203.

2007. 'The Principate – Lifebelt or Millstone around the Neck of the Empire', in: O. Hekster, G. de Kleijn and D. Slootjes (eds.), *Crises and the Roman Empire*. Leiden; Boston, 67–74.

2019. *Nero: Emperor and Court*. Cambridge.

Drogula, F. K. 2007. 'Imperium, Potestas, and the Pomerium in the Roman Republic', *Historia* 56 (2007), 419–52.

Duindam, J. 2016. *Dynasties: A Global History of Power, 1300–1800*. Cambridge.

2018. 'Rulers and Elites in Global History: Introductory Observations', in: M. van Berkel and J. Duindam (eds.), *Prince, Pen, and Sword: Eurasian Perspectives*. Leiden; Boston, 1–31.

Dvornik, F. 1966. *Early Christian and Byzantine Political Philosophy. Origins and Background, Dumbarton Oaks Studies*, IX, 2. Washington, DC.

Eck, W. 1996². 'The Emperor and His Advisers', in: A. Bowman, E. Champlin and A. Lintott (eds.), *CAH*. Vol. 10. Cambridge, 195–213.

1997. 'Der Kaiser, die Führungsschichten, und die Administration des Reiches', in: W. Eck (ed.), *Die Verwaltung des römischen Reiches in der hohen Kaiserzeit* Vol. 2. Basel, 3–145.

1999. 'The Bar Kokhba Revolt Roman Point of View', *JRS* 89: 76–89.

2002. 'Imperial Administration and Epigraphy: in Defence of Prosopography', in: A. K. Bowman, H. M. Cotton, M. Goodman and S. Price (eds.), *Representations of Empire. Rome and the Mediterranean World*. Oxford, 131–52.

2004. 'Lateinisch, Griechisch, Germanisch ...? Wie sprach Rom mit seinen Untertanen?', in: L. de Ligt, E. Hemelrijk, and H. W. Singor (eds.), *Roman Rule and Civic Life: Local and Regional Perspectives*. Amsterdam, 3–19.

2007. 'Krise oder Nichtkrise – das ist hier die Frage. Köln und sein Territorium in der 2. Hälfte des 3. Jahrhunderts', in: O. Hekster, G. de Kleijn, and D. Slootjes (eds.), *Crises and the Roman Empire*. Leiden; Boston, 23–43.

Eck, W., and G. Foster. 1999. 'Ein Triumphbogen für Hadrian im Tal von Beth Shean bei Tel Shalem', *JRA* 12: 294–313.

Eckert, A. 2016. *Lucius Cornelius Sulla in der antiken Erinnerung. Jener Mörder, der sich Felix nannte*. Berlin; Boston.

Edmondson, J. 2022. 'Domestic Servants in the Imperial Court', in: B. Kelly and A. Hug (eds.), *The Roman Emperor and His Court, ca. 30 BC–ca. AD 300. Volume 1: Historical Essays*. Cambridge, 168–203.

Edwards, C. 1994. 'Beware of Imitations: Theatre and the Subversion of Imperial Identity', in: J. Elsner and J. Masters (eds.), *Reflections of Nero: Culture, History, & Representation*. Chapel Hill; London, 83–97.

Eich, P. 2016. *Gregor der Große. Bischof von Rom zwischen Antike und Mittelalter.* Paderborn.

— 2020. 'Quod Prosperum Nobis Utile Rei Publicae sSt. Senatorische Macht und Ressourcenkontrolle im Italien Theoderichs', in: H.-U. Wiemer (ed.), *Theoderich der Große und das gotische Königreich in Italien.* Berlin; Boston, 193–222.

Elkins, N. 2015. *Monuments in Miniature: Architecture on Roman Coinage.* New York.

— 2017. *The Image of Political Power in the Reign of Nerva, AD 96–98.* Oxford.

Ellis, R. (ed.). 1888. *Poetae Christiani Minores. Corpus Scriptorum Ecclesiasticorum Latinorum XVI.* Vienna.

Ellithorpe, C. 2017. *Circulating Imperial Ideology: Coins as Propaganda in the Roman World.* PhD University of North Carolina.

Elsner, J. 1994. 'Constructing Decadence: The Reputation of Nero as an Imperial Builder', in: J. Elsner and J. Masters (eds.), *Reflections of Nero: Culture, History, & Representation.* Chapel Hill; London, 112–30.

— 1995. *Art and the Roman Viewer. The Transformation of Art from the Pagan World to Christianity.* Cambridge, 1995.

— 2006. 'Perspectives in Art', in: N. Lenski (ed.), *The Cambridge Companion to the Age of Constantine.* Cambridge, 185–220.

— 2007. 'Physiognomics: Art and Text', in: S. Swain (ed.), *Seeing the Face, Seeing the Soul. Polemon's Physiognomy from Classical Antiquity to Medieval Islam.* Oxford, 204–24.

— 2018². *The Art of the Roman Empire AD 100–450.* Oxford; New York.

— 2021. '100 Years of Dura Europos', *JRA* 34, 764–84.

Elsner, J., and J. Henderson. 2017. 'Envoi: A diptych', in: M. Squire and J. Wienand (eds.), *Morphogrammata. The Lettered Art of Optatian. Figuring Cultural Transformations in the Age of Constantine.* Paderborn, 495–515.

Elsner, J., and M. Squire. 2016. 'Sight and Memory. The Visual Art of Roman Mnemonics', in: M. Squire (ed.), *Sight and the Ancient Senses.* London; New York, 180–204.

Escribano Paño, M. V. 2013. 'Bishops, Judges and Emperors: CTh 16.2.31/ CTh. 16.5.46/ Sirm. 14(409)', in: A. Fear, J. Fernández Urbiña and M. Marcos (eds.), *The Role of the Bishop: Conflict and Compromise.* London; New York, 105–26.

Esposito, A. 2019. *Performing the Sacra: Priestly Roles and Their Organisation in Roman Britain.* Oxford.

Evans, E. C. 1969. *Physiognomics in the Ancient World.* Philadelphia.

Evans, R. J. 1994. *Gaius Marius: A Political Biography.* Pretoria.

Evers, A. (ed.). 2023, forthcoming. *Religion, Power, and Politics in Late Antiquity: Bishops, Emperors, and Senators in the Collectio Avellana, AD 367–553.* Leuven.

Evers, A. 2010. *Church, Cities and People. A Study of the Plebs in the Church and Cities of Roman Africa*. Leuven.
    Forthcoming. 'Someone else's robe? Emperor Gratian's refutation of the imperial title Pontifex Maximus'.
Fanning, S. 2003. 'Odovacer "rex", Regal Terminology, and the Question of the End of the Western Roman Empire', *Medieval Prosopography* 24: 46–55.
Fantham, E. 2006. *Julia Augusti: The Emperor's Daughter*. London; New York.
Färber, R. 2014. *Römische Gerichtsorte. Räumliche Dynamiken von Jurisdiktion im Imperium Romanum*. Munich.
Faust, S. 2012. *Schlachtenbilder der römischen Kaiserzeit. Erzählerische Darstellungskonzepte in der Reliefkunst von Traian bis Septimius Severus*. Rahden.
Fears, J. R. 1975. 'Nero as the Vicegerent of the Gods in Seneca's de Clementia', *Hermes* 103: 486–96.
    1977. '*Princeps a diis electus*'. *The Divine Election of the Emperor as a Political Concept at Rome*. Rome.
    1981. 'The Cult of Jupiter and Roman Imperial Ideology', *ANRW* II.17.1: 3–141.
    1981. 'The Theology of Victory at Rome: Approaches and Problems', *ANRW* II.17.2: 736–826.
Fejfer, J. 2008. *Roman Portraits in Context*. Berlin.
    2021. 'The Image of the Emperor: Seeing Domitian', in: A. Raimondi Cominesi, N. de Haan, E. M. Moormann and C. Stocks (eds.), *God on Earth: Emperor Domitian. The Re-invention of Rome at the End of the 1st Century* AD. Leiden, 73–82.
Fejfer, J., M. Moltesen and A. Rathje. 2015. 'Introduction', in: J. Fejfer, M. Moltesen and A. Rathje (eds.), *Tradition: Transmission of Culture in the Ancient World*. Copenhagen, 9–16.
Fernández, S. 2020. 'Who Convened the First Council of Nicaea: Constantine or Ossius?', *Journal of Theological Studies* 71: 196–211.
Ferris, I. 2000. *Enemies of Rome. Barbarians through Roman Eyes*. Thrupp; Stroud.
    2003. 'The Hanged Men Dance: Barbarians in Trajanic art', in: S. Scott and J. Webster (eds.), *Roman Imperialism and Provincial Art*. Cambridge; New York, 53–68.
Filippini, A. 2016. 'Fossili e contraddizioni dell' "era costantiniana": i dignitari del culto imperiale nella Tarda Antichita e il loro ruolo nelle "riforme religiose" di Massimino Daia e Giuliano', in: A. Kolb and M. Vitale (eds.), *Kaiserkult in den Provinzen des Römischen Reiches. Organisation, Kommunikation und Repräsentation*. Berlin; Boston, 409–75.
Fink, R. O., A. S. Hoey and W. F. Snyder. 1940. 'The Feriale Duranum', *Yale Classical Studies* 7: 1–222.
Fischer, E. A. 1978. 'Theodora and Antonina in the Historia Arcana: History and/or Fiction?', *Arethusa* 11: 252–79.

Fischer, R. A. 1999. *Fulvia und Octavia: Die beiden Ehefrauen des Marcus Antonius in den politischen Kämpfen der Umbruchszeit zwischen Republik und Principat*. Berlin.

Fishwick, D. 1987–2005. *The Imperial Cult in the Latin West. Studies in the Ruler Cult of the Western Provinces of the Roman Empire*. Vol. I.1–III.4. Leiden; Boston.

  1988. 'Dated Inscriptions and the Feriale Duranum', *Syria* 65: 349–61.

  2007. 'Numinibus Domus Divinae', *ZPE* 159: 293–6.

Fittschen, K. 1971. 'Zum angeblichen Bildnis des Lucius Verus im Thermen-Museum' *Jahrbuch des Deutschen Archäologischen Instituts* 86: 214–52.

  1972. 'Das Bildprogramm des Trajansbogen zu Benevent', *Archäologischer Anzeiger* 87: 742–88.

  1977. 'Siebenmal Maximinus Thrax', *Archäologischer Anzeiger*: 319–26.

  1979. 'Juba II und seine Residenz Jol/ Caesarea', in: H. G. Horn and C. B. Rügen (eds.), *Die Numider. Reiter und Könige nördlich der Sahara*. Cologne, 227–42.

  1993. 'Das Bildnis des Kaisers Gallien aus Milreu: zum Problem der Bildnistypologie', *Madrider Mitteilungen* 34 (1993), 210–27.

  1996. 'Courtly Portraits of Women in the Era of the Adoptive Emperors (98–180) and Their Reception in Roman Society', in: D. E. E. Kleiner and S. B. Matheson (eds.), *I Claudia. Women in Ancient Rome*. New Haven, 42–52.

  2015. 'Methodological Approaches to the Dating and Identification of Roman Portraits', in: B. Borg (Ed.) *A Companion to Roman Art*. Hoboken, 52–70.

Flaig, E. 2019². *Den Kaiser herausfordern. Die Usurpation im Römischen Reich*. Frankfurt a. Main.

Flower, H. I. 2006. *The Art of Forgetting. Disgrace and Oblivion in Roman Political Culture*. Chapel Hill.

  2020. 'Augustus, Tiberius, and the End of the Roman Triumph', *Classical Antiquity* 39: 1–28.

Flower, R. 2015. '*Tamquam figmentum hominis*: Ammianus, Constantius II and the Portrayal of Imperial Ritual', *CQ* 65: 822–35.

Foubert, L. 2010. 'Literary Constructions of Female Identities. The Parallel Lives of Julio-Claudian Women in Tacitus' "Annals"', in: C. Deroux (ed.), *Studies in Latin Literature and Roman History*. Vol. 15. Brussels, 344–65.

  2016. 'Crowded and Emptied Houses as Status Markers of Aristocratic Women in Rome: The Literary Commonplace of the *Domus Frequentata*', *EuGeStA* 6: 129–50.

  2016. 'The Lure of an Exotic Destination: The Politics of Women's Travels in the Early Roman Empire', *Hermes* 144: 462–87.

  2018. 'Men and Women Tourists' Desire to See the World: "Curiosity" and "a Longing to Learn" as (Self-) Fashioning Motifs (First–Fifth Centuries c.e.), *Journal of Tourism History* 10: 5–20.

Fournier, E. 2006. 'Exiled Bishops in the Christian Empire: Victims of Imperial Violence?', in: H. A. Drake (ed.), *Violence in Late Antiquity. Perceptions and Practices*. London; New York, 157–66.

Francis, J. 2020. 'Classical Conceptions of Visuality and Representation in John of Damascus' Defense of Holy Images', *Studies in Late Antiquity* 1: 284–308.

Francis, J., and G. W. M. Harrison. 2003. 'Gortyn: First City of Roman Crete', *AJA* 107: 487–92.

Frank, R. I. 1969. *Scholae Palatinae. The Palace Guards of the Later Roman Empire*. Rome.

Fraser, T. E. 2006. *Hadrian as Builder and Benefactor in the Western Provinces*. Oxford.

Frend, W. H. C. 1952. *The Donatist Church: A Movement of Protest in Roman North Africa*. Oxford.

Frier, B. W. et al. 2016. *The Codex of Justinian. Based on a Translation by Justice Fred H. Blume*. Cambridge.

Friesen, S. J. 1993. *Twice Neokoros: Ephesus, Asia and the Cult of the Flavian Imperial Family*. Leiden; New York; Cologne.

Fuchs, M. 1990. 'Römer in Götter- und Heldenpose', *JRA* 3: 279–85.

Fuhrmann, C. J. 2012. *Policing the Roman Empire: Soldiers, Administration and Public Order*. Oxford; New York.

Gabelmann, H. 1984. *Antike Audienz- und Tribunalszenen*. Darmstadt.

Galimberti, A. 2014. *Erodiano e Commodo. Traduzione e commento storico al primo libro della Storia dell'Impero dopo Marco*. Göttingen.

Galinsky, K. (ed.). 2014. 'Memoria Romana', *Memory in Rome and Rome in Memory*. Ann Arbor.

Galinsky, K., and K. Lapatin (eds.). 2015. *Cultural Memories in the Roman Empire*. Los Angeles.

Gambash, G. 2015. *Rome and Provincial Resistance*. New York; London.

Gangloff, A. 2019. *Pouvoir imperial et vertus philosophiques: l'évolution de la figure du bon prince sous le Haut-Empire*. Leiden; Boston.

García Ruiz, M. P., and A. J. Quiroga Puertas (eds.). 2021. *Emperors and Emperorship in Late Antiquity: Images and Narratives*. Leiden; Boston.

García Sánchez, M., and M. Albaladejo Vivero. 2014. '*Diademas, tiaras y coronas de la antigua Persia: formas de representación y de adopción en el mundo clásico*', in: C. Alfaro Giner, J. Ortiz García and M. Antón Peset (eds.), *Tiarae, Diadems and Headdresses in the Ancient Mediterranean Cultures: Symbolism and Technology*. Valencia, 79–94.

Garipzanov, L. 2018. *Graphic Signs of Authority in Late Antiquity and the Early Middle Ages, 300–900*. Oxford.

Garnsey, P. 1988. *Famine and Food Supply in the Graeco-Roman World*. Cambridge; New York.

Gasperini, L. 1968. 'Su alcuni epigrafi di Taranto romano', in: M. Raoss (ed.) *II miscellanea greca e romana II*. Rome, 379–97.

1971. 'Ancora sul frammento "cesariano" di Taranto', *Epigrafica* 33: 48–59.

Gehn, U. 2017. 'Late Antique *Togati* and Related Inscriptions – A Thumbnail Sketch', in: K. Bolle, C. Machado and C. Witschel (eds.), *The Epigraphic Cultures of Late Antiquity*. Stuttgart.

Gelzer, T. 1999. 'Das Gebet des Kaisers Theodosius in der Schlacht am Frigidus (Socr. h. e. 5, 25)', in: E. Campi, L. Grane and A. M. Ritter (eds.), *Oratio. Das Gebet in patristischer und reformatorischer Sicht*. Göttingen, 53–72.

George, M. 2022. 'Imperial Villas', in: B. Kelly and A. Hug (eds.), *The Roman Emperor and His Court, ca. 30 BC–ca. AD 300 Volume 1: Historical Essays*. Cambridge, 239–66.

Ghini, G. 1999. 'Thermae Agrippae', in: *LTUR* 5, 40–2.

1999. 'Thermae Neronianae/ Alexandrinae', in: *LTUR* 5, 60–3.

Gibson, B., and R. Rees (eds.). 2013. *Pliny the Younger in Late Antiquity*. Baltimore (= *Arethusa* 46 (2013), 141–7).

Gillet, A. 2001. 'Rome, Ravenna and the last Western Emperors', *PBSR* 69: 131–67.

Gilliard, F. D. 1984. 'Senatorial Bishops in the Fourth Century', *Harvard Theological Review* 77: 153–75.

Ginsburg, J. 2006. *Representing Agrippina: Constructions of Female Power in the Early Roman Empire*. Oxford; New York.

Giuliani, L. 1986. *Bildnis und Botschaft: hermeneutische Untersuchungen zur Bildniskunst der römischen Republik*. Frankfurt am Main.

Given, J. 2014. *The Fragmentary History of Priscus: Attila, the Huns and the Roman Empire, AD 430–476*. Merchantville.

Goette, H. R. 1989. *Studien zu römischen Togadarstellungen*. Mainz.

Gordon, R. L. 1990. 'The Veil of Power. Emperors, Sacrificers and Benefactors' in: M. Beard and J. North (eds.), *Pagan Priests. Religion and Power in the Ancient World*. London, 199–231.

Gozalbes García, H. 2016. 'La corona cívica en la moneda provincial de la Hispania romana', *Espacio Tiempo y Forma. Serie II, Historia Antigua* 28: 75–96.

Gradel, I. 2002. *Emperor Worship and Roman Religion*. Oxford.

Graham, E. J. 2009. 'Becoming Persons, Becoming Ancestors: Personhood, Memory and the Corpse in Roman Rituals of Social Remembrance', *Archaeological Dialogues* 16: 51–74.

Grierson, P. 1991. *Coins of Medieval Europe*. London.

Grierson P., and M. Mays. 1992. *Catalogue of Late Roman Coins in the Dumbarton Oaks Collection and in the Whittemore Collection. From Arcadius and Honorius to the Accession of Anastasius*. Cambridge [Mass.]; London.

Griffin, M. 2002. 'Sociocultural Perspectives on Visual Communication', *Journal of Visual Literacy* 22: 29–52.

Grig, L. 2012. 'Deconstructing the Symbolic City: Jerome as Guide to Late Antique Rome', *PBSR* 80: 125–43.

Grig, L., and G. Kelly. 2012. 'Introduction: From Rome to Constantinople', in: L. Grig and G. Kelly (eds.), *Two Romes. Rome and Constantinople in Late Antiquity*. Oxford; New York, 3–30.

Grigg, R. 1979. 'Portrait-Bearing Codicils in the Illustrations of the *Notitia Dignitata*', *JRS* 68: 107–24.

Gros, P. 2002. 'Hadrien architecte. Bilan des recherches', in: M. Mosser and H. Lavagne (eds.), *Hadrien empereur et architecte. La villa d'Hadrien: tradition et modernité d'un paysage culturel*. Geneva: 33–53.

Grüner, A. 2013. 'Die kaiserlichen Villen in severischer Zeit: Eine Bestandsaufnahme', in: N. Sojc, A. Winterling and U. Wulf-Rheidt (eds.), *Palast und Stadt im severischen Rom*. Stuttgart, 231–86.

Guest, P. 2019. *The Transition to Late Antiquity on the Lower Danube. Excavations and Survey at Dichin, a Late Roman to Early Byzantine Fort and a Roman Aqueduct*. Oxford.

Guidetti, F. 2021. 'Between Expressionism and Classicism: Stylistic Choices as Means of Legitimisation in Late Fourth-Century Imperial Portraits', in: M. P. García Ruiz and A. J. Quiroga Puertas (eds.), *Emperors and Emperorship in Late Antiquity. Images and Narratives*. Leiden; Boston, 139–76.

Gurval, R. A. 1995. *Actium and Augustus. The Politics and Emotions of Civil War*. Ann Arbor.

Guyot, P. 1980. *Eunuchen als Sklaven und Freigelassene in der griechisch-römischen Antike*. Stuttgart.

Haake, M. 2016. 'Trophäen, die nicht vom äußeren Feinde gewonnen wurden, Triumphe, die der Ruhm mit Blut befleckt davontrug …' Der Sieg im imperialen Bürgerkrieg im ‚langen dritten Jahrhundert' als ambivalentes Ereignis', in: H. Börm, M. Mattheis and J. Wienand (eds.) *Civil War in Ancient Greece and Rome*. Stuttgart, 237–301.

Habinek, T. 2008. *Ancient Rhetoric and Oratory*. Malden [Mass.]; Oxford.

Haegemans, K. 2010. *Imperial Authority and Dissent: The Roman Empire in AD 235–238*. Leuven.

Haensch, R. 2007. 'Apokrimata und Authentica. Dokumente römischer Herrschaft in der Sicht der Untertanen', in: R. Haensch and J. Heinrichs (eds.), *Herrschen und Verwalten. Der Alltag der Administration des Römischen Reiches in der Kaiserzeit*. Vienna, 213–33.

2007. 'Die Rolle der Bischöfe im 4. Jahrhundert: Neue Anforderungen und neue Antworten', *Chiron* 37: 153–81.

Hagedorn, D., and K. A. Worp. 1980. 'Von *kyrios* zu *despotès*. Eine Bemerkung zur Kaisertitulatur im 3/4. Jhdt.', *ZPE* 39: 165–77.

Hahn, J. 2013. 'Schenute von Atripe, die kaiserliche Religionspolitik und der Kampf gegen das Heidentum in Oberägypten', in: F. Feder and A. Lohwasser (eds.), *Ägypten und sein Umfeld in der Spätantike: vom Regierungsantritt Diokletians 284/285 bis zur arabischen Eroberung des Vorderen Orients um 635–646*. Wiesbaden, 81–108.

2015. 'The Challenge of Religious Violence Imperial Ideology and Policy in the Fourth Century', in: J. Wienand (ed.), *Contested Monarchy: Integrating the Roman Empire in the Fourth Century* AD. New York, 379–404.

Hahn, J., and V. Menze (eds.). 2020. *The Wanderings of the Holy Man. The Life of Barsauma, Christian Asceticism, and Religious Conflict in Late Antique Palestine*. Oakland.

Halfmann, H. 1979. *Die Senatoren aus dem östlichen Teil des Imperium Romanum bis zum Ende des 2. Jahrhunderts n. Chr.* Göttingen.

1986. *Itinera Principum: Geschichte und Typologie der Kaiserreisen im Römischen Reich*. Stuttgart.

2001. *Städtebau und Bauherren im römischen Kleinasien*. Tübingen.

2022. 'Imperial Journeys', in: B. Kelly and A. Hug (eds.), *The Roman Emperor and His Court, ca. 30 BC–ca. AD 300 Volume 1: Historical Essays*. Cambridge, 267–87.

Hallett, C. H. 2005. *The Roman Nude. Heroic Portrait Statuary 200 B.C.–A.D. 300*. Oxford.

Hammond, M. 1956. 'The Transmission of the Powers of the Roman Emperor from the Death of Nero in A.D. 68 to that of Alexander Severus in A.D. 235', *Memoirs of the American Academy in Rome* 24: 63–133.

Hannestad, N. 1986. *Roman Art and Imperial Policy*. Aarhus.

Harker, A. 2011. *Loyalty and Dissidence in Roman Egypt: The Case of the Acta Alexandrinorum*. Cambridge.

Harlow, M. 2004. 'Clothes Maketh Man: Power Dressing and Elite Male in the Late Roman World,' in: L. Brubaker and J. M. H. Smith (eds.), *Gender in the Early Medieval World*. Cambridge, 44–69.

2005. 'Dress in Historical Narrative: The Case of the Historia Augusta', in: L. Cleland, M. Harlow and L. J. Llewellyn-Jones (eds.), *The Clothed Body in Ancient World*. Oxford, 143–53.

2018. 'Satirically Sartorial. Colours and Togas in Roman Satire', in: M. García Sánchez and M. Gleba (eds.), *Vetus Textrinum: Textiles in the Ancient World. Studies in Honour of Carmen Alfraro Giner*. Barcelona, 185–95.

Harper, K. 2017. *The Fate of Rome: Climate, Disease and the End of an Empire*. Princeton.

Harries, J. 2013. 'Men without Women: Theodosius' Consistory and the Business of Government', in: C. Kelly (ed.), *Theodosius II. Rethinking the Roman Empire in Late Antiquity*. Cambridge, 67–89.

Hartmann U. 2008. 'Das palmyrenische Teilreich', in: K.-P. Johne (ed.), *Die Zeit der Soldatenkaiser: Krise und Transformation des Römischen Reiches im 3. Jahrhundert n. Chr. (235–284)*. Berlin, 343–78.

Hauken, T. 1998. *Petition and Response. An Epigraphic Study of Petitions to Roman Emperors 181–249*. Bergen.

Havener, W. 2014. 'A Ritual against the Rule? The Representation of Civil War Victory in the Late Republican Triumph', in: C. Lange and F. J. Vervaet (eds.), *The Roman Republican Triumph. Beyond the Spectacle*. Rome 2014, 165–80.

Havé-Nikolaus, F. 1998. *Untersuchungen zu den kaiserzeitlichen Togastatuen griechischer Provenienz. Kaiserliche und private Togati der Provinzen Achaia, Creta (et Cyrene) und Teilen der Provinz Macedonia*. Mainz.

Hayes, C. 2020. 'Roman Power through Rabbinic Eyes: Tragedy or Comedy', in: K. Berthelot (ed.), *Reconsidering Roman Power. Roman, Greek, Jewish and Christian Perceptions and Reactions*. Rome, 443–71.

Head, C. 1980. 'Physical Descriptions of the Emperors in Byzantine Historical Writing', *Byzantion*, 50: 226–40.

Heather, P. 2006. *The Fall of the Roman Empire. A New History of Rome and the Barbarians*. Oxford.

— 2018. *Rome Resurgent: War and Empire in the Age of Justinian*. Oxford; New York.

Heather, P., and D. Moncur. 2001. *Politics, Philosophy and Empire in the Fourth Century. Select Orations of Themistius*. Liverpool.

Heijmans, S. E. 2010. 'Temples and Priests of Sol in the City of Rome', *Mouseion* 10: 381–427.

Heijnen, S. 2020. 'Living Up to Expectations: Hadrian's Military Representation in Freestanding Sculpture', *BABESCH* 95: 195–212.

— 2021. 'Statues in Dialogue: Visual Similarities in "Grown" Roman Imperial Statue Groups from the Greek East', *Ancient Society* 51, 123–56.

— 2021. *Portraying Change. The Representation of Roman Emperors in Freestanding Sculpture (ca. 50 BC – ca. 400 AD)*. PhD Nijmegen.

Heijnen, S., and E. M. Moormann. 2020. 'A Portrait Head of Severus Alexander at Delft', *AA*: 163–70.

Heijnen, S., O. Hekster, and T. Hermsen, 2022. 'Roman Imperial Statue Portraits Dataset', *Research Data Journal for the Humanities and Social Sciences* 7, 1–14.

Heinzelmann, M. 1976. *Bischofsherrschaft in Gallien. Zur Kontinuität römischer Führungsschichten vom 4. bis zum 7. Jahrhundert. Soziale, prosopographische und bildungsgeschichtliche Aspekte*. Zürich; Munich.

Hekster, O. 2001. 'All in the Family. The Appointment of Emperors Designate in the Second Century A.D.', in: L. de Blois (ed.), *Administration, Prosopography and Appointment Policies in the Roman Empire*. Amsterdam, 35–49.

— 2002. *Commodus. An Emperor at the Crossroads*. Amsterdam.

— 2007. 'Fighting for Rome: The Emperor as a Military Leader', in: L. de Blois and E. Lo Cascio (eds.), *The Impact of the Roman Army (200 BC–AD 476): Economic, Social, Political, Religious and Cultural Aspects*. Leiden; Boston, 91–105.

— 2007. 'The Army and Imperial Propaganda', in: P. P. M. Erdkamp (ed.), *The Blackwell Companion to the Roman Army*. Oxford, 339–58.

2008. *Rome and Its Empire,* AD *193-284*. Edinburgh.
2009. 'Honouring Ancestors: The Dynamic of Deification', in: O. Hekster, S. Schmidt-Hofner and C. Witschel (eds.), *Ritual Dynamics and Religious Change in the Roman Empire*. Leiden; Boston, 95-110.
2010. 'Reversed Epiphanies: Roman Emperors Deserted by Gods', *Mnemosyne* 63: 601-15.
2011. 'Imagining Power. Reality Gaps in the Roman Empire', *BABESCH* 86: 111-24.
2015. 'Left Behind in Translation? The Image of Augustus in Asia Minor', in: M. Derks, R. Ensel, M. Eickhoff and F. Meens (eds.), *What's Left Behind, The Lieux de Memoires of Europe beyond Europe*. Nijmegen, 176-82.
2015. *Emperors and Ancestors. Roman Rulers and the Constraints of Tradition*. Oxford.
2017. 'Identifying Tradition. Augustus and the Constraints of Formulating Sole Rule', *Politica Antica* 7: 47-60.
2017. 'Religion and Tradition in the Roman Empire: Faces of Power and Anchoring Change', *Journal of Ancient Civilizations* 32: 13-34.
2019. 'Emperors and Councillors: Imperial Representation between Republic and Empire', in: H. Kaal and D. Slootjes (eds.), *New Perspectives on Power and Political Representation from Ancient History to the Present Day: Repertoires of Representation*. Leiden; Boston, 11-25.
2020. 'Hadrian and the Limits of Power', in: C. Gazdac (ed.), *Group and Individual Tragedies in Roman Europe. The Evidence of Hoards, Epigraphic and Literary Sources*. Cluj-Napoca, 277-87.
2020. 'Imperial Justice? The Absence of Images of Roman Emperors in a Legal Role', *Classical Quarterly* 69: 247-60.
2020. 'Ruling through Religion? Innovation and Tradition in Roman Imperial Representation', in: R. Dijkstra (ed.), *The Early Reception and Appropriation of the Apostle Peter (60-800): The Anchors of the Fisherman*. Leiden; Boston, 26-40.
2020. 'When Was an Imperial Image', in: A. Russell and M. Hellström (eds.), *The Social Dynamics of Roman Imperial Imagery*. Cambridge, 274-88.
2021. 'Epilogue: Continuity and Change at the Roman Imperial Court', in: B. Kelly and A. Hug (eds.), *The Roman Emperor and His Court, ca. 30* BC*-ca.* AD *300. Volume 1: Historical Essays*. Cambridge, 479-97.
2021. 'Les Contraintes posées par la tradition dans la création de l'image impériale', in: P. Ledoze (ed.), *Le Costume de Prince. Regards sur une figure politique de la Rome antique d'Auguste à Constantin*. Rome, 87-112.
Forthcoming. 'Provincial Emperors AD 98-235', in: D. Potter, N. Lenski and N. Rosenstein (eds.), *The Oxford History of the Roman World*. Oxford.
Hekster, O., S. Betjes, S. Heijnen, K. Iannantuono, D. Jussen, E. Manders, and D. Syrbe. 2019. 'Accommodating Political Change under the Tetrarchy (293-306)', *Klio* 101: 610-39.

2022. Forthcoming. 'The Fame of Trajan: A Late Antique Invention', Klio 104.
Hekster, O., and R. Fowler. 2005. 'Imagining Kings: From Persia to Rome', in: O. Hekster and R. Fowler (eds.), *Imaginary Kings: Royal Images in the Ancient Near East, Greece and Rome*. Stuttgart, 9–38.
Hekster, O., and J. W. Rich. 2006. 'Octavian and the Thunderbolt: The Temple of Apollo Palatinus and the Roman Tradition of Temple Building', CQ 56: 149–68.
Hellenkemper, H. 2013. 'Anatolische Riviera: Byzantinische Kaiserpaläste in Bithynien', in: E. Winter and K. Zimmermann (eds.), *Neue Funde und Forschungen in Bithynien*. Bonn, 61–81.
Hellström, M. 2020. 'Epigraphy and Ambition: Building Inscriptions in the Hinterland of Carthage', JRS 110: 57–90.
  2020. 'Local Aspirations and Statues of Emperors in Roman North Africa', in: A. Russell and M. Hellström (eds.), *The Social Dynamics of Roman Imperial Imagery*. Cambridge, 159–79.
Hellström, M., and A. Russell. 2020. 'Introduction: Imperial Imagery and the Role of Social Dynamics', in: A. Russell and M. Hellström (eds.), *The Social Dynamics of Roman Imperial Imagery*. Cambridge, 1–24.
Hemelrijk, E. 2005. 'Octavian and the Introduction of Public Statues for Women', Athenaeum 93: 309–17.
  2015. *Hidden Lives, Public Personae. Women and Civic Life in the Roman West*. Oxford; New York.
Herrmann-Otto, E. 1998. 'Der Kaiser und die Gesellschaft des spätrömischen Reiches im Spiegel des Zeremoniells', in: P. Kneissl and V. Losemann (eds.), *Imperium Romanum. Studien zu Geschichte und Rezeption. Festschrift für Karl Christ zum 75. Geburtstag*. Stuttgart, 346–69.
Herz, P. 2001. 'Das römische Heer und der Kaiserkult in Germanien', in: W. Spickermann, H. Cancik and J. Rüpke (eds.), *Religion in den germanischen Provinzen Roms*. Tübingen, 91–116.
Heuchert, V. 2005. 'The Chronological Development of Roman Provincial Coin Iconography', in: C. Howgego, V. Heuchert and A. Burnett (eds.), *Coinage and Identity in the Roman Provinces*. Oxford, 29–56.
Heucke, C. 1994. *Circus und Hippodrom als politischer Raum*. Hildesheim.
Hexter, J. H. 1979. *On Historians: Reappraisals of Some of the Makers of Modern History*. Cambridge [Mass.].
Hind, J. G. F. 2003. 'Caligula and the Spoils of Ocean: A Rush for Riches in the Far North-West?', Britannia 34: 272–4.
Hintzen-Bohlen, B. 1990. 'Die Familiengruppe – ein Mittel zur Selbstdarstellung Hellenistischer Herrscher', JDAI 105: 129–54.
Hobsbawm, E. 1983. 'Introduction: Inventing Traditions', in: E. Hobsbawm and T. Ranger (eds.), *The Invention of Tradition*. Cambridge, 1–14.
Hodgson, L. 2016. *Res Publica and the Roman Republic: 'Without Body or Form'*. Oxford.

Højte, J. M. 2005. *Roman Imperial Statue Bases: from Augustus to Commodus*. Aarhus.
Hölscher, T. 1967. *Victoria Romana. Archäologische Untersuchungen zur Geschichte und Wesensart der römischen Siegesgöttin von den Anfängen bis zum Ende des 3. Jhs. n. Chr.* Mainz.
— 2004. 'Images of War in Greece and Rome: Between Military Practice, Public Memory and Cultural Symbolism', *JRS* 94: 1–17.
— 2006. 'Greek Styles and Greek Art in Augustan Rome: Issues of the Present Versus Records of the Past', in: J. I. Porter (ed.), *Classical Pasts: The Classical Traditions of Greece and Rome*. Princeton, 237–59.
— 2008. 'The Concept of Roles and the Malaise of "identity": Ancient Rome and the Modern World', in: S. Bell and I. L. Hansen (eds.), *Role Models in the Roman World. Identity and Assimilation.* Ann Arbor, 41–56.
— 2014. 'Historical Representations of the Roman Republic: The Repertory of Coinage in Comparison with Other Art Media', in: N. T. Elkins and S. Krmnicek (eds.), *'Art in the Round'. New Approaches to Ancient Coin Iconography.* Rahden, 22–37.
— 2018. *Visual Power in Ancient Greece and Rome: Between Art and Social Reality.* Oakland.
Holum, K. G. 1982. *Theodosian Empresses: Women and Imperial Dominion in Late Antiquity.* Berkeley; Los Angeles.
Hopkins, K. 1978. *Conquerors and Slaves. Sociological Studies in Roman History. Volume 1.* Cambridge.
Horster, M. 1998. 'Ehrungen Spätantiker Statthalter', *Antiquité tardive* 6 : 37–59.
— 2007. 'The Emperor's Family on Coins (Third Century). Ideology of Stability in Times of Unrest (291–310)', in: O. Hekster, G. de Kleijn and D. Slootjes (eds.), *Crises and the Roman Empire.* Leiden; Boston, 291–307.
Hotalen, C. 2020. *Embodying the Empire: Imperial Women and the Evolution of Succession Ideologies in the Third Century.* PhD University of South Florida.
Howgego, C. 1995. *Ancient History from Coins.* London; New York.
Huchthausen, L. 1974. 'Herkunft und ökonomische Stellung weiblicher Adressaten von Reskripten des *Codex Iustinianus* (2. und 3. Jh. u. Z.)', *Klio* 54: 199–228.
Hug, A. 2021. 'The Imperial Family', in: B. Kelly and A. Hug (eds.), *The Roman Emperor and His Court, ca. 30 BC–ca. AD 300. Volume 1: Historical Essays.* Cambridge, 60–84.
Hug, A., N. Bernstein and B. Kelly. 2022. 'Court Relationships', in: B. Kelly and A. Hug (eds.), *The Roman Emperor and His Court, ca. 30 BC–ca. AD 300. Volume 2: A Sourcebook.* Cambridge, 79–131.
Humphrey, J. H. 1986. *Roman Circuses. Arenas for Chariot Racing.* London.
Humphreys, M. 2013. 'The "War of Images" Revisited. Justinian II's Coinage Reform and the Caliphate', *The Numismatic Chronicle* 173: 229–44.
— 2003. 'Roman Senators and Absent Emperors in Late Antiquity', *Acta ad archaeologiam et atrium historiam pertinentia* 17: 27–46.

2015. 'Emperors, Usurpers and the City of Rome. Performing Power and Contesting Monarchy from Diocletian to Theodosius', in: J. Wienand (ed.), *Contested Monarchy: Integrating the Roman Empire in the Fourth Century* AD. New York, 151–68.

2020. 'Romulus and Peter: Remembering and Reconfiguring Rome's Foundation in Late Antiquity', in: R. Dijkstra (ed.), *The Early Reception and Appropriation of the Apostle Peter (60–800): The Anchors of the Fisherman*. Leiden; Boston, 172–87.

2021. 'Valentinian III and the City of Rome (425–55): Patronage, Politics, Power', in: L. Grig and G. Kelly (eds.), *Two Romes. Rome and Constantinople in Late Antiquity*. Oxford; New York, 161–82.

Hunnell Chen, A. 2014. *From the Seed of the Gods: Art, Ideology and Cultural Exchange with the Persian Court under the Roman Tetrarchs, 284–324 CE.* PhD Columbia.

2016. 'Rival Powers, Rival Images: Diocletian's Palace at Split in Light of Sasanian Palace Design', in: M. Peachin and D. Slootjes (eds.), *Rome and the World Beyond Its Frontiers*. Leiden; Boston, 213–42.

2018. 'Omitted Empresses: The (Non-)Role of Imperial Women in Tetrarchic Propaganda', *Journal of Late Antiquity* 11: 42–82.

Hurlet, F. 2000. 'Les Sénateurs dans l'entourage d'Auguste et de Tibère: un complément à plusieurs syntheses récentes sur la cour impériale', *RPh* 74: 123–50.

2002. 'Le *Consensus* et la *concordia* en Occident (Ier-IIIe siècles ap. J.-C.). Réflexions sur la diffusion de l'idéologie impériale', in: H. Inglebert (ed.), *Idéologies et valeurs civiques dans le monde romain. Hommage à Claude Lepelley*. Paris, 163–78.

Huttner, U. 1995. 'Marcus Antonius und Herakles', in: C. Schubert and K. Brodersen (eds.), *Rom und der Griechische Osten. Festschrift für Hatto H. Schmitt zum 65. Geburtstag*. Stuttgart, 103–12.

Iannantuono, K. 2020. 'La monumentalizzazione del potere nelle Alpi Cozie all'indomani della conquista romana. Una "descrizione densa" dell'arco di Susa', *SEGUSIUM* 58: 11–48.

2021. 'A Christian Emperor between Pagan Gods: Accommodating Imperial Representation and Religious Change in Late Antique Ephesus'. *Journal of Applied History* 3: 3–46.

2022. Forthcoming. 'Artemis, Trajan and the Demos in Parade. A Reinterpretation of the Reliefs at the So-called "Temple of Hadrian" at Ephesus'. *Jahreshefte des Österreichischen Archäologischen Institutes in Wien* 90.

Icks, M. 2011. *The Crimes of Elagabalus: The Life and Legacy of Rome's Decadent Boy Emperor*. London.

2017. 'Turning Victory into Defeat. Negative Assessments of Imperial Triumphs in Greco-Roman Literature' in: F. Goldbeck and J. Wienand (eds.), *Der römische Triumph in Prinzipat und Spätantike. The Roman Triumphal Procession in the Principate and Late Antiquity*. Berlin; Boston, 317–34.

2019. 'Agrippina, Theodora and Fredegund as Evil Empresses in the Historiographic Tradition', in: S. A. Samoilenko, M. Icks, J. Keohane and E. Shiraev (eds.), *Routledge Handbook of Character Assassination and Reputation Management*. New York, 183–95.

2020. 'Keeping Up Appearances. Evaluations of Imperial (in)Visibility in Late Antiquity', in: E. Manders and D. Slootjes (eds.), *Leadership, Ideology and Crowds in the Roman Empire of the Fourth Century AD*. Stuttgart, 163–79.

Icks, M., D. Jussen and E. Manders. 2020. 'Generaals in de groei: De militaire representatie van de kindkeizers Gratianus en Honorius op munten en in lofdichten', *Tijdschrift voor Geschiedenis* 132: 541–58.

IIIS. 2020. *The Military Balance 2020*. London; New York.

Imrie, A. 2018. *The Antonine Constitution. An Edict for the Caracallan Empire*. Leiden; Boston.

Jaeschke, V. 2020. 'Architecture and Power. Defining Tetrarchic Imperial Residences', in: E. Manders and D. Slootjes (eds.), *Leadership, Ideology and Crowds in the Roman Empire of the Fourth Century*. Stuttgart, 19–33.

Johnson, M. 2009. *The Roman Imperial Mausoleum in Late Antiquity*. Cambridge.

Jones, A. H. M. 1964. *The Later Roman Empire, 284–602*. Oxford.

Jones, C. P. 2013. 'Elio Aristide e i primi Anni di Antonino Pio', in: P. Desideri and F. Fontanella (eds.), *Elio Aristide e la Legittimazione greca dell'Impero di Roma*. Bologna, 39–67.

Jones, L. 2018. 'Taking It on the Road. The Palace on the Move', in: S. Tougher (ed.), *The Emperor in the Byzantine World*. London; New York, 322–40.

Joska, S. 2019. '"Show Them that You Are Marcus's Daughter" The Public Role of Imperial Daughters in Second-and Third-Century CE Rome', in: J. Rantala (ed.), *Gender, Memory, and Identity in the Roman World*. Amsterdam, 105–30.

Jussen, D. 2019. 'Enduring the Dust of Mars: The Expectation of Military Leadership in Panegyric to the Child-Emperor Gratian', *Arethusa* 52: 253–73.

2022, Forthcoming. 'Leading by Example: Historical Exemplarity in Fourth-Century Imperial Panegyric', *Talanta* 54.

2022. 'The Marks of a Ruler: The Face of the Roman Emperor in Fourth-Century Imperial Panegyric', *Hermes* 149, 304–25.

Kaizer, T. 2001. 'Introduction', in: D. Praet, T. Kaizer and A. Lannoy (eds.), *Franz Cumont: Doura-Europos. Bibliotheca Cumontiana. Series Minora VII*. Turnhout, xi–xcviii.

2002. *The Religious Life of Palmyra*. Stuttgart.

- 2006. 'A Note on the Fresco of Iulius Terentius from Dura-Europos', in: R. Rollinger and B. Truschnegg (eds.), *Altertum und Mittelmeerraum: Die antike Welt diesseits und jenseits der Levante*. Stuttgart, 151–9.
- Kalas, G. 2015. *The Restoration of the Roman Forum in Late Antiquity. Transforming Public Space*. Austin.
- Kaldellis, A. 2015. *The Byzantine Republic. People and Power in New Rome*. Cambridge [Mass.]; London.
- 2016. 'The Forum of Constantine in Constantinople: What Do We Know about Its Original Architecture and Decorations', *GRBS* 56: 714–39.
- Kampen, N. 2009. *Family Fictions in Roman Art*. Cambridge; New York.
- Karanastasi, P. 2012/2013. 'Hadrian im Panzer. Kaiserstatuen zwischen Realpolitik und Philhellenismus', *JDAI* 127/128: 323–91.
- Kelly, B. 2011. *Petitions, Litigation, and Social Control*. Oxford, 150–9, 167–8.
- 2020. 'Court Politics and Imperial Imagery in the Roman Principate', in: A. Russell and M. Hellström (eds.), *The Social Dynamics of Roman Imperial Imagery*. Cambridge, 128–58.
- 2021. 'Conceptualising the Roman Court', in: B. Kelly and A. Hug (eds.), *The Roman Emperor and His Court, ca. 30 BC–ca. AD 300. Volume 2: A Sourcebook*. Cambridge, 10–31.
- 2022. 'Introduction', in: B. Kelly and A. Hug (eds.), *The Roman Emperor and His Court, ca. 30 BC–ca. AD 300. Volume 1: Historical Essays*. Cambridge, 1–15.
- Kelly, C. 2004. *Ruling the Later Roman Empire*. Cambridge [Mass.]; London.
- 2013. 'Stooping to Conquer. The Power of Imperial Humility', in: C. Kelly (ed.), *Theodosius II. Rethinking the Roman Empire in Late Antiquity*. Cambridge, 221–43.
- Kelly, G. 2013. 'Pliny and Symmachus', *Arethusa* 46: 261–87.
- Kemmers, F. 2006. *Coins for a Legion: An Analysis of the Coin Finds from the Augustan Legionary Fortress and Flavian canabae legionis at Nijmegen*. Mainz.
- 2011. 'Out of the Shadow: Geta and Caracalla Reconsidered', in: S. Faust and F. Leitmeir (eds.), *Repräsentationsformen in severischer Zeit*. Berlin, 270–90.
- Kent, J. P. C. 1992. 'Coin Inscriptions and Language', in: D. F. Clark, M. M. Roxan and J. J. Wilk (eds.), *The Later Roman Empire Today*. London; New York, 9–18.
- Khrustalev, V. K. 2017. 'The Image of the Egyptian King Ptolemy XII Auletes in Cicero's Speeches', *Journal of Ancient History* (Вестник древней истории) 77: 91–105.
- Kienast, D., W. Eck and M. Heil. 2017^6. *Römische Kaisertabelle. Grundzüge einer römischen Kaiserchronologie*. Darmstadt.
- Kierdorf, W. 1986. '"Funus" und "consecration". Zu Terminologie und Ablauf der römischen Kaiserapotheose', *Chiron* 16: 43–69.
- Kiilerich, B. 2001. 'The Image of Anicia Juliana in the Vienna Dioscurides. Flattery or Appropriation of Imperial Imagery', *Symbolae Osloenses* 76: 169–90.

King, C. 1999. 'Roman Portraiture: Images of Power', in: G. Paul and M. Ierardi (eds.), *Roman Coins and Public Life under the Empire. E. Togo Salmon Papers II*. Ann Arbor, 123–36.

King, C. W. 2020. *The Ancient Roman Afterlife: Di Manes, Belief, and the Cult of the Dead*. Austin.

Kiss, Z. 1989. 'Représentations de barbares dans l'iconographie romaine impériale en Egypte', *Klio* 71: 127–37.

Kleiner, D. E. E. 1992. *Roman Sculpture*. New Haven; London.

Klose, D. O. A. 1987. *Die Münzprägung von Smyrna in der römischen Kaiserzeit*. Berlin.

Kneissl, P. 1969. *Die Siegestitulatur der römischen Kaiser. Untersuchungen zu den Siegerbeinamen des ersten und zweiten Jahrhunderts*. Göttingen.

Kolb, A. (ed.). 2018. *Literacy in Ancient Everyday Life*. Berlin; Boston.

Kolb, A. 2010. 'Augustae – Zielsetzung, Definition, prosopographischer Überblick', in: A. Kolb (ed). Augustae. *Machtbewusste Frauen am römischen Kaiserhof? Herrschaftsstrukturen und Herrschaftspraxis II*. Berlin, 11–35.

Kolb, F. 1987. *Diokletian und die erste Tetrarchie. Improvisation oder Experiment in der Organisation monarchischer Herrschaft*. Berlin.

2001. *Herrscherideologie in der Spätantike*. Berlin.

Koldt, C. 2001. *Bescheidene Größe. Die Herrschergestalt, der Kaiserpalast und die Stadt Rom: Literarische Reflexionen monarchischer Selbstdarstellung*. Göttingen.

Koortbojian, M. 2006. 'The Bringer of Victory: Imagery and Institutions at the Advent of Empire', in: S. Dillon and K. E. Welch (eds.), *Representations of War in Ancient Rome*. Cambridge, 184–217.

2013. *The Divinization of Caesar and Augustus: Precedents, Consequences, Implications*. Cambridge.

2020. *Crossing the Pomerium. The Boundaries of Political, Religious and Military Institutions from Caesar to Constantine*. Princeton; Oxford.

Körner, C. 2017. 'Monarchie auf Zypern im 5. und 4. Jahrhundert v. Chr.: Herrschaft von König und Polis?', in: S. Rebenich, *Monarchische Herrschaft im Altertum*. Berlin; Boston, 217–44.

Kousser, R. 2006. 'Conquest and Desire: Roman *Victoria* in Public and Provincial Sculpture', in: S. Dillon and K. E. Welch (eds.), *Representations of War in Ancient Rome*. Cambridge, 218–43.

Kreikenbom, D. 1992. *Griechische und römische Kolossalporträts bis zum späten ersten Jahrhundert nach Christus*. Berlin.

Kroll, J., and B. Bachrach. 1993. 'Justin's Madness: Weak–Mindedness or Organic Psychosis?', *Journal of the History of Medicine and Allied Sciences* 48: 40–67.

Kropp, A. J. M. 2009. 'King – Caesar – God: Roman Imperial Cult among Near Eastern "Client" Kings in the Julio-Claudian Period', in: M. Blömer, M. Facella and E. Winter (eds.), *Lokale Identität im römischen Nahen Osten: Kontexte und Perspektiven*. Stuttgart, 99–150.

2013. *Images and Monuments of Near Eastern Dynasts, 100 BC–AD 100*. Oxford.

2013. 'Kings without Diadems – How the Laurel Wreath Became the Insignia of Nabataean Kings', *Archäologischer Anzeiger*: 21–41.

Kröss, K. 2017. *Die politische Rolle der stadtrömischen Plebs in der Kaiserzeit*. Leiden; Boston.

Kruse, M. 2020. *The Politics of Roman Memory. From the Fall of the Western Empire to the Age of Justinian*. Philadelphia.

Kuhn-Chen, B. 2002. *Geschichtskonzeptionen griechischer Historiker im 2. und 3. Jahrhundert n. Chr.* Frankfurt am Main.

Kuhoff, W. 1979. *Herrschertum und Reichskrise. Die Regierungszeit der römischen Kaiser Valerianus und Gallienus (253–268 n. Chr.)*. Bochum.

Kulikowski, M. 2019. *The Tragedy of Empire. From Constantine to the Destruction of Roman Italy*. Cambridge [Mass.]

2020. 'How to End a Dynasty: Rehabilitating Nero', *London Review of Books* 42.

Kunst, C. 2008. *Livia. Macht und Intrigen am Hof des Augustus*. Stuttgart.

Kurt, A. 2020. *Minting, State, and Economy in the Visigothic Kingdom: From Settlement in Aquitaine through the First Decade of the Muslim Conquest of Spain*. Amsterdam.

Kuttner, A. L. 1995. *Dynasty and Empire in the Age of Augustus. The Case of the Boscoreale Cups*. Berkeley; Los Angeles; Oxford.

L'Huillier, M.-C. 1992. *L'Empire des mots. Orateurs gaulois et empereurs romains, 3e et 4e siècles*. Paris.

La Rocca, E. 2017. 'Nero's Image: The Four Portrait Types' in: S. Bartsch, K. Freudenburg and C. Littlewood (eds.), *The Cambridge Companion to the Age of Nero*. Cambridge, 354–8.

LaFollette, L. 1999. 'Thermae Decianae', in: *LTUR* 5, 51–3.

Lahusen, G. 1999. 'Zu römischen Statuen und Bildnissen aus Gold und Silber', *ZPE* 218: 251–66.

Lambert, D. 2012. 'Salvian and the Bacaudae', in: S. Diefenbach and G. M. Müller (eds.), *Gallien in Spätantike und Frühmittelalter: Kulturgeschichte einer Region*. Berlin; New York, 255–78.

Langford, J., and C. Hotalen. Forthcoming. 'Mater Castrorum: A History of Imperial Women and Succession Ideology', in: L. L. Brice and E. M. Greene (eds.), *Women and the Roman Army*. Cambridge.

Laniado, A. 1991. 'Some Problems in the Sources for the Reign of the Emperor Zeno', *Byzantine and Modern Greek Studies* 15: 147–74.

Laporte, K., and O. Hekster. 2022. 'Herodian, Memory and Judgement: Emperors and Their Death', in: A. Galimberti (ed.), *Herodian's World: Empire and Emperors in the Third Century*. Leiden; Boston, 88-109.

Lavan, M. 2020. 'Devastation: The Destruction of Populations and Human Landscapes and the Roman Imperial Project', in: K. Berthelot (ed.), *Reconsidering Roman Power. Roman, Greek, Jewish and Christian Perceptions and Reactions*. Rome, 179–205.

Leader-Newby, R. E. 2003. *Silver and Society in Late Antiquity: Functions and Meanings of Silver Plate in the Fourth to Seventh Centuries.* Aldershot.

Le Bohec, Y. 2021. 'L'Empereur et l' armée sous le Principat', in: P. Ledoze (ed.), *Le Costume de Prince. Regards sur une figure politique de la Rome antique d'Auguste à Constantin.* Rome, 437–64.

Lee, A. D. 2013. *From Rome to Byzantium* AD *363 to 565: The Transformation of Ancient Rome.* Edinburgh.

2013. 'Theodosius and his Generals', in: C. Kelly (ed.), *Theodosius II. Rethinking the Roman Empire in Late Antiquity.* Cambridge, 90–108.

Leeb, R. 1992. *Konstantin und Christus. Die Verchristlichung der imperialen Repräsentation unter Konstantin dem Grossen als Spiegel seiner Kirchenpolitik und seines Selbstverständnisses als christlicher Kaiser.* Berlin.

Lehnen, J. 1997. *Adventus Principis. Untersuchungen zu Sinngehalt und Zeremoniell der Kaiserankunft in den Städten des Imperium Romanum.* Frankfurt am Main.

Lendon, J. E. 1997. *Empire of Honour. The Art of Government in the Roman World.* Oxford.

Lenski, N. 2015. 'Constantine and the Tyche of Constantinople', in: J. Wienand (ed.), *Contested Monarchy: Integrating the Roman Empire in the Fourth Century* AD. New York, 330–9.

Leone, S. 2020. *Polis, Platz und Porträt: die Bildnisstatuen auf der Agora von Athen im Späthellenismus und in der Kaiserzeit (86 v. Chr.–267 n. Chr.).* Berlin; Boston.

Leppeley, C. 1979. *Les Cités de l'Afrique romaine au Bas-Empire.* Vol. 1, *La permanence d'une civilisation municipal.* Paris.

Leppin, H. 1996. *Von Constantin dem Großen zu Theodosius II. Das christliche Kaisertum bei den Kirchenhistorikern Socrates, Sozomenus und Theodoret.* Göttingen.

Leuenberger-Wenger, S. 2019. *Das Konzil von Chalcedon und die Kirche. Konflikte und Normierungsprozesse im 5. und 6. Jahrhundert.* Leiden; Boston.

Levene, D. S. 2012. 'Defining the Divine in Rome', *TAPA* 142: 41–81.

Levick, B. 2009. 'The *Lex de Imperio Vespasiani*: The Parts and the Whole', in: L. C. Colognesi and E. Tassi Scandone (eds.), *La Lex de Imperio Vespasiani e la Roma dei Flavi.* Rome, 11–22.

2010. *Augustus: Image and Substance.* Harlow.

2017². *Vespasian.* London; New York.

Lewis, N. 1984. 'The Romanity of Roman Egypt: A Growing Consensus', in: *Atti del XVII Congresso Internazionale di Papirologia.* Naples, 1077–84.

Liebeschuetz, J. H. W. G. 2001. *Decline and Fall of the Roman City.* Oxford.

Liebs, D. 2023, forthcoming. 'From the Archives of the City Prefecture in Rome: Collectio Avellana 1–40 (AD 367–420)', in: A. Evers (ed.), *Religion, Power, and Politics in Late Antiquity: Bishops, Emperors, and Senators in the Collectio Avellana,* AD *367–553.* Leuven.

Lindberg, N. 2019. 'The Emperor and His Animals: The Acquisition of Exotic Beasts for Imperial Venationes', *Greece and Rome* 66: 251–63.

Lintott, A. 1999. *The Constitution of the Roman Republic*. Oxford.

Lipka, M. 2009. *Roman Gods. A Conceptual Approach*. Leiden; Boston.

Liverani, P. 1998. 'Introduzione topografica', in: P. Liverani (ed.), *Laterano 1. Scavi sotto la basilica di S. Giovanni in Laterano. I materiali*. Rome, 7–16.

2007. 'Dal trionfo pagano all'adventus cristiano: percorsi della Roma imperiale', *Anales de arqueología cordobesa* 18: 385–400.

2007. 'Victors and Pilgrims in Late Antiquity and the Early Middle Ages', *Fragmenta* 1: 83–102.

2014. 'Per una "storia del colore". La scultura policroma romana, un bilancio e qualche prospettiva', in: P. Liverani and U. Santamaria (eds.), *Diversimente bianco. La policromia della scultura romana*. Rome: 9–32.

Lobur, J. A. 2008. *Consensus, Concordia, and the Formation of Roman Imperial Ideology*. London; New York.

Lorenz, K. 2018. 'Writing Histories from Roman Imperial Portraiture: The Case of the Julio-Claudian Princes', in: C. M. Draycott, R. Raja, K. Welch and W. T. Wootton (eds.), *Visual Histories of the Classical World: Essays in Honour of R. R. R. Smith*. Turnhout, 171–80.

Luther, A. 2008. 'Das gallische Sonderreich', in: K.-P. Johne (ed.), *Die Zeit der Soldatenkaiser: Krise und Transformation des Römischen Reiches im 3. Jahrhundert n. Chr. (235-284)*. Berlin, 324–41.

Luzzi, A. 1996. 'Per l'identificazione degli imperatori bizantini comme morati nel Sinassario di Costantinopoli', *Rivista di Studi Bizantini e Neoellenici* 33: 45–66.

Lyne, M. 2003. 'Some New Coin Types of Carausius and Allectus and the History of the British Provinces AD 286-296'. *The Numismatic Chronicle* 163: 147–68.

MacCormack, S. 1981. *Art and Ceremony in Late Antiquity*. Berkeley; Los Angeles; London.

Machado, C. 2019. *Urban Space and Aristocratic Power in Late Antique Rome: AD 270-535*. Oxford.

MacIsaac, J. D. 1975. 'The Hand of God. A Numismatic Study', *Traditio* 31: 322–28.

Mackie, N. K. 1986. 'Res Rublica Restituta. A Roman Myth', *Studies in Latin Literature and Roman History* 4: 303–40.

MacMullen, R. 1959. 'Roman Imperial Building in the Provinces', *HSCP* 64: 207–35.

1964. 'Some Pictures in Ammianus Marcellinus', *Art Bulletin* 46: 435–55.

1982. 'The Epigraphic Habit in the Roman Empire', *The American Journal of Philology* 103: 233–46.

1984. *Christianizing the Roman Empire: (A.D. 100-400)*. New Haven.

Maderna, C. 1988. *Iuppiter, Diomedes und Mercur als Vorbilder für römische Bildnisstatuen. Untersuchungen zum römischen statuarischen Idealporträt*. Heidelberg.

Magalhães de Oliveira, J. C. 2020. 'Late Antiquity: The Age of Crowds?', *Past & Present*, 249: 3–52.

Magdalino, P. 2011. 'Court and Capital in Byzantium', in: J. Duindam, T. Artan and M. Kunt (eds.), *Royal Courts in Dynastic States and Empires. A Global Perspective*. Leiden; Boston, 131–44.

Maier, F. K. 2019. *Palastrevolution. Der Weg zum hauptstädtischen Kaisertum im Römischen Reich des vierten Jahrhunderts*. Paderborn.

Makhlaiuk, A. V. 2020. 'Emperors' Nicknames and Roman Political Humour', *Klio* 102 202–23.

Malloch, S. J. V. 2001. 'Gaius on the Channel Coast', *Classical Quarterly* 51: 551–6.

Malone, C. W. 2009. 'Violence on Roman Imperial Coinage', *Journal of the Numismatic Association of Australia* 20: 58–72.

Manders, E. 2011. 'Communicating Messages through Coins: A New Approach to the Emperor Decius', *Jaarboek voor Munt- en Penningkunde* 98: 17–38.

2012. *Coining Images of Power: Patterns in the Representation of Roman Emperors on Imperial Coinage, A.D. 193–284*. Leiden; Boston.

2020. 'Macedonius, Constantius and the Changing Dynamics of Power', in: C. A. Cvetković and P. Gemeinhardt (eds.), *Episcopal Networks in Late Antiquity*. Berlin; Boston, 249–66.

Manders, E., and O. Hekster. 2011. 'Identities of Emperor and Empire in the Third Century AD', in: S. Benoist and C. Hoët-van Cauwenberghe (eds.), *Figures d'empire, fragments de mémoire. Pouvoirs (pratiques et discours, images et représentations) et identités (sociales et religieuses) dans le monde romain impérial (Ier s. av. J.-C.–Ve s. ap. J.-C.)*. Villeneuve-d'Ascq, 153–62.

Mango, C. 1990. 'Constantine's Mausoleum and the Translation of Relics', *BZ* 83: 51–62.

Mango, C., and R. Scott. 1997. *The Chronicle of Theophanes Confessor: Byzantine and Near Eastern History AD 284–813*. Oxford.

Maniscalco, F. 1997. *Ninfei ed edifice marittimi severiani del Palatium imperial di Baia*. Naples.

Mar, R. 2005. *El Palatí: la formació dels palaus imperials a Roma*. Tarragona.

Marien, B. 'Symmachus' Epistolary Influence: The Rehabilitation of Nicomachus Flavianus through Recommendation Letters', in: K. C. Choda, M. S. de Leeuw and F. Schultz (eds.), *Gaining and Losing Imperial Favour in Late Antiquity*. Leiden; Boston, 105–24.

Marlowe, E. 2006. 'Framing the Sun: The Arch of Constantine and the Roman Cityscape', *The Art Bulletin* 88: 223–42.

Marsengill, K. 2014. 'The Christian Reception of Sculpture in Late Antiquity and the Historical Reception of Late-Antique Christian Sculpture', *Journal of the Bible and Its Reception* 1: 67–101.

Martin, G. 2006. *Dexipp von Athen. Edition, Übersetzung und begleitende Studien*. Tübingen.

Massner, A. K. 1982. *Bildnisangleichung: Untersuchung zur Entstehungs- und Wirkungsgeschichte der Augustusporträts (43 v. Chr. – 68 n. Chr.)*. Berlin.

Mathews, T. F. 2016. *The Dawn of Christian Art in Panel Paintings and Icons*. Los Angeles, 74–83.

Matthews, J. F. 1975. *Western Aristocracies and the Imperial Court*. Oxford.
   2000. *Laying Down the Law: A Study of the Theodosian Code*. New Haven.

Mattern-Parkes, S. P. 2003. 'The Defeat of Crassus and the Just War', *Classical World* 96: 387–96.

Mazzucchi, C. M. 1982. *Menae Patricii cum Thoma Referendario de Scientia Politico Dialogus*. Milan.

McClanan, A. 2002. *Representations of Early Byzantine Empresses: Image and Empire*. New York.

McCormick, M. 1986. *Eternal Victory*. Cambridge, 80–3.

McCoy, M. T. 2014. *The Responses of the Roman Imperial Government to Natural Disasters 29 BCE–180 CE*. PhD University of Arkansas.

McEvoy, M. 2010. 'Rome and the Transformation of the Imperial Office in the Late Fourth-Mid-Fifth Centuries AD', *PBSR* 78, 151–92.
   2013. *Child Emperor Rule in the Late Roman West, AD 367–455*. Oxford.
   2016. 'Becoming Roman? The Not-So-Curious Case of Aspar and the Ardaburii', *Journal of Late Antiquity* 9: 483–511.
   2018. 'Dynastic Dreams and Visions of Early Byzantine Emperors (ca. 518–565 AD)', in: B. Neil and E. Anagnostou-Laoutides (eds.), *Dreams, Memory and Imagination in Byzantium*. Leiden; Boston, 99–117.
   2019. 'Celibacy and Survival in Court Politics in the Fifth Century AD', in: S. Tougher (ed.), *The Emperor in the Byzantine World*. London; New York, 115–34.
   2019. 'Leo II, Zeno, and the Transfer of Roman Imperial Rule from a Son to His Father in 474 CE', in: J. W. Drijvers and N. Lenski, *The Fifth Century: Age of Transformation*. Bari, 197–208.

McFadden, S. 2015. The Luxor Temple Paintings in Context. Roman Visual Culture in Late Antiquity, in: M. Jones and S. McFadden (eds.), *Art of Empire. The Roman Frescoes and Imperial Cult Chamber in Luxor Temple*. New Haven, 105–33.

McIntyre, G. 2016. *A Family of Gods. The Worship of the Imperial Family in the Latin West*. Ann Arbor.
   2019. *Imperial Cult*. Leiden; Boston (= Ancient History 2.1 [2019]).

McKitterick, R. 2004. *History and Memory in the Carolingian World*. Cambridge.

McLynn, N. 1994. *Ambrose of Milan: Church and Court in a Christian Capital*. Berkeley; Los Angeles; London.

Meier, M. 2003. *Das andere Zeitalter Justinians. Kontingenzerfahrung und Kontingenzbewältigung im 6. Jahrhundert n. Chr.* Göttingen.

2010. 'Ariadne – Der "Rote Faden" des Kaisertums', in: A. Kolb (ed.), *Augustae. Machtbewusste Frauen am römischen Kaiserhof? Herrschaftsstrukturen und Herrschaftspraxis II*. Berlin, 277-91.

2011. 'Roman Emperors and "Natural Disasters" in the First Century AD', in: A. Janku, G. Schenk and F. Mauelshagen (eds.), *Historical Disasters in Context: Science, Religion, and Politics*. London; New York, 15-30.

2017. 'Der Monarch auf der Suche nach seinem Platz. Kaiserherrschaft im frühen Byzanz (5. bis 7. Jahrhundert n. Chr.)', in: S. Rebenich (ed.), *Monarchische Herrschaft im Altertum*. Berlin; Boston, 509-44.

Meier, M., and S. Patzold. 2010. *August 410 – Ein Kampf um Rom*. Stuttgart.

Mennen, I. 2011. *Power and Status in the Roman Empire, AD 193-284*. Leiden; Boston.

Meshorer, Y. 2001. *A Treasury of Jewish Coins: From the Persian Period to Bar Kokhba*. Nyack.

Méthy, N. 2003. 'Une Critique de l'optimus princeps: Trajan dans les "Principia historiae' de Fronton"', *Museum Helveticum* 60: 105-23.

Meyboom, P., and E. M. Moormann. 2013. *Le decorazioni dipinte e marmoree della Domus Aurea di Nerone a Roma I-II*. Leuven.

Michel, A.-C. 2015. *La Cour sous l'empereur Claude: les enjeux d'un lieu de pouvoir*. Rennes.

Michels, C. 2018. *Antoninus Pius und die Rollenbilder des römischen Princeps. Herrscherliches Handeln und seine Repräsentation in der hohen Kaiserzeit*. Berlin; Boston.

Migl, J. 1994. *Die Ordnung der Ämter. Prätorianerpräfektur und Vikariat in der Regionalverwaltung des Römischen Reiches von Konstantin bis zur Valentinianischen Dynastie*. Frankfurt am Main.

Mikocki, T. 1995. *Sub specie deae. Les impératrices et princesses romaines assimilées à des déesses: Étude iconologique*. Rome.

Miles, R. (ed.). 2016. *The Donatist Schism. Controversy and Contexts*. Liverpool.

Millar, F. G. B. 1984. 'State and Subject: The Impact of Monarchy', in: F. Millar and E. Segal (eds.), *Caesar Augustus. Seven Aspects*. Oxford, 37-60.

1992[2]. *The Emperor in the Roman World (31 BC-AD 337)*. London.

2000. 'The First Revolution: Imperator Caesar, 36-28 BC', in: A. Giovannini (ed.), *La Révolution romaine après Ronald Syme. Entretiens sur l'Antiquité Classique* 46. Geneva, 1-30.

2006. *A Greek Roman Empire. Power and Belief under Theodosius II (408-450)*. Berkeley; Los Angeles.

Milner, N. P. 2015. 'A New Statue-Base for Constantius II and the Fourth-Century Imperial Cult at Oinoanda', *Anatolian Studies* 65: 181-203.

Mitchell, S. 1987. 'Imperial Building in the Eastern Roman Provinces', *Harvard Studies in Classical Philology* 91: 333-65.

Mlasowsky, A. 1996. '*Nomini ac fortunae caesarum proximi*. Die Sukzessionspropaganda der römischen Kaiser von Augustus bis Nero im

Spiegel der Reichsprägung und der archäologischen Quellen', *JDAI* 111: 249–388.

Moatti, C. 2011. 'Historicité et altéronomie: un autre regard sur l'histoire', *Politica Antica* 1: 107–18.

2018. *Res publica. Histoire romaine de la chose publique*. Paris.

Moffatt A., and M. Tall. 2012. *Constantine Porphyrogennetos: The Book of Ceremonies*. Leiden; Boston.

Mols, S. T. A. M., E. M. Moormann, and O. Hekster. 2016. 'From Phidias to Constantine: The Portrait Historié in Classical Antiquity', in: V. Manuth, R. van Leeuwen and J. Koldeweij (eds.), *Example or Alter Ego? Aspects of the Portrait Historié in Western Art from Antiquity to the Present*. Turnhout, 19–63.

Mols, S. T. A. M. 2003. 'The Cult of Roma Aeterna in Hadrian's Politics', in: L. de Blois et al. (eds.), *The Representation and Perception of Roman Imperial Power*. Amsterdam, 458–65.

Moormann, E. M. 2020. Nerone, Roma e la *Domus Aurea*. Rome.

Morgan, T. 1998. *Literate Education in the Hellenistic and Roman Worlds*. Cambridge.

Mosco, V. 2015. 'The Political Economy of Communication: A Living Tradition', in: L. Albornoz (ed.), *Power, Media, Culture. A Critical View from the Political Economy of Communication*. London; New York, 35–57.

Moser, M. 2018. *Emperors and Senators in the Reign of Constantius II. Maintaining Imperial Ruler Between Rome and Constantinople in the Fourth Century* A D. Cambridge.

Mouritsen, H. 2011. *The Freedman in the Roman World*. Cambridge.

Musiał, D. 2014. 'The Princeps as *Pontifex Maximus*: The Case of Tiberius', *Electrum* 21: 99–106.

Mylonopoulos, J. 2009. 'Divine Images versus Cult Images. An Endless Story about Theories, Methods, and Terminologies', in J. Mylonopoulos (ed.), *Divine Images and Human Imaginations in Ancient Greece and Rome*. Leiden; Boston, 1–19.

Naerebout, F. G. 2021. 'Domitian and Religion', in: A. Raimondi Cominesi, N. de Haan, E. M. Moormann and C. Stocks (eds.), *God on Earth: Emperor Domitian. The Re-invention of Rome at the End of the 1st Century* A D. Leiden, 147–51.

Naismith, R. 2014. 'Gold Coinage and Its Use in the Post-Roman West', *Speculum* 89: 273–306.

Neil, B., and P. Allen. 2020. *The Letters of Gelasius I (492-496): Pastor and Micromanager of the Church of Rome*. Turnhout.

Neri, V. 2019. 'The Emperor as Living Image in Late Antique Authors', *RIHA Journal* 0223, 30 September 2019: www.riha-journal.org/articles/2019/0222-0229-special-issue-paradigms-of-corporeal-iconicity/0223-neri.

Niemeyer, H. 1968: *Studien zur statuarischen Darstellung der römischen Kaiser*. Berlin.

Nixon, C. E. V., and B. Saylor Rodgers. 1994. *In Praise of Later Roman Emperors: The Panegyrici Latini*. Berkeley.

Nock, A. D. 1947. 'The Emperors' Divine *Comes*', *JRS* 37: 102–16.

Noreña, C. 2011. *Imperial Ideals in the Roman West. Representation, Circulation, Power*. Cambridge.

— 2015. 'Ritual and Memory: Hellenistic Ruler Cults in the Roman Empire', in: K. Galinsky and K. Lapatin (eds.), *Cultural Memories in the Roman Empire*. Los Angeles, 86–100.

Norton, P. 2007. *Episcopal Elections 250-600. Hierarchy and Popular Will in Late Antiquity*. Oxford.

Olovsdotter, C. 2011. 'Representing Consulship. On the Concept and Meanings of the Consular Diptychs', *Opuscula* 4: 99–123.

Olson, K. 2017. *Masculinity and Dress in Roman Antiquity*. London; New York.

— 2022. 'Dress, Adornment and Self-Presentation', in: B. Kelly and A. Hug (eds.), *The Roman Emperor and His Court, ca. 30 BC–ca. AD 300 Volume 1: Historical Essays*. Cambridge, 461–78.

Osborne, R. 2018. 'Introduction: For Tradition as an Analytical Category', *World Archaeology* 40: 281–94.

Osborne, R., and C. Vout. 2010. 'A Revolution in Roman history?', *JRS* 100: 233–45.

Osgood, J. 2016. 'Cassius Dio's Secret History of Elagabalus', in: J. Madsen and C. H. Lange (eds.), *Cassius Dio: Greek Intellectual and Roman Politician*. Leiden; Boston, 177–90.

Packer, E. 1997. *The Forum of Trajan in Rome. A Study of the Monuments*. Berkeley.

Palmer, A. N. 2020. *The Life of the Syrian Saint Barsauma. Eulogy of a Hero of the Resistance to the Council of Chalcedon*. Oakland.

Palombi, D. 1999. 'Thermae Aurelianae', in: *LTUR* 5, 48–9.

Pandey, N. B. 2019. *The Poetics of Power in Augustan Rome: Latin Poetic Responses to Early Imperial Iconography*. Cambridge.

Parani, M. G. 2008. 'Defining Personal Space: Dress and Accessories in Late Antiquity', in: L. Lavan, E. Swift and T. Putzeys (eds.), *Objects in Context. Objects in Use. Material Spatiality in Late Antiquity*. Leiden; Boston, 495–529.

Pardini, G. 2011. '*Signa* et *insignia* nell'iconografia numismatica', in: C. Panella (ed.), *I segni del potere. Realtà e immaginario della sovranità nella Roma imperial*. Bari, 77–122.

Parnell, D. A. 2017. *Justinian's Men. Careers and Relationships of Byzantine Army Officers, 518-610*. London.

Parsi, B. 1963. *Désignation et investiture de l'empereur romain*. Paris.

Paterson, J. 2007. 'Friends in High Places: The Creation of the Court of the Roman Emperor', in: A. J. S. Spawforth (ed.), *The Court and Court Society in Ancient Monarchies*. Cambridge; New York, 121–56.

Peachin, M. 1996. *Iudex Vice Caesaris. Deputy Emperors and the Administration of Justice during the Principate*. Stuttgart.

Pekáry, T. 1985. *Das Römische Herrscherbild*, III, *Das Römische Kaiserbildnis in Staat, Kult und Gesellschaft, dargestellt an Hand der Schriftquellen*. Berlin.

1986. 'Das Opfer vor dem Kaiserbild', *BJ* 186: 91–103.

Penders, S. 2021. *Empire of Virtue? Normative Language and the Legitimation of Power in the Roman North Africa*. PhD Leiden.

Peppard, M. 2011. *The Son of God in the Roman World. Divine Sonship in Its Social and Political Context*. Oxford.

Pfanner, M. 1989. 'Über das Herstellen von Porträts. Ein Beitrag zu Rationalisierungsmassnahmen und Produktionsmechanismen von Massenware im späten Hellenismus und in der römischen Kaiserzeit', *Jahrbuch des Deutschen Archäologischen Instituts* 104: 157–257.

Pfeiffer, S. 2010. *Der römische Kaiser und das Land am Nil. Kaiserverehrung und Kaiserkult in Alexandria und Ägypten von Augustus bis Caracalla (30 v. Chr.–217 n. Chr.)*. Stuttgart.

2012. 'The Imperial Cult in Egypt', in: C. Riggs (ed.), *The Oxford Handbook of Roman Egypt*. Oxford, 83–100.

Pfeilschifter, R. 2013. *Der Kaiser und Konstantinopel. Kommunikation und Konfliktaustrag in einer spätantiken Metropole*. Berlin; New York.

Pflaum, H. G. 1961. 'Les Gendres de Marc-Aurèle', *JS* (1961), 28–41.

Pflug, J. 2013. 'Die bauliche Entwicklung der Domus Augustana im Kontext des südöstlichen Palatin bis in severische Zeit', in: N. Sojc, A. Winterling and U. Wulf-Rheidt (eds.), *Palast und Stadt im severischen Rom*. Stuttgart, 181–212.

Pflug, J., and U. Wulf-Rheidt. 2022. 'The Imperial Palaces on the Palatine Hill: Architecture as a Reflection of Social Practices and Imperial Authority', in: B. Kelly and A. Hug (eds.), *The Roman Emperor and His Court, ca. 30 BC–ca. AD 300 Volume 1: Historical Essays*. Cambridge, 204–38.

Pina Polo, F. 2011. 'Public Speaking in Rome: A Question of Auctoritas', in: M. Peachin (ed.), *The Oxford Handbook of Social Relations in the Roman World*. Oxford, 286–303.

Piranomonte, M. 1999. 'Thermae Antoninianae', in: *LTUR* 5, 42–8.

Pitsakis, L. 2011. 'Sainteté et empire. À propos de la sainteté impériale: formes de sainteté "d'office" et de sainteté collective dans l'Empire d'Orient?', *Bizantinistica* 3: 155–227.

Pollini, J. 2012. *From Republic to Empire: Rhetoric, Religion, and Power in the Visual Culture of Ancient Rome*. Norman.

2020. 'Die Umarbeitung römischer Kaiserbildnisse: Deutungsprobleme und neue Lösungsansätze mit Hilfe digitaler Technologie', in: T. Greub, *Revisionen des Porträts. Jenseits von Mimesis und Repräsentation*. Leiden; Boston, 243–70.

Popkin, M. L. 2016. *The Architecture of the Roman Triumph. Monuments, Memory and Identity*. Cambridge.

Potter, D. 2004. *The Roman Empire at Bay. AD 180–395*. London; New York.
    2010. 'The Unity of the Roman Empire', in: S. McGill, C. Sogno and E. Watts (eds.), *From the Tetrarchs to the Theodosians. Later Roman History and Culture, 284–450 CE*. Cambridge; New York, 13–32.
Powell, A. 2009. 'Augustus' Age of Apology: An Analysis of the Memoirs – and an Argument for Two Further Fragments', in: C. Smith and A. Powell (eds.), *The Lost Memories of Augustus and the Development of Roman Autobiography*. Swansea, 173–94.
Price, R., and M. Gaddis. 2005. *The Acts of the Council of Chalcedon*. Vol. 1. Liverpool.
Price, S. F. R. 1984. *Rituals and Power. The Roman Imperial Cult in Asia Minor*. Cambridge.
    1987. 'From Noble Funerals to Divine Cult: The Consecration of Roman Emperors', in: D. Cannadine and S. Price (eds.), *Rituals of Royalty. Power and Ceremonial in Traditional Societies*. Cambridge; New York; Melbourne, 56–105.
Purcell, N. 1986. 'Livia and the Womanhood of Rome', *PCPS* 32: 78–105.
Pury-Gysel, A. D. 2017. *Die Goldbüste des Septimius Severus: Gold- und Silberbüsten römischer Kaiser*. Basel.
Quinn, J., and A. Wilson. 2013. 'Capitolia', *JRS* 103: 117–73.
Radtki, C. 2016. 'The Senate at Rome in Ostrogothic Italy', in: J. Arnold, M. S. Bjornlie and K. Sessa (eds.), *A Companion to Ostrogothic Italy*. Leiden; Boston, 121–46.
Raedts, P., and M. Derks. 2015. 'Introduction', in: J. W. Buisman, M. Derks and P. Raedts (eds.), *Episcopacy, Authority, and Gender. Aspects of Religious Leadership in Europe, 1100–2000*. Leiden; Boston.
Raepsaet-Charlier, M.-T. 1975. 'La Datation des inscriptions latines dans les provinces occidentales de l'empire romain d'après les formules "IN H (ONOREM) D(OMUS) D(IVINAE)" et "DEA DEAE"', *ANRW* II.3: 232–82.
Raeymakers, D., and S. Derks (eds.). 2016. *The Key to Power? The Culture of Access in Princely Courts, 1400–1750*. Leiden; Boston.
Raimondi Cominesi, A. 2018. 'Augustus in the Making: A Reappraisal of the Ideology behind Octavian's Palatine Residence through Its Interior Decoration and Topographical Context', *Latomus* 77: 704–35.
    Forthcoming. 'From Villa to Palace: The Creation of a Palatial Culture in Rome under the Severans'.
Rapp, C. 2012. 'Death at the Byzantine Court: The Emperor and His Family', in: K.-H. Spieß and I. Warntjes (eds.), *Death at Court*. Wiesbaden, 267–86.
Raschle, C. R. 2016. 'Bis wann bleibt der Kaiser "Kult"? Die Verehrung des Kaiserbildes als Akt der Zivilreligion in der Spätantike', in: A. Kolb and M. Vitale (eds.), *Kaiserkult in den Provinzen des Römischen Reiches. Organisation, Kommunikation und Repräsentation*. Berlin; Boston, 477–96.
Rawson, E. 1975. 'Caesar's Heritage: Hellenistic Kings and Their Roman Equals', *JRS* 65: 148–59.

Rebenich, S. (ed.). 2017. *Monarchische Herrschaft im Altertum*. Berlin; Boston.

Rebenich S., and J. Wienand. 2017. 'Monarchische Herrschaft im Altertum. Zugänge und Perspektiven', in: S. Rebenich (ed.), *Monarchische Herrschaft im Altertum*. Berlin; Boston, 1–41.

Rees, R. 1993. 'Images and Image: A Re-Examination of Tetrarchic Iconography', *Greece & Rome* 40: 181–200.

2005. 'The Emperors' New Names: Diocletian Jovius and Maximian Herculius', in: H. Bowden and L. Rawlings (eds.), *Herakles and Hercules. Exploring a Graeco-Roman Divinity*. Swansea, 223–39.

Reeves, M. B. 2004. *The Feriale Duranum, Roman Military Religion, and Dura-Europos: A Reassessment*. PhD Buffalo.

Reinhold, M. 1970. *History of Purple as Status Symbol in Antiquity*. Brussels 1970.

Reynolds, J. 1982. *Aphrodisias and Rome. Documents from the Excavation of the Theatre at Aphrodisias Conducted by Professor Kenan T. Erim Together with Some Related Texts*. London.

Riccardi, L. A. 2000. 'Uncanonical Imperial Portraits in the Eastern Roman Provinces: The Case of the Kanellopoulos Emperor', *Hesperia* 69: 105–32.

Ricci, M., G. Pardini and C. Panella. 2011. 'Galleria di immagini', in: C. Panella (ed.), *I segni del potere. Realtà e immaginario della sovranità nella Roma imperial*. Bari, 250–77.

Rich, J. W. 1996. '*Augustus and the* Spolia Opima', *Chiron* 26: 85–127.

1998. 'Augustus's Parthian Honours, the Temple of Mars Ultor and the Arch in the Forum Romanum', *PBSR* 66: 71–128.

2012. 'Making the Emergency Permanent: "Auctoritas, Potestas" and the Evolution of the Principate of Augustus', in: Y. Rivière (ed.), *Des réformes augustéennes*. Rome, 29–113.

2015. 'Consensus Rituals and the Origins of the Principate', in: J.-L. Ferrary and J. Scheid (eds.), *Il princeps romano: autocrate o magistrato? Fattori giuridica e fattori sociali del potere imperiale da Augusto a Commodo*. Pavia, 101–38; 115.

Richlin, A. 2006. *Marcus Aurelius in Love. The Letters of Marcus and Fronto*. Chicago.

Richter, D. 2004. *Das römische Heer auf der Trajanssäule. Propaganda und Realität*. Mannheim; Möhnesee.

Ridley, R. T. 2005. 'The Absent *Pontifex Maximus*', *Historia* 54: 275–300.

Rietbergen, P. 2018. 'Not of This World . . . ? Religious Power and Imperial Rule in Eurasia, ca. Thirteenth – ca. Eighteenth Century', in: M. van Berkel and J. Duindam (eds.), *Prince, Pen, and Sword: Eurasian Perspectives*. Leiden; Boston, 129–296.

Ripollès, P. 2005. 'Coinage and Identity in the Roman Provinces: Spain', in: C. Howgego, V. Heuchert and A. Burnett (eds.), *Coinage and Identity in the Roman Provinces*. Oxford, 79–93.

Ritti, T. 2002-2003. 'Antonino Pio, "padrone della terra e del mare". Una nuova inscrizione onorario da Hierapolis di Frigia', *Annali di archeologia e storia antica* 9-10: 271-81.

Rives, J. 1999. 'The Decree of Decius and the Religion of the Empire', *JRS* 89: 135-54.

Robert, L. 1977. 'La Titulature de Nicée et de Nicomédie: la gloire et la haine', *HSCP* 81: 1-39.

Rock, I. E. 2017. *Paul's Letter to the Romans and Roman Imperialism: An Ideological Analysis of the Exordium (Romans 1:1-17)*. Cambridge.

Roddaz, J.-M. 1984. *Marcus Agrippa*. Rome.

Rodríguez Gervás, M. 2020. 'Teodosio, construcción de una vida y muerte ejemplares', *História* 39 [online, cited 2020-12-10], e2020052.

Rohr, C. 1995. *Der Theoderich-Panegyricus des Ennodius*. Hanover.

Rollé Ditzler, I. 2019. *Der Senat und seine Kaiser im spätantiken Rom. Eine kulturhistorische Annäherung*. Wiesbaden.

Roller, M. 2003. *Constructing Autocracy: Aristocrats and Emperors in Julio-Claudian Rome*. Princeton.

2018. *Models from the Past in Roman Culture. A World of Exempla*. Cambridge.

Roman, Y., B. Rémy and L. Riccardi. 2009. 'Les Intrigues de Plotine et la succession de Trajan. À propos d'un aureus au nom d'Hadrien César', *REA* 111: 508-17.

Rose, C. B. 1997. *Dynastic Commemoration and Imperial Portraiture in the Julio-Claudian Period*. Cambridge.

2021. 'Reconsidering the Frieze on the Arch of Constantine', *JRA* 19: 1-36.

Roth, J. P. 2007. 'Jews and the Roman Army', in: L. de Blois and E. LoCascio (eds.), *The Impact of the Roman Army (200 BC-AD 476)*. Amsterdam, 409-20.

Rothe, U. 2020. *The Toga and Roman Identity*. London; New York.

Rothenhöfer, C. 2020. 'Emperor Tiberius and His *praecipua legionum cura* in a New bronze tablet from AD 14', *Gephyra* 19: 101-10.

Roueché, C. 1984. 'Acclamations in the Later Roman Empire: New Evidence from Aphrodisias', *JRS* 74: 181-99.

Rowan, C. 2011. 'The Public Image of the Severan Women', *PBSR* 79: 241-73.

2012. *Under Divine Auspices. Divine Ideology and the Visualisation of Imperial Power in the Severan Period*. Cambridge.

2013. 'Imaging the Golden Age. The Coinage of Antoninus Pius', *PBSR* 82: 211-46.

2018. *From Caesar to Augustus (c. 49 BC-AD 14). Using Coins as Sources*. Cambridge.

Rowe, G. 2013. 'Reconsidering the Auctoritas of Augustus', *JRS* 103: 1-15.

Roymans, N. 2019. 'Conquest, Mass Violence and Ethnic Stereotyping: Investigating Caesar's Actions in the Germanic Frontier Zone', *JRA* 32: 439-58.

Royo, M. 1999. *Domus imperatoriae: Topographie, formation et imaginaire des palais impériaux du Palatin (IIe siècle av. J.-C.-Ier siècle apr. J.-C.)*. Rome.

Rubin, Z. 1975. 'Dio, Herodian, and Severus' Second Parthian War', *Chiron* 5: 419–44.

Ruck, B. 2007. *Die Grossen dieser Welt: Kolossalporträts im antiken Rom.* Heidelberg.

Rüpke, J. 2005. *Fasti sacerdotum. Die Mitglieder der Priesterschaften und das sakrale Funktionspersonal römischer, griechischer, orientalischer und jüdisch-christlicher Kulte in der Stadt Rom von 300 v. Chr. bis 499 n. Chr.* Stuttgart.

    2007. *The Religions of Rome.* Cambridge; Malden [Mass.].

Russell, A. 2019. 'Inventing the Imperial Senate', in: J. Osgood, K. Morrell and K. Welch (eds.), *The Alternative Augustan Age.* Oxford, 325–41.

    2019. 'The Augustan Senate and the Reconfiguration of Time on the Fasti Capitolini', in: I. Gildenhard et al. (eds.), *Augustus and the Destruction of History: The Politics of the Past in Early Imperial Rome.* Cambridge, 157–88.

Rutledge, S. 2012. *Ancient Rome as a Museum: Power, Identity, and the Culture of Collecting.* Oxford.

Sághy, M. 2020. 'Damasus and the Charioteers. Crowds, Media and Leadership in Late Antique Rome', in: E. Manders and D. Slootjes (eds.), *Leadership, Ideology and Crowds in the Roman Empire of the Fourth Century* AD. Stuttgart, 117–33.

Salomies, O. 2000. 'Some Interesting Expressions Found in Late Antique Honorific Inscriptions', in: G. Paci (ed.), *Epigraphai. Miscellanea epigrafica in onore di Lidio Gasperini. Vol. 2.* Tivoli, 931–42.

Salomonson, J. W. 1956. *Chair, Sceptre and Wreath. Historical Aspects of their Representations on Some Roman Sepulchral Monuments.* PhD Amsterdam.

Salway, B. 1994. 'What's in a Name? A Survey of Roman Onomastic Practice from c. 700 BC to AD 700', *JRS* 84: 124–45.

    2006. 'Equestrian Prefects and the Award of Senatorial Honours from the Severans to Constantine', in: A. Kolb (ed.), *Herrschaftsstrukturen und Herrschaftspraxis. Konzepte, Prinzipien und Strategien der Administration im römischen Kaiserreich.* Berlin; New York, 115–35.

    2007. 'Constantine *Augoustous* (not *Sebastos*)', in: J. Drinkwater and B. Salway (eds.), *Wolf Liebeschuetz Reflected. Essays Presented by Colleagues, Friends, and Pupils.* London: 37–50.

    2013. 'The Publication and Application of the Theodosian Code. NTh 1, the *Gesta Senatus*, and the *Constitutionarii*', *MEFRA* 125 (2013), 327–54.

Santamaría Álvarez, M. A. 2017. 'The Sceptre and the Sickle. The Transmission of Divine Power in the Orphic Rhapsodies', in: A. Marmodoro and I. F. Viltanioti (eds.), *Divine Powers in Late Antiquity.* Oxford, 108–24.

Sarris, P. 2011. *Empires of Faith. The Fall of Rome to the Rise of Islam, 500–700.* Oxford.

Sartre, M. 2001. 'Les Manifestations du culte imperial dans les provinces syriennes et en Arabie', in: C. Evers (ed.), *Rome et ses provinces. Genèse et diffusion d'une image du pouvoir. Hommages à Jean-Charles Balty.* Brussels, 167–86.

Sawiński, P. 2021. *Holders of Extraordinary Imperium under Augustus and Tiberius: A Study into the Beginnings of the Principate.* Abingdon; New York.

Schade, K. 2003. *Frauen in der Spätantike – Status und Repräsentation. Eine Untersuchung zur römischen und frühbyzantinischen Bildniskunst.* Mainz.

Schäfer, T. 1989. *Imperii Insignia. Sella Curulis und Fasces. Zur Repräsentation römischer Magistrate.* Mainz.

    2014. 'Ciclo di rilievi Medinaceli', in: E. LaRocca et al. (eds.), *Augusto.* Rome, 321–3.

Scheid, J. 1998. *Commentarii Fratrvm Arvalivm qui svpersvnt. Les Copies épigraphiques des protocols annuels de la confrérie Arvale (21 av.–304 ap. J.C.).* Rome.

    2001. *Religion et pieté à Rome.* Paris.

Scheidel, W. 2009. 'Sex and Empire: A Darwinian Perspective', in: I. Morris and W. Scheidel (eds.), *The Dynamics of Ancient Empires: State Power from Assyria to Byzantium.* Oxford, 255–324.

Schlösser, R. 1989. 'Römische Münzen als Quelle für das Vulgärlatein', *Quaderni Ticinesi* 18: 319–35.

Schneider, R. M. 2003. 'Gegenbilder im römischen Kaiserporträt: Die neuen Gesichter Neros und Vespasians', in: M. Büchsel and P. Schmidt (eds.), *Das Porträt vor der Erfindung des Porträts.* Mainz, 59–76.

Schoolman, E. M. 2017. 'Vir Clarissimus and Roman Titles in the Early Middle Ages: Survival and Continuity in Ravenna and the Latin West', *Medieval Prosopography* 32: 1–39.

Schöpe, B. 2014. *Der römische Kaiserhof in severischer Zeit (193–235 n. Chr.).* Stuttgart.

Schowalter, D. N. 1993. *The Emperor and the Gods. Images from the Time of Trajan.* Minneapolis.

Scott, A. G. 2015. 'Cassius Dio, Caracalla, and the Senate', *Klio* 97: 157–75.

    2018. *Emperors and Usurpers. An Historical Commentary on Cassius Dio's Roman History.* Oxford; New York.

Sear, D. R. 2014. *Roman Coins and Their Values.* Vol. 5. London.

Seelentag, G. 2004. *Taten und Tugenden Traians. Herrschaftsdarstellung im Principat.* Stuttgart.

    2017. 'Antoninus Pius und die Herrschaftsdarstellung des 2. Jhs.', in: C. Michels and P. F. Mittag (eds.), *Jenseits des Narrativs. Antoninus Pius in den nichtliterarischen Quellen.* Stuttgart, 19–30.

Segal, C. 2001. 'Jupiter in Ovid's *Metamorphoses*', *Arion* 9.1: 78–99.

Settis, S. 1985. 'La Colonne trajane. Invention, composition, disposition', *Annales* 40: 1165–94.

Shaw, B. D. 2011. *Sacred Violence: African Christians and Sectarian Hatred in the Age of Augustine.* Cambridge.

Sherwin-White, A. N. 1979². *The Roman Citizenship.* Oxford.

Sigmund, C. 2014. *'Königtum' in der politischen Kultur des spätrepublikanischen Rom.* Berlin; Boston.

Simić, K. 2018. 'The Byzantine Augustus', in: P. Goodman (ed.), *Afterlives of Augustus,* AD *14–2014.* Cambridge, 122–37.

Simpson, C. J. 1996. 'Caligula's Cult. Immolation, Immortality, Intent', in: A. Small (ed.), *Subject and Ruler. The Cult of the Ruling Power in Classical Antiquity.* Ann Arbor.

Singor, H. 2003. 'The Labarum, Shield Blazons, and Constantine's *Caeleste Signum*', in: L. de Blois et al. (eds.), *The Representation and Perception of Roman Imperial Power.* Amsterdam, 481–500.

Sirks, A. J. B. 2013. 'The *Episcopalis Audientia* in Late Antiquity', *Droit et cultures,* 65: 79–88.

2015. 'Status and Rank in the Theodosian Code', in: A. Kuhn, (ed.), *Social Status and Prestige in the Graeco-Roman World.* Stuttgart, 291–302.

Skovmøller, A. 2014. 'Where Marble Meets Colour: Surface Texturing of Hair, Skin and Dress on Roman Marble Portraits as Support for Painted Polychromy', in: M. Harlow and M.-L. Nosch (eds.), *Greek and Roman Textiles and Dress: An Interdisciplinary Anthology.* Oxford; Philadelphia, 279–97.

Sloan, M. C. 2018. 'Augustus, the Harbinger of Peace. Orosius' Reception of Augustus in *Historiae Adversus Paganos*', in: P. Goodman (ed.), *Afterlives of Augustus,* AD *14–2014.* Cambridge, 103–21.

Slootjes, D. 2023, forthcoming. 'Dynamics of Power at the Imperial Court: Theodosius II, Pulcheria, Nestorius, Cyril and the Council of Ephesus of 431', in: C. Davenport and M. McEvoy (eds.), *The Roman Imperial Court. Pathways from the Principate to Late Antiquity.* Oxford.

2006. *The Governor and His Subjects in the Later Roman Empire.* Leiden; Boston.

Sluiter, I. 2017. 'Anchoring Innovation: A Classical Research Agenda', *European Review* 25: 1–19.

Smith, R. R. R. 1987. 'The Imperial Reliefs from the Sebasteion at Aphrodisias', *JRS* 77: 88–138.

1988. *Hellenistic Royal Portraits.* Oxford.

1999. 'Late Antique Portraits in a Public Context: Honorific Statuary at Aphrodisias in Caria, A.D. 300–600', *JRS* 89: 155–89.

2000. 'Nero and the Sun-God: Divine Accessories and Political Symbols in Roman Imperial Images', *JRA* 13: 532–42.

2016. 'Aphrodisias', in: R. R. R. Smith and B. Ward-Perkins (eds.), *The Last Statues of Antiquity.* Oxford, 145–59.

2016. 'Statue Practice in the Late Roman Empire: Numbers, Costumes and Styles', in R. R. R. Smith and B. Ward-Perkins (eds.), *The Last Statues of Antiquity.* Oxford, 1–27.

Sonnabend, H. 1999. *Naturkatastrophen in der Antike: Wahrnehmung- Deutung- Management.* Stuttgart; Weimar.

Spawforth, A. J. S. 2012. *Greece and the Augustan Cultural Revolution. Greek Culture in the Roman World.* Cambridge; New York.

Speidel, M. A. 1986. 'Maxentius and His *Equites Singulares* in the Battle at the Milvian Bridge', *Classical Antiquity* 5.2: 253–62.

Speidel, M. P. 2000. 'Commodus and the King of the Quadi', *Germania* 78: 193–7.

Squire, M. 2016. 'How to Read a Roman Portrait? Optatian Porfyry, Constantine and the "Vvltus Avgvsti"', *PBSR* 84: 179–366.

— 2017. 'Optatian and His Lettered Art', in: M. Squire and J. Wienand (eds.), *Morphogrammata. The Lettered Art of Optatian. Figuring Cultural Transformations in the Age of Constantine.* Paderborn, 55–120.

Squire, M., and J. Wienand (eds.). 2017. *Morphogrammata. The Lettered Art of Optatian. Figuring Cultural Transformations in the Age of Constantine.* Paderborn.

Srirangacher Ramesh, D., S. Heijnen, O. Hekster, and L. Spreeuwers. 2022. 'Facial Recognition as a Tool to Identify Roman Emperors. Towards a New Methodology', *Humanities and Social Sciences Communications* 9.78; www.nature.com/articles/s41599-022-01090-y

Stäcker, J. 2003. *Princeps und Miles: Studien zum Bindungs- und Nahverhältnis von Kaiser und Soldat im 1. und 2. Jahrhundert n. Chr. (Spudasmata 91).* Olms.

Steel, C. 2020. 'Sulla the Orator', in: A. Eckert and A. Thein (eds.), *Sulla. Politics and Reception.* Berlin, 19–32.

Steinberg, A. 2020. *Weaving in Stones: Garments and Their Accessories in the Mosaic Art of Eretz Israel in Late Antiquity.* Oxford.

Stephens Falcasantos, R. 2020. *Constantinople: Ritual, Violence, and Memory in the Making of a Christian Imperial Capital.* Oakland.

Stephenson, P. 2009. *Constantine: Unconquered Emperor, Christian Victor.* London.

Stepper, R. 2003. *Augustus et sacerdos. Untersuchungen zum römischen Kaiser als Priester.* Stuttgart.

Stevenson, W. 2014. 'Exiling Bishops: The Policy of Constantius II', *Dumbarton Oaks Papers* 68: 7–27.

Stewart, P. 2003. *Statues in Roman Society. Representation and Response.* Oxford.

Stoll, O. 2007. 'The Religions of the Armies', in: P. P. M. Erdkamp (ed.), *The Blackwell Companion to the Roman Army.* Oxford, 451–76.

— 2001. *Zwischen Integration und Abgrenzung: Die Religion des Römischen Heeres im Nahen Osten. Studien zum Verhältnis von Armee und Zivilbevölkerung im römischen Syrien und den Nachbargebieten.* St Katharinen, 367–79.

Stolte, B. 2019. 'Law Is the King of All Things? The Emperor and the Law', in: S. Tougher (ed.), *The Emperor in the Byzantine World.* London; New York, 171–8.

Stone, D. 2020. 'A Diachronic and Regional Approach to North African Urbanism', in: L. de Ligt and J. Bintliff (eds.), *Regional Urban Systems in the Roman World, 150 BCE–250 CE*. Leiden; Boston, 324–49.

Stout, A. M. 1994. 'Jewelry as a Symbol of Status in the Roman Empire', in: J. L. Sebesta and L. Bonfante (eds.), *The World of Roman Costume*. Madison, 77–100.

Strobel, K. 2007. 'Vom marginalen Grenzraum zum Kernraum Europas. Das römische Heer als Motor der Neustrukturierung historischer Landschaften und Wirtschaftsräume', in: L. de Blois and E. LoCascio (eds.), *The Impact of the Roman Army* (200 BC–AD 476). Leiden; Boston, 207–37.

Strocka, V. M. 1972. 'Beobachtungen an den Attikareliefs des severischen Quadrifons von Lepcis Magna', *Antiquités Africaines* 6: 147–72.

Strootman, R. 2017. 'Eunuchs, Renegades and Concubines: The "Paradox of Power" and the Promotion of Favorites in the Hellenistic Empires', in: A. Erskine, L. Llewellyn-Jones and S. Wallace (eds.), *The Hellenistic Court: Monarchic Power and Elite Society from Alexander to Cleopatra*. Swansea, 121–42.

2022. 'Hellenstic Influences on Roman Court Culture', in: B. Kelly and A. Hug (eds.), *The Roman Emperor and His Court, ca. 30 BC–ca. AD 300. Volume 1: Historical Essays*. Cambridge, 16–34.

Stutzinger, D. 1986. 'Das Bronzebildnis einer spätantiken Kaiserin aus Balajnac im Museum von Nis', *Jahrbuch für Antike und Christentum* 29 (1986), 146–65.

Sünskes Thompson, J. 1993. *Demonstrative Legitimation der Kaiserherrschaft im Epochenvergleich: zur politischen Macht des stadtrömischen Volkes*. Stuttgart.

Swain, S. (ed.). 2007. *Seeing the Face, Seeing the Soul. Polemon's Physiognomy from Classical Antiquity to Medieval Islam*. Oxford.

Syme, R. 1958. 'Imperator Caesar: A Study in Nomenclature', *Historia* 7: 172–88 (= *Roman Papers* I, Oxford 1979, 361–77).

Szidat, J. 2010. 'Usurpator Tanti Nominis', *Kaiser und Usurpator in der Spätantike (337–476 n. Chr.)*. Stuttgart.

Tacoma, L. E. 2020. *Roman Political Culture. Seven Studies of the Senate and City Councils of Italy from the First to the Sixth Century AD*. Oxford.

Talbert, R. 1987. *The Senate of Imperial Rome*. Princeton.

Tatarkiewicz, A. 2012. 'Caenis. Augusta in All but Name', *Classica Cracoviensia* 15: 223–9.

Tatum, W. J. 2008. *Always I am Caesar*. Oxford; Malden [Mass.].

Thienes, E. 2015. *Remembering Trajan in Fourth-Century Rome: Memory and Identity in Spatial, Artistic, and Textual Narratives*. PhD University of Missouri.

Thomas, C. 2004. 'Claudius and the Roman Army Reforms', *Historia* 53: 424–52.

Thonemann, P. 2012. 'A Copy of Augustus' Res Gestae at Sardis', *Historia* 61: 280–8.

Tomei, M. A. 2011. 'Nerone sul Palatino', in: M. A. Tomei and R. Rea (eds.), *Nerone: Catalogo della Mostra (Roma, 13 Aprile–18 Settembre 2011)*. Milan, 118–35.

2013. 'Le residenze sul Palatino dall'età repubblicana all'età antonina', in: N. Sojc, A. Winterling and U. Wulf-Rheidt (eds.), *Palast und Stadt im severischen Rom*. Stuttgart, 61–83.

Tomei, M. A., and M. G. Filetici. 2011. *Domus Tiberiana: scavi e restauri 1990–2011*. Milan.

Tommasi Moreschini, C. O. 2016. 'Coping with Ancient Gods, Celebrating Christian Emperors, Proclaiming Roman Eternity: Rhetoric and Religion in Late Antique Latin Panegyrics', in: Maijastina Kahlos (ed.), *Emperors and the Divine – Rome and Its Influence*. Helsinki, 177–209.

Torres, J. B. 2023, forthcoming. 'Concerning John Chrysostom: *Collectio Avellana* 38 and His Controversy in the West', in: A. Evers (ed.), *Religion, Power, and Politics in Late Antiquity: Bishops, Emperors, and Senators in the Collectio Avellana, AD 367–553*. Leuven.

2021. 'Purple and the Depiction of Constantine in Eusebius and Other Contemporary Panegyrical Works', in: M. P. Gracía Ruiz and A. J. Quiroga Puertas (eds.), *Emperors and Emperorship in Late Antiquity. Images and Narratives*. Leiden; Boston, 76–92.

Tougher, S. 2018. 'Julian Augustus on Augustus: Octavian in the Caesars', in: P. Goodman (ed.), *Afterlives of Augustus, AD 14–2014*. Cambridge, 87–102.

2020. 'Eusebia and Eusebius: The Roles and Significance of Constantinian Imperial Women and Court Eunuchs', in: N. Baker-Brian and S. Tougher (eds.), *The Sons of Constantine, AD 337–361*. Cham, 185–220.

2020. *The Roman Castrati. Eunuchs in the Roman Empire*. London; New York.

Traina, G. 2007. *428 dopo Cristo. Storia di un anno*. Rome.

Trillmich, W. 1993. 'Hispanien und Rom aus der Sicht Roms und Hispaniens', in: W. Trillmich and H. Schubert (eds.), *Hispania Antiqua*. Mainz, 41–70.

Trimble, J. 2014. '*Corpore Enormi*. The Rhetoric of Physical Appearance in Suetonius and Imperial Portrait Statuary', in: J. Elsner and M. Meyer (eds.), *Art and Rhetoric in Roman Culture*. Cambridge, 115–54.

2017. 'Communicating with Images in the Roman Empire', in: F. S. Naiden and R. Talbert (eds.), *Mercury's Wings. Exploring Modes of Communication in the Ancient World*. Oxford, 106–27.

Trombley, F. R. 2011. 'The Imperial Cult in Late Roman Religion (ca. A.D. 244–395): Observations on the Epigraphy', in: J. Hahn (ed.), *Spätantiker Staat und religiöser Konflikt. Imperiale und lokale Verwaltung und die Gewalt gegen Heiligtümer*. Berlin, 19–54.

Trombley, F. R., and S. Tougher. 2019. 'The Emperor at War', in: S. Tougher (ed.), *The Emperor in the Byzantine World*. London; New York, 179–95.

Tuori, K. 2012. 'Greek Tyrants and Severan Emperors: Comparing the Image', *BICS* 55: 111–19.

2016. *The Emperor of Law*. Oxford.
Turner, A. 2016. 'The Importance of Numa Pompilius: A Reconsideration of Augustan Coins', *Open Library of Humanities* 2: http://doi.org/10.16995/olh.58.
Turpin, W. 1991. 'Imperial Subscriptions and the Administration of Justice', *JRS* 81: 101–18.
Unruh, D. B. 2015. 'The Predatory Palace: Seneca's Thyestes and the Architecture of Tyranny', in: A. M. Kemezis (ed.), *Urban Dreams and Realities in Antiquity: Remains and Representations of the Ancient City*. Leiden, 246–72.
Van Dam, R. 2007. *The Roman Revolution of Constantine*. Cambridge.
  2011. 'Bishops and Clerics during the Fourth Century: Numbers and Their Implications', in: J. Leemans, P. Van Nuffelen, S. W. J. Keough and C. Nicolaye (eds.), *Episcopal Elections in Late Antiquity*. Berlin; Boston, 217–42.
Van der Blom, H. 2011. 'Pompey in the Contio', *CQ* 61: 553–73.
Van Ess, H. 2017. 'Konzeptionen monarchischer Herrschaft im frühen China', in: S. Rebenich, *Monarchische Herrschaft im Altertum*. Berlin; Boston, 401–12.
Van Haeperen, F. 2003. 'Des Pontifes païens aux pontifes chrétiens. Transformations d'un titre: entre pouvoirs et représentations', *RBPh* 81: 137–59.
Vanderspoel, J. 1995. Themistius and the Imperial Court. Oratory, Civic Duty, and *Paideia* from Constantius to Theodosius. Ann Arbor.
  2012. 'A Tale of Two Cities. Themistius on Rome and Constantinople', in: L. Grig and G. Kelly (eds.), *Two Romes. Rome and Constantinople in Late Antiquity*. Oxford; New York, 223–40.
Vankeerberghen, G. 2021. 'Of Gold and Purple: Nobles in Western Han China and Republican Rome', in: H. Beck and G. Vankeerberghen (eds.), *Rulers and Ruled in Ancient Greece, Rome, and China*. Cambridge, 15–68.
Varbanov, I. 2005–2007. *Greek Imperial Coins and Their Values*. Bourgas.
Varner, E. R. 2017. 'Incarnating the Aurea Aetas: Theomorphic Rhetoric and the Portraits of Nero', in: S. Blakely and E. Olin (eds.), *Gods, Objects, and Ritual Practice in Ancient Mediterranean Religions*. Atlanta, 75–115.
  2020. 'Innovation and Orthodoxy in the Portraiture of Constantine and His Sons', in: N. J. Baker-Brian and S. Tougher (eds.), *The Sons of Constantine, AD 337–361. In the Shadows of Constantine and Julian*. London, 97–132.
  2004. *Mutilation and Transformation. Damnatio Memoriae and Roman Imperial Portraiture*. Leiden; Boston.
Versluys, M. J. 2015. 'Haunting Traditions. The (Material) Presences of Egypt in the Roman World', in: D. Boschung, A. Busch and M. J. Versluys (eds.), *Reinventing the Invention of Tradition? Indigenous Pasts and the Roman Present*. Paderborn, 127–58.
  2017. 'Object-Scapes. Towards a Material Constitution of Romaness?', in: A. van Oyen and M. Pitts (eds.), *Materialising Roman Histories*. Oxford, 191–9.

2021. 'Art', in: R. Osborne (ed.), *A Cultural History of Objects in Antiquity*. London, 115–33.

Vervaet, F. J. 2004. 'The Lex Valeria and Sulla's Empowerment as Dictator (82–79 BCE)', *Cahiers du Centre Gustave Glotz* 15: 37–84.

2010. 'Arrogating Despotic Power through Deceit: The Pompeian model for Augustan *dissimulatio*', in: A. J. Turner, K. O. Chong-Gossard and F. J. Vervaet (eds.), *Private and Public Lies. The Discourse of Despotism and Deceit in the Greco-Roman World*. Leiden; Boston, 133–66.

Vervaet, F. J., and C. Dart. 2016. 'Last of the Naval Triumphs: Revisiting Some Key Actian Honours', *JRA* 29: 389–410.

Veyne, P. 1976. *Le Pain et le cirque. Sociologie historique d'un pluralisme politique*. Paris.

1988. 'Conduct without Belief and Works of Art without Viewers', *Diogenes* 36: 1–22.

Viscogliosi, A. 1999. 'Porticus Octaviae', *LTUR* 4, 141–5.

Vitale, M. 2017. *Das Imperium in Wort und Bild. Römische Darstellungsformen beherrschter Gebiete in Inschriftenmonumenten, Münzprägungen und Literatur*. Stuttgart.

von den Hoff, R. 2011. 'Kaiserbildnisse als Kaisergeschichte(n): Prolegomena zu einem medialen Konzept römischer Herrscherporträts', in: A. Winterling (ed.), *Zwischen Strukturgeschichte und Biographie. Probleme und Perspektiven einer römischen Kaisergeschichte (Augustus bis Commodus)*. Munich, 15–44.

Vorderstrasse, T. 2009. 'Coinage of Justin II and Its Imitations. Historical, Papyrological, Numismatic and Archaeological Sources', *Anatolica* 35: 15–35.

Vout, C. 2006. 'What's in a Beard? Rethinking Hadrian's Hellenism', in: S. Goldhill and R. Osborne (eds.), *Rethinking Revolutions through Ancient Greece*. Cambridge, 96–123.

2007. *Power and Eroticism in Imperial Rome*. Cambridge.

2012. *The Hills of Rome: Signature of an Eternal City*. Cambridge.

2017. 'Art and the Decadent City', in: S. Bartsch, K. Freudenburg and C. Littlewood (eds.), *The Cambridge Companion to the Age of Nero*. Cambridge, 179–94.

2021. 'Portraiture and Memory Sanctions', in: A. Raimondi Cominesi, N. de Haan, E. M. Moormann and C. Stocks (eds.), *God on Earth: Emperor Domitian. The Re-invention of Rome at the End of the 1st Century* AD. Leiden, 175–80.

Wallace-Hadrill, A. 1982. 'Civilis Princeps: Between Citizen and King', *JRS* 72: 32–48.

1996. 'The Imperial Court', in: A. K. Bowman, E. Champlin and A. Lintott (eds.), *The Cambridge Ancient History: The Augustan Empire, 43* BC–AD *69*, revised edition, Vol. X. Cambridge, 283–308.

2008. *Rome's Cultural Revolution*. Cambridge.

Wang, Z. 2015. *World Views and Military Policies in the Early Roman and Western Han Empires*. PhD Leiden.

Ward-Perkins, B. 1993. *The Severan Buildings of Lepcis Magna: An Architectural Survey*. London.

2006. *The Fall of Rome and the End of Civilization*. Oxford.

2012. 'Old and New Rome Compared: The Rise of Constantinople', in: L. Grig and G. Kelly (eds.), *Two Romes. Rome and Constantinople in Late Antiquity*. Oxford; New York, 53–80.

2014. 'A Most Unusual Empire: Rome in the Fourth Century', in: C. Rapp and H. A. Drake (eds.), *The City in the Classical and Post-Classical World*. Cambridge, 109–29.

2016. 'The End of the Statue Habit, AD 284–620', in: R. R. R. Smith and B. Ward-Perkins (eds.), *The Last Statues of Antiquity*. Oxford, 295–307.

Ware, C. 2019. 'Panegyric and the Discourse of Praise in Late Antiquity', *JRS* 109: 291–304.

Washburn, D. 2006. 'The Thessalonian Affair in the Fifth-Century Histories', in: H. A. Drake (ed.), *Violence in Late Antiquity. Perceptions and Practices*. London; New York, 215–24.

Watts, E. J. 2018. *City and School in Late Antique Athens and Alexandria*. Berkeley; Los Angeles; London.

Wei, R., and B. Kelly. 2022. 'The Roman Aristocracy at Court', in: B. Kelly and A. Hug (eds.), *The Roman Emperor and His Court, ca. 30 BC–ca. AD 300. Volume 1: Historical Essays*. Cambridge, 85–114.

Weisweiler, J. 2012. 'From Equality to Asymmetry: Honorific Statues, Imperial Power, and Senatorial Identity in Late-Antique Rome', *JRA* 25 (2012), 319–50; 332–35.

2015. 'Domesticating the Senatorial Elite Universal Monarchy and Transregional Aristocracy in the Fourth Century AD', in: J. Wienand (ed.), *Contested Monarchy: Integrating the Roman Empire in the Fourth Century AD*. New York, 17–41.

2015. 'Making Masters, Makings Subjects: Imperial Ideology and Memory Policy in the Early Roman Empire and the Later Roman State', in: K. Galinsky and K. Lapatin (eds.), *Cultural Memories in the Roman Empire*. Los Angeles, 66–85.

Whitmarsh, T. 2013. 'Resistance is Futile? Greek Literary Tactics in the Face of Rome', in: P. Schubert, P. Ducrey and P. Derron (eds.), *Les Grecs héritiers des Romains: huit exposés suivis de discussions*. Geneva, 57–85.

Wickert, L. 1954. 'Princeps (Civitatis)', *REAL* 22: 1998–2296.

Wickham, C. 2005. *Framing the Early Middle Ages. Europe and the Mediterranean 400–800*. Oxford.

Wieber, A. 2010. 'Eine Kaiserin von Gewicht? Julians Rede auf Eusebia zwischen Geschlechtsspezifik, höfischer Repräsentation und Matronage', in: A. Kolb (ed.), *Augustae. Machtbewusste Frauen am römischen Kaiserhof? Herrschaftsstrukturen und Herrschaftspraxis II*. Berlin, 253–75.

Wiedemann, T. 1994. *Cicero and the End of the Roman Republic*. London.

— 1995. *Emperors and Gladiators*. London; New York.

— 1996. 'Tiberius to Nero', in: A. Bowman, E. Champlin and A. Lintott (eds.), *CAH*. Vol. 10. Cambridge, 198–255.

Wienand, J. (ed.). 2015. *Contested Monarchy: Integrating the Roman Empire in the Fourth Century* AD. Oxford; New York.

Wienand, J. 2015. 'The Empire's Golden Shade. Icons of Sovereignty in an Age of Transition', in: J. Wienand (ed.), *Contested Monarchy: Integrating the Roman Empire in the Fourth Century* AD. New York, 423–52.

Wienand, J., F. Goldbeck and H. Börm. 2017. 'Der römische Triumph in Prinzipat und Spätantike. Probleme – Paradigmen – Perspektiven', in: F. Goldbeck and J. Wienand (eds.), *Der römische Triumph in Prinzipat und Spätantike. The Roman Triumphal Procession in the Principate and Late Antiquity*. Berlin; Boston, 1–26.

Wilker, J. 2020. 'Modelling the Emperor. Representations of Power, Empire, and Dynasty among Eastern Client Kings', in: A. Russell and M. Hellström (eds.), *The Social Dynamics of Roman Imperial Imagery*. Cambridge, 52–75.

Wilkinson, K. W. 2010. 'Palladas and the Foundation of Constantinople', *JRS* 100: 179–94.

Winsor-Leach, E. 1990. 'The Politics of Self-Presentation. Pliny's "Letters" and Roman Portrait Sculpture', *ClAnt* 91: 14–39.

Winterling, A. 1999. *Aula Caesaris: Studien zur Institutionalisierung des römischen Kaiserhofes in der Zeit von Augustus bis Commodus (31 v. Chr.–192 n. Chr.)*. Munich.

— 2011. 'Die Freundschaft der römischen Kaiser', in: A. Winterling (ed.), *Zwischen Strukturgeschichte und Biographie. Probleme und Perspektiven einer römischen Kaisergeschichte (Augustus bis Commodus)*. Munich, 207–32.

Wiseman, T. P. 2019. *The House of Augustus: A Historical Detective Story*. Princeton; Oxford.

Wolters, R. 2003. 'Die Geschwindigkeit der Zeit und die Gefahr der Bilder: Münzbilder und Münzpropaganda in der römischen Kaiserzeit', in: G. Weber and M. Zimmermann (eds.), *Propaganda – Selbstdarstellung – Repräsentation im römischen Kaiserreich des 1. Jhs. n. Chr.* Stuttgart, 175–204.

Wolters, R., and M. Ziegert. 2014. 'Umbrüche – Die Reichsprägung Neros und Domitians im Vergleich', in: S. Bönisch et al. (eds.), *Nero und Domitian. Mediale Diskurse der Herrscherrepräsentation im Vergleich*. Tübingen, 43–80.

Wood, S. E. 2016. 'Public Images of the Flavian Dynasty: Sculpture and Coinage', in: A. Zissos (ed.), *A Companion to the Flavian Age of Imperial Rome*. Malden [Mass.]; Oxford, 129–47.

Woolf, G. 1994. 'Becoming Roman, Staying Greek: Culture, Identity and the Civilizing Process in the Roman East', *The Cambridge Classical Journal* 40: 116–43.

1998. *Becoming Roman. The Origins of Provincial Civilization in Gaul.* Cambridge.

2012. 'Divinity and Power in Ancient Rome', in: N. Brisch (ed.), *Religion and Power: Divine Kingship in the Ancient World and Beyond.* Chicago, 235–51.

2020. 'The Rulers Ruled', in: K. Berthelot (ed.), *Reconsidering Roman Power. Roman, Greek, Jewish and Christian Perceptions and Reactions.* Rome, 85–100.

Woytek, B. 2014. 'Heads and Busts on Roman Coins. Some Remarks on the Morphology of Numismatic Portraiture', *Revue numismatique* 171: 45–71.

Wrede, H. 1981. *Consecratio in Formam Deorum. Vergöttlichte Privatpersonen in der römischen Kaiserzeit.* Mainz.

Wright, N. 2005. 'Seleucid Royal Cult, Indigenous Religious Traditions, and Radiate Crowns: The Numismatic Evidence', *Mediterranean Archaeology* 18: 67–82.

Wueste, E. 2017. 'The Costumes of Late Antique Honorific Monuments: Conformity and Divergence within the Public and Political Sphere', in: M. Cifarelli and L. Gawlinski (eds.), *What Shall I Say of Clothes? Theoretical and Methodological Approaches to the Study of Dress in Antiquity.* Boston, 179–201.

Wulf-Rheidt, U. 2013. 'Die Bedeutung der severischen Paläste für spätere Residenzbauten', in: N. Sojc, A. Winterling and U. Wulf-Rheidt (eds.), *Palast und Stadt im severischen Rom.* Stuttgart, 287–306.

Yarrow, L. 2018. 'Markers of Identity for Non-Elite Romans: A Prolegomenon to the Study of Glass Paste Intaglios', *Journal of Ancient History and Archaeology* 5.3: 35–54.

Yegül, F. K. 2014. 'A Victor's Message: The Talking Column of the Temple of Artemis at Sardis', *Journal of the Society of Architectural Historians* 73: 204–25.

Yon, J.-B. 2002. *Les Notables de Palmyre.* Beirut.

Zanker, P. 1987. *Provinzielle Kaiserporträts. Zur Rezeption der Selbstdarstellung des Princeps.* Munich.

1988. *The Power of Images in the Age of Augustus.* Ann Arbor.

1995. *Die Maske des Sokrates: das Bild des Intellektuellen in der antiken Kunst.* Munich.

2004. *Die Apotheose der römischen Kaiser.* Munich.

2009. 'The Irritating Statues and Contradictory Portraits of Julius Caesar', in: M. Griffin (ed.), *A Companion to Julius Caesar.* Malden [Mass.]; Oxford, 288–314.

Ziegler, R. 1993. *Kaiser, Heer und Städtisches Geld. Untersuchungen zur Münzprägung von Anazarbos und anderer ostkilikischer Städte.* Vienna.

Zimmermann, M. 2011. 'Die Repräsentation des *kaiserlichen Ranges*', in: A. Winterling (ed.), *Zwischen Strukturgeschichte und Biographie. Probleme und Perspektiven einer römischen Kaisergeschichte (Augustus bis Commodus)*. Munich, 181–205.

2015. 'Die Darstellung des kaiserlichen Status und seines Prestiges', in: A. Kuhn (ed.), *Social Status and Prestige in the Graeco-Roman World*. Stuttgart, 189–203.

Zink, S. 2012. 'Old and New Evidence for the Plan of the Palatine Temple of Apollo', *JRA* 25: 388–402.

Zink, S., and H. Piening. 2009. '*Haec Aurea* Templa: The Palatine Temple of Apollo and Its Polychromy', *JRA* 22: 109–22.

Ziosi, F. 2010. 'Sulle iscrizioni relative alla ricostruzione di Cirene dopo il "tumultus Iudaicus", e sul loror contesto', *ZPE* 172: 239–48.

Zoja, L. 2017. *Paranoia. The Madness that Makes History*. London; New York.

Zuiderhoek, A. 2009. *The Politics of Munificence in the Early Roman Empire*. Cambridge.

2014. 'Controlling Urban Public Space in Roman Asia Minor', in: T. Bekker-Nielsen (ed.), *Space, Place and Identity in Northern Anatolia*. Stuttgart: 99–108.

Zwierlein-Diehl, E. 2007. *Antike Gemmen und ihr Nachleben*. Berlin; New York.

Index of Persons and Places

Actium, battle of, 108, 118
Aelia Flaccilla, 89
Aelius Antipater, 219
Aelius Aristides, 288–9
Aelius Caesar. *See* Ceionus Commodus, Lucius
Aeneas, 143, 194
Aetius, Flavius, 128, 130, 224
Africa, 127, 133, 196, 316, 319, 321
Agamemnon, 105
Agricola, 131
Agrippa (king of Judea), 320
Agrippa II (king of Judea), 321
Agrippa Postumus, 243
Agrippa, Marcus Vipsanius, 108, 245
Agrippina the Younger, 22, 228–9, 237, 239–40, 248, 258, 321, 329
ALBINUS, CLODIUS, 81
Alexander of Seleucia, 219
Alexander the Great, 55, 115
   as an example, 48, 54, 56, 90, 129, 178
Alexandria, 198, 202, 206–8
Amalasuntha, 252
Ambrose, 141, 202–3
Ammianus Marcellinus, 39, 57, 66, 77, 124–5, 230, 249
ANASTASIUS, 42, 139, 155, 240–2
ANTHEMIUS, 62, 268
Antinous, 320
Antioch, 202, 206–9, 276
Antonia the Younger, 239
ANTONINUS PIUS, 37, 74, 112, 176, 178, 224, 246, 284, 299–300
   as an example, 179
Antony, Mark, 24, 70–1, 110, 118, 218
Aper, 247
Aphrodisias, 286
Apollo, 82, 152
   emperors associated with, 85, 142, 182, 274
Aquileia, 202
Arbogast, 130, 225

ARCADIUS, 42, 77–9, 128, 198, 200, 204, 210, 284
Areus of Alexandria, 218
Ariadne (empress), 240–2, 252
Arles, 185, 202, 219
Armenia, 112, 122
Arrian, 47
Artemis, 180, 311–12
Asia Minor, 26, 47, 288, 307, 311
Aspar, Flavius Ardabur, 67
Assyria, 122
Athalaric, 252
Athens, 218
Attila the Hun, 129–30
Augustine, 202, 204
AUGUSTUS, 1, 11, 14, 24–7, 31, 48–51, 57, 59, 64, 67, 70, 82, 84, 92, 94, 96, 108–10, 115–16, 118, 135, 141, 146, 153, 156–7, 165, 176, 184, 187, 237, 243, 245, 248, 273, 299–300, 326, 328–9, 332
   and Apollo, 85, 142–3, 146, 182, 274
   as an example, 22, 49–51, 53–4, 56, 102, 108–9, 135–6, 157, 178–9, 182, 331
   Divus, 61, 85, 93
   Res Gestae, 109, 156, 184, 288, 299
AURELIAN, 80, 125
Ausonius, 218, 250
Autun, 289

Bacchus, 152
Baiae, 275
BALBINUS, 127, 136, 189, 222, 247
Barsauma, 220–2
Basil, 63
BASILISCUS, 226, 240
Batavians, 261–2
Belisarius, 79, 133, 252, 269
Boethius, Manlius, 68
Boniface (pope), 201–2
Britain, 110, 114, 295, 319
Britannicus, 243, 246, 248
Brutus, Marcus Junius, 24

393

Caenis, 231
Caesar, Gaius (grandson of Augustus), 31, 51, 237, 245
Caesar, Gaius Julius, 1, 8, 24, 28, 48–9, 67, 69–71, 82, 91, 110, 133, 135, 178, 222, 248, 269, 298, 326, 332
   Divus, 61, 135, 146, 150
   as an example, 107–9, 135
Caesar, Lucius (grandson of Augustus), 31, 51, 237, 245
Caesarea, 162, 206
CALIGULA, 1, 14, 51, 71–2, 74–5, 109, 114–15, 136, 152–3, 167, 171, 176, 178, 186, 189, 222, 230, 237, 239, 294, 332
Callistratus, 263
Calpurnia, 228
Calpurnius Bibulus, Marcus, 133
CARACALLA, 40, 65, 76, 87, 89, 112, 137, 154, 174, 215, 219, 222, 226, 229–30, 237, 244, 246, 248–9, 306
Carthage, 202, 206, 263, 290
Cassiodorus, 42, 192
Castor, 134
Cato the Elder, 26, 122
Ceionus Commodus, Lucius, 246
Ceres, 235
Chalcis, 134
Chrysostom, John, 200
Cicero, Marcus Tullius, 26, 57, 90, 107, 109, 141, 144
Claudian, 41, 129, 148, 252
CLAUDIUS, 4, 39, 51, 59, 95–6, 109–10, 112, 114, 136, 147, 150, 157, 171, 174, 213, 229–30, 239, 248, 290, 295, 299, 319
CLAUDIUS GOTHICUS, 148
Cleander, 267
Cleopatra, 24, 119, 218
Clodius Pulcher, Publius, 228
COMMODUS, 74, 95, 111, 116, 142–3, 154, 177, 219, 244, 248
Concordia, 235
Ὁμόνοια, 238
CONSTANS, 124
CONSTANTINE, 9–10, 39, 41, 56, 88–9, 104, 114, 116–17, 124, 138, 148–9, 158, 166–7, 193–4, 198–9, 205, 223–4, 248, 266, 276, 278, 289, 315, 327, 332
   and Christianity, 14, 100–1, 139–41
   as an example, 22, 53, 56, 150, 181, 232
CONSTANTINE II, 88, 167
Constantinople, 187, 193–4, 202, 206, 235, 264–9, 275–85, 328
   Church of the Holy Apostles, 141, 200

Column of Justinian, 282
   as episcopal see, 207–8
   Forum of Arcadius, 282
   Forum of Constantine, 279
   Forum of Theodosius, 67, 179, 282
   Hagia Sophia, 265, 283
   Hippodrome, 265, 267–9
   as New Rome, 207–8, 264, 279, 276–7, 279
CONSTANTIUS CHLORUS, 144, 148
CONSTANTIUS II, 66, 88, 124–5, 138, 149, 173, 191, 193, 200, 230, 315
Corbulo, 131
Corinth, 219
Corippus, 148
Crassus, Marcus Licinius, 110

Dacia, 65, 303–5
Danube, 108, 111, 119, 223, 262, 307
David, 79
DECIUS, TRAJAN, 87, 138, 147
Dexippos, 125
DIADUMENIANUS, 249
Diana, 72
DIDIUS JULIANUS, 267
Dio, Cassius, 39, 122, 160, 179, 186, 189, 215, 231, 248–9, 287, 295
DIOCLETIAN, 9–10, 30, 39, 74–5, 89, 117, 144, 154, 332
   and Jupiter, 144–5
   reforms of, 76, 105, 168, 215–16, 253, 324
Dionysius of Halicarnassus, 287
Dionysus, 320
DOMITIAN, 53, 71, 95–6, 116, 120, 131, 142–3, 171, 174, 177, 222, 226, 230, 246–7, 272, 302
Drusus (son of Tiberius), 213
Dura Europos, 147, 311–14

Egypt, 108, 119, 161, 211, 282, 287, 295–8, 310
Elagabal (deity), 142
ELAGABALUS, 39, 74, 89, 112, 142, 174, 215, 249, 284, 332
Ennodius, Magnus Felix, 138, 155
Ephesus, 287
   Parthian Monument, 299–300
   temple of Hadrian, 180
Ethiopia, 244
Eudoxia, 102, 198, 200, 220, 230, 242
EUGENIUS, 225
Eulalius (pope), 201–2
Euric, 35
Eusebius (courtier), 217

Index of Persons and Places 395

Eusebius of Caesarea, 100, 140, 158, 180, 266, 278–9
Eutharic, 252
Eutropius, 30, 178, 217, 230, 258, 307
Eutropius (courtier), 210, 217

Fabius Maximus, Paullus, 26
Fausta, 89, 248
Faustina the Elder, 231
Faustina the Younger, 75, 239
Favorinus, 219–20
Felicitas, 235
Flaminius, Titus Quinctius, 134
FLORIANUS, 247
Fortuna, 142
Frontinus, 287
Fronto, 47, 74, 157–8, 178, 218
Fulvia, 228

GAIUS. *See* CALIGULA
GALBA, 1, 84, 142, 213, 222, 224, 306
GALERIUS, 144, 215
Galla Placidia, 128, 232, 251
Gallic Empire, 54, 307
GALLIENUS, 54, 75, 89, 117, 119–20, 138, 189, 237, 307
GALLUS, TREBONIANUS, 148
Ganymede, 214
Gaul, 222, 292, 298, 300, 307–8, 319
Geithion, 134
Gelasius (pope), 138
Gemma Augustea, 92–4
Genius Senatus, 98
Germania Inferior, 307
Germania Superior, 120
GETA, 65, 76, 112, 174, 243, 246, 248
Glabrio Faustus, 323
GORDIAN, 127
GORDIAN II, 127
GORDIAN III, 111, 127, 131, 237, 247
GRATIAN, 44, 128–30, 139, 192, 218, 249–50
Greece, 47, 134
Gregory of Nazianzus, 69, 316

HADRIAN, 47, 53, 65, 86, 96, 112, 122–4, 160, 162–3, 167, 174, 211, 219–20, 246, 261–2, 275, 286–7, 295–8, 304–6, 332
    as an example, 54, 179, 181
Hadrian of Tyre, 218
Helena, 89, 231
HERACLIUS, 292
Hercules, 134, 142, 144–5, 152, 154
    emperors associated with, 129

Hermes, 320
Herodes Atticus, 218, 287
Herodian, 148, 158, 179, 208, 231
Historia Augusta, 116, 215, 222
Homer, 181
HONORIUS, 41, 105, 128–9, 148, 191, 200–2, 204, 232, 250–1, 275
Horace, 26, 41
Hormisdas (pope), 196, 268
HYPATIUS, 268

Isidore of Seville, 98
Italy, 79, 133, 190, 284, 292

Jerome, 262
Jerusalem, 125, 202, 206, 220, 310
Jesus Christ, 35, 88, 125, 140, 154
JOANNES, 129
Juba II (king of Mauretania), 320
Julia (daughter of Augustus), 237, 245
Julia Domna, 65, 76, 222, 229, 231, 237–9, 242
Julia Maesa, 237
Julia Mamaea, 239–40
JULIAN, 41, 56–7, 59, 69, 71, 104, 128, 138, 182, 218, 316, 329
    The Caesars, 128, 165
Julius Caesar. *See* Caesar, Gaius Julius
Juno, 235
Jupiter, 91–2, 134, 144–5, 152, 174, 214, 311
    emperors associated with, 92–8, 143–5, 327
JUSTIN, 113, 223, 267
JUSTIN II, 130, 194, 226
JUSTINIAN, 9, 29, 79, 133, 145, 154, 163–4, 182, 194–5, 197–8, 207–8, 252, 268–9, 282–3, 285, 324, 327–9, 332
JUSTINIAN II, 35
Juvenal, 116

LEO, 58, 62, 102, 223, 240, 268
Leo (pope), 100, 196, 232
LEO II, 240
Lepcis Magna, 22, 61, 65, 239, 289
Libanius, 41
LIBIUS SEVERUS, 102–3
LICINIUS, 59, 249, 276
LICINIUS II, 59, 249
Livia, 74, 227–8, 231, 234, 239–40, 242
Lusius Quietus, 295

Macedonius, 199
MACRINUS, 54, 112, 174, 189, 249, 319
MAGNENTIUS, 124
MAGNUS MAXIMUS, 62, 130, 203

Malalas, John, 182, 192, 285
Mamertinus, 158
Marcellus, Marcus Claudius, 245
MARCIAN, 22, 36, 220-2, 232-3
Marcianopolis, 238
MARCUS AURELIUS, 47, 59, 74, 157-8, 160, 174, 178, 189, 209, 218, 224, 244, 246, 248, 288-9, 306
  as an example, 165, 179
  Meditations, 165
Mardonius, 218
Marius, Gaius, 48, 107
Mars, 146
Martial, 73, 95, 214
Matidia the Elder, 240
Matidia the Younger, 240
MAURICE, 223
MAXENTIUS, 100, 117, 140, 223, 270, 276
MAXIMIAN, 89, 144, 148, 158
MAXIMINUS THRAX, 127, 148, 158
Mehmed II, 244
Menander Rhetor, 160
Mesopotamia, 112, 122
Milan, 191, 202
Minerva, 142, 174

Naulochus, battle of, 118
Neptune, 25, 152
NERO, 14, 51, 71, 74, 87, 95, 109, 115-16, 131, 136, 142, 144, 157, 174, 177-8, 213, 229-30, 239, 246, 248, 274, 295, 330
NERVA, 89, 112, 136, 171, 174, 181, 189
  as an example, 165, 179
Nicaea, 209, 276, *See also* church council
Nicomedia, 209, 276
Numa, 194
NUMERIAN, 247

Octavia the Younger, 231, 237
Octavian. *See* AUGUSTUS
Odaenathus, 307
Odoacer, 2, 192
OLYBRIUS, 192
Optatian, 41, 278
Orosius, 180
Ostrogoths, 133
OTHO, 112
Ovid, 95, 104, 145

Pacatus, 155, 179
Palmyra, 54, 307, 311
Palmyrene Empire, 54, 307
Parthians, 110, 112, 116, 179

Paul (apostle), 282
Paulinus of Nola, 202, 232
Pax, 111-12, 235
  pax deorum, 108, 134
PERTINAX, 174
PESCENNIUS NIGER, 209, 267
Peter (apostle), 206, 282
PETRONIUS MAXIMUS, 192
Pharsalus, battle of, 269
PHILIP ARABS, 111-12, 249
PHILIP II, 249
Philo of Alexandria, 152
Philostorgius, 149
Philostratus, 219
Pietas, 235
Pinarius Valens, 247
Plato, 181
Plautianus, 210
Pliny the Elder, 82, 185, 213
Pliny the Younger, 41, 144, 158, 314
Plotina, 246, 258
Plutarch, 39
Polemon of Laodicea, 320
Pollux, 134
Pompeia, 228
Pompey the Great, 48-9, 107, 144
Pompey, Sextus, 118
Poppaea Sabina, 239
Porphyry (bishop), 198
POSTUMUS, 307
Priscian, 155
Priscus of Panium, 130, 324
Probus (noble), 268
Procopius, 39, 230
PROCOPIUS, 77
Ptolemy (king of Mauretania), 71
Ptolemy XII Auletes, 90
Pulcheria, 22, 221, 232-3, 238, 243
PUPIENUS, 54, 127, 136, 189, 222, 247

Quirinus, 146

Ravenna, 191-2, 202, 328
  Basilica of San Vitale, 79, 240, 328
Rhea, 279
Rhine, 119, 223
Rhoemetalces of Thrace, 320
Ricimer, 102
Roma (goddess), 264, 275
Rome (city), 124-5, 141, 187, 189-92, 235, 263-7, 269-75, 284
  Anaglypha Traiani, 160
  Ara Pacis, 64, 70, 165, 187, 328

Arch of Claudius, 295
Arch of Constantine, 65, 116–17, 125, 165–6, 223
Arch of Septimius Severus, 65, 125
Arch of Titus, 65
Arco di Portogallo, 160
Basilica Nova, 270
Basilica of Marcellinus and Peter, 224
Baths of Agrippa, 270
Baths of Diocletian, 270
Circus Maximus, 266–7
Colosseum, 266
Column of Marcus Aurelius, 20, 65
Column of Trajan, 20–1, 65, 74, 270
Curia Julia, 192
Domus Aurea, 274
as episcopal See, 206–8
Equus Traiani, 66
Forum of Augustus, 270
Forum of Caesar, 269
Forum of Nerva, 270
Forum of Trajan, 66, 179, 270, 328
Forum of Vespasian, 270
Forum Romanum, 144, 147, 272
Gardens of Maecenas, 274
Lateran Basilica, 223
Mausoleum of Augustus, 60
Palatine, 272–5
porticus Octaviae, 237
sack of (410), 192, 206, 262
Santa Maria Maggiore, 79
Temple of Castor and Pollux, 153
Temple of Quirinus, 146
Temple of Venus and Rome, 270
Romulus, 27, 145–6, 194
ROMULUS AUGUSTULUS, 2, 35, 42, 192, 324

Sabina, 65
Salonina, 237
Salus, 121, 235
Sasanians, 54, 56, 90, 111, 127, 168–9, 215–16, 233, 307, 329
Scipio Africanus, 26
Securitas, 236
Sejanus, 210
Sempronius Rufus, 215
Seneca, 144, 218
Serdica, 276
SEVERUS ALEXANDER, 112, 174, 215, 231, 237, 249, 275, 284
Severus III. *See* Libius Severus
SEVERUS, SEPTIMIUS, 22, 40, 44, 59, 64, 75–6, 81, 84, 89, 116, 119, 163, 165, 174, 176, 209–10, 237–8, 244, 246–8, 274, 289, 306, 311, 328, 331
Shapur, 112, 119, 307
Shenoute of Atripe, 262–3, 323
Sicily, 319
Sidonius, 148
Smyrna, 320
Sol, 85, 88
Solomon, 283
Sozimus, 232
Spain, 133, 179, 240, 300, 307–8, 319
Stilicho, 128–9, 250–2
Suetonius, 57, 74, 157, 213, 231, 272
Sulla, Lucius Cornelius, 48, 107, 133
Symmachus, 129
Synesius of Cyrene, 105

TACITUS, 4, 39, 80, 116, 121, 148, 157, 179, 213–14, 243, 247
Tarquinius Superbus, 23
Tertullian, 196
Themistius, 178, 193
Theodahad, 252
Theoderic I, 42, 129, 155, 192–3, 252, 292
Theodora, 230, 240, 242, 285, 329
Theodoret, 199, 206
THEODOSIUS, 41, 58, 62, 77–9, 89, 130, 148, 155, 163, 179–81, 192, 203, 207, 251
THEODOSIUS II, 40, 57, 128–30, 148, 204, 220, 232–4, 238, 284, 323
Thessalonica, 276
TIBERIUS, 1, 39, 51, 61, 92, 96, 109, 136, 153, 176, 189, 210, 239, 245, 288, 319
TIBERIUS II, 223, 226
TITUS, 53, 89, 112, 176, 246–7
as an examplee, 179
Tivoli, 275
TRAJAN, 21, 41, 47, 96, 112, 120, 144, 158–60, 174, 185, 212, 246, 270, 299, 302–4, 314
as an example, 53, 56, 58, 66, 177–81, 282, 331
Tranquillina, 237
Tropaeum Alpium (La Turbie), 300
Tropaeum Traiani (Adamklissi), 302–4
Troy, 105, 206

Vaballathus, 307
VALENS, 101, 201, 257, 284
Valens (slave), 212
VALENTINIAN, 59, 128, 249–50
VALENTINIAN II, 77–9, 128, 130, 192, 203, 225, 250, 257

Index of Persons and Places

VALENTINIAN III, 36, 128, 130, 191, 224, 233, 250, 284
VALERIAN, 54, 89, 119, 138
Vandals, 35, 133, 263, 316
Venus, 235
Vergil, 143
Verina, 240
VERUS, LUCIUS, 158, 160, 179, 244, 246, 306
VESPASIAN, 32, 38, 52–3, 176, 231, 246–7, 274, 299, 306, 327
Vesta, 235
Victoria (mother of Victorinus), 239

VICTORINUS, 239
Victory, 108, 113–14, 152, 233, 235–6
Visigoths, 35, 133, 308
VITELLIUS, 71, 80, 112, 214

Xerxes, 178

ZENO, 223, 226, 240, 332
Zenobia, 54, 307
Zosimus, 139
Zosimus (pope), 201

General Index

adventus, 118, 265-6
arches. *See also* Rome (city)
   Arch at Susa, 302
   Arch of Claudius (Cyzicus), 295
   Arch of Hadrian (Tel Shalem), 124
   Arch of Septimius Severus (Lepcis Magna), 65
   Arch of Trajan (Benevento), 96
attributes
   labarum, 100-1, 141
   sceptre, 24, 100-2, 327
      cruciform, 90-102
Augusta (title), 239, 243
Augustus (title), 3, 32, 34, 37-8, 42, 45, 69, 104
   appropriation under Tetrarchy, 43

bishops, 8, 195-210
   emperor as special bishop, 209

Caesar (title), 31-2, 34, 38, 41-2, 327
   appropriation under Tetrarchy, 43
censor, 248
Christianity, 63, 138, 140-1, 145, 149-50, 220-2, 231-3, 278-9, 329, *see also* bishops, imperial cult
   appropriating imperial symbols, 79-80, 125-7
   impact on emperorship, 14, 35-6, 62, 100-1, 113-14, 138-41, 154-5, 182, 315-17
   persecution of Christians, 138, 180
Church council
   of Chalcedon (451), 206-7, 221, 232
   of Constantinople (381), 207
   of Constantinople (553), 203
   of Ephesus (449), 206, 221
   of Nicaea (325), 203, 206, 224
   of Tyre (335), 199
civilis princeps, 157, 166, 168, 181, 288
coinage, 5, 20, 24, 28-9, 35, 48-9, 64, 84-9, 92-3, 97-8, 100-3, 112-14, 122-3, 134, 136-8, 158-9, 162, 165-6, 170-7, 246, 255-6, 264-5, 304-7

   empresses on, 89-90, 229-30, 235-7, 239-40
   legends, 31-2, 35-6
   provincial, 5, 38, 162, 229, 236-7, 321, 324
   Republican, 24
Constitutio Antoniniana, 83, 319
consuls/consulate, 68, 91-2, 98, 167, 194-5, 242
   abolition of, 9, 194
   emperors as consul, 32-4, 42, 92, 158, 248
crowns. *See* headgear

dictatorship, 3, 107
diptychs, 68, 242, 250-2
divus/divi, 61, 85, 135, 145-50, 180
Dominus Noster (title), 32, 34, 105
dress, 69-81
   capite velato, 73, 136
   chlamys, 77-80, 240
   cuirass, 112, 114, 123, 127
   laticlavum, 77
   paludamentum, 80, 89, 123
   paludamentum, 240
   stacked toga, 73
   toga picta, 71
   toga praetexta, 71-2
   toga purpurea, 69, 71
   toga virilis, 249
   tunica palmata, 30

empresses/imperial women, 89-90, 228-44, 250-2, 329-30
epigraphy. *See* inscriptions
equestrians, 8, 16-17, 188-9, 194, 211, 217, 219, 222, 266, 269
eunuchs, 213-18, 257-8

Felix (title), 32, 34

guards
   equites singulares Augusti, 223, 269
   Excubitors, 223, 267
   Germanic, 223
   Praetorian Guard, 127, 222, 269

guards (cont.)
    Scholae Palatini, 223
    Varangian Guard, 223

headgear, 81–90
    corona civica, 82, 84–5
    corona etrusca, 85
    corona laurea, 83
    corona triumphalis, 82, 84–5, 327
    diadem, 24, 56, 69, 81, 88–90, 104, 240, 327
    radiate crown, 85–8, 327

Imperator (title), 32, 34, 38, 42
imperial cult, 150–1, 290, 310–17
    and Christianity, 151, 154–5, 198, 316–17
inscriptions, 35–9, 88, 96–7, 161, 212, 321

justice (as an imperial virtue), 161–4, See also laws

kings
    Hellenistic, 23, 28, 48, 85, 89–90, 100, 134, 153, 255, 261, 287–8
    kingship problematic in Rome, 23–7
    of client kingdoms, 84, 320–1
    of successor kingdoms, 35, 42
    Old Testament, 79, 164, 283
    Parthian/Sasanian, 56, 90, 134, 164, 168–9, 215–16, 329
    pharaohs, 134, 170, 261, 310

laws, 62, 162, 194, 204, 208, 278, 291, 315
    Digest, 145, 182, 263
    Justinian Code, 61, 77, 164, 194, 211, 315
    Lex de Imperio Vespasiani, 34
    Theodosian Code, 61, 164, 194, 211, 315, 323

magister militum, 102, 128, 130, 250–1
mater castrorum, 233, 239
memory, 17–22, 121, 331
memoryscape, 19, 260, 331
monuments, 5, 19–21, 64–6, 120–1, 190, 192, 238, 245, 260–1, 269–75, 293–304, 323, 331, See also Constantinople, Rome (city)

nomenclature, imperial, 30–45

panegyric, 9, 16, 41, 63, 104, 121, 148, 155, 158, 178–9, 181–2, 194, 252, 261, 275
papyri, 38–9, 211, 295
pater patriae, 42, 184, 264
pharaohs. See kings
Pius (title), 32, 34

Pontifex Maximus, 32, 36, 43, 107, 135–40
    and Christianity, 138–40, 327
portraiture, 5, 45–69, 112, 122–3, 136–8, 173, 316, 324
    coin, 24, 28, 48–9, 62, 64, 134, 326
    importance of material, 58–60
    private, 67–9, 83
    Republican, 48
Praetorian Prefect, 185, 210, 216, 222, 224, 247–8
praetors, 98
princeps (title), 24–8, 31, 42, 105
    princeps iuventutis, 167, 245
proconsul, 42, 167
profectio, 265
proskynesis, 15, 168
purple (as an imperial colour), 59, 71–5, 77

reliefs. See portraiture
rex (title), 24, 35, 37
roads, 287
    Via Appia, 42
    Via Julia Augusta, 300
    Via Sacra, 270

sceptres. See attributes
sculpture. See portraiture
senate/senators, 4, 8, 11, 16–17, 22–3, 42, 64, 67, 70, 77, 80, 110, 116, 127, 152, 157–8, 162, 164, 168, 178, 184–97, 199, 201, 203, 206–7, 210, 216, 219, 222, 224, 228, 239, 249, 255–9, 266, 268, 299, 331
    emperor as special senator, 157, 209
statuary. See portraiture
synods. See church council

Tetrarchy, 43, 54–5, 138, 254, 276, See also Diocletian
    associated with Jupiter and Hercules, 96, 144–5
titulature, imperial, 30–45
togas. See dress
tradition, 333
    definition of, 14–17
    local, 43, 295, 304, 310
    Roman, 156, 276, 279
        as a framework for rule, 29
        suspicion to change, 4
tribunicia potestas, 32, 34, 42, 167
triumph, 83, 92, 94–5, 101, 111, 114–20, 247

victory titles, 117, 120

wreaths. See headgear